The English Students

Singularly Sensational Boomers

# of B-1

The English Teacher

Dr. Judith T. Witmer

(aka Judith Thompson Ball
[JTB] from 1959 to 1972)

B-1

The English Student: I always wondered if you intentionally created such a sheltered space for us or whether it evolved as the relationships among what you later termed the exceptional boomers deepened among ourselves and between us and you. Was it our presence that ignited the big bang that occurred there or was it more an evolution of relationships that continued long after we had left B-1?

The English Teacher: My own experiences in high school are part of it, as is my wanting to be a part of your education and your lives, but more than that, it was my intuitive gyroscope that came out of a Liberal Arts education, spiced with my anger of having a high IQ but lacking guidance/opportunity to consider another career path. My only intellectual stimulation at LD was through discourse in the class and preparing you for opportunities that had not been open to me.

... we to them will speak
A lasting inspiration, sanctified
By reason, blest by faith: what we have loved
Others will love, and we will teach them how;
Instruct then how the mind of man becomes
A thousand times more beautiful than the earth
On which he dwells ...

The Prelude
William Wordsworth

About the Author

Dr. Judith Thompson Witmer is a prolific writer on a wide range of topics. Her professional books include the first guidebook written for women in pursuing advancement in educational administration (*Moving Up*), a book on service learning (with shared authorship of Carolyn Sandel '65), and one on team-based professional development.

Her research passion, however, is personal and social history as evidenced by her wide-range of publications, beginning with a biography of Rodrigue Mortel, MD (*I Am from Haiti*) who rose from abject poverty to becoming a renown gynecology oncologist and philanthropist. This was followed by *Jebbie: Vamp to Victim*, the true story of a young woman who went from being the stunning and stylish girl with all the gentlemen callers to becoming a town legend, until she fell prey to her niece, leading to deceit and tragedy.

All the Gentlemen Callers: Letters Found in a 1920s Steamer Trunk is a companion publication to Jebbie in the form of narrated love letters from Jebbie's suitors. The book offers a first-hand account of life in a gentler time and displays emotions familiar to all generations as revealed through the more than 100 letters written by her many suitors.

Published in 2012 is *Growing up Silent in the 1950s: Not All Tailfins and Rock 'n' Roll*, an investigation of the factors that created the Silent Generation. Its historical framework is enlivened by personal reflections by members of this generation through diaries, scrapbooks, interviews, and other memoirs, as well as the author's investigation of the factors that created a generation that, despite the suppression of the times, history has shown to be responsible and productive.

Loyal Hearts Proclaim (2013), the 500-page social history of Lower Dauphin High School is the first of its kind, containing anything one would want to know about this hidden treasure of a successful high school that was unusual in its early support of the faculty (half of whom were first-year teachers) to introduce innovative courses and approaches to teaching and learning. It also includes narrative reflections from each class (1961-2010) and the name of every person who worked at the school during these often glorious first fifty years.

Her more recent books include a biography of her parents (*Kate and Howard*) and a narrative genealogy of the lineage of four sisters (*The Thompson Sisters*) through their two sets of grandparents from the time these ancestors landed in the 17th Century on the east coast of America; in 2016, she produced *Letters from a Son to His Father, WWII*, the story of William Calhoon, a young soldier from Hummelstown who spent three years in the Philippines, faithfully writing letters home to his widowed father. In 2017 she traced the story of an enduring friendship and belated romance in *I Have Always Loved You*. Her most recent book is *The English Students in B-1*, a celebration of the Baby Boomers who were graduated in the 1960s from a newly-formed high school with uncommon energy, that provided them a fresh canvas for discovery.

In addition to the number of books she has written, Judith Witmer has published numerous articles in professional journals, a cover feature in *Penn State Medicine*, newspaper columns, monographs, national speeches, and book reviews. Dr. Witmer holds a B.A. in English Literature, an M.S. in Science and Humanities, and a Doctorate in Administration, as well as post-doctoral credits from Harvard University. As a change of pace, she also has been a professional musician, featuring piano and vocals in "Recapture the Romance, Music of the 20th Century."

ISBN 978-0-9977956-3-9

Published in the United States by Yesteryear Publishing.

Books are available at www.amazon.com as well as through the author: jtwitmer@aol.com.

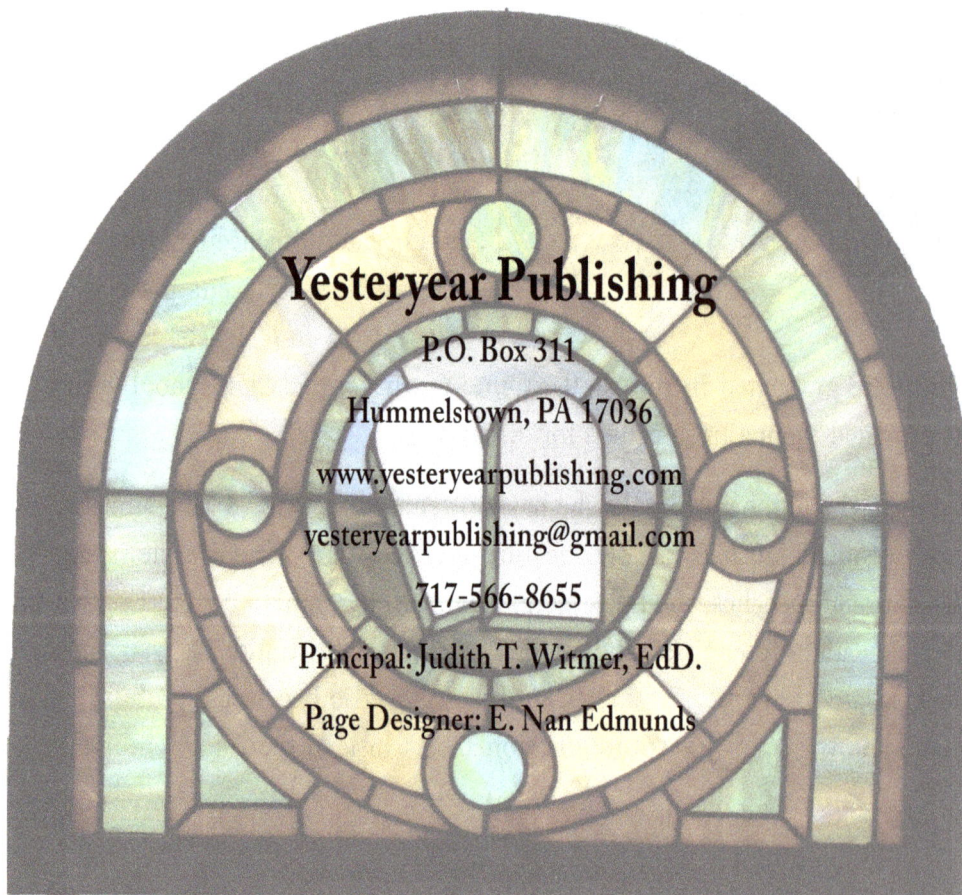

Yesteryear Publishing

P.O. Box 311

Hummelstown, PA 17036

www.yesteryearpublishing.com

yesteryearpublishing@gmail.com

717-566-8655

Principal: Judith T. Witmer, EdD.

Page Designer: E. Nan Edmunds

In Appreciation

Book Design and Layout
E. Nan Edmunds

First Reader/Reviewer and Preface Writer
The Reverend Barry L. Stopfel '65

Editorial Contributors
Ann Landis Kopp '65
Susan Irene Petrina '65

Researchers for HHS Parents
Barbara Olson Bowser '62
Betty Musser Radle '62

Materials/Memorabilia
Marilyn Menear Demey '66
Jeannine Lehmer Groff '69
Jan Brightbill Heckenluber '72
Esther Engle Hivner, HHS
Alan Larsen '68
William Minsker, Faculty
Sandra Naples Lockerman '74
Faye (Hughes) and Edward Parmer '67

Draft Reader/Reviewer
Nancy L. Hivner '72

Chart of Parents/Children
Elaine Mader Royer '65

Table of Contents

Preface   xii

Dedication   xiv

Introduction   17

   Chapter 1   Heritage of the Baby Boomers   29

   Chapter 2   The 1950s: Forerunner to the Boomers   61

   Chapter 3   Cycles of History and Generations   91

   Chapter 4   The 1960s: Passages and Defining Moments   111

   Chapter 5   High School in a World Turned Upside Down   131

   Chapter 6   Leaving   163

   Chapter 7   Adjusting   203

   Chapter 8   Maturing   247

   Chapter 9   Changing   279

   Chapter 10   Metamorphosing   313

Reflections   343

Scrapbook   405

B-1 was not just a room. It was a different universe.

Beach Boys, in my room...

As I write I wonder, "How did this come to be?" Age 70, that is. With all the aches and pains, twists, turns, successes, failures and wisdom that comes with a life lived day-by-day until one is, well, 70. How can this be?

I am a graduate of the class of 1965 at Lower Dauphin High School. I am one of the Boomers about whom so much has been written and about whom the "English Students" is a chronicle.

I believe we do ourselves a disservice if we underestimate what we meant to each other during our years at LD. It was a time of being born and shaped. No insignificant matter. And to share that experience is more than we can describe because words are sometimes inadequate. It truly is beyond rhetoric and heads toward, "You had to have been there."

In the intervening years we were born and shaped by so much else in life beyond the years at LD. The phrase "time flies," and that ever-present reminder from our parents, "You'll see how fast time seems to go when you are older," no longer seem to be innocent clichés.

Psychologists say that if we reminisce with abandon we live longer and happier lives. So let's have at it with a reflection on an iconic room, B-1.

If we think about it, all of our lives have a narrative. A story line composed of time, place, and context. In that light I see B-1 as both a place and a metaphor for one part of our narrative.

B-1 was home base. It was social, academic, personal, a place to return to in order to get one's balance and begin again; a place of primary concern for school work like studying, tests, and grades; a place for shaping relationships between student and teacher; where the training of our minds was implicit and where academic rigor was demanded; where human kindness and respect flourished.

B-1 frequently was a haven for some on the margins of thought who had the freedom to speak openly about what troubled or concerned them, a workshop to sort through intellectual ideas that fell outside the box. And often it was a sanctuary for some who, if they were true to themselves, couldn't possibly color within the lines; and sometimes a place of healing and hope for students who were bullied, taunted, and rejected. It was a truly safe place long before such a place became widely known as a necessity for some in our present world.

It was a significant place for creating opportunities for our collective lives. We were urged on to as much creativity as we could muster—proms, newsletters, after school clubs of all descriptions to attract the students to fully participate.

It was our own special universe, our Kingdom, a mystical place, yet a place for senior class executive committee business. We intuitively—and by observation knew—that B-1 was where it all happened—play rehearsals, tutoring, prom match-making (notices posted as to who was still available to be invited), practicing music, a haven for choir ex-patriates, using a piano that had found its way to B-1, script-writing for our Commencement choralogues, seeking advice, rehearsing speeches to be delivered in Speech Class the following day, critiquing of term papers, repository for "primary sources" to substantiate those term papers, and, often, just collecting ourselves to face whatever challenges elsewhere awaited us. It was where even the more confident of us stopped by when we were troubled, under the universal guise of "Do you have a minute?"[1]

As a metaphor I think of B-1 as a kind of birth. A moment when one is shaken awake; where one takes a deep breath and dives into a whole new experiment in life. Each of us in that place began to grow at what now seems an alarming pace. More than being born in a particular year, it was the experiment that we began that made us Boomers.

In a perfect world I suppose all classrooms should or could be a place of an expanding universe, a place where nothing worth imagining is too far and where exploration beyond the conventional and institutional can be commenced. Perhaps more of us than we can know longed for that universe. And perhaps, after we left, other students also discovered it at LD and more specifically in B-1.

It was certainly that for me so I may have a bias. But I do know a portal into the spectacular unknown when I experience one. What comes to my mind is, "was blind, but now I see." It was in B-1 that I, and to the extent that it is true, "we" learned to see further than we thought we could.

As we recall the remarkable memories from that place let us not forget that our vision, honed there in so many ways, remains strong and there are more discoveries to be made. Seventy or not, we are Boomers. From the beginning we were intrepid. And so we remain.

Barry L. Stopfel
Class of '65

To the members of the Lower Dauphin High School Class of 1965 who are part of the larger American High School Class of 1965, deemed by birth to be the largest cohort of the 1960s and by history to be the most representative cohort of the decade—

The Baby Boomers

This work is a celebration of all Baby Boomers, those who were members of the Classes graduated from Lower Dauphin High School in the 1960s, and especially to a specific class in a distinctive high school. The Class of 1965 was not only a singular sensation in and of itself, but was in a very special place which in many ways seems to have been built especially for the Boomers, providing just the nurturing they needed to come of age.

To The Class

While every class thinks it is special—and well it should, history confirms that your Class of 1965 was the most representative class of that decade—more than just being the largest. Little did you know that, being thrown together in eighth grade, you as a cohort born in 1947 were to make history. And where better to make it than in a newly created high school district, with no entrenched customs, wide open for you to create your own.

You didn't know one another, except for the few who had been your cohorts in your small classes sprinkled among the five separate schools from which you were being sent. A large number of you had been together in seventh grade in the local junior-senior high school, but most were coming directly from rural elementary schools (Grades 1-8) with little experience in leadership or sense of rebellion that was to be your destiny by virtue of being born in a particular time, a time that was ripe for being re-defined.

There was an uncommon energy at this new school known as Lower Dauphin. This partly was because of the youth of the teachers—at least half of whom were in their first or second year—and partly by the arrangement of the junior high grades (7th, 8th, 9th) in separate "wings" of the building where each grade was free to shape its own identity. Importantly, this school was a fresh canvas and everyone was poised to share in a newly designed adventure.

There were no traditions when in the fall of 1960 you arrived as eighth graders. The school colors (blue and white) had already been decided, possibly in tribute to the nearby Olmsted Air Force Base, which was the inspiration for selecting the falcon bird as the mascot, or maybe because no other school in the surrounding area was using these colors. The music for the Alma Mater had been composed that summer by the new band director and the lyrics selected as a result of a contest held in the school; everything else would be designed or decided as the first year of the new decade unfolded. Each person—teachers and students alike—would be part of making those choices, through a sense of common purpose, which also was not yet clear to everyone.

Lest you think there was chaos with 1300 students coming to a new school district, there was not. Far from it. Rather, there was a mood of camaraderie. It may have been a bit frightening as well, because of the trepidation of both students and teachers of facing experiences never yet ventured. Nonetheless—and perhaps without fully realizing it, everyone was on the cusp of an adventure they all could help direct. And they did. In the doing, everyone, with or without knowing, became part of the "singular sensation" that is Lower Dauphin High School.

None of the students in that building during its first year (Classes of 1961, 1962, 1963, 1964, 1965, and 1966) would have had a thought that their generation would write history as the **Baby Boomers,** and most certainly, the Class of 1965 could not have known that they would have a standing in history as the most representative group of the 1960s decade.

For most of the students, however, just getting through the first day of meeting new teachers, as well as 80 percent of their classmates that they had not known before, was challenge enough. And they accepted the challenge, perhaps not seeing it as a trial any greater than getting through the first day.

Poise, Success, and all that Pizzazz...

One singular sensation
Every little step they take
One thrilling combination
Every move that they make
One moment in their presence
And you can forget the rest
For the class is second best to none
They really are the one!

They walk into a room and you know
They are uncommonly rare, quite unique
Peripatetic, poetic and chic
They walk into a room and you know

From their maddening poise, effortless whirl
They are the special class strolling
Can't help all of their qualities extolling
Loaded with charisma they are jauntily
Sauntering, ambling, shambling.

One moment in their presence
And you can forget the rest
For they are second best to none
So give them your attention
Do I really have to mention
They really are the one![1]

Introduction

It has been almost six decades since the Baby Boomers (without yet knowing they would bear this generational designation) entered Lower Dauphin, filling it to capacity even in its first year. All were strangers—teachers, administrators, support staff, "cafeteria ladies," custodians, and students. Overwhelmed with schedules, new faces, lack of desks and an insufficient number of books, the teachers—with six classes (plus an activity period) a day, many classes with more than thirty students, and the students—awed by the building and how to find their classrooms as well as the gymnasium and the lavatories—spent one of the longest and shortest days they had ever experienced. It took weeks to remember the names of everyone, and nearly as long to remember the order of each day's schedule.

In retrospect, we remember with incredulity the few real problems we had. Parents were quietly supportive, a Parent-Teacher Organization was formed, the equipment for the vocational shops and the bass drum—as well as band uniforms—finally arrived, and the day came when we remembered *everyone's* name.

We soon had a championship football team (with previous high school opponents now on the same team), an eager, cohesive marching band, 35 students vying to work in the library, and students asking for schedule changes so they could join the choir—especially once it was announced that the director would be producing a musical! The commitment by the School Board to provide late afternoon ("activity") busses made it possible for any student (with parental permission) to participate in a myriad of after school programs during every season.

All who were in this adventure together hold special memories in their hearts, and it continues to be surprising when a former student reaches out ten, twenty, or even fifty years later to confess a prank or, more often, to say "thank you." That scenario is not unfamiliar, but it always catches one by surprise. So does the fact that most teachers have "unforgettable" and/or "favorite" classes—not always the same!

The special bond with particular classes occurred for various reasons, not always easily explained. Often classes for which a teacher is the Advisor were memorable because students and teachers worked together on a fund-raiser or a play or a team. Teachers also remember classes with fondness because of acts of kindness, or with overcoming a common obstacle. Some students are memorable because they, for a variety of reasons, are in that teacher's class for more than one particular subject or for multiple years. And some are unforgettable because of the friendships that endure for a lifetime.

Little did any of us know what a very special class those who entered the eighth grade in the fall of 1960 would become, not only to me personally but to everyone who has any knowledge of the Class of 1965. Whether it was the time in history or the "chemistry" among them or the fact that many of them initially were strangers to one another or the excitement of beginning a completely new high school, or whether it was simply the combination of the right people coming together at the right time, the important result is a group of friends who are part of history, not just as "Boomers" but as trend-setters and leaders in every walk of life.

In speaking to the Class of 1965 I would add the following:

It is your class that led me to really understand the phrase "born ten years too soon," for I saw in you many things that were not possible for my own high school classmates. Even as adults we lived under United States presidents, such as George Herbert Walker Bush, who were more than a decade older than our generation, to ones who were a decade younger, such as Bill Clinton and George W. Bush, never seeing a president who was of our cohort age. (We are the only generation to not have one of our own as President.)

As teenagers (Incidentally the one claim to social history my class shared is that we were the first generation universally to be referred to as "teen-agers."), my classmates and I found ourselves (without knowing it at the time, of course) in the middle of two notable historical periods. Our cohort class was stuck in the middle, *dismissed* as the "Silent Generation." We were sandwiched between the WWII generation and the "Baby Boomers" and were, as a group, overlooked partly because there were so few of us and partly because we didn't understand that we could protest about this. We were brought up to "be good," to not question adults, and to obey the rules. And we did.

We also were a high school class at a time when women in general were not expected to attend college, even though our teachers gave as much time and attention to the girls in class as to the boys. I believe they saw in us some potential, but society wasn't quite ready for us. Another oddity for 1955 was that all seven of the high honor students in my class were female. (Two of us later earned doctorates—three, if we count the one who was not on the high honors list.) Two males [not high honor students] also claim medical degrees—although this is too small a sample from which to draw any general conclusions.

What strikes me most clearly in your generation, only later to be known as the "Baby Boomers," is your ease with one another, particularly your ability to establish and maintain friendships. I am sure, like young people since time immemorial, you had your moments of doubt (your letters from college attest to that), but there was always a sense of confidence not seen in previous generations of youth. Part of it was the fact that your parents had lived through the hard times of World War II, becoming part of what is now called the "Greatest Generation."

What I do believe is that your parents instilled in you the idea of *possibilities*, that you would have choices they never had. They also were the first generation of parents who could begin to enjoy their offspring, to provide for them, and clearly to voice their expectations of them.

High school teachers saw you as energetic, bright, ambitious, and—an observation they had not previously encountered—they saw you as very comfortable with one another, a social phenomenon no previous generation had enjoyed to the extent that yours did. Prior to the 1960s (with the possible exception of some of the Jazz Age cohort) young people had demonstrated few or no skills in just being "friends" with the opposite sex.

In the 1950s, there were boys and there were girls, and few, if any, groups of friends contained both males and females who gathered in clans. In my class a group of boys and girls would rarely, if ever, travel together to a movie or a football game. Even with a borrowed car, the passengers would have been of only one gender (and most certainly of only one race). In stark contrast to this, the high school students of the 1960s found opportunities to form many friendships, perhaps in part because, again, there was such a large pool of you from which to find many friends in common.

The 1960s also saw real per capita income increase by 41 percent, resulting in prosperity for many workers. This new affluence neatly coincided with the impact of the bumper crop of post-World War II baby boomers coming of age just in time to be indulged by their parents who (many for the first time) found themselves with discretionary income. More parents were able to provide a car (or at least to loan the family car), money, and permission for their young to "go have fun." Thus, the decade of the sixties became a time of optimism, especially for the privileged young who believed there were no limits to how comfortable and powerful and healthy and happy they could be.

I don't know how many of you remember my telling you that your generation would rule the world. And you do. I was struck in particular (but not really surprised) by the number of persons named in various articles in the November 14, 2005 issue of *Time* whose age was given as 58, also your age at that time.

That power and desire to make your own way on your own terms has not changed. You have lived through some of the most wonderful discoveries of humankind and some of the most terrible. You watched John Glenn's first orbit in space and Neil Armstrong's first walk on the moon, and you watched with fear and helplessness when friends succumbed to the scourge of AIDS.

Samuel Huntington, in his book *American Politics: The Promise of Disharmony* about the 1960s, discussed why some generations are different from the norm. He explained that most generations in history have been organizational ones, preferring to motor along in their daily grooves, directed by others. The 1960s, however, constituted what he called a "creedal passion period," something that erupts every few generations in Anglo-Saxon culture and has its roots in England's seventeenth-century Civil War. Despite the indulgences found in the 1960s generation which he readily acknowledged, Huntington viewed you as essentially Puritan, upset that **institutions were not living up to ideals.**

This, I believe, is the essence that others admire in your class. You are idealists, but willing to work to achieve those ideals. And most of the time you have succeeded. More importantly, you give back to your community, and, yes, to your Alma Mater. You truly have taken a part of your heritage with you and left a part of yourselves in the roots of that heritage. I thank you for allowing me to be a part of that legacy. It has been quite an adventure!

"Time It Was and What a Time It Was"[2]

When you entered a new high school in the fall of 1960 as eighth graders, you may or may not have felt what upperclassmen and faculty felt—a sense of uncommon energy in this new school not usually seen in educational institutions. Perhaps part of it was the youth of the staff or perhaps it was the fact of a shared new adventure for both staff and students that made such a powerful impact on this new school which still had the paint drying and flooring in some rooms not yet finished.

Teachers were supported, trusted in their judgment, and encouraged to try new approaches to learning. With six classes a day, some with up to 39 students in a class, innovation was welcomed. The result was academic excellence. The pace was set and we never looked back.

In football, aspiring lettermen were easily recognized by the LD on their helmets and their low cut shoes with white stripes. The practice field was affectionately called The Dust Bowl and a seven-man sled was added to make practice more effective.

There were 75 million of you (only later termed the Baby Boomers) born between 1946 and 1964, according to the U.S. Census Bureau. However, according to the Strauss–Howe generational theory (See Chapter 3), Baby Boomers are defined as those born between 1943 and 1960, which would include those who were between 58 and 75 years old in 2018. Others view the Baby Boomers as those who were graduated from high school between 1960 and 1977, although those in the latter years more likely identify with Generation X.

With maternity wards filled to capacity, it was a sea of babies with many of you spending your first days of life neatly tucked away in hospital hallways, operating suites, even boiler rooms—one crib after another lined up in a seemingly endless line of babies.

Being born in a child-focused society, there was always someone looking after you. While you may not have welcomed the inoculations, you benefited by the sweeping advances against childhood illness, diphtheria and polio, and fluoridating the water to protect teeth.

Even today your generation has the perception of being very different from other generations. You were reared to believe you were "special" and you enjoyed the most secure family life in American history; even today you retain strong family ties.

Under Dr. Benjamin Spock you grew up with national optimism shining on you. Parents wanted you to live in modern houses and provided these as much as possible; they saw you being on the fringe of a golden era. No wonder you were viewed as adorable babies, cute grade schoolers, and strikingly handsome teens. After all, you were!

You were also what was termed the first **standardized** generation—with similar kitchens, houses, curricula in school, and atomic bomb drills.

Again, because there were many more of you than cohorts in the previous decade, the crowding you endured in nearly every aspect of your lives created a deep need for privacy and a striving for individual distinction. You disliked being labeled and were committed to individualism, self-reliance, and introspection.

As you were growing up, your future appeared to be happy, easy, uncomplicated, and prosperous. To most of you, poverty, disease, and crime were invisible or, at worst, temporary inconveniences. You did not expect painful challenges or tragic outcomes, because overall everything was good. This became your normal.

Because your lives on the whole were free from danger, your cohort felt free to cultivate strong inner lives. The main difference, however, between your generation and earlier ones is that what previous generations thought of as privileges, Boomers viewed as rights.

More of you were able to complete high school and go to college than any other generation before you; however, you expected to have the same things when you walked out of college or trade school that your parents didn't have until they were 35 or 40 years of age.

However, again because there were so many of you, you experienced more competition for jobs and promotions, with fewer opportunities to get ahead. This gave you even more reason to concentrate on the development of the inner self.

You sought economic security through college, your own rooms, your own homes, automobiles, air conditioners and refrigerators with no worry about economic survival.

You still

1. Seek instant **gratification** and products that reflect your uniqueness.
2. Are more likely to **reject traditional moral principles** governing the consumer market.
3. Usually have a well-thought-out sense of **priorities.**
4. Are typically **separated** from traditional, social, and political roles.
5. **Reject traditional social labels**, choosing to go through life as individuals.
6. **Do not like descriptive labels of yourselves.**

Most of you never knew an environment in which there wasn't a television set. Because of this, you did not have a chance to gradually <u>learn about ideas from adults</u>. Instead, information was blasted at you without your having the skills to analyze or reflect upon what you were hearing and watching.

Television affected you as it taught you how to be an adult without intervention from your parents. It also presented a world in which there was remarkable similarity of all things no matter what channel you watched. You were also the first childhood generation to be target-marketed by advertising agencies.

Think about this: your first contact with the real world was television. You, therefore, had <u>less</u> time hearing stories written for children, less time playing alone or with other children, and less time spent in conversation and family interaction, all privations of sentient experience.

Your world, for the most part, was crowded with others your own age. Because you shared a degree of social and academic overcrowding unknown to previous generations, you could not be handled as individuals; there were too many of you. Thus, you found (or created) new limits (without understanding it, of course, as this was your "normal") on individual achievement.

While you may not have noticed because it was your conventional mode, in schools your generation was packed together like no other generation in history. Not only were there more students per classroom but the sheer number of you also led to a teacher shortage. From 1960 through 1969 your cohort class was larger than any other in the decade. At Lower Dauphin High School, there were 129 in the graduating class of 1961 and double that at 265 in the Class of 1965.

Another forfeiture your cohort experienced was losing an important chance to learn how to participate, because you couldn't all be in the play or a cheerleader or on a first string sports team. Such situations led to some enterprising high schoolers to form additional groups so that more of you could participate. For example, in Lower Dauphin because there were not enough uniforms for more majorettes, several of the girls decided to form a marching-unit dance group on their own, make their own uniforms, and become a part of the marching band as the Falconettes.

As a generation you are guarded and you demand your own personal space; you believe the government has no business meddling in your lives; and you generally don't care where the car comes from as long as it works. (Some specific exceptions for burgundy Pontiacs, of course, were true.)

And did you ever think, in the 1990s when the prediction was made, that the decaying public infrastructure would be the single greatest threat to your economic future and that this would directly impact you some day? (Count the number of decayed bridges in the United States, or even in Pennsylvania only.)

WHEN YOU WERE ONLY 16

On August 28, 1963, 250,000 people gathered at the Lincoln Memorial to support the civil rights legislation the President had proposed and, instead, heard the iconic "I have a dream" message. You never forgot.

WHEN YOU WERE IN 11-12TH GRADES

- The Beatles appeared on Ed Sullivan (thus being given a public stamp of approval in the entertainment realm, if not by parents).
- Barry Goldwater was nominated, setting an angry new tone for politics.
- Inner cities unleashed the first of many long, hot summers.
- The "Free Speech Movement" at Berkeley took aim against the Academic Establishment.
- On December 2, 1964, after Mario Savio had addressed thousands of rallying students at Berkeley, they walked into Sproul Hall and held a sit-in against the university's refusal to grant them political freedom. Police arrested the students and 773 of them were hauled away, the largest mass arrest in California history.

WHEN YOU ENTERED COLLEGE

Most of you who entered college in the fall of 1965 missed the opening of The Raven in nearby Swatara Township. The Raven was a dance club for teens, housed in a building that looked like a castle. Of the 14,000 teens who held membership cards, on a given night the club drew about 2,000 young people.[3]

WHEN YOU WERE COLLEGE FRESHMEN WRITING HOME

Much to my disbelief, I am really here.

"Everything here seems so fascinating. There's so much to experience and to explore."

Brother, I am hiring me a secretary. This correspondence is getting me down. This makes the twelfth letter I have written tonight. I hope I can finish The Fountainhead in 2 weeks.

I have all this afternoon and this evening to do what I want. I have never experienced such confused feelings in my life. The city is absolutely overwhelming. I'm entranced with the idea of being a college student and yet I'm as sad and lonely as I've ever been. The worst part of it is that I couldn't leave the city if I had to. It's everything I've ever dreamed of.

I feel like a seventh grader again.

No one HERE ever heard of Lower Dauphin.

It is now 2:20 a.m. The other guys decided to do the wash so I went along so we could stick all of it in one load. We have nine washers and dryers for six hundred guys.

Every day I become more sure that this is where I belong, yet it seems that there is no one around that I can express that feeling to.

You know, I'm still scared to invest any money in a college sweatshirt or jacket for fear that I'll flunk out and then won't be able to wear it.

This is my first distress call. I'm homesick. And in all my stupidity, I'm looking at it objectively.

I wish there was another method of cheap communication besides letter writing.

I was thinking lately, "What would I have done in high school if I had studied as I do now?"

Tomorrow is last day of classes. My bags are all packed, but I don't want to leave. This is where I belong now. I can't imagine being anywhere else.

WHEN YOU WERE COLLEGE JUNIORS

In October 1967, 50,000 protesters marched on the Pentagon. Six hundred were arrested for trespassing and 47 were hospitalized after being tear-gassed.

On a lesser scale, there was also picketing on college campuses against the computer-punch-card with protesters carrying signs, "I Am a Student! Do not Fold, Spindle, or Mutilate!

WHEN YOU WERE COLLEGE SENIORS WORRYING ABOUT THE DRAFT

In August 1968 the most militant antiwar demonstrators massed in Chicago to protest against the Democratic convention. Police clubbed protesters, shoved them through plate-glass windows, sprayed them with Mace, and beat them. Richard Nixon vowed to the American people that he would hear their voices.

AFTER YOU WERE GRADUATED FROM COLLEGE

In the summer of 1969 three dramatic national events occurred:

- July 18, the incident at Chappaquiddick
- July 20, the moon landing of Apollo 11
- August 1969, the largest civilian generational gathering in American history at Woodstock of 400,000 youths in their late teens and twenties.

You also were dealing with Vietnam. Although America had entered the war on a limited basis from 1964 to 1969, the year 1969 is viewed as a symbolic date in the Vietnam conflict when Nixon decided to end the war.

What made Vietnam different is that it was so public, viewed every day on the news. It also was hard for most citizens to understand its purpose. Lies were told to convince the American public that "we" were winning as more people began to question authority—on all fronts.

On October 15, 1969, a national teach-in against the war occurred. As many as 10 million Americans were involved in this, the largest public protest ever held in America. Thousands of teach-ins and sit-ins were held throughout the country.

The draft system created a wide split between Boomers who went to Vietnam and those who did not. For many, this rift has never healed.

This division regarding America's presence in Vietnam was one of the reasons for the many riots, protests, and disregard for authority, the likes of which America had never seen before. Counter cultures sprang up everywhere, but the first, biggest, and most visible occurred in the Haight-Ashbury area of San Francisco. Haight-Ashbury was the first community in America to be founded on making, taking, and selling drugs. Social historians say that consumption and distribution of illegal and experimental drugs, more than any other single factor, was responsible for the creation and development of America's many countercultural enclaves.

WHEN YOU WERE IN YOUR MID-TWENTIES

In your mid-twenties you remained detached, many of you showing an emotional intensity older generations found strange, even compulsive.

- Exercise faddists searched for the "runner's high."
- Backpackers with graduate degrees sparked a back-to-nature movement unlike anything seen since the turn of the nineteenth century.
- Meditative diet faddists triggered "the century's Second Golden Age of Food Quackery."
- Those of you who were born to be serious were seeking meaningful careers or starting small, eclectic businesses.

WHEN YOU APPROACHED MIDLIFE

You took it upon yourselves to grow into a new sense of responsibility and self-denial.

You saw (and still see) yourselves as the embodiment of moral wisdom. On matters of right and wrong, you care little for the opinions of others, older or younger, nor do you emulate them.

AS YOU TURNED SEVENTY

In addition to going into denial, as a cohort you have a generational persona, different from people born at another time. You share a zeitgeist, a spirit of your times that shapes your direction from youth through old age. You have a common location in history and common beliefs. You share attitudes about family, life, gender roles, politics, lifestyle and the future. In your case you have had a search for self and a culture of narcissism, having difficulty reaching consensus and mobilizing as a unit.

Your quest has always been how to live individually in this crowded society, rather than how to change it collectively. This is the natural order of your generation to be an individual while being crowded in a group. Hold on to this trait that makes you who you are….

To dream the impossible dream
To fight the unbeatable foe
To bear with unbearable sorrow
To run where the brave dare not go

To right the unrightable wrong
To love pure and chaste from afar
To try when your arms are too weary
To reach the unreachable star.

…this is our quest, to follow that star
No matter how hopeless, no matter how far…[4]

Introduction Endnotes:

1. Adapted from "One Singular Sensation," from *Chorus Line.*

2. Paul Simon.

3. It was open on Tuesday, Friday, and Saturday evenings in summer and on Friday and Saturday evening during the school year. Would teens today believe that such a place existed that attracted name entertainers such as Little Anthony and the Imperials, The Vibrations, The Ronnettes, The Drifters, Major Lance, Mary Welles, The Impressions, Isley Brothers, Martha and the Vandellas, and The Four Tops!

4. "The Impossible Dream," from *Man of La Mancha.*

Chapter 1

Heritage of the Baby Boomers

O joy! That in our embers
Is something that doth live

Ode on Intimations of Immortality
Wordsworth

Education in Hummelstown
1764 - 1960

While not all members of The English Students spent their childhood in Hummelstown, the community is the base for and the origin of the Lower Dauphin School District. Thus, to understand the heritage shared by all graduates of Lower Dauphin High School, we start our quest of understanding *why* you are *who* you are by beginning our journey in this small town that provided the core for what became the legacy of all graduates, not the least of which are the Baby Boomers of the 1960s.

Locations and Buildings

While there were various locations for the schools in Hummelstown, the first building of record was one of logs erected on ground donated by the founder of Hummelstown, Frederick Hummel, circa 1764. In 1790 the school room was moved to a second log structure west of the present Lutheran Parish House.

In 1845, as the population grew, the school community was divided into three small "districts." Following that distribution, a single, central school was established which occupied all three floors of the rear of the building which later housed Smith's Hardware Store on Main Street. In 1892 a new school building, later to be known as the Elizabeth Price School, was built on Water Street.

In 1926 a two-story brick building was erected on the corner of Short and John Streets. This would be known as the High School and would be used as such until the fall of 1960.

Not only have the pupils been given the advantage of a building built and equipped along the most practical and scientifically up-to-date lines, but the community at large has also found the new school a most desirable place in which to congregate on special occasions.

In the summer of 1930, the high school building was enlarged and a "splendid gymnasium" was added with parallel bars, a horizontal bar, jumping standards and other equipment. Wrestling and boxing also were introduced, along with calisthenics, indoor baseball, basketball, and volleyball games, with the medicine ball and dodge ball designed for the girls.

> *Without the townspeople there would be no school as we have it; there would be no gymnasium as well constructed as ours; there would be no additions to the building. …there would be no football, basketball or baseball. …there would be no athletic field—the pride of Hummelstown.*

Class Sizes at Hummelstown

Since 1875 Hummelstown has provided a complete high school program. Its first graduating class, in 1878, consisted of eight members; its last class, 1960, includes portraits of 47 seniors in its final yearbook, *The Tatler*, which tied with the Class of 1958 as the class with the largest number of students.[1]

Like in most American small towns, the schools in Hummelstown were central to the community and were a microcosm of America. Their buildings provided space for community gatherings for programs or meetings, and were central to the education of the children of the community. Also similar to most small towns, Hummelstown was multi-generational and the history of the town can be followed through its schools.

Yearbooks

Second only to local newspapers in following the history of generations is the yearbook, an annual publication of the schools, itself displaying an American-style history. Yearbooks are the record of a particular set of students all of the same age who (often) traveled 12 years together. And like most high school traditions, yearbooks also imitated traditions often first seen in college yearbook formats.

Most sources agree that the first college yearbook was created and published by Yale College in 1806. While class photographs were not widely available until years later in the mid-19th Century, the National Museum of American History has in its collections an early 1860 yearbook from Rutgers, New Jersey with photographs.

College Yearbooks

Pennsylvania's Ursinus College published its first yearbook to include photographs in 1896. This yearbook, known as *The Ruby*, was produced by the Junior Class for the Senior Class, as was the *Quittapahilla* of Lebanon Valley College in Annville. However, the practice of class portraits was not common until the early 20th Century. One pioneer, for example, is the *1902 Yale Banner*, particularly noted for including profile pictures of the graduating class.

1902

High School Yearbooks

The first high school yearbook, "The Evergreen," was published in 1845 in Waterford, New York; however, yearbooks were not mass-produced until 1880 when the letterpress allowed for printing the books at an affordable cost.

Many high schools had started newspapers in the 19th century and it was these that were expanded into yearbooks. Hummelstown's earliest publication was a newspaper titled *The Tatler*. Because the first issue to which this author had access is dated Vol II, No. 4, 1919, it can be presumed that this school newspaper originated in 1918 with Vol I.

When in 1930 offset printing made yearbooks affordable for smaller high schools, Hummelstown High School published its first yearbook, *The Tatler*, fifty-two years after its first class had been graduated.

Most early high school yearbooks had soft covers, similar in texture to heavy weight blotting paper. Publications then gradually moved to hard covers, except for the years during WWII when many returned to a soft cover because of cost and rationing of materials; during this time Hummelstown's covers were spiral-bound with a metal or plastic coil.

Yearbooks allow for communities to remember the students and the activities of the schools of the past. For example, a central Pennsylvania high school class in 1920 wrote in its yearbook,

"This takes us back to the day when as freshmen we proudly waved goodbye to

Victor Jones,[2] who left with his brother, Worrell, to fight in the World's War.

Vic was our class president, and we miss him. Although only a freshman, Vic was

one of the first in our school and community to enlist. One of the first boys across,

he was in all of the big and decisive battles of the war. He was twice wounded,

once in the Argonne drive. He has a record to be proud of and the Class of 1920 is

proud to say that he was once one of our members."[3]

Pre-1930s

A review of the 1920s shows that a totally democratization of nearly all aspects of American life occurred during that one decade. The following changes mainly affected young people:

1. **Education.** There was a large increase in the number of co-educational colleges.

2. **Transportation.** The Model T Ford made it possible for more people to afford a car.

3. **Dress and Fashion.** All classes of society began wearing the same kind of clothing, thus blurring the traditional indicators of wealth; further, young women especially were wearing more and more revealing clothing.

4. **Recreation.** More people attended movies and listened to the new radio, recently being offered for sale to the public. There were also more public parks, tennis courts, and golf courses available to all.

5. **The Marketplace.** More goods were available to the general public and the job market kept people in jobs.

Both Boy Scouts and Girl Scouts have a long history in Hummelstown, with the first Boy Scout Troop formed in 1917 (registered in 1921) and soon was followed by at least half a dozen others. Girl Scout troops were first formed in Hummelstown in 1921. Both organizations have had a very positive influence on the youth of Hummelstown and are still very popular.

In the nineteen-twenties America became a leader in world affairs. Automobile sales boomed to nearly 4.6 million, and nearly 43.3 percent of the world's manufactured goods were made in America, an indicator that America had become the greatest financial and creditor nation in the world.[4]

Americans began to enjoy a profitable economy and soon began learning about investing in stocks and bonds. Later generations often mistakenly assumed that "everyone" in the 1920s was playing the stock market and buying on margin. However, the reality is that in a population of 120 million citizens, there were only 1.5 million investors and around 600,000 speculators,[5] not at all the entire nation.

In the last year of the 1920s decade, the number of investors reached its peak as stock prices zoomed out of sight and credit was stretched to help attract more buying. Then, a breaking point occurred on October 24, 1929, the day known in history as "Black Thursday." In a word, the stock market crashed.

Speculators—many of whom had bought on margin[6]—rushed to unload their stocks as the market took a plunge; however, most of them were too late to get rid of their holdings. Within weeks, 1.5

million investors had lost $30 billion in what later was referred to as the Great Crash—a monetary amount equal almost to a third of the entire year's Gross National Product. A panic swept banks and brokerage houses that had financed the investing when the realization dawned on the American public that the nation had experienced the most devastating financial collapse in its history.[7] This did not bode well for the country on the cusp of a new decade in which there would be a world war.

The following are excerpts from some of the early *Tatler* newspapers/magazines from 1919-1929 (Note: While not stated in any earlier publication, there is evidence of a Boys Basketball Team [six members pictured in uniforms] in 1916).

1919

Vol. II, No. 4., Leta Hitz, Editor

- Literary Society program, December 23, 1919.
- High school dance, November 29, held in the Masonic Hall (thought to be in the building on the southwest corner of High and Water, also at one time housing the Junior Order of American Mechanics. The Masonic Order is also said to have met on the 2nd and 3rd floors of the Farmers Bank building.).[8]
- Suggestion made to start a skating club.
- Ten pages of ads, including one from Morris M. Engle.

Vol. II, No. 5, January 30, 1920. Leta Hitz, Editor

- The area of town west of Landis Street was called Landisville.
- First hotel was the Zerfoss Hotel.
- In 1870 the population of Hummelstown was 837.

Vol. II, No. 9, June 3, 1920. Esther Miller, Editor

- A tribute made to the eight graduating seniors.
- The school purchased a piano "on bond" for $225.

Vol. IV, Nos. 17-18-19, November 24, 1921. Martha Brinser, Editor

- 12 seniors, 22 sophomores.
- An editorial on the state of the school building, poorly equipped for school purposes… with a call for improvement.

In 1923 Hummelstown High School had an active Girls Basketball Team and, while not noted in any school publication, an attempt was made in 1923 to organize a football team. A number of boys turned out on the first day, but later lost interest. In 1924 enough interest from the boys led to their playing two games and in 1926 a squad was formed and continued for the remainder of the decade but without a winning season.

Vol. VI, No. 5, Commencement Number, June 2, 1924. Ruth Clark, Editor

- Senior Class Play, noted by its reviewer to be "the best ever given in Hummelstown."

Vol. VIII, No. 5, June 1926. Russel Etter, Editor

- Third annual May Day Celebration.[9]

Vol. IX, No. 2, 1926-27 school year. Russel Etter, Editor

- Editorial asking for an auditorium.
- A photo of the new high school.

Vol. IX, No. 4, 1926-27 school year. Russel Etter, Editor

- Senior Class held a food sale and oyster supper.
- "A successful school paper indicates an energetic school body and the *Tatler* alone is enough to prove that the Alma Mater is the 'giver of all things fine.'"

Vol. IX, No. 5, May 25, 1927. Virginia Gingrich, Editor

- Committee being formed to select a standard school ring.
- Juniors ordered their class pennants.
- J. M. Brightbill advertises "Insulite" to replace lath and plaster.

Vol. X, No. 1, 1927-28. Virginia Gingrich, Editor

- "In Memoriam" tribute for a senior killed in a July 4th lighting fireworks accident.
- "School spirit! Every year it is customary for articles to be written, speeches delivered, and pep meetings held in order to instill into the students of Hummelstown High a greater love for their Alma Mater and more spirit in upholding her traditions."[10]
- The Alumni Association voted that the old seal of the high school be abandoned and the new seal be that selected for the standard high school ring.

Vol. X, No. 2, 1927-28.

- Alumni Association helped fund improvements at the athletic field.

Vol. XI, no. 1. no date given, 39 pages.

- Nine of the eleven senior men enrolled (in school) were on the football team.

- The school board provided a "tackling" dummy.

Vol. XI, No. 4, 1929. Robert Nissley. Editor

- Senior Class trip to DC by train, on the Reading Railway.

1930s

Hummelstown's Bell Telephone system celebrated the new decade by switching to a two-person operator system, after beginning 29 years earlier with 18 customers serviced by one telephone operator. The town would wait for 25 years for the next improvement —a dial system.

The bad economic times of the 1930s brought a rise in high school secret marriages nationally, as well as a drop in divorces. For others who couldn't afford to marry, secret or not, the postponement of marriage and the growing frankness regarding sexual matters led to an increase in premarital scx.[11]

Also gaining strength in the 1930s was the dating-and-rating system initiated by 1920s youth.[12] This idea of a rating standard was promoted by magazines, such as *Scholastic* with its column "Boy Dates Girl." By the mid-1930s *Scholastic* had established itself as the arbiter of high school mores.[13] Because the magazine professed to not discuss the intimate phases of dating, it was viewed by adults as appropriate reading material for youngsters.

Early in 1930 a "wait and see" attitude concerning the economy prevailed; thus, many of the events of the year were not reflective of the terrible times yet to come. Rather, in many quarters of the nation there was a sense of "normalcy" with only occasional flashes of concern reported.

Sinclair Lewis won the Nobel Prize for Literature in 1930 for his satire on middle class life and values in the person of George Babbitt (*Babbitt*, 1922). While many readers took exception to Lewis's indictment of the superficiality of the middle class, others said they recognized the shallow characteristics of George Babbitt *in people they knew.*

The best films of 1930 addressed concerns of the times, including the Academy-Award-winning *All Quiet on the Western Front* based on the book by Erich Maria Remarque.[14] The book (published in 1929) describes the extreme physical and mental stress of the world war. Other notable films of

1930 were *The Blue Angel*, providing a glimpse of decadent pre-Nazi Germany, and *Anna Christie*, a story of redemption, based on the drama by Eugene O'Neill, winner of the Pulitzer Prize for Drama for 1922.[15]

The number of weekly movie-goers in the United States in 1930 increased to 115 million, and the new pastime of miniature golf was introduced with great success in Florida, followed the next year by the installation of driving ranges. Golf had been increasing in popularity and the quadruple triumph ([1] British Amateur, [2] British Open, [3] US Open, and [4] US Amateur) of Bobby Jones at age 28 inspired more words of cabled news than any other individual exploit during 1930.

Early in September of 1930 the United States Stock Exchange began to crack. The Market quickly recovered only to fall again, rise, and fall yet again, until on the morning of October 24, it broke wide open. The leading bankers of New York met to form a buying pool to keep the Market from collapsing and for a few days there was a hopeful rally on the exchange.

However, it soon became obvious that nothing could stem the tide of potential disaster. Telephone lines began to clog with trades, and the ticker was running late in projecting any trends. Within hours, the Stock Exchange's entire system was unable to cope with the emergency of record-breaking trading. As a result, on October 28 the Stock Exchange collapsed and US securities lost $26 billion in value.

The following day, when over sixteen million shares of stock were thrown on the market, was described as "the most devastating day in the history of the New York stock market which may have been the most devastating day in the history of (all) markets."[16] It was not until more than two weeks later on November 13 that a semblance of order was restored to the Stock Exchange.

Shortly after the stock market collapse, still early in 1930, a "wait and see" attitude prevailed in the country. Many citizens still felt a sense of normalcy, holding barely a memory of the short-lived Great War (WWI). Most people in the 1930s still had only occasional flashes of concern for world affairs and America as a nation was still focused on remaining insular.

On the other hand, those who married and planned to start a family during the depths of the Great Depression likely stood in fear of turmoil in Europe, with many of them stating an apprehension of bringing children into such a world. This was reflected in the overall low birthrate for this period—(a birthrate not to be repeated until their children, who would become known as the Silent Generation, produced their own offspring). And, even with the faint rumbles of turmoil in Europe, American families in the 1930s could have had no idea of another world war yet to come.

On the lighter side, radios became popular, both for the news and the music of the big bands, leading to rising sales in musical instruments and, for the first time, the growing number of schools who organized bands and orchestras. This drew large numbers of the students into the novelty of performing.[17] In some schools, "a new idea was introduced with the presentation of the high school operetta" in addition to class plays.[18]

In the center of Hummelstown one of the landmarks of the square was a fountain, later moved to High, Rosanna, and Railroad Streets when a large wooded arch was constructed in the Hummelstown Square by John Bieber as an advertisement for Indian Echo Caverns. The first electric trolley from Hershey was routed to Hummelstown through the arch on the square. However, trolley cars had barely enough room to pass through the arch.

The first yearbook produced by Hummelstown High School was in 1930, edited by H. Cynthia Goshert, with 27 graduating seniors some of whom were part of the first Student Cabinet in the school. Notably among the seniors were Paul Deimler, Kathryn Witmer (Sandel), Carroll Porter, and Sara Jane Buser (Seavers). This class also had been the first freshman class to enter the new high school building. The operetta featuring this class was *Tulip Time*, presented two nights in Hummelstown's Orpheum Theatre.[19]

1931

In a display of national optimism, President Herbert Hoover switched on the lights of the Empire State Building in New York City for the first time. This skyscraper was viewed as the loftiest structure on earth and had been put up in a single year at a cost of $52 million. In contrast, the tailspin of the economy in general began that same summer and continued until mid-1932 when nearly 12 million people—about 25 percent of the workforce—were **unemployed**.

In many cities (usually not so in small towns) soup kitchens, breadlines, and shanty towns became common while jobless men began picking through the refuge of nearby dumps for building materials. These they used to construct makeshift shacks in common areas they named Hoovervilles. On cold nights many of these homeless men covered themselves with newspapers they mockingly called their "special Hoover bed sheets."

As might be expected, the country blamed President Hoover for the state of the economy, and the Empire State skyscraper that had been illuminated earlier that year instead became a symbol for the collapse of capitalism.

Farmers were particularly hard hit by the failing economy as they faced foreclosure on their farm lands. In desperation, some armed themselves with shotguns, dumped milk on the highways, and allowed their crops to rot in the fields because prices for milk and grain did not cover the cost of hiring the workers needed for harvesting.

Many unemployed men of all classes were reduced to selling apples on the streets or, in despair, to begging for food. Luxury hotels were empty and Pullman trains made many scheduled runs without a single passenger. In his syndicated press column in January 1931, former president Calvin Coolidge made one of his characteristic understated comments, "The country is not in good condition."[20]

The *1931 Tatler* is notable in that even in the midst of a failing economy, a smiling—and resilient —school marching band is shown in their new uniforms paid for by community fund-raising. The band held the spotlight in the Memorial Day parade and a new instrumental program boasted a budding orchestra.

The school also produced a musical comedy/operetta (as did many schools in the early 1920s). Hummelstown High School presented *Purple Towers*, a popular operetta. In addition, in any given year, there was an annual Junior Class Play and a Senior Class Play, along with a Senior Card Party and Dance. Two popular clubs were La Bonne Ami Club for girls and the Student Christian Association for boys.

1932

In the spring and summer of 1932, a major protest, later to be known as the Bonus March on Washington, began when nearly 10,000 veterans of World War I camped out all summer on the capital grounds and environs, rallying Congress to pass the veterans' bonus bill. These veterans, who also set up shantytowns across the Potomac River from the city, refused to leave (most had no jobs to which to return and saw this protest as necessary to call attention to their plight), even on orders of President Hoover. Finally, General Douglas MacArthur was ordered to take care of the problem, which he did by sending military troops into the area, forcing the veterans out by setting fire to the shacks.[21]

Near the end of 1932 the entire economy was snowballing downhill as consumer buying declined sharply and citizens hid their currency in home safe-deposit boxes or under their own mattresses. During the next several years every business in the country suffered and millions of workers were furloughed. Many of the jobless defaulted on their installment payments and were forced to use their life savings for daily expenses of survival. Many people had nothing to fall back on except to move in with relatives.

Things were calmer in small towns such as Hummelstown, although the marriage rate was lower than usual because of the economy.

1933

Nineteen thirty-three saw the worst year of the Depression as well as the inauguration of Franklin Delano Roosevelt. Even with banks throughout the country failing, a self-confident Roosevelt proclaimed a four-day bank holiday, essentially closing all banks in the nation. He also called Congress into special session to enact legislation to launch what he called his New Deal.

By the end of the year there would be 4,004 bank closures, a steady 25 percent unemployment, and a shutdown of 31 percent of the nation's productive capacity.[22] Small towns struggled, but managed to keep youth programs going, particularly sports, because school boards believed sports and music were necessary for young people, especially in hard economic times.

Despite limited funding, L. Bruce Henderson, first as a coach and later as a principal at Hummelstown High School, probably did more to establish football firmly at the school than anyone else did. In 1933 he coached the first "Bulldog" team to win the regional Lower Dauphin County title, later helping the schools get lights for night football. He also was one of Hummelstown's most winning coaches. The outstanding teams in the 1930s were the following:

1933: E: Don Thomas, Frank Shuey, Melvin Davidson, John Mosser, Dave Keller, Carroll Lentz, R. Allemann, Merle Shaffer, Harold Hainley, Carroll Zerfoss, Russell Wolf, William Fenner, Wilson Bieber, Ken Walters, Wendell Johnson, Tom Peterson, Ed Ludwig, Mick Mauro, Don Ludwig, Carl Stoner, and Don Jacobs.

1939: E: Richard Eckenroth, Russ Erby, T. Earl Handwerk, John Hall, John Ebersole, Charles Brandt, Chester Martin, John Dillon, Warren Strite, Rudy Petrina, John Hummel, Harold Kreiser, Harry Miller, and Harold Smith.[23]

The Federal Emergency Relief Act and the Civil Works Administration of 1933 soon had over four million people building roads, schoolhouses, airports, parks, sewers, and other public works. The Public Works Administration funded projects on reforestation, flood control, rural electrification, water works, sewage plants, schools, and slum clearance.

During the same year (1933) the Emergency Farm Mortgage Act was charged with halting foreclosures against farms, providing federal refunding of mortgages while the Home Owners Loan Corporation refinanced small mortgages on private dwellings. The Civilian Conservation Corps (CCC) helped to restore the nation's natural resources and to give unemployed young men useful work.

In Hummelstown, *The Tatler* staff was busy producing an impressive edition of their legacy. This book is larger than that of 1932, with an Art Deco style (there is no doubt this is a 1930s book!), creative writing, especially the clever style used in commenting on events of the school year (Is the writer Fern Fromm?).

1934

The 1934 Tatler staff rose to the unspoken challenge of its predecessor with a very classy frontispiece and divider pages. Their dedication to "The Townspeople" is well-written and the entire publication well done. This is an impressive class whose members were the undisputed champion of Dauphin County in football (fall season 1933)—undefeated and untied. The Mixed Glee Club was huge in size, which is likely why the operetta was double cast. The La Bonne Ami and Students' Christian Association were both outsize.

As other yearbooks had done, the staff of '34 kept a running record of their year with quips:

- ✓ Oct. 7 – HHS consecrated Middletown's new Athletic Field by burying Middletown under it in a 12-6 victory (first bonfire).
- ✓ Nov. 6. Drive began for the fence fund.
- ✓ Nov. 13. The fence!! We're going to get it.
- ✓ Nov. 25. VICTORY OVER HERSHEY, 7-6.
- ✓ Nov. 27. Squad gets day off.

As a fillip, the student artist provided skilled cartoon caricatures of seniors sprinkled throughout the advertising pages. This staff set the bar high for local high school yearbooks.

1935

At the beginning of the year Amelia Earhart flew solo from Hawaii to California. February saw the introduction of the board game Monopoly in the United States. Other notable events included the conviction of Richard Hauptmann for the kidnapping and murder of Charles Lindberg's toddler son; the discovery and development of Prontosil[24], the first broadly effective antibiotic; and the banning of airplanes from flying over the White House.

March 22 marked the world's first television program from Berlin, Germany, and in April the "great dust storm" hit eastern New Mexico and Colorado, with western Oklahoma the hardest affected.

May brought the New Deal which created the Works Progress Administration. On a lighter note, on the 24th the first nighttime Major League Baseball game was played between the Cincinnati Reds and Philadelphia Phillies at Crosley Field in Cincinnati, Ohio. At the end of the month, Babe Ruth appeared in his last career game.

On August 14 President Franklin D. Roosevelt signed the Social Security Act into law. On September 13 Howard Hughes set an airspeed record of 352 mph in his Hughes H-1 Racer, and on the 30th of the month President Roosevelt dedicated the Hoover Dam.

November witnessed the creation of the Congress of Industrial Organizations (CIO) which pushed the cause for industrial unionism in North America. The final marvel of 1935 was the delivery of the first airmail cargo across the Pacific Ocean.

1936

Harrisburg was hard hit by the Flood of 1936 ("St. Patrick's Day Flood"), with the Susquehanna River cresting at 29.23 feet with many local areas affected. In June a major heat wave struck North America setting high record temperatures.

On June 10 Margaret Mitchell's epic *Gone With the Wind* was published and in 1939 the movie version was released and would become an all-time classic.

In August Jesse Owens won four gold medals at the Berlin Olympics, which dashed the German claim of Aryan supremacy; less than two weeks later the Summer Olympics was held at which the United States men's national basketball team won its first ever Olympic basketball tournament in the final game over Canada, 19–8.

In November the San Francisco-Oakland Bay Bridge opened to traffic. In the same month *Life* magazine began publication as a weekly news magazine.

Closing the year, the United Auto Workers union began its sit-down strike in Flint, Michigan.

Following its predecessors, *The Tatler* utilized a full page to thank the community for its support, particularly for the athletic field and the addition to the building.

Girls' basketball won the Lower Dauphin County Championship after a triple tie for first place followed by a series of play-offs. Jane Strite was the highest scoring forward.

The 1935 Hummelstown Track Team (from the previous spring) was District Champs and runner-up for the State Championship. Ken Walters and Donald Thomas placed in the 100-yard, 220-yard, and 440-yard Dash, with Walters winning first place in the 440 in 52 seconds as well as winning first place in the low hurdles.[25]

1937

The broadcast in 1937 of the crowning of George VI, following his brother Edward's abdication announcement, was the first worldwide radio program heard in the United States, and it can be presumed that millions tuned in for the broadcast.

1937 also saw the completion of the Golden Gate Bridge, the death of millionaire-philanthropists Andrew Mellon and John D. Rockefeller, the Hindenburg dirigible disaster by fire, and the loss of Amelia Earhart on a flight over the Pacific. It also is marked as the year the first supermarket opened in Queens, New York.

An editorial in *Good Housekeeping* (January 1937) offered this advice, "It is characteristic of the American voter to be strongly partisan; …it is also characteristic to concede to the victor the qualities that leadership requires and to admit that the country will continue in its appointed way. …We are a *nation*."

The *1937 Tatler* included a full page to honor "School Spirit," stating that, "The old-time spirit of H.H.S. is once more returning to the cherished position it once held."[26] This page explains, "…steps were taken to increase the flame of that spirit and plans were made…. More time was spent in cheering during assemblies and pep meetings."

Forerunner of Internet shopping: *Good Housekeeping* (January 1937) magazine offered a service by which a shopper called, asked the operator what company sells a particular product; the operator then provided names and addresses of the appropriate retailers.

Likely the most tactful and most beneficial move for school spirit was the organizing of the "Student Spirit Society "(who)…march with the band to football games and participate in organized cheering." It boasted more than **120 members.**

A long-term School Board member was William E. Habbyshaw whose namesake nephew, a member of the senior class, later honored his uncle by establishing the William E. Habbyshaw Award to the outstanding member of the graduating class. (This tradition continued at Lower Dauphin and lasted into the 21st Century.)

Also noted was the eighth annual Bazaar (which raised funds for the Athletic Association). The candid senior pictures included the smallest and tallest girls as well as the *stoutest* and *thinnest* girls in the high school(!!)

Further, 1937 is the birth year for the most representative cohort of the Silent Generation, ten years before the birth of the most representative cohort of the Baby Boomers.

1938

1938 brought with it the House Un-American Activities Committee, the Lambeth Walk, and the Benny Goodman band, foreshadowing the "big band" sound that would become the hallmark of 1940s music.

The Pulitzer Prize for literature was awarded to *The Yearling* (Marjorie Rawlings) and for drama to Thornton Wilder's *Our Town.*

Following protracted negotiations, Congress passed legislation that set a 40-hour work week for clerical workers, a 36-hour week for industrial workers, and a minimum wage of 40 cents an hour. This legislation also abolished child labor. The forty-hour week gradually became standard and offices began to close on Saturdays, providing the underpinning for "free" week-ends.

The event for which 1938 most often is remembered, however, occurred on Halloween Eve with the radio broadcast of Orson Welles' "War of the Worlds," resulting in a short-lived but intense panic gripping the country. Despite reminders that this was a fictional program, many listeners truly believed that Earth was being invaded by aliens from another planet.

An interesting note in the *1938 Tatler* is that one particular senior male won 30% of the list of attributes such as "most popular," "best socializer," and "most influential." Class President was Philander Rainey, later to be the father of five Lower Dauphin graduates. Senior Maynard McKissick formed an orchestra for which he was widely known for many years yet to come.

1939

As clouds of conflict gathered on the world's horizon near the end of the 1930s, in only one year's time Hitler brought under his rule Austria and the Sudeten Germans. In 1939, breaking solemn promises he had made to heads of state in Europe, Hitler sent the German army into Prague, dividing the remainder of Czechoslovakia into two German satellites.

At the same time, the Japanese militarists were building an empire in East Asia, driving American and European missionary, educational, medical, and cultural activities out of China. Japan captured Shanghai, and Germany attacked Poland. Two days later Britain and France declared war on Germany, initiating World War II and changing life forever.

As the decade drew to a close, Christmas 1939 brought difficulties to many families, both in finding gift items and having the money to purchase them. Fearing war in Europe and not knowing when the country would come out of the Depression, many parents had to keep the spirit of Christmas with family traditions rather than with gifts.

Despite the difficult financial bind for a high percentage of Americans, something as frivolous as nail polish was gaining popularity, and traveling lecturers were speaking to women's groups on the etiquette of cigarette smoking, demonstrating ways to use smoking "as a means to reflect social graces."[27]

On a happier note was the opening of a roller skating rink in Middletown named Skater's Paradise. (It closed in 1960, later to be purchased by the Yoder family who re-opened it in 1962 under the name of Le Patin D'or (The Gold Skate).[28] It retained this name until 1991 when Charles Yoder '70 took over the operation of the rink and (re)named it Doc's Roller Rink/Doc's Family Fun Center in honor of his father.

High school socials included roller skating parties (which, in addition to Skater's Paradise, were the Rainbow on the West Shore, Capital in Harrisburg, and Mt. Gretna Rinks) and dances.

There is evidence to suggest that at one time there was a roller rink in the Band Hall at the northwest corner of Second and Water Streets. This large frame building, according to the *Hummelstown Bicentennial* book, also served as a theatre for home talent shows and traveling shows and as an auditorium for the Chautauqua Circuit programs.[29]

However, in the 1930s dancing still was the main social activity. A yearbook from a school in central Pennsylvania notes that during their school year of 1939-1940, "We danced for three solid hours to the music of popular records played over the recently-purchased amplifying system; students and faculty danced from eight 'til eleven to some of the latest recordings; and this social was made more successful by the addition of several new records to our increasing store."[30]

1940s

Despite all of the destruction to lives and property that wars bring, the Second World War is unique in the history of the United States in that it captured the spirit of an entire country in an effort more united than at any other time. Most would agree that it is likely the economic hardships of the Great Depression that steeled the country's resolve to get through the adversities of war.

While perhaps that spirit of determination is identified more clearly in retrospect, persons of any age who lived during the time of World War II will say that "people banded together" and the whole thrust of living focused on the war effort, from factories retooling their machinery to create what the military needed, to women joining the Armed Forces, and from the children's contributions with silkweed drives to composers creating the music of wartime. It was a very intense time, but recalled as a time when citizens were instilled with a deep sense of service to others. Even so, nearby Elizabethtown College still had separate Men's and Women's Student Councils.

1940

In 1940 Franklin Roosevelt signed into law the first peace-time draft in the country's history. Under the Selective Training and Service Act, all males between twenty-one and thirty-five years of age were required to register for the draft. The government selected men through a lottery system and those drafted served for twelve months. The *1941 Tatler* notes that on October 16, 1940 no classes were held in the afternoon because of the draft registration. It also confirms that early in February 1941 the Hummelstown High School Band gave the second group of draftees from the town and surrounding townships "a great send-off."

Because America was a major industrial power, machinery could be converted from domestic needs to the tools for war—tanks, jeeps, ships of all sizes, submarines, small-bore rifles, and large artillery pieces. And convert they did.

To support the war effort, six and a half million women went to work in factories, 350,000 joined the Armed Forces, and countless others assumed leadership roles in the community as the men marched off to war. Children went on a modern crusade, gathering everything from scrap metal to newspapers and silkweed. They also bought defense stamps once a week at school and donated toiletry items, packing them in Junior Red Cross boxes to send overseas.

Everyone, young and old, realized that the way of life they had known was forever changed. With factories concentrating on the needs of war, the entire population of the country found they could "make do" without new products. Rationing became a way of life and coupon books determined what wearing apparel could be purchased and what menus could be planned. Many children didn't realize that their favorite dessert, Junket, was really a way mothers had to not waste any pasteurized milk.

Most inspiring, however, was the dedication of an entire generation. Those living at the time viewed this spirit of national cooperation as being normal, and this era is viewed as one of the most secure times in which to grow up in small town America.

Betty Alleman, a member of the *1940 Tatler* staff, was the Senior Editor of the well-written Class History to which she added humor (Example, "Dec. 5: Miles Early is late.") It is not surprising that her classmates also voted her as "wittiest."

Also from this *Tatler*:

September 11, 1939 — all boys must wear ties to school.

November 3, 1939 — Senior Class hay ride and wiener roast.

In the fall of 1939, the Class of 1940 also enjoyed an exciting football season, writing that this was "one of the finest and greatest football teams in the history of HHS."

Rudy Petrina scored the first—and the second—Hummelstown touchdowns against Hershey in the first game played between the two rivals on the new Hershey High School Field in the fall of 1939. In school the next day was heard the following comment, "Boy, that Hershey Stadium is some layout!" On September 25, at a pep meeting Captain Petrina (also captain of the basketball and baseball teams) presented the game football to Coach Sponagle.

On April 13, 1940 Geraldine Huss advanced to the state oratorical contest after winning in districts. On April 25 high school entrance exams were held for the current eighth grade.

1941

In August 1941 the federal government established the Office of Price Administration (OPA) and in May 1942 the OPA opened War Price and Rationing Boards in every county across America to monitor government-issued coupon books. Rationing of goods began almost immediately, regulating purchases of nearly every consumable. Menus were devised around available food products and clothing purchases were limited.

In the initial years of rationing, worn automobile tires had to be turned in before ration cards were issued for replacements. However, as the war dragged on, rubber was so scarce that no new tires or recapped tires were available even with the ration cards. If an automobile blew a tire and the owner had no spare, the car either sat out the war or the car owner would try to find a spare tire from a kind relative or neighbor.

Those who were young children in 1941 likely did not remember the quiet Sunday afternoon in 1941 when news of Pearl Harbor began to leak or that same evening when Mrs. Eleanor Roosevelt took her husband's place for his usual "Fireside Chat" because the President was in session with his advisors.

The following day the President spoke to the nation, concluding with these words, "I ask that the Congress declare that since Sunday, December 7, 1941, a state of war has existed between the United States and the Japanese Empire."[31] While the children might not have understood all the words in his address, they all heard the simplistic summary made by adults, "We are going to war."

Early in the decade, people's daily lives remained fairly routine in most towns and cities that were not populated by government offices. In the schools there was little discussion about war (or any other current event), as adults were not comfortable with in-depth discussions of contemporary world events because of their own limited knowledge and their belief that children should not be troubled by what was happening outside their immediate experience. Many homes did not subscribe to a city newspaper, only perhaps a local weekly, the county daily, or "The Grit," a folksy weekly broadsheet aimed at rural and farming communities and published in Williamsport, Pennsylvania.

"Teen age" began to emerge as a term for adolescence during the early 1940s, although the use of "teenager" in its current designation didn't occur until a bit later.[32]

The Evening News, Harrisburg, PA, September 6, 1941. "Teen-Age Dancers Step Out at Harrisburg Country Club. Dancing provides summer entertainment and pleasure for younger members of the Harrisburg Country Club and their guests."

In addition to dancing, these teen-agers were also patrons of roller skating rinks as confirmed by the records of activities kept in the yearbooks of the time. Time and again are notations such as the following: "January 15: Senior Class held a skating party at the Rainbow." On February 5 were two notations: "The faculty will soon be experts on skates" and "The seniors held their second roller skating party. On March 11 the sophomores also held a skating party." Of course, there were also a number of dances held throughout the school year.

The high school band had grown to 55 members, one of which was the new position of drum majorette.

Another entry in *The Tatler's* Class Diary (February 25, 1941) reveals more than it states, an underlying commentary on the lack of males who were attracted to participating in the current year's high school operetta: "Did you notice the lack of he-men in the high school around this time?" The answer was also provided, "...very few who wish to portray cowboys in the operetta."

1942

By 1942 sixty percent of all civilian food items had been rationed, and hardship from the lack of goods was being felt in every corner. Everyone learned to re-use items rather than discard them. Little girls who had practiced ironing on handkerchiefs were shown how to iron wrapping paper and ribbon so that these could be re-used. Hair curlers were fashioned from the covered wire closures that came on coffee bags.

Teen-agers in the 1940s had no luxuries because there weren't any. Even fabric for a prom gown was hard to come by, to say nothing of the scarcity of an escort for the event. Even so, a 1942 yearbook from a school in another Pennsylvania county described their prom in alluring terms, "The quiet charm of a rose garden inspired one of the most glamorous and bewitching proms ever held in this school." Such hyperbole could come only from the young.

Those of high school age during the 1940s saw their classmates heading to war instead of college, as the excitement and aura of "serving one's country" overrode the fear that the some of them might not return. Many young soldiers tried to hold onto their ties to their classmates as evidenced by an excerpt from a letter sent by a serviceman, "…when are Class Night and the rest of the social events that go with graduation? I'll sure be thinking of you kids the night they give out diplomas."[33] While the term "you kids" would have been meant affectionately, it gave a message that, while all were classmates, the young soldier had become a man.

With gasoline rationing in effect, passenger traffic on the Pennsylvania Turnpike, which had opened in 1940, fell by more than 70 percent. Military convoys, however, found this new highway of great benefit as there was so little civilian traffic that the convoys could travel great distances in a very short time. Many drivers—and their passengers—whose first glimpse of the turnpike from a parallel road found it startling to suddenly see a four-lane empty highway through the trees, and children found it almost terrifying when the explanation given was that this had been built "for the army to use."[34]

As rationing continued, hoarding of items began. Sugar and coffee in particular were hoarded and some grocers were forced to limit purchases of coffee to ten pounds. One of the oddities is that many people who were not coffee drinkers hoarded it only because it was scarce.

During the first year of the war more people remained at home in the evenings listening to the radio. The number of listeners increased 20 percent and remained at high levels. Parlor games also rose in popularity; sales of checkers and chess sets zoomed; and sales were up 1,000 percent for playing cards.[35]

Adults were attracted to bridge clubs because of the skill of the game and because it was inexpensive for couples to take their turn hosting a table or two. Occasionally the bridge games had to halt abruptly when the air raid siren sounded. Even though it was only a drill, the rules were in effect and the lights had to be turned off until the "all clear" signal was sounded.

Blackouts became a familiar occurrence in more populated areas. Blackout curtains, light-opaque window shades, and blackout candles became familiar accessories in homes, while in New York City's Times Square no exterior theatre lights were allowed to be lit, and theatre-goers had to find their way through the theatre district in the dark.

Membership in State Guard units, geared to provide assistance should there be an attack on the United States, was open to draft-age men with deferments and to men whose age was above draft age. These groups met weekly to train and to plan for ways to boost civilian morale.

On Memorial Day most parade watchers stood in solemn tribute as they viewed the veterans pass by, followed by the boys who had enlisted in the service and, in many cases, would be leaving a few days after their graduation. Everyone knew these young men, and a hush fell over the crowd as the boys passed by, most of whom could not possibly comprehend what was in store for them.

Wartime also raised hard-to-answer questions about a teenager's place in the world. In time of economic depression when jobs were hard to come by, teenagers were viewed as children who had to be sheltered from the adult world of work. In time of war, however, teens were expected to be capable of victory on the battlefield, to make production in defense jobs, and to show self-discipline. Most responded with gallantry.

Senior Classes of 1942 saw as many as 40% of their male classmates leave school before graduating in order to enlist in military service. Senior class plays were modified to re-cast male roles. However, the school band in Hummelstown grew to 60 members.

"Hand-me down" articles of clothing became more common in most families and women who made some of their family's clothing used white cotton lawn fabric for undergarments, because neither silk nor rayon was available. While many children viewed the garments as second-rate because they were "homemade," in later years many came to understand the generosity and love demonstrated by these gifts.

The *1942 Tatler* was dedicated to Mr. Paul Hershey, a faculty member "in service." The yearbook also included a list of "Boys in Service" and noted Lieut. Ralph E. ("Bucky") Walter, Jr. as the first war casualty to that date.

1943

The 1942-43 school year saw an all-out war effort in schools. The Tri Hi Y Club collected clothes for the Red Cross, repaired and distributed toys to needy children at Christmas, sold defense stamps throughout the year, and helped the VFW sell poppies for Memorial Day. The younger children packed boxes of small toys and supplies for the Red Cross to distribute to the Allies, and students made a great effort to gather all the silk they could find to be used as a replacement for scarce kapok[36] in the lining of life jackets.

With patriotism at fever pitch, War Bond Drives were popular in both cities and smaller towns. Hollywood personalities brought publicity to the larger fund-raising efforts and personal appearances guaranteed a large turnout and record bond sales.

By 1943 full skirts, knife pleats, and patch pockets had been banned from manufacturing because of the amount of fabric needed. Shoes were rationed and were limited to six colors: black, white, navy blue, and three shades of brown—when they were available. Leg make-up replaced stockings, even though its application required a steady hand and the make-up often rubbed off on clothing or furniture.

In most households it was typical to have the same meal a particular day of the week, such as meat loaf, macaroni and cheese, creamed dried beef, hamburgers, scrambled eggs, chicken, or soup weekdays with hot dogs on Saturday and a pot roast on Sunday.

Rationing was hard on everyone with families standing in line "in shifts," with the children fearing they would not know what to select if the line moved too fast and their "turn" came before a parent arrived. In 1943 canned goods were added to the list of rationed foods so that one not only had to wait in line, but also had to present a ration stamp for every food purchase. This was followed by the five percent "war effort" tax, ingeniously named the "Victory tax."

A motto, "Use it up, wear it out, make it do, or do without" was coined to encourage the public to tolerate rationing. More encompassing, however, was the stock answer to almost every question as to how long the shortages and rationing, the blackouts and the boys overseas, would continue. It was always the same: "For the duration." Everything, it seemed, was for the duration.[37]

The number of males in both high schools and colleges dwindled as males left their studies to defend their country. The Elizabethtown College yearbook noted "When the class returned in nineteen forty-three it was to find their class reduced in male members as the draft boards had played havoc with our class enrollment."[38]

The *1943 Tatler* listed 150 names (seven of whom were women) of those from Hummelstown High School who were at the time in the armed forces. Four faculty were also named. Noted separately were five who had made the ultimate sacrifice.

The Class of 1943 had many challenges as the captives of wartime austerity. Their Class History reflects their graceful stoicism:

Junior Year: "The war really made itself felt as the Junior year arrived (fall of 1941). Numerous social events were canceled and the entire student body became war-minded. Nevertheless, the social high-spot, the Junior-Senior Reception, went off on schedule with exceptional success."

Senior Year: "No fun, no Washington trip, very few parties. Courses were intensified and stress was laid on preparing students to take their places in a wartime world. Salvage Committee, Victory Corps, and additional aviation courses claimed all leisure time. Class Day, Commencement, and the Junior-Senior Reception were not as cheerful as in former years. In the face of these trying conditions, we go forth prepared to defend that freedom and democracy which have educated us."

By October air raid drills were common, causing unspoken fear to first graders who didn't understand their purpose, but intuitively accepted that this must be something important because the adults responded so immediately to the air raid signal. It was troubling because, while the little ones felt the nameless fear, they did not understand it. Stories of war were vague to their understanding, as was the loss of life.

By November 1943 Christmas catalogues were restricted in number of pages and many listed items were stamped with the words, "Sorry, not available." Thus, even those who had money found that many items could not be purchased and small children struggled to understand that Santa could not produce items tagged "Unavailable."

Life for everyone was unusual and World War II was particularly uncommon in the unusual unanimity that the country seemed to feel for the rightness of the war. The result is that children took this harmony to be the natural way for a country to feel about wars. They had no skills to interpret events; thus, they accepted whatever was occurring as the norm.

Teens suddenly were expected to be capable of victory on the battlefield. Even the term "boy" went from designating a male child to the honorable designation through the usage in references such as "our boys over there."

High schools established clubs called Victory Corps in which students participated in physical fitness programs and wartime activities including scrap drives, bond rallies, and stamp sales. School yards were heaped with scrap materials collected by zealous young people.

There was a great scarcity of manufactured goods of any kind. Automobiles were not being built, toys were very limited, and the clothing shortage increased with each successive year of the war, with men's suits in particular being hard to find. However, young people were inventive in trying to follow or create trends, one notable one being wearing slacks (no jeans yet) rolled up to mid-calf length.[39]

Courses were streamlined to better prepare students to be useful for the armed forces and war industries. Commercial training turned more practical; military forms, nomenclature, rules, law and practices were emphasized; and a "pre-induction radio" course became popular.

The Girls Basketball team won the Lower Dauphin[40] County Championship—their first since 1936 and the Bulldogs also enjoyed a very successful football season in winning the Dauphin County Class B Championship.

Notable members of this class included Marian Auchenbach, James Birchfield, and Esther Engle (Hivner) who became local teachers. Also to be mentioned are Charles Frederick Hummel, Louis Rathfon, and philanthropist Donald Reed, the latter remembered through the Donald A. Reed Plaza at the local library.

1944

By 1944 everyone was "hunkered down" for the duration. There were hints that the Allies would not lose this war, but without guarantees of total victory, rationing with its accompanying shortages of goods and services increased in severity, making a normal life difficult. There was even a shortage of alarm clocks. Many more social activities such as the county fair, picnics, and dances were canceled.

In winter, sledding was quite popular as children from all the nearby streets gathered on Quarry Road[41] or Duke Street, the latter having a slope just right for younger children and their older siblings ordered to watch them, because a sled could speed the whole way to the bottom and possibly across the bridge (if not side-railed in a gutter); and the incline was not too steep to pull the sled back to the top.

The war dragged on through the minutiae of daily living on the home front, the federal amusement tax was raised from 10 to 20 percent while the cost of living rose almost 30 percent. Wages were frozen, and a new Victory tax was imposed.

Automobiles ceased to be used for pleasure because of gas rationing, and the unavailability of replacement parts for cars led to their not being driven unless necessary. "Sunday drives" were suspended for the duration.

Musical activities were restricted in 1944 when the Pennsylvania School Musical Association[42] canceled all district and state band, orchestra, and chorus festivals for the duration. Photos from high school proms show a preponderance of girls in attendance with scarcely a male visible on the dance floor.

The high spot was the local roller-skating rink, although a new phenomenon in many towns, including Hummelstown, was the establishment of teen clubs, places where high school students could dance to music from a jukebox stocked with the latest records.

During the winter of 1944-45, the bitterest in years, an acute fuel shortage left Americans in the eastern half of the country shivering in their homes. Overburdened railroads, manpower shortages, and blizzards were to blame. A brown-out was ordered throughout the nation, and the use of neon signs[43] was prohibited. Stores closed at dusk.

Families living in Hummelstown were affected by rising costs for the coal needed for furnaces. Many whose heating systems had pipes only to the first floor, counting on a dispersal system through a ceiling vent to heat the second floor, vowed they would install new systems following the war.

With only three football team members returning from the previous season, the Bulldogs still managed to win four of their 10 games. This 1944 class had spent all of its high school days living in a country engaged in war, with nothing being "normal."

1945

On May 2, 1945 Germany surrendered to Russia and five days later signed an unconditional surrender with the Allies. On August 6 the first atomic bomb was dropped on Hiroshima. On August 9 a second bomb exploded over Nagasaki. Emperor Hirohito surrendered on August 14, ending the war in the Pacific.

By summer Hummelstown was a microcosm of what was happening throughout the entire country where thousands of men and women began to return home—some to resume their lives and some to discover that "home" as they remembered it no longer existed, because they had changed, people they knew had changed, or the town had changed. Most veterans headed back to their hometowns with the goal to create a better life, assisted in some part by a grateful nation. Jobs were waiting for the majority of the veterans and life in the many small towns offered the promise of some normalcy.

Gearing up for peacetime, most town events and celebrations were reinstated and new ones initiated. On November 11, Armistice Day 1945, originally established to commemorate World War I, took on a greater significance as the end of World War II led the citizenry to the realization that once again they had paid a high price for liberty. It is likely that every head was bowed in silence at 11:00 a.m.

Christmas 1945 in general was a happy time in the United States, at least in homes to which the servicemen returned. Some families had kept their Christmas tree trimmed until spring when their son, father, or husband was discharged. While children thought it odd to see the tree still in place in March, the adults understood perfectly.

Post-WWII

The period following World War II, like most post-war eras, was viewed as a time for solidarity and direction. Well into the nineteen-fifties "planned orderliness" became the method by which to create a new age of security following a stressful period of war.[44]

1946

In September 1946 the town held a huge, three-day "Welcome Home" party with a parade, a Dedication of Honor Roll, a Memorial Plaque, a football game, band concert, dog show, a vaudeville act, and two public dances.

However, during this year after the war women were suddenly being told their primary task was parenting and that they should go home and stay home. A promotional advertising campaign then was initiated to convince women to concentrate on the needs of husbands and children. Government child care facilities were closed, leaving mothers with small children to face even more pressure to remain home.

And colleges were still using patronizing descriptions such as the following, "Strict foul rules ... two-dribble limit ... restricted zones ... that's girls' basketball and the Bluebirds play it with all the feminine know-how that makes for spectator appeal."[45]

As usual children were protected from the after-effects of war. They didn't hear what the war had done to families, the losses suffered by these families and the country, the women who went to work or war, or the divorces when the soldiers came home. As Franzosa wrote, "The war had simply disappeared."[46] ...and families were headed back to Strite's Orchard for fresh produce.

The post-war era for adolescents was very much their own time and by 1946 an active social life had become the measure of success for teenagers, and the quest for popularity assumed new importance.

There was no stopping the teen-age market once adolescents were targeted as ideal consumers who not only had the time and interest to try out new products, but also tended to spend their money freely. What was happening, of course, is that the adolescents believed everything they read and heard, not understanding they—and all generations to follow—were being groomed to be a new category of consumers.

Children still had only few opportunities to learn how to interact with the opposite sex. Segregated by gender in most activities, girls made friends only with other girls. Children's birthday parties were gender-based—with all girls or all boys.

Boys played in groups or teams, whether they were in organized sports or simply playing pick-up games. Participating in such groups validated and solidified masculine solidarity, game rules, and maleness itself. Because of this, everything boys did was from the perspective of playing a game—and learning how to win.

The emphasis for girls was *exclusivity*, shutting out other girls. Boys flocked; girls rarely congregated in groups. Because boys were teammates and had learned "one for all and all for one," they rarely quarreled. Because girls were **not** teammates but separate individuals they often quarreled over what to do, when to do it and who was whose best friend.

1947

Nineteen forty-seven saw the arrival of the Bell Laboratories' transistor, probably Bell's most important invention ever, and it also marks the date that a United States airplane first flew at supersonic speed. *The Diary of Anne Frank*, written by a young Jewish teenager in hiding from the Nazis, rivaled *Hiroshima* of the previous year in its personal account of the effects of war on the individuals. On the stranger side, the sighting of flying saucers was first reported in this country.

Overall enrollment in colleges and universities was more than two million, the largest number of students ever enrolled; of these, approximately one million were veterans of World War II who were receiving financial aid under the G. I. Bill.[47]

Teen-agers were tasting the flavor of what high school was without the cloud of war and could enjoy their junior and senior years with a lighter heart. Teens flocked to Nisley's Dairy Dell while Rintz's enjoyed the patronage of younger children.

However, in nearby Annville at Lebanon Valley College, the May Day pageant was aptly described as "strictly a war-time production…"[48] and plans were made to discontinue it.

Hummelstown High School teachers of this year who later became part of the foundation for Lower Dauphin High School included Miss Janet Ausmus, Miss Kathryn Zeiters, Mrs. Louise Schaffner, Miss Mary Jane Strite, and Mrs. Mary Alice Lewin.

The Hummelstown Class of '47 was also the core of the football team (fall of 1946) who "emerged with the Class B Championship, led by legendary Tony Orsini" under the auspices of Coaches Bulota and Freeland, returned veterans. In basketball the boys were Class C Champions.

And, yes, Homecoming was not instituted by Lower Dauphin High School, but was a tradition at Hummelstown with a senior parade and a flag presentation at the athletic field prior to the game.

In the fall of 1946 a school roller skating party was held at the Rainbow Rink. The fundraiser by the Senior Class was holly wreaths and laurel roping and the Girls' Club continued the practice of sending Christmas boxes to alumni in the military service. In basketball the team played a game with alumni, as normalcy continued.

A field trip in January 1947 saw the seniors attending a County Court session and the entire high school traveling to Hershey by bus to attend a Town Hall meeting. March saw the Interscholastic Student Council, in its second year, sponsor a dance for all member schools at the Madrid Ballroom in Harrisburg. The culminating event for seniors was their resumed traditional three-day trip to Washington, DC in April.

Also, while the Class of 1965 is self-noted as being the first to call in a bomb threat, the favorite prank in 1947 was to ring the fire alarm in the winter and watch classmates shivering in the cold.

Most important, the year 1947 marks the birth year for a cohort that would leave its mark on everything its members touched.

1948

1948 saw the beginning of television for homeowners even though most of the screens were very small. The first color newsreel of the Tournament of Roses Parade and the Rose Bowl game was filmed on January 5.

On April 3 President Harry S. Truman signed the Marshall Plan which authorized $5 billion in aid to 16 European countries. On the same date ABC began its television services on WFIL-TV in Philadelphia.

The Berlin Blockade during the Cold War began on June 24 and the first World Health Assembly of the World Health Organization was held in Geneva.

The "witch hunt" for Communists began its hearings in August with the appearance of Whittaker Chambers before the House Un-American Activities Committee (HUAC) and on the 25th held the first-ever televised Congressional hearing.

It was a cold winter again in Pennsylvania and the ice on Kellick Run had frozen. A few skaters ventured on to the solidly frozen areas near the shoreline and other areas where the water did not run deep. Others went to Swatara Creek near the quarry, but more children preferred sled riding.

High schoolers were thrilled with the opening of the Chatterbox while still thronging to the popular Dairy Dell, both of which provided areas to gather and dance. And who could forget Dave's

Dream with curb service!

Alas, however, that the Bulldogs' football season could not match that of the fall of 1947 even though "for the third time in the history of Hummelstown High School and the first time in eight years, the Bulldogs won over Hershey, 27-6, with the first score coming in the first quarter when Quarterback Wally Witmer ran 87 yards for a touchdown, Charles Eisenhour ran 53 yards for a second score, and a 22-yard pass to Witmer earned yet another.

Sadly *The Tatler* was lean in text (only 56 pages, where earlier editions had been 88 pages.) Its patrons included the following:

Bell's Meat Market
Deimler Insurance
E. B. Smith Hardware
East End Restaurant
Engle's Garage
Farmers Bank
Fasnacht's
Fromm's Dairy
Funk's
Handwerk
Hauer's Department Store
Hoffer's Appliances
Hummelstown Sun

Indian Echo Caverns
Lynn's Grocery
National Bank
Porter's Grocery
Press Dress Factory
Rhan's
Rintz's
Smith's Tires
Spire Electric
Stanford's Drugstore
Warner Motors
Warwick, National, Keystone Hotels
Wolf's

1949

This was the year the 1948 model of the Volkswagen Beetle arrived in the United States and went on to become the greatest automobile phenomenon in American history.

It was also the year of a Hummelstown baseball team's unexpected state championship, likely the finest team ever. They won 37 of 42 league games, seven of seven in district level, in state play six of seven, and in national competition they won one of three. Thus, their season record was 51 wins and only eight losses.[49]

March 2 marks the date of the first non-stop, around-the-world airplane flight; on June 24 the first television western ("Hopalong Cassidy") aired on television; and on June 29, the last U.S. troops withdrew from South Korea.

The Capital Roller Rink, holding its grand opening on September 3, 1948, arrived just in time for the Class of 1949 to enjoy. According to the October 16 issue of "The Billboard," "More than 1,000 skaters and 300 spectators attended the opening outside the city limits." The large building (with a skating surface of 88 by 193 ft.) later became a part of AMP, Incorporated,[50] then years later bought out by Tyco.

As was universal at the time, "dress regulations were required, in order to maintain the rink's standards: Men to wear sport shirts with or without ties…ties to be worn with a dress shirt. Sweaters permitted if worn over sport or dress shirt. Dungarees or T-shirts not allowed. Ladies to wear dress slacks, skating costumes finger-tip length, or street clothes. Blue jeans, pedal pushers, and shorts not allowed." Smoking was not permitted on the skating area. General admission was 25 cents.

The selling of ads spiked to a full signature of sixteen pages in the *1949 Tatler* and included the following Hummelstown businesses (in addition to those listed in the group above):

A&P
Achenbach Insurance
American Legion
Ames & Landis
Aungst Insurance
Bair Insurance
Bubs Jewelers
Bucciarelli Café and Gas
C.S. Shope
Capital Roller Rink
Drs. Horn, Stanford, Springer
Drs. Dietz, Karmany, and Berkheimer
Fisler Shop
G.S. Morelock
Habbyshaw (tax collector)

Hetrick's Bakery
Hummelstown Beverage
Hummelstown Building Supply.
J. M. Brightbill
John Bordner
John R. Shope
Lash Motors
Le Fever
Mickey's Drycleaning
Mutual Fire Insurance
Ruof Florist
Strite's Café
VFW
Winnie's

By the dawn of the next decade, the 1950s, the Baby Boomers were learning many things for survival without realizing these were essential skills they would hone for the next two decades.

Chapter 1 Endnotes:

---

1. *The Tatler*, 1960, Hummelstown High School, p. 5.
2. He can't have been more than age 16 at the time. (Some high schools offered three, rather than four, years of instruction: freshman, junior, and senior years.)
3. *The Breeze*, 1920, Clearfield High School, p. 40.
4. Evans, *The American Century*, p. 182.
5. Evans, p. 231.
6. Purchasing securities with borrowed money, using the shares themselves as collateral.
7. *Life Bicentennial Issue*, 1976, p. 33.
8. *Hummelstown Bicentennial*.
9. Another indication that high schools copied what colleges were doing.
10. The beginning of many such movements through the years.
11. Lynd and Lynd, *Middletown in Transition*, p. 152.
12. Palladino, *Teenagers: An American History*, p. 8.
13. Schrum, *Some Wore Bobby Sox*, p. 3.
14. The author was a German veteran of World War I.
15. The film starred Greta Garbo, and was marketed using the slogan "Garbo Talks!", as it was her first talkie.
16. Evans, p. 228.
17. Schrum, p. 126.
18. *1939 Echo*, Curwensville High School.
19. (Author's note: Guessing by the date and the fact that the movie theatre on Main Street was known by several other names, this particular reference may be in reference to a theatre said to be in the Band Hall at the northwest corner of Second and Water Streets. Or perhaps the students simply named its stage in the gymnasium "The Orpheum Theatre" for this operetta. Further, the *1940 Tatler* notes their operetta was held in the gymnasium.)
20. Morison, *History of the American People*, p. 944.
21. Bailey, T., *Voices of America*, p. 382.
22. *Life Bicentennial Issue*, 1976, p. 35.
23. A list that had been prepared and distributed by Gerald R. Zinn.
24. An antibacterial drug discovered in 1932.
25. "The splendid showing of Hummelstown High's track team at the PIAA State Championship Meet terminated one of the most successful seasons the school has ever achieved with our team Champion of District 3 and runner-up for the State Championship."
26. (This was a surprise to this author based on the near dazzling yearbooks of 1933 and 1934 [although perhaps the class of '37 had a stronger remembrance of the Classes of '35 and '36]).

Chapter 1 Endnotes continued:

27 "Clubwomen Get Lessons in Cigaret (sic) Smoking," *Life 50 Years,* Special Anniversary Issue, Fall 1986, p. 87.

28 Ad shown in *Falcon Flash,* February 20.

29 Reported in Wikipedia to have "just about run their course by 1940s." Nonetheless, I attended these in Clearfield, PA into the 1950s. (Author)

30 *The Echo, 1940.*

31 Evans, p. 309.

32 Breines, *Young, White, and Miserable,* p. 93 and Schrum, p. 18.

33 *The 1942 Echo.*

34 The author's own experience on a family trip.

35 Lingeman, *Don't You Know There's a War On?* p. 284.

36 The floss of the kapok, a large deciduous tree of the Amazon rain forests, is resistant to water and decay, and prized for the filling of life jackets.

37 Duration was a new term used to mean for however long it took to win the War (Wakefield, *Under the Apple Tree,* 1982, p. 48).

38 *The Etonian,* 1944, Elizabethtown College, p. 16.

39 *The Ingot,* 1946, Steelton High School, p. 32.

40 It should be noted that the name Lower Dauphin was not devised with the formation of the new high school.

41 This long before the highway cut through the incline of the road.

42 Later, the Pennsylvania Music Educators Association.

43 Neon signs were relatively new for smaller businesses at the time because of the expense; I can remember seeing one for the first time and asking about it.

44 Strauss and Howe, *Fourth Turning,* 1947, p. 147.

45 *The Etonian,* 1949, p. 29.

46 Franzosa, *Ordinary Lessons,* 1999, p. 207.

47 *Etonian,* 1947, p. 11.

48 *Quittapahilla,* Lebanon Valley College, 1947, unpaginated.

49 G. Boyer, H. Bricker, A DeLucia, H. DiJohnson, H. Eckenroth, G. Finney, M. Gasper, G. Gasper, P. Gasper, H. Graybill, B. Hermansader, P. Keim, H. Kreiser, G. Malehorn, P. Martin, J. Meyers, M. Miller, M. Neidigh, R. Petrina, F. Saksek, B. Stricker, C. Westheafer, and Howard Lash (sponsor).

50 (AMP was the very first building in the Harrisburg area that I entered when I first came to the area to student teach in the fall of 1959.)

Chapter 2

The 1950s: Forerunner to the Boomers

I stood among them, but not of them—
in a shroud of thoughts which were not their thoughts.

Childe Harold, Canto iii
Lord Byron

1937 Birth Cohorts:
The Epicenter of the Silent Generation

The Silents were young in an era when age was respected and old in a time when youth was revered.

While the Silent Generation has been called "the last truly educated Americans," Time magazine called them the "oldest young generation in the world."

The Birth Cohort of 1937 arrived as depression babies, dramatically fewer in number than in previous or following years. In 1933 the birthrate for women in their prime childbearing years had dropped to the least ever recorded in the United States and remained there for several years, including 1937 when 2,413,000 babies were born, the first American generation to be born mainly in hospitals. They were also part of a group that increased the population by only seven percent, the *lowest decade growth rate in American history.* The life expectancy for those born this year was 60 years of age. (For those born ten years later (1947), the life expectancy was 66.4 years of age.)

Members of this generation are known as both (1) a **decade cohort**, meaning they are a group whose members are very similar in many ways, and (2) a **historical generation** as based on year of birth. The members were born in the central year (1937) between 1932 and 1942 (the span of the Silent Generation era), which placed them as most representative of the era. Thus, **the Class of 1955 most exemplifies the Silent Generation, as the Class of 1965 in various ways best typifies the Baby Boomers.** Facts about this Silent Generation are striking, despite their "silence": (1) They represent the characteristics of success; (2) they overcame challenges of low expectations to become high achievers; and (3) they have led fulfilling lives.

From a historical perspective of this generation, the first worldwide radio program heard in the United States was the broadcast in 1937 of the crowning of George VI. In addition, 1937 saw the completion of the Golden Gate Bridge, the death of millionaire-philanthropists Andrew Mellon and John D. Rockefeller, the Hindenburg dirigible disaster by fire, and the loss of Amelia Earhart on a flight over the Pacific. It also is marked as the year of the first supermarket, which opened in Queens, New York.

The road to their unheralded success began in childhood where they were taught to become responsible members of their world, whether in their own family or in the wider world they would later enter. Their up-bringing provided the determination they needed to find their own way in the world. They were taught to postpone gratification as they looked for ways to improve themselves. They worked toward a goal (not always clear, but most of them knew they wanted *something*) and, **relative to their aspirations, history shows they achieved greater success than any other generation has before or since.**

There were various groupings of these classmates during their twelve years in school, both during the school day and in spending time in sports, musical groups, dancing lessons, scouts, and church activities. There were different pairings of friends, short-lived "secret clubs," many combinations of best friends, a few best friends who never varied or wavered, and some dating pairs. They were each other's teammates, steadies, competitors, nemeses, and, perhaps later, lovers. They laughed, shared private jokes, harbored secrets, kept things from each other, but rarely betrayed one another.

As children they were a generation who, for the most part, were cherished, who were watched over by the town; who were cared for, taught, and guided by the same corps of teachers; who were influenced by peers and adults; and who generally remained true to themselves and true to one another.

They were, like all cohorts, shaped by their own time and they share the destiny of that time and place. As a cohort they were unique in that all of them, from the time of their birth, encountered the same national events, moods, and trends at the same time. They developed a sense of collective identity and, in many ways, a common personality with boundaries "fixed" by that personality. And, like any cohort, as they aged, their inner beliefs retained a consistency, a collective inner compass, much like the personality of an individual growing older.[1]

Most of them chose their high school program (limited though it was) with a goal in mind—business, college, or a trade. They aimed toward a target, even though most had to figure out for themselves how to reach it since there did not seem to be anyone to ask for advice or direction.[2]

Notably, most of them continue to be contributors to society. They volunteer their resources to the betterment of our communities, they follow the rules, and they help their neighbors. For the most part they are not the leaders, but the second-in-command, the dependable ones who get the job done and don't expect a reward. They are an impressive group still laughing at the experiences they shared in high school and, more importantly, still caring about their classmates as demonstrated in the fact that many hold reunions, which is the best indicator of their affection for one another.

They held a common age location and they reacted to history as a cohort, that is, they generally all responded in the same way, but in a way that was different from another age cohort. For example, while D-Day empowered those of the GI generation, it intimidated the Silent Generation. The GIs remember the bombing of Pearl Harbor as the call to their country's service; the Silents saw this same event through the eyes of the awe-struck children they were, trying to figure out just who Pearl Harbor was.[3]

Boomers regard Pearl Harbor as the possible reason for their large number (fathers returning home from the war eager to procreate), the Generation Xers view Pearl Harbor Day as simply a part of ancient history, and the Millennials probably would shrug and say they have no idea, then think themselves clever for this comment.

The Silent Generation would become the conformist "Lonely Crowd," Peace Corps volunteers, and middle managers of an expanding public sector, later coming to realize that they had come of age too late for historical fame or notoriety. Most were too young for combat in Korea and too old to feel the heat of the Vietnam draft.

All points of reference for the members of the Silent Generation are in terms of their predecessors, the G. I. Generation, more recently called the Greatest Generation. The benchmarks of the Greatest Generation's World War II are the benchmarks of the Silents' point of reference as well, because the Korean War was not historically important enough to qualify to belong to the Silent Generation.

The members of the Greatest Generation were the unmatched heroes of the Silents in all regards—war heroes adulated, football players and majorettes emulated, and later, the country's leaders followed. The Silents realized early on that the Greatest Generation was an impossible act to follow. Who could ever match such legends as they? Certainly not a generation that had been silenced!

Strauss and Howe (*Generations*) placed those born in 1937 in the generational category of Recessive Adaptive (more on this in Chapter 3), characterized as a generation that grows up overprotected, is suffocated in youth during a secular crisis, matures into risk-averse conformists, produces indecisive midlife leaders who act as arbitrators, and who maintain influence (but garner less respect) as elders.[4]

This cohort was both pampered and commanded, their worlds regulated with the "heaviest hand of the twentieth century,"[5] but they enjoyed the lowest child labor rate to that date. They also were the earliest marrying and earliest baby-producing generation in American history, but marked less by what they themselves did than by what those older and younger did.[6]

They were the last generation of Americans to suffer the dread diseases of childhood—and to survive them without antibiotics, penicillin, or even the sulfa drugs that went to the war effort and not to them.[7]

Feeling disquieted by their lack of connectedness, those of the Silent Generation were less successful in forging a sense of national or personal direction than any other generation in living memory, leaving this generation with what Gail Sheehy calls "resignation, a vague dissatisfaction with jobs, families, their children, and, most of all, themselves."[8]

The result of their acquiescence is a wounded collective ego, what Daniel Levinson described as "a silent despair and fear of becoming irrelevant."[9] The board game *Sorry* that was so popular with them may serve as an appropriate metaphor for what they were.[10]

Perhaps most telling is that their cohort group has scored highest of all groups in geometric reasoning, second in logical reasoning, but last in "word fluency."[11] It is troubling to consider that it was believed there was no need for this generation to have language fluency, only acquiescence resulting in silence.

The parents of this cohort of Silents wanted their children to be obedient, to behave courteously, to feel close to the family group, and to be religious. Character training was a deliberate parental task with the focus on keeping the child from being a nuisance to the adult world. These parents were strict about manners, toilet training, sex education (or lack thereof), and gender behavior. As children they were "brought up" rather than, as some would say, "loved up," then continued to bring themselves up, feeling throughout life that their characters were something to be worked on.[12] There was an insistence by all adults that they be "normal" children, with normal being defined as cooperative, congenial, well-adjusted, conforming, and adaptable.

Their mothers conscientiously kept their children clothed at all times because nudity was "not nice." This, of course, resulted in prudishness, particularly in little girls. As might be expected, there was also a stricter prohibition regarding sexual activity in children that was stronger among mothers of girls. Boys were allowed more aggressive behavior, but girls were expected to be clearly feminine. The emphasis on daughters needing to be "ladylike" was united, with a strong emphasis on good manners, especially table manners. Chores were gender-geared and, in general, boys were held to a higher expectation than were girls to achieve scholastically.

1950s

While the 1950s in sum is remembered by many as rather dull and complacent, history shows otherwise, at least on the national and international scene. Historians view the 1950s as a time of relative peace because many of the historical events did not change the world in the way the Great Depression of the 1930s or World War II in the 1940s did.

Those peaceful times are reflected by Hummelstown High School's *Tatlers* as well, with the yearbooks of the 1950s doing just what would have been expected of them—they are neat and correct, following the prescribed pattern, but with no individuality such as a running commentary of the year and nothing to distinguish them from their shared blandness except for a changing of the dates—from one year to the next.[13]

For this generation every Christmas was the perfect Christmas with memories of snow, whether or not there actually was a snowfall. Every house in town, it seemed, had at least a lighted candle in the window, and often families would drive through the streets of town to see the various houses, brightly, but not elaborately, lighted. Hauer's Department Store, in the center of Hummelstown, had a special section of Christmas decorations with ornaments in sectioned cardboard boxes, real tinsel, fiberglass snow and the new bubble lights.

Fathers would sometimes take their children to Hauer's or to one of the drugstores—or perhaps even the Hershey Department Store—to select a gift for their mothers, sometimes "Blue Waltz perfume" (usually found in the Five and Tens—"dime stores") with its pungent, distinctive fragrance of cheapness still identifiable today to those who purchased this for their mothers, not realizing its very poor quality. Perhaps there would even be a stop at Dunkelberger's Dairy Dell for ice cream, and the children could always count on their respective Sunday Schools for Christmas candy in a small, squared or bucket-shaped box, sporting a limp string handle and filled with hard candies and two treasured, cream-filled chocolate drops.

1950

At the beginning of this quiet decade, the Korean War began when North Korean troops invaded South Korea. Two days later President Truman sent 35,000 "military advisors" to South Vietnam to give military and economic aid to South Vietnam.

The census count in the United States in 1950 was more than 150 million people, a 14% increase since the previous census in 1940, with New York as the most populous state, followed by California.

1951

In 1951 Senator Kefauver submitted a preliminary investigative report on organized crime, focusing on gambling, and the Rosenbergs were found guilty of conspiracy of wartime espionage, their sentencing of execution still being debated.

On a lighter note, the first trans-continental television broadcast was sent and in December a patent was filed by Buckminster Fuller for construction of a geodesic dome. This led the way for a flutter of short-lived domed houses.

1952

In November 1952 the first hydrogen bomb was exploded in the Pacific Ocean, causing great alarm as to its potential, and providing even more interesting commentary on the newly elected President Dwight D. Eisenhower, a career military man.

In addition to the high number of portable record players being sold, 1952 marks the year when church membership was the highest in the history of the nation, only to be surpassed three years later by a record 61 percent membership with attendance reaching 49 percent of the population, the highest on record before or since that time.[14]

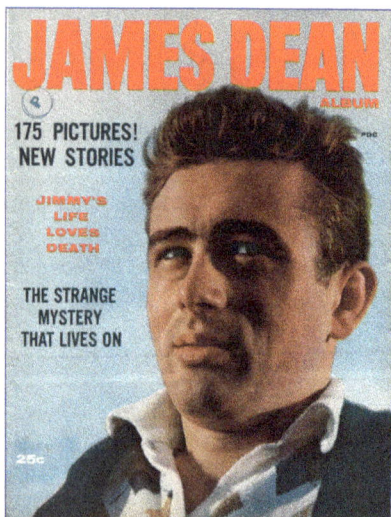

The literary world of 1952 is known for producing the brilliant work of Ernest Hemingway (*The Old Man and the Sea*), John Steinbeck (*East of Eden*), and Edna Ferber (*Giant*), with these latter two novels later becoming major movies, both starring James Dean, one of the few stars to have a special edition fan magazine devoted entirely to him.

Cinerama, a new motion picture process, was described by the *New York Times*, "…as if one were seeing motion pictures for the first time."[15] It also was the first time in memory to that date that a film review appeared on the *front page* of this esteemed newspaper. Cinerama used three synchronized projectors to place the picture in three sections on an extra-wide screen which was deeply curved and nearly three times as wide as it was tall. The soundtrack was recorded in seven-channel stereo, nearly unheard of in the early fifties. Only seven Cinerama movies were ever made, but those who traveled to one of the theatres built in major cities especially for Cinerama never forgot the experience.

1953

CinemaScope made its debut this year, with its wide, curved screen, of a size possible to fit into smaller theatres. Movies filmed by this new process were larger, clearer, and brighter than the standard movie, and the theatre managers remarked with relief that CinemaScope "brought the audiences back to the movies."

The movie that most attracted the public, however, was the forgettable one, "Bwana Devil," notable only because it was the first movie in color in three dimensions (3-D). In April 1953 smaller theatres had premiered the 3-D "The Man in the Dark" to packed houses whose audiences willingly donned the required cardboard-framed glasses which provided the illusion of a three-dimensional screen. The only difficulty for some patrons was trying to fit these cardboard glasses over regular glasses, not an easy task without tearing the cardboard.

Great excitement in the science and medical research field occurred with the discovery of the double helix DNA molecule, later (1962) resulting in a Nobel Prize for Dr. James D. Watson of America.

The theme of the *1953 Tatler* was music, with the yearbook being dedicated to choral director, Mrs. Grace Aston. The classes tended to be small enough in number that quite personal descriptions were written for the 24 seniors. The Girls Basketball Team, under Coach Jane Strite, with a total of 12 wins and only one defeat, had one of the best records in the school's history, including winning the Championship of the Lower Susquehanna League.

Hummelstown saw its first public library installed in a basement room on the northwest corner of "The Square" and three years later moved to 215 West Main where volunteers managed it. In 1958 Mrs. Kathryn Sandel became a part-time hired (certified) librarian; in 1960 the library needed larger quarters and was moved to 15 South Rosanna Street with the closing of the Teen Club for which the structure originally had been built.

An armistice was signed regarding the Korean War following a visit by President Eisenhower to that country and, to the excitement of many American citizens, the first color television went on sale right after Christmas 1953.

1954

Early this year school children were offered vaccinations against polio.[16] That spring another landmark occurred when racial segregation in public schools was declared unconstitutional. And in Hummelstown the *Tatler* editor confused comptometers with typewriters.

Sections in the yearbook were typical, with good-natured kidding in the descriptions of the seniors and a delightful rendering on the cover of the front door of the high school building, true to its design, but with a whimsical touch that a reader today might question. The entrance design is accurate as to its classic broken pediment, with the letter "H" in the open space between the two sides, but with the center emblem greatly resembling a bulldog, not seen as such in other photos and drawings!

Sociologists denote 1954 as the year movies began to reshape mass attitudes. More than any other factor, the movies made youth realize "that truth, whatever it was, was something they had all their lives been protected from. Reality had been kept in quarantine so they could not become contaminated."[17] But there was neither reality nor experience for youth to be had in the mid-1950s.

At Shippingport, Pennsylvania, ground was broken for the world's first non-military atomic power plant which would open three years later, two months following a reported UFO sighting near the plant.

1955

In 1955 the United States government agreed to train South Vietnamese troops, opening a sad chapter in American history. In contrast, this is the same year as the opening of Disneyland in Anaheim, California.

Life magazine quizzically called the Class of 1955 "The Luckiest Generation," declaring that since there was no war and fewer babies had been born during the nineteen thirties, it was expected that the males of this birth cohort would have their pick of jobs upon entering the job market.

By 1955 the average age of marriage was twenty years for women and twenty-two years for men (down from 20.4 for females and 22.9 for males in 1951[18]).

The price of a main floor ticket to *Cinerama Holiday*, exclusively shown at Eitel's Palace Theatre in Chicago, was a then-highly-priced $2.75.[19]

Popular gifts that year included the original Schwinn Black Phantom bicycle, newly readied for the mass market.

The postal service upset a number of citizens when mail delivery was reduced from twice to once a day.

The Hummelstown Bulldog Football Team (Class of 1955, season of 1954) was undefeated and untied, setting the bar high for the following season.

1956

For the first time the number of white-collar jobs outnumbered blue-collar ones and America officially became a postindustrial, service economy.

President Eisenhower signed the Interstate Highway System Act, changing travel for future motorists, while the Hummelstown High School Class of 1956 delayed the publication date of its yearbook in order to include a group photo of their graduating class in academic regalia.

The Hummelstown Class of 1956 (football season 1955) saw the second consecutive undefeated and untied football season with Captain Norton Seaman chosen for the second team all-state squad. According to the *Tatler* "This has been the greatest team Hummelstown ever had." Eleven seniors on the team would be lost to graduation. With that it might also be asked, "Was anything said to the yearbook staff when it was noticed that girls' athletic teams were completely absent from mention in the 1956 yearbook?"

The Glenn Miller Orchestra played for the Junior Prom at Penn State where likely most of us in attendance did not fully appreciate the history of this big band, one of a number which had originated in the 1930s and 1940s with great jazz and swing music evolving from the 1920s.[20] We just took these "big name" bands for granted, even though historically they made almost as much impact on dancing in the 1930s and 40s than Rock 'n' Roll did in the late 1950s.

After WWII and the advent of television, live music lost its popularity as well as its live audience who had traveled to large venues to dance to music with a full sound. The public, however, wasn't willing to pay the price of attending a venue with a big band; thus, many of the bands had to reduce the number of musicians it preferred and travel the smaller circuits such as Sunset Ballroom in Carrolltown, the Oriental Ballroom in Gallitzin, and the Hershey Park Ballroom.

The music of the 1950s was lifeless and, with boring melodies without even a good beat, there was nothing to entice dancers to be as innovative in their dancing as the youth of the 1940s and those of the 1960s. In a phrase which may have an even broader connotation, *we could not feel the rhythm....*

1957

Federal troops were sent to Little Rock, Arkansas after Gov. Orval Faubus had called out the National Guard to prevent nine black students from attending previously all-white Central High School.

While the public was still reeling from Little Rock, a greater fear arrived in the form of a "beep, beep, beep" in A-flat coming through radios and television sets. The signal came from several hundred miles above the Earth, generated by a 184 pound aluminum sphere the size of a beach ball.[21] This was Sputnik I, the first Russian space satellite.

An organization by the name of SANE (The Committee for a SANE Nuclear Policy) was quickly formed as a "ban the bomb" organization.

1958

The National Aeronautics and Space Administration (NASA) was established to administer scientific exploration of space (and to catch up with the Russians).

Explorer I, the first U.S. space satellite, was launched at Cape Canaveral in January and three months later the first major World's Fair since the end of WWII opened in Belgium, becoming best known as the origin for the worldwide love of Belgian waffles.

In December jet airline passenger service was inaugurated by National Airlines with a flight between New York City and Miami, Florida.

1959

As the 1950s decade drew to a close in 1959, John Galbraith's *The Affluent Society* provided Americans a good profile of who they were, while Vance Packard's *The Status Seekers* revealed a profile of Americans as others saw them.

The European Common Market was in its fledgling year, and the American Express credit card made its debut in the face of the recession rate of 7.7 per cent of the total labor force, the highest rate since 1941.

The threat of the science supremacy demonstrated by Russia was the deciding factor in Alaska's becoming the 49th state, followed by Hawaii the next year (each because of its strategic location), making the United States an even 50 states.

Americans cheered when the nation regained some of its defense status as the US nuclear submarine, *The Nautilus*, passed under the icecap at the North Pole.

In April of 1959 NASA selected seven military pilots to become the first ever US astronauts. The names of the original Mercury Seven are now legendary: Gordon Cooper (the youngest), Scott Carpenter, John Glenn, Gus Grissom, Wally Schirra, Alan Shepard, and Deke Slayton.

At the beginning of the decade television had been essentially unknown in most households. As the decade ended, 86 percent, or 46 million, of the country's households had television sets, and average Americans were watching it almost six hours a day.[22]

By 1960 the gross national product had increased by 250 percent and per capita income was 35 percent higher than in 1945, the most recent prior boom year.

This new affluence neatly coincided with the impact of the bumper crop of post-World War II "Baby Boomers" coming of age just in time to be indulged by their parents who—many for the first time—found themselves with discretionary income. Thus, the Decade of the Fifties made it possible for the Decade of the Sixties to become a time of optimism, especially for the privileged young who believed there were no limits to how comfortable and powerful and healthy and happy they could be.

The Silent Generation of the 1950s

With parents who had lived through a national depression followed by an unexpected World War, perhaps the only result could be a generation of offspring of the Lost Generation who would be reared with caution, eventually earning the soubriquet of "Silent."

From 1925 through 1942 nearly 50 million of this new generation were born to parents of the "The Lost Generation" who had come of age during the Great Depression. This new generation would be caught between the generation who became their early role models—The Greatest Generation— and the Baby Boomers with whom, it is often said, they had little in common. In turn, the Boomers were *shaped* by the events of the 1950s as experienced by the Silent Generation who themselves suffered the disdain of the GIs.

As the unobtrusive children of the Depression (1930s) and World War II (1940s), the Silent Generation had come of age too late for combat in Korea and too early for the first and strongest heat of the Vietnam draft. Further, we lived in a humorless decade. We never learned to laugh at ourselves. We lived in slow motion, always looking into what would be in the future rather than what was going on around us.

As the first American youth since 1930 to come of age in peace and prosperity, we had more of everything[23]—and we had it sooner—than any generation before us: more education, younger marriages, and producing more babies than in any other time in the nation's history.[24] Thus, we were expected to live happily ever after.

Instead, our lives were filled with social upheaval and marital strife, greater expectations, higher achievements and bigger disappointments than that experienced by any other Americans in the twentieth century.

Part of the reason for this unsettled existence was that **real life for us was always placed in the future, never in the present.** We were always told that "life will be exciting *when* you are in college or find the ideal job or marriage and *when* you find out what sex is like (when you are married, of course)." We were constantly reminded, "Your time will come."

However, **it never did,** because personal success was not set as a priority for the Silents; faith, family, and duty were to come first. And they did. Remarkably our generation was the last one in history not to question what they were told.

Notably, where practically every society can recognize a distinct "coming-of-age moment"—a historic rite of passage, this cohort of the 1950s did not have one identified. **Unlike that of other specific cohorts, the history of the Silent Generation shows no single event that would impact everything around us forever after.** Thus, our generation was said to have no landmark.

Fear of Not Doing Right

The Silents were led to believe there was something special about the classes who had gone before us, and, in particular, we learned to pay deference to GIs. The Silents were not expected to achieve greatness because the GIs had already done that. All we could do was listen to adults rearing us to be perfect, or at least rearing us to be right, as defined by the adults. As clueless Silents we didn't realize we had a choice **not** to be right.

Likely what most bothers members of this generation is that the 1950s as a distinct era of time is generally *ignored*. In books about generations and of defining moments in history, our Silent Generation is not even mentioned. Rather, we were *dismissed* from history.

In those growing-up years during the 1950s there also was always something for us to fear: the beginning of the Korean Conflict; the spread of Communism in Europe; the Soviet blockade of Western Berlin; the infiltration of Communism in the United States; McCarthy and the spy trial of the Rosenbergs; Russia's successful atom bomb; and Truman's newer hydrogen bomb. As a result, we were honestly and quietly **terrified** of the possibility of the bomb hitting the United States, and we shared a deep sense that something terrible could happen *at any minute* to all of us. (At the same time we also wondered why our parents were not building a fall-out shelter to protect us, and to ask would have been viewed as rude.)

No matter what we did, there was a vague sense of uneasiness that something wasn't quite right. We were always anxious about something with a fear that there would be no future.[25]

We also lived with a feeling that, while we were waiting, there was a life going on *somewhere* that we didn't know about. (I remember believing that when we reached the age of 21 someone—possibly a church elder—would explain everything to us, but that, of course, did not happen.)

Because we had no forum for speaking freely, we learned early not to show passion, enthusiasm, or any other intense feelings. We were skillful at covering negative emotions such as anger, jealousy, fear, or grief, just as we harbored our anger, resentment, rebellion, and, in a very few cases, rage.

The saddest truth was that the youth of my generation didn't even seem to know we were *young*.

The only lightness was that we had friends, school, movies, music, and (sometimes) cars. And that is what caught the attention of the advertisers—potential for consumer dollars. And because teens were naïve, malleable, and ripe to be targeted as consumers, astute marketers began to cater to them/us by focusing on what teens found important. We never saw this capture coming.

It was easy to convince us that **appearance** was everything. Easily swayed, we teens focused on the belief that popularity was based on how we looked, what we wore, and everything else we did. (While this kind of advertising is widespread today, at that time we were naïve about such exploitation.)

All that we teens had wanted was helpful information about emotions, sensations or sexuality because we had no one to ask. As a result, we never did get the information we were seeking.

Looking for Answers

Because parents had no answers for the advice sought by their offspring, we turned to magazines. We were ALWAYS measuring ourselves against someone else's categories and testing ourselves against every new set of criteria in *Seventeen* magazine.

We were well aware of our lack of knowledge of ourselves, and we searched everywhere for information. What we couldn't find in magazines we sought from books. However, in many small towns there was no public library and no book store.

Regardless of how we tried (or worse, didn't know how to try), we remained confounded by what role we were to play in a society that had *never before had a distinct category of teen-agers*.

Music, Television, and Movies

In general, the music of the 1950s was the music of everyone, not categorized as being adult music or youth music, likely because radios and phonograph records in working-class homes belonged to the family and not to an individual. Even into the early 1950s young people danced to the same music as did their parents, because there wasn't yet any specific teen-age music.

Nonetheless, music ruled our world, with the name "Hi Fi"[26] becoming the most evocative term of the 1950s. Suddenly, everyone wanted a Hi-Fi and we teens were ripe to buy into the culture everyone had said was ours. We had discretionary funds from allowances or gifts or baby-sitting, and soon sales of Hi-Fi record players jumped seven fold between 1953 and 1957, helped by millions of us who "had to have" a **Hi Fi!**

Then, in the 1960s, along came transistors which made short work of Hi Fi. (Sigh—just another sign of this generation's being at the wrong place....)

While the 1950s marks the decade of the television take-over, historians did not identify it as the life-altering incident for the Silent Generation that it actually was because television was a *gradual* change. Further, because not all teens of this generation had television in their homes, we were not all affected by the programming and its accompanying advertising.

However, it should be noted that television projected the same kind of authority and integrity as did the early browsers and websites of computers in the early 1990s. Thus, the viewers believed everything they were told.

Movies in the mid-1950s continued to be far more important to teens than did television for the following reasons: (1) the movie theatre was not in someone's home, and (2) it provided a safe place for teens to be together and share an experience that they could possibly mention the next day at school. More importantly, **movies helped us imagine we were—or could be—someone else.** An added positive factor is that movies also offered a darkened theatre, possibly suggestive music, and the entire "ambience" of the theatre seating—an ideal place for those dating.

The movies also provided the education that no one talked about—dating, romance, and how to interact. Because no one told us and magazines didn't provide instructive photographs or diagrams, we focused on the techniques we saw on the screen to learn about candlelight settings, positioning of the head when kissing, and "setting the mood" by playing love songs.

For teens, watching movies was all about trying to understand the mysteries of sex (although we never used that word), an ongoing subtext to everything else we did.

The memorable teen-age movies included Pat Boone's *April Love*; the surprise smash hit

Blackboard Jungle; Elvis's *Jailhouse Rock* and *Love Me Tender*; *Rock Around the Clock* with Bill Haley and the Comets; *Marjorie Morningstar*; *Peyton Place*; *A Summer Place*; *The Young Stranger*; *The Young Don't Cry*; Brando's *The Wild One*; and the iconic *Rebel Without a Cause*.

Rebel Without a Cause was **venerated** among teenagers, giving those graduating in the mid-1950s the momentum to begin to understand the latent yearnings we had felt throughout high school. In some ways this movie empowered us and in other ways it made us long for a second chance to go through school asking more questions and perhaps challenging the adults for more interaction and information—except for the fact that we didn't know what questions to ask.

Rebel was a stark[27] reminder to us of how repressed and compliant we had been. Most importantly, the movie marked our cohort as being a generation that may have been waiting for an opportunity to rebel and hadn't yet verbalized it even to ourselves. Rather, we had chosen to remain silent because *we weren't sure how many of our peers felt the same way*. And so we repressed even the angst brought by *Rebel*.

Thus, it wasn't Jim Stark (James Dean) who changed lives at that time because we didn't know what to do with this revelation; instead, it was Elvis Presley who changed life forever for those who were teens in the later years of the 1950s. With the arrival of Elvis, teenagers and music would never be the same.[28]

While parents weren't sure how to react to rock 'n' roll in general, their reaction to Elvis Presley was clear. They called him vulgar, sensual, and, finally, trashy, the strongest pejorative term a parent at that time could make.

High School as All

Everything else aside, however, the moment in history that belongs to all youth of the 1950s was high school. Looking back at our scrapbooks and diaries suggests that we had much more personal freedom than we may have thought or recall now. It was rare to have a curfew—partly because there was little to do late at night and partly because we were so ingrained with doing the right thing that stated restrictions were not necessary. Our parents trusted us, which was an indication that even in high school this cohort of 1950s teens began to take on middle age characteristics.

In high school we all learned the skills we would need in our future families, such as cooking and sewing for the girls and woodshop for the boys, but what no one ever gave us was the skills to question either peers or adults. Thus, what we were internalizing was the expectation to *maintain the overall status quo of the 1950s family*.

The goal was to dress the part, play the role, and blend into the crowd as *typical Americans*. We even maintained a silence among ourselves, not wanting to raise issues about any differences among us and never asking each other about anything personal or sharing any personal concerns or societal fears.

Teens typically did not invite their friends to their homes, partly because the houses were not large enough for entertaining. Few homes had "rumpus rooms" in finished basements. Nor was there wide-spread use of telephones between and among teens, as there would be little privacy to have a conversation that would not be heard by others in the room; thus, interaction with friends primarily took place in the schools (with, of course, the note-passing which was constant.)

In towns where there was community sponsorship, Teen-Age Centers/Teen Clubs became the teens' haven and social hub. Most teens didn't realize that these clubs were available because of the generosity of the townspeople; rather, they assumed that their Teen Club was just part of what most towns had.

Hummelstown was one of the towns to provide this facility for its youngsters. The Teen Club was organized in November 1954 when a committee of citizens rented, restored, and furnished a storage building, at the corner of Rosanna and West Second Streets, with recreational equipment and furniture. A year later a fire destroyed everything on the property. For two years the VFW generously offered space for the teens to meet while a fund-raising campaign led to building a Teen Club on the corner of John and Short Streets. It opened in October of 1957 and was enjoyed for many years— until a number of teens no longer wanted to be bound by the rules and neighbors objected to the noise, at which time it was decided to convert the space to a much needed larger community library.

Above all else, however, cars ruled teen culture. Cars were essential for dating and freedom from adults. Riding for the sake of riding and of being with friends; riding to avoid being home and being anywhere else except there; riding to go to the movies, to the library, to shop, to get to practices and rehearsals; riding to show off the car; and riding to a hidden "parking" destination—all were extremely important, even essential, to their lives.

Without wheels, there was no social life. Having a car positively influenced one's standing, and obtaining a learner's permit became the main rite of passage. Further, a car provided a convenient way *to not have to talk*. It honored the prevailing practice of silence.

Second only to the rush found in driving cars was high school football and being a part of the thrill and excitement of the sport as it once was in small towns across America. Those who grew up in these towns especially looked forward to the fall football season, the focal point of the school year, pushing the prom and graduation to second and third place. Even today, most graduates continue their silent support of their hometown teams regardless of where they live.

Football was king—the glory of the battle, the being part of an event, the camaraderie, the excitement of a competition, and the pride of place, emotions focused on the wins and losses. Anyone who was a part of this—whether player, cheerleader, pep squad, band member, alumnus/a, or a spectator in the stands—we all knew the cheers used at the football games and, even today, many of us can still chant them word for word.

Dating was so complicated it can't be summarized. Interaction with friends was all-important. And it has never stopped. The Silents don't give up; we keep hoping forlornly to win the love of our classmates all through life. Maybe that is why we hold class reunions….. and maybe that is why this generation was described as "the first men and women in history to be allotted so much time alone together with so little intimacy to show for it."[29]

Further, a girl didn't have a way to become *friends* with a boy, whether or not he might become a *boy*friend, because there were no opportunities for girls and boys to develop conversational skills. It was particularly difficult—if not impossible—to talk intimately about dreams, fantasies, or the future, and because of the need to be "cool," it was impossible to talk at all about personal fears and problems.

Boys didn't know how to talk with girls and we girls didn't know how to talk with either girls or boys. Thus, both girls and boys typically talked past each other. Most of what the boys uttered seemed cryptic to us girls who, while we had no clear idea of what any of the boys' incomplete remarks meant, were afraid to let on that we didn't understand what the boys were saying.

Growing up, boys communicated by saying something funny or sarcastic, which they used as a put-down or one-upmanship among themselves. And while the barbs were brief, they were constant throughout their school years. The second style of discourse was used by boys when a guy realized he liked a girl; he simply shut down and offered no useful information at all.

Boys often were confused by how to present themselves—should it be patterned on an image based on a mixture of James Dean, Marlon Brando, and the Beatniks—all described as "men of few words but intense emotions, expressed through a grunt or a flick of the eye, always on the run?"[30]

Some guys tried to emulate this brooding persona as they stood with their shoulders against the wall, hips forward, eyes narrowed but opened, with all motion toward any possible listener or observer being held back, guarded, and silent. In some men, this stance returns at class reunions without their even realizing it.

We girls were sure that, because of this silent but outwardly confident posture, the boys knew things about male-female relationships that we didn't. The girls also assumed boys were better informed than the girls were because they talked a lot among themselves. We girls were wrong on both counts.

This particular conversational style can still be recognized at Class Reunions, often through hearing only a single phrase, the passing utterance going unnoticed by anyone other than classmates. Younger or older spouses of their classmates totally miss the subtle eye contact, body language, or personal connection.

Early in the dating process the girls reported to one another about their dates, but after the first kiss was admitted and described to one's girlfriends, no one asked any more details and none were offered. The subject simply became off-limits.

The trend of going steady flew in the face of parental understanding; however, teenagers themselves saw it as both security and a sign of popularity. In most high schools going steady became the linchpin of the whole system of teenage relationships, with a 1959 poll finding that 57 percent of American teens had gone or were going steady. Maybe this was just an attempt to make connections that didn't seem to be happening within families.

Our parents were warned by magazine articles that demonstrating too much affection could create in their daughters an excessive appetite for love that could lead them to seek physical demonstrations of affection in their teen years. Heeding this advice, many parents stopped showing any affection at all to their children.

This advice backfired, resulting in many teens of this generation being unable to demonstrate affection or to express strong feelings for another person. Even today hugging and verbally expressing affection do not come easy to us, and we hear from one another plaintive comments such as "My dad never hugged me" or "I never heard my mother say, 'I love you.'"

In today's world of almost too much information it is hard to relate to the lack of information faced by the teens of the 1950s. We didn't ask our parents or each other about anything personal and other pathways were quite limited. For example, it would have been unthinkable to ask the high school librarian for a book on sex education—first, because no one would have uttered the word "sex," second, because of embarrassment, third, because there weren't any such publications, and fourth, because the librarian would not have released such material even if there were such.

The library also likely would not have had any medical books on the shelves. Further, teens would not have known how to make an appointment to talk to a doctor about personal matters nor would doctors be likely to discuss such matters with a minor.

Magazines were filled with instruction to girls on ways to deflect personal "advances," such as advising their female readers, "If a boy is forward (translated, "if he makes a pass"), change the subject of the conversation." (This advice was NOT helpful.)

Further, because we lacked conversational skills, most of us girls were lost as to how to change a subject when there was no conversation to begin with. Girls didn't even know how to ask one another for information, let alone what to say to a boy. They wouldn't know how to frame questions and everyone would end up being embarrassed.

All told, the teens of our time lived in a world of confusion. All we knew is that we felt rudderless because sexual customs that had guided young people of earlier generations had no definite hold on us. Because nothing concrete had replaced those earlier mores, we were left in a muddle. Later, we realized that we had been—and still are—the last generation to hold onto outdated social and sexual patterns.

Graduation and Higher Education

Commencement

The events that probably were most important in high schools at the time were the end-of-year activities, particularly the Graduation Events held by all public schools. However, my high school had many traditions, including senior-written and senior-produced programs. All of the workings of the ceremony were ours to plan, even the colors for the academic regalia had we wanted to. Like everything else in our lives at that time, however, we took for granted all of this additional attention by the faculty to create a personal Commencement for each class.

A part of the long-standing senior end-of-year tradition was what we called Shelf Day, produced by the graduating class. This included an assembly program with an original skit, along with the reading of the Class Will, Class Prophecy, and the yearbook dedication. Following the program, seniors then headed to an offsite Class Picnic which concluded in the evening with a square dance (in the mid-fifties when square dancing held short-lived, but intense popularity, to say nothing of the fact that it was easy to follow, and, as a "group dance," would engage more of the class members).

The irony in this is that as the newly graduated Class of 1955, the class which later was deemed most representative of the Silent Generation, found themselves having to be grown up by eighteen, just as the rest of the world began to become caught up in going "teen-age." Once again, the Silent Generation found that their timing was wrong and that they had missed their own party.

Preparation for College

On the a whole, studies have shown that **high school students of this generation earned higher achievement scores than any generation before or since,** even though they received lower numerical grades from their teachers (before the days of grade inflation).

All of us who expected to attend college had enrolled in the academic course in high school, but no adults ever talked about how we would get to college, what program we should take once we got there, and how we might pay for it.

"No one told me how to get from where I was to where I might have wanted to go," wrote Magna Gere Lewis. "It's like there was information there about how to prepare for a career and that there were important things I needed to know but no one ever told me. And by the time I figured it out it was too late. …The boys in the class seemed to know what to do; it's like they already had the information."[31] I often wondered if they did. Was someone guiding them? We would never ask.

While it appeared on the surface that we were being prepared for some kind of future, there were silent messages (at that time not fully interpreted) that the future lives of us girls would be nothing like the futures of the boys in our class. Sadly, few high schools were set up to help females in their college path and career choices, and even fewer higher education institutions were interested in helping women complete a basic degree, let alone enter a professional school. It wasn't until fifty years after high school graduation that I finally had the courage to ask my best male friend what kind of help he had in applying to colleges. "Not much," was his reply; however, his "not much" was still far beyond what I had had. Perhaps without his realizing it, from my perspective he was being mentored by professional men in our town who were ham radio operators and drew him into their circle.

One large advancement the Silents did make, however, was achieving a different kind of success, a self-fulfillment completed to an extent much greater than that of the Greatest Generation or any other prior or succeeding generations. This cohort made the single largest leap forward in mass education of any generation in the 20th Century[32] in that our high school graduation cohort rate of the Silents was 62.3 percent in 1956.[33]

Further, more than three-quarters of the men of the Silent Generation finished high school and a full one-fourth of them were graduated from college, more than double the share of male college graduates of the Greatest Generation.

Unfortunately, however, women of this generation did not match this achievement. While about the same number of men and women were graduated from high school, women lagged far behind the men in college attendance and graduation. In fact, the deficit in college education among our generation of women compared to men surpassed that of any other generation during the twentieth century, but, of course, we didn't know that or perhaps we individually would have had more pride in our accomplishment.

Twenty percent of my own class entered college (the national percentage was 45 percent in 1959, the first year such records were kept), becoming a part of the 1950s college culture that was conservative, a microcosm of the larger society, and entrapped in the Cold War mentality of the decade.

Both women and men were afraid to speak out in their college classes for fear of acquiring a reputation for being radical, an identification that could jeopardize our futures. Further, many of the young men on campus at that time were on military draft deferment and did not want to risk losing that status by going near anything controversial.

Professors taught by example that life was safer if students had no politics, not sharing with the students their own reactions—or anyone else's reaction—to the headlines. As a result, we students absorbed nothing of weight, only bare facts. In general the women were viewed as being not very interesting. We didn't feel disliked, just not very welcomed in the classrooms. Much of the time we went around feeling like we should be apologizing for taking up space.

Most men and women did not believe we had any rights, and certainly no right to criticize the authorities at a university. Further, we would never think of attaching ourselves to a social movement or protest. William Manchester was right when he said there had never been a generation as silent as ours.[34]

Nobody talked about either stress or anxiety.[35] Dissemblance was our answer to cover any concern or worry. We students learned to not show passion, enthusiasm, or intense feelings of any kind, particularly not anger, jealousy, fear, or grief. We learned to cope by becoming compliant. What most surprises later generations about the Silent Generation is that individual pleasure was not a priority and rebellion was not in our field of vision. We were puzzled and confused at times, but with no skills or confidence to question anything we read or heard.

I felt surrounded by those who, I thought, were more confident and sophisticated than I was. The other girls in the Thespian productions, the boys in my classes, the sorority sisters (for the very brief time I belonged to one), and members of the honor societies—all seemed to know what they were doing. If they didn't, I had no way of knowing.

For the most part, professors were not very helpful either; in fact, they often were dismissive. We co-eds thought it somehow was our own fault. I will never forget how surprised I was to find a comment a professor had written on the post card sent to me with my grades. He complimented me on my response to a question, then added, "I wish you would have come to the office to discuss this."[36]

I had not realized we were allowed, let alone expected, to do so.

Women, in particular, were handicapped because of general assumptions that it was not important for them to have an education or profession. Paul Goodman in his landmark *Growing Up Absurd*, was very specific, "…a girl doesn't have to achieve, as she is not expected to make something of herself."[37]

On college campuses most women remained in the dark because no attention was paid to the lack of recognition for women's professional work and accomplishments. Most co-eds just continued to solidify the label of "silent" as we buried our heads in our textbooks, almost all of which were written by men.

Poet Adrienne Rich says of her experience at Radcliffe, "I never saw a single woman on a lecture platform, or in front of a class, except when a woman graduate student gave a paper on a special topic. The 'great men' talked of other 'great men,' of the nature of man, the history of mankind, [and] the future of man…. Women students were simply not taken seriously."[38]

Female college students wondered where this left us and we constantly asked ourselves (without sharing the concern with our cohorts) if we could be successful career women without jeopardizing our role as wife and mother or if we simply had the faith that our futures would somehow work out. We had not yet heard of Betty Friedan or of Simone de Beauvoir, so we had no frame of reference for Friedan's comment about her own growing up without ever having known any woman who (1) used her mind, (2) played her own part in the world, (3) loved someone, and (4) had children.[39]

Further, even in college there were no images or vocabulary that would have made it possible for women to reveal themselves to each other, and few ways for them to interact with one another except through sororities—an entirely different story. Thus, most kept to themselves, never intruding, only observing while remaining powerless and silent.

So there we were, left alone in our dorm rooms, not knowing how to fit in. No one expected much from us because we didn't seem to be expecting much from ourselves. Because for most of their lives females had been reared to believe that the fault for anything about them was their own, they did not want to call attention to the possibility of their own weaknesses, particularly with people who did not know them well. That included everyone.

There were constant reminders that we women could not measure up to whatever the ideal was supposed to be. Therefore, we couldn't compete professionally in a society which prevented some of the best and the brightest of us from pursuing professional careers by greatly limiting access to professional schools. Medical schools made no secret of limiting the number of women admitted to five percent, and law schools' quotas were even lower.[40]

However, our loss was the gain for high schools and those we taught, and I will never forget Mr. Staver telling me that the classes during the earlier years of Lower Dauphin were taught by the brightest of women to whom most other professions were closed.

College or not, couples raced into marriage, perhaps seeing it as a kind of safety from the political situation and the fears of the mid-fifties (including the anti-Communist hysteria and the threat of atomic and nuclear weapons). Others may have been attracted to marry because of the affordable single family homes in suburban developments made possible through federal funds. Or maybe it was simply that they believed what they were being told on all sides, that *marriage would fix everything*.

More than one-third of the males entered professions or became managers (many without a college education), particularly rising up through the new corporate organizations, going on in unprecedented numbers to successful careers in these fields.[41] This was the largest single education attainment of any generation, and no other American generation, from age 20 to 40, ever attained such a steep rise in real per-capita income and household wealth.

Further, the men of this generation were the only generation in American history to have an active military draft hanging over their heads almost the entire time they were of military age. Thus, men of the Silent Generation were given a mixed blessing: as a cohort they were more likely than previous generations to finish high school and be graduated from college while at the same time they were more likely to be drafted into the military.

This national cohort also stands out as being more likely than any other generation of the twentieth century to own guns and keep them at home, in their cars, or on their persons. As a cohort they continue to demonstrate a love for firearms that is unusual in terms of the historical context that shaped us.[42] It is the author's belief that this interest was the result of two factors, (1) the hunting pastime that was prevalent in many areas of the country and (2) as children, spending Saturday afternoons watching cowboy movies. At that time we all, girls and boys alike, wanted to be the hero with the gun, prizing—and comparing—our cap pistols.

In addition, the media pushed the idea that if a woman worked before marriage she likely would become dissatisfied with her family and hence cause emotional damage to both her husband and their children. Commentators were never clear on what females might do with this dissatisfaction other than create disharmony in the home. Popular magazines, therefore, promoted the idea that to keep the home harmonious, it was the job of women to defer totally to their husbands on every decision.

This dilemma of role expectation was very real for women who wanted a college education but worried that a degree could be a negative factor in a marriage. The choice of marriage or career was compounded for many who wanted to go to college yet maintained a vague sense that maybe they should not.

When *House and Garden* reported that suburbia had become the national way of life, it became the norm to marry young, and policymakers, popular culture, and advertisers all began pushing for traditional roles for women and touting age twenty-one as the "healthful" age for marriage. By 1955 the average age of marriage was twenty for women and twenty-two for men (down from 20.4 for females and 22.9 for males in 1951).[43]

Further, nearly one-third of all American women gave birth to their first child before reaching their twentieth birthday. Everyone seemed to be marrying and procreating, and it became the norm to have a child promptly and to have one's own home, the latter being widely regarded as fulfilling a very high purpose.[44]

As might be expected, the college women generally were inept job-hunters. In interviews we would wait for the employer to draw us out, much the same as we always had responded to adults, having been taught—even warned—not to brag or initiate comments.

We evidently thought the interviewers were going to discover our hidden talents or we naively believed that the interviewers already knew our skills, as we sat there in our quiet, unassuming demeanor which we had been reared to hone—a demeanor which only made us look stupid. *We did not know we had only ten minutes to make an impact or to lean forward and provide information to show we were bright and eager job-seekers.*

There we sat—in interviews or in our rooms and later in homes and in our jobs—waiting for opportunities, but never thinking to create them. After all, we had been brought up to believe that we should not seek success. We were told repeatedly, "If you deserve success, it will seek you."[45] We were resigned to our fate even before we knew what that fate would be.

More important were the essential characteristics the Silents shared but had not thought about: we were cautious and dutiful, disliked conflict, regarded our lives as personal and private, and were guided by what Mead called "silent respectability."[46]

However, it likely was that silent respectability was also a deterrent for any advancement. For example, most of us postponed making changes in our professions and pursuing advanced degrees, only to realize too late that we should have started on these paths earlier. By waiting, we put ourselves in competition with the Baby Boomers whose youthful assertiveness gave them an advantage over the Silents in attitude and in interviews.

Other general characteristics the Silent Generation women shared, such as lack of spontaneity, joy, or fun in our lives, also were deterrents in our "catching up." One particular characteristic of the Silents (that often was misinterpreted by those who weren't) was the fact that, in general, we don't laugh readily, we often don't take long or expensive vacations, and we don't very often reward ourselves—and if we do, we feel guilt or remorse. Our motto in life has been *"Do what you <u>need</u> to do before you do what you <u>want</u> to do."* Rewards were and still are viewed as occurring in the future.

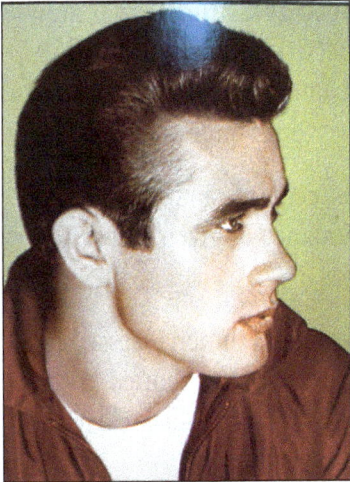

The Nexus

While we never saw it coming, it was the transcendent James Dean in *Giant, East of Eden,* and *Rebel Without a Cause* (all released months after our graduation in 1955) who indirectly had more impact on those of us growing up in the 1950s than even Elvis Presley.

Dean's heart-stopping portrayal as Jim Stark in *Rebel Without a Cause* was quietly revered among us for unwittingly giving us the momentum to begin to understand the latent yearnings we had felt throughout high school. In some ways understanding those unfulfilled longings empowered us and in other ways it made us long for a second chance to go through school asking more questions and perhaps challenging more of the unwritten rules.

Rebel Without a Cause was the complete and blatant reminder of how repressed we had been and how compliant we still were. Mainly, the movie marked us as being a generation that may have been waiting for an opportunity to rebel and hadn't yet verbalized it even to ourselves, but rather had chosen to remain unresisting and silent because we weren't sure how many of us felt the same way.

What also is notable was the story line (perhaps not intentional) of *Rebel*, establishing that three teens who had not known each other well were completely able to relate in harmony. A viewer who paid attention to this could not help concluding that the unintended message of the film reinforced the feeling of *generational solidarity.*[47]

Jim Stark was the first screen character that we knew for certain was who we were, and a cult (albeit, of course, a silent one) was born. While we didn't completely understand the epiphany, we knew something had happened to us.

When I first saw *Rebel Without a Cause* in Chicago on November 25, 1955, I recall not being able to move or speak at the end of the movie. I was stunned by the performance, the message, and the sudden realization that this was a movie that was ours, one that distinguished who we were. Another memory, just occurring as I write this, is that I did NOT want to discuss what I had just seen. And my date and I did not speak of what we had just viewed.

Fifty years later it struck me that **this movie had been the defining moment of our time** that all historians had missed.

....

And it was this defining moment that was to be the lure—not understood at the time—that drew a few of us in our twenties to serve as advocates for the delineating impact the youth of the 1960s would be making on the world. We just didn't know in what capacity. We knew only that we wanted to be a part of making some kind of difference or impact that would answer our search for ourselves.

The conundrum was how to do this in a world that did not welcome educated women. While we were "allowed" to choose a major in college, we were not provided with guidance or given a review of our aptitudes with suggestions made accordingly.

The Kudor Preference test that had been administered to us as high school freshmen assessed my aptitude as "mechanical," and all I could envision was repairing machinery; thus, I just scoffed at this result. As a freshman in college, despite my earning the highest grade in the class in College Algebra, no one ever asked if I ever had considered applying to the College of Engineering.

While this may sound corny or melodramatic, what I knew in the core of my being was that I simply wanted to go to college to *learn*; I wanted a broad-based education and I did not want to be in the College of Education. A "liberal arts" education, whatever that might be, sounded like a good fit, although, again, no one ever asked me what I wanted "to be" or even explained to me just what "liberal arts" meant.

By the end of my Junior Year at Penn State, I realized that my English Literature major in the School of Liberal Arts wasn't going to lead me to a job. Thus, in the fall of my junior year I began to take electives to meet the minimum requirements for a teaching certificate.

My diary entries captured this decision, "I called Mimi (the older sister of my best friend) and she told me where to go tomorrow."[48]

Years later I recounted that next day, "Any doubts I had about my ability to succeed academically in college were laid to rest with a visit to the College of Education to have my grades reviewed for possible transfer from Liberal Arts. Miss Hunter, with whom I met, telephoned Dr. Free (Department Chairman) at home, saying to him, "When I saw Judith's record, I was going to lock the door and keep her here."

I was somewhat taken aback both by her eagerness and assumption that I was seeking admission to the secondary education program. While flattered by her comments, I couldn't help wondering if the students they enrolled were not as academic-centered as I and, if not, then did I want to be part of this program. I was not looking for easier courses, just a plan by which I could find a job after graduation. I left the room determined that I would remain in Liberal Arts and continue to take the minimum requirements for a teaching certificate as electives.

I found some colleagues of like mind when I began teaching and as we watched our budding high school students with all of their exuberance, we were confirmed (although individually) in our beliefs that, yes, we were different from our own peers; we just didn't know why. And because some of our cohorts viewed us as aloof and not outgoing socially, we had a sinking feeling that this emerging culture that was destined to make a huge impact on society had come too late for us to be a part of.

Then the *possibility* to be part of the adventure came when some of the Baby Boomers gave us an unspoken invitation to join them in the breaking of new ground, a chance to grab onto the defining moment that had first cracked open through a 1955 movie.

I later realized that Donald Campbell was right. My own high school cohort had been the "oldest young generation in the world" and likely the last truly educated Americans. Our legacy is that we provided the eccentric loners, isolated, quietly competent, and creative people who somehow managed to assemble the most progressive and exciting society and culture the world has ever seen.

We are most certainly Martin Scorsese's Most Creative Generation in American History,[49] setting in motion major changes in American society to create a new society.[50] We don't brag about it or flaunt it. Rather we just do what we do.

Chapter 2 Endnotes:

[1] Strauss and Howe, *Generations*, p. 66.

[2] Author's note: There was a guidance counselor, but no one seemed to know his role in the school, not even he.

[3] Some of us thought this was a person because of the song lyrics, "Let's remember Pearl Harbor; How she died for liberty!"

[4] Strauss and Howe, *Generations*, p. 74.

[5] Strauss and Howe, *Generations*, p. 286.

[6] Strauss and Howe, *Generations*, p. 281.

[7] Eisler, *Private Lives*, p. 31.

[8] Sheehy, in Strauss and Howe, *Generations*, p. 292.

[9] Levinson, in Strauss and Howe, *Generations*, p. 292.

[10] Strauss and Howe, *Generations*, p. 292.

[11] Strauss and Howe, *Generations*, p. 50.

[12] Reisman, *The Lonely Crowd*, p. 61.

[13] I say this as the editor of my own high school yearbook in the 1950s as well. Nothing distinguished our year from most of the others (although we thought it did), even though our yearbook took first honors designated by the Columbia University Press Association.

[14] Elwood, *The Fifties Spiritual Marketplace*, p. 103.

[15] Bruce Handy, "This is Cinerama," *Vanity Fair*, April 2001, p. 260.

[16] The author remembers the fear of this inoculation administered by a family friend, a nurse, who brought this serum to their home. The author was the last hold-out in the family to allow the inoculation.

[17] Foreman, *The Other Fifties*, p. 60.

[18] "Picture This: 1951," *Temple Review*, Fall 2002, p. 48.

[19] The author spent Thanksgiving week-end in 1955 attending (1) Cinerama, (2) "Guys and Dolls" with Marlon Brando and Frank Sinatra, and (3) the newly released "Rebel Without a Cause" with James Dean, along with an evening at the Black Orchid nightclub. It certainly beat the house parties at PSU.

[20] I personally surely did not realize this!

[21] Evans, *The American Century*, p. 476.

[22] Evans, p. 151.

[23] Author's note: I can't say I would agree with the phrase, "more of everything," for the examples are quite narrow in focus, and, from my point of view, not necessarily positive.

[24] Eisler, flyleaf.

[25] They still do!

[26] In the 1950s, audio manufacturers employed the phrase high fidelity as a marketing term to describe records and equipment intended to provide faithful sound reproduction.

Chapter 2 Endnotes continued:

27 Intended pun.

28 This partly was due to Sam Phillips's echo chamber recording technique that gave the music its distinctive sound and "beat." (Gitlen, *The Sixties: Years of Hope, Days of Rage*, p. 37)

29 Eisler, p. 160.

30 Foreman, *The Other Fifties*, p. 61.

31 Lewis, *Without a Word*, p. 63.

32 Carlson, *The Lucky Few*, p. 48.

33 Kett, *Rites of Passage*, p. 245.

34 Strauss and Howe, *The Fourth Turning*, p. 162.

35 Eisler, p. 72.

36 It was common practice to provide a self-addressed post card to the professor who then would write our course grade on the card and mail it to us.

37 Goodman, *Growing Up Absurd*, p. 13.

38 Kaledin, *Mothers and More*, p. 48.

39 Kaledin, p. 49.

40 Kaledin, p. 54.

41 Carlson, p. 95.

42 Carlson, p. 135.

43 "Picture This," *Temple Review*, Fall 2002, p.48.

44 Modell, *Into One's Own*, p. 257.

45 Miller and Nowack, *The Fifties: The Way We Were*, p. 128.

46 Wakefield, *New York in the Fifties*, p. 3.

47 Jezer, *The Dark Ages*, p. 245.

48 Diary entry.

49 Campbell, *Silent Celebration*, p. 147.

50 Campbell, p. 151.

Chapter 3

Cycles of History and Generations

Whether 'tis nobler in the mind to suffer
The slings and arrows of outrageous fortune
Or to take arms against a sea of troubles
And by opposing, end them.

Hamlet's Soliloquy
Shakespeare

The Theory of Generations

For many years history has identified people by the generation in which they were born and to which they belong, a generation being defined as collectively all of the people born and living at about the same time. The length of a generation is described as about 25 years, the period during which children are born, grow up, become adults, and begin to have children of their own.

"Generations" as a particular area of study is fairly new, emerging as a subset of sociology. There is evidence and ongoing research to show that a generational approach to understanding society and groups of people is scientifically acceptable, as it is well-grounded in good social science. The best up-to-date research into generations is being generated by sociology and practical theology departments of top universities, with an emphasis on understanding how value shifts impact societal institutions, including religious institutions.

The study of the cyclical nature of history and generational development is not new, having begun in Biblical times. However, the first modern scholar to investigate this phenomenon and to describe generational values development was Karl Mannheim, a German sociologist and founder of the sociology of knowledge which deals with social influences on individuals' lives. Mannheim believed that young generations are imperfectly socialized because of a gap between the ideals they have learned from older generations and the realities they experience.

He believed that young people learn values from their parents and communities, and often share similar core ideals throughout their lifetimes. However, as they become aware of the world around them, they experience society differently than through the eyes of their parents and they adapt the value systems they have received for the realities they experience. These collective values continue to influence their behavior throughout their lives.

Even with distinct individual experiences, however, every generation, including the Baby Boomers, has its own name and place in history. Many historians/researchers hold to the belief that what a person's generation is at birth—and what they collectively become—is destiny, not choice, a most interesting thought.

Generational theory as we view it today was most popularized by the work of William Strauss and Neil Howe, two of the best-known historians in the study of generations in the 1990s. Since that time most researchers and others writing about generations use the terms relative to this theory designed and made popular by these two scholars.

Most of what is cited here comes from the work of Strauss and Howe who collaborated on two books, *Generations* (1991) and *The Fourth Turning* (1997). Only Howe survives and has continued in this work begun by the two authors.

Below is a listing of the generations in the United States that have been identified, from the mid-19th Century Missionary Generation to the present adult generation generally known as Generation X, and the newest generation, currently termed Millennials.[1] The terms here are not universally used, but are those most recognizable to general readers.

Great Power Sacculum

Generation	Type	Birth Years	Formative Era
Missionary Generation	Prophet (Idealist)	1860–1882 (22 yrs.)	High: Reconstruction/Gilded Age
Lost Generation	Nomad (Reactive)	1883–1900 (17)	Awakening: Missionary Awakening
G.I. Generation	Hero (Civic)	1901–1924 (23)	Unraveling: World War I/Prohibition
Silent Generation	Artist (Adaptive)	1925–1942 (17)	Crisis: Great Depression/World War II

Millennial Sacculum

Generation	Type	Birth Years	Formative Era
Baby Boomers	Prophet (Idealist)	1943–1964 (17)	High: Superpower America
Generation X[2]	Nomad (Reactive)	1965–1983 (19)	Awakening: Consciousness Revolution
Millennials		1984–2004	Unraveling
Next Unnamed		2005–	Crisis

A Generation:

▶ The average life of a person in a generation is 80 years, and consists of four periods of 20 years each:

❖ Childhood → Young Adult → Midlife → Elderhood

▶ A generation is an aggregate of people born approximately every 20 years:

❖ The Silent Generation → Baby Boomers → Generation X → Millennials

▶ Each generation experiences "four turnings," one approximately every 20 years:

❖ High → Awakening → Unraveling → Crisis

▶ A generation is considered either "dominant" or "recessive" according to the turning experienced as young adults. As any youth generation comes of age and defines its collective persona, an opposing generational archetype is in its midlife peak of power:

❖ Dominant: independent behavior + attitudes in defining an era

❖ Recessive: dependent role in defining an era

Dominant Generations of young adults include the following (terms defined by Strauss and Howe):

❖ **Prophets:** Experience an Awakening as young adults. An awakening is defined as a time when institutions are attacked in the name of personal and spiritual autonomy.

❖ **Heroes:** Experience a Crisis as young adults. A crisis is defined as a time when institutional life is destroyed and rebuilt in response to a perceived threat to the nation's survival.

Recessive Generations include the following:

❖ **Nomads:** Experience an Unraveling as young adults. Unraveling is defined as a time when institutions are weak and distrusted, while individualism is strong and flourishing.

❖ **Artists:** Experience a High as young adults. High is defined as a time when institutions are strong and individualism is weak.

It is the cycle itself, and not the individual members, that determines the fate—as well as the personalities, of each generation or cycle. Not all members of a generation are identical, but most of them share the same traits and have the same experiences, the same frame of reference, the same lifestyle, and are likely to make similar choices. Thus, it could be said that **all identified generation members are predestined to have certain characteristics, make certain decisions, and live a particular way of life (as a cohort).**

The characteristics of a generation are not chosen by the group, but are predestined by the cycle of history into which a cohort is born. Thus, while we can describe particular generations or eras or cohorts, we can also predict what the characteristics in future generations will be, as these generations/eras/cohorts/groups appear in history in sequence. We also can have certain expectations of each new generation as to personality features the members will have in common.

As an example, Generation X is the name given to the demographic cohort following the Baby Boomers generation.[3] Generation X members were born between the early-to-mid 1960s and the late 1970s to early-to-mid 1980s. Generation X is a relatively small demographic cohort[4] sandwiched between two larger ones, the Baby Boomers and the Millennials.

Members of Generation X were children during a time of shifting societal values and as children were sometimes called the "latchkey generation" because they had less adult supervision than those of previous generations, due to increasing divorce rates and mothers who were more likely to be in the workforce at a time when there were not many childcare options outside of the home. As adolescents and young adults they were sometimes referred to as the "MTV Generation," and characterized as slackers and as cynical and disaffected. In midlife, they have been described as active, happy, and as achieving a work-life balance, as well as being credited with entrepreneurial tendencies.

(See Addendum in this chapter for a recent [2017] assessment of Generation X.)

Strauss and Howe state that every two decades or so Anglo-American society enters a new era which Strauss and Howe call "a new turning" and that at the beginning of each turning, people (as a cohort) change how they view themselves, their culture, the nation, and the future. Strauss and Howe have identified four turnings, the total of which spans the approximate length of a long human life, roughly eighty to one hundred years. The following identifies the descriptive name of each of the four turnings that a cohort will experience together:

First Turning: High   Third Turning: Unraveling

Second Turning: Awakening   Fourth Turning: Crisis

The First and Second Turnings (High and Awakening) are part of the Great Power Saeculum (a saeculum is the length of time approximately equal to the potential lifetime of a person), covering, in our example, the cohort's birth years of 1901–1942. The Third and Fourth Turnings (Unraveling and Crisis) are part of the Millennial Saeculum and, in our example, cover the birth years of 1943–1983.

First Turning

The First Turning (High, which follows the Crisis of the previous generation) is a time when institutions are strong and individuals weak. Collectively, society is confident as to where it wants to go, although those outside the center of the society often feel stifled by the conformity they sense. The most recent High Cycle (First Turning with birth years of its cohort members, known as The **G.I. Generation** [later changed to The **Greatest Generation**] being between 1901 and 1924) occurred during the presidencies of Truman, Eisenhower, and Kennedy and ended with the assassination of President Kennedy.

Strauss and Howe described that the public in general (including the Baby Boomers) brims over with optimism, in which smart people accomplish big projects and impossible dreams are freshly achievable. Strauss and Howe describe this as a time when (1) "the moon is reachable, poverty can be eradicated, Tomorrowland is a friendly future with moving skywalks; and (2) life is filled with pastel geometric shapes, Muzak, and well-tended familics.[5]

Second Turning

The Second Turning (Awakening) is an era in which institutions are attacked in the name of personal and spiritual autonomy and, just when society is reaching its high tide of public progress, people tire of the social discipline and want to recapture a sense of self-awareness, spirituality, and spiritual poverty. The most recent Awakening included from the time of the college campus revolts of the mid-1960s to the tax revolts of the late 1980s.

People during this turning have new spiritual agendas and social ideals, and try utopian experiments, seeking to reconcile total fellowship with total autonomy.

There is a high tolerance for risk-prone lifestyles in this turning, while public order deteriorates and crime and substance abuse rise—all representative of disorder alternating (1) between perfection and disaster and (2) between utopias celebrating love and dystopias annihilating everything. This also is a time when self-expression takes precedence over self-control. (The birth years of the current Second Turning are between 1925 and 1942. Their generation name is the **Silent Generation**.)

Third Turning

The Third Turning (Unraveling) is a time when the center does not hold. By this point people in this cohort have had their fill of spiritual rebirth, moral protest and life-style experimentation. It is a time of national drift and institutional decay in which institutions are weak and distrusted, while individualism is strong and flourishing.

Pleasure-seeking continues, co-existing, however, with a declining public tolerance for aberrant personal behavior. While the sense of collective and personal guilt reaches a zenith at this time, the cynical alienation from it hardens into brooding pessimism. The birth years of the current Third Turning cohort are between 1943 and 1964. Their generation name is the **Baby Boomers**.

The most recent Unraveling in the U.S. ranged from the late 1980s and was projected through the middle of the 2000s. However, since the Strauss and Howe book was published in 1997 there is no date in this book for this particular Unraveling occurrence.

Fourth Turning

The Fourth Turning (Crisis) is an era (1) in which institutional life is destroyed and rebuilt in response to a perceived threat to the nation's survival and (2) when people begin to locate themselves as members of a larger group. We are currently in the Fourth Turning (approx. 2007–2030) in which it was predicted that America would suffer a historical event commensurate to the American Revolution. This current Fourth Turning cohort is known as **Generation X** (initially named by Strauss and Howe as the 13th Generation) and identifies those born between 1965 and 1983.

A Fourth Turning era can end in either apocalypse or glory. "The nation could be ruined, its democracy destroyed, and millions of people scattered or killed, with the means to inflict unimaginable horrors and, perhaps, adversaries who possess the same."[5] Or it could enter a new golden age as predicted by 1950s forecasters who predicted America's future would be filled with well-mannered youth, a wholesome culture, an end of ideology, an orderly conquest of racism and poverty, steady economic progress, and plenty of social discipline. This crisis could destroy us as a nation and people, or it could ennoble our lives. (At the time of this writing, we are about halfway through the modern Fourth Turning.)

Strauss and Howe also say that in the areas of social interaction there is the following pattern in periods of time:

High eras **promote** income and class **equality**;

Awakening eras **change** that equality;

Unraveling eras **promote inequality**; and

Crises eras **change** that inequality.

In another delineation of the Four Turnings, Strauss and Howe describe the following:

First Turning (High) is a time when people want to **belong**.

Second Turning (Awakening) is a time when people want to **defy**.

Third Turning (Unraveling) is a time when people tend to **separate**.

Fourth Turning (Crisis) is a time when they want to **gather (preparing for the next "belonging").**

With each new Crisis, which is the end point of a cycle, a society typically will rejuvenate and replenish its culture as it is cleansed, censored, and then harnessed again to new goals (if it is not destroyed).

Strauss and Howe clarify that the cycles themselves have no power. They are merely descriptors of a cadre of people going through changes, each cycle being a time when most people in a particular cycle will want to push their own lives more in one direction than in another.

A fallacy which needs to be addressed, however, is that "only a one-minute delay in birth separates the new-born babies at the end of one cycle (for example, a person born December 31, 1942 is considered a member of the Silent Generation), from those born the first minute of the following cycle (for example, a person born January 1, 1943 is considered a member of the Baby Boomers)—a critical tick of the clock that can have interesting consequences, such, for example, creating a lasting cohort bonding—or a boundary—between, again for example, the Silent and Baby Boomer generations.[6]

Turnings for the Boomers

The Boomers First Turning (A High, 1946 - 1963)

This span of years combined optimism, technology, and prosperity. At the same time that the **G.I.s** (Greatest Generation) were settling in on midlife conformism, the **Silents** were fulfilling their destiny as adaptable helpmates, and the **Boomers** were continuing to enjoy new indulgences.

Based on the Generations Theory all that was happening was inevitable, regardless of what people did. Whether the American First Turning was good or bad is not the point. In theory of the seasonal rhythms of history, the First Turning is a *necessary* era, cleaning up from the Crisis that came before the new First Turning and setting the stage for the Second Turning (An Awakening) to follow.

The High era also marks the new cycle phase (which, remember, follows a Crisis of the previous cycle). In this particular High, heroes move into midlife, and parents (in this orderly post-Crisis world of the High era) can safely devote more time to child raising and offer new freedoms to this new generation.

G.I.s

American schools enjoyed an all-time peak of confidence during this time, partly through a support network between mothers and teachers (beginnings of PTOs/PTAs) who had a close partnership to provide the best for the children. Importantly, the G.I. generation saw to it that Boomers were taught critical thinking, instilling in them what was later described as an "orientation to principle."

Silents

In the first years of this particular High (late 1940s), the early collegians of the Silent Generation found themselves surrounded by G.I. vets who got the best grades and subsequent job offers. In contrast, the Silents seemed to be dreary as they were described as having clothing, manners, and lifestyles that were scaled down versions of what adults had. (Boring.) They were expected to—and did—behave impeccably in school. Their major discipline problems were gum chewing and cutting in line—and perhaps among the girls, passing notes.

As noted in Chapter 2 of this book, the high school Silents received lower grades (grade inflation started with the next generation), but *earned higher educational achievement scores than any generation before or since their time.* And by the time the last of the Silents completed college, they had achieved the nation's greatest two-generation advance in the number of years of schooling.

They excelled at arts and letters while searching for someone to confide in, something they sought for most of the years of their lives. This factor in and of itself has not been addressed head-on, but certainly explains the way life was/is for them.

The only way most mainstream Silent Generation members bent the rules even a little was by "cultivating refined naughtiness."[7]

Refined Naughtiness

From my personal experience, an example of this "refined naughtiness" is my wearing in the classroom a pair of earrings with the insignia of the Playboy Bunny I had bought at the Playboy Club in New York City.

Importantly, the overall compliance to rules learned and followed by the Silent Generation would not be of interest to the Boomers, and the Boomers themselves soon would be enjoying every perk possible.

Boomers

The Boomers were enjoying being cosseted, but would not yet have, at this point, been verbalizing or even considering that the ideas held by the G.I.s were becoming stale.

Boomers would be reared according to Dr. Spock and their own G.I. parents who wanted their children (the Boomers) to be self-focused enough to resist peer pressure and to become "modern kids of a modern age." A best-selling book at the time advised parents to continually give to their children; otherwise, they would not be viewed as loving parents.

Presumed to have a bright future, children in this High era were *encouraged to demand much of life.* (What is most fascinating is that the behavior of each generation contrasts sharply with its predecessor's behavior at the same age. And every time it seems to catch society by surprise!)

Another factor in this High era (1946–1964) is that few women worked outside the home, particularly not mothers of pre-school children. During this time scientists also conquered childhood diseases, as well as fluoridating the water. No other generation of children had had more inoculations or surgeries, including millions of circumcisions and tonsillectomies that in today's world would not be performed.

Boomer children in neighborhoods were made to feel welcome at almost all homes, and adults watched out for all the neighborhood children. In addition, with the more affluent society in which the Boomers were children, towns offered libraries, recreation centers, and other civic entities to engage children and youth. All of this helped to develop a sense of entitlement in the Boomers.

Further, at no other time in the twentieth century did the mainstream culture show such a peaceful, unfearful world view to its children; however, they were not being prepared for challenges or tragic outcomes. For example, from the mid-1940s to the mid-1950s, the average daily hours a household spent watching TV rose from four to four-and-a-half hours. Thus, it was the Boomers who were the first child market to be targeted by advertising agencies.

Overall, the period in which the Boomers were adolescents was described by Robert Samuelson as "a period of high optimism when people believed that technology and society's best minds would guarantee social improvement." It also should be noted that as the 1960s dawned, California State University-Berkeley's president Clark Kerr (who had served in WWII) commented that the entering college classes would be easy to handle. "There aren't going to be any riots," he mistakenly predicted.....[8]

The Boomers Second Turning (An Awakening, 1964 - 1984)

These awakening years bring skirmishes of several movements that developed during those twenty years. America entered the Awakening with what became known as the Consciousness Revolution.

During this Awakening Era the G.I.s were entering elderhood, the Silents were entering into midlife, and the Boomers were reaching their teens and young adulthood.

G.I.s

The G.I.s entered the Awakening at their height of public power, their energy and collective purpose, not slowed down by their aging. This spurred them to ever grander constructions. When they were challenged by young zealots (the Boomers) the G.I.s at first battled against the Boomers' new values, but they later acceded to them.

Many of the G.I. Generation were troubled by what they viewed as a lack of respect and appreciation from the Boomers.

For the G.I.s it was a time of disappointment, humiliation, and angry division as they watched the society (that they had so painstakingly cleaned up) transform into something they didn't much like.

Silents

The Silents saw the Awakening as times of personal "passages" when their lives became more turbulent and adventuresome. Somewhat indecisive as to their role in society, they brought expertise and process to improve society while doing their best to calm the often excessive passions of the young. As mediators, they guided the Boomers while still honoring the G.I.s. The Silents often deflected argument by compromising or postponing unpleasant choices. They worked toward moderation which helped keep the Awakening from turning into social chaos.

According to Strauss and Howe, the assassination of President Kennedy left a larger imprint on the Silents than on any other generation and, with the loss of this generation's own Martin Luther King and Robert Kennedy, the Silents never again felt as confident in or uplifted by public life.

Further, they felt stuck between the "can-do" G.I.s and the self-absorbed Boomers, and found themselves asking, "Is this all there is?" They completely understood the lyrics of Bob Dylan, "Ah, but I was so much older then, / I'm younger than that now."

While some Silents tried to convince Boomers that they understood them, others supported the fury of the Boomers by becoming their pied pipers, leading the way for them. Some of the Silent

Generation also began resisting the G.I.s because of their own feeling that they (Silents) themselves had been repressed by being sandwiched between the G.I.s and the Boomers and perhaps were noting that the G.I's had no time for them.

More traumatic, it suddenly dawned on many of the Silents that they had spent their lives doing what they were "supposed to do," and realized in midlife that they had spent their lifetimes waiting for the right time for them, which never arrived.

Boomers

The Awakening laid out a lifetime agenda for leadership by the Boomers, which likely is why the Boomers recall this era most favorably. Self-absorbed, the Boomers (not having experienced a Crisis era yet), took for granted the comforts and indulgences of the new secular order.

Nurtured by adults to be creative thinkers, they cultivated their own inner lives, viewing themselves as holding spiritual authority and as serving as the arbiter of new values. They often burst forth with angry challenges to what they viewed as the narrower constructions of the G.I.s and Silents, and did not seek the advice of the G.I.s on basic life decisions.

The 1960s Boomers wanted to rebuild, were often impatient, and were willing not only to upset apple carts, but also to destroy protesters they didn't agree with. Unlike the Silents, they did not fear any results such as "blotches on their permanent records." They were savvy enough (which the Silents, being used to following orders, did not) to realize that no one was giving them black marks.

Most sociologists who studied the Boomers agreed that they were fundamentally revolting against their G.I. father figures, mocking them with the two-fingered peace sign, the defiant wearing of khaki, and the desecration of the American flag. The Vietnam War gave the Boomers the perfect cause by which to protest their rage.

The Boomers also avoided being drafted through any means possible, and only one in every sixteen male Boomers ever saw combat. Ten times as many Boomers committed draft law felonies as were killed in the war. The long-lasting result was a major division between those Boomers who fought in Vietnam and those who did not.

Following the Vietnam War, some Boomers found the economy a barrier in finding employment, and some rationalized that working was "beneath" them. A Dartmouth valedictorian declared, "I have made no plans because I have found no plans worth making." His peers cheered.

Large numbers of the Boomers dabbled in various kinds of self-religion, insisting on engaging in only "meaningful" careers. It was also reported that many Boomers left their own young families to do "what I want to do." Because the Boomers deliberately didn't purchase much, America's decades-long productivity surge ended when Boomers turned away from brand loyalties.

In general, the Boomers remained expressive in their own way and many agreed with fellow Baby Boomer Hillary Rodham (Clinton) when in her college valedictory speech she announced that she and her colleagues would be "…choosing a way to live that will demonstrate the way we feel…" Things were, indeed, a-changing.

The nation moved from Leslie Fiedler's "cult of the child" in the 1950s to Landon Jones' "cult of the adult" in the 1970s when sacrificing one's own happiness for the sake of one's children became passé in the views of many. In fact, adults were advised by many "experts" to teach small tots about "consequences" rather than teaching them about right and wrong.

The Boomers Third Turning (Unraveling, 1984 – 2005)

This period was also referred to as the Culture Wars (a description of America's niche group conflict), opening with individualism and then moving to pessimism. Personal confidence remained high but the public was still concerned with growing violence and uncivility, widening inequality, distrust of institutions, and a debased popular culture.

G.I.s

During this Third Turning the G.I.s remained in leadership positions but had begun to vacate the culture, instead worrying about a society whose new spiritualism they found alien.

Silents

The Silents entered into their midlife adulthood, and sensing that the old order had been repudiated, began to expand their own realm of personal choice.

Boomers

The Boomers entered midlife feeling confirmed in their earlier discovery of personal truth, deciding they wanted to change society from the inside out.

In the early part of the Third Turning many were discovering that they were comfortable—for the moment. Americans had survived the Awakening when rebels (Boomers) had attacked the fortress, and most of them expected that the victors (themselves) would end up ruling.

Niche groups began to form and before long any argument or idea or observation outside one's own group became suspect. There was no central public opinion, as public discourse became more "tribal" and less cordial.

This then led to a division over what kind of country America was and what was meant by "The American Way of Life," as American ideals began morphing into ideologies. The only commonalty of these niche groups was the agreement that the institutional order was not working and perhaps was not worth defending.

Generation X

The new Generation Xers (whose earliest members were born in the 1960s) were in the childhood-young adulthood age. Somewhat cynical in this world of powerless adults, they learned to distrust the rules and to prepare to make their own way on their own terms.

All Generations

Americans at all levels soon became cynical, and conspiracy theories abounded. The result was that a system, which had only looked corrupt from the outside during the Awakening, now looked that way from the inside as well. Polls showed that nine of ten people agreed that "at an earlier time people in America felt they had more in common and shared more values than Americans do today."

This unraveling changed American life in ways no one had predicted and by the mid-1990s fiscal excess had become a political way of life. Three in four adults believed the United States to be in moral and spiritual decline.[9]

Uncivility became the norm.[10] This was completely opposite to what was seen in the "High" era when the concept of communal chaos and rampant individualism would have been unimaginable.

Hard as it may be to believe when one is embroiled in an unraveling, Strauss and Howe stand by their study of these cycles. However, what may make this more troubling to the reader is that each cycle that civilization goes through seems to become more frightening and unfathomable.

The Boomers Fourth Turning (Crisis, 2005 - 2025)

The Silents are now the elders, still trying to be the peace-makers. The Boomers are entering elderhood, reaching their apex of leadership in this Crisis period. Born in the aftermath of one Crisis, the Boomers will be fomenting the next Crisis.

Generation X will step up as the pragmatic midlife managers of the Crisis, and the (new) Millennials will become the young-adult soldiers.

Based on past history, Strauss and Howe offered five possible scenarios as to what could happen in this new Fourth Turning (whose center point was 2015, so that we are now in the second half of this Fourth Turning).[11] (Also bear in mind that Strauss and Howe wrote their books in the 1990s.)

1. The government will lay claim (or has laid claim) to its residents' federal tax monies.
2. A global terrorist group will bring (or has brought) down an aircraft and announces it possesses portable nuclear weapons.
3. An impasse over the federal budget reaches a stalemate.
4. The Centers for Disease Control and Prevention announce the spread of a new communicable virus.
5. Growing anarchy throughout the former Soviet republics prompts Russia to conduct training exercises about its borders.

Strauss and Howe's forecast will likely be correct here, that sometime in the middle of one of these crises (or a different scenario crisis), some action will ignite a new mood of national urgency. This would then set off a chain reaction of further emergencies rooted in debt, civic decay, and global disorder. At home and abroad the event will reflect the tearing of the civic fabric of America at points of extreme vulnerability.

At the same time each generation's approach will be a reminder of how unprepared the nation is for the future. Strauss and Howe expect(ed) the following:

1. The Boomers' old age will loom, exposing the lack of private savings and the unsustainability of public promises to support their needs (such as Social Security).
2. Generation Xers will reach their make-or-break peak earning years, realizing at last that they can't all be lucky exceptions to their stagnating average income.
3. The Millennials will come of age facing debts, tax burdens, and two-tier wage structures that older generations will declare intolerable.

This Unraveling will have left the government so fiscally overcommitted that whatever they propose will lack credibility. The economy could be on a brink of a depression.

With this and other complicating factors, the system will further unravel. This national issue will affect the shape of American life. Any number of scenarios could lead to any number of events. Eventually all of the separate problems will combine into one giant problem and the people *may* coalesce to focus on "this one big problem." Or they may not.

Any number of serious crises could occur, including total war; however, whatever the outcome, American society will be transformed over time into a new emergent society, and the Fourth Turning will close in either glory or ruin.[12]

One possible scenario in the middle of the Unraveling that could close the Fourth Turning in ruin is the following as projected by Strauss and Howe, a haunting, but believable scenario considering that this was written by them in 1997 twenty years before *The English Students* (2018):

A severe recession has erased a decade's worth of Dow Jones gains and, according to some economists, promises to deliver yet another "lost decade." Global trade is shrinking for the first time in a half century. Protectionism looms. Households are retrenching as they adjust to the "new normal." America has swelled with a new vein of Tea Party rebelliousness and political anger. Washington, DC is humming with plans to overhaul on a vast scale—from banks to health care, energy, schools, cities, and transportation. Meanwhile, the nation is waging ground wars in two Asian nations and wages proxy wars on terror in over a dozen others.

Inevitably, according to the Strauss-Howe theories, the Boomers will pursue new late-life careers, often in non-paid emeritus positions, becoming part professor and part spiritual guide in a reinvention of the university. In churches, elders will deliver fierce homilies while younger adults take up the collection, the reverse of what is today's custom. Talk radio will be their bastion of elder reflection.

Boomers, as elders of the tribe, predictably will become the wisdom keepers who will use their intuition to become prophets who guide the long-term reclamation project. These Elder Boomers will be viewed as spiritually gifted and likely will *relish* being authentically *old* people.

True to themselves, Boomers will do what they have done with every earlier step of the aging process:

1. First, resist it.
2. Then, dabble in it.
3. Ultimately, devise a plan to glorify it.

They will do this with serenity as the traits of slow talking, walking, and driving will become badges, not of physical decline, but of *contemplation*.

Samuel Huntington's Theories

It also should be noted that Strauss and Howe, while the best known, are not the only theorists of generations and eras. Samuel Huntington, lauded for his theory, explained in his 1996 book, *The Clash of Civilizations and the Remaking of World Order*, says that the American Revolution was the finest—and perhaps most dangerous hour in politics,[13] because it (1) was episodic (at sixty year intervals); (2) was associated with reaffirmation of traditional American values, but not a change in ideologies; and (3) had as its purpose to bring (American) political institutions and practices into accord with the prevailing values and beliefs.[14]

Huntington explains that prior to each sixty-year period is the concentration of power away from the political values of the American Creed. In addition to his findings, the key element for the 1960s power was in numbers, an increase of 13.8 million in the youth population which was greater than the total increase in the youth population–12.5 million–during the seventy years prior to 1960.[15]

Importantly, Huntington further says that the power of the 1960s was characterized by intense and widespread political activity, supported by a series of emerging new forms of **media.** He explains that during the Revolutionary War years of this country it was the **pamphlet** that helped the Colonies' cause; in the Jacksonian era it was the **newspaper**; during the Progressive years, **mass popular press and cheap magazines** proliferated; and in the 1960s, **television** exploded.

Huntington's point is that <u>it was the method as well as the message</u> that served as the catalyst to change society; that is, pamphlets, newspapers, and magazines changed the way information was shared, as well as being the instrument of information. (Author's note: Consider the power wielded today by social media, with a close second being web-based news sites.)

Huntington further mentioned (and this is important in understanding the 1960s) that his example of creedal political activity was demonstrated in the **1930s** by the abolitionist movement; in the **1950s** by the rights of blacks; and in the **1960s** by the civil rights movement and black consciousness, and he particularly noted that *the media as the means of exposure played a far more influential role in American politics than in the politics of any other society.*

Further, the 1960s was ripe for change when the complacency of the post-WWII country began to deteriorate at the end of the 1950s, particularly with Sputnik. There existed in the country at the time, as John Steinbeck commented, "a nervous restlessness, a thirst, a yearning for something unknown—perhaps morality."[16] And researchers wanted to learn that unknown.

Huntington also expected that the wave of the future would be under the leadership of America because the United States was relatable to the Western nations of Europe. This gave the US a diplomatic status of some significance. However, Huntington added that the United States is alien to the Eastern cultures and would need to consider that factor and decide direction accordingly.[17]

Generation X, Next-in-Line

Because Strauss and Howe's work ended in the late 1990s and even more so because Generation Xers are, in general, the offspring of many of the Boomers, this addendum is being offered as general interest to the reader.

The full article from which this information came is "The Bestest Generation," found in *Vanity Fair*, September 2017, pp. 152-154. The author, Rich Cohen, was born in 1968 and his view is the best description that I have read to date about Generation X, the offspring of many from the Baby Boomer generation and the Silent Generation. Interesting, but not surprising, if Strauss and Howe's theories are to be believed, is that the Gen Xers mirror many of the facts known about the Silents, one important one being that, as a generation, there were few of them, sandwiched in-between much larger groups, in this case the multitudinous Boomers and the even more numerous Millennials.

Cohen[18] brings a viewpoint from Generation X that begins with the following noteworthy description of the Boomer generation, "We Gen Xers grew up in the world of the Baby-Boomers simply because there were so many of them. They were the biggest, easiest, most free-spending cohort the planet had ever known. What they wanted filled the shelves and what filled the shelves became our history. They wanted to dance so we had rock 'n' roll. They wanted to open their minds so we had LSD. They did not want to go to war so that was it for the draft."

Cohen's book, *The Sun and the Moon and the Rolling Stones* (2016) is one of the best accounts ever written of the Rolling Stones, partly because the band was surprisingly open to his traveling with them. However, he himself was clear that he was not "of" the Stones. I identified with his wistful realization, one he called an epiphany while traveling with them in 1994—"Time would always separate me from these guys, from this generation. I'd missed everything: 1964, 1969, 1972—those were the years that mattered. I'd been born too late.[19] Whatever happened had happened already. I'd spent my entire life trying to reach this party. By the time I got there, everyone was old. …Above us, the baby boomers, who consumed every resource and every kind of fun. Below us, the millennials, who've remade the world into something virtual and cold.[20]

Cohen continues, "We will grow old in the world and in the mind of the Millennials because there are even more of *them*. Because these Millennials don't know what they want, the culture will be scrambled and the screens a never-ending scroll. They (Millennials) are not literally the children of the Baby Boomers but might as well be because here are two vast generations, linking arms over our heads, akin in the certainty that what they want they will have, and that what they have is right and good." Strauss and Howe very likely would agree.

Cohen suggests that the Gen Xers have been "squeezed" between two generations, one (Boomers) of which is demanding that they (the Gen Xers) grow up and move away and the other (the

Millennials) wanting the Gen Xers simply to grow old and die. In both cases, the Boomers and the Millennials would like the Xers to "get out, delete your account, kill yourself."

However, the fascinating point Cohen makes is that if our nation has any chance of survival and of carrying its traditions far into the 21st century, it will be because of Generation X who are "the last Americans schooled in the old manner, the last Americans that know how to fold a newspaper, take a joke, and listen to a dirty story without losing their minds." The Gen Xers are the last outpost in a world gone mad, Cohen says, and will be "the last light in in the last saloon on the darkest night of the year."

He further believes that the philosophy of the Boomers is based on a misunderstanding and that they were not in rebellion against Nixon, the Viet Nam War, or the conformity of the Silents, but were against their own fathers who, some believed, had hidden themselves from action in World War II. The Boomers were wrong in their assumption, he says, the real truth (Note: supported by historians) being that the WWII fathers were far from hiding; instead they were seeking peace, tranquility, and stability.

Cohen also comments on the likely fact that there were never enough of the Gen Xers to become the focus of advertisers and notes that they also display a kind of detachment, as well as an aversion to the "older brother still in a peace shirt."

While Cohen doesn't exactly believe in the designation of "generation" in the sense that Strauss and Howe use it, he does agree that "a generation is the creation of shared experiences, the things that happened, the things you (a group) all did and listened to and read and went through and, just as important, the things that did not happen."

He adds that his own generation of Gen Xers are the last Americans to have an old-time childhood, "wherein you were assigned a bully along with a classroom teacher. Our childhood was closer to those childhoods of the 1950s than to whatever the children are doing today. It was coherent, hands-on, dirty (out-of-door activities), and fun."

Cohen concludes that while *The Breakfast Club* was not one of his favorite movies, it is said to define his generation. In the movie the teacher (the only adult in the movie with a major role) speaks to the school janitor, and Cohen says the words of the teacher trouble him, "Now, this is the thought that wakes me up in the middle of the night, that when I grow older these kids are gonna take care of me." Yes, that can strike fear, as it likely has for each generation thinking its future is with its own children.

What most struck me, however, is stated in the middle of the article, much as Generation X itself is stuck between the refined pomposity of the Boomers and the overblown arrogance of the Millennials, as noted by Cohen,

"Though much derided, members of my Generation X turn out to be something like Humphrey Bogart in Casablanca—we've seen everything and grown tired of history and all the fighting and so have opened our own little joint at the edge of the desert, the last outpost in a world gone mad, the last light of the year. It's not those who stormed the beaches (Greatest Generation) and won the war, nor the hula-hooped millions (Baby Boomers)[21] who followed, nor what we have coming out of the colleges now; rather—**it's Generation X that will be called the greatest.**"

Chapter 3 Endnotes:

1   Australian Professor Dan Woodman submits that there is a new micro generation which he terms Xennials, born between 1977 and 1983, a mix of Gen X and Millennials. Since this may be only a passing designation and at best is being viewed as a sub- or micro-generation, this Xennial group within the Millennial designation is not being addressed in this book.

2   Early work of Strauss and Howe [1990s] uses the term "13th Generation," rather than   Generation X, for this cohort.

3   Partly because they are for the most part the children of the Silence Generation.

4   Strauss and Howe, *Generations*, p. 101.

5   Strauss and Howe, *The Fourth Turning*, p. 10.

6   Strauss and Howe, *The Fourth Turning*, p. 66.

7   *The Fourth Turning*, p. 165.

8   *The Fourth Turning*, p. 169.

9   Ibid., p. 206.

10   Ibid., p. 206.

11   Bear in mind that this book you are holding was written in 2017–2018.

12   *The Fourth Turning*, p. 278.

13   Huntington, *American Politics*, p. 129.

14   Huntington, p. 131.

15   Huntington, p. 144.

16   Huntington, p. 174.

17   Huntington, p. 240.

18   Rich Cohen is a contributing editor at *Vanity Fair* and *Rolling Stone* magazines. He is co-creator, with Martin Scorsese, Mick Jagger and Terence Winter, of the HBO series *Vinyl*.[1] His works have been *New York Times* bestsellers, *New York Times* Notable Books, and have been collected in the *Best American Essays* series. One of his most recent publications is *The Sun and the Moon and the Rolling Stones*, highly recommended to the Gen Xs.

19   Just as I, as a member of the Silent Generation, had been born too soon (Author's comment).

20   *The Sun and the Moon and the Rolling Stones*, p. 7.

21   Author's note: Oh, dear, here we are again; Cohen skips right over the Silent Generation.

Chapter 4

The 1960s: Passages and Defining Moments

Bliss it was in that dawn to be alive,

but to be young was very heaven.

The Prelude
Wordsworth

Part I: Microcosm (Hummelstown)
        ….when you're tired of…

Part II: Macrocosm (The Larger World)

Part I: The Microcosm of the 1960s

The term "boom," used long before Baby Boomers had arrived on the scene, means any sudden rise or increase in whatever is being described. Thus, the term "baby boom" was fitting to describe the increase in the national birth rate almost exactly nine months after World War II ended.

As historian Landon Jones[1] described "…the cry of the baby was heard across the land when more babies were born in 1946 in the United States than ever before, making it clear that America was going to experience the birth of 3.4 million babies which was 20 percent more than in 1945. Another 3.8 million were born in 1947, a year in which one American citizen was added to the population every eleven and a half seconds;[2] 3.9 million were born in 1952; and more than 4 million every year from 1954 until 1964 when the "boom" finally tapered off. By that time there were 76.4 million baby boomers, making up almost 40 percent of the nation's population. Totally, more babies were born between 1948 and 1953 than in the previous thirty years combined.[3]

Included among the more than 76 million babies born in the United States between 1943 and 1964 were those who were born in 1947 and would become part of the **Class of 1965, the class considered by sociologists and historians as most representative of that decade**—most of whom when infants were part of a sea of babies in maternity wards filled to capacity, many of them spending their first days of life neatly tucked away in hospital hallways, operating suites, even boiler rooms— one crib after another lined up in a seemingly endless line of newborns.

The two main sources for this major increase in births at the time were (1) parents who had postponed marriage and having a family because of the Great Depression and World War II and (2) young married adults who were eager to start families. Another factor of the high birth rate was the confidence adults had that the future would be one of comfort and prosperity and that they would be able provide for their families all the material things that they themselves had gone without.[4] These families were about to become part of the richest nation the world had ever seen, with the expectation that prosperity would continue. In fact, the economic wealth coming out of the 1950s was the single most important factor in shaping the 1960s.[5]

In early 1964 the American Red Cross reported that the Chase Manhattan Bank announcement that the characteristics of families having an income of over $10,000 a year were changing and that three out of four heads of households worked for someone else rather than being self-employed as was previously. Further, this five-figure income was spreading into jobs that hadn't seen such high wages before. While 51% of these salaries were earned by those in managerial and professional occupations, 15% were currently going to craftsmen; 12% to operators, service workers and laborers; 7% to salesmen; and 5% to clerical workers. The Bank also announced that trends indicated that one-third of all families would be making over $10,000 annually by 1970.[6]

One clear fact about the Baby Boomers is that they were totally unlike any generation that had come before them. They were completely alien to the societal norms that the Silent Generation followed. The Boomers also were viewed by sociologists as "standardized," meaning they were more like one another than like any other generation ever had been, and they also were more unlike any other generation before or since. They were, in fact, a **singular sensation**.

Before they had read their first book or watched their first movie, they all had watched the same television programs and commercials. Almost without exception they never knew a living environment in which there wasn't a television set. As a result, most of their expectations of life were shaped not so much by their family experiences in their home, but by television, both its stories and its advertising.

When the first Boomers were small children in the 1950s, most parents viewed a "good life" as including a well- furnished house, a new car in the driveway, a good white-collar job for the husband, and well-adjusted and successful children who were taken care of by a full-time, stay-at-home wife and mother.

For the most part, the Baby Boomers were reared by parents who were working hard to build a prosperous and secure country. In addition, taxpayers at the time were generally agreeable to build and equip new schools to accommodate this large—and somewhat sudden—increase in enrollment.

Many of the parents followed the advice of Dr. Benjamin Spock who wanted to teach mothers exactly how to rear their offspring. Dr. Spock's method of child-rearing likely aided in Baby Boomers' developing the attitudes they still hold about family, life, gender roles, institutions, politics, religion, lifestyle, and the future.

"Spock babies" were expected to be optimistic, if not idealistic. They were the modern kids of a modern age. "Spock parents" were told to practice democratic discipline and deal with their children "thoughtfully, reasonably, and kindly." Mothers were to coax, not threaten, their recalcitrant children and to use an "on demand" feeding schedule. Childhood diseases were nearly eradicated, water was fluoridated, and inoculation became a matter of course. As a bonus, Parent and Teacher Associations/ Organizations promoted a strong link between parents and schools.

An interesting trend of the time was that adults were paying close attention to what their Boomer-era children were saying, and this "pleasing the children" approach became a very important goal of parents. The future that was spread out before these children was viewed as happy, easy, uncomplicated, and prosperous. There was no need to prepare them for difficult challenges or tragic outcomes because negative challenges and outcomes were not expected to happen.

In general, the Boomers were made to feel welcome by entire communities. Concern for the children's welfare and enjoyment led to increasing the number of local libraries (that would welcome young people), teen centers, and other civic entities that once had been the domain of only parents.

All of this focus on the well-being of Baby Boomers in childhood gave them a very nonthreatening worldview. Since there were no threats, they were free to develop strong inner lives. This was viewed as very positive.

On the other hand, it was also a time when many families were no longer following what had been traditions. This left the Boomers, in some cases, with little sense of family history, or even knowing what behaviors were expected or without understanding "why" holidays such as Memorial Day and Armistice Day were celebrated.

All Boomer children who attended elementary school during the 1950s remember hearing the siren or bell in the school which was the signal that had them "dropping to the floor, trying to balance in a position that required kneeling, clasping hands behind necks, and covering eyes with an elbow so that the imminent atomic flash wouldn't turn their little faces to ash." Other instructions were to keep their eyes closed following the blast and to wear cotton clothing in light colors to help shield against the heat. Yes, really.

Civil defense manuals were available, but only added to the feeling of helplessness. These pointless defenses frightened everyone, and those involved became the first generation to fear not only the possibility of nuclear war, but also the end of the world. As Light noted, the question was not whether they could get to the head of the class the next day, but whether there would be any next day.[7] Thus, the boomers became the first American generation compelled from infancy to fear not only war, but the end of the world. Some may still cringe at the command to "Take cover!"

A few families (and some corporations) built fallout shelters, complete with water, food, cots, and blankets. A high school in Battle Creek, Michigan was said to have a fully equipped fallout shelter for 1200 people. Anyone who came to school would be permitted to enter, but once the doors were closed, no one could leave. Fortunately, they did not have to test the security or their resolve.[8]

With all this being said, however, the central problem with the large number of Boomers was very basic. They were born into a society which very simply was not prepared to accommodate them; thus, this generation shared a degree of social crowding unknown to previous generations. This meant not only needing physical space in homes and Sunday Schools and playgrounds and schoolrooms, but also in school activities and in local Little Leagues and Scouts, and, in some instances, finding a piano teacher who had an open time slot.

However, with all of this attention came a sense of entitlement, and what previous generations had thought to be privileges, Boomers saw as their right. This assumption would have consequences in the future, one of which is that most people would be blindsided and filled with disbelief that the political protests of the late 1960s could possibly be influenced by the darling Boomers!

Consumer goods, including telephones, televisions, refrigerators, and electricity to run everything, were available and affordable to most households. In middle and upper class America cars and inexpensive gasoline became commonplace throughout most of the country.

It was indeed a time of abundance, ripe for the introduction of credit cards and installment buying, with the result that many consumers were caught up in the perception of wealth, not realizing that using credit cards could lead to a different set of problems.

It wasn't long before Baby Boomer children couldn't help but notice how attentive adults were to whatever they said or did. This extra "attention" they received was thus internalized by the children, leading them to believe that they truly were important people. No wonder the Silent Generation was puzzled by these upstart newcomers, wondering why these Boomers didn't seem to have to listen to adults, but had license to do as they pleased.

In 1969 John Aldridge, a member of the Silent Generation, noted, "By now the young people have so intimidated us with their sheer clamorous and moral presence that some of us have been almost persuaded to believe that our primary obligation to society is to die as quickly as possible, so that the Boomers can inherit the earth without further delay."[9]

A decade later, Paul Sann added, "There was such a dramatic contrast between the Silent

Generation and the Baby Boomers that there was nothing in the 1950s culture to prepare us for the 1960s."[10] Sann's Silent Generation cohorts agreed—they were not in any way ready to compete with this huge, exuberant group that was moving toward them like a tidal wave.

By 1960 the number of high school teenagers had increased from 5.6 million to 11.8 million, a little more than doubling. Everyone asked, "What do we do with them?"

By the time the high schools were filled with Boomers, the country brimmed over with optimism, with the possibility of a bustling future in which to "dream the impossible dream" would be the norm. Coming into that cycle, some even believed that going to the moon was within the grasp of the Boomers, poverty was on its way out, and the land of tomorrow would be friendly and utopic. Of course, the ever-proliferating television commercials were promoting "a world where anything could happen, but it all would be good."[11]

As they entered high school, the Boomers were being viewed as confident, stylish, "in-the-know," having indulgent parents, and engaged in a wide selection of activities. The Boomers became more like the happy and confident teenagers who had been depicted in *Calling All Girls* (founded in 1941) and *Seventeen* (1944) magazines than the "Silents"—or the last teens of the Greatest Generation—ever were. Further, bringing more students together, the teen-agers were becoming more savvy.

There were more choices in everything—from churches to movie theatres, and from choices of courses in school to private lessons outside of school, extra-curricular activities, and the confidence to make things happen. As noted, freedom for teens in the 60s was far broader and, in general, held more opportunities than had been dreamed of in the 1950s world.

Families with teenagers in the 1960s were quite different from those families of the 1950s. The 1950s family was headed by the archetypal white, middle-class suburban or working class male with little or no political bent, few opinions, and no notable connection with the world around him. It was a structured patriarchal, nuclear, suburban middle-class unit. Three children would be typical. The G.I. fathers, of course, were hard workers and ever so grateful just to be back to normalcy with all thoughts of war service behind them.

In contrast, the 1960s families were smaller in number and often without close kinship units of extended families. There also was a growing paranoid fear in these parents of the outside world, with an exaggerated sense of privacy, particularly among the new affluent and middle classes.[12]

Good as life was, however, in both the 1950s and the 1960s, an underlying fear permeated everything, that being the possibility of a nuclear war. As Wallech noted, "When you grow up and your whole life is focused on getting ready for a nuclear war, a pervasive fear clouds everything you do."[13] It becomes a person's "normal" without his realizing it.

Even so, in the fall of 1960, those entering the new Lower Dauphin High School held only one concern—the basic fear of "not knowing what awaited them" in what appeared to be a huge high school where many of them did not know very many of the others. They also could not have known that they would be coming together for an adventure no one possibly could have envisioned.

At the school's opening in the fall of 1960, students were more concerned about finding their way through the building than envisioning possible adventures, completely unaware that they were being identified and catalogued and referred to by the year of their expected graduation:

- The Class of 1961 were seniors
- The Class of 1962 were juniors
- The Class of 1963 were sophomores
- The Class of 1964 were freshmen
- The Class of 1965 were in 8th grade
- The Class of 1966 were in 7th grade
- The Class of 1967 were in 6th grade
- The Class of 1968 were in 5th grade
- The Class of 1969 were in 4th grade (the latter three classes still attending Hummelstown or their township elementary schools).

The seventh graders, reminded by their teachers that they would be the first class to spend all six years in the new high school, were gearing themselves to rule the school. Without even knowing there had been a Silent Generation, they were poised to achieve what their predecessors had hoped they themselves *would* be, but *could not* be: confident, stylish, "in-the-know," indulged by parents, engaged in a wide selection of activities, and, most coveted, possessing a hint of savoir faire. All in all, the Boomers in general had the chutzpah to make things happen; Strauss's more colorful description was that they resembled the yapping and multiple puppies in "101 Dalmatians."[14]

In general, larger schools have less social interaction among their students, limiting their opportunities for participation. Typically, large numbers of students must place limits on individual achievement with so many vying for the position of team captain, the lead in the school play, solos in the concerts, and academic awards. Some in the spectrum became sidelined, limited in what they might otherwise achieve. The result was that many in this wider Boomer generation lost an important chance to learn how to participate and how to lead.

However, Lower Dauphin was a notable exception as adults and students alike were able to create activities and events so that more students could be a part of the school offerings. For example, as early as their sophomore year, leadership came from the Class of 1965 to form a dance troupe as part of the marching band when many girls wanted to be a part of the band, and majorette positions were filled. The result was "The Falconettes," self-formed, self-taught, and successful.

Another academic accommodation was made for several males in this class by the director of guidance, the exceptional Kenneth Staver, who created a program by which identified students in the Vocational Program could also have a full complement of academic courses. And the school district did provide (late) "activity bus" transportation so more students could participate in after school programs. Teachers were encouraged to provide after school clubs of all descriptions to attract the students to fully participate.

The biggest surprise, however, and what yet may not have been realized by either the general public or school faculties, is that the Boomers were a force to be reckoned with, compounded by the fact that in general they could not be handled as individuals because there were simply too many of them.

Everywhere they turned, there were more like them. Thus, most not only had to find a niche among their own peers, but also needed to commit themselves to searching for space and opportunities that in previous years would have been open and looking for people to fill them. The crowding of the Boomers thus would lead to an assertiveness, even a boldness, that in any other time would not be needed (or tolerated).

To repeat for emphasis, it just wasn't possible for Baby Boomers to be handled as individuals because of their numbers. Even guidance counselors sometimes had to meet them in small groups rather than individually.[15] This crowding on every side thus created in many of them a lifelong commitment to individualism and they began a search for space and opportunity as soon as they could.

What many adults didn't realize at the time (having had no prior experience with a massive generation of children and youth) is that to the extent that crowding increases, so does the need for individual space and privacy. This is particularly risky with those individuals who have aggressive tendencies, for people who feel aggressive under high density conditions often then become even more aggressive in confining spaces or circumstances. Of course, not many of the students understood this, either.

Other results of crowding also needed to be considered, such as the fact that people typically withdraw when a situation becomes one of "overload," and they try to get away both physically and mentally.

Crowding also affects personal relationships, increasing personal irritation, the number of arguments, and the level of physical violence. On a very basic level, children in a crowded household are less likely to have a place to study or think; thus, they spend more time outside, just to be alone.

Further, it is said that for the rest of their lives this cohort looked for individuality. Even today most of its members don't like crowds, for it was the crowding in every activity they experienced that created a deep personal need for privacy and individual distinction.

The impact on public schools was enormous, beginning with the decisions local governments needed to make, such as raising taxes to build new schools and debating how to balance the very real possibility that once the Boomers moved on, there might be empty classrooms for following generations.

While all of the discussions about space were occurring, those in this generation had no choice but to remain packed together in schools—as elsewhere—like no other generation in history. That meant not only more children to teach but also a teacher shortage. (The number of emergency teaching certificates greatly increased.) Another problem was the question of where the additional professional staff (and classrooms) would be placed.

Administrative and public planning continued as some high schools went on split shifts, while classes in elementary schools were held wherever space could be found in churches, library meeting rooms, historical societies, club rooms, and perhaps even fire halls.

Even when new schools were built in the late 1950s and early 1960s (Lower Dauphin High School being only one of them), the class sizes were large, the average being 33 students per classroom, with even more in some classes during the highest periods of enrollment in the early and mid-sixties.

Also needing to be factored into the education system is that the Boomers overall were staying in school longer. By the mid-60s three out of four of all age-eligible students were being graduated from high school and by the mid-60s about half of all students attended a program of higher education. (Just imagine the impact of 38 million youngsters during the period seeking further education or training following high school.)

However, a new advantage for girls growing up in the 1960s is that business schools, colleges and professional graduate schools were beginning to open their gates wider to females, and young women who had any connections at all likely could gain acceptance. Granted, competition was keen because of the large numbers, but the possibility for many more opportunities—particularly for females—was also widening.

What even high-ranking students faced was not being offered admission to the top tier colleges or even their first choice of college because of their numbers. They were, however, usually welcomed to their second choice.

The most interesting sociological fact in the 1960s is that this vast increase in matriculating students meant that a much greater percentage of young people stayed together in the same youth-centered institutional system far longer than any previous generation had. The result was a working formula that created a force in numbers. This national cohort of Baby Boomers had years together to develop their own world, all 76 million of them co-participants in a new world of their own making.

Paul Light suggests that even those who grew up in stable families shared the fervent desire to find a "community of peers" outside the family to take seriously and by whom to be taken seriously.[16] Thus, they were more influenced by their cohorts than by parents, a fact that helped them more easily enter the larger world.

Part II: The Macrocosm of the 1960s

If we use the spectrum of historical significance that was defined by Strauss and Howe (Eras in cycles of four: High, Awakening, Unraveling, and Crisis), the cohort that became known as the Baby Boomers was already marked by its order in the cycle to be a generation who, as children, would enjoy the most secure family life in American history.

This did not surprise those who study generations and cycles. To review, what Strauss and Howe identify as the **First Turning** (A High) is the cycle of history that began in the mid-to-late 1940s under the leadership of Truman, Eisenhower, and Kennedy. The country was confident, yet very conformist and spiritually complacent.

The **Second Turning** (An Awakening) of the cycle began with the campus protests and revolts of the mid-60s with a cultural divide separating anything that was thought or said "after" the revolts from anything thought or said "before" them.

Strauss and Howe termed the **Third Turning** (An Unraveling) the "Culture Wars," which was an era of national drift and institutional decay (beginning in 1984).

At the time of the book's publication, the <u>Fourth Turning</u> was expected to begin around 2005 which, they had predicted, would bring a sudden event that would be the beginning of a new crisis mode for this cohort. Strauss and Howe further predicted that in this Crisis mode there would be a high risk of catastrophe and a greater rate in the technology of destruction and mankind's willingness to use it. They predicted that this Fourth Turning (Crisis) should end around 2030.

In short, according to Strauss and Howe, each new generation develops an adherence to a *Weltanschauun,*[17] which also becomes the worldview of every individual in that cohort. Importantly, the researchers also identified that the common beliefs and behavior of the members of a given generation are different from those of a generation born either earlier or later.

Add to this Strauss and Howe's findings that the post-World War II period likely will continue to rank in history as the **all-time pinnacle of a most positive and joyful national mood.** With findings like this, who would not have wanted to be part of this cohort?

Politics of the Boomers

The beginning of the 1960s saw the political campaign of Kennedy and Nixon in a race in which for the first time both presidential candidates had been born in the 20th century.[18] This offered a comparison of birth cohorts (Silents compared to Boomers) that also likely explains why the Eisenhower administration was described as dull, unpoetic, and unimaginative while the style of the Kennedy leadership was viewed as slapdash, informal, and spontaneous. Farber describes the presidential victory in 1960 and the following administration of John F. Kennedy as being disorderly with no one seeming to know who was responsible to whom.

Kennedy had run as the candidate of economic growth, blasting the Republicans for not having the energy and talent to make America even stronger and richer than it already was.[19] The theme of Kennedy's inaugural address was "inspiration and possibility." He connected American prosperity to American mission, saying that "Americans are the ones destined to carry out God's work on earth[20]— just what the country was ready to hear.

Kennedy's good looks and his skill in using television to his advantage were also factors in his success. Through carefully crafted publicity, he was viewed by most citizens as a "cool" hero. Few disputed that Kennedy was exciting and fun to watch, engaged in activities others only wished they could be part of.

President Kennedy's administration is credited for laying the groundwork for social programs because the Ford Foundation reached out with funding to join forces with him. This support for civic programs was the beginning of a wave of community action[21] and ultimately provided the seeds for Lyndon Johnson's "Great Society."

While youth often profess to be totally bored by politics, the political elements of a generation did play a major role in shaping their world. Even today we must stand in awe of their sheer numbers which made the shaping not only possible, but necessary, for the sake of management. The increase (13.8 million) in the youth population (ages 14 to 25) during the decade of the 1960s was greater than the total increase (12.5 million) during the seventy years prior to 1960. This particular fact should be impact enough on anyone who tries to shrug off the Baby Boomers.

The Baby Boomers (born in the High era), were the youth and young adults of the Awakening. Huntingdon's description of Awakenings is that it was a time when "society deviated too far from the moral and religious understandings that legitimized authority in church and state."[22] As an example, he described the most recent Awakening as "…the civil rights demonstrations, the campus disturbances, and the urban riots of the 1960s all combined. Further, the Awakenings were characterized by mass organizing (See Alinsky below).

Awakenings, as explained in Chapter 3, are times of changing structures of authority and power as well as a division between those who "saw the light" and those who did not. Awakenings are also characterized by mass organizing and religious passion, both adding to the politics of the time.

Specific to the 1960s and 1970s, which were the young adult years of the Boomers, the following major political movements took hold:

- The February 1, 1960 Woolworth **sit-in**, said to be the fire-starter of the protests to come.

- The dominant tone of the period that included unrelenting questioning of and **opposition to authority** in almost any form. These oppositions then became organized protests, which reached a peak in August 1974.

- The **desegregation of a society**, with the resignation of a President (Nixon) and the dismantling of an intelligence system, added to the period's assault on inequality, authority, hierarchy, and secrecy.

- The **assassination** of John F. Kennedy.

Two distinct crises occurred during this period, the first beginning in the summer of 1965 which may have been the breaking point for many Americans when 28 separate events left a stain on this generation, beginning with Selma and continuing through Vietnam.

The first crisis saw twenty-seven million men coming of draft age in the 60s and 70s, one-third of them drafted, and less than 10% of these going to Vietnam, but the war divided them all, seared them, wounded them, and left lasting scars, physical, psychological, and/or guilt from those who dodged the war. And the Watergate political scandals between 1972 and 1974 brought down a presidency.

The second crisis was the collapse of the American family with divorce and the end of the "breadwinner as male." Further, until this time adults had rarely changed jobs and if families could not afford luxuries, they didn't buy them. Men, almost exclusively, had held all of the economic power in the household as well as in society.

The assassination of President Kennedy had led to the coalescence of these two crises, as the country was knocked back on its heels. Here were the Boomers, in the most sensitive moment of their life cycle, faced with their world turned upside down as they transitioned from their almost perfect childhood to a completely confusing adolescence and young adulthood.

During this Awakening period it was also widely supposed by most citizens that whatever America believed in would later be what the entire civilized world would believe in. However, in reality, Americans, while clearly identifying with the Western nations, did not connect well at all with Eastern cultures.

It also should be noted that while it is the American Baby Boomers that are most recognized as a distinct group in western civilization, they did not own the distinction. There also was a post-World War II baby boom in Britain, Denmark, Sweden, the United Kingdom, the Netherlands, France and Switzerland. In all of these countries, the birth rate approximately doubled during 1939–1948, with the rates peaking in 1947–1948.

However, in the European countries, there was no collective experience like Vietnam that united or divided them. Further, the timing of the Baby Boom across Europe, together with all the different social, economic, and political contexts of nation states, complicates the task of being able to identify a specific European baby boomer generation, and the increase in births in Europe is not comparable to the huge impact the Boomer generation had on the United States.

As far as political influence in the United States, Baby Boomers represented one out of every five potential voters in 1972 (which is not to say they all voted), and by the 1980s the Boomers trailed in voter turnout and appeared to have abandoned party identification and loyalty. As Light noted, "The challenge for the political parties was how to get the Baby Boomers engaged in the political process when they were so actively engaged in *themselves*."[23]

There also seemed to be a general estrangement between the Boomers and the mainstream officials over the following issues: (1) the effects of Watergate; (2) the assassination of Martin Luther King; (3) the My Lai massacre; and (4) having a low draft number, which would have far more impact than might appear on the surface.

Saul Alinsky

A further effect on politics both at the time and to come in the future, was the groundwork laid by Saul Alinsky in the 1930s. Alinsky's initial influence in organizing local communities was the beginning of what would become a squad of community organizers infiltrating and politically influencing multiple publics.

History has shown that many of these community organizers later realized that they were no longer organizing around small, specific, immediate and realizable issues, but were guiding a full-blown social movement. What is troubling in this *social movement* is that its mission was to help others *to reinvent the ideas of commitment and engagement.* The goal was a new "designed truth" (based on doctrine) rather than long-standing beliefs of the communities. It should also be remembered that while Alinsky was active in the 1930s, the changes in the 1960s had their roots in these experiences of the 1930s in which the seeds originally were planted.

Media

The emergence of a "national press," which later would determine what was news, and then would set the model for how events should be covered and interpreted, got its initial foothold during this time when more families subscribed to one of the city papers and believed what they read. However, the growing influence of television brought an unexpected impact on how people received news. What is sometimes forgotten is that initially television, like print news, simply reported the news; however, before long, mainly in the 1960s, news was "produced" for television to fit the length of the newscasts which had begun as 15 minutes and grew to fill an hour or more. And many citizens found it easier to listen to the news being "delivered" than to read the news on a printed newspaper page.

Soon careers in the media began to attract larger numbers of college graduates, especially from the better and more prestigious liberal arts colleges which were known for teaching skills in writing. Before long, the press changed from passive observer and recorder of what was happening to becoming a participant/leader in the news through investigating and interpreting, *often from their own perspective.* According to Huntington, during this time the overall impact of the media, particularly television, was to *undermine the legitimacy of government.*[24]

In the early 1960s about 92 percent of all American households owned more than one television set (most of which were black and white, although some families did have "a color tv"), which a majority of families viewed six hours a day. By 1962, for the first time ever, a majority of Americans said they received most of their news from television. Thus, television became the source by which most children learned more than they did from print media.

While the young people were not the largest group of viewers, they watched television "with a special avidity," learning from television much of what previous generations had learned at the movies. Thus, television became the medium whereby most of the young learned about what they believed to be their world.

Because television had been a part of their environment since birth, the young were more comfortable with it than the older generation was. The young didn't see commercials as interruptions, only as a part of the program. Nor did they fully realize that television was in the business of making money and that the young were being targeted because they had money of their own to spend (and would be the voters of the near future).

For all of television's attraction, however, the effects on the young of watching so much was troubling. First, television programs separated children and youth from traditional social connections of families, and, second, it taught them intimate lessons about being an adult without any discussion with their own parents or teachers.

Another troubling effect of television is the disconnectedness of the story, with scenes jumping from one to another, without any depth of feeling or complex ideas displayed. The interruptions by commercials—many commercials—also made it difficult for those still learning (how) to make thoughtful connections in a story or idea.

Unfortunately, television helped to reinforce an entire generation's separation from both peers and families. For some small children, television was the first contact with what they believed was the real world. And, worse, the programs took time away from parents reading stories to their children and time for children to play alone; further, it reduced time spent in conversation and family interaction.

In addition, television likely influenced young people's political views more than families did, providing the first contact most children had with such events as the war in Viet Nam. Light suggests that television was to the Baby Boomers what comics were to the parents of the Boomers—with one important difference: Television introduced children to a very adult world very quickly and, for good or ill, the Baby Boomers entered adulthood with a much clearer sense of the risks they would be facing in life.

The 1960s

Nineteen-sixty signified a demographic watershed when the age at marriage began to rise after decades of decline. The birthrate began to dwindle, and within a decade, the birthrate was at an all-time low and still plummeting. The marriage rate also declined, as more people remained single or lived together as couples, families, and households without marriage. The divorce rate, after more than a decade of stability, began to rise gradually in the early sixties and then dramatically in the late sixties, skyrocketing to unprecedented heights in the early 1970s.

While not often noted in accounts of the 1960s, in 1962 the Supreme Court ruled that children in public schools could no longer begin their day with a prayer. This authority taken by the federal government's intrusion into every classroom began to erode the old way of doing things, including traditional beliefs and patterns of behavior. This edict was personally memorable to this author who was the person who every morning used the public address system to read a short scripture passage, followed by the pledge to the flag and morning announcements.

While school segregation was not an issue in the small town of Hummelstown and its surrounding townships, the civil rights movement was exploding throughout the country and on August 28, 1963 a sprinkling of students from this area were part of the 250,000 followers who gathered at the Lincoln Memorial in Washington, DC to hear the immortal "I have a dream" speech of Martin Luther King, Jr.

Members of the 1960s middle-to-upper-class were generally optimistic about the future, with a self-assurance that expected life to be comfortable and rewarding. This confidence is, in part, a testament to the sense the middle class retained that *good things were a birthright.*

On the other hand, *Look* magazine interviewed teens, asking them what they feared, accepted, resisted, dreamed of, or dreaded. The following is a sample of their responses:

- We are less outspoken in believing we can change the world because we do not focus our efforts. We will make our own patterns. We seldom stand still.
- We are concerned about the bomb, but it doesn't worry us.
- We have choices that previous generations did not have.
- We mature at age 12, become world weary with boredom at 16.
- We are moving along accepting the possibility of nuclear war, without counting on the world's being here long enough for us to live in it.
- We hold a fear of becoming anonymous. We wonder how we will keep our individuality.
- We, like all other generations, are a secret society within ourselves that refuses to share its private mysteries.[25]

With all of the attention focused on them by the media and most adults, the Boomers were the first teenage generation to take the concepts of individual choice and personal identity for granted. They had an unprecedented belief in their own importance as a group and their place in the postwar world. However, throughout the Cold War they did greatly benefit by the focus of society on a rigorous education.

It also should be noted that by 1960 there were approximately 11.7 million girls in America between the ages of 12 and 18, opening an even wider market aimed at convincing the girls that by buying (whatever was being sold), their lives would be more fun and they more popular. The marketing plan was to convince the girls that they were a new, privileged generation whose destiny was more open and exciting than that of their parents.[26] And it was!

In the 1960s middle class teenagers also dominated the rock and roll music market, recasting the genre as teenage pop music. The Beatles were able to reinstate the 1950s teen-age spirit that hadn't been seen since the days of Elvis Presley's reign.

There was even a resurgence of folk music in the 1960s, but with a modern twist, with the result that most teens in the 1960s were fans of both rock and folk music. The Weavers had been one of the earliest and the best in folk music in the mid-1950s and when in 1958 The Kingston Trio recorded "Tom Dooley," the folk "revival" surged.

According to a member of a high school class of 1965 (far from Hummelstown, Pennsylvania), "I always had a sense that our generation was bigger and better than any that had come before. [27]

Those of the 1960s who were aspiring flower children quickly aligned with Allen Ginsberg, one of the gentle "Beat Poets," who was at least a generation older than many of them. Ginsberg's poem "Howl," published in 1956 ("I saw the best minds of my generation destroyed by madness....") is considered to be the trigger for the social and political consciousness that reached full bloom in the 1960s.

In some odd way, Ginsberg's poetry of the 1950s helped the Boomers to realize that some of the Silents actually shared their interest in the Beat Poets and, in some cases, had been the very ones to introduce the Beat Poets to the English classes of the Boomers.

To those who ask what happened in society to change some of the nineteen-fifties generation from watching life from the sidelines to become activists of the nineteen sixties, Benita Eisler, author and historian, replies, "I think some of us were always activists at heart. We just didn't have any place to go with how we felt."[28] The 1960s opened that door.

Author Barbara Ehrenreich, also a member of the Silent Generation, had a similar response, "It wasn't permissiveness that opened the doors. Rather, it was the influences that poured in through television, radio, records, and music. While most of the influences were bland, they were a kind of signal for us to begin to think of ourselves as a new, distinctive social group, with a rebellious agenda of its own—something we once had to hide."[29]

Debi Unger blamed the change of public focus away from members of the Silent Generation on what she termed the "de-legitimatizing" of all sources of authority—governments, universities, parents, critics, experts, employers, the police, families, and the military.[30] Further, as the Boomers began to realize that they heavily outnumbered and outflanked the Silents, they began to wield their own authority "over the Silents."

This taking over did not go unnoticed, as magazines began to focus on this concern and, in its December 1964 issue, *Show* magazine ran an article addressing the effect on the country by its huge population of teen-agers.

In "The Teen Scene: A Hard Year's End," Paul Brodeur wrote a semi-satirical article with his classic description of the teens, noting, "In 1964 the teenage establishment burst into a full bloom of muffin-faced heart throbs bearing such names as Bobby Vee, Bobby Vinton, Bobby Sherman, and Bobby Rydell who breathlessly beat out songs with such titles as "Baby, Baby All the Time," "Baby, Baby, Where Did Our Love Go," "Baby Be Mine," "Baby, I Need Your Loving," "Baby, Don't You Do It," and "Baby, Don't Look Down."[31] This, of course, was a sign of just who was determining the music market.

Again, it also must be said that at this time the teen establishment had a membership of nearly 22 million (in a country of nearly 92 million), *nearly a quarter of the total population* of the United States. One could not help but notice them. In the article cited above, Brodeur called attention to both the *affluence* of the teens (a total annual income of $12 billion, derived largely from allowances and part-time jobs, ten percent of which was spent on entertainment) and their *influence* (both given to and received from "a galaxy of disc jockeys, movie makers, record dealers and showmen, who started out with the idea of directing the tastes of this group while developing the enormous market potential of these youth."[32])

Author Grace Palladino, noted, "We were the chosen, we were going to make the world right… We had the luxury of free time and economic security… We could just go in any direction we wanted.[33]

And so those teens in the lower section of Dauphin County did choose a different direction, taking over the entire Junior-Senior High School, led by the Classes of 1961-64, with mixed emotions, trying to cram in all the changes, different from what they had to date experienced of high school, making new friends from former rivals of the neighboring school, excited to create new patterns that would become traditions, yet at times missing the familiarity of Hummelstown High School and Hershey High School (some of the townships had allowed students to go to either high school). Those from Hummelstown were eager to have more space after being in the crowded halls of their high school, while those who came from the four townships were simply hoping this change would work out.

All who entered this new building had been readying themselves in one way or another for the changes. Little did they know what was in store for them, the freedom, yet the restrictions; the freedom, along with the confusion; the restraint of being overwhelmed with everything in their lives; the freedom for and the stress of too many choices; the angst as to where to turn, with the choice to turn anywhere.

Those who were waiting to enter the doors of a brand new day—and a brand new school, trying to find a place, trying to find themselves, not knowing where the country was going—or where they themselves were going, pulled on all sides, told to be good, told to be daring, hoping to find one's niche, wanting desperately to fit in, but not knowing what that meant, knew one thing

—they needed to be ready and it would be better to be ready by banding together.

Chapter 4 Endnotes:

1   Landon Jones is a former managing editor of *People* and Money magazines and the author of *Great Expectations: America and the Baby Boom Generation.*

2   Katz, *Home Fires,* p. 44.

3   Gitlin, *Years of Hope,* p. 13.

4   www.history.com

5   Farber, David, *The Age of Great Dreams,* pp. 8-9.

6   *American Red Cross Journal,* January 1964, p. 8.

7   Light, *The Baby Boomers,* p. 137.

8   Wallechinsky, *Midterm Report,* p.158.

9   Aldridge, *In the Country of the Young,* p. 16.

10 Sann, *The Angry Decade: The Sixties.*

11 Bell, *The End of Ideolology,* p. 16.

12 Jezer, *The Dark Ages,* p. 220.

13 Wallechinsky, p. 159.

14 Strauss and Howe, *The Fourth Turning,* p. 166.

15 Later, some students recalled that they felt ignored or neglected as one of the early guidance counselors seemed to "have no time for us as we were interested in training in the professional health field, not college."

16 Light, p. 57, although he makes this point throughout his book.

17 A person or a group's conception, philosophy or view of the world

18 Farber, *Good Times,* p. 25.

19 Farber, p. 27.

20 Farber, pp. 33-34.

21 Joseph, p. 30.

22 Huntingdon, *American Politics,* p. 161.

23 Light, p. 145.

24 Huntington, p. 218.

25 "Face of the Future," *Look,* December 25, 1964, p. 73.

26 Douglas, *Where the Girls Are,* p. 26.

27 Palladino, *Teenagers,* p. 194.

28 Eisler, *Private Lives,* p. 295.

29 Ehrenreich, *Fear of Falling,* pp. 91-92.

30 Unger & Unger, *The Times Were a Changin',* p. 1.

31 Brodeur, p. 48, *The Teen Scene: A Hard Year's End,* SHOW, December 1964.

32 Brodeur, p. 48.

33 Palladino, p. 194.

Chapter 5

High School in a World Turned Upside Down

We look before and after,

And pine for what it not;

Our sincerest laughter

With some pain is fraught;

Our sweetest songs are those

That tell of saddest thought.

Ode to a Skylark
Percy Bysshe Shelley

1960—1961

One of the early opportunities in the newly created school was broader program offerings, such as the Public Speaking class initially taught by Mr. Douglas Stauffer—almost certainly the first opportunity any of the students had to take such a course, one not often taught in public schools. The highlight of the first year in this class was a trip to Olmsted Air Force Base in December where the students were given an opportunity to speak through a microphone and record their voices, a first for most students.

Overall, the new school provided broader educational experiences than most students had had in their smaller schools. However, while most of the focus was on the high school, there were many advantages to having all six higher grades in the same building. The largest class in the school's opening year was 8th grade, 320 strong, who would parlay the advantages provided by this school and leave a lasting legacy. The new structure was filled with what would later be noted as the best decade of Baby Boomers and was the decade that was represented by each class in writing its own story in the publication telling the history of the first fifty years of Lower Dauphin High School.[1]

The sports headline the morning following the new school's first football game said it all, **"Lower Dauphin's Last Play Makes New School First."** The game-winning score came on the last play to win the game (7-0) before a crowd of approximately 6,500 spectators. The winning touchdown resulted from a quarterback sneak play from the one-yard line by sophomore Mike Shifflet.

This first football team set a fast pace and never faltered. The news coverage tells the story and is included here (1) to demonstrate the impact this original team had—a team composed of players of opposing teams in all the years of football prior to the creation of Lower Dauphin High School—and (2) as a record for their progeny and for the school:

- 9/16/60 (Unidentified news clipping).[2] Lower Dauphin is still undefeated, but for the second straight week the outcome was very much in doubt until the final whistle. Last night Mike Shifflet, 170 pound sophomore quarterback, ran 44 yards for a touchdown midway in the third period to provide the margin of victory as the Falcons downed Camp Hill 13-7. … After being halted earlier on the eight, LD got a break less than one minute later when Harry Menear, 211 pound center, recovered a fumble on the 12. Barry Broadwater then gained a yard and Shifflet made a first down on the two when he faked and then bored through the middle. … Four plays later Broadwater plunged the final two yards on his third straight carry. … Broadwater was easily the outstanding ball carrier as he spearheaded the Lower Dauphin attack. The work of Glenn Ebersole, Captain, and Ken Epler, senior linebacker who made 17 individual tackles, drew praise from Coach Osevala. "Not bad for an opener." The home crowd was thrilled.

- 9/22/60 (*The Hummelstown Sun*). In the third quarter Glenn Ebersole blocked a Camp Hill punt on their 25 and John McCormick scooped up the ball and carried it to the 14. The Falcons drove to the 2 from where Barry Broadwater went over for the touchdown. … After driving 19 yards in five plays, Mike Shifflet scored the winning touchdown on a spectacular 44-yard run. Barry Broadwater passed to George Emerich for the extra point and LD was out in front 13-7.

- 11/4/60 (*The Evening News*). Lower Dauphin reigns supreme today in the Capital Area Conference…with a hard-earned victory over Palmyra. A win-whipped[3] crowd of 4,000 saw John McCormick race 12 yards with a screen pass for the lone touchdown of the game with only 1:50 minutes remaining in the fourth period. …McCormick's 12-yard run was accomplished behind fine blocking by his teammates and climaxed a 38-yard drive that started with six minutes remaining. …LD punched out four consecutive first downs moving from their own 47 to the Palm four. …The biggest gain in the advance was a 12-yard pass from Wyld to Emerich. Broadwater got loose once for 11 on an end run. "I don't want to pinpoint anyone, but the play of Harry Menear was terrific at center in going both ways. Lew Cobaugh and Pete Costelli did a fine job at the guards and Tom Duck and Glenn Ebersole were tough at the tackles. We got good end play from Emerich and Dennis Shertzer, too," noted Coach Barney Osevala. Broadwater was the leading ground-gainer for the Falcons with 55 yards on 15 carries.

- 11/12/60 (*Harrisburg Patriot*). Led by Barry Broadwater, who figured in the scoring of 16 points, Lower Dauphin defeated Middletown 28-20 to complete a perfect record season in the CAC Conference last night with 3,000 frozen fans in the stands. The 145-pound halfback scored touchdowns on runs of one and eight yards in the third quarter, and added three extra points by placement and threw a pass to end George Emerich for a fourth PAT (extra point.) Broadwater accounted for 145 yards of the 186 gained on the ground by the Falcons. He carried 20 times for an average of 7.2. …Glenn Ebersole and Tom Duck stood out as the defense limited Middletown to only 27 yards rushing.

The very first big dance was the Christmas Ball on December 17, 1960 with music by the Fred Harry Orchestra for students in the Senior High. The other big December announcement was from Mrs. Sandel, the librarian, that "books on the shelves, most from Hummelstown High School, include 606 fiction books and 446 non-fiction." Limited service for students would be available in the library beginning in January 1961.

An unidentified handwritten basketball record reveals the following about a powerhouse basketball team as well:

- Most points scored: George Emerich, 348
- Most field goals in one game: George Emerich, 13
- Consecutive fouls made: Barry Broadwater, 7
- Most fouls made in one game: Barry Broadwater, 8

In March the auditorium was filled for the Dedication Ceremony of the new school. Mr. Emerich had sent a very diplomatic letter to every employee about the importance of making a good showing. Now, that was impressive!

Another first for the new school was fielding a baseball team, as, until this point, conference scholastic baseball was only forming. There were only two seniors, Barry Broadwater, outfielder, and John Moyer, pitcher and outfielder. A junior, George Emerich, served as catcher.

In April 1961 Karl Bell took first place in Physical Science in the Junior High Science Fair; Gary Gearhart in Earth Science, Donald Page in Biology, and Jeff Davis in Mathematics were noted. Audrey Roland, only a freshman, took first place in the grander Capital Area Science Fair.

Carol Flocken and John Hall will be remembered as the first students to be recognized as National Merit Finalists; the first prom, May 5, 1961, was called the Junior-Senior Dinner Dance; and, as the ribbon on the package, the Joint School Board approved an After-Prom Party, sponsored by the Junior Chamber of Commerce.

On May 20, 1961 the school's first musical was performed with great gusto. Jane Mellin Smith, the director, had selected "Good News" because there was no budget for costumes and the students, with some improvising, could wear their own street clothes.

1961—1962

The Hummelstown Sun, September 1, 1961, noted that the high school would be "strained to capacity" when it opened for its second year on September 5. The newspaper was spot on!

Hope was high for another good football season. Some citizens noted that we spent too much on sports, but not many spectators agreed.

On September 17, 1961, the *Sunday Patriot-News* noted, "If Randy Kahler is any indication of what the sophomore class at Lower Dauphin has to offer, the Falcons will roost high in area grid circles for some time. Kahler paced Lower Dauphin to a 32-13 victory over Camp Hill yesterday with four touchdowns as 3,100 fans looked on in the Lion's home den. The October 27 issue of *The Evening News* reported the Falcons' first victory in the league, naming in particular Jim Hertzler, Larry Behney, and Bruce Wyld for delivering four TDs and three extra points."

However, the newspaper erroneously noted that Lower Dauphin's Falcons had been named for a space-age missile, a mistake made by more than one person, particularly after Olmsted Air Force Base gifted the school with an actual (deactivated) missile.

Football season closed as *The Hummelstown Sun* noted that "the leading scorer for the Falcons was Randy Kahler who accounted for half of his team's touchdowns against Middletown."

In the fall of 1961 Mr. Roy Campbell was called to service during the Berlin Crisis after the USSR issued an ultimatum demanding the withdrawal of Western armed forces from West Berlin, culminating with the East German erection of the Berlin Wall. As a result of this crisis, an issue was raised at the school board meeting regarding fallout shelters and/or the evacuation of the school in case of aerial attacks (*The Hummelstown Sun*, October 6, 1961).

Future Farmers of America

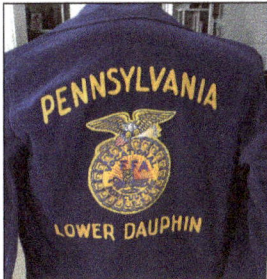

The Vocational Agriculture Program and its accompanying Future Farmers of America (FFA) was on its way to being one of Lower Dauphin High School's most successful and highly regarded programs. Considered a premier offering, vocational agriculture had been an inherent part of the planning for this new high school. Located at the end of F-wing, "Vo Ag" was more than a program; it was a vocation, a lifestyle, and a home for those enrolled. The Lower Dauphin FFA was at the heart of the school for more than thirty years with a vast number of accomplishments that resulted in many successful alumni.

During the 1960s Keystone Farmer Degrees were conferred on the following LD Future Farmers of America members: Jay Kopp '62, Doley Cave '62, Kenneth Zell '63, Doug Hancock '63, Galen Kopp '63, Jay Brandt '64, Russel Cassel '65, Dave Coble '65, Dale Good '65, Mike Hubler '65, and Rodney Teets '66.

Later, Jay Brandt, Doley Cave, and Russel Cassel earned the coveted American Farmer Degree. Russel also was the only FFA member to hold a state office, being elected state vice-president.

Some years later a news article noted that Keystone (Pennsylvania) Farmers Degrees had been earned by 20% of the Lower Dauphin FFA students while the national average was only 2%.

Lower Dauphin had 23 tuition students that year, four of whom were children of military personnel at Olmsted Air Force Base. Later during school year 1965-1966, the school board would rule that children of parents who were being transferred to other AF bases could continue at Lower Dauphin, a ruling also attractive to the increasing number of professional families who were moving to the area to work at the Penn State Hershey Medical Center.

And who remembers participating in the Physical Education Demonstration, performed for the public on April 28, 1962?

Also in the spring of 1962, while the brilliant Spanish dancer Jose Greco performed at the imposing Hershey Theatre, the 9th grade Modern Theatre Club presented a one-act play during activity period with students from study halls invited as the audience. The spring of 1962 will also be remembered for its second school musical, "The Boyfriend," another hit and the highlight of all things musical at LD.

The school year 1961-62 will also be remembered as the year of the Jazz Club, Booster Buttons, School Pennants, LD Metal Club's making and selling LD license plates for $1.25, completion of a track and field site for home meets, and learning to spell Xanthopoulos.

Nearby Gretna Playhouse, a perennial favorite for summer stock, was particularly exciting for LD as its Choral Director, Mrs. Smith, and several students performed in *Damn Yankees* and *Leave It to Jane*. What a thrill for Carol Kasbee '62, Donna Walmer '64, George Wagner and Barry Stopfel, both '65.

1962—1963

1962's main local event in the late summer/early fall was Hummelstown's celebration of its own Bicentennial, August 27-September 2, fondly remembered by teens who were part of the event, particularly the pageant.[4]

What a surprise to the school district when Mrs. Smith did not return in the fall of 1962—a near scandal, as she simply did not show up! Later we discovered that Jane had had an offer to join the Lambs Club, part of the widely-known New York Actors Guild.

In the fall of 1962 Fred Shope and Ralph Espenshade launched a rocket, following a record-breaking launch that Ralph had completed in April 1960; that rocket had traveled 15,000 feet at a speed exceeding 760 mph, breaking the sound barrier and resulting in a sonic boom.[5]

In a football win over Susquehanna, Larry Behney had his greatest game of the season and in their final game with Middletown, a perennial rival, "the team drove for their first touchdown with Clayton Smith going the final nine yards. Bruce Wyld intercepted a Raider pass to start another Bird drive, going nine yards to notch the score himself after engineering the drive on a series of passes."

The Sophomore Class sponsored a Christmas Dance, December 22, with music by the then-favorite local dance band, El Dantes.[6]

In the January 26, 1963 issue of *The Saturday Evening Post*, former President Dwight D. Eisenhower took stock of what he considered national concerns: (1) patriotism being viewed as outdated, (2) many young people not learning responsibility by having assigned tasks in their homes, (3) the need for alternatives to four-year colleges, (4) the need for a responsible press, and (5) limited terms in Congress.[7]

On January 29, 1963, a fund-raiser for the Girls' Athletic Council featured one team of girls opposing the Senior High Male Faculty and a second team facing the Junior High Faculty.

LOWER DAUPHIN HIGH SCHOOL ATHLETIC ASSOCIATION
presents

WHITETTES	Fouls	1st	2nd	3rd	4th	Total
Jan First						
Patricia Miller						
Sandra Rider						
Betty Roe (Capt.)						
Marilyn Shertzer						
Nancy Fabian						
Jane First						
Mildred Goss						
Darlene Herr						
Vera Hetrick						
Carolyn Templin						
SENSATIONS						
Romaine Engle						
Jane Harper						
Beatrice Hosler						
Mary Ann Umberger						
Nancy Werner (Capt.)						
Betty Bellaman						
Helen Clare						
Nancy Smith						
Sylvia Snyder						
Gloria Verdelli						

JUNIOR HIGH FACULTY	Fouls	1st	2nd	3rd	4th	Total
Mr. Heiss						
Mr. Capitani						
Mr. DeLiberty						
Mr. Seacrist						
Mr. Cassel						
Mr. Kahler						
Mr. Bernitsky						
Mr. Swartly						
Mr. Zeiters						
Mr. McClure						
Mr. Belser						
Mr. Staver						
Mr. Curry						
Mr. Longreen						
Mr. Balmer						
Mr. Faden						
SENIOR HIGH FACULTY						
Mr. Sehan						
Mr. Richards						
Mr. Stanitski						
Mr. Musket						
Mr. Peck						
Mr. Heistand						
Mr. Murdocca						
Mr. Goepfert						
Mr. Brittain						
Mr. Bishop						
Mr. Strait						

key for scoring: 2 = basket made   0 = attempted foul shots   ⌾ = foul shots made   one stroke = a foul

During the 1962-63 schoolyear the fund-raiser for the Junior Class was candy sold during lunch and after school (unwittingly competing with Student Council's Snack Bar), hoping to fill their coffers for the Junior Prom. The fundraiser for FBLA[8] was selling peanuts; Future Farmers sold home-made apple cider and geraniums; and the cheerleaders held a gigantic sub sale.

During this same year the Guidance Department published a "book of facts" which provided a variety of information about all school activities; the *Falcon Flash*, under the guidance of Miss Myers, was in its second year of publication.

In the spring of 1963 Robert Gibble became LD's first National Merit Winner, after sharing finalist honors with Vivian Lewin. In track Tom Sheaffer won the mile, breaking a Conference record.

The marching band went to the Cherry Blossom Festival in DC, one of the many competitions the band attended and continued to enter.

With Best Wishes
Your Congressman
John C. Kunkel

Also in the spring, Junior High students, as only they can do, sent birthday cards to teachers. Bruce Meyerhoffer, a Junior in the high school, hand-delivered a card, on which he had written, "To my favorite 9th grade teacher. Sorry this is late; I couldn't make it down."

The second week in July, Judy Sener, Barry Stopfel, and I went to see Jane Smith in *The Student Prince* at St. John Terrell's Music Circus in Lambertville, NJ, where Jane was doing summer stock. We discovered New Hope.

In August Lynn Sandel sent a post card from Gillette Castle State Park in Connecticut. Her family was on their way to see a Shakespearean play in a theatre replica of The Globe Theatre; I also received two post cards from teaching colleague Jack Harry who was traveling in Uganda and Egypt!

Construction began on an addition to the high school, the building exceeding capacity from the first day it opened.

WASHINGTON TRIP Apr. 6 —

1. MAKE SURE ALL YOUR BELONGINGS ARE LABELED & ON
2. ON SIGNAL, LOAD BUSES & GET NAME CHECKED OFF.
3. WHEN $\frac{1}{2}$ HR. OUT FROM WASH. GO TO REST-ROOM ETC.
4. <u>1st Stop</u> — tour of Supreme Court Bldg.
   & Capitol Blds.
5. 2nd Stop — Hotel — PickUp SuitCASE & uniform —
   uniforms will Come off travel in Following order.
   1. Specialties
   2. Falconettes — High Numbers First.
   3. Band uniform — High Numbers thru Low.
6. Report to Hotel Room — Key in Room — Report to
   Chaperone Room to Pick-up Caps - Hats etc.
   <u>Rooms 800 — 714 — 504 — 105</u>
   take Cap etc. to Hotel Room — check uniform —
   make sure its yours & you Have <u>everything</u>.
7. UNPACK — DRESS for MEAL — WAIT till CALLED.
8. EAT.
9. Report to Buses for tour.
10. WHEN back from tour — Report <u>Direct</u> to Hotel
    Room & RETIRE.
11. ARISE at time to be Established.
12. DRESS in <u>Full</u> uniform — Report for Breakfast
    on Signal. Any uniform or Dress troubles
    See Chaperone immediately.
    BUSES — Approx 10 AM. — travel to
    off on signal — Put

1963—1964

The Original Falcon
Mascot 1963

In the fall of 1963, Miss Margaret Gluck formed a Glee Club and Mrs. Lee Finkenbinder formed a Junior Classical League, while Harold Snyder continued as the Falcon mascot in the hand-made costume with fabric feathers that had been cut with pinking shearers.

I moved to the high school to teach College Prep English (Senior British Literature) and found my "first year students" (then Freshmen, now Seniors) sitting at their desks before me. I also greeted Juniors in the "top section" of College Prep English (Junior American Literature), the second year of the three years I would be teaching them as well.

Student Council's Snack Bar was replaced by refreshment machines, available for use after school and for home games. "Glazed sweets" from the cafeteria became the running joke of the year.

Anyone watching the high school football games that fall would agree that the Falcons made the greatest comeback effort in their four-year football history as they defeated Cumberland Valley 26-13. With less than two minutes to play, "Randy Kahler took the Eagles' kickoff and went 69 yards before being forced out of bounds by the last remaining defender at the 11. On the third play thereafter, the hard-driving Falcon fullback plunged over from the three-yard line. Soon after, Ted Klinger intercepted a CV pass and raced 36 yards to make the score 13-12. LD took the lead and added the clincher in the final period when the Eagles were afflicted with a disastrous series of fumbles."

The cheerleaders sent invitations to the faculty to join the students in a Snake Dance to start from the school, wind through Hummelstown, then proceed to Borough Park where a large football rally would be held. The first Cross Country team was formed this year and the thin-skins earned the CAC championship with a perfect 4-0 record, while the Senior Class was busy with their Class Play, *Curtain Going Up.*

"THE PRESIDENT HAS BEEN SHOT!"

On Friday afternoon, November 22, 1963, I was overseeing a study hall in B-1 when near the end of the period there was a light tap at the door. I opened it to find Sally Walters, a senior. She motioned me to step outside the room as she proceeded to whisper the frightening information coming out of Dallas, Texas. "The President has been shot," she said solemnly, adding that she had been sent to notify all faculty in B-wing. It was understandable that such news be delivered personally and not announced over the PA system and I thought later of that wise choice made by Mr. Curtis Taylor, the high school principal. Sally appeared to be calm, entrusted with her heavy burden, but no doubt was in as much shock as those to whom she had been instructed to deliver her staggering news. Little did we know we were in the tragedy that would be most identified with this decade and this generation.[9] Shortly thereafter we were called to report to the auditorium. Word of the shooting had begun to spread, but not all students had yet heard the details. Teachers were exchanging glances of disbelief, sorrow, and fear, for none of us had ever faced a national event of such import.

We faculty were filled with our own thoughts as well as how we would handle the students. Of course, none of us had any more information than what Sally Walters had delivered, and we were hoping to learn more at the assembly.

The principal didn't need to ask for silence. We already had been struck dumb by the gravity of the situation. Mr. Taylor, with overwhelming sadness evident in his face, announced that the president had been "mortally wounded." Later many of the students said they had not known what "mortally wounded" meant and were left in even more perplexity. Ann Landis '65 recalls being in Spanish class when they first heard the news and later the classmates looked at each other wondering what this term meant. As Dr. Janet Calhoon '66 recalls, "Heading home that day were two girls walking in front of me asking what 'mortally wounded' meant; they truly did not know and did not grasp that the president was dead."

Mr. Taylor gave us the information that he had and asked us to pray for the country. As no other news was available and it was near the end of the day, the students were directed to go to their lockers and get what they needed to take home, as no one yet knew what the next steps would be.

Grief-stricken, the faces of most of the adults were ashen. We just looked hopelessly at one another, or bowed our heads. The silence was deafening until Mr. Seitzinger raised his baton and, as the students stood to leave, we all were startled to hear the full force of a rousing John Philip Sousa march, as disquieting as the news of the death of our president.

Later we learned that Mr. Seitzinger had collected as many band members as he could find and quickly assembled them on the stage.

It was not until years later that the realization struck me that Prowell Seitzinger had purposefully selected "The Stars and Stripes Forever" to play following the startling news of the President's assassination because it was the National March of the United States. What a splendid choice.

The reaction to this loss throughout the country and worldwide was almost paralyzing. A writer who had been a student at a large urban high school recalled that on hearing of the assassination, "We were dismissed when Mr. Brown threw himself against the blackboard and cried, his shoulders heaving. We were dismissed, all five thousand of us in Newton High. It was a silent dismissal. The eerie part was that no one had told us to be silent. The world fell apart after that."[10]

With heavy hearts and evident perplexity, Lower Dauphin students returned to school after an extended Thanksgiving recess, not quite sure to what extent their own lives would change. They were encouraged to resume school activities.

On December 5, 1963, LD played John Harris HS in basketball with one of the bright spots being George Chellew "who put on a one-man scoring rally that ended with his scoring 32 points to take high point honors for the game. His rundown for the night was 13 field goals and 6 fouls. Lee Moyer had 12 and Dale Broadwater 10."

It was likely a toss-up between the marching band and Future Farmers for having the most imaginative fundraisers this year—the band with its Christmas trees, followed by Kool School Stools. and home-made cider sold exclusively by the FFA.

Student Council promoted Christmas spirit with holiday displays in showcase windows at the end of the various Wings, trees in front of the auditorium, a nativity scene, and a scene composed of a fireplace with Christmas stockings hung on its mantle.

After the last student had boarded the last bus out prior to Christmas break, the Faculty Christmas Party began in the back room of B-Wing Faculty Room where a large gold ball had been hung from the middle of the ceiling above a round table on which was a spread a holiday buffet. As there were few occasions for teachers to share their fellowship, the high school faculty looked forward to this "once a year day," and the event would become a tradition lasting nearly twenty years.

In addition to Cross Country's perfect 1963 fall season record, basketball achieved its best record to date, the first Girls Basketball team was well underway in its season, and wrestling went undefeated. LD could boast six Sectional Wrestling Champions: Bobby Hess, Randy Kahler, Jim Rhone, Jim Sanders, Harold Shellenhamer, and Randy Umberger.

February 6, 1964 saw 1,400 fans watch the unbeaten Falcons chalk up an additional Conference win and eleventh win in a row in overall competition, with five undefeated wrestlers: Bill Pinkerton, Rhone, Sanders, Shellenhamer, and Umberger.

On February 20, 1964 the *Press and Journal* reported a perfect overall record for the wrestling team of 14 wins and no defeats, sweeping the first seven of the 12 individual matches...a brilliant season, the only undefeated team in the Greater Harrisburg area.

On the same date the LD basketball team recorded what was undoubtedly the biggest upset of the 1964 Capital Area season as they trounced Milton Hershey 62-56. Both Dale Broadwater and George Chellew played one of the best games of their careers.

The local press did a feature article on George Chellew (basketball) and Jim Rhone (wrestling), while in other news Bill Stump won second place in the Tri-County Fiction Contest. The standing tagline continued to be "Glazed Sweets!" for anything possible.

The February 20, 1964 issue of the *Falcon Flash* noted that Peter, Paul, and Mary had appeared at the Zembo Mosque in Harrisburg on January 11 and another article in this school newspaper explained to the readers who/what the Beatles were. **WHAT?!**

As the date for the Junior Prom neared, a Bulletin Board appeared in B-1 to encourage a higher attendance, even to attend as a group (an unheard of choice at the time). As a further incentive, and trying to add some fun to the process, there was a list of names (both male and female) of those who were "still available," a subtle suggestion of "match-making." Most important, the point was also made that those without escorts were as welcome as those with.

This year's school board did not approve a request for an after prom party for the Junior Prom. Nonetheless, the prom itself was well-attended. Held at the Palmyra American Legion on April 4, music for dancing was provided by the Mello-Macs.

The Senior Prom was held May 1, and according to the *Falcon Flash*, prior to the event, ..."after which there are various parties being held at students' homes."

The April 17 issue of the *Flash* noted that music would be accompanying the daily morning meditations. I was skeptical since I was the one delivering the readings.

On June 19, 1964 The Rolling Stones (still relatively unknown) appeared at the Harrisburg Farm Show where three hundred people showed up.[11] Were you one of them? The Stones were on a 12-day tour across America; tickets were $5.

And at this early point the cards and letters from students began to arrive in my mailbox, one of the first being sent from Ocean City, July 28, 1964: "Hi, I'm having a real panic, but the ocean is colder than the blue blazes. Today was my first day on the beach and I got myself thoroughly fried. I'll try to not get into too much trouble."

The Assassination of JFK: Excerpts

Juniors and Seniors in B-1 were asked to respond to the tragedy of the death of JFK by choosing a theme from the following: Democracy, Responsibility, Martyrdom, Tragedy, Hate, Complacency, or Disrespect. The following are excerpts.

- If ever the term "martyrdom" should be applied to any person, it is now. John Kennedy was one who did not have to run for President; he had wealth, heroism in war, and success in his work. This would be enough for any ordinary man, but John Kennedy was not ordinary. (Rick Glocker '64)

- When compared to most other English words, the word Hate is very small, but it has caused more ruthless destruction and death than one could ever list. This force has cost the world a man of peace and a man of young ideas. (Kathy Verdelli '65)

- John F. Kennedy was a martyr, giving his life in service of his country. …Even our Cold War adversaries admit we lost a good leader. Never since World War II has there been as much prayer, as much church attendance, and a national revival for unity and the value of freedom. (Larry Geesaman '65)

- His words will remain through the words of others, his ideas in their minds, and his love in their hearts. (Kathleen Convery '64)

- Hate is defined as an intense dislike, abhorrence, detestation, abomination, or loathing. This intense emotion was released last Friday by millions. People in every corner of the globe united in sorrow for the death and hatred for the assassin of John F. Kennedy. (Bill Stump '65)

- Hate ran very high for the assassin of the United States as many people wondered how anyone could murder the President. Yet, if they themselves every once criticized or downgraded Kennedy, they too had a role in his assassination. They also are to blame for this national tragedy. (Carol Kauffman '65)

- This past week-end brought much hate into the hearts of many Americans, directed largely to one man, Lee Harvey Oswald. (Audrey Roland '64)

- Lee Harvey Oswald not only showed disrespect for his country, but also for human life and for the reputation of Americans to be fair and just. (Louise Davis '64)

- During this last weekend our basic system of government, a democracy, has been tried and tested by various events over which we had no control. …If we were to have any other type of governing then we have, our country might find itself in complete ruin. (Bill Campbell '65)

- John Kennedy stood as a symbol of hope, of man's indomitable spirit and of man's search for freedom. To many Americans his death was a severe blow which knocked us, and the world, to our knees. (Judith Sharp '64)

- "America." "America, the home of the free and the brave." "Only in America may a boy grow up to be President." "Only in America, Land of Opportunity." (Carol Zerfoss, '65)

1964–1965

The fall of 1964 marked the third year I would serve as the English teacher for those senior students in the top academic section. There were 31 students in this section, and for special events two other students joined us for a total of 33—a full house! This included Linda Lash who also audited Senior English, at the request of her parents, while taking American Literature her Junior year, as Linda had been accepted to begin college in Florida a year early in the fall of 1965.

My being the teacher with these students was viewed as a culmination in many ways, and also included a huge caseload with many papers to read, correct, and grade, because I was also teaching academic English for other college prep sections, for both the junior and the senior classes. This was the difficulty—and one that hasn't changed in public education—the standard that teachers are assigned the same number of classes, regardless of the preparation and complexity of the course and/or the necessary writing assignments to review, edit, and confer with students. While it was considered to be the premium assignment, no one took into account the work load.

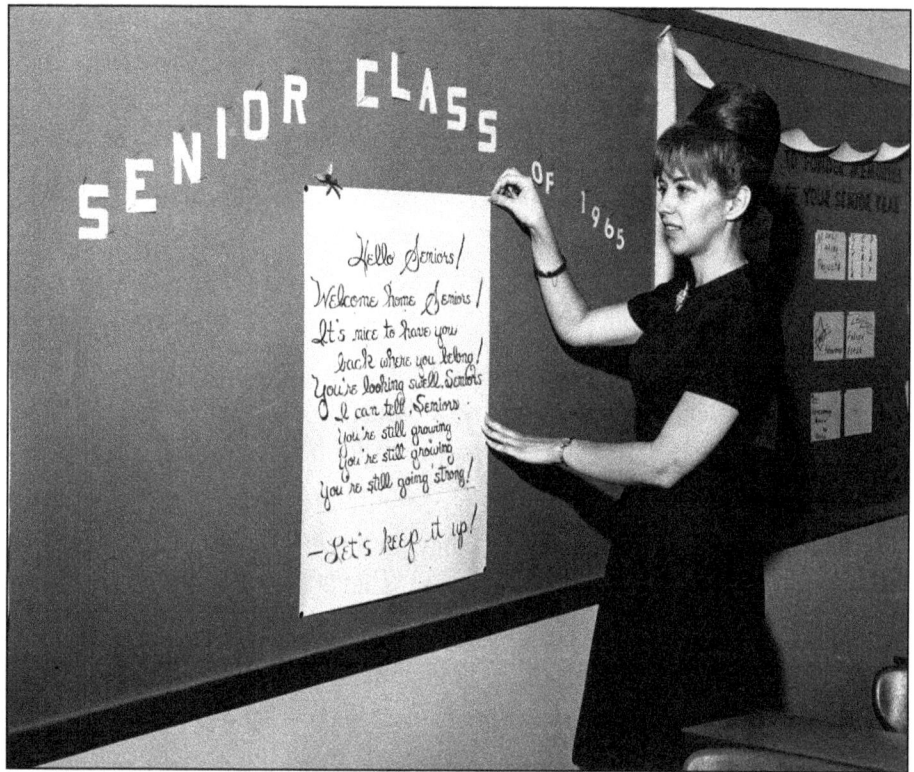

Welcome Class of 1965 Bulletin Board - B-1

The Evening News of September 8, 1964, reported that an additional wing had been added to the west side of the high school at a cost of $254,000. Known as H wing, it was located next to A wing and far removed from F and G wings. The article stated that the school capacity was now 1,800. Many classrooms were still too full.

The Seniors had a good time determining how to market their ingenious fund-raising product. Before the end of September, they had conducted a bubble bath blitz to fill the treasury depleted by their Junior Prom. Twelve hundred bottles were sold, giving the class a profit of $800.

Class officers shown discussing their fund-raising bottle of bubble bath

Dick Clark's success and influence hosting the national program AMERICAN BANDSTAND led to programs such as Lancaster's WGAL Dance Party (Channel 8) which debuted on October 14, 1961. As some of the readers will recall, each week a different Susquehanna Valley high school, including Lower Dauphin, was invited to send students to the Saturday afternoon program in Lancaster where the teens danced to pop tunes recorded on 45 rpm records. Those with really good memories may remember the names of the hosts on this local Dance Party: Terry Abrams and Ginny Lou. (And you do remember Justine on American Bandstand, don't you?)

Joining the craze for "dance parties," in the fall of 1964 WCMB Radio sponsored an area dance party contest. To win required making calls (234-3005) to the station the most times during the time period of the contest. All classes in the junior-senior high school accepted the challenge to participate and they willingly manned the telephones. Lower Dauphin won the contest which included a dinner and free night of skiing at Ski Roundtop for the football team, coaches, and principal. A dance for the entire student body was also part of the prize and on January 30, 1965 Gabriel and the Catalinas provided entertainment at the high school for a record attendance. The crowning touch was an appearance by selected Lower Dauphin students on WGAL's Dance Party.

This also marked the year Field Hockey made its debut and girls who lettered were welcomed into the Varsity Club.

November 20 and 21 were the dates of the Senior Class Play, *The Skin of Our Teeth* by Thornton Wilder. This was not the typical high school play; rather, it was a learning process that allowed the students to select a complicated play and take the responsibility for it, with the leadership of Stage Manager Lois Downes, Director Barry Stopfel, and Publicity Chairman, Lynn Taylor. The local paper did a feature article on "behind the scenes" with the Manager who was in charge of prompters, props, make-up, and ushers, and the Student Director whose duties went …"from helping to select the play last summer to directing and taking part in the actual production."[12]

In December Bethanne Bojanic, Editor of *The Falcon Flash*, announced a format change to the publication from a newspaper to a magazine and that the production would include using Varitype, with the assistance of Miss Strite. The magazine's first issue featured what would turn out to be the only time the word **computer** occurred in the school newspaper during the 1960s, with the innocent, understated, and prophetic closing sentence of *"The whole field of computer programming is a rapidly expanding and attractive field for business students."*

A student program was broadcast on December 21 on WCMB radio, as part of the radio station's plan to feature high school students and give them an experience in broadcasting. Nancy Bolash, Bethanne Bojanic, Barry Stopfel, and Kirk Seibert participated.

On January 21, 1965 the Future Teachers of America representatives (President Mike O'Donovan, Sandra Morrow, Sharon Bistline, Steve Schell, and Dave Heueisen) attended a conference in Camp Hill with other local clubs.

Wrestling had an outstanding season!

In early March an examination in British Literature had to be postponed because of my absence. The class sent me three pages of very creative handwritten messages, in four languages, an example of their confidence that the creativity and humor would be welcomed.

On March 13, the Juniors presented Thornton Wilder's Pulitzer Prize-winning *Our Town*, with Joe Gonglowski in the lead role as the Stage Manager/ Narrator. Audiences were quite supportive (perhaps intrigued) at the drama choices made at LD, not typical high school plays, but which provided opportunities for discussion and challenges for the student actors.

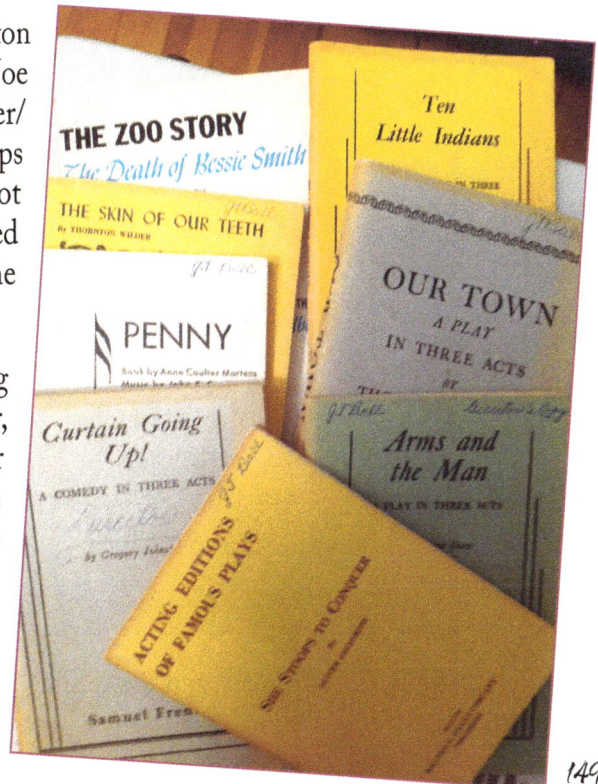

Among the many memorable moments in Spring 1965 were Joe Mateer's trophy as best foul shooter, Ray Yohe's as Mr. FHA Dance, and the least-stellar operetta, produced by Miss Margaret Gluck. Miss Gluck had a difficult time with the show and was the second choral director (to follow Jane Mellin Smith) who found Jane a hard act to follow, as no one could match her skill, talent, actual stage experience, and boundless energy. Further, Miss Gluck likely was the only choral director who ever banned a student from an LD chorus; he found a welcome in B-1 with his classmates.

Another first for the Class of 1965 was the use of photographs in color in some sections of their yearbook. There is also evidence that the first bomb scare prank was the work of this class and, for certain, they turned a pigeon loose in the auditorium during the Senior Awards ceremony.

Spring 1965 brought a Seniors Only Talent Show whose main attraction was Edward Albee's "The Sandbox," a one-act play. Because this was a Theatre of the Absurd drama, it was risky to perform, particularly in a high school assembly where anything can happen. Students in the audience were totally unfamiliar with the play, and likely no more than a handful of teachers had ever heard of it. The young student director was courageous to direct this play, even though it was only fifteen minutes in length. Longer, it might have invited noise from the audience, but all were respectful.

What many of us found so delicious is that an Albee play could be staged one week and the next week the same students could participate in a super conservative, mainstream, old-fashioned Arbor Day Event on April 30 at which time the Student Council held a traditional tree-planting ceremony which was given a double page spread in the 1966 *Falconaire*.

How did we ever have time (or the interest) to do periodic LOCKER INSPECTIONS?

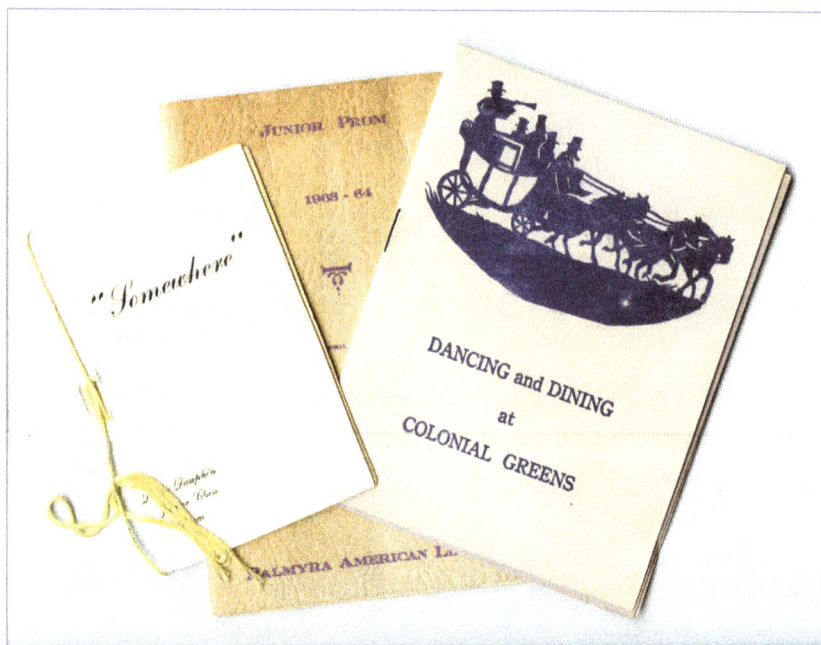

The Senior Prom also took on a very formal tone and theme, "Dancing and Dining at Colonial Greens." The gardenia corsage was worth remembering.

One of the final assignments of the British Literature students was to write a letter to themselves which would be mailed in 1970.[13]

The last day of classes for seniors included a party in B-1, complete with bulletin board, streamers, and the reading of *Ode Written Upon the Occasion of the Graduation of Friends*.

The final event, aside from Baccalaureate and Commencement, was a Class Picnic, the first of its kind at Lower Dauphin, and open only to the Class and totally separate from the Senior Prom. It was designed as an informal gathering where the Class Will and History could be read and enjoyed. The picnic was held at the Farm Bureau Picnic Grounds not far from "The Farm" of Symposium fame.

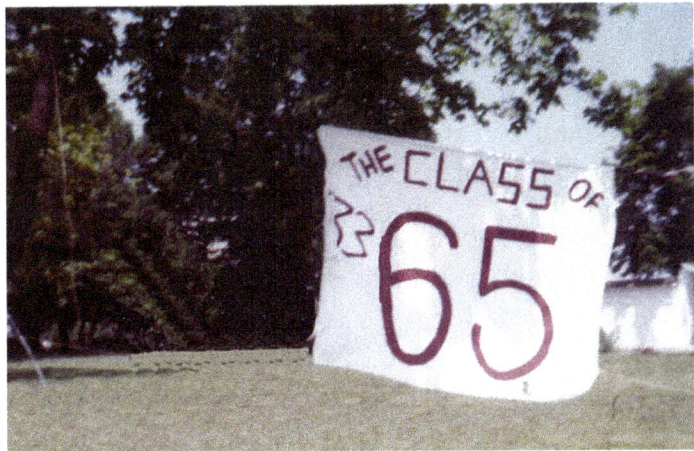

Following graduation of this class, I held a luncheon for the top female students and gifted them with *The Readers' Guide to Literature* or *Merriam-Webster's Collegiate Dictionary*. A note from one of the recipients was typical of those written by each of them, "Your gift will always have value for me, not only as a useful reference book, but also as a reminder of the past four years and our association."

I felt confident that the English Students were prepared for the next chapter of their lives. However, none of us had any idea of the world they would be facing, far more complex than mine had been ten years earlier. And as only a tiny indicator that perhaps they still had reservations about their preparedness for college life in general, the National Honor Society saw the need for more direction for those attending college and sold booklets, "Off to College," as a service to those who were college-bound.

Information about college life and expectations was not easy to come by and one of the class members wrote me that summer, asking me to try and find for her a copy of a book a friend of hers had suggested, *Making the Most of College*.[14] I did.

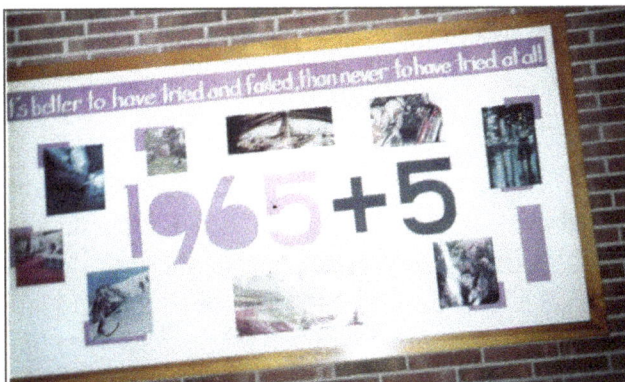

All members of the Class of 1965 faced two distinct national crises during the summer of 1965 following graduation. The first was the occurrence of 28 separate events causing political turmoil which left their mark on this generation and the second was the collapse of many families (nationwide) because of divorce and the resulting loss of the household breadwinner.

The political turmoil was personal to this cohort in that 27 million Baby Boomer men came of draft age in the 60s and 70s and, while less than 10% went to Viet Nam, the war divided the Boomers, leaving lasting scars, real and psychological, including a feeling of guilt by some who had "dodged" the war. The other political scandal was that of Watergate and the resulting further loss of trust in the national government.

The collapse of families that began this decade was a new social challenge, as to this time in history husbands had controlled most of the economic power in families, and now more women needed to earn a living to sustain themselves and, in many cases, their children. This led to the unspoken expectation for the young women of this teen-age group to gain training and an education to be able to support themselves and to not be dependent on anyone. This was parallel to the studies showing that longevity for women was increasing.

All of these factors coalesced with the deeply felt loss by most citizens following the death of President Kennedy as these events came together at the most sensitive moment in the life cycle of the Baby Boomers, while this group transitioned from childhood to adolescence and to young adulthood.

As a cohort Baby Boomers revered "the new" and avoided "the old." They wanted to be different, to be recognized. Even if they didn't realize it at the time, they were living in an era of optimism when there was the desire to follow new opportunities and make one's own pathway.

And as one of them said decades later, "We thought we were cool because we had a crystal ball suspended from the cafeteria ceiling for the school dances."

1965—1966

The Class of 1966 was quite different from the Class of 1965, with their snappy belief that, in their own words, "We were a class with things to do, places to go, and people to meet." That included the Hob Nob, the place to go to be seen, even though the favorite snacks (M&Ms and Sugar Crisps) of this group were not served at the eatery.

Located across from the high school, the Hob Nob served the purpose of a hangout until the highway was reconfigured. To a lesser extent devoted to teens, the Towne & Country Restaurant also was a popular gathering place following events such as football and basketball games. Dave's Dream, too, was a favorite spot, but it was a mile out of town. All three eatery hang-outs offered standard fare such as hamburgers, and they all welcomed young people.

As the first class to have spent all six years in the new high school, the Class of 1966 cohort had made their mark in seventh grade as being fun and having a good sense of humor—the kind of kids who made teachers laugh. In high school they populated most of the dances, particularly enjoying the Milton Hershey Spartan Dance Band and listening to "Eve of Destruction," "I Hear a Symphony," and "Over and Over" by the Dave Clark Five.

This class in particular felt the juxtaposition at Lower Dauphin, with Future Farmers picking through fallen apples to make and sell cider while at the same time those in Vocational Agriculture were—and had a reputation of—breaking precedents and winning academic honors. The same description of collocation may be used for most of the Class of 1966 with their penchant for disruptions, yet producing some very fine scholars and success stories.

This class sold friendships bonds and coin purses to raise funds for a Team Board in the Gymnasium on which to place the names of the home players. And how many knew at the time that Ken Willis, one of their classmates, was the only student ever lost by the Drivers' Education teacher?

Occasionally their quest for fun became a problem such as missing senior class play rehearsals for *Ten Little Indians*. But, unless I am mistaken, they are laughing about this, their usual defense.

Other memories shared by this class would include the months of the daily cafeteria menu item of black olives (usually left on the plates until the day there was the black olive missile war [15]).

They crowed about their senior hook day, assured that they were the first to have this idea, but their best prank was the pre-arranged dropping of marbles to roll down the slope of the auditorium during their Senior Awards Assembly. I can still see in my mind's eye several of the clever perpetrators, led by cool Harold Johns. (Was that really Lester I saw helping with this? Lester??!)

They were also the first LD Class to enjoy the newest trend of Teen Age Dance Clubs, the first in this area being The Raven, established in the fall of 1965, and located in Swatara Township. On a good night it drew about 2,000 of the 14,000 teens who held membership cards. The club attracted name entertainers such as Anthony and the Imperials, The Vibrations, The Ronettes, The Drifters, Major Lance, the Isley Brothers, Martha and the Van Dellas, and the Four Tops.

Color television sets were becoming affordable and many teens enjoyed "The Man from UNCLE" and, of course, debuting on January 12, 1966, "Batman" in color!

On January 29, 1966 the high school band sponsored a dance with music by the on-going favorite local band, El Dantes. And noting that imitation is the sincerest form of flattery, the Service Club sponsored a talent show during the winter with all three grades invited to audition. Mrs. Venus Connelly, a devoted guidance counselor with only a short tenure, led this effort, following the precedent set by the Seniors Only Talent Show of the previous year.

The front page article in the March 1966 issue of the *Falcon Flash* was the Junior Prom. Page two featured an article by Kitch Lee on "Apathy." Page three's column "The Falcon's Tracks" chastised the boys for not inviting girls to the Junior Prom with this header, "...Event of all Events—the social occasion of a lifetime—The Junior Prom!"

The article continued, "Please note that we use the past tense...for sadly enough, the Juniors have had their enthusiasm dampened by some extremely apprehensive prospects. You see, the Junior Class has a problem—perhaps the most grave and serious ever to befall the young damsels of any school... namely, the difficulty of the Junior boys! You may ask, 'What's so new about that?' Well, granted, more often than not they are confusing our lives, but this time they have apparently out-done themselves. In short, these fine examples of chivalry and gallantry have taken it upon themselves **not** to invite the girls *of their own class* to the Prom!"

On April 4, 1966 the Joint Board of the Lower Dauphin School District rejected a proposal from the PTA to hold a post-prom party, saying students should not be encouraged to stay out until 5 a.m. and that midnight was late enough for high school Juniors. They just couldn't win.

However, the first Art Show (sponsored by the Service Club) was held in May.

And the Class of 1966 likely will count the number of words in this description of themselves to compare it to that of the Class of 1965, as they loved annoying their predecessors with this teasing, "She always liked you best."

1966–1967

There are cliques in many classes, but the Class of 1967 is remembered for its four honor students, self-named the Culture Creeps, who chose their own company as they sat by themselves at lunch every day discussing literature and music. As one of them later wrote, "Among other things, we discussed music and literature, art and the theater—things that nourished our minds and spirits as much as food nourished our bodies. We reveled in the power of words, in emotional and intellectual responses to books, scripts, song lyrics, poems, speeches. Of course, we also talked about our classes. Memorizing and performing Hamlet's soliloquy for English class was more than a demanding course requirement. It was a brief chance to immerse ourselves in the mind of a tormented young Danish prince. Whatever the substance of our talks, perhaps we were practicing for one of life's sweet pleasures: quiet conversation and food shared with close friends."

"Who will ever forget Friday, November 11, 1966 when 1,000 stunned spectators watched one of the greatest nights in L.D. history as the Falcons destroyed Middletown's hopes of the CAC crown, marching 80 yards in 70 seconds... in what has to be one of the best high school games ever played in the area." (*Hummelstown Sun*)

The short-lived International Club announced it would be sponsoring a Slave Day on November 23, according to the November 18, 1966 issue of *The Sun*....We heard no more of this.

The arrival of the Blue Guard Movement was a surprise to all except its own members. The *Falcon Flash* announced "a new organization has been born at LD, and the school hasn't been the same since.... Those involved call themselves the Blue Guard and can be seen en masse at all school sponsored activities. Their purpose is to support the school and heighten school spirit. Not only have these boys designed and made their own insignia arm bands, but they have given the school paper some hot competition by creating their own underground newspaper with the irreverent banner of *The Flush Gazette!*" According to Alan Larsen '68, "It had the simultaneous virtues of ticking off the administration and ramping up school spirit. The identities of its authors and how it miraculously appeared in the hallways remain a secret to this day."[16]

The Blue Guard announced that anyone was welcomed to join the resurgence of school spirit. In political terms they would have been on the side of conservativism and they prided themselves as being respectful and mainstream. Several imitator groups emerged, but none had the brio and confidence as did the leaders of this original movement.[17]

Nevertheless, a shadow group was soon formed in opposition to the Blue Guard. The Warriors seemed to have appeared overnight as a protest that the Blue Guard had taken school spirit to the extreme. This group was short-lived as it was not as well-organized as the Blue Guard.

Most of the adults believed the Blue Guard held a lot of promise and could have continued as a positive force with some adult guidance. As a letter to the *Falcon Flash* editor from an anonymous writer in December 1966 notes, "...The Blue Guard, under capable leadership, could turn into one of the best organizations our school has seen."

Another instance of the varied and not typical events shared by this class occurred Saturday evening, January 14, 1967, when more than 1100 fans left the Lower Dauphin gymnasium confident that they had just witnessed humanity at its finest. This was the evening when the Faculty Basketball Team played Wilmington, Delaware in a fund-raising event to help defray the medical expenses of and to pay tribute to Mr. G. William Peck who had been transported from his hospital bed by ambulance to be in attendance at this event. The sum total raised at this emotionally powerful event was more than twice the goal.

As a result of a call for more student-sponsored assemblies, the National Honor Society responded to the challenge, sponsoring various topics held during the end-of-day activity period which were identified as *Lyceums*.

The designation of a class "spirit stick" was instituted by this class[18] and they were the first to break out with an original Commencement program guided by the program's advisor. We wrote a choralogue based on their class motto, *Nils mortalibus arduum est* (Nothing is too high for the daring of mortals) and delivered it through a speaking choir. The program was recorded and made available in an LP recording, a first!

The Hob Nob continued to be a favorite hangout. Located directly across the school on Hanover Street, it was a safe place for students to stop after school events; it was also a convenient place for parents to pick up their teens.

In May, the *Falcon Flash* announced that an eighth period was being added to the high school schedule to be used for all special interest activities such as seminars and research, advanced studies, special interest clubs, remedial and correctional instruction.

The 1967 *Falconaire* staff fell short on identifying photos and it appears that some homerooms were missed entirely. However, the class memorialist made up for this by recalling that their "one constant that almost everyone learned to treasure was class friendship."[19]

1967–1968

The summer of 1967 was a pivotal one and may have been the catalyst for the many diverse changes at Lower Dauphin yet to come. One of these major changes occurred when Mr. David C. Smith was made Director of the Lower Dauphin School District Federal Project, Title I of the Elementary and Secondary Education Act, a milestone in public education. Lower Dauphin was awarded a Federal grant of $27,845 (close to $200,000 in today's dollars) to improve science education in grades K-12. More than 160 students and 50 teachers were involved in the project at LD and spent the summer working to develop a logical, sequential curriculum plan for K-12 science. A large number of course guides were developed and became the cornerstone of an exceptional science program in the district.

Returning for their senior year in the fall of 1967, the Class of 1968 saw the announcement in the September 1967 issue of *Know Your Schools* that individualized scheduling, using the McBee data processing system, would be instituted at the high school. This required far more administrative effort than the then current scheduling process, and initially students were bewildered, but it was in the best interest of the individual students as it gave them more flexibility in selecting classes. The seniors were glad they would have been graduated and would not have to deal with it.

Field hockey held a 22-game winning streak as they wrapped up the League Title for a third straight year, this time with its first undefeated team. The fall of 1967 also marked the beginning of gymnastic interscholastic competitions. Prior to this time, gymnastics had been only an intramural activity.

The December issue of *Know Your Schools* reported that a Student Forum had concluded that students and teachers show pride in each other and that the forum members like the close connection between the student body and faculty.

Those in the Lower Dauphin choir and/or marching band were very proud to be a part of the first half-time program to present a salute to Veterans' Day (during the last home football game, November 11, 1967). This program included both the LD choir and the marching band. Such a tribute to veterans had never before been presented by Lower Dauphin or by any other school in the area.

Also in November the Electronics Club developed a jamming device to interfere with Mr. Longreen's radio during the World Series. The device was then offered to the Athletic Department to jam opponents' walky-talkies during football games. They declined!

This was also the year of the Carol Channing hoax on February 27, 1968.[20]

A major milestone was reached in varsity basketball when Lee Seibert was honored with the Capital Area Conference crown as the high scorer in the entire Conference membership.

Other ground broken by this class was a result of disappointment that there had been no high school musical produced since 1965. Thus, a cadre of students determined to revive the musical on their own! A team of band officers worked for months organizing, writing, and then producing "It's a Big, Wide, Wonderful World," under the direction of band president Elaine Bell and the choir director, Mr. William Nixon. Delivered in the spring, the program showcased several soloists along with choreography to accompany the music. There was no charge for admission.

Mainly, however, the Class remembers their high school years as history does, as a time of turmoil and changes. Assassination of President John F. Kennedy, Martin Luther King, Jr., and Robert F. Kennedy all occurred during the high school years of this class, more trauma than teen-agers should have to deal with. As they noted, "Where earlier classes had the Beach Boys, we had U2's "Early morning, April four, a shot rings out...."[21]

The members of this senior class should have been thinking about their last chance to goof off or pull a prank before getting a full time job or going to college, and not having to be worrying about being drafted under the looming shadow of the Viet Nam War.

A very special event almost forgotten, but should be noted, is the Second Annual All Sports Banquet held on May 28, 1968. The featured speaker was the popular young head coach of the Penn State Nittany Lions Football Team, Joe Paterno.

The Class of 1968 was the last class to hold their Commencement in the auditorium.

Alan Larsen remembers, "It was quite a journey that brought us all to that springtime of 1968 as we entered the auditorium for the last time in the spring of 1968, remembering that the Beach Boys "Good Vibrations" was the apt sound track for our 9th grade year. But now—with the assassinations and the escalating war, the dizzying redefinition of everything we thought we knew, at the very moment when seniors, those rulers of the hallways, usually are fully convinced they do actually know it all—the new soundtrack for us was Dylan's "The Times, They are a Changin'."[22]

1968–1969

Members of the Lower Dauphin marching band had spent a week of the summer at their first band camp held at Elizabethtown College!

The 1st LD Band Camp at Elizabethtown College

The summer weekly band rehearsals were over, and on August 19th BAND CAMP began. It wasn't until that morning that everyone realized just what it really was. Band members were ready to joke, work, eat, sleep and live band for a solid week.

The fun began in trying to get everything organized. I do believe there were more suitcases than band members ... AND THE GIRLS!!! All the stuff they brought. A kitchen sink? No, but oh, the curlers, hair dryers, radios, clocks, irons, etc. ...

And so we arrived ... EAGERLY??? Let's say cautiously, and got things in some order ...QUICKLY? Well, once things got under way, they never stopped. The newer band members began to fit in and we began to hear the names "Saltzer, Ricker, Scalise!!!!

By the second day we were in the groove of things, having to walk everywhere. By nightfall we were ready to collapse and would have had a good night's sleep except the "elementary school" college boys kept the girls awake and the giggling girls kept the boys awake.

For the rest of the week we walked, talked, marched, played, swam, ran, ate, slept, and then sang in a daze. The 8 ½ hours of drills had their effect. We (at least half the band) easily feel asleep by 10 and were up at 6:30.

Things feel into place; the saxes were always perfect; the tubas were too lazy to carry their own tubas; the drums had laziness down to an art; the clarinets were trying to out-blow the trumpets; while the first trumpets out-blew the entire band and the third trumpets didn't even know there was a band camp.

Remember: how poorly we did the first day; the happy faces and tired feet; "Warfel, what are you doing? Warfel, get in line; WARFEL, are you catching grasshoppers?"

...the odd feeling when the girls had to go through a door marked MEN to get to the women's assigned locker room. ...after hours running through the sprinklers ..."Where's Heisey?" ...Karol explaining her sprained ankle, "Well, see, me and Mr. Nixon were in the shower room, and...."

And we left with looking forward to next year!

The band featured competition-winning head majorette Jeannine Lehmer who was also chosen as solo head majorette for the Sweet 66 and the featured performer at the half-time ceremonies at the Big 33 football game the summer of 1969. Jeannine's final high school performance was a baton-dance combination during the spring band concert. She was also known as one of the finest majorettes in the state, having appeared with the Sweet 66 since 1966. After graduation Jeannine entered Franklin and Marshall College—as a member of the first freshman class to admit women—where she majored in science and became the lead majorette in the college marching band.

One would be hard pressed to find anywhere else the variety of scholastic programs offered at Lower Dauphin High School, particularly in the early years when most high schools offered only the typical tracked courses in College Prep, Business, and General. In the spring of 1968 students had been advised of a new method of scheduling based on individual ability and interest, and the Class of 1969 would be the first to use this system that was instituted and managed through a data processing system, a very new idea at the time.

Arena scheduling followed soon after, a lesson in controlled chaos. As long as there were several sections of any given course taught by more than one teacher, this process could be made manageable. However, offering "singletons"—courses with only one section and one designated teacher—complicated the process of scheduling both classes and students, and it wreaked havoc for the person who did the scheduling, for these singletons needed to be scheduled "by hand." Nonetheless, development of new courses and new programs was encouraged in every subject area, and this brought richness to the depth of the course offerings, ranging from mini-courses[23] which might be taught only once ever to programs that required a two- or three-year student commitment. This huge philosophical and actual change gave rise to courses such as English Enrichment, Longitudinal Studies, and Archaeology in the early 1970s.

The November 1968 issue of *The Flying Falcon News*[24] reports a Victory Dance held to close the football season. LD grad Tom Hughes, a music major at West Chester, served as the disc jockey. This issue of the paper also contains a letter to the editor asking for the students to keep the cafeteria in better order.

Craig Tritch, who wrote the memoir for his class in *Loyal Hearts Proclaim*, set the tone for this end of the sixties decade by opening his remembrance piece with "You haven't yet heard from the Class of '69 because they, like me, lived high school through the years of turmoil when this great nation nearly came undone."

This very well captures the late sixties as he continued, "Spirited discussions in Mr. Croll's Problems of Democracy class contrasted harshly with the bucolic, peaceful lives that we all came from. American cities were in flames because of race riots, students took to the streets to protest the Vietnam War, and those of us who remained loyal wondered why our government had lied to us." This was, indeed, a powerful comment.

He continued, "In football our six seniors had to learn from losing, and yet lose with dignity. One of my teammates played with a broken arm until he broke his leg. Such efforts surely are worthy. Every LD athlete has the feeling of walking in the steps of giants who came before. Wrestlers could not imagine letting down our beloved coach. Every week Mrs. Ball faithfully posted the latest LD sports headlines on the front of her lectern for all of us to see with pride.

"Some will never know what it's like to wait in a locker room and listen to the fans screaming [during the JV matches/games] at such a volume that the varsity wonders 'Will they have anything left for us?' They did, and provided even more! No LD athlete ever took the floor, field, or mat without knowing that fathers and farmers, mechanics and mothers, lived and died with their efforts those nights.

"No mentioning by name could ever do justice to the teachers (Bill Linnane), counselors (Pat Lanshe), coaches (Cleon Cassel), and superintendent (Doc) who had a profound impact on our lives. If they'd only known how much their guidance meant to us….

"Our lives are marked by a few special events …including the reunion with classmates and sad remembrances of those who are gone. We who walked the halls of LD and lived full and wondrous lives are blessed beyond measure."

The end of the sixties was captured in Rosak's *Counter Culture* and the struggle with technocracy based on the premise that the vital needs of man are purely technical and everything can be analyzed. And, now, nearly fifty years later, what Rosak predicted is eerily near the mark, "*In a technocracy, totalitarianism is perfected because its techniques become progressively more subliminal.*"[25] An early and continuing concern is that this counter culture included reducing all information to a form that a machine is able to use, in simplifying (some would say "dumbing down") the language used for the machine to operate.

Spanish Guitar and Strat-O-Matic Football both were new—and popular—this year, as was LD's Outdoor Education Program at Camp Hebron for which high school students could volunteer as counselors for the 5th grade's week away at camp. A bit more exotic in the high school, the summer of 1969 saw Mr. David C. Smith's launching student travel programs by which chaperoned groups of students could travel to Europe.[26]

July 1969 brought man's first walk on the moon; and November 15 delivered the first nationwide Viet Nam War Moratorium held in Washington, DC with an estimated 600,000 demonstrators. It is widely viewed as the largest march in the history of the United States to that point. The march and all-day rally on the Mall culminated a week of protests throughout the city.

Surely the 1960s qualified for being the best example of a world turned upside down in only ten short years and a decade that showed the potential power of youth.

Chapter 5 Endnotes:

[1]   See "Class Reflections," *Loyal Hearts Proclaim*. p. 108.

[2]   Likely either *The Patriot* or *The Evening News*. The *Sun* account is also included to provide additional information on the same game.

[3]   Pun intended in the newspaper report.

[4]   Recounted by Classmates (1962) Barbara Olson Bowser and Betty Musser Radle.

[5]   Paul Beers, "Reporter at Large," *The Patriot*, September 26, 1962.

[6]   In Spanish, Italian, and Latin, the word means lasting or enduring. Another source suggests that El Dantes could mean "The Dances."

[7]   pp. 16-17.

[8]   Future Business Leaders of America.

[9]   See student written reactions in the Scrapbook.

[10] Farber, David. *Age of Great Dreams*, p. 47.

[11] Cohen, *The Sun and the Moon and the Rolling Stones*, p. 109.

[12] *The Hummelstown Sun*, fall 1964.

[13] One letter yet remains to be sent and if someone reading this book knows where Fay Zeiders is, please let one of the editors of this book or a class officer know and the letter will be mailed to her. The letter remains unopened and bears a 3¢ stamp.

[14] Richard A. Kalish, Wadsworth Publishing, 1959.

[15] *The Falcon Flier*, June 1961, p. 4.

[16] *Loyal Hearts Proclaim: The First Fifty Years of Lower Dauphin High School*, p. 119.

[17] For more details see *Loyal Hearts Proclaim*, p. 372.

[18] In the fall of 1966 a new "tradition" emerged—the awarding of a spirit stick, a practice that had its roots in a cheerleading camp in 1954 when its director was so impressed with a squad that, while not the best performers, had "incredible enthusiasm, dedication, and spirit." He broke a branch of a tree and handed it to the squad, dubbing it the "spirit stick." High schools picked up on this innovation, using manufactured sticks often painted the school colors and awarding them at pep rallies to the class dubbed the most spirited.

[19] Larsen, "Reflections," pp. 120-121, *Loyal Hearts Proclaim*.

[20] See "The Ultimate Prank," *Loyal Hearts Proclaim*, p. 362.

[21] Larsen, Ibid.

[22] Larsen, Ibid.

[23] Mini-courses are a story for the 1970s. One listing included 108 individual courses.

[24] (This evidently is a short-lived rename of the school newspaper.) This may have been the second year for this name since this issue is identified as Vol. II, no. 2. With student management it is difficult to confirm the issues.

[25] Roszak, *The Making of a Counter Culture*, p. 9.

[26] *Know Your Schools*, Lower Dauphin School District newsletter, June 1969.

Chapter 6

Leaving

April to December 1965

In that sweet mood when pleasant thoughts
bring sad thoughts to the mind.

Lines Written in Early Spring
Wordsworth

The letters from The English Students began to arrive in the summer after the Class of 1964 had been graduated. I began saving these and other letters in the spring of 1965, adding them to the letters I initially had kept from Judy Sener, Class of 1963. With the correspondence I began to realize my affection for these remarkable young people and my desire to follow their careers, interested as to where life might take them. Judy Sener was a close friend to one of the key figures in this story and was also active in the musicals as the teenage baby sitter for "Pammie," Jane Mellin Smith's young daughter.

Most of the letters used here are from students in the Class of 1965; second in number are from the Class of 1964, and third, from the Class of 1966. Further, not all of the letter-writers were in college; several had entered the military and likely needed a tie to an adult friend back home who was not one of their own parents, and maybe who simply was a connection to their school days.

Excerpts from this collection of letters are offered here to the English Students as a way to return, if only for a moment, to a time when you first stepped out into the world away from friends and family, Lower Dauphin High School, and Hummelstown, and, to some degree, even away from the person you had become to that point in your life.

Most of you previously had not set foot on the college campus (or military base) to which you were pledging your attendance. Some, but not all, colleges had sent basic information to you, although very few colleges had included photographs of the rooms in the dormitories. Some of you had exchanged letters with your future roommates, but not many had exchanged photos of yourselves.

When you arrived on your respective campuses nearly everything was unfamiliar. You experienced anxiety, anticipation, excitement, trepidation, and, most of all, bravado, for you certainly were not going to admit anything even resembling *FEAR*.

This was the first time for many of you to be away from home for an extended period of time. I could identify with your thoughts, many the same as mine ten years earlier—although I was only twenty miles from home, at DuBois University Center of Penn State, living alone in a rooming house. Thus, I shared your excitement vicariously, feeling the apprehension, as well as the excitement, as, one-by-one, you left home and you left Hummelstown.

Among us we used a phrase, coined by 18th Century author and lexicographer Samuel Johnson, to laugh away any inner fears of leaving the familiar. If you recall, Dr. Johnson expressed his love of London by noting, "When you are tired of London, you are tired of life." We adapted this for our own use as a tag to ward off the anxiety of leaving: "When you are tired of Hummelstown, you are tired of life."[1] Laughing made the leaving easier, in a way that you understood Hummelstown would always be home.

In your fears you likely were not much different from most of your peers in the United States. Many of you had never shared a bedroom and now you had a roommate or, in some cases, roommates. However, only one of you would return home because of homesickness; the others toughed it out, laughed it off, cried in private, or changed schools at the end of the first year.

The following excerpts from your letters were selected as being representative of what most of you were experiencing, even though the particulars of the incidents were not identical. A few accounts are included because the style and/or the experience of the writer is distinctive; others because they show reassurance in the mundaneness of money, friends, classes, music, movies, books, and school activities. Each letter is identified by date and place. The silhouettes indicate the following:

- a male (both students and adults)

- the teacher and author

- a female student

Was there any better time in history than to be eighteen and heading off to college in the mid-1960s? Even fifty-plus years later the excitement continues to reverberate from your early college letters. Emails and texting can't begin to compare....

1965

April 6, Collegeville

Thank you so much for sending the Faulkner material so promptly. It arrived just in time. Tomorrow we have an in-class comp. on "The Bear." Your information has been most helpful, especially the genealogy. I was really confused about that part. I assure you that I will not allow anyone else to have your material. I am quite familiar with the results of friendly loans. We received our mid-semester grades. I was very pleased I got B's in English and French. What really surprised me was the grade on symbolism. I got an A. I didn't give the modern interpretation that he prefers, but he said my arguments for what I had were well organized so I was rather pleased. Thus, I thank you even more so for the material as that made the difference. I appreciate it very much. Sincerely.[2]

Summer in Europe

At first I didn't like Venice because of all the water. Being an American, I like to get around fast, but you just can't do it with all the water.

Florence, Pisa, Naples, but Rome was my favorite city, then on to Paris which I find wonderful. I like it more and more. My room has class and is the kind in which one could write a famous novel or paint a masterpiece.

I also visited Pigalle where the life of Paris is, such as Bal du Moulin Rouge. I hope to go on a side trip of my own to Germany. I have to wait for permission from home. My aunt has been very good to me, but I would like to get out on my own a bit now that I am acclimated to the European travel.

July 26, Shippensburg

I owe you a note for the much appreciated box of peanut butter cookies I received today.[3] They're very good, and my roommate agrees. Thank you very much. I was in New York again on Friday. The Fair[4] was still there and as great as ever. I'd write more, but I will be home this weekend. I'll see you then.[5]

July 30

I would like to thank you very much for getting me tickets to the Baccalaureate and Commencement and inviting me to the senior class picnic. It sure was wonderful to see you and all my classmates again, and it was one trip I'll never forget.[6]

The first letter specifically from the Lower Dauphin High School Class of 1965 came from one who was the youngest in her family, her three older siblings having been on their own for years.

June 8, Hummelstown

I wrote this the night of graduation, but I waited to give it to you. I know you understand why. How do I express my appreciation in return for a friendship well cherished? I owe you so much already and as the years will pass I'll no doubt realize my indebtedness to you even more. These past four years, with all their joys and sorrows, will not be taken lightly and I shall carry this friendship wherever I go, for I hold with me tonight a treasury of "little, nameless, unremembered acts of kindness and of love"[7] that you have given to me.

July 6, Canadensis

Everything here is fascinating. There's so much to experience and explore. The first day I thought of B. and how he would die if he had to put up with these people. I can't even believe myself. Most of the people who come here to the lodge are older, as I had suspected. There was one elderly man who loved to read historical novels. We sat and talked most every afternoon. I really enjoyed him, but he's gone now. I've lost track of all time. Though I have written only one letter to you, I think of you often. I think of what you might say or feel about something I have seen or read.

July 9, Canadensis

This place is dead at nights. What I need is a car.

July 24, Canadensis

The owner here says I receive more mail than the hotel. When you come, start early in the morning and bring a picnic lunch. Do you like southern fried chicken? Mother could make it. And the usual stuff like your brownies. We could do something around here, like golf, horseback riding, tennis. (Forget relaxing! I can hardly wait to get my hands on the wheel!)

Thanks for recommending the movie, *The Sandpiper*. Not likely that I'll see it around here. The nearest movie house is still playing *The Swan* with Grace Kelly. Got my hip-riders from Mom. They fit nice and snug, but they don't ride on the hips that much.

I selected my courses for next year. Don't know how they're going to be, as I took what they suggested. A total of 16 semester hours; this is average.

I like the sound of your innovation for next year's class. It's bound to produce some excitement. Here I was worried about you.

I'm going to have to find a new place for my tips. After the stash got too big for my wallet, I used an envelope, then a Band-Aid box. Now what?

Would you do me a favor? There's a book Dale has called *Making the Most of College*. It's the size and shape of the spelling book you gave me. Would they have it in a book store? Would you look sometime? I'd appreciate it immensely.[8]

July 26, Shippensburg

I thought I owed you a note for the much appreciated box of peanut butter cookies I received today. They're very good, and my roommate agrees. Thank you very much. I was in New York again on Friday. The Fair was still there and is as great as ever. We also saw the Phillies lose to the Mets, 3-2 in 10 innings. Shea Stadium is really beautiful.[9] There were 40,000 there Friday night.

August 4, Canadensis

Good morning! Just walked down to the crossroads to mail a letter. Felt mighty good outside, nice and brisk, and quieter than a tomb. You're right. The mornings are wonderful before the people are up and on their merry way. Now that you know that all roads lead to Canadensis, you must come and see me more often. Surprise me!!! That was a genuine surprise yesterday! From all indications I was certain you wouldn't be here. And when I saw you all standing in the doorway—you made it!!!! But it seemed like you were here and gone before I knew it, and a better day than I ever expected.

August 11, Canadensis

I am hiring me a secretary. This makes the twelfth letter I have written tonight. Believe me, they were short! I take it that you all are coming up again in two weeks? I also investigated into an overnight stay in the motel unit, $16 a night.

Will you please bring my copy of the French Boot Shop catalog? Oh, yes, I received your copy of *Life* today. Gracious!! I couldn't agree with you more. The color combinations are just atrocious even though they are the typical Bobby Brooks style!

Lois on the steps, Canadensis

Any information on the house? Though I like it more than most, I can't see you living anywhere except someplace secluded.

I did manage to read 150 pages of *Marjorie Morningstar*. It took me all summer just to read the first 98 pages! Things are looking bad when I can stay with a thick book.

Sent for a season ticket to five celebrity shows on campus, including Erroll Garner, "Stop the World I . . .," the Highwaymen, Glenn Yarbrough, and Los Trovadores de Espana. Five shows for $12. I can see it coming—four years of starvation.

My roommate's name is Cheryl and we have a room in one of the older dorms—but it's handy—near the chapel. I'm so excited, I can hardly wait. What I'd like to accomplish is some good study habits. I hope I won't find it hard to fit in, but if it means I might jeopardize my own ideas of loyalty, etc., forget it. I'd much rather be a loner. I don't always relish having hordes of people around.

August 17, Canadensis

Saw *The Sandpiper*. ... would you do a favor? Buy me 2 yds. of pink satin ribbon, if you have a chance... no dire need... just finished the 565-paged monstrosity of *Marjorie Morningstar*... could you bring something else to read... be expecting you...

August 25, Canadensis

You've been gone at least a whole ten minutes by now. Brother! Oh, how I dread the thought of tomorrow, so I'll just think of all the good things we all did today. It was a splendid day, you know. Most of all I enjoyed just being with my friends.

I hope I can finish *The Fountainhead* in 2 weeks. Like I have anything else to do. And funny this guy on the radio says so many familiar things, and is now talking about James Dean.

I'm looking at those post cards Cheryl sent. Just think in three weeks I'll be walking on those grounds. I get chills all up and down every time I think of it. Four whole years of growing, experiencing, absorbing, living. Oh, I can hardly wait. I feel like a small child at the expectation of an amusement ride. Full of wonder and sure of a thrill.

August 31, Shippensburg

I again thank you for sending me the fudge. I just tested it and it's very good! The cookies were crumbled a little bit, but they were still good. I would send you something but our cafeteria food isn't too great!

September 13, Springfield

I can't trust myself to say too much, so this letter will be brief. Much to my disbelief, I am really here. Realized this even more after I saw how much they have to offer. Room is more than I expected.

I guess it's safe enough to say that I'm overwhelmed. Unpacking, tours, tests, convocations, assemblies, visits, rallies, meetings and more meetings. Wish I could share it with someone who appreciates the same things I do. Perhaps, vicariously, I can. Couldn't have a better roommate. I am being slow at making friends—like to look them over first. This way I tend to keep the friends I seek.

Last night groups of about 14 of us visited different professors. We met at Dr. Call's home—professor of English. There's a phoniness about his knowledge or maybe it was because a table with marble-designed paper-covering was being passed off as marble.

Have a problem explaining why I chose this college. Feel like a seventh grader again. I would get the beanie that doesn't even fit. Mr. Fickes' address, please. ....

September 13, Boston

Well, my first day of orientation is over. I have never experienced such confused feelings in my life. The city is absolutely overwhelming. I'm entranced with the idea of being a college student and yet I'm as sad and lonely as I've ever been. The worst part of it is that I couldn't leave the city if I had to. It's everything I've ever dreamed of.

My room is a suite of 3 rooms and a bath. Four of us share the place. I have a private entrance to the bath and more than adequate closet space. Only 3 of us have shown up. The 4th must be an upperclassman. Both roommates have high college boards. Mike is the wealthiest. I'm not sure what his father does but they drove a Buick Riviera and his brother goes to Brown University. Both of them are in Public Communications. The other boy and I are in Basic Studies.

Last night Mike and I went into Boston Commons via the subway. We had a complete riot. We checked out Kennedy's which is advertised in *Esquire* and *Playboy*. We also had some fun with 2 girls soliciting in front of the subway station. I'll bet they followed us for three blocks.

I'm sorry I can't tell you everything I want to in a letter; it would take 15 pages. I think what's so terrible is that there is no one around to really express my feelings to. I can see what you meant when you said that I would never have the close friendships I had in high school.

It's unbelievable how strange it is not to have K. bombing around. Every time I see a burgundy Pontiac, I forget myself and wave. I really started the day off great. I was late for registration this morning.

The ratio of girls to men up here is 3 girls to every man. Wahoo!!!

Kim, my other roommate, is pretty wild. He has a car here which is illegal, and he also has a bottle of gin. He and Mike had orange drink and gin last night before going to bed. I didn't indulge. I'm not taking any chances.

September 15, West Chester

Well, my father "jammed" everything into the car. Of course, my clothes were a wrinkled mess but evidently they didn't give that any consideration. Found out that we don't have any classes Monday so guess I might as well come home.

Wanted you to be among the first to know that Tim wants to pin me. That's one reason why he wants me to go up to State as soon as possible. Hate to admit it but I believe I might be in love with him. Question: How can one be sure?

September 16

Your call last night was the brightest spot I've had since all of you left. It seemed so normal—just as though you were calling from the Farm. I am happy to hear that you like school. OK so I've said it. And I am!

We're going to L.D.'s football game tomorrow night, movies (*Darling* Saturday night, and last night *Once a Thief*). I'm even going to watch TV tonight because there's an intriguing movie on, *The Manchurian Candidate*.[10]

P.S. Don't destroy or sell your term paper. I want it back to keep with all the others from your class.

September 17, Springfield

I love it here. And somehow I sense that I won't regret saying it either. It's the little things I love—like the chapel bells that ring every quarter-hour, the squirrels that scamper freely across the campus grounds, all the little things that don't mean much in themselves.

Walked downtown this afternoon. There are many beautiful rambling homes on wide tree-lined streets that I know you would just love. We didn't have too much time when we arrived to look around. I felt like I had been dropped from an airplane.

They're doing *J.B.* in October. The facilities are very poor. But the freedom! They're also doing *Oh Dad, Poor Dad*. In the final scene girl climatically seduces boy on stage! Suppose it's not unusual for college, but for me ---!!!! Imagine what we could have done in high school with freedom like that!!! I mean constructive things.

My roommate went to the Freshmen Mixer tonight. So the room is all mine for the first time. Secondly, could you recommend a dictionary? I'd like to buy a really good one.

September 19, Boston

Hi!!!!!!!! It is now 2:20. The other guys decided to do the wash so I went along so we could stick all of it in one load. First we put 20 cents in the washer and it starts out in the rinse cycle. We wait for it to finish so we can put another 20 cents in. We do and the machine blows up. Sparks flew all over the place. Naturally we have to take all the wet clothes out and put them in another washer. What a panic. Right now Kim is running all over the place looking for someplace to get change.

Send Mrs. Kramer's address to me, please. I've got to check the wash so I'll be back later.

I'm sorry if I seemed to be in a hurry last Friday but I knew if I stayed any longer it would be twice as hard to leave. Believe me, if I could have I would have hidden you in one of my suitcases. You'd fit in perfectly up here.

Last night a couple of us checked out one of the coffee houses but it had a $2.25 cover charge so needless to say we didn't go in.

I went to Chapel this morning. The organ is terrific. I'd love to get my hands on it.

September 20

I saw a fine movie Saturday night—*Darling*. Sort of an English *La Dolce Vita*. I hope to see *The Pawnbroker* as it had great reviews in *SHOW* magazine. Started to read *Boys and Girls Together*. Very powerful. Absorbing!

Disastrous defeat in football at the hands of Carlisle, 55-7.

I just turned the fan on in study hall—my own I brought from home. You should see the little heads pop up—one by one as they feel the breeze.

Sent from Delaware, Ohio to Boston, forwarded to Hummelstown.

Rushing is the biggest farce and front job I have ever seen. It makes me sick. I will not go to a fraternity that is athletic and I'm sick of hearing how much beer one can drink.

September 21, Delaware, Ohio

Today I finished the first complete day of classes. Tonight I tried reading the introductory material in the chemistry book text and I couldn't wade through the second paragraph. It is really bad news.

No one ever heard of Lower Dauphin or Union Deposit for that matter. Regretfully I must say that I hail from Hershey, the Chocolate town. Most of the freshmen come from private schools so they can't begin to imagine a "hick" high school. Ironically, next door is a boy from Elizabethtown. My roommate is from Baltimore and is not that bad to live with. Also he brought his own stereo.

My only disappointment so far is that I did not receive a bid from any of the fraternities. It was partly my fault for out of 14 frat houses I only like four, and I did not receive a bid at any of these, so now I am an Independent and happy. I still say get your Masters and come on out to teach here.

September 21, West Chester

Received a letter from Ohio and K. says he really likes the place; doesn't have to go to Chapel. Honestly, these guys don't realize how lucky they are. There's a possibility that Tim will be able to come down here for "Rampage Weekend."

Betsy bought that *Boys and Girls Together* book so I guess I'll read that one after *The Fountainhead*. Anyway, the temptation is hard to resist.

September 22, Boston

Received your letter today. It was really quite a gift in the condition I'm in, which is pretty low today for some reason. I think it's the weather (It's miserably hot up here too.) The weather reminds me of summer and leads to the farm, which in turn leads to depression. I wish you were here because you always helped me get out of little fits of this sort. It would be different if I were homesick because then I have a possibility of going home, but I can't return to the farm.

Our 4th roommate finally got here. Believe it or not he is a transfer from Hershey Junior College. I almost fainted.

I'm on the staff of the dorm newspaper. I do reviews on the movies that are shown here. We have some pretty decent but older movies, such as *Psycho, La Dolce Vita, Breakfast at Tiffany's*.

I'm not going to get much studying done till later tonight when it cools off. I'll probably go over and sit along the river. In case I haven't told you I do have my director's chair up here.[11] Fits perfectly. I bought a print at the Union, Degas' *Absinthe Drinkers*.

I'm really going to enjoy Humanities. We're reading D. H. Lawrence, James Joyce, Billy Faulkner, and guess who? Jean Paul Sartre. Monday and Tuesday nights I spent 5 hours studying, which is really an accomplishment for me.

I can't wait to describe to you the building I have classes in. It was built in 1868. I'll wait to tell you the rest when I get home. I couldn't do it justice in a letter.

In your next letter, give me some hints on how to study. It seems that for all the time I study I'm not getting very far.

P.S. They put Pepsi in the drink machine downstairs. So every day after class I also have a Pepsi and read my mail. If I'm not with you in person I'm with you in Pepsi spirit!!!

September 24, Boston

Surprised to hear from me so soon? Well, I can't help it. I just heard Andy Williams sing "Tender is the Night" and that did it.

I don't really have anything new to tell you since I only talked to you 6 hours ago. Say hello to Tom!!!! Tell him the women up here are fantastic. They're all over the place.

I can't wait for the brownies. Something to cherish from Hummelstown.

September 27, Boston

I was the only one who got mail today. (4 letters and a package!) My roommates keep asking where it all comes from. I guess I'm just fortunate to have such great friends.

I found out today that one of the musicals playing here now is based on the play *Picnic*. If I can afford it I'd like to see that and *On a Clear Day You Can See Forever*. It would be like heaven for me.

6:15. Hi!! I'm back again. Dinner was delicious. We had pork chops and French fries. The Union has the book *The Prophet* which I had been looking for. As soon as I have enough money I'm going to buy it. It only comes in the hardback edition.

As far as explaining your coming here, why couldn't you just say you're coming to see me and see a show since that is what it is? I think it'll be good for you to get up here. You'll be in your kind of town with your kind of people. You'll love it.

September 29, Boston

At this moment I'm sitting here eating my brownies. They're great. Thanks so much. I've had four since 3:15. I was looking for a letter with them but when I saw the Krackel bar it said the same thing as a letter.

Tomorrow ends one of the most important months in my life. I'm still scared to death that all this is going to fall out from under me. And every day I become more sure that this is where I belong, yet it seems that there is no one around that I can express that feeling to. Right now, I'm reminded of a quote that I learned from you which goes something like this, ". . . when pleasant thoughts bring sad thoughts to the mind."[12]

You know, I'm still scared to invest any money in a sweatshirt or jacket from the university for fear that I'll flunk out and then won't be able to wear it. It might seem funny but it's a horrible feeling.

October 1, Delaware, Ohio

What a surprise. Thanks so much for the goodies! They're delicious. I guard those precious sweets more than my dink. It may seem greedy, but I won't offer them to anyone here. They're mine, all mine! I appreciate your thoughtfulness.

I will have been here three weeks Sunday. I have recovered from the fraternity fiasco.

The GDI's[13] aren't too bad! Last nite I attended a mixer party and was surprised to see how many girls were also Independent. 150 pledged, 200 didn't.

I am finally getting the pros and cons of frats. Their policy on religion and race really alarmed me. Maybe I'm naïve, but to see a great guy be turned down by fraternities because he is colored really shocked and irritated me. The Jewish students are also hit hard by blackball clauses. Unfortunately, the university is over the barrel with its fraternity system as they are needed for housing and eating facilities.

The second term starts in January. There will then be an opportunity to pledge if I so desire. Right now being an Independent is great. I have more time for studying and adjustment. Maybe it was Divine Intervention after all.

Just finished rereading your letter for the nth time! Thanks for all the included news. I'm still laughing about your landlord stories.

Three cheers for *Ten Little Indians*! When are tryouts? I bet the senior girls will complain.[14] Tough!

Tonight I'm going to see the French film, *The Suitor*. It is part of a lecture/movie series which features foreign films plus lectures by such notables as Phillip Burton, Stephen Spender, Louis Fischer, and Arthur Schlesinger, Jr. The ticket for the season costs only $5.50. Real bargain!

Yes, we had to buy all ten books! For this term I have to read de Tocqueville's *History of the French Revolution*. Your English notes are great for my English history class.

I must devote the rest of this afternoon to studying. I appreciated the long and informative letter and also the brownies. (I am eating one piece now. Yum, yum). Be kind to your senior students.

October 1

About ten minutes to go in this impossible study hall. It's in B-Audion with **70** roughnecks who have nothing to do but talk. They won't even go to the library. The quota for this room (to go to the library) is 35, but the most I've had go is 5. Apparently most of them have another free period later in the day and are waiting to go then, as a student (except honor roll and special permission) can use the library but once a day.

Rain, rain, rain—so discouraging. Perfect Thomas Hardy day—or, more so, a perfect Rachmaninoff Second Concerto evening!

Guess I'd best finish this letter before you completely disown me. I went up to C-ville after class on Saturday and spent a pleasant 23 hours. It was relaxing in its own unique way. Saw Walt Disney's *Those Calloways*—impossible movie, but Jeanie loved it! We even stayed for the cartoon.

I got back here at 6:00 p.m. in time to see J. before she left. She was wearing Tim's pin. I had tried to talk her out of it Friday evening because she had such reservations, but to no avail. She's not sure about coming home next week-end since it is W.C.'s (sounds like water closet, doesn't it?) big Rampage Week-end.

I'm waiting for Mr. Stauffer who wants to borrow my notes on Chaucer. He borrowed them once before, then just this week he loaned his set to another colleague. Hope my facts are accurate—otherwise half of Harrisburg Area Community College will be given misinformation. Perish the thought!

Check the October 9th *Saturday Evening Post* for an article on the Taylor-Burton-Nichols' *Who's Afraid of Virginia Woolf*.[15]

You asked about the class play and that if I need any pointers I'm to ask. OK, so I'm asking, as I need a dependable, capable, endearing student director. Any suggestions or shall I forget the whole idea? Try-outs are this week after school.

Do hope you get home this week-end. You have much to tell and I want to hear it all.

October 2, Meadville

First report from the ivy-covered halls of northwestern Pa. I'd have written before but there hasn't been time. This term I'm taking English, psychology, political science, and phys. ed. I was terrible at first with English of all things, but it's improving—that is, it's getting more challenging. Our teacher is somewhat disappointing when compared to the ideal professor we were told to expect. Psychology will be interesting—our professor has a sense of humor and a lot of background from his own experiences, which he brings into his lectures. Political science is a seminar-type class with a different approach. Finally, I'm taking modern dance in PE, but only because it's required.

October 3, Springfield

Just settling down for another one of those dreaded Sunday afternoons. It's so beautiful out today, such a lovely fall day to take a walk. It's just sheer torture to spend such a day studying. Usually, I end up not doing much of anything I <u>want</u> to do or anything I should do, which only proves to make me more regretful.

Friday was bad news. We better skip that day. Saturday was much better. I got up (Oh, the alarm didn't go off, so I didn't get a chance to study as I had planned; therefore, I flunked my test.). Then I scurried around the library looking for a print that I ended up spending my last penny for in the bookstore, which I later found in the library. Other than that it was a good day, for at least I feel normal again.

In the evening I went to the football game. We lost. I'm so crushed. The first game I went to and they lost, which further strengthens my belief that I'm jinxed. It was their first defeat after 32 consecutive wins! Imagine!!!

This morning I went to Communion, and directly after, I went to dinner. The meals here are excellent unfortunately. No fried mush or the like. We have a choice of 6 salads, 6 desserts, 2 hot vegetables, 2 platters, beverage and extras—all we want: four different flavors of ice cream at each meal!!! I haven't had the same thing twice yet. I have a problem of selecting a balanced meal; such a conglomeration. Atmosphere is pleasant, except for Tillie, a big, shaggy mutt who wanders among the tables.

Now I intend to study some before I go to an invitational tea by some of the fraternities.

Oh, I got this pathetic crush on some guy—a freshman, who comes from Switzerland! His shoulders (I hope no one saw me staring) must be a yard wide, tho' he's not what you'd call a muscle man. As it turns out, I'm not the only heart he flutters.

(Later)

I think I'll pledge a <u>fraternity</u>. Can't say much for the guys, but I like their taste. The one I saw is like a novelty shop. I could have spent all day looking in their rooms. Each room on the second floor has a theme—the deck, the trophy room, the hub, the playboy room (you can imagine what the walls were like) and on third floor (the attic) all the beds, bunk beds. And in the basement was their rec. room. Really neat.

P.S. I went to the second Theater Guild meeting Friday and signed up for stage crew.

Sometime in early fall, Springfield

1. Received the book. Had forgotten all about it. Thanks. Will settle account later.

2. Won first football game this season!!!!, 27-6. Otterbein – opponents.

3. Saw Erroll Garner Friday night. Fab-u-lous. Lifted me from mundane stagnation.

4. Roommate home this week-end. Glad to see her go. Missed her while she was gone. Wished she hadn't come back. Beats me! Guess I really do like people, just can't live with them.

5. Also attended lecture of John Ciardi, poetry editor of *Saturday Review* and considered expert on Dante. Talked about the "Inferno." Good speaker – witty.

6. Got an A on first psych test. B- on theme. I don't think I deserved even a C, so I came directly back to the room and wrote a revision just to prove I could.

7. Curious as to why my mother thinks I belong here. My first reaction was I didn't, but that's a spontaneous reaction I always have to her. You really think I do?

8. Don't think you have to keep up with my spastic letter writing. Your schedule is just as busy as mine.

9. I ditched my beanie. Looked like a dumb dope with it. And I'm not, you know. (See #6.)

10. You'll be glad to know I use the book (*Readers' Guide*) you gave me for graduation quite a lot when reading assignments.

11. Oh, reminds me, acquired new interest. The bookstore.

October 2, Shippensburg

I'll bet you were beginning to think I was never going to return the book and papers. I really enjoyed *Huck Finn* and your notes were quite helpful in reading *Crime and Punishment*. Thank you.

College really puts one to the test in more ways than one. In the beginning, I had an easy English, but now I have a new prof., and I don't particularly care for his ideas on life. On my themes, usually my grammar is correct, but he always notes in BIG RED letters, NO IMAGINATION. So now I am struggling to expand his idea of an imagination.

I have talked to several people, and have done a lot of thinking about switching my field of study. Now, I am almost certain that second term I'll be going into Elementary Ed. with a history or Spanish sequence. We were told that about 200 will be asked to leave in November. Forty-one have left already. I miss LD and all the classes and activities.

October 5, Springfield

SOS, SOS, SOS. My first distress call. I'm homesick. And in all my stupidity, I'm looking at it objectively. I'm rather surprised; after this summer I was certain I could never be homesick. I've thought about fighting it. Actually, it's the only way out, but what's bothering me is the time I'm wasting. I spent this whole evening (a valuable 4 hours) just figuring out how far away Christmas vacation is. I know you know how disturbing it is to waste time.

Why am I homesick? I'm not sure. Besides I'm sick of figuring the reasons out for things. I've thought about calling home, but I know I'd start crying. So, not one word of this to my mother. Writing this letter helps. You probably never expected me to say this; well, neither did I. Pretty soon I'll be selling you my soul. Well. I couldn't think of a nicer soul to sell it to. Ah, next week I'll probably be crying for help for some other reason. I think I'm going to try sleeping. I keep telling myself it'll look different tomorrow.

P.S. One consolation is knowing Delaware is only 53 miles away. Imagine! Finding a classmate as a consolation.

October 5, West Chester

It seems that the whole damn dorm had to come see my pin. I thought my parents accepted the pinning quite well. In a way, I'm glad and happy I have it. (I know I'm contradicting myself once again.) Like I said before, I have 2 years to decide what I want and a lot can happen between now and then.

The State Department doesn't want to give us any heat in the dorm until November. They said they can't afford to do it sooner. We signed a petition last night requesting heat NOW.

My first graders were nothing but brats today. I've decided that I don't want to make elementary phys. ed. my career. High school better prove to be more enjoyable or else!

October 10, West Chester

Tim didn't write so I sent him a nasty letter. (I'm in a mean mood.) I also told him I had a great weekend even though he didn't come down. (CUT!)

Didn't get to see the prince before I left. I said something to the effect concerning his weekend coming up and nearly got my head chopped off. By the way, it's none of my business whether or not he misses school on Friday. I'm not allowed to cut one damn class down here! Oh, well, better shut up or else I'll lose my well-known temper.

I have one class Tuesday at 8 a.m. Damn! I might decide to cut and stay in bed. (Don't tell the War Party.)

October 12, Boston

I read a great short story tonight for Humanities, "The Lottery" by Shirley Jackson. If you're not familiar with it, try to read it. Maybe you can get it from the library.

It was great not having classes today. I studied all afternoon but it was still nice. Monday night Rita and I walked on the beach. There was a full moon on top of it all.

We had some fun and games here at the dorm tonight. The fire trucks went down Bay State Road and stopped at one of the girls' dorms. Well, needless to say all of Myles went charging down the street. Eventually things got a little out of hand in the dorm and outside. Guys were throwing water out of windows and guys in the streets heading for a panty raid on Charlesgate. They were halfway up the street when one of the advisors got the mob stopped. Kids all over the place, traffic jammed up, the works. After a while riot trucks came bombing up the street. I can see how riots start. See what these kids are missing by going to small colleges.

October 12, Springfield

I had to write and tell you about this picture I'm painting for the house you don't have yet. (Maybe you can use this approach with Tom.) Anyway, it's going to take a special room for this masterpiece. No ordinary house, or even "237 Park Avenue," could ever withstand the impact. I'm kidding, of course, about its being a masterpiece, but I wish you could see it. I was going to surprise you with it, for the wall at the bottom of the staircase.

I said to myself, "You gotta be kidding!" I used the brightest colors I could create – reds, purples, yellows, blues, oranges – all intense and vibrant. You can almost see them knocking each other off the canvas. I patterned it after the drapes hanging in your living room, but I'm afraid my colors overcome even the drapes.

Our art center is in a reconverted home. Downstairs is a lecture room, a small office, and a lounge with a huge, gigantic fireplace that works and a coffee pot going all the time. Upstairs are two large rooms and a small sitting room where we take our paintings to view critically. The attic, with large gables projecting out from four sides, is where many students paint. I like it a lot.

P.S. Went to a Grumby dance (Levis and sweat shirts and sandals) Saturday. Met this guy, but I forget what he looks like. We only danced together all night! Same thing happened this summer. Imagine! I really let loose after a week of studying. I put everything I had into the jerk or whatever it's called. Didn't realize what I was missing.

October 14, Boston

2:30 a.m. I've been in the worst state of depression since I've been here. I couldn't study so I tried to cheer myself up a little. I walked down to Shelton to see Rita thinking maybe that would help. I get to her dorm and find that it closed early tonight because of some dorm meeting. I walked around for a while, then as a last resort I went to Bill's apartment. That was a big mistake. There was another guy there that was telling Bill that this will be his last semester because he's flunked 2 science courses. Of course, this increased my desire to jump off the roof of the phallic symbol building. You'll understand the humor in that sentence in a few minutes.

I told you Bill was odd. Well, believe me, I was right. He offered me a beer and I sat down. First thing he asked me if my roommate had told me what had happened the Sat. night of the party when he slept there to help clean up in the morning. I said "No, he didn't" and forgot about the question. A half an hour later when I said I had to go, he offered me a shot of Scotch for the road. Unsuspecting, I went out into the kitchen with him to get it. He poured the drink, handed it to me, then, (get this), he pinched my cheek and asked me how I've been. I almost shit!!! In fact, I almost puked, too. I didn't know what to do. Talk about being dumbfounded!!! Face it, I'm just not accustomed to guys of this sort. I stayed only long enough to borrow his Rachmaninoff record and then got the hell out of there.

I have to return his record Sat. night. He said emphatically that he'd be home alone Sat. night. Needless to say, I'm taking Rita along. It seems pretty funny now but earlier this evening I was shaken. The shame of it is he throws great parties. I guess I'll still go since there will be 20 or so other people there. The funny part is that I would have stayed if I hadn't had to walk Rita home. Man, what a piece of Divine intervention. And that concludes chapter one of Suggestive Tales of a Virgin College Student. Serially[16], I was scared. Homelyville[17] is nothing compared to this place.

October 16, Springfield

So much excitement here with Homecoming I'm ready to jump out of my skin. Hordes of people yelling in the streets all night. Saturday was Open House, so the halls were filled with all sorts of simple souls running around. Excitement climaxed with afternoon game with Baldwin-Wallace, 31-7!! (We won). Ohio Wesleyan, here we come – tramp, tramp, tramp! Dance that night for which most guys asked girls back home and girls asked guys from back home and for which I asked no one and certainly no one asked me. Can't decide whether I'm crushed or not. Really no need for pity—wouldn't have missed it for all the apples in China!

I'm afraid my body will never recover from this summer. This college life is bound and determined to make me fat and sassy. Send your care package on ahead. Might as well do it well or not at all. Serially, though, my tongue has been hanging down to my navel waiting for my turn to come. That's all my classmates from LD write about—your unending virtues and the care packages that you send.

October 18

Dear Virgin in Boston,

Yes, there is a Santa Claus ~~ (I will explain this statement later, if necessary.) If you're not ready to run home to Homelyville now, then I think you'll be safe for the duration!

I read as far as your reference to the phallic symbol and guessed what had happened. Continuing the reading, I discovered that my suspicions (& fears?!) were correct. So, now you've been "approached." I can't wait to see your parents' faces when I tell them. (Footnote: Did I scare you there for a second?)

As it's now Sat. night, I can't help but wonder how you're making out at Bill's. (Sorry, that was the wrong expression, wasn't it?) Better not ever go there alone (as if I have to tell you that). Weren't you saying once how great Bill was? Surprise. Incidentally, don't trust anyone—roommates included!

Oh, BTW, the *Falcon Flash* is doing an article on former L.D. grads' comments and thoughts about college life. OK if I let them quote your letter just received?

Mid-October, West Chester (second student at West Chester)

Thank you very much for the literature you gave to me for use in preparing my speech. I think our discussion group made out pretty well on our debate. Your speech course that I had in high school really proved to be quite an asset. Thank you again and I hope to see you over Christmas vacation.

Undated, from Delaware, Ohio to Boston, forwarded to Hummelstown[18]

Well, I bet you thought I had forgotten about you, didn't you? Honestly, tonite[19] is the first free time since I got here.

My roommate is fine, with loads of money. He is from Baltimore & brought his own stereo & records. How's that? Seriously he is not bad or hard to get along with. I guess, however, he thinks I'm a penny pincher because I don't throw it around like he does. And his clothes, god, put mine to shame.

Next door is a guy, Rick Barr, from Elizabethtown, Pa. A real good kid. Most of the frosh aren't bad except rich as hell, smart—most of them coming from private schools! They can't believe the hick school I come from.

Back again from a meeting with the Dean, then to the bank and finished by buying a $54 sports coat. You were wise getting yours before going to college. Prices are hellish! I need one so I had to get one.

October 19

At play practice—on break. I am going insane with pounding and hammering for sets being made. Seems worse this year for some reason. Could it be that I'm suffering from battle fatigue?

Most of the play cast are going to Allenberry tomorrow night to see "Ten Little Indians." It's supposed to be quite good. This way the students will also see the continuity of the plot.

Did you make reservations yet for your parents' visit? I hope you have a few activities mapped out—like the zoo, the public library, the museum, the squirrels in Boston Common, and Jordan Marsh!

Enjoy all the smiling-type parents this week-end. I have enclosed an article for you on LSD which I had mentioned to the English classes when I first heard about it last year. Sounds bad.

Boston (AP) – Doctors are concerned about a spreading black market in powerful "consciousness-expanding" drugs that they say can lead to schizophrenia or suicide if improperly used. Dr. Max Rinkel, who introduced the drug popularly known as LSD to the States, says its dangers when obtained on the black market are frightening. "I have a number of patients who took LSD at parties and who suffer from panic anxiety, feelings of unreality, illusions, hallucinations or delusions," he said. "The truth is we don't understand the chemical effect on the brain and some of the hallucinations are eerie and lurid.

"...drugs have become readily obtainable in student areas or artist colonies. Sugar lumps drenched in LSD may be bought at Harvard Square for $5," he said.

October 20, West Chester

Called my parents on Sunday while at my cousins' home and they said to come home Friday so I'll give you a call or stop sometime that night. I can hardly wait to hear what the Prince has to say concerning Miami U.

October 23, Chicago

I was glad to hear from you. I really miss you and the sixth period class. Chicago is really interesting to me; the people just go their own way, you never see them again; that's really funny, to me. The weather is nice, not too cold or hot; just right. I really like school. I'm holding a 97.4 average, the third in the class of 130 students, but I study!

Read? Boy, do I know what that word means now. Mrs. Ball, just keep making those kids read and read, because it will help when they are out of school. I know. It sounds like you hear that all the time, "If I would have studied in school I could go to college or get a better job." Hah!

Love, xx.

P.S. Forgive me, the way I signed the letters. I forgot I was writing to you. But I don't think that matters or does it, but it's true. Please write soon.

October 23, Springfield

WAIT A MINUTE. Stop the world. I want to get off. Now I remember why I never let people know my feelings because it leads to things like this. I'm not homesick and I never was. I missed not one of you. (Sorry about that.) I did miss you to the point that I recognized your absence, but not to the point that I wanted to come running back. I love it here! Here is where I want to stay.

I don't know why I am spouting off to you, except that you're more likely to appreciate my situation than anyone else!! You have sense enough to let me bare my soul and go on about your business as if you had seen nothing. Thanks.

Wednesday evening was very nice at dinner hour. There's a secret organization called the "Shifters" here on campus. Well, every once in a while they march around the campus (even in dorms) in single file with their thumbs in the air singing, "Shifters, Shifters, Shifters."[20] Imagine this taking place while we were having a candlelight supper.

October 25, Boston
HAPPY HALLOWEEN!!!

Just taking a break between history and humanities. I don't know if I should say this or not but I wish you were coming up next weekend. That's enough said about the subject. It just gets me worrying when I think about it.

I have a humanities test tomorrow. I'm learning all kinds of interesting facts in that class. For instance, in Katherine Mansfield's "Bliss" I learned that the candle is a phallic symbol and that the flowering pear tree represents Bertha's blossoming sexuality. I missed all that when I read it. I must be reading these stories all wrong.

. . . I'm now working on a research exercise in footnotes. Thank God I've had to do research papers for your class.

I picked up an extra Playbill for you from *The Devils*. *The Times* said it got terrific reviews. Today at lunch I saw a girl standing in line reading Albee's *Who's Afraid of Virginia Woolf*. I couldn't believe my eyes. Couldn't you see that happening at LD?

October 25, West Chester

Went to see *The Hill* at the Uptown Saturday night, then called Tim when I got home. He's going to try to get home Thanksgiving Day. We're going to try and get his mother and my parents together.

Mrs. Erdman is trying to start a sex education program at LD. She called a special meeting for anyone interested for November 8. She's really going to have a rough time convincing the parents. From what I understand she's pretty much on her own with the whole program.

October 26, Shippensburg

I am still here and things are going as well as can be expected. However, right now, I am a bit disturbed with my English prof. This was the fourth class he did not show, or bother to leave a message. So the class waited the 15 minutes due him, and then all left mumbling and grumbling.

My grades are fairly good, except history. I went to see my prof. last week, and he told me I had studied for an objective test and he gave an essay question—and there is always so much material, I don't know where to begin. All I can do is study more ideas than facts for the next exam, and pray, too.

I received a letter from Lauren yesterday, and she is seriously thinking of transferring to Penn State next year. Also, Kathy became extremely homesick and had to drop out of Michigan State. She hopes to apply to Penn State now. I understand that Lo won't be home till Christmas. I couldn't stay away from home that long.

Last week-end I came home, because we went out of the dairy business. There are no more cows on the farm. It made me sad to see some of my favorite ladies (cows) walk onto a strange truck and leave.

P.S. Our English prof was very disturbed with our vocabulary. So he gave us a surprise exam, and I received the highest score. So that makes me feel that all those Thursday nights in high school spent studying vocabulary lists were well spent!

October 26

Rehearsals for *Ten Little Indians* are now in full swing—so far, so good. Act I was to have been memorized for last night and all went well. Most of the cast went to see the play at Allenberry last Wednesday. Their report was that the set was pretty poor and the acting average with a couple of very good characters. Mr. Fickes is doing our set in very modern style, even using some of this own furniture.

J. was home from West Chester this past week-end. We drove out to the Farm, but didn't go in.

October 28, Delaware, Ohio

An apology is in order for not writing you sooner. However, I was studying for my midterms these past two weeks. They all came in the course of two days so this last week has been quite hectic.

Thanks also for the enclosed article on *The Loved One*. I enjoyed it very much. Yes I read the book last spring. Speaking about other books made into movies, at this point I am the only one who hasn't seen *The Collector* yet. Isn't it funny the one who got the most out of the book hasn't even seen the movie yet? Chances are slim that it will ever come to the Delaware theatre house.

You asked whether I have had an occasion to refer to de Sade. Since I have no comp course I haven't had the opportunity to refer to it. But the first night I was here several of us were discussing something insignificant and the question of sadistic people came up. I was quite in the know as we discussed it, although no one was really impressed. But sometime somewhere I will be able to refer to it constructively! Just Wait.

Next week I am going to explore Columbus for a day. I have been stuck in Delaware for about two months now and I think it is time I get away even if it is only for several hours. But you know I need to get away from it all once in a while, so this will be my big excursion of this year. The Big City.

Look out civilization, here I come.

L. and I are going to try and see each other this Saturday at the football game here in Delaware. She is coming on the Booster Caravan. We don't know when she arrives as no one seems to know about the buses, so at this point I am scared as to whether I will find her or not in the crowd. I need some Divine Intervention.

Well, I am up to my old tricks again: hibernation. These past few days the temperatures in Delaware have been colder than those in Boston. All the leaves have fallen by now, and the place really looks winterish! Tonite the temperature is already down in the 30's. Brrrr. My roommate thinks I am crazy because I have the heat turned all the way up but I AM COLD! We haven't even had snow yet, and I am complaining. My favorite stunt is keeping the blinds closed. That way my room is nice and warm as well as cozy.

Thanks for the suggestions on birthday presents but as you probably heard I spent my wad on calling him on that special Sunday. But I am going to buy *Playboy* for him as a Christmas present. He gets the biggest kick out of that magazine and I think he should have it if at all possible.

You mentioned Eliot's "Hollow Men." But I can't remember the last word. "Not with a bang but with a - - - "?[21] What is it? Also where is this line from, "When pleasant thoughts bring sad thoughts to the mind?" I use it quite often when talking to myself. But I can't remember where I read it! Please help.

October 30, Springfield

Left here at noon by bus and got there by 1:30. Everybody either slept or talked on the way. Not me! Lapped up every mile. Almost missed the bus as I had overslept, so you can imagine the rushing around. However, I do think I managed to impress him properly. Wore my red coat, red suede shoes, red headband with white gloves and neck scarf, and my shades. Wish I could be at your end of this deal to compare the two versions. Anyway we talked and talked and talked some more. Don't even remember the football score. He showed me all around campus (this was during the game—we only had four hours). Seems to be quite contented (I think the place is gloomy, but then I might be biased, huh?).

He "fits in" but in a different way than I am used to seeing. To me he is definitely the fraternity type, but somehow I'm glad he isn't—the feeling is so vague I can't grasp it with words. Whatever it is, I like it. (I keep thinking of things I wanted to tell him!)

This week was really harrowing (3 mid-term exams plus one theme); how was yours? Can't believe play practices are becoming a drag. How are the sets coming? Might drop Mr. Fickes a note of encouragement, sympathy, or whatever he might need at the moment. Can't see how he can go through it without me there to help with the sets.

Bulletin board does sound colorful. As you were describing it I thought to myself, "I hope she hasn't overdone it," and then you come up with the same ending. I had to laugh.

I have a feeling that my family and I have different ideas about college. I have no thought, at this time, of preparing for a profession or whatever. All I'd like to do is soak in as much as possible, which if continued will leave me out in the cold afterwards.

October 31, Boston

Homecoming weekend is almost over. At 4 o'clock our Open House ends. Five minutes ago I finally got rid of Rita. She's beginning to get on my nerves. I'd like to take one of her roommates out. That sort of gets pretty sticky. I'll have to see what I can do.

Only three weeks till Thanksgiving. Can't wait to see you again. We'll have to go out to the farm. Our host is still hanging in there and will be home for T-giving. It'll be a lot of fun when we all get together again.

I went to the Homecoming Ball Friday night. It was held at the Sheraton Plaza. A beautiful place. The Ball reminded me of our prom. Was sort of sad. Afterwards we went to the float-building festivities. The girls had 3:00 a.m. curfews. Saturday we won our game.

Saw Stan Getz last night. Really great.

I'm freezing to death in this room. My radiator leaks so I have no heat. I came in Friday night and there was water all over my floor.

Did you get *Status* in place of *Show*?[22] I got *High Fidelity*. It made me mad. I guess I'll have to buy *Status* on the newsstand. I hope you can get it.

Five-thirty and it's dark already. If that isn't depressing I don't know what is. I can see the fire flickering in the fire places in the frat houses. Makes me think of the farm.

My history mid-term is Wed. I'm scared to death. We're going to have two essay questions; 25 minutes each. He gave us a list of 11 questions, 2 of which are the ones on the test. Started going up to the 17th floor of the education building to study. A beautiful sight at night. It is also much quieter than the dorm. Must get back to studying so I'll close. Say Hello to Mrs. Kramer for me. Write when you get a chance.

November 1, West Chester

Received a letter from Boston today. He seems quite concerned that you didn't mention anything about not going up. Let him worry!

Last week on 2nd floor the telephone fell off the wall. The housemother accused the seniors of deliberately taking it down and she took all their extensions (hours) off for a while. The new Dean is threatening to move in over here because she feels the seniors need disciplined. The phone actually fell by itself. The whole situation is really funny.

November 4

Well, tonight I did it. I walked out of play practice. First, only one person had his costume there tonight. Second, by 7:10, four of the eleven cast members were not there. A few minutes lateness has been the rule for some of them right along. I did not become angry. Just put on my coat and left. The sad part is that practice has been rather dull all week—not knowing lines, not staying in character, "walking" through their parts—so I had decided that tonight I would reverse tactics and, instead of scolding, would give an encouragement speech. I haven't been as aggressive perhaps as I should be. But you know me—I won't battle them. I've never done this before, walked out.

Zeiters' house has a "Sold" sign. I really liked that house. The house (on end of the street) across from us goes on sale by auction next Saturday. I looked at it. Too small. Purcell's house is advertised in *The Sun* today! Would truly love it!! $27,900 – Ugh. Rumor has it that Herb Schaffner bought it, yet it is still listed. Trying to convince Tom to call Purcell tomorrow. Three hour exam on Saturday. Must dash.

November 5, Delaware

A double whammy if I ever saw one! Your letter arrived yesterday (Thursday) and tonite I got your Care Package. You score 10 points! Thank you so much. I just sampled the fudge and the cookies; they are delicious. However, it really took every inch of my self-control to contain myself, for I was capable of eating all the contents of the box.

Nothing really exciting happened this week except a little raid the male population of Wesleyan pulled off last Sunday. Apparently it is a traditional thing, and in any event it was a wild evening. I must say the girls had as much fun as we did, but most of them won't admit it. Anyway the "raid " made the *Delaware Gazette* if that means anything.

I found out today that I am in the wrong French course. Because I got over 500 on my French Achievement Test I should have been placed in the fourth level. However, the review in third has done me good—at least that is what I keep telling myself.

Also Mastrangie Baby pulled a fast one on us. This week we started reading Moliere's so-called masterpiece. The prof admits that it is too hard for us, but then in the same breath she screams at us for not completing the assignment. The poor soul reminds me of Mrs. Finkenbinder. She told us that she has "the passion for Ringo Starr!" I try to understand my teachers and profs, but I actually choked when she said that!

If I didn't learn anything else this week I am now "in the know" about bagels. This was a new food for me, however. All my Jewish friends say there is nothing finer. In my care packages I get cookies and brownies. The Jewish kids get bagels. This is not a joke.

Thanks so much for explaining Wordsworth and Eliot to me. I almost forgot you are still plagued with book reports every week, aren't you?

Last week-end it was so good to see Lo! Contentment is in her smile, her voice, her whole personality. Incidentally, she is still cutting me up and it is wonderful. That night she wrote me and said "The girls still think you're cute, no matter what I told them!" She comes through, doesn't she?

Happy Holiday is only 17 days away, Yes, I've given in, I'm coming home. And I am soon to get the pictures of the farm; I can't wait. I am going to paste one of them on the ceiling, so when I am in bed I will see the farm in front of me.

Tonite I finished at least half of the chocolate chip cookies. Where is my self-control? However, if I eat them no one else will. I again thank you so much for the Care Package. Your letters are well appreciated too. I close with fondest regards and in good spirits.

November 9, Springfield

I hadn't planned to write tonight, but I feel in such a great mood I couldn't let it go to waste. Went to see The Highwaymen this evening. So very enjoyable, quite humorous. Always makes me feel so crushed after hearing such music. I love it so, yet I can't sing a note.

Last Friday night I ushered for the play, *J.B.* Enjoyed it. Acted so poised I even impressed myself. Very much captivated by the acting and it made me wish we were all back at LD working together once again.

November 9, West Chester

On Saturday night one of the sorority officers held a party at her home after induction. I had sense enough not to go. Thank goodness. The party got out of hand and the recreation room was completely ruined. The police came, and what's worse three co-eds were caught by the housemother. They will probably get suspended from college for a few weeks and there's a possibility that one of those three will be expelled for good.

More excitement: Saturday night a couple of guys broke into our dorm through the windows and took a large number of 45 records and three clock radios. Sunday night a Peeping Tom was caught looking in windows in the same hall where the stuff was taken. This place isn't safe to live in!

I'd like to see *Virginia Woolf* so if you want some company, order four tickets.

November 11, Boston

Just finished listening to Rachmaninoff and was inspired to write. Nothing new has happened recently. I've been very busy with mid-terms this week. Tomorrow, chemistry is my last and I'm going to flunk it.

Dammit, I'm going to say it. I miss you like crazy. It takes every bit of my will power not to call you. The time till Thanksgiving seems like an eternity. There, it's said.

J. said you've been very busy; don't let it get you down. I'm thinking of you. I guess I sort of miss you to run to when I'm unhappy or depressed. Sometimes I get pretty lonely and then other times I am as content as ever. Hope everything is OK with the play.

November 10

I am glad to say the play is going much better. Must say that the reaction I got after Thursday's walk-out was not at all what I had expected. We had a talk-it-out Monday night. It seemed to help. Things are going much better since—at least to all outward appearances.

Don't be too credulous about all the phallic symbolism in short stories. Much of it is imposed upon the stories by the critics and not necessarily intended by the author.

Thanks for getting me the program for *The Devils*. I'll put it in the faculty room and let them wonder where a Playbill came from.

November 12, Harrisburg

This past week-end I saw the announcement in *The Hummelstown Sun* about the class play and I got a terrible "pang" in my heart! I really miss those plays and rehearsals we had at school, especially since I'm here at the hospital where things like that are "taboo" on your time off. When I saw the article, I dreamed of the days when I had only one term paper a year and one test a day!!

I really like nursing school and almost all of my subjects. I'm planning to come to the play and I'll give you an evaluation after it is over! P.S. If anyone gets sick at the last minute just let me know. I'll be glad to come and fake my way through for you!

November 13, Boston

Just got back from a date with Rita. Went to a nice mixer at her dorm and then for something to eat. Decided I really don't like her. I don't know why I take her out. Her one roommate I want to take out was there. She's one of the "in crowd" in New York City. Very wealthy; her parents gave her one of those "coming out" parties or whatever you call them. Her parents wanted her to go to Radcliff.

It was great to hear from you. The difference in this letter and the last one is unreal. Sounds like your spirits are a little better. Glad to hear it.

Want very much to see ... *Virginia Woolf*. Please make the arrangements – get the middle-priced tickets, not the cheapest ones. I don't think I'd like sitting on the sides. That is unless you don't want to spend the money. It will be great to go with the gang. I'll be getting in Tuesday night.

Please do me a favor—try to dig something up for me in the way of a critical analysis of D.H. Lawrence's short story "The Rocking Horse Winner." Thanks.

I don't know if I told you, but my Communications professor asked me to do the theatre reviews for the CBS newspaper! Quite flabbergasted; I hope I can handle it.

November 13, Springfield

Feeling real groovy tonite. . . the end of a perfect week – hah!. . .guess they got the news back home about my grades. . . . .

Loved your letter which I got today...could just see you—sharpening your claws, your hair raising... one of your many moods that I miss so... I can always tell what has happened that day after reading the first couple lines... never anything put on (that's the way I like them)...enjoyed the *Grump* magazines... thought some of the others in the dorm would, too... but I don't think they appreciated the humor... when I read something aloud they just looked at me, like I was some perverted soul or something... missed the point entirely... boy, one sure can get in a groove in college... never read the newspaper, seldom hear the news, sure appreciate the news of the world my mother sends... this college is really out of it—really....

Got a real tingling feeling hearing you talk about play practice. Can't imagine such excitement. You really walked out? Loved to have been there (as a spectator, of course).

You know what I feel like doing tonite? … skipping over to your house, listening to some barbra streisand records, chomping on some ice, doing much of nothing… you know what would be the neatest… putting all the good things of the past together with the good things of the present… .

Christmas vacation begins 5:00 p.m. Friday, December 17, 1965. I'll be coming home on a bus chartered for students in central Penna. area. Only $30 round trip… besides sounds like fun… busload of kids… I believe they leave at 5:00, so we're home early Sat. morn. I'm glad you're an early riser. If I have to stop to ring your doorbell—heaven forbid, I don't think I'll be able to restrain myself in a proper lady-like manner. Glad to do anything—even clean. Am not planning anything. Safer that way.

November 14, Alaska

It's been a long time since I wrote, but I just can't find time to write. The weather is real nice here, about 30° to 10° and is it windy. Boy, you should be here. You would love Alaska. Ha Ha. School is OK. I took my finals and got a 96%; that's not too bad, for 12 weeks. Don't you think so? How's school and the students? Did you ever hear from Jim or Lynn? Did they marry like they said they would when she turned 18? I didn't receive any mail from him, so I don't know! Well, I have to go now. Have to iron, "Boy, is it fun!"

P.S. Please write, You're about the only one who writes. Thanks for writing to me; it's nice to receive mail once a week, even if it's my English teacher.

November 15, Harrisburg

I can hardly wait to come home to see the play. I'm making it a special point to come back early and soothe everyone's nerves. Shall I wear my nurse's uniform?

November 16, West Chester

Tim wrote and said he'll be home next Wednesday night and Thursday only, so I don't believe I'll be able to go to the Arena House with you. I'd like to spend as much time as possible with him since our time together will be limited. I'll call you when I get home Friday to find out the details for your get-together with the cast—that should be around 5:30 p.m.

Guess you heard Susan Petrina wrecked a car. She wasn't hurt, just bruised. Richard Gourley had just bought an MG and smashed it.

November 17

It's now 12:30 a.m. and as I must face the dawn at 6:00, this will be brief. This really has been some busy month. I haven't even gotten around to changing the desk calendar. According to that, it's still October.

Called in our reservations yesterday for *Virginia Woolf*. Best in the house. Center section, $3.00.

Set another precedent tonight at play practice. Replaced a member of the cast. Rick wasn't in school today. I was sure he wasn't sick and Steve verified my suspicions. I expected him at play practice anyhow as he pulled the absence-from-school excuse once before. And this is the final week. Mike (Student Manager) couldn't reach him by phone so he went to his house with the message that if he wanted to be in the play he was to get to practice. He didn't show; Mike's taking the part.

November 21, Harrisburg

Congratulations! The play was marvelous! However, it makes a big difference when you're sitting in the audience and you know what's going on behind those curtains! I thought the casting was well done. Walt Sener actually portrayed the real Walt Sener.

Well, I'm back in this "hole" for another three days. I got a letter from B. and he said he can hardly wait, too! I wish he could have seen the play. I know exactly what he would have said. "We were never allowed to cuss like that!" I was so excited Saturday night that I had to take a placidyl capsule to get to sleep! Again, congratulations for a job well done! Always.

November 28, Harrisburg

Friday evening BLS called me and asked me to go out with him. We went to the farm. I just can't get over how different all of the kids are. I can't figure out who has changed the most. What was so interesting is that they are all so happy and really like college. When I compare my life here it just makes me sick. We aren't allowed to do anything! I really feel like "Prudence Pots!!"

The gang can't get over how strictly our school is run and right now neither can I. I'm ready to forget the profession of nursing and go to college to be a teacher. I really think I'm missing life and it's making me sick. I am tired of people acting like I'm some kind of saint for being a nurse!

I guess what I'm trying to ask you is, do you think it is really worth three years of hell to be a nurse? Right now I don't think it is. Thanks for your shoulder.

November 28, Springfield

This is to let you know that I am back on campus. I had such a good time. Cheryl's family is so nice. They asked me to come back for Christmas, but Cheryl told them that not even God could drag me back to Celina for Christmas. She knows how anxious I am to see everyone back home. I went everywhere, saw everyone, did everything. Had dates with three different guys. Hit all the hot spots of Celina. It got pretty funny. We'd get all fixed up for a date, come back in about 2:00 in the morning, sleep till noon, look like sick cows all day, and start all over again that night. We went out every night from Tuesday to Saturday. I still can't believe it. I never ran around so much in my life. Loved every minute of it. Missed all my buddies back here at school. It's funny—this is where I belong now. I can't imagine being anywhere else. We had a big reunion in our room. Something about our room everybody likes. Write and tell me all the kids you saw during break.

November 29, Springfield

Well, my bags are all packed (have been for the past five days) and I couldn't be more ready! Haven't felt so alive in weeks! Just can't seem to stay very long in one place. Gotta keep on the move.

Cleaned our room, then sat down to read your letter. Sometimes I just can't believe you and me. I started reading the clipping, didn't get beyond the first paragraph and thought, "Who wrote this?!" It wasn't until I finished reading that I noticed your comment. Couldn't help but smile when I read your account of the "237" gathering after the play.

November 30, Meadville

Midnight last time I looked! I feel like a rat not answering your letters sooner, after you persevered with 2 of them, and this will be a spastic one for sure.

The canoe trip was canceled because of rain (which we only get about 95% of the time). MODERN DANCE CLASS IS OVER!!!!!!!!!!!!!!! Today I finished my last assignment, a 5 to 8 minute dance. Guess what I did mine to—"Night on Bald Mountain" --- remember in 9th grade you had us write a story about the music?

About my courses: Eng. Prof. knows what he's talking about but can't present it right – he's illogical – skips from one topic to another – you can imagine how that would drive Yours Truly completely mad. Mad. Mad. Psych would be good but it's too general a course. We've hardly touched on the really interesting part (abnormal psych). I must admit I've learned a lot, though, and the prof's lectures are interesting.

You wondered about Margie. She likes Millersville a lot, but is (1) switching to elementary ed.

instead of liberal arts (She got a little annoyed at me for asking "Why?") and (2) is going steady with Russel.

Heard the Senior Class Play (capital letters used since you're the director) was excellent. Congratulations.

Thanks for the poems. They're different but I like them. We have 2 confirmed e. e. cummings fans on the floor—thought that might interest you.

We have to read 3 Albee plays (*Sandbox*, *Death of Bessie Smith*, and *Zoo Story*) for the English final and we don't go over them in class. If you know anything helpful concerning any or all of them, I'd appreciate the info.

December 2, Gettysburg

I thought that I had better soon write a letter to you or else you would think that I had taken some decisive measure such as leaping from the third floor of our palatial dorm.

I am sure that by this time you must have heard dozens of stories about the difficulty of the courses and about the realization of what studying really means to a "green" college freshman.

I do not have an English course this semester and I must say that my exemption from English can be ascribed to the instruction of this inspiring English teacher I had for about three years of high school. But not only has this helped me in this respect but also in my other courses such as contemporary civilization, especially with those discussion questions at testing time. I realize it and have heard it spoken often, that a student who lacks at least some writing ability suffers the consequences in almost every course he takes.

December 2, Miami, Ohio

I got your letter and the picture of Walt yesterday. I can't thank you enough for it. It is really a good shot. Of course, look what a handsome subject Joe had to work with! Ha!

My folks saw the play and said it was quite good. I sure wish I could have seen it.

Speaking of LD productions, I hear our charming, talented Miss Gluck is putting on a junior version of "The Messiah." You can bet I am going to try and get back for that. I am anxious to hear what she will pick for a spring musical. It scares me to even guess what it might be, after doing "The Red Mill."

Grade-wise I am doing well here but as you probably know I am going to transfer next year. It

is one mass exodus because of all the changes. It is really a shame, too. You wouldn't believe how beautiful this place is. It is like a setting out of Paramount studios.

Needless to say, I can hardly wait to get home for Christmas. I am looking forward to your Open House on the 19th. I will also see you at school. Until then, keep your "little darlings" hopping with the lit.

December 3

I've been listening to records for the past hour and a half, including Phaedra, Rachmaninoff, and, of course, Streisand. This naturally tends to make me more than somewhat moody. Wrote to J today, telling her I hadn't heard from you yet and that I can't understand why. Actually, I can think of a myriad reasons, but which one fits?

I don't know why I seem to be at a loss for words at the moment. Perhaps the lateness of the hour or the moodiness. Or maybe, more likely, it's the shield I sense that you've placed yourself behind. There seemed to be a feeling of uneasiness the short time we were together when you were home for T-giving. I'm afraid I don't quite understand. I'm still me, you know. Don't put me on. You don't have to be Harry High School from Homelyville around me. At the risk of sounding pedantic, may I repeat to you the advice Polonius gave to his son Laertes, "To thine ownself be true...."

God—I just read the last paragraph and **I** sound like what I am trying to tell **you** not to be: Stuffy. I miss you, good buddy.

December 3-4, Boston

Just got finished writing my second rough draft for my term paper. I'm still not satisfied with the damn thing. It sounds elementary and some of my transitions are pretty sloppy. Just have to work on it some more tomorrow.

It has been a miserably slow weekend. Friday night I went downtown to see the Christmas decorations. They're indescribable. Jordan Marsh has a whole floor devoted to an enchanted village with life-size animated figures. It has a huge revolving Christmas tree in the middle. Boston Commons is also decorated. They have Santa's reindeer—real ones. Also have people in an animated house.

Hope to get tickets to see "The Messiah" next Sunday. Can't wait, and I hope they aren't sold out. Must get some sleep. Write when you get a few minutes.

December 5, Harrisburg

First of all, thank you so much for your letter. It really did help. It also made me feel good to know that you appreciated me as a student. I guess I should tell you that I was questioning nursing before I started school. There hasn't been one day for the past two years that I haven't wondered whether I really did want nursing.

We're educated, but only in the sciences and that is what really gets me down. I've always enjoyed reading good books once in a while and even poetry. The other day I borrowed a book of poems from one of the girls but I always feel guilty reading poetry when I should be studying anatomy or microbiology.

My roommate has given me her opinion about this mess. She said she thinks I'd make a wonderful teacher, too, but not in a public school. She said she really admires the way I "function" as a nurse and she thinks I should finish nursing and go on to college and study to be a nursing instructor. Just let it up to my roommate to combine everything and come up with a fairly logical answer. I never really thought about teaching nursing. I mean it never entered my tiny brain. What do you think of this suggestion?

I was going to call you over the week-end, but my brother just got out of the Army. He hadn't seen me since I went on my diet and I thought he was going to have a CVA (stroke) when he saw me. He said he thinks I look sick! For one year and three months I've waited so see him and surprise him, so he tells me I look sick!

December 8, Springfield

Yesterday I was packing my trunk (yes, my trunk) and it was all I could do from jumping in myself. Last Saturday Cheryl and I went downtown and came back with a bundle of Christmas decorations. Talk about overdoing—our room is plastered!!! Or it was. Seems scotch tape doesn't stick too well and we awoke one morning to find ourselves lying in a mass of crepe paper. Cheryl brought back the family's stereo at Thanksgiving, so every night we fall asleep to Christmas carols. If I have ever looked forward to Christmas, it's certainly this year.

I'm nearly bursting with talk. Do you think two weeks will be sufficient time to get it all out? Mom's being real decent about not planning my time over the holidays. We're going to the farm for Christmas. I haven't been there since last spring when I went by myself. And let me tell you, I miss the old place almost as much as home.

Guess when I'm expected in Harrisburg? <u>2:30 Sat. a.m.</u> I thought for sure I wouldn't get there 'til at least 9:00. Are you still going to leave your doors open? This is terrible. I'll have to wait 4 whole hours until it's a decent hour to see you. I might as well be home now. I'm hooked. The next 8½ days are shot. Down the drain. I won't rest until I'm on that bus 4:30 Fri. afternoon, 8 whole days from now. I wish I could control myself a little more, but I'll sure be happy to see you guys and I don't care who knows it.

Funny; it will be dark out. I slipped out of Homelyville Sept. 10 with fog so thick I didn't know I was leaving and now I'll slip back in during the night. Woman of mystery, just think when I wake up Sat. morn, that's if I go to bed. There I'll be, little ole me. Back in Hummytown, PA. Love ya.

On December 8, 1965 the lead story in *The Marble,* the newsletter from Boston University College of Basic Studies, was "Students Voice Opinions of Viet Nam," featuring articles from two students with complete opposing views. On the back page of the newsletter was an article giving advice on deferment from the draft which included what draft deferment appeals would be acceptable and which had to be filed not later than ten days after receiving the draft notice.[23] The article further warned the students that *protesting* U.S. policy in Viet Nam could *lose* their deferment, with a reminder that the Director of Pennsylvania's Selective Service had announced that deferment is *not* for the benefit of the student, but for the benefit of the nation.

December 10, Harrisburg

My Christmas vacation starts Dec. 17 and I can hardly wait to get next week over with. As far as I know, I can come to your Open House. It really sounds great!

This week we got our grades from the first week in Sept. until Nov. 17. I have an 84 over-all average. Four of the girls in my class and five juniors were asked to leave.

Next week I'll be getting my clinical evaluation. After this morning, I don't want to see it. I had a wretched time! My instructor told me I get too flustered and frustrated. I even made a bed wrong this morning. I also had a patient who was going to the OR and we made an anesthesia bed for when the patient returns. I felt like a fool because I couldn't remember how to make it.

P.S. Your taking the classes to the State Library is a good idea. At least you know that the students will do some research! It also gives you a chance to help them with it.

December 10, Boston

Thank God it's Friday!!! Got another test out of the way today—psychology. I don't think I did too well. I'm really discouraged. I'm trying so damn hard and not getting anywhere. It seems I'm in a "C" rut. Sort of makes me feel like giving up, but I have too much to lose.

I'm going to see *Phaedra* tonight. It's at one of the art theatres. A bit of luck there. Also, next

Thurs. night I'm seeing *Luv*, with Dorothy Loudon and Tom Bosley. Tried to get tickets for "The Messiah" over the weekend but I was a day late.

Check *Time* issue week of December 10th for picture of Christmas decorations in Boston Commons. Must get going. Will continue later. I'm stunned. *Phaedra* was magnificent. As you already said, I agree that the love scene was the most beautiful I've ever seen. Guess what record I'm buying next?

I'll be getting in Friday night about 9:30 or 10:30. I'll be over sometime. Don't know when; you understand the circumstances.

It was sort of ironic that last Sat. night we were both writing letters probably about the same time and you were wondering why I hadn't written. We always manage to stick together somehow.

December 12

Just five days to go until the Open House! I baked cookies again today. Sure hope I've calculated near enough. I, of course, have no idea how many people to expect.

Gave a miserably difficulty test to College Prep on Thursday on the Victorian Period. Actually there were a few questions on material they hadn't been spoon-fed that always throws them into a panic. I also had a few matching with no answers. I have to awaken them somehow. Took 50 of them to the State Library on Wednesday. Well worth it.

Have you heard Petula Clark (other than "Downtown")? Pretty good.

I've been meaning to ask you. Have you received any issues of *Grump* yet?

Judy gave Tim's pin back to him last night.

I've been working like crazy all week-end. One set of (long) book reports to go. Had hoped to maybe practice the piano for a while, but guess that's out. Must finish papers, esp. since I have stacks of tests at school awaiting their turn to be graded.

Does the Prudential Building (where you have been studying) have an observatory floor or some place from which you can look all over Boston? Mrs. Connelly mentioned a place that sounded like that.[24] You must meet her. Top drawer; grew up in Boston!

Questions: 1. Did you finish your term paper? 2. How did it go? 3. I loved *Hud*. What did you think of it? 4. Don't you have your own bedroom where you can seclude away from your card-playing friends?

December 14, Springfield

Last Friday Cheryl and I decided (in one of our lighter moments) to decorate our telephone, which hangs on the wall. We put a box over it and wrapped it like a present. When we finished, Cheryl stepped back and said, "Maybe now we'll get some phone calls." And didn't you call that very same night. You never saw a box torn off the wall so fast in your whole entire life.

Three more days, yet time still ticks off, minute by minute. Then again, sometimes I can't believe that it's only three days. I'm sure it's just some cruel joke. I feel like a little kid, hanging on to a well-worn, slobbered-over, chewed-up toy, afraid someone will grab it away from him. Silly 'ittle kid!

Last night we had a dorm Christmas party. So pretty with a big fire in the fireplace, and Christmas tree lights and gifts and million dollar fudge and entertainment and singing and even Santa Claus (a pregnant one at that!).

I'll always remember Marsh's last letter right before he was discharged from the AF. At the time he was stationed in Spokane, Wash. He wrote, "Fix your eyes to the West and keep a sharp lookout for a two-tone Chevy, a dual exhaust, and a hearty 'Hi, Ho, Silver.' I'm headin' home." Well, I guess that sums it up. Homelyville, here I come!

Chapter 6 Endnotes:

1   "You find no man, at all intellectual, who is willing to leave London. No, Sir, **when a man is tired of London, he is tired of life**; for there is in London all that life can afford." Samuel Johnson, quoted (September 20, 1777) in *The Life of Samuel Johnson, LL.D.* (1791) by James Boswell.

2   Class of 1964.

3   During the time members of my 1960s classes were in college, I sent those who corresponded food packages, cookies, homemade fudge, and Krackel bars.

4   The World's Fair.

5   Class of 1964.

6   Class of 1965 whose military family had moved prior to his senior year.

7   Wordsworth, "Lines Written a Few Miles Above Tintern Abbey."

8   See Chapter 5.

9   Built in 1961.

10   *Show* magazine; personal archives and also from rogerebert.com: "The title of *The Manchurian Candidate* has entered everyday speech as shorthand for a brainwashed sleeper, a subject who has been hypnotized and instructed to act when his controllers pull the psychological trigger. In the movie, an American patrol is captured by Chinese communists during the Korean War, and one soldier is programmed to become an assassin; two years later, he's ordered to kill a presidential candidate. That such programming is impossible has not prevented it from being absorbed as fact; this movie, released in 1962, has influenced American history by forever coloring speculation about Lee Harvey Oswald. Would the speculation about Oswald's background and motives have been as fevered without the film as a template?"

11   My graduation gift to him.

12   Wordsworth, "Lines Written in Early Spring."

13   Students who did not join a sorority or fraternity but are declared "Independent." At some colleges the Independents were as well organized as the fraternal groups.

14   Most of the leads in this play are male.

15   Personal archives.

16   Our word for "Seriously."

17   A term we sometimes used for "Hummelstown."

18   The initial letter writer from Delaware found it expedient sometimes to send a letter and ask the receiver to send it on.

19   This was the common spelling in this geographic area.

20   A secret society formed in Wittenberg perhaps in the 1930s.

21   …but a whimper."

22   *Show* magazine, a wonderful, but short-lived publication described elsewhere in the book, offered the best reviews on all the arts and entertainment. Their articles were outstanding! It was published from the early 1960s; the last copy I have is May 1965. The magazine was initially so popular that they had plans to open a private club without the bunnies! When it folded, the publisher offered a choice of substitute publications to SHOW subscribers.

23   Personal archives.

24   This is the Prudential office tower, built in 1965. Its Skywalk Observatory is on the 50th floor. The totally enclosed space offers 360 degree views of the city.

Chapter 7

Adjusting

January to June 1966

Farewell! A word that must be, and hath been—
A sound which makes us linger; yet—farewell!

Childe Harold's Pilgrimage, Canto iv
Lord Byron

As I read these letters some fifty years later, bringing a catch to my throat, a few tears, and much laughter, these memories are again made fresh, and I am *there*.

How ardent the English Students were, loving one another. They were—and still are, much more open with one another than my classmates and I ever were.

In this set of letters I see a clear difference in the tone of their letters, with more of a lilt in their voices than there was during their first semester as freshmen. I also can sense their growing in all respects, particularly in confidence.

January 3, Boston

I wish I could talk to you personally about what I have to say, but since I feel it necessary to get it off my mind before exams, I must say it in a letter. I assume you had guessed I have been told by now that your actions New Year's Eve were rude, humiliating, insulting, and, worst of all, disappointing.

I can't understand for the life of me how you could imply that drinking was going on inside the house. Of all the times you've been out to the farm you have seen that we would not permit any drinking while there is a party there. I realize what was going on outside, but that we couldn't control. But you must know us better than to think that we would permit it inside. Even by your questioning it, it was a direct blame at our integrity, our whole policy of keeping the farm decent, a place to go and relax and be with one's closest friends. You must realize that by implying what you did that you were being no better than the people who had started the rumor about the farm.

I can't think of a reason why Lo wouldn't go in. People whom I had met for the first time were invited by kids we had invited. I hate to say all of this, but I wanted you to know that I am hurt. I have no idea what this will do to our relationship. I hope to God nothing. Please write and let me know what your feelings are. Enough said about that subject.

My trip back was rainy and depressing. Boston had 4 inches of snow to greet us. We got in about 2:45 a.m. Must read Chekov's *The Cherry Orchard* yet tonite, so I'll close.

Love, and send me some luck for my exams.

January 6, Hummelstown

You know, I've always felt a special feeling existed between us. Friendship, yes, but deeper than general friendship. Call it rapport, empathy, or mutual admiration, but it was there, wasn't it? It's now like I'm watching you slowly drifting away. Of course, I expect you to change because of new experiences, but these experiences should strengthen the bond, not weaken it. Your education should help to narrow the gap in age and experience that does exist between us.

You call my action New Year's Eve rude, humiliating, and insulting. I thought things were conducted very quietly. Who besides the host witnessed (or cared about, for that matter) our arrival and abrupt departure?

I am sorry if you think that I implied there was drinking going on inside the house. I don't believe I said that. The scene that greeted us was of strange cars and strangers. It didn't look like the usual gathering of the clan. Then, what do we see but people drinking in the cars. True, this is not in the house, but to an outside observer (not me) it would imply "drinking at the party." Then you tell us that there is "spiked punch" in the house and that no one is to touch it. How naïve and foolish you sounded. Why hadn't you disposed of it? Also, you had told me earlier in the week that you fellows were having your drink(s) before the guests arrived.

However, the main point and reason for our not going inside was that we were afraid of what the outside drinking would lead to. It only takes a few people, bold with drink, to start things rolling that your rules couldn't control. Too, Carol's vodka was there somewhere, wasn't it? What if she had decided she wanted it? After all, she most certainly lacked the modesty befitting a young woman as she strolled around the parking lot clutching a cigarette in one hand and her abdomen in the other. If she were "not feeling well," why didn't she just stay home, or, at least not flaunt that she was indisposed!

I very much resent being categorized with those who rumored about the farm. I repeat: I did not imply that there was drinking inside the farm. I was only afraid of what it might lead to, particularly with strangers and some who would jump at an opportunity to "prove their college maturity."

I am sorry you're disappointed. So am I.

January 4, West Chester

Wish that damn stuffed tiger[1] would stop staring at me. I'm trying to think of an appropriate name for it—have any suggestions?

Got all my history reports back—overall grade was A+. I think I'll frame them.

Hated to say farewell to everyone —April seems far away. Wouldn't mind going out to Ohio over spring vacation in March or maybe Washington's Birthday week-end.

I checked out the care package. Thanks again! All kinds of little goodies.

January 4, West Chester

My exam schedule is all mixed up. Hope my parents allow me to have the car just for that day. I'll get more studying done at home than here.

Do me a favor (please)—save me your *Look* magazine for this week. I understand it contains some good articles on the American woman.

My supervisor talked to me about assistantships. Sounds inviting but I'm not thoroughly convinced yet. I would have to apply next fall at the latest so I guess I'll have some thinking to do in the next few months.

January 7, West Chester

Seeing as this evening is a waste, I might as well write a letter. It's Friday night already. I find myself trying to remember what it was like being home. Once again I'm caught up in the whirl of college life. Exams will be coming soon, undoubtedly too soon.

My sore throat hurts sufficiently enough to move me to the infirmary. I stayed just long enough to stock up on pills, tablets, spray, and lozenges. Sandy came down with Mono.

I'm in the process of selecting courses for next semester. If I can get my schedule accepted, I will have neither Saturday classes nor 8 o'clocks. Dreamer.

Hear from big stuff yet?

January 8, Boston

Thanks very much for writing back and letting me know how you feel. It shows me that you care and do consider what I have to say.

First, I must comment on your letter. Regarding the punch (eggnog) – it was given to us by Miss Lentz. As of New Year's Eve, K. is permitted to drink at the farm. Big Doc approved of the spiked eggnog. However, the point is that he will not drink or let anyone else drink while there are other people there who might themselves drink but whose parents would not approve. About having our drinks before the party—I told you Doug was going to drink before the party to become "more sociable." I'm not trying to tell you that none of us drink when we're there by ourselves. You know yourself that we have done it. Since when have you disapproved of drinking? [always]

The only thing I have left to say about the party is that I sincerely wish you would have been there. The farm looked nice. You would have liked it. Very Christmassy. You also add "class" to our parties.

In your next letter please explain "... and some who would jump at an opportunity to 'prove their college maturity.'" I wish you wouldn't define or analyze my attitude. Not yet at least. Here at college for the first time in my life I'm forming my own life, ideals, and attitudes without any past influences. I'm not sure what I am myself, let alone someone else telling me or judging me. What is considered OK or socially acceptable up here is not considered so at home. Thus, explaining part of my double life.

I'd explain the rest of how I feel but it would take all night, so I promise to talk to you over intersession. This time there won't be as many distraction and friends.

You gave me part of my outlook on life. You gave me almost everything I'm working for in college. How could you feel that I'm drifting away from you? Don't you think the rumors and attacks we went through my senior year would almost cement our relationship?

I'm very sorry that you got the impression that I was trying to be Mr. Importance. I'm very, very proud and lucky to be going to B.U. It has given everything I've dreamed of. It gives me everything and every ideal you and I have shared. I hope this feeling (my feelings) isn't blossoming into a Mr. Importance. If anything, I've always felt below you. Although as you said in your letter, this gap is becoming more narrow. I hope so. If I have given you this impression, I'm sorry – I didn't realize it.

I'm pretty confused about my whole life at this point. Just bear with me. Remember, you have already experienced the "college confusion."

It's been snowing up here all day. We now have about 4 inches and it's expected to continue through the night. The frat house across the street has built, out of snow, a ten-ft. bottle of Southern

Comfort. It's really wild.

Thanks again for the thought of good luck and say hello to Mrs. K. for me. I expect to be home the 18th. Will let you know later about definite plans.

January 9, Harrisburg

Last Friday I got back a term paper I wrote for Nursing I. I had the highest grade in the class! I'm really very proud of my "masterpiece" and some weekend I'd like you to read it. The reason I'm telling you about this is to prove that the preparation I had in your English class has really helped me. You can put an extra feather in your hat after this one! By the way, I had a 95 on it. This is the highest grade that you can get on a term paper or a Care Plan. P.S. Don't get me wrong, I still detest writing term papers!

January 10, Shippensburg

Just to let you know I was in a big hurry Sunday. My Dad wanted to leave early so he could get back before dark. I'm sorry about the cookies. Save them and I'll eat them no matter what condition they're in. School is fine, but the first week back was a bit of a drag. I'm not sure when I will be home. My parents didn't go away, so no party at my house for the guys. Write if anything exciting happens.

January 11

A reply by letter is so inadequate because it's one-sided. I know each of us is misinterpreting some things the other says, no matter how clear it seems to the writer.

You are so right in most of what you've said in your last letter. In fact, you're so canny it's a bit disconcerting to me. You thank me for replying and letting you know how I feel. You say it shows you that I care. Dammit! Of course I do. If I didn't, all of these little petty things wouldn't bother me.

Sorry if my analysis of your attitude offends. I can understand how you feel. I realize you're just beginning to find yourself. I should understand—I'm still trying to clarify my own beliefs. For example, in a section of your letter you asked, "Since when have you disapproved of drinking?" I think basically I really do disapprove of it. I think that's why I can't develop a taste for it. I can't bear anything that is false, a crutch, so to speak. I like to be completely dependent upon myself. Like social drinking—I want to talk to people as they are, not through liquor. Sounds perhaps like Miss Prude. Yet, I don't think so.

In other areas my beliefs are quite open—yet there is a bit of the "old Protestant ethic" hovering. I now know what is meant by the expression "born 10 years too early." I'm in a state of flux, perhaps even more so than you.

You also realize, don't you, that regardless of my enigmatic life, you really know me much better than most people do. I'm sure you found out last year that you can't "explain" me to other people. I don't always act like "me" around others, especially people I don't feel sure of. That's why at the farm I'm different, depending upon who is there. I realize I don't always "fit."

In the line "some who would jump... to prove... maturity" – I did not mean you.

I seem to have tried to explain a lot that perhaps isn't explainable. Let's just try to accept each other for what we are because of and in spite of each other.

I'll be with you in spirit during your exams.

January 11, West Chester

Even though you received a nasty letter from him, you should feel honored because I haven't heard from him at all. He at least wrote and asked me to explain my actions so I did—he probably won't answer for a while because I told him how I felt. Leave it to you-know-who to put his foot in his mouth. Guess I didn't make our actions too clear to him before he left for school. I am glad you put him in his place, as I can't imagine him writing like that.

I have a ride home this Friday (14th). My parents are allowing me to drive down Wednesday (19th) for my last two finals. This will give us a chance to plan our action-attack on our mutual friend when he comes home. I don't know what to say to him after his writing that letter.

January 13, Springfield

I just finished your letter. I wish there were another method of cheap communication besides letter writing.[2] Right now I'm frustrated; I don't know where to begin. Maybe, they'll send us to the same sanitarium.

I remember deliberating as to whether I should or should not bring up my painting in my last letter, but I can't remember why I let it go. As you probably suspect, I'm still working at it. I'm dissatisfied mostly with the exposed body areas of the girl. When I inquired about the due date, he said he would rather I take my time and get it right, than do a rush job. Sooo, I'm taking my time. Someday I'm going to do a painting like I want to. That is, I'm going to do it in one sitting and after

I get up, I'm never going to touch it again. I think I know what the problem is now. I work on them too much for the effect I want.

Couldn't wait until I wrote you this week to see if you got a letter from either of "them." I hadn't. Then today up pops a letter from the younger one. Pooh, he's not mad. I wasn't going to write first, but I figured later I could always use the excuse of exams. He had no excuse, so I was anxious to see what move he would make. At the end, he says, "I hope you're not angry with me, you know how hard I try to be in good graces with everyone." That made me mad. He never puts up a fight. He always gives in to me. If I were he, I'd tell me off one of these days.

Actually, there's no reason for me to be angry with him. Just because I act like I am . . . I'm impossible, I know. My trouble is I always react oppositely. It's a natural tendency which I can't help. I sure could hit myself sometimes though. Now I don't know what to think about the other one. I won't do anything foolish with him, because there I have a chance of losing his friendship. I'm not sure if that prospect bothers me or not.

Things are sure going to be fun around here for the next two weeks. Prior to exams, we have study emphasis week. Absolute silence 24 hours a day. Rest assured; I'll be thinking of you. I don't know which will get me, the silence or the studying.

January 14, Boston
The count now stands at 3 finals down and 2 to go. So far everything is under control.

I'll be home very late Tues. night. Probably not until 2:00 a.m. or after, so I'll wait till Wed. afternoon to see you. Wouldn't want to ruin your image in the classroom.

Went to Jordan Marsh today after my finals and bought *Phaedra*. There were two left. I also bought the music (soundtrack) to *Zorba the Greek*. It's by the same composer. Thought if you can't find it at Korvette's, I could get it for you up here. It will be more expensive here though.

I'm going to see *The Loved One* tonight so I'd better get ready. Will give you a report when I get back.

11:00. *The Loved One* was so morbid, sarcastic, satirical, and disgusting that it was great!! Anybody with a weak stomach in religious (bigot) victims should never see it. It truly has "something to offend everyone." You must see it. It's so sacrilegious it's pathetic, but yet hilarious. It's typical Terry Southern and Tony Richardson. One of the first lines was a guy explaining the initials AID on his passport, "Artificial Insemination Donor." I couldn't believe what I was hearing!

I liked your wax seal on the letter. You should have heard my roommates laughing and mocking about that one.

P.S. For my second semester research topic I show Jean Paul Sartre as a dramatist. Thought you would be glad to hear that. If I start acting "abnormal" over this vacation please let me know. There are so many things we must talk about. It'll be good to have the "air cleared." We never were a pair for hidden emotions, feelings or ideas. Enough said till next week.

Midnight, January 15, Springfield

I spent the last two and a half hours reading an impossible paperback on the "Renaissance Debate," so I am glowing inside with a pleased-with-myself feeling. It's times like this that I feel especially kindred to your soul. I say to myself, "Now I know what she must feel. This is what she is trying to convey to others." Then I feel all pleased with myself, because I know you would be pleased. It's so exciting knowing that I am really learning something, however small and insignificant it may be, and because it is due to my own effort. Just thought I'd let you know.

Tomorrow begins the long-awaited week. I feel I must offer a prayer at this thought: "Lord help me." Tuesday I find out what my psy. grade is and if it's satisfactory to me, I'll not take the exam. That would leave only four exams, one of which is speech. So, depending upon whether or not I take the psy. exam, finals will begin Thursday and end the following Monday and I have the feeling I mentioned all this before.

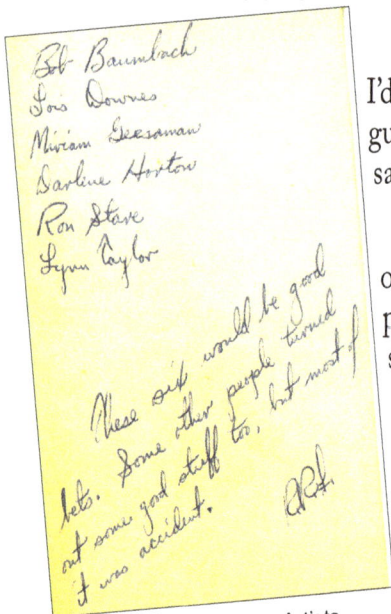

As you would probably like to know, I got the official letter Friday. I'd be the first to scoff at the idea that I'm modest, but really --- me? I guess I don't have to explain to you how I reacted. Don't worry; I'm quite satisfied that you had no direct influence on the choice.

I suppose I'm rather frightened by the thought of proving myself or something. One question, how many pictures does the class plan to purchase? Approximately, what is your guess? And what would be some suitable subjects? This is all I can allow myself to say on the subject.

Would you believe it if I told you we had filet mignon for supper? I didn't think you would. The other day we had Waldorf salad and you will be most pleased to know that it didn't compare to yours. In fact, I didn't finish it—most unusual for such a "chow-hound" as I. Has the car come yet? As the night is still young, I'll do some more studying.

Bob Baumbach
Lois Downes
Miriam Geesaman
Darlene Horton
Ron Stave
Lynn Taylor

These oils would be good. Some other people turned in some good stuff too, but most of it was accident.

Selected Senior Artists

January 15, Shippensburg

Last year at this time I was poring over my term paper! I just happened to remember that. Of course, that was a week-end I shall never forget! I still think the most interesting themes we ever wrote in English were the ones we wrote the Monday the papers were due. By the way, how are the kids doing this year with their abstract projects?

Besides being "fed up to here" with my roommate, and having a terrible time with my math course, things are great! Only five more weeks till term break. By the way, this weekend I'm working on a report speech from the *Quarterly Journal of Speech*, titled "Elizabethan Stages and Open-Air Performances in America, a Half-Century Ago." So far, I think, I'll be over the time limit by just repeating the title!

Last night we went to see *The Cardinal*, which was shown (free) by the College. I had seen it before, but was too young to understand it. After the movie, we went to the Raider Room, and met Harold. He was feeling rather low, because he had had three tests during the day. However, he did say something about receiving a "care package" from Hummelstown. I believe it was from Mrs. Santa!

Speaking of Santa, did dear little Jean receive what she wanted from Santa? She looked so sweet the night of your Open House, which I enjoyed so much along with the rest of us who were there.

Next week, I believe the Zerfoss twins, Slez, and Sip all are coming up for the weekend. That should prove to be interesting, at least I hope. This place is like a morgue especially on the weekends. It seems like the whole campus moves out.

January 17, Delaware, Ohio

Today is Monday which means another week. Ugh! I am fortunate, however, in that my only class today is at 1:00 p.m. That means by the time I get up, the day is half over. Currently Delaware is experiencing its first real snow. God, that is all I need for a Monday.

I have been here only two weeks. It seems like Christmas was months ago. However, I do have the memories of that fabulous vacation and I want to thank you for your part in making it so enjoyable. Your "reunion" party was very nice, and I was glad I got home in time for it.

At this point I wish I were on a 2-semester plan. It really hurts to think the rest of the crew will have a vacation coming up this weekend and here I sit studying. We go for 10 straight weeks with finals, too! I shudder to think of it. Ten weeks in my opinion is awfully long!

My courses for this term are English composition, French, and theatre appreciation. Each of these fulfills one of the requirements for a Wesleyan degree (a language, one fine arts course, and proficiency in writing). French Level IV is turning into a real stinker. But at least I was able to transfer into another class. Reason…. Incompatibility of personalities. Sounds scientific, doesn't it? Anyway, now I have a twelve o'clock class with Mademoiselle Divers. (Age 23). She is really hard, but at least she smiles, has an interest in her students and I can understand her. So, time will tell how I do, but at least I can stomach the prof!

I also wanted to tell you that Barbra Streisand was named to the "Best Dressed Women" poll for 1965. I found a fellow freshman who has all her records and thus have access to all her albums. Last weekend I listened to *Funny Girl.*

I must tell you about the Theatre Appreciation course which I have this term. We are studying the development of the theatre in America with emphasis on the 20th Century. I actually am fascinated with it. Mondays we discuss a particular period of drama such as the Twenties, the Transitional Period, etc. Thursday we consider one playwright. Included in this part is the assignment of reading two of his plays and Friday the prof. lectures on Contemporary Theatre (Anything from critics to Little Theatre). This week we are reading Arthur Miller's *Death of a Salesman* and *All My Sons.* The course is hard test-wise, but I enjoy it so much. (Note: Our one textbook cost $10. I practically fainted in the Book Store!) There is also one assignment I won't have to read (because of the senior class play)—Thornton Wilder!

It seems so strange not to have a science this term. Whenever I get low with a course, I just have to say, "At least it is better than chemistry!" and I immediately feel better!

P.S. Would enjoy hearing from you and I need no explanation concerning New Year's Eve.

January 18, State College

I made it to the library last week, before I got your letter. I was going to look around for something to read, but I ended up studying. It's a bit rougher this term than it was last term. It's such a good change from last term that I have even grown accustomed to studying and I enjoy it!

I'll probably be home Jan. 29, and I'll stop back then. I'm glad to hear that you changed the pillow covers, but to pink?! Well, at least it's a start. I guess the pink looks alright on the white couch, and I'm sure it looks better than the last ones.[3]

There was a terrific gymnastics meet up here on Saturday. Springfield was down for the meet which was predicted to show the Eastern Division Champion. State was predicted to win by .3 of a point. The actual final score was Penn State 176.75 to Springfield 176.70. It was quite a meet, with a record crowd in Recreation Hall.

January 25, Springfield

Well, it's over. Except for my red, squinty eyes and the biggest small blister on my little finger, I'm still here laughing it up. All of us have become somewhat better acquainted having to share such an ordeal. Dinner hour has become immensely pleasurable, food and conversation-wise. All of us don't know whether to laugh or cry. We're just up to here with studying. You should see the study room they rigged up in the laundry room, which is soundproof. Blankets and pillows and books.

I can't study with people because I become fascinated with them and they distract me, so I hid among the piles of trash, books, and clothes in our room. No wonder I never saw Cheryl, except for dinner. Well, at least I feel good about studying, even if my grades will only be just passing. The tests were rough and I was scared like I haven't been since 7th grade. I feel especially hopeful about my English and history exam. I wrote for 4 hours on Monday.

I finally got the scrapbook I wanted. Boy! I had fun last night. You should see it. I used 2 bottles of Elmer's glue; ¾ of the book is my senior year – the rest covers the other 17 years of my life.

P.S. I checked out *Atlas Shrugged*. Gosh, big one, isn't it?

January 25, Harrisburg

I read your letter just before anatomy and physiology lab. It gave me the lift I needed. This morning I did a coronal dissection of a sheep kidney. It was really terrific. Miss Pierce kept the kidney I did to show the other group.[4] I mean to tell you, I'm really getting good with my "trusty scalpel" and forceps!

It is now 12:35 and I must prepare myself to go to chemistry lab. (Barf.) I shall continue this letter at 3 p.m. if I don't have any deadly accidents!

3:25. I have returned and I'm still in one piece! I did albumin tests on urine. Oh! The fun and games of nursing!

In reference to your letter, I did see B. and J. As a matter of fact, he came up for me last Friday evening and ran his "bus" to Hummelstown. It was really great to see him again, but it makes me sick to have to stay here during the week.

Concerning my next vacation, well, you see it's like this. I have a two week vacation the end of

July! I wince every time I think about it. However, capping is April 28th and we have the 29th off plus the week-end. I mean these people are all heart.

February 2, Boston

I have a few minutes before I make my mad exodus to the library so I thought I'd start your letter. My impression of the first two days of the second semester is HELP! It looks like a lot more work. The rat race begins again.

I didn't get in until Monday night. I guess you were snowed in up at your home also. My train ride back was a real nightmare. I felt like some lost immigrant herded onto a cattle car. The trains were jammed with all kinds of "stupid" people. NEVER AGAIN.

11:35. Just downstairs and had a Pepsi. What else? Five students in my section were asked to leave. One was a pretty good friend of mine. Sure is a strange feeling seeing all the kids dropping like flies.

I received a letter of invitation from the Inter-Fraternity Conference and their Rush Dates. Don't think I'll go. Mike got a special letter from one of the frats. He isn't going either. Nothing new really happening. Just wanted to let you know that I miss you and that I'm thinking of you.

February 2

How in God's name did you get back to Boston? (I'm here assuming that you did return.) Did you have a momentary feeling of panic and terror that you might be trapped forever in Homelyville? In the midst of my own predicament on Sunday I was mainly concerned for your escape to the outside world.

We never made it back at all on Sunday. Got as far as 5 miles this side of State College when we hit the blizzard. Impossible to see. Cars abandoned all over the road. We had to stop numerous times because of cars and drifts. During one such "stoppage" a car plowed into the rear of the Buick. We saw it as it approached, but were powerless to halt it. As that car's radiator got bashed in, we rescued the passengers—a young couple from Philadelphia, and traveled back to Clearfield.

February 5, Boston

Received your letter today. Thanks for writing so soon. Well, I'm back in "my" life again. It seems as if I've never been home. Time flew so damn fast. I spent this afternoon in the public library looking for research paper material.

I finally got the issue of *Grump* today – really great. Thanks.

Right now I have this terrible headache.

On the other hand, some good news: CBS has this CIS which is the Communications Independent Studies. In the CIS you have no classes, no final, and must write 2 research papers a semester. You must be recommended by your prof. I was told on Friday that I'm being recommended. I was completely floored. However, there is a catch. I must achieve dean's list this semester. That bit of news sort of deflated me. To be recommended is a great honor but I don't feel I can fulfill the rest of the qualifications. It's nice to dream!!

Two more Excedrin down the hatch. Saw the movie *Umbrellas of Cherbourg* tonite. It was quite good. It was in French with subtitles. It was all sung, no speaking.

Was just reading your last letter before vacation and thinking. At one point you said, "I don't want to drive you away, yet it's probably inevitable." Please explain. This is one of the things I wanted to talk to you about over vacation and didn't get around to it.

I'm quite bewildered over our relationship. I can't describe my feelings. The more I try to define them to myself, the more confused they become. Enough of that topic.

February 6, Springfield

"When I woke up this morning, you were on my mind." The lyrics of this song motivated me to write this letter.

One girl, who went to Harrisburg on the bus at Christmas break, went home again for semester break. It took her approximately 26 hours to get back. Well, there better be no snow the 26th of February when I come flyin' home. Yep. Elinor called last Tuesday nite to ask me to be her attendant at their wedding. Yep. Sure is nice. Yep. Sure am happy—it's about the nicest thing I could ever wish to happen to me. You can imagine how proud I am.

Poor Paul. All he could say after Elinor and he went to talk to Pastor Trump was, "It all seems so permanent." "So you see," Elinor said, "we need you. If he goes, there I go." Boy! They sure picked a good one (me) to hold them up. But I'll be there.

Yesterday, Cheryl and I went uptown to look at some dresses. Well, we didn't see any dresses. We did see some goldfish, which we bought. After traipsing all over town and not finding anything, well, we just had to buy something to lift our spirits. So, now we have two goldfish: Able and Willing. Willing and Abel. I don't know. Just nuts, I guess.

Semester break certainly was a change. Got a letter from Cheryl's mother saying she missed our "beautiful, sleeping bodies and sweet, hungry faces" already. I guess four college girls can be a traumatic experience for the average family household. We awoke at one o'clock every afternoon. We spent the remainder of the day watching television. I mean from 1:00 p.m. to 1:00 a.m. Between times, we attended to acute attacks of hunger. We ate everything from jelly and peanut butter to coconut (the package kind for cakes) until the cupboards were bare. TV! I still see visions of *Batman* – WHAM. If you ever get a chance, don't miss it. You'll die laughing from either shock or disbelief.

Also watched the National Health Test which was a lucky bit of chance. First day back in hygiene class, the prof gave the same test, so I zipped right through it, laughing all the way. And *Peyton Place*. I picked up the story right where I left it a year ago. There was one show, *Fort Apache* or something, we saw three times in that one week. It (TV) got pretty hilarious by the end of the week. The commercials—they were the best. Just ghastly. The one for Crest toothpaste just tore us apart every time we saw it.

We did manage to venture outside once in a while. Sunday afternoon we went sleigh riding, only we used the hood of a car, padded with burlap and strung with a rope. Sleigh riding in Ohio is pretty much a farce as this land is as flat as a pancake. We had to go 30 miles till we came to this ravine. God, I almost croaked when I looked down. Daring little devils, these guys! I was chicken and you bloody well better know it. My first and last trip was a real thriller. Somehow we got turned around; we were going down backwards! It was fortunate that it didn't overturn. Besides the bank didn't have much snow on it, just a little ice and frozen, slicked-down mud. At the bottom of the Grand Canyon is a lake. We went zooming across and ended up in a snow bank, covered with snow we were. Below zero temperature didn't help. Went home with this girl who lives in a log cabin (just beautiful) and had hot chocolate and hamburgers. Two hours later, we were at a dance.

Saturday night, Mr. and Mrs. Lammers took us out for dinner. It was pretty special in that we had southern fried chicken made with a beer batter and Kellogg's cornflakes. Scrumptious. We also went out that evening and the hit of the night was this kid Marvin who asked me to dance. Repulsive as his name. The only thing that kept us apart was my hand. Finally when that wasn't suggestive enough, I excused myself. What really got me was later we found out that he was in eighth grade. Sick! Sick! Sick!

Well, this time I did do it. Doesn't look quite as blonde as this piece I sent you here, however. We had nothing better to do, so we decided to experiment on me.

Thanks for the pictures from the farm!! Really like the one of you; glad you sent them.

I had seen the article on situationism[5] when I was working on Tom's folder. Interesting to find you noticed it, too.

Did Mom tell you what my point average ended up as? You'll be proud to know that my only two Bs were in English and public speaking. The rest were C's. I was pleased with the results. I can honestly say I worked to get them. I pulled both religion and western civilization up with my final exam. It takes a lot of hard studying, but at least I know now that it can be done. I plan to work even harder this semester. In English, we're starting off with a research paper.

Went to hear Mr. Hayakawa this week. Very good. His wit was very entertaining. You might get your sign (quote by Dante) printed yet. Lettering class is fun.

I'd like to finish *Atlas Shrugged* before I comment on it. Finished the first of three parts. Wait a minute. It's the phone.

(2 hours later – long minute) Oh, rudder guts. I hate when things get complicated. I'll have to cut my Friday afternoon class to get home. Plane leaves Dayton at 1:45. Arrives in Pittsburgh at 3:30, where I'll have to wait two hours for Allegheny hop to H-burg. Hopefully I'll be there by 6:30 –rehearsal at 7:30. Can't you just see that weekend? I like to take my time and enjoy it. To top things off, I can't find a dress I like.

Haven't heard from the guys; I think I'll send them Valentines and make them feel like heels.

February 9, Meadville

You'll never believe what just happened! We got back our latest paper in English on "The Bear," and I got an <u>A</u>. I was so surprised! He said he really liked it because it was forceful and accomplished what I set out to do. Right now I'm working on a paper on Kafka's *The Trial*. Have you read it? In class we're reading poems and letters of John Keats. I can't imagine doing a 5-7 page paper on <u>him.</u>

You know, astronomy's not as bad as I thought it was going to be. I had an 87% on the first quiz and, unfortunately, a 77% on the second, which I didn't study for enough. (I studied for College Reading all that day). The problem with astronomy up here is that we haven't had one clear night to look at the stars yet! The neatest thing we've learned so far is how to find the right ascension of everything in the sky. The right ascension of the sun today is 21 hours, 16 minutes and when you get this letter, it will be 21 hours, 24 minutes. How meaningful, how fascinating, how useful (to be stated in a monotone).

French (I'll have to break this news to Miss Meyers) is undoubtedly the hardest thing I have ever attempted. My mid-term grade will be a C- if I'm lucky. You see, at LD everyone took German, and up here, everyone has taken French, so it's naturally rough. Especially the speaking; it rather shook me up the first day and still does occasionally. I barely, and I mean barely, passed the oral exam with the second lowest grade out of 19 in the class. I await your congratulations (or consolation)!

Thanks for the Faulkner material. It was a big help to compare my knowledge (?) with someone else's.

February 9-10

Your words arrived at an introspective time for me, as I sense some of the students here are disgruntled. The top section just finished writing biographical sketches of each other (in pairs) which are revealing. Many seem to believe they are not getting a "quality education" here at LD. Apparently they believe the faculty should be doing more. While agreeing with their argument to some extent, in defense I hear myself saying, while they complain about what they are not getting, they complain as well when worthwhile offerings are made. Oddly enough, even before I read these bios, I had decided to try something new for next year. I ran this by Mrs. Sandel and have requested a time to meet with Mr. Staver. What I want to propose is a Humanities program, strictly voluntary, no credit, one evening a week.

As for "us," (and you shouldn't revisit old letters), what I was trying to say is when I wrote "it's probably inevitable," is that the friendship/magnetism we seem to share will come to a crossroads. I may have been thinking that when the point is reached of seeing each other strictly as a man to woman, that would drive us apart, out of fear, or some other common sense.

You know, we did/do have an unusual simpatico, almost unique; that's why no one quite understood it. We didn't try to define it because we never felt the need to question it; we just accepted it. No need to fret about it. Let's just be honest with each other and remember that we are *still* us.

February 12, Millersville

I guess this is a surprise! I know you told us that if there was anything you could help us with to let you know, so here goes. We are doing term papers for English this semester and I'm doing one on pornography. My English prof. is very much in favor of this topic. I must compare 2 books, one which condones and allows pornography (I can use *Pornography and the Law* for that) and now I must find a book published recently against pornography or for censorship but which deals with pornography in detail. I have tried MSC's library, but without success.

I hope to do some research at the State Library when I'm home at the end of February but in the meantime I must find out whether such a book exists or not. I must let my prof. know on the 22nd or before. So, if you know of any such book or where I could find out about one would you please let me know as soon as possible.

February 12, Springfield

Gee! Batman in COLOR! That would even be super! You certainly have the words for it – "utterly unbelievable." Whatever happens on the 25ᵗʰ, I must see that color TV. You know I've never seen one—not even in the stores.

You ALMOST tricked me into explaining about the snow bank (being inconsistent with the blizzard). But I won't bite—even if I do have a good explanation.

I came up with this real original term paper idea. I haven't narrowed it down sufficiently as of yet, but I hope to do something about **set designs**. We had to give her a choice, so I put it down to fill up the list, and wouldn't you know, she thought that was THE perfect topic. So, unless I can come up with something better, it looks like that's it. Hey! Maybe I could use my last year's term paper. Oh, don't be so horrified, I was only kidding.

You're dying to know what I think about *Atlas Shrugged*, aren't you? No comment until I finish. I want to be fair about it.

Tonight I plan to hear Glen Yarborough, the guy of "Baby, the Rain Must Fall" fame. I like his style, so I am eager to hear him in person. Do you know of William Schuman, the composer?[6] He was here this week. I missed him. Thought you'd like to know.

Gee, I hope you hadn't thought that I mentioned to Tom about the pool table beforehand. I couldn't do that. You know what I think about surprises. Obviously he was thrilled with it. I know what you mean about wanting to play well. I had similar feelings with Marsh. The more stupid I was about something, the more elaborate his illustrations. They were so exaggerated that I'd start laughing at him and he'd get mad. I'm afraid I wouldn't be too good at pool, but I must try it sometime. Maybe if you crowd Tom's living space, he'll be more receptive about buying a new house.

We (girls) were talking about our first impressions of each other. Quite funny. They were all scared to death of me. Imagine!

The wedding is Saturday afternoon. I made plane reservations yesterday. If it weren't for the fact that I have never been off the ground before, I'd nix flying. It is going to take me as long to get to the airport as it will to fly home. I'm not sure how I am getting back, but I would like to leave late Sunday evening and get in here early Monday morning.

I'm all excited; every time I hear a plane go overhead now, I get goose bumps. Can't you see me playing the woman-of-the-world role? There I'll stand, lost and forlorn amidst a throng of sophisticated people. At least I'll have plenty of time to enjoy the trip.

It's rained for the last three days. No great flood waters, just a constant drip, drip, drip.

February 12, Delaware

Thank you ever so much for your Valentine "surprise." I appreciate your thinking of me. Have munched on the brownies all weekend. They're great, just like the donor. Also concerning the use of your name "for everything except checks." What can I say, but again thank you; I am much obliged.

Big news of the week! I finally saw *The Pawnbroker*. I remember that you wrote me back in the fall that this movie was a must to see. Well, it took me four months, but by damn I finally saw it. It was well worth the wait though! Decent. Last nite I heard the Ramsey Lewis trio in a Wesleyan concert. They made the LP "in crowd." Well, this musical trio really was tremendous. They didn't play/cater to the rock 'n roll set; they played jazz and classical music too. Trés extraordinaire! One number in particular appealed to me—*West Side Story* songs.

Six weeks of this term are complete. Four more to struggle through and then finals, and so it goes week after week, bluie after bluie. I wanted to say the seal on your last letter was cool. The message, incidentally, is posted above my desk. Your comment about LD kids being "snowed" on hearing it brought back memories of class plays, meditations, and English lit. The "happiness" one to me is so true, at least this is what I have found. You never know until it's past.

Talked to Lo last week-end. Was all types of moody the week before so I thought I would call her. I wanted to hear a familiar voice. She told me about Elinor's forthcoming wedding and her plans to fly home for it! She sounded real keyed for the trip – her first in an airplane. Well, needless to say, I shared her enthusiasm even though I can't go!

Barbra Streisand has a new LP out, "Where Am I Going?" B. informs me that she will have another special on TV at the end of March. I only say this because I am currently playing her records.

The group seems to have done well with their first term/semester in college. It makes me really glad to have such serious goal-seeking friends. Lo's grades were good, was proud to hear she did so well. Jean missed the Dean's List by a .7 she told me. As for B., I have received no news. But as I tell him, those grades, whatever they are, are good because he did his best. The amount of studying which he does puts me to shame. So much for college.

Theatre Appreciation is fine. Hard as h---, but I am having the time of my life with this course. Thanks for being concerned, but I have no problems with it as yet! Here's hoping. Our text (main one) is Theatre, USA by Bernard Hewitt which cost $10. But worth it. If I have the room, I will bring it home with me come Spring Vacation. I think it is the only text to date that will be useful as a reference/reading for later years. I am sold on the course, am so glad it fit my schedule.

Back (gosh, I am skipping around, aren't I?) to French topic. You are correct; this is my final course in French, on passing it (which is at least likely now) I will have completed my language requirement. I say it is likely I'll pass it because there was a time at the beginning of the term when things did look bleak. But since I switched professors, at least I am passing. My feelings at this point are confused. I only wish I had had more background in high school because I do enjoy it. My goal is to use it someday, to visit France.

I imagine you have been busy with your science course. I am sympathetic as you know only too well. Chemistry first term has drained me of all initiative to take another science course. Unfortunately, Wesleyan thinks differently. I still have two more courses to take so that means next year I take Botany. Must start preparing a schedule for third term. However, I register the last day so it is inevitable the course I want will be filled!

The last nite home Mr. Deimler did ask me about LD. I told him about choir which I thought he was aware of.

Could you do me a favor? If you believe you can't or it's unprofessional I'll understand. But I want to know how Lee did the second marking period. Honor roll (yes or no) is fine. I sit here and worry as usual. The hour is late, so I will close. Look out, world. Spring's coming. Enjoyed the letter, the message, the brownies. I am grateful to you. Write when you can.

February 15

I found a few more notes on Sartre; I hope these are not a repeat of what you already have.

We had a bomb scare! At 8:00 we were evacuated to the parking lot and were told to remain until further notice. About 8:30 three of us got into my car; Mrs. Lanshe then joined us, bringing with her a freezing Harold Johns who had given his coat to someone else. An hour later we were given the order to return to classes.

There is also a sniper loose in the area; he has been shooting a high power rifle. I hope the volunteer Humanities course I am offering Monday evening will have the same effect.......

February 15, Shippensburg

Thanks a lot for the "care" package. Again it came in handy (and how)! I can't believe the work I have to do this week and next week. Finals are next week. I'll be home Thursday, February 24 for term break. I can't wait. I'm going to Baltimore this weekend with some brothers for some sundry activities. Well, I have Am. Lit. to read for tomorrow and a health test. Hoping everyone's well.

February 17, Boston

Received your letter with enclosed notes. I sure do appreciate your letters. They sort of keep me going. With the work I have now I find it extremely hard to find time to write to everyone. Keep writing and just bear with me. When Judy is home please say Hello for me and tell her I'll write as soon as I find time. The amount of work is almost unbearable. I'll be much gladder for spring vacation than Thanksgiving. Only 4 weeks. Wahoo!

I'm not sure when I'll be home. I have a final in meteorology on the 18th and maybe a social science mid-term. If I can't get a flight Friday night, I'll probably be in as early as I can on Sat. the 19th. Sure hope I can make it the 18th.

My humanities prof. said today that we will be discussing *Phaedra* after vacation. Sure glad I finally saw the movie. Here's some news on the "Rocking Horse Winner"—the boy had an Oedipal complex. The riding on the rocking horse symbolizes sexual intercourse with his mother. It also symbolizes masturbation. I couldn't believe it! I almost refused to regurgitate it to him on the test. You should have heard the kids discussing that. Still say he's a dirty old man. He's ruining Humanities with his sex-obsessed mind.

February 19

K. relayed that you are busy, etc. Just wanted to tell you that your humanities prof. is warped in his thinking. D. H. Lawrence simply calls a spade a spade. He doesn't play games. Stick with the text. The child is riding his horse to a trancelike state as in his trance he seems to have the ability to predict winners in horse races and the theme is to what lengths do we go and for whose approval.

February 19, Springfield

Guess I really did a job on my last letter. Thought I better get things straight before I come home. No, I didn't lighten my hair. One day Suchee was over here cutting someone's hair (blonde), so I thought I'd see what kind of a reaction I could create.

And it wasn't a coincidence that my term paper was about set designs. You had told me about Richard Lyter's topic at Christmas. I was using that idea. But my topic's changed now. I'm writing about the effect historical events have on furniture styles.

I finally got my dress. Since I can talk to you confidently, I don't really like it. It looks nice on a hanger, but not on me. It has a high empire waistline, but it doesn't hang as nicely as my prom gown. I do like the color. Oh well, I'm not going to fuss.

Included is an article on "camp."[7] Thought of you.

February 23, Boston

Just a few lines to let you know I'm thinking of you. I have ¾ of my research finished. I will have about 20 pages. I'm pleased with it so far. One of the best student writers here asked me for some advice so maybe I'm coming up in the world, like a Nobel Prize!!

Last Friday night I went to see the premiere of the movie *The Oscar*. I saw Elke Sommer, Edie Adams, Stephen Boyd, Eleanor Parker, Joseph Levine, and Edith Head. They sat in the row across the aisle from us. It was just like TV—gowns, minks, limousines, spotlights, cheering, pictures, etc. I wished so much that you were here. I could just see myself with you in one of your long gowns and your hair piled up on your head. You would have fit so well. It was truly your kind of life. The movie theatre was fantastic. Plush carpet, maids and butlers for the restrooms, moving seats. I wanted you here so bad. It was sort of depressing taking MTA back to a dormitory.

While I'm on the subject of you—I'm not sure what game you're talking about that I'm supposed to be playing. If it's about our relationship I have only one thing to say. Some day, some where I'm going to meet you man to woman. When that happens, if it does, it will be the happiest day of my life. I have decided to let whatever is between us, take its course, and I'm not going to question it. Maybe that old feeling will come back again. 'nuff said. Must get to work. Write soon. Your letters are very much appreciated.

February 25

Your letter arrived today; I realized you are swamped and can't write often. Just don't stop altogether.

Sunday J. and I went for a drive—house-hunting! Lo-babes just called; she is on a flying week-end for Elinor's wedding.

Town is buzzing with your father's resignation; he will be a hard man to replace.

Harold stopped by early this evening, relieved that the semester is over.

How did you manage to get tickets for a movie premier?! I can just see you there, completely at home in your environment. (Color me washed-out Homelyville.) I would have savored every minute of it. At the risk of sounding completely unaware, who is MTA? Your date of the evening?

February 28, Delaware

I have finally convinced father that Lee must go out of LD and Union and attend a private school. On my excursion home, the good doctor agreed a change of atmosphere —intellectually and social—would be best. So come spring vacation I start the second maneuver of the operation.

Two more weeks of classes. A real test. Tomorrow the first of two "hurting" bluebooks, French and theatre. Well, your message has comforted me somewhat. As usual I am in at the midway point in grades. I have a 79% test average & 75% quiz, so it's all or nothing come exams.

Can't wait to hear about your Humanities symposium project! By spring vacation you'll probably know whether the effort is worthwhile and the '66ers who are benefiting.

Well, I think you have noticed that this letter is very bumbled and confusing. Too many interruptions. But I did want to send greetings and meta beaucoups.

March 1, West Chester

This will be a short letter since I'm on my only break for the day. We leave to play at 2 p.m. Two basketball teams, 2 swimming teams, and 1 gymnastic team—all on the same bus. Where they plan to put everyone is beyond me but I'm refusing to stand (manager privilege).

Walt spoke with Penn State Dean of Admissions who confirmed his rejection for the fall semester. The Dean suggested he put 2 years in at HACC and try to get in again after then. Guess he feels kind of bad about the whole mess but it was bound to happen. Mom suggested West Chester but I know he hasn't a chance down here. Our campus is rather selective. I was just lucky to get in because my field of work is in demand.

March 2

Am listening to Rachmaninoff—a bad choice if I expect to get anything done tonight. Occasionally it's possible to ignore the schoolwork, but the nagging inner voice is always there, reminding….

Ron Stare was drafted; he stopped by to tell me. Also saw Herman Snyder who had just finished basic training; he looked in his element.

Harold Snyder and John Burtner were here to try the pool table out on Saturday. I actually won a game!

Anyone up there reading *Last Exit to Brooklyn*? At the risk of sounding prudish, I'll just say it's unbelievably gross.

March 5, Boston

It's a rainy, damp, dull, depressing and boring Saturday evening. I must spend this evening catching up in history because I was sick a couple of days last week. (sore throat and cold, running a temp.) Needless to say, I wish I was home or better yet here living it up!! Wahoo!!

Just interrupted by a fire. Second trash can fire in two weeks. On my floor no less. I am doomed. I'm flying in on the 18th at 9:15 p.m. Since your final is the next day, I'll save my visit for Sat. unless you want me to come over Friday night. It'll probably be about 12:00, since I'm obligated to my parents for a couple of hours.

I bought *My Name is Barbra* today. Over vacation I promise to treat you to a chocolate milkshake at the Hob Nob if you take the 'Vette. In fact I'll treat you even if we go in the Studebaker. Just think, the Seniors will have something to talk about. They can go to hell—I'm not a student anymore.

By the way, MTA means Mass. Transit Authority; better known as the subway, only sometimes it comes out of the ground. I had to laugh when you asked. Sorry!!

I have a ticket to see the Vienna Boys Choir tomorrow. That should break up a usually depressing Sunday afternoon.

Check the Arena House; sounds like a good idea. *Ivanov* is playing in Boston now with Vivian Leigh and John Gielgud. Wanted to see it but I don't have time.

I'm glad my dad quit his job. Let Harleysville sweat awhile. Needless to say none who criticized him will apply for the job. Detect much resentment? He was also being considered for LD Business Manager. I'm glad he took the engineering firm job. More money.

For my second research topic I was considering "George Eliot's *Middlemarch* and Lewis' *Mainstreet*: Criticism of a small town." Boy, could I write on that! Instead my topic is "Artificial Insemination in Humans." That's a knee slapper, isn't it? So far it's quite interesting.

March 9, Shippensburg

I thought I'd better write and let you know about my grades. The miracle of the year goes to me. I went into my Structure of English final with a D or F. Guess what I got in the course – a **B.** Unbelievable? Who's to argue with fate? I also got B's in Am. Lit. and Philosophy. My lone C was in Health, a 2-credit course.

March 10, Millersville

I want to thank you for your help. I got *A History of Pornography* in a paperback. I only started to read it, so I can't give any opinion of it. I had to write a composition comparing my two books from reviews I've read. I managed to get an 88 on it, which was the highest in my class. That really made me happy. I hadn't done very well on my first composition and now this one will pull up my average.

Please thank Mrs. Sandel also. I will return those papers on pornography, when I'm home at Easter. Thank you very much.

March 12, Boston

A very boring Saturday evening. It's snowing right now. We have about 3 inches now. Sort of ruins the image of "spring" vacation. Thank God I have only two more tests. I've about reached my capacity for work and pressure. I've decided after spring vacation I'm definitely going to the Cape or NY for a weekend about two weeks before finals. I can't go into finals in the frame of mind I am now.

I saw *Juliet of the Spirits* Friday night. I can see why it's called a masterpiece & Fellini's joke. It uses all the traditional symbols but <u>none of them mean anything</u>. My humanities prof would go crazy. Remind me to tell you about it. It also had a typical Fellini party.

I read Joseph Conrad's *Heart of Darkness* tonite. I didn't like it. He's the most verbose writer I've ever come across. He's worse than my history prof.

I broke down and got a haircut today. The first thing that was said to me when I got back to the dorm was, "You look like hell with your hair cut!" I came up to the room and Mike said, "Shit, you look funny!" I was about ready to have a mental trauma.

Can't believe I'm getting a cooked meal tomorrow. Polished my shoes, a haircut, brushed my jacket—have to impress the parents, you know. I'll probably spill something on the table, floor, or my lap. At times I can be a real klutz. I hate to think when they'll ask me where I'm from. Then they'll know I'm a klutz. Maybe I'll tell them my Dad is a Gladstone[8] candy "magnate." That sounds impressive.

<u>Our</u> paper strike is still on. The kids from New York are making wise cracks on the subway (MTA) about all the New York papers. You should see the people wince. Ken always says, "Well, for a change they're reading a good paper!" The papers up here are rather poor. I'd better get to bed if I want to get up at 12:30 tomorrow!

March 12, Springfield

It's that time of the year again when it would be better if people would all disappear. I really can't blame them. I get more disturbed with myself. I know what will happen, but I let myself fall in the same trap. When college started I thought oh, boy, here's my chance to start anew. I really like people; it's when I get up so close to them, I see and know and understand too much. I try to stand back, but they always lure me close in the end.

Things around here have become stale. I think I could find a retreat in Vicki's friendship, but her center of life is focused on this guy she likes and knowing this, I could not force myself into her circle. I wish I were there at "237" today, maybe to help sort notes or just watch you in the kitchen. I'll always find your friendship refreshing—like one yellow rose.

Gosh, this doesn't sound like a happy-type letter, does it? I'm really not that miserable. When "friends" get me down, there's cheer in knowing I have a "friend." Sooo, enough of that. I am keeping myself busy not even counting the 20 more days left until vacation.

Monday in English we will be beginning lit. for the first time. I'm all enthused with our book, a composite entitled *Fate of Innocence* with such works as *The Tempest, Comus, Daisy Miller, Billy Budd* and *Songs of Innocence and Experience*. I even read the fifteen page intro without its being assigned. Would you have any supplementary notes on these pieces that I could review at Easter time? Especially William Blake's poems which were so hard to understand in high school? Did I tell you I saw the movie *Billy Budd*? It was one of these last minute dates so frequent at colleges. This girl was describing how choice this guy was, but when she mentioned *Billy Budd*, I thought, "Now, Lois, it's not every day you get to see a free movie." Besides, I heard Harold always talking about it last year and I wondered what it was all about. It was very good, though I'm sure that guy will never ask me out again.

I think I'd like to read *The Collector* over vacation. I'm also planning on sewing my Easter outfit. Don't ask me why I feel so ambitious all of a sudden. I do hope to get to see you—I see that you have school until Friday. Mother will be happy—I'll have all day to spend with her and I won't be "running over to Mrs. Ball's house all the time."

Is Tom leaving, left, or coming back? From the Bahamas. I wonder if he knows that the Fountain of Youth is supposedly found on the Isle of Bimini? I know he doesn't believe in such folderol, but he could bring some back for the rest of us.

Thanks for your envelope of goodies. Got it Monday. Cut this small clipping out of *Status* for Tom. It was from an article entitled "Status—anything but—Quo" in which it listed a number of things "in" and "out." You're right about my research topic. It is dumb. Do you always have to be right? Got a nice letter from Ann today. Guess I'll mosey on over to the library.

March 12

A beautiful day with nowhere to go. The 'Vette is sitting out front rarin' to go. Maybe I'll run down to the Post Office with this letter. I drove out to the Farm Thursday evening. Didn't go in, of course; just wanted a bit of nostalgia.

Last evening a group of us went "pool hall" hopping. First to the Hitchin' Post on Paxton Street (crummy floor; country-style "live" music, including a banjo-player) then to the Rising Sun in Campbelltown which was really lively.

Next week-end Hershey Theatre is doing *She Stoops to Conquer*. I'd like to see it since I am considering using it for a class play. And how would you like to go with Judy and me to see *Rashomon* at the Arena House on the 23rd. *Life at the Top* is playing at the Uptown Theatre this week. Would love to go, but probably won't. Come join us in an escape from oblivion.

March 17, Elizabethtown

I was reading the Lancaster morning paper today and I saw an article which amused me. Last year in English class we talked about the verb "graduate."[9] I don't know how authoritative this article is, but I'll bet you read it.

After last semester's final exams, I made a few resolutions—to study harder. I had a 3.0 average, all B's. This semester the work is twice as difficult and the marks are not coming much easier. This semester in place of English composition, I am taking Survey of English Literature. The professor handed back our tests yesterday, and he wasn't too happy. The test was divided into two parts, short answer on Friday, and an essay Monday. The average score on the short answer was 16 out of 69 points, so you can see it was a dilly. The essay saved me. We were tested on the Romantic Period, concentrating on Blake, Wordsworth, Coleridge, Byron, Keats, and Shelley. I was home last weekend and I looked at last year's English notes.

I was thinking lately, "What would I have done in high school if I had studied as I study now?" I know I would have had very close to an all A average. Right now I am catching spring fever. It is very contagious and has no antidote. Along with spring fever, I think I am catching a cold, my first one all winter. Well, I still have to write letters to Ann and Ruth Ann at Ship. I might be around Easter vacation; it all depends on how much painting my father has for me. The Class of '65 misses LD as much as LD misses '65.

Early Spring, Delaware

On checking my application for summer employment I have discovered I will need references. May I please use your name? This is in regards to applying for a job as counselor at a crippled children's camp. I would appreciate this favor very much.

I imagine that Homelyville also got some snow this weekend. I like to think what the farm looks like, the thoughts are very appealing!! Big news—someone just walked in and said his friend got classified 1-A for the draft! This guy was one (like me) who had just turned 18 and registered. That's all I need to worry about—what my classification is.

March 20, Shippensburg

This afternoon I read *Oedipus Rex* and my mind kept wondering off to the literature I read in high school. I'm anxious to see how the prof. will handle it tomorrow in class. She said she had an oral test planned. It should be interesting!

This term I like my courses much better than last term. I have "Early History of U.S. and PA," which I think is fascinating, English II, Health, and Speech II. My speech professor has accepted a position at the University of California. I'm frightened of him. He seems to know everything about anything, and I think he enjoys making a fool out of a student. The first thing he told us was to forget about the *Readers' Guide, Time, Post, Newsweek*, and such magazines cannot be trusted! I just keep thinking, "Be of good faith and this, too, shall pass!" By the way, I have to do a research paper concerning Ancient Greece.

I heard from Larry Geesaman yesterday, and he said something about sending you an article about the verb "graduate." I'm puzzled. Last Monday night I went to a Formal Rush of Zeta Beta, a service sorority. There were about 60 girls there, and the sorority is only taking 12 to 15 pledges. This should be exciting!

Last evening, Jay came up to see me and we went to see *Diamond Head*. It was so good. Next week-end, he's coming up and we're going to the Freshman-Sophomore Dance. Then I'm going to the Hill Climb at Hershey on Sunday. I'm really looking forward to that. I still have my heart set on a Jaguar when I graduate from here!![10]

Yesterday, I was a time-keeper for an Inter-Collegiate Debate. I kept time for two fellows from Elizabethtown College and two from Messiah. I really enjoyed it.

How is Mr. Peck? I haven't heard any news concerning him.

I have a new roommate for next year; she graduated from Dover High School. She's more alive than this one I have now! Also, she loves wrestling!

I suppose by now all the term papers are in, and the public speaking kids are doing their debates for other classes. Reminiscing once again…

March 24, Springfield

Hi! How'd your test go? Bet you "aced" it. I'm in my usual frantic state with research paper due soon. Nobody to make me coffee or bring me brownies. I won't let myself think about this coming week and I don't dare think about the following week. Right now there are at least three different pop songs out, all including some phrase about "Homeward Bound" or "Wish I Were Going Home," or "I Want to Go Home." What's with it? Don't they know I can't go home till I'm through with this paper?

All those plans I had for vacation about reading and sewing and whatever! I don't feel so enthusiastic about them anymore. I just wanna go home. . . .Do you ever get the idea I have a one-track mind?

This weather around here is enough to make anybody want to leave. It's crazy, absolutely and completely. It's snowing today. Yesterday it was raining. I nearly drowned on my way to class and when I got there I felt like I was sitting in a puddle. You'd never be able to take it. The wind is about the only neat thing around here. But then when I get to class, I spend the whole entire period pushing the hair from one side to the other.

Are these mimeographed papers you're sending from seminar class? I especially liked the last one, "Why please people?" How'd it go this past Monday? Did he come?[11] Wished I'd been there. Was he a special speaker? What was the topic? Cripes! Why do I miss out on everything!

Noticed you devoted two whole sentences to the Junior Class Play.

You're right; that 'vette is a hunk of metal. Even told K. that the Catalina comes in second place now. (I bet that got him where it hurts.) I luv it, the 'vette. Wished it was parked outside my door. I heard you were running around—in the car. When Mom called one Sunday, she noticed you getting into it. Would it have been neat going to school in that!

I got an "A!" I got an "A!" in lettering. I was pretty proud of the plate, too. I had only done it about 6 times over. The next assignment is to write "symposium" in three different styles. I know what "symposium" is. It's marshmallow battles and Grandma's farm, and special requests for songs. It's fun!

Boy, I'm really sloppin' this together. If you see Jude, give her a peace offering, will ya? I owe her a couple of letters. Don't have too much fun while I'm not there. Save some room for me and my bag of funnies. Anxious for your next letter. Already.

Oh, in case of future reference you can report that on the 24th of March, 1966, I was still very much alive. See ya in a week, ifin' I'm around and not gone underground. I've decided I'm really going to start working harder. Maybe I can even pull an "A" in something. First, I'll start with Western Civ. Got a "D" on latest test. Made up for it in Soc. Got an "A" in that. OOOh, I feel ambitious – today. Hope some kind soul wrote me a letter today, though I couldn't imagine who fits that category.

March 31

What did you think of La Streisand? Hate to admit it, but I became bored and didn't watch the last twenty minutes. I did let the set on so I could listen; I (1) didn't think the selections were as good as last time, (2) thought the format became tiresome, (3) dislike her severe haircut (longer hair softens her features), and (4) she was too dxxx pleased with herself.

Lo arrives home tomorrow, around midnight. Tom offered to pick her up at the station in the 'Vette. She'll love it!

If you get a chance, check an article on "Puritanism," *The Saturday Review*, March 26th. It may be related to your telling me about students' (college kids?—what shall I call all of you?) ideas of "sex for sex's sake," "sex without love," and so forth.

April 3, Boston

Just back from the Sheraton-Boston. Carol is staying there tonite. I have a test tomorrow so I had to come back. Can't see her tomorrow either. So this big week-end is finished. I spent $28.50 this week. My parents will not be happy.

Tomorrow the concentrated studying starts. Up until the 25th of April I have 2 tests, 1 mid-term, 3 term papers, 1 speech and regular reading assignments. Guess you can tell I'm quite worried about the whole mess. Only 7 more weeks! Wahoo! I'm very sorry I didn't write sooner. Tuesday night I was up all night waiting in line for room reservations for next year. What insanity!!! I got #928. Great view!

Last night at the apt. there was a fight. Some kid had a big gash over his eye. Two girls had 20 guys in their apt. and things got out of hand. Ah, the joys of Marlboro Street!!

2:30: Surprise!! Still didn't get anything done. Studied for about 30 min. until the room turned into a looney bin. Then Carol called. I got feeling bad about her being up here and me deserting her so three of us at midnight decided to go over to the Sheraton. Did see a good Laurel and Hardy movie. My self-control has been nil since I got back. What am I doing to myself? Damn. I've got to start studying!!! P.S. Write!

Friday, Boston

Here it is Friday and what am I doing? STUDYING! I have to go to the Medical School Library to do some research. It's in Roxbury which is Boston's Harlem. Fun & games!! Sorry I haven't written, but I'm up to my neck in work. I'm sure you can understand. My communications prof. told me not to plan on sleeping too much the rest of the semester. That was encouraging. Just bear with me. I do appreciate your letters. They sort of keep me sane. It's at times like this when I begin to wonder if it's all worth it.

I enjoyed the Streisand show very much. I can't criticize it, though, because I get in a trance every time I see and hear her so I miss everything else. That's a helluva thing, isn't it? It's what the psych dept. calls a mystic experience.

I've had 3 letters from J. which surprised me because I only sent her one. I was a little disappointed in her when she didn't bother coming home in time to see me before I left after spring vacation. Did she ever mention anything to you about her mood over vacation? I've been feeling so removed from her. Don't know what's wrong. Maybe she's getting senioritis already. Hope she doesn't start playing the mature role on me.

Seems funny being up here at Easter. I am going to Church Sunday and out to dinner. More money!! Last week I spent $30. I had a great week-end. Carol and I stayed at the apt. Sat. night. (Mum is the word.) When we got there, a rumble was in action. Some kid was running around bleeding all over the place. Took him to the hospital. The joys of Marlboro Street.

We haven't seen spring up here yet. I got a jay-walking ticket!! Man, was that a panic. Let it up to me! I think it's the only damn law in this city that is enforced. Write.

April 14, Boston

Color me frantic!! I've been working 2 days straight on my research paper. Cutting classes—the works. It's not near as good as the last one. I must have it to my typist by noon on Sat. At this point I might have to rewrite the whole middle section. HELP!

Received both of your extremely cheery letters today. Each letter contained at least two different attitudes and moods. Sorry about repeating news about my "grown-up weekend." Besides that, the reason I told you not to say anything about Carol staying at the apt. is because of her parents. She'll say something if she wants to. I thought your remark concerning that subject was very unfair. Give me a break, huh?!

Talk about repeating info—you've mentioned the "wedding" in the last 3 letters and I still don't know what the hell wedding you are talking about, or for that matter whose wedding. Besides, I said WRITE because I enjoy getting your letters even though sometimes I can't return the favor as often as I'd like, mainly because I have a "helluva" lot of work to do, and because I want to keep my 2 A's, 1 B & 2 C's. Surprise!!

Enclosed is a cocktail napkin (from a glass of Chianti) from the place I ate Easter dinner.

Thanks for the goodies. I've been spending too much. $60. in 2½ weeks.

P.S. Why the "attack" all of a sudden?

April 15, Boston

Must write and apologize for my much too hasty letter written yesterday. I've been hanging on a cliff lately with all the pressure and work, and I guess the indefinite tone of your letters just pushed me off. You do have a right to be edgy with the house, the work, the town, and your comprehensives. I should have taken that into consideration. Please accept my apologies.

I cut two classes today to study for my psych. test at 3:30. My term paper is only half finished with the second draft and I must have it to the typist by tomorrow noon. Looks like I'll be up all night tonite. Sunday I have to study for an astronomy test on Monday. Then I must start on my psych self-analysis due Wed. I got this test result rating how much my friends are like me. Out of a possible 20 you, Jude, and some kid up here had a 19. At least we have one thing going for us. One point of interest is that my mother and Miss Gluck both had 11. IMPOSSIBLE!!

Spring finally arrived in Boston today. Yesterday it was 92° and today 62°. Last night I was thinking about the summer which for me is only 5 weeks away!! I'm looking forward to us playing pool and bombing around in the 'Vette. I also had another "evil" little thought. If Tom wouldn't take you to the Sr. prom wouldn't it be a panic if I would. Damn, would that be fun!! Although, I think at heart I'm a coward. Maybe I could just drop you off? P.S. Please interpret WRITE as a plea!

April 15, Springfield

Received your letter, just as you promised. You should have seen me strut up the hall toward that mailbox. I knew you couldn't let me down. (Such confidence.)

I think this week-end is just what you need to lift you out of the mundaneness of everyday living. Such special occasions always made living more tolerable for me. The trouble with most people—as I hang my shingle over the door—is that they reason this way: if a little is good, more will be twice as better. To me, variety is the panacea.

I had a marvelous time last week. Home is more appealing now that I don't have to look at it every day. I really don't think I could survive with married life. You say you're hard to live with; I'd be impossible. Really very sorry that you don't consider this one of your better years.

I think it is one of my better ones. It even says in my horoscope that "This is a year when you begin to "break through," to see the light of greater happiness...that without happy family members, success will mean little or nothing ... which means it is up to you to strive for a happy, constructive compromise." I think both Kirk and I realize this finally. (How's that for a well-constructed paragraph?)

Bar's letters make me stop and think of what mine must sound like sometimes. Actually I always was conscious of this aspect. I often wondered what Marsh thought of my letters. They're always chockfull of me and "what I have been doing lately." Your letters are the easiest to write. We understand each other, don't we? At least, they're the most fun to write. I can skip here and there and I know you'll eventually understand me. Must be that sixth sense all you teachers are endowed with.

Guess what it was doing here when I got back? Yep. I told Mother at the station, ten-to-one it would be raining. It's what you call a sure thing. Poor Kirkus hasn't seen sunshine for 16 days straight. I found out there is no such thing as a spring formal at Wittenberg. Cripes! Instead, some morning—no one knows exactly when—they'll play the "Fight Song" on the chapel chimes at 7:30. That day we have no classes and, I guess, there's water fights and battles and things like that. Sound like my kind of fun, huh? Guess I'll have him down some weekend anyway.

Got something in the mail yesterday that sounds like a pretty good deal.[12] You fill out a test questionnaire and send it in with $3. Operation Match. They dig up five guys compatible to your personality. I ought to send it in just for spite. Wouldn't they have fun scrapin' up five guys for me? I don't think I'm that desperate yet.

Hey, guess what? I had a tennis test yesterday. Did ya ever hear of anything more ridiculous? And me, coordination plus. We had to bounce the ball with the racket one hundred times without flubbing, then one hundred times in the air, then alternating five up and five down. I was there one whole hour. I ought to have the tiniest wrists around after that. At least I'm not afraid of the ball anymore. Really, I have more control with that exercise.

Thursday we went out for dinner. It was Jeffery's birthday. Too bad we don't have birthdays every day. They give people an extra sheen. Watching her all aglow made me feel good. I wonder if I acted so "bubbly." Everybody had steak. I had spaghetti. Jeff asked me if I wanted to room with her next year. Imagine, someone actually asked me.

Went to a poetry reading last night. Galway Kinnell[13] was the poet. He read some of his own poems, as well as the old masters. I had mixed feelings. In one way, I feel only the poet (or artist, musician, etc.) should read his own poetry, no one else. But then, that sort of puts him on the spot. It's an uncomfortable feeling to me, one I try to avoid.

I really feel like sitting down and doing some serious studying. But I don't know what to do with all these people. I honestly don't. Was thinking how Tom would love to be here today. There's a deck full of babes outside our window soaking in the sunrays. And these babes wear nothing but two-piece-ers!

With bunches of love.

April 17

Dear _____Frantic, _____Terse,_____Hurt (check appropriate square)

Are we picking again? Let's not.

I trust you made your term paper deadline. Sorry you had to cut classes in order to do it, and sorry I can't send help—moral support will have to suffice.

If any remark of mine annoyed you, by all means delete it.

April 22, Boston

Thanks for the candy bar. It means a lot. It's strange how something as insignificant as a Krackel bar can mean so much. I am currently working on my humanities paper. The topic is "Discuss the symbolism in Chekhov's *The Seagull*." I understand the play, but since Chekhov has a habit of being very complex, I'm having trouble with organization. This is the 4th time I've tried to write the damn thing. I'm about half-way finished.

Today was a fairly interesting day. We had to take a reading comprehension test for Communications Class at 3:30. We had a 1½ hr. break before the test. About 10 guys got bombed and one got sick in the middle of taking the test. What a mess. A panic even!! I was laughing so bad I think I got a score of about a −2. It was the funniest thing I've ever seen. Two rows of guys juiced to the gills and one throwing up.

Ken and I went for a walk downtown after dinner since it was so warm today—trees, flowers, green grass, and seven boats on the lake. SPRING!! I'm looking forward to going into New York next weekend. Jane is moving to her new apt., so I won't be able to stay with them at all. I hope to see her sometime during the weekend.

I'll explain my philosophy when I see you also. It's like a new lease on life!! I'd better get back to seagulls. Please say hello to Mrs. Kramer for me.

April 26, Delaware

Hope you haven't disowned me; I do apologize for not writing sooner. To get up to date, thanks so much for the Batman comic book. Six weeks from tonight, well, I think you know. I'm finished. A wonderful thought, n'est-ce pas? But lots to do before June 7. Tonite's work has shown me that! Am currently preparing a persuasive speech, studying for a literature mid-term, and reading about perception.

As for next year—it is time to select courses again. I hope to make it psych (again), history and zoology. Yes, it is science requirement time again. I can just see father; of course he will think I am secretly planning to become a veterinarian.

I also plan to rent a room for my sophomore year and I save $200. Incidentally next year (if things go as planned) my address will be a Park Avenue! However, the name Delaware ruins the effect.

Perhaps Lo has told you—I am going to visit her the weekend of May 14. It will give me a needed break before the panic of exams.

I keep remembering things to tell you! Last weekend I couldn't believe the cultural events that I attend! I mean Delaware and OWU really shocked me. I saw the movie *A Patch of Blue* as well as the Wesleyan Players' production of *Romeo and Juliet*.

April 26, Harrisburg

Are you ready? I mean are you really ready? I passed my finals and I'll get my cap Thursday evening!! Hallelujah! It really feels like a ton has been lifted from my shoulders. No more sciences! Wheee!! Along with all this, I got my clinical evaluation and the instructor gave me an "EXCELLENT!" I'm the only freshman who received an excellent rating all year! I guess I don't have to tell you that I'm really flying high!

Right now my roomie and I are so silly it's sinful! The tension last week during finals was unbelievable and this week we're experiencing the "calm." It really is a terrific relief. I hope I have time to visit you and model my sexy organdy cap. I'm seriously thinking of visiting LD Friday and talking to "Clara Barton" (the school nurse).[14] Don't be surprised if an "angel of mercy" bops in for an English class!

April 26

We made an offer on the Fromm house. We looked at the place on Saturday. It has a lot of potential. Beautiful grounds. And **private**—a prime consideration. A couple from Baltimore also bid on it.

Hey, have a great week in NYC—say Hello to Jane and Wesley for me.

April 27

Went to Shippensburg for a meeting for supervisors of student teachers. Spent some time with Stevie and Harold whom we met in the Raider Room.

April 29, Boston

Just back from a movie and local delicatessen. Saw DeMille's *Ten Commandments*. Quite fantastic. No, I didn't go for the "message." This week in Harvard Square the Brattle Theatre is running a James Dean film festival. Thinking about you.

Found out today that I got an A+ on my second research paper. Highest in the section. Finally achieved my goal. Came out on top of one of the best writers in the Freshman Class. My talents doth amaze me!! Knowing me has been the greatest experience of my life. Serially, I was very shocked.

Surprise!! I'm not in New York. Last minute changes in testing plans forced us into going next week. Besides Ken's parents have been in Las Vegas, at the Sands no less, for the last week and a half, so next week will be more convenient for them.

Found Rachmaninoff music, but it was for two pianos. I want it for one piano if there is such an animal. Boston Pops is doing this in their program this week. Unfortunately I couldn't get tickets. I hope to see them when my parents come up.

On May 21st I take the draft test. That has me a bit concerned. You know, I can't help feeling a little resentment. It's kids like me that have to work their asses off to get grades and then are the ones to be drafted.

It's good to hear that Tom is considering another house. With a little bit of luck you will get your "dream."

Had a little bit of excitement here Thursday night. Some robber shot a cop one block down the street from the dorm. There was then a bulletin that he was loose in Kenmore Square, the Square right outside our front door. Finally caught him on a roof on good ol' Marlboro Street.

I have been very tense and high-strung these past 2 weeks. I try to slow down, but it seems as if internally my body is going a mile a minute. It's the strangest feeling. As for my mind, complete impotency. The atmosphere in the room is also very tense. Mike and I were even at each other's throats. First time all year. May 20th, where are you?

Was sitting in the library study room last night when I realized they possess a three-foot statue of The David. I'd confiscate it for you, except for one problem, it's solid marble.

Come to CBS; you can get a job in the Humanities Department. Say Hello to Mrs. Kramer for me. I miss you. Love.

April 29, Springfield

The house? The house? Did you get the house? Sure did get me excited with that unexpected letter. Guess I'm as anxious as you are for you to have a place of your own. The only Fromm place I'm familiar with is the one past Beth's house. Is this it?

Before I forget, I got your chocolate bar. Thanks. Krackels are my favorite. Also, if you see or write to Harold, tell him I got his book. It's going to help a lot on my next theme. Our English final's going to be based on some book we read out of class dealing with the theme innocence or experience, as *Lord of the Flies* or *Of Human Bondage* or *The Tempest*, or something else that sounds good.

I was thinking the other day, How come it is I learn the best or easiest when I have someone to run and tell? Here I am—getting a liberal education when all I want is all the culture, social relations, and aesthetic courses I can cram in.

I'm sending the paintings home by bus this weekend. Thought they would be better handled this way. Mom will bring them over.

You know what would be fun to do this summer? For you, Tom, Barry, and I to do something together, or go somewhere. Did I tell you Elinor is coming out for me Memorial Day week-end? My last exam is Memorial Day.

If you've ever had doubts about yourself, listen to this. One night having read 2 chapters of

Western Civilization and on the verge of climbing the walls, I sat down to a pile of construction paper and scissors. I cut out over 150 flowers. Now our ceiling is covered with 150 flowers of all shapes and sizes; each flower is somebody! You're purple with a yellow center. At night, I lie here and muse over my flowers. Now I'm twice as disturbed.

K. is coming down the weekend of May 15th – Friday, Saturday, and Sunday! He offered to take me out to dinner and do anything I want. Cheryl and I are going to see Paul Newman as *Harper* tonight. I feel in the mood for being thrilled and Paul Newman thrills me. Saw *My Fair Lady*, I think I told you. Liked her costumes best of all. See where "Shadow of Your Smile" made best song of the year. Now they'll probably play it to death like they did "Moon River."

May 1, Harrisburg

A telegram from Hummelstown to Harrisburg! I was really surprised and delighted, too!! Thank you so much for caring. The capping ceremony was really beautiful. I just wish that all of the group could have been there. Thanks again for the telegram.

May 1

Hey! I survived the comprehensive yesterday. What a relief—I am sure you can empathize.

How was the Big City? Or did you decide to remain there forever? I never made it to the Prom.

May 4, Springfield

Today was the day! Awoke with the same thrill as on Christmas morn. Chapel bells rang a full 15 minutes. Played "Happy Days Are Here Again," and "Dixieland" plus others. By 9:00 we were out lying in the sun. Closest thing to a nudist camp I've seen yet. Came in at 3:00. Am now sitting on a soft, downy pillow. Burnt the back of my legs and belly. Rest of me is an off shade of white. A Sing-along, dance, and movies tonight.

May 6

Good morning!

Thought that greeting would excite you, expecting that you'll receive this letter on Monday at which time you'll probably be exhausted after your week-end (5 pts. if you can diagram that sentence.).

What a beautiful week-end for NYC. I'll bet you're glad you waited. Wish I were going, but the time has come to concentrate on correcting Term Papers.

Yearbooks came out today. The seniors aren't getting theirs early as is custom. Some of them came to me yesterday at 2:30 asking if I could do anything. I went and spoke to Mr. Schan, but it was to no avail. I asked if the seniors could at least get theirs in the morning, but he said, "NO."

The *Falconaire* is very nice. Especially like the cover. The last page is the Last Will and Testament of the Class of '66, mainly bequeathing to faculty, for example, "To Mrs. Ball, Another Class of '65!" I was actually laughing and told Harold Johns (Editor) that I was delighted. It is a cut, of course, and they thought I would be angry. Quite the contrary. I shall thank all of the senior classes on Monday.

I knew you had many latent talents, but an A+ on your research paper. Magnifique! My most sincere compliments. It's a good feeling to be in the top bracket, isn't it?

Are you saying that Ken's parents want to be there when you visit? I understand that The Sands is quite lush.

May 7, Lehigh

I thank you very much for considering me as a possible applicant for the summer lab jobs at AMP and for giving me a chance to get a job in a field of science which can help me in training for my future profession. If the job does not require much formal electronic training, I feel I could handle it, and this work experience in electronics can be of use in any field of science. John Miller got a summer job with a contractor, so this should give him experience in his planned Civil Engineering major.

I bet you will not believe me if I tell you all the books I have read this semester! In English II we have read parts of *The Canterbury Tales*, all of *The Great Gatsby, Gulliver's Travels, Antony and Cleopatra, The Iliad,* and selections of poetry from Shakespeare, Donne, Pope, Wordsworth, Keats, Browning, Dickinson, Housman, Yeats, Robinson, Frost, and Eliot. By the way I got a "B" in first semester English.[15]

I am in an honors history section. In there we have read *The Second Treatise of Civil Government* by Locke, *The Social Contract* by Rousseau, *On Liberty* by John Stuart Mill, *The Communist Manifesto* by Marx and Engels, *Communism* by Meyer, and *The Outbreak of WWI* by Lee. For next week we have to read *Civilization and Its Discontents* by Freud, and for the following week *The Rebel* by Camus. So you can see I have been doing quite a bit of important reading!

Have fun grading the Senior English finals!

May 8, Boston

Needless to say, I'm on cloud nine after my week-end. That city is so fantastic. It was great seeing Jane again. Their new apartment is very nice. It's on the 33rd floor. It has a terrace with a beautiful view of the city. On the roof of the building are a cocktail lounge and swimming pool. Wesley just bought a Jaguar sedan, with fold down decks in the back and bar type things. You walk into the lobby of their building and have the door opened by a little man in a Charles de Gaulle-style uniform. In the entrance hall they have one of those gigantic crystal chandeliers. Very impressive.

I spent Sat. evening at Jane's. Stayed till about 2:30 a.m. She is still the same old Jane. She's as happy as a little kid at Christmas over that apt. In fact, she's not doing summer stock because she likes it so well. Wesley's 3rd play[16] is now being read by someone who's associated with David Merrick. He hopes possibly it'll make Broadway. Who knows?

Ken's place was also out of this world. Six-room apt. overlooking the Hudson River on Fort Washington Ave. French door knobs, chandelier in hallway, French provincial furniture, gold carpet, maid. Just unbelievable. Also met his grandparents. His grandmother is really cool. She had this ring that looked like it weighed 5 lbs., about $5,400 worth. She had a broach ($3,500). I couldn't believe it. You'll go crazy when I tell you about the particulars of the whole weekend. Remind me to tell you about it. It seemed like it couldn't be true. Little 'ol Homelyville me, with "those" people. Right now I'd better stop drooling and go to bed. I'll continue tomorrow.

Monday, Boston

Just back from classes. Received your letter. The Batman sticker was killing. Of course, there were the usual roommate questions to answer. They just don't understand. The joke, well, methinks there is personal implication. It is hysterical. Passing it to Lois is a cute little trick to get me to write. I do dislike being subjected to writing against my will. But for you – the world!!

Found out 2 bits of very depressing news today. One, no maid service next year. In order to keep the room and board at the same fee they have to cut out maid service. Two, my one friend tells me that my humanities prof. overheard me telling him (my friend) that he (the prof) looks like the toad on Walt Disney. He really does; it's quite remarkable. I don't think he heard me though because he was busy talking.

Ken's dad made $20,000 on the stock market this year but when it dropped 15 pts. last week he lost some of it. Don't know how much, but needless to say he was a little upset over the weekend.

I agree that the "cut" in the yearbook is complimentary. Poor souls just don't understand you yet. When you thank them they'll be completely befuddled. Saw *Patch of Blue* in the city. Very good. The girl was a close second for Julie Christie. I could have never made the decision.

Friday the Thirteenth of May

Hurray! I got a letter from you. Yet in spite of the pleasure felt, I found your letter to be somewhat unsettling. I'm not quite sure just why; it's just a general feeling I had after I had read the letter. Here I go, introspecting again.

Does your Tensor light "hum?" Mine does and it's driving me crazy.

If possible, reserve May 31st (in the evening). I'm throwing a paper-correcting party. Exams for seniors begin May 27th, but social studies wins again as the first exam to be given.

Well, you'll no doubt wonder why I didn't spring this news first. It's probably because it doesn't seem real to me yet. Are you ready? (No, I'm not pregnant.) I think we have a house. Yes, a real place in which to live! It's in—get this—South Hanover Twp. It's the Fromm place I rejected about six weeks ago. I didn't like the outside so I wouldn't even look at it as a possibility. Plus the price was too high. About three weeks ago I happened to casually ask about it. The price had dropped; in addition, I was becoming more desperate with the impossible conditions here. We looked at it. I fell in love with the grounds and the location. The house itself is in good condition. Two floors. It has potential (for building on to, etc.) and it's private.

The front yard reminds me of the farm. Big trees. I rashly promised to keep the grass mowed. Tom also gets the big bedroom (21 x 12) but I get the dining room for a library/study. Funniest thing is that we've only seen the place once! I don't even know when we get the key! Fromms have moved, but we haven't signed anything yet. I don't know how long such transactions take. We won't move for at least a month. To say "I can't wait" is a gross understatement.

May 14, Boston

Just back from the esplanade studying social science. It's a very warm day but the breeze coming off the river is pretty cool. Hope to play tennis late this afternoon at the Boston College courts.

Had a date last night. My last fling in Boston. It'll be good to get away from the work and get home to see you and the rest of the gang but I hate to leave Boston. Rita and I went out to dinner at the Café Almafi. Then to Paul's Mall, a jazz night club. Enclosed is the swizzle stick. Only problem is it was in a ginger ale. Depressing, isn't it?

Yesterday we had our art final. I got the 4th highest grade in the section. But, alas, a "B" on a theme.

I couldn't get tickets for the Boston Pops next Sat. night so I don't know what I'm going to do with my parents.

I heard a Judy Garland record this afternoon on which she sang "My Man." Streisand's style is quite similar, although I think Streisand has a better voice quality than Garland.

At this point I'm desperately trying to resist calling you. But self-control is a virtue and I must learn, be virtuous and pious.

I guess by now you're starting to concentrate on your final. We're in this together, baby! I think Rachmaninoff for two sounds like fun also. If we had two pianos we could have a little project over the summer "Playing and passion go together like a horse and carriage. . ." Well, if I don't buy it, we can always work on the passion. I'm probably better at passion than playing anyhow. Speaking of Rachmanioff, I'm going to the Deli-Haus for lox and bagels. Will continue later.

May 15, Boston

Well, it's later, isn't it? I'm diligently studying social science today. How would you like a 4,000 word dissertation on Social Darwinism as applied to radical nationalism in post-war Prussia? Or how about Pan-Slavism? Ecch!

Since finals are approaching this dorm is like a morgue. Very enjoyable. Nothing else new so I shall leave you where I did last night. Off to the Deli-Haus for dinner. See you soon.

May 17, 1966, a card sent to Barry

The front cover of the card has a cartoon little girl saying, "The minute I looked into those big brown eyes …. I knew I liked you…… why don't you follow me home sometime…..

(inside) and I'll ask your mother if I can keep you."

May 17, West Chester

For some reason I feel there's a new type relationship being established between parents and daughter. I can finally communicate with them. Don't know what's come over me but it's a heck of a good feeling. Daughter must be opening her eyes to a few things. Took a long time to realize this but I'm glad it's not too late. I'm probably not making myself clear so I'd like to explain it to you sometime soon.

Received a letter from bls yesterday. Evidently he had a great time in NYC. Also seems to be spending more time and money at the exclusive places in Boston.

May 18, Springfield

Hi! Thought it time to write. Had a dream about you last night. Something about graduation. Appropriate time of year?

I am most anxious for studies to be over, but I fear I shall miss this life. I suddenly realized how I have grown used to having someone around. Sort of a quiet companionship I enjoy. I am still undecided about boarding arrangements for next year. Jeff wants me to room with her in the Christus House (an honorary dorm with time set aside for devotions). All very well and good, but I prefer to pray on my own time, thank you. Considered a single room, but they are so few.

I cut my hair today. Quite short. Got some Summer Blonde, but I haven't quite convinced myself yet.

Had a letter from K. today. He has a certain knack for saying the same thing in a thousand different ways. Something like Harold and his "thank you's." I did enjoy the week-end. By Sunday I was completely exhausted. Friday night we went bar-hopping (Beat him at pool!); Saturday we "toured" the campus; had a picnic (filched food from the Union); walked through Snyder Park and Ferncliff Cemetery (unbelievably beautiful); rented a tandem bicycle (what a stitch!); went out for dinner (took a taxi and had veal scaloppini); and saw *Patch of Blue* (fell in love with Sidney Poitier).

Sunday I took him to chapel (communion even) and to dinner. Afterwards we took a long walk in our Sunday duds and found the most beautiful homes. Without a doubt, here is what you have been looking for. I'm so glad Kirk was along, to testify to their magnificence. Since he was so impressed with Springfield and Wittenberg, I am convinced more than ever that you must come out.

I am wondering if anything further has developed with the house since you wrote on Thursday. I really wish you wouldn't put so much store in whether I like it or not. Is it really going to matter whether I do or not? The house has potential, as you said. I'm sure you can make it very appealing. The location is fine. What are the chances of development around it? Apparently it has the essential things you want. You really can't expect Tom to be wild about any house (other than a dream home). It's not his nature. It would be nice, I know. But you ought to be used to that by now. I know you're anxious about a new home and I'm anxious for you.

Now that I have written this epistle, I feel like tearing it up. But I can't do that, because I'd never get another one off. Let me know about the house.

One of the Great Ones of '65

May 24, Springfield

Tomorrow is the last day of classes. How sad. Really gonna hate myself next week after I ace all my exams. I'm being inconsistent again. My bags are all packed, but I don't want to leave. Things are just getting interesting.

May 28, Springfield

Me? Tired of studying? Heck, no. Weather is superb. Has captured my soul. Tomorrow at this time I'll be sitting on the porch waiting to be picked up. Comin' home! Thanks for the card. Done cheered me up. Ready or not, here I come. Suppose I'll find everything in boxes. Hope you missed me.

Late Summer, before the move to Grandview, a note was left at Park Ave.[17]

Sorry I couldn't make it over today. It's about this mean ole Mommie I have. How was it today anyway? I want to say good-bye, but I can't; I want to say thank you for the last 2 weeks, for just being you, but to what avail; I want to say I love you, but I don't know how. One "comfort" is knowing that I'll always be a part of this house and this house will always be a part of me.

Sorry I had to be melodramatic, but I couldn't just leave. Time's getting short and a few "courtesy calls" yet to make. I'm trusting that you will read this and understand.

P.S. Would you see that Tom gets the pink note?

Chapter 7 Endnotes:

---

[1] A gift we had given her, after she had admired one like it in Tom's car.

[2] This, of course, was written long before email was available.

[3] The new pillow covers were pink velvet; the ones they replaced were very colorful and matched the bright, 60s colors, colors Lois later tried to capture in a painting she created to give me as a gift.

[4] I can't help wondering if anyone ever suggested to this young nursing student to switch to pre-med.

[5] The theory that behavior is chiefly response to immediate situations. The source I found gave the date for the development of the theory as 1968, but that can't be accurate.

[6] Twice winner of the Pulitzer Prize, founding president of Lincoln Center and president of the Juilliard School.

[7] Camp is an aesthetic style and sensibility that regards something as appealing because of its bad taste and ironic value. Originated in the 1960s; similar to "kitsch."

[8] Gladstone manufactured lollipops in Hummelstown.

[9] As in "one is graduated from;" one does not "graduate from."

[10] And some years later she did!

[11] Captain William Allen.

[12] Forerunner to online dating services.

[13] In 1983 he won a Pulitzer Prize for his work.

[14] The name of the school nurse really was Mrs. Barton.

[15] One of three Valedictorians in his class, Karl always made it very clear that he didn't like English courses.

[16] Two of St. John's plays were "The Acting Lesson" and "The Naked King."

[17] Lois lived with her parents two houses from me.

Chapter 8

Maturing

September to December 1966

... For I dipt into the future far as human eye could see:
Saw the vision of the world and all the wonder that could be.

Locksley Hall
Alfred, Lord Tennyson

There were no letters exchanged over the summer, as most of The English Students were in residence in the Hummelstown area, some with summer jobs, including restaurants, a few at Hershey Park, and the Hershey Chocolate Factory, the latter considered the best-paying, but with the least cachet.

In the Fall of 1966, The Class entered their Sophomore Year. Some, including the writer below, made one last trip "down the shore," the typical place for students to collect before heading back to their respective colleges which, at that time, didn't open until mid-September.

September 7, Ocean City, Maryland

A postcard:

I think this existence beats almond bars.[1] Thought you'd appreciate this card full of humanity. Weather has been great. Judy arrived today so the mayhem keeps mounting.

September 15

Hi, there, already. Think of me Saturday night. I really and truly and professionally have a job, playing piano. I'm scared ghost white! Know why? Cause it's in Homelyville. Don't laugh. I'm on at the American Legion from 10 to 2. All by myself.

Luv from the piano player at your friendly neighborhood bar.

September 17, Boston

All I have to say is the American Legion isn't the Ritz but it's a start. Needless to say, I'm very happy to be back in the city. Millions of college students on the corners again. When I left the place last May, it was deserted.

I picked up my books on Friday. My humanities (philosophy) course looks great—Plato, More, Hindu, Skinner (*Walden Two*). It looks pretty thick, especially the religion, but it'll be good to get a taste of that end of things.

My room is a bit small but very homey. You know—something more than bed, desk, and chair.

Jude is really psyched about teaching. I hope she doesn't get too disillusioned before the end of the semester.

I like the view from my room.[2] We can see Fenway Park. We can also hear the loud speakers ("and number 42…"). Help! Of course every 15 minutes we hear 2 sets of chimes—the bank clock and our chapel chimes. Well, adversity builds character. Funny we didn't hear either of these chimes when we looked at the apartment. Last night was an apartment party—no furniture. It was different. Tonite is *Dr. Zhivago*.

I'll be thinking of you tonite as you are performing. You'll give the Legion some class. Write some encouragement next week when my classes start. You know how lazy I am. Say Hello to Lo for me.

September 19

I just had a few minutes reading marginal notes I wrote during my Chaucer course while an undergraduate at PSU. A fellow and I were exchanging comments after class. Shades of high school!

Did you ever find the references for "The Love Song" from *Tristan and Isolde* in October's *Playboy*? I came across it yesterday and had to smile to myself.

Saturday at the Legion went fine. How was your week-end?

September 22, Boston

Tomorrow is Friday! Just couldn't believe this week. My courses are great but difficult. I'm having a helluva time getting back in the routine of studying. As usual I'm apprehensive about the semester. You know I want to do well, but I dread that "C" rut.[3] Ah, to be brilliant!

Glad to hear things came off all right at the Legion. I'm proud of you!! (gush!)

Ken's dad sent him a $2,000 check to buy a VW this spring. Of course I applauded him, became violently ill, and then cried in private.

I have a date tomorrow night. Don't know what is on for the remainder of the week-end. Last weekend was a real blast with the usual partying and reacquainting.

I've been spending money like crazy. Well, I must keep up with the rest of the "big time" spenders up here.

I'd appreciate any notes you could send me on naturalism. My rhetoric course is based on that subject. What was the quote you told me about naturalism and realism? Something about a back porch and a garbage can, maybe?[4] Thank God, I have only two classes tomorrow. Must study before I go to bed, so I'll close. Miss you!

September 23

I have a good class planned for tomorrow. We're starting the Renaissance and I brought in my gorgeous books on Michelangelo and da Vinci, plus the album of Spanish music from the Renaissance.

Almost forgot—this letter was supposed to encourage you in your studies. OK: Study hard and you, too, can be an adult with frustrations. Be good, dammit. I'm thinking of you.

Luv, Teach

September 25, from Jack Harry, a former teacher at LD

May I have your autograph? Seriously, it sounds like great fun. What do the powers that be say about your appearing at the Legion? How many weeks are you working? Does this mean every week-end is tied up?[5]

Talking about week-ends, it looks as though I won't get to the shore this fall either (Either alone or with company.).

No, my brother Tom isn't living with me. He met a girl last spring and is getting married November 4. She is very nice but oh, so young. She just graduated from high school last June.

I am coming up this week-end. The plan is thus: Friday evening I will meet Tom in Harrisburg to get measured for a tux and do some of the other things that always need to be done. Saturday evening I am going up to State College to visit friends. I thought we might visit Friday after I finish the errands in Hbg. If I don't hear from you this week, I'll assume you will be home Friday and I will call you, O.K.?

September 26

Feel in a pretty good mood tonight, so I thought I'd better quickly write before it passes. Finally the wall in the study here is covered with my framed pictures. It took 3 hrs. Saturday and 5 hrs. tonight.

I've decided to do *Arms and the Man* (G.B. Shaw) as the Senior Play, mainly based on casting. There is a new student who has possibilities. Very good looking—a real smoothie.

September 27, Arizona

Hi! Arizona is beautiful. Wouldn't mind living here. Colors are so vivid, intense. Marsh drove us 100 miles north to Flagstaff Sunday. Different terrain. Large Ponderosa Pines. Up there the weather is perfect—thin and cool-warm. Had a delightful picnic. Today Virginia took us to a mall to shop. Almost went wild at the things you could buy.

Tonight M. said he'd take us and "cruise Central" (main drag in Phoenix) lined with palm trees and police cars. Elinor and I had a ball flying out. Marsh met us at airport. Forgot all about my grand exit from the plane because I was so excited. Wished you could have seen the city as we flew in at night. Nothing but lights for miles. Something like LA, I guess. Marsh just came home from school. He's exhausting — wants to show us everything. Going over to Scottsdale. Already I don't want to leave. Greetings from Cloud Nine.

September 28, Boston

I'm thinking about you now as you sit in school with "them" (the difficult section). Poor soul!

One more class for me today at 1:30. We're having discussions on Schopenhauer and naturalism. Hope someone else on my panel knows what they're talking about.

I saw the movie *The Wrong Box*[6] last weekend. Liked it even though the critics cut it up. Must be poor critics!

Been studying in the new library. It has 2 tons of red carpet in the place. Study room for 5,000 students, audio-visual rooms, listening rooms, faculty library, and graduate library.

Found out yesterday that I can transfer to SPC (TV production and directing) with no lower than a 2.3. I should be able to manage that.

There was a big discussion last night in our room about student-teacher relationships at the high school level. Most of the guys seemed to have the strange notion that a first name basis symbolizes or is the criteria for a friendly relationship. What asses! Of course, I straightened them out.

Have you heard from Lo? I imagine she is higher than a kite over her trip.

Thanks for the encouragement in the last letter. I can't wait to become an adult. By the way, you'll have to explain the quote by Eliot about the birds. Sorry! ("Go, go, go, said the bird: human kind cannot bear very much reality.")[7]

Must get going. Write when you can. Miss you.

September 30, Boston

Just got this awful urge to sit in a hayloft on the farm so I thought I'd write. What really provoked the letter was Rachmaninoff.

I have a miserable sore throat and cold. That's why I'm not out tonite. Stayed in and saw the dorm movie, *The Prize*. Next week is *Lolita*. Haven't seen that yet.

You've heard of Dr. Shepard, the man who was accused of killing his wife? Well, his son is a freshman in this dorm. Two of my better friends are out drinking with him tonight. I imagine I'll eventually get to meet him.

Currently I'm worried about my philosophy course. Doesn't seem to be my cup of tea. Would appreciate any tip on how to study that type of thing.

Homecoming weekend is rapidly approaching so I have to start planning for Oct. 15. We're having Charlie Byrd and Astrud Gilberto for a concert. Should be very enjoyable. Well, I must take care of my body so I'd better get to bed. Will continue tomorrow.

September 21, Boston

It's a cold, rainy, ugly Saturday in Boston. I went downtown to see if I could spend some money. Jordan Marsh was complete mayhem because Al Martino was autographing records. My roommate bought oil painting supplies because that's his new hobby. I bought a burgundy poor boy sweater in Kennedy's. I'm gonna frame the register slip. The joys of being "in." Do you think I'm too thin for a mod belt? I think I ought to have one.

Yesterday I received the *Grump* mag you sent. Thanks, but I have that issue. Anna has it right now. Do you want it sent back?

Read the Sept. 23 issue of *The Sun* if you can (Letters to the Editor). Ken wrote an answer, which will probably appear next week. Things could get pretty amusing. Off to dinner. Love, b.

October 2

What's all this about the use of first names? You mean your cohorts believe that if you use a person's first name you automatically become friends?

Have you heard Andy Williams' "When I Hold You in the Arms of Love?" Very, very smooth. Also I am wild about Damita Jo's "If You Go Away."

October 4, West Chester

I can well imagine how you feel about the comments in the *Falcon Flash* concerning student-teacher relationships. I was rather annoyed myself—what happens if I write a reply and give a student teacher's point of view? I could even force myself to be "nice" and honest concerning the blast to new teachers. Over confident—ha! That's a joke! If some students would only know what we go through to become professional.

I think a few teachers and possibly the certain ones referred to in the article should definitely reply and defend themselves. Something's lacking when teachers must "defend" themselves to students for their actions. Can't students think of something more constructive? I'd really like to write a letter to the *Falcon Flash*! It's too bad that the students can help make or break a teacher and for that matter, the whole faculty. 'nuff said!

October 4, Boston

Dear Fragile,

For God's sake, don't resign, although I do agree with your attitude. Just please wait until the end of the year and then please get out. As I have said time again, you do not belong there. Come to Boston University (to be said in a theatrically passionate voice) Meanwhile, cool it!

Thanks for the little gift. Enclosed is me in return. Although it'll probably be miserably smashed, remember the thought.

Right now I'm very depressed and worried about my studies. Plato is getting worse by the day. The pressure to transfer is getting worse. I'm beginning to realize that physical therapy was only a fantasy which also confuses me. Public Communications is becoming more a reality. I need a 2.3 to get in and the way my subjects are going, I'm beginning to wonder about that possibility. As always, "be of good faith…" Will continue later.

Back from the library. I suffered my way through Marx and Plato. I feel completely mentally sterile. The willpower it takes to read *The Republic*!

About the first name stuff—I meant that the attitude was that if a teacher and student became friends one of the prime factors in that relationship was to be able to call the person by their first name. Hope that's a bit more clear. Looks like my communications course didn't sink in.

I've decided to leave the indignation and get my hair cut next week. I always need a few days to build up courage. However, I must prepare for the big social event. Big deal!

Was just thinking that last year at this time I was preparing to come home for my birthday. Then it seemed like I had been here for years. Now it seems as though I've only been here for a few days. I'm not at all sure I like things moving that fast.

Last week in psych. class we were discussing something to the effect that often times we don't have people to share peak experiences with. In other words, to whom do we, or can we go, when we have just had an experience of complete ecstasy. For instance, last year when I first came to college I was so overwhelmed and so perfectly content with my surroundings that I couldn't express the emotion in words. The point is that you were the first person I called because I knew that you would be the one to most appreciate that feeling. I think that's one of the things that we have in our relationship that is so indefinable, and yet so evident. I don't think I'm making myself clear....

October 7, Springfield

I just now realize that I've missed you. (Thanks a whole bunch, huh?) Really, I've been one constant flutter for the last two weeks. I'm finally getting me and my belongings situated. My trunks didn't arrive until Wednesday which caused all sorts of problems. Anyway, my room is beginning to take on that lived-in look. Wish you were here to admire it with me. Rather proud of it.

It's oh-so-good to be back, though actually it seems like I never left. Already I'm two weeks behind—the same old hole I was in last spring. Biology, logic, theater arts, and archery. How does that sound? Building towards a new body and a new mind, although I'm beginning to think my old body and mind weren't so bad after all.

About Arizona. Well, I certainly saw enough of it to know that if I ever got to California, I wouldn't want to come back, although Marsh tells me California is older looking. There's not a shed, house, or building in Phoenix that isn't spanking new. Sort of nice to see a city that is clean and neat. I'm sure I saw all there was to see. Marsh took us out every day, but he was disappointed that we didn't have a full weekend out there. He wanted to take us to Disneyland. He's such a perfect guide; he has a commentary about everything, and funny. Reminds me of how Barry tells about working in the Hershey factory.

Our flight back was beautiful. Land looks sort of funny from 3,000 ft. up, and it looks like that fairyland you always read about above the clouds. The pilot even stopped to talk to Elinor and me. As I left (1 hour before E.) I really felt sorry for her. She looked so alone. And there I was—surrounded by 6 men and seated right behind the pilot room.

You know I really didn't mind saying goodbye to Marsh. It was like I had to make that trip, to see for myself that he was all right, that he hadn't changed, and was happy. Now I'm satisfied that he is all three.

As I gaze out my window, my heart goes all to pieces as I see this neat little white 'Vette zip by. Can you imagine having a white 'Vette on a college campus?

October 8, Boston

Just in from a rather uneventful Sat. night. We doubled (Ken and I)—went to play pool in the Union and then downtown to the Pewter Pot Muffin House. The two girls are pretty "notorious" but we felt like that type tonight. Meanwhile, I got jilted tonight by the girl with the Streisand eyes that I told you about.

It has been a helluva weekend. Last nite I was sick and today lapsed into a fit of miserable depression. I've been waiting for someone to call (even my parents); I expect they will for my birthday. By the way, my number is 267-6600, ex. 454. Sometime when you feel wealthy, call. It's one of those times when I think if I don't get out of this dorm room I'll go crazy.

We were walking down Marlborough St. tonight (with our dates) watching the drunks, prostitutes, and LSD groups when much to my surprise I heard Rachmaninoff blasting out of an apartment window. When I mentioned it, our "In" girls sort of looked at me like I was crazy.

My first test is on Tuesday, biology, no less. Hope I'm in the right frame of mind for studying. We had discussion panels on Malthus and Schopenhauer in Rhetoric last week. By some bit of luck I managed an A-. The professor made a comment that I had good understanding of the philosophers. That was news to me.

We bought a 39-cent frying pan today in Woolworth's. It's a nifty ashtray. Did you read the two letters to the editor in this week's *H-town Sun*? The first one was the laughing stock of the 9th floor today. Believe it or not, I was extremely embarrassed. I have friends who come from small communities like Shaker Heights outside of Cleveland. They assume H-town is the same wealthy suburb-type town. It blew the whole image. I've got to move.

October 9

Dear First-Name-Basis-Friend,

I wore my earrings from the Playboy Club to school on Friday. A number of students commented on them, but the choice remark came at noon from Mrs. Sandel who, after saying she liked them, added that they reminded her of the play *Harvey*.

Tuesday evening I plan to go to the Forum to see John Ciardi, sponsored by HACC. I've seen him before. Good.

How do you like Streisand's "Free Again?"

I selected the play cast which includes Anne Granzow (she is good) and Charles Raisch—romantic lead, good-looking newcomer smoothy who wears Playboy cufflinks and who is not at all abashed by me. Betsy Sandel is the Stage Manager.

Regarding how to study philosophy, just read as much about it as you can. Summaries are excellent (see Will Durant's *Story of Philosophy*). Even encyclopedia information on the philosophers themselves usually is helpful.

You are not too thin for a mod belt. Hope you got one.

You make your point very clear in what you said about our friendship. It is a kind of empathy, a "connection" if you prefer. Who else but you, for instance, could have understood that day we took Kirk to the airport?

October 10, Boston

A beautiful day in Boston. Temp is about 75°. Of course this kind of weather always makes me feel like studying....

That little fiasco in the *Falcon Flash* sure was poor. I don't blame you at all for getting upset. It takes guts for high school kids especially, to write something like that.

October 12

Nice, quiet study hall this year, in my own room. Such a relief after last year.

I wish my whole class could have heard John Ciardi. He said so much of what I (like to think I) try to convey to my students. His topic was "Why Read?" Excellent. He made many allusions to *Hamlet* which we're currently studying. He used "empathy" a lot, implying that no one used the word or has ever heard of it. Surprise! He also stressed vicarious experiences through reading; one example was to know Emma Bovary between the covers of a book rather than just between the covers.

I'll be playing at the Holiday Inn Town and I'm trembling with excitement. Decided on a stage name.

October 14, Boston

Received your picture yesterday. Thank you very much. I felt all kinds of honored and pleased that you would send 2 large as well as 2 smaller ones to me. Both of them are great. I think they perfectly create the image you want. Especially the one with the black dress. The other is more you. At least the "you" I know. I think the one in the white dress would be best for the yearbook. I don't think you should be too daring. Went to Sears today to look for some kind of a frame for one of the big ones. Couldn't get what I wanted so I'll look elsewhere.

Ken was glad to hear you appreciated his article. I've told him a lot about your genius and he's very impressed with you. So coming from him, the comment means a lot.

Tonight is my birthday celebration. Ken has rented a room at the hotel and we're throwing a party for about 10 people. We have champagne (my present, since I've never had any) and J&B Scotch. After we get feeling good we're all going to the all-university float building. Wish you were here to celebrate with us.

I had no classes today so it was fun and games all day. Our building was being dedicated. Meanwhile, my favorite course right now is sociology. Must get to dinner. Will write tomorrow.

October 16, Boston

A rainy, ugly day. The weekend was great. The champagne was very good. We didn't even get thrown out of the hotel. Saturday we lost our Homecoming game 17-14. In the 4th period we were about 5 inches from the goal and time ran out. It was a real disaster.

The concert last night was great. Astrud Gilberto's[8] breathy voice really tears me up. Then there is today. Sociology and biology to read. What a contrast.

I received a gift from Jean yesterday. She likes the idea of your being a cocktail pianist. She "admires" you for it. I like the name you picked out and also agree that it was necessary. Tonite you start at the Holiday Inn Town. I'll be thinking of you. Wish I were there to see your opening night. Maybe you'll be playing somewhere over Thanksgiving or Christmas vacation.

John Ciardi sounds like he's on the ball. Like his poetry. I've been showing everyone your pictures. No one can believe you're a teacher. That's what is so great. Miss you.

October 16, Springfield

Someone asked me if you were a movie star. Someone also asked me if you were my sister. Needless to say, your picture is framed and hanging. I had wanted a wallet size and was thoroughly deluged with the enlarged print. I suppose my admiration is thank you enough.

Holiday Inn Town!! How exciting for you!! I hope over Christmas vacation that I can see you play. I really wish I were around now to share in the fun. I'd even be content to stand outside the spotlight.

I'm interested in hearing whether your sister was thrilled or disappointed with seeing Europe. Someone shot down my expectations of Europe this summer and I keep hoping they were wrong.

Yes, I saw *Arms and the Man* with you. I think it was on my 18th birthday. I wonder what kind of a charm you'll get to correspond with this play. For my theatre arts class I have to read or see a play every week. Perhaps I can come home to see it. While I'm on the subject, what good plays can you recommend for me to read?

John Ciardi. Remember he's the one I wrote home to you about and proceeded to tell you all about him like he was the world's biggest unknown. (Duh) Speaking of names, ever hear of Dr. Dobzhansky?[9]

Gee, I'm having a rough time with my subjects this year. Last year I ate them up. But biology and logic just aren't appealing to a romantic like me. I just can't seem to force myself.

Only thing I've heard about K. is that he flew home the weekend of Oct. 7th. Mail isn't too abundant this year—going either way. Most of it's a lot of poppycock anyway. Well, I wouldn't want to starve myself into a nice figure, so I better get ready for supper.

P.S. Besides the Christmas parade in H-burg, what else is happening Nov. 19? I got lost in your letter.

October 16, Delaware

I thought since I wasn't so keyed to study I would proceed to send my greetings to you out there in the country of South Hanover. I can imagine your view of the valley is spectacular now that fall is upon us.

Things are coming along fine here in Delaware. Nothing has really changed. I am living in an off-campus room and I find I like the quietness of the place. My friends here say the décor is ghastly, but I find it livable and conducive to studying, and that is important.

I have two great courses this term, and one is rather so-so. My history course is probably my favorite—at least the professor is. Zoology for some reason is proving fascinating. I mean I never got excited over the molecular construction of DNA before. As for psychology of adjustment I really am disappointed. But I will bear with it anyway.

It has been a good fall, though. I had the opportunity to return to Union Deposit several weekends ago so that did break the monotony somewhat. Things at home are going rather well and for the time being we will not be moving. Apparently the draft board is after my brother. At any rate the farm is supposed to be sold.....But as I tell Barry after a year and a half of all this who knows and who cares.

I also have sent for applications for transferring. I bet you are saying right now something to the effect that it is about time! My only problem is OWU isn't exactly willing to help. But I consider it my little project of the year. I have no real preference of other schools at this point. Unless a miracle occurs, I hope by next summer to be finished with Delaware, Ohio.

I hope you will write me about yourself. I remain,

Your friend

P.S. I saw an ad in *The Sun* that you were playing somewhere. Is your newest interest working out?

October 18
Dear Barrance,

Kay was full of stories about her trip to Europe. Her movies were like professional travelogues. She brought me an original water color of *The Bridge of Sighs*. Very touching and a reminder of Byron's haunting poem.

We got the new garage doors finally—white with small windows in the center.

October 20, Boston
Well, here I am communicating. Or maybe radiating?

Received your postage due letter today; no problems. I like the folder on Dauphin County. I burned it immediately.

Right now I am taking a break from baby-sitting my dryers. Despise doing laundry.

You received another compliment on your pictures tonite. Of course people can't help but notice them since they're all over the room. I now have a total of 8 different pictures of you. In every one you look different. Eve revisited! Anyhow I was asked who the girl was in the pictures. Quote, "God, she looks glamorous!" He said you look like one of those girls who sing in cocktail lounges. Looks like you've conveyed the image you want. I just keep saying it's a friend back home. The English teacher bit sort of ruins it. Anyhow, it feeds my ego just sitting there. (The picture that is.) Wish I knew what the hell I was saying.

Enclosed is an article you might be interested in. There has been a lot of trouble lately in BU with drugs. FBI investigations—the works. There is a lot of pot circulating in the dorms.

The kid next door just got a raccoon coat. I've decided I have to have one. I want to go down to Goodwill Industry. This weekend.

Certainly am glad you called this week. It's just what I needed. Thanksgiving can't come any too soon. Only 4½ more weeks.

Anna is considering BU for nursing graduate work. I think she'd like it very much.

Found out some reassuring information about the draft. 93% of the college students in Mass. who took the deferment test received above the passing percentage. It was the highest in the country. Says a lot for the caliber students up here and the quality of the colleges. I'm beginning to believe the statement that a degree from a New England or Massachusetts School has a lot of weight. It also means that the competition is very tough. Therefore, a 2.6 at these schools means more than that in another school in another part of the country. I think maybe I am rationalizing!

2:30 a.m. Finally finished with laundry. I don't like Streisand's English version of "Non C'est Rien." Words are too trite.

My sociology prof. made an interesting observation today. If all college students would play the role of an intellect they would be better students. So beware. At Thanksgiving I'll be an intellect. Listen—anything will help. Miss you.

P.S. Got your Krackel bar – thanks.

I CARE!

October 22

What a marvelous letter—full of compliments for me! I loved it. It filled my ego to its zenith. Love to all your friends and you. Just one pin prick which nearly burst my puffed head. After you said all of those nice things you concluded thus—"Wish I knew what the hell I was saying." Did you mean in regard to the whole thing, or just the last part which dealt with my (not) being "your woman?" I got a charge from your statement, "Too bad I can't say 'that's my woman.'" I do believe you're halfway serious. As usual, I'm flattered.

Any luck in finding a raccoon coat?

You're right about colleges in the Northeast. They do have a high rating—a certain "class" as well as academic rating. I had read about the 93% draft deferment. Impressed and reassured.

Your sociology prof is right about students "playing the role" of an intellect. We become the role we begin by playacting. Look what happens to little girls who play house!

Have you seen the Plymouth car ads? So Freudian. Please check (the ads, not me.)

I finally did that obnoxious set of essay tests. Felt very virtuous. Gee, if it is that easy to gain virtue!

October 23

Spent close to four hours this Sunday afternoon on one set of book reports. Two more sets to go yet today.

Have you heard "Winchester Cathedral?" …kind of different. Speaking of different, I prepared a Cornish game hen for dinner. How does that sound?

October 25, Boston

Dear woman, So, I'm a scatterbrain; I was born that way. The article is enclosed this time, honest.

Hey, good news—I got an A- on my sociology mid-term. Happiness is…

While I write this letter I'm eating the last hunk of Krackel bar.

Pressure is still on with mid-terms. The damn GPI determines whether or not I stay with the "in crowd." My Dad thought it would be a good idea to apply to Syracuse just in case. I'd hate like sin to leave BU. You know I'm a social climber (whether that be good or bad). There is just that atmosphere here that I couldn't leave.

My parents gave me the word that I can buy more Farmers Bank stock. Shareholders get some type of option on new issuances of stock. It's up to $40 now. Looks like they're not hurting too bad keeping me in school.

Miss you something terrible right now. Was thinking last night that I don't even think about "home" anymore or the goodbyes. Everything happens so fast.

Here is part of a song from "Fiddler on the Roof" which I think is beautiful and describes my feelings now about us and my life.

Sunrise, sunset, sunrise, sunset,
Swiftly flow the days,
Seedlings blossoming into sunflowers even as we gaze.
Sunrise, sunset, sunrise, sunset,
Swiftly fly the years,
One season following another,
Laden with happiness and tears.

Love, b.

Following is an article by a University senior who expresses his point of view on use of marijuana on campus.

"The **NEWS** plans to publish articles studying the extent and causes of drug use on campus later in the semester, but in the meantime offers this student's opinions for consideration and to open the debate. Campus opinion articles do not necessarily reflect the opinion of the **NEWS** Editor."

"Student pot smoker asserts his preference"

(*Boston University News*, Thursday, October 13, 1966, page 9.)

BY SEBASTIAN DANGERFIELD

Many are the analogies which have been drawn between the problem of pot on today's campuses and alcohol on the campuses of the thirties, and to some extent they are valid. Pot has certainly replaced alcohol as the extra-legal means by which students today carry on their tireless search for "kicks."

Pot is undoubtedly a symbol of rebellion to many of its devotees. In the numerous Dariens[10] and suburbias of present-day America, alcohol has become an accepted part of a teenager's growing-up process. Few parents would be disturbed to learn that their son or daughter had spent Saturday night at a party where drinks were served, but these same parents would be horrified if the drinks were replaced with "joints."

Smoking pot is also a fine way to make friends. Take a few drags and you have a ready-made set of friends, a code language to talk to them with, and a place to go on Saturday night, along with the world or in the lives of our television or cinema heroes, takes on an extra-realistic quality. The intelligent individual who is "high" on pot begins to perceive that we are living in a **prefabricated** world that has been structured to make it as easy as possible for an individual, be he intelligent or otherwise, to accept a role whose basic values he need not question....

To the serious individual who is after more than kicks (or at least kicks of a different sort), and there are many such people, pot is more than a way to lose your inhibitions, to forget about your problems, or to endow your date with a more lenient attitude about spending the evening in bed. It is, purely and simply, a new way to perceive things.

During a good Saturday night drunk, you lose your inhibitions, but this loss is accompanied by a numbness of body and a dullness of mind. While smoking pot, the opposite occurs. You have a heightened sense of perception and your body becomes sensitive to the slightest touch.

Because of a heightened sense of taste, eating becomes much more than a mundane, everyday chore; it becomes a highly sensuous, pleasurable act.

The great value of pot, however, lies in this reoriented sense of perception. *It reduces the logical arrangement of the world around us....*

Certainly in an **ideal** situation we should be able to have this kind of perception without pot. We should be able to explore our own values, to send questions into the recesses of our minds and have the answers come echoing back without needing psychedelic stimulation. But, many of us need something to make this "investigation of consciousness" a bit easier. So we smoke pot. it is not addictive, it is less harmful than alcohol or cigarettes, and it is instructive as well as fun. So we choose, in the words of Timothy Leary, to "turn on, tune in, and drop out."

October 26, West Chester

I applied for a loan and am waiting to hear whether or not it's approved. My uncle said that there's an opening at a brand new high school in the Cumberland Valley district next fall. My father hopes to work in Washington, DC starting January which means he'll only be home weekends and since Walt's at E-town I might live at home until the loan is paid off. At least I'll apply in the Harrisburg area for now and see what happens.

October 27

The last two nights of play practice went much better. Worked on Act II, in which Charles doesn't make an appearance until the end. I felt again like I am working with a real play cast as the other students are such a pleasure to work with. They follow directions, they agree, they smile, and they thank me when I make a suggestion. This evening felt great without Charles' obstinacy and last year's animosity.

In class yesterday I played the Burton *Hamlet*. The contrast is noticeable.

I received a letter from the Dean of Lebanon Valley; they have no openings, but he suggested that I call to schedule an appointment with him.

Good news on your sociology test. Rather whets your appetite, eh? Keep it up!

Yes, I agree on the "Sunrise, Sunset" song. It's frightening how fast things move. Yet in that speed is packed much living and loving. It has always bothered me that it can't be packaged—the past, that is. I want so much to hold on to certain moments, yet they're even more elusive than the sad moments. I'm left with only feelings about things that have happened. Romanticist that I am, I fear that I really only live for those special moments. I find it difficult, sometimes, to become involved in day-to-day living.

Thinking of you.

October 29, Boston

Just finished reading material on Aristotle that I hadn't read yet. My test is on Monday. Methinks I am going to bomb it.

Finally bought a frame for one of your pictures. I can switch them occasionally. You got another compliment today from my R.A., the "big wheel" on the 9th floor. I told him you were my English teacher. His mouth dropped. He wondered why I have a picture "like that." I always end up saying, "We became very close friends." It never fails; they usually look at me and say, "I'll bet." It's really strange.

I met a girl last week at a mixer. I've fallen madly in love. It's disgusting. She's very attractive (big blue eyes), intelligent, Jewish and wealthy from Long Island. Can't see her this weekend because her parents are up for mommy and daddy weekend. Parents here are swarming all over the place.

Only 3 weeks and 3 days until Thanksgiving. Anything interesting at the Arena House over vacation? I'll be home the evening of the 22nd. I'll probably see you Wed. after school at your place.

Just like summer today in Boston at 71°. Anna wrote and said Kirk was home last weekend. Did he stop in at your place?

Hope play practice is improving. Hope Mr. Big[11] has settled down or improved. Please send me dates of the play. I forget what they were. Are you having an opening night party this year? Wish I could be there. Sort of makes me all kinds of nostalgic.

Maybe we can go to The Beachcomer[12] again during vacation. Trouble is, it's so damn expensive.

I got the supreme compliment this week, "You dress well for a hick." That assessment came from a New York (White Plains, the #1 Machismo Place) "In" person.

Nothing else really new. Hope you're managing to get yourself out from under the pile of papers.

Heard anything from the colleges?

Love,

The Intellectual

October 31, Springfield

The big week-end is over! Mother, Elinor, Emily and Leon arrived Friday night around ten. We went out for coffee and talked awhile. Saturday morning I showed them the campus and around S-field. We had lunch with Jeff, my friend. Elinor needed sunglasses, so that meant a trip downtown. We got back in time for the football game with number one arch-rival, Ohio Wesleyan! It was Leon's first football game. Imagine! We won (27-0). I showed them my room and later they returned to the motel to rest.

In the meantime, the most exciting thing in any whole college career happened to me. Three boys stumbled into my room! I was on the phone talking to Jeff. The door was open and people were wandering in and out. Three guys, going down the hall, asked where room 305 was. Someone answered, "around the corner" to which I added, "but we have cookies and cake in this room."

That's all I needed to say. I had three guys sitting in my lap. It was pretty funny because everyone came in to see them and my room isn't much bigger than the one I had in the Poconos. In the confusion, the cookies dropped all over the floor and the telephone cord got all wound around. My bed was heaped with things Mother had brought out. And that shaft of wheat you gave me, that had been hanging on the wall, fell. They literally ransacked the room, trying to get in or out, while I sat back and laughed at the whole state of confusion.

Later, while I was cleaning up, two of the guys came back. They wanted to look out my window. Sure they did, but they were just having fun and I played along. Anyway, someone, out of deep concern for my welfare, went and "told" an RA. Which teaches me a lesson—thinking makes it so. They thought it was terrible of me, and so it was terrible of me. And they spoiled my fun and I think that is criminal.

That night Leon took us out to dinner. Sunday we went to chapel and dinner afterwards. Such a long trip for such a short visit, but I'm so glad they came (esp. Mom). I had promised myself this weekend last year at Homecoming. And my family "done me proud;" everyone looked so nice.

And if Saturday night's experience with the 3 guys wasn't enough, Sunday night's was even better. Every year the Phi Psi fraternity goes through the girls' dorms at Halloween spooking the heck out of them. These guys really go out of their way to look horny. Ugly, green, scarred, candle-dripped faces and clutching hands and unearthly moans that drive nails up and down your spine. Nothing fakey about it. I screamed along with the rest of them. You can hear them progress through the dorm as the blood-curdling (and that's exactly what it is), blood-curdling screams get louder. So that anybody with an ounce of imagination is in a highly excitable state by the time they pass by their rooms.

I'm not sure from where I gathered my courage (or insanity, if you wish), but I was going to take a picture of them. I stood in the middle of the hall in order to get a good shot. They kept coming closer, but I just couldn't push the button. By this time I couldn't even scream. Somebody must have pushed me into a room, I don't remember. I do remember looking up and this horrible freak came right into my room. I never expected that. He walked right over to me and then there was this brilliant flash of light. If I was ever close to fainting, it was then. Of course, they didn't dare lay a hand on me, but just the same, it might as well have been out and out rape. That's what I call a thrill!

Found out later that the light was a home movie camera. Great. Just real great. It was nice to know that the guys didn't escape without some casualties. In North Hall, one guy was grabbed and thrown in the shower. On our first floor, one guy was jumped and held till Mrs. S., our house mother, was called. She's a real fuddy-duddy about 60 years old, but a good joe nevertheless. She played the part to the hilt. She terrorized the heck out of the guy. They said he was so red and so hot, you couldn't touch him. I wouldn't have been in his place for anything. What had started out as a harmless joke ended up ruining his whole college career, or so the poor guy probably thought.

November 3, Texas

It was great to hear from you, and now, especially, since I haven't received any mail for about a week. Getting a "first timer" like your letter makes mail call even more eventful.

I've got to tell you about my ex-girl now! Things went on as usual for about a week after I came back to Texas. Then one day we went shopping together and tensions were gradually building up inside of me. We then went out to dinner and on our way out of the restaurant I bought a *Playboy* magazine. We drove to her house and sat in the car; talked for a while. Still sitting in the car, I pulled out my *Playboy* and started to look at—but not read—it! She got just a bit mad and said that I was too young to have a book like that. Well, that about did it. What an opportunity to start a fight, so I did, she was gone, and finis! We haven't seen each other since. Even though I don't love her I think of going to see her again, well, even a thief returns to the scene of his crime quite often! Enough "True Confessions" for right now.

How are you and your brilliant young students getting along? So you're doing *Hamlet*. Shenfeld hated that kind of stuff, he always complained about it. But come to think of it he complains about everything. The last letter I had from him he said he's coming here to see me, but I doubt it. The next leave I take will probably be late in May. I want to be home for Mary's graduation. I hope she can get me a ticket, or maybe you could swing it. That's officially asking a favor of you.

It's getting late now and I guess my sergeant will be wanting to touch me in, so words end here.

Militarily yours, Jon
P.S. Grammatically, too many I's in this letter, but it's not error. It's conceit!

November 6, Springfield

And how is my world?
Funny you should ask.
As frustrated as your world.
Isn't it a gas!!!

Like to compare notes, chum? …to bring my account up to date, it's about these three disturbed hours of sleep I had and this one cold fish dinner I should not have had. But even better than that, there was the joy and the delight of counting one-hundred and thirty-two FRUIT FLIES over ten times in order to separate the dumpy-winged Drosophila from the wild-typed Drosophila, remembering **not** to breathe on them and **not** to squash them and **not** to entangle them in the culture media and **not** to, MOST OF ALL, let them escape, while remembering to count them (the original task) and how to distinguish dumpy from wild and to re-etherize them occasionally but **not** enough to kill them. And managing to live though that delightful experience, I went on to count each and every individual kernel of corn on a cob to discover which of the purple full waxy were really purple shrunken starchy.

But wait! There's more! With my trusty little knife, I hacked away at a fragile little bean, made chromosomal maps and worked out genetic problems and graphed the dosage of radiation lethal to 50% of the population of wheat and barley plants and made Chi-squares and recounted my corn kernels. And then for fun, I planted six little beans in a cottage cheese container, filled it with sand, and took it "home" to make a day by day report of the progress and growth of a bean plant. So after spending from 11:30 to 5:30, a total of six delightful hours in the bio lab all day, I rush "home" with my planted bean pot, grab my ID, rush over to the Union (just as they are closing the doors), gulp down my cold fish dinner with a lump, only to rush back to my dorm and fall ker-plunk on my bed.

Your letter that I received today was timely. Nothing like another frustrated individual to pull yourself out of your own frustrations. Which is not to say I am using you, but to say you are helping me. Let's face it; we need each other to climb out of this "frustrated" world-pool-like whirlpool. I'm not sure if you wanted me to comment or not on your letter. If, in fact, you did, I do have some comments to make. In fact, I had a whole page full of comments which I promptly tore up.

Thanks for the booklets. Do appreciate. Was really surprised to wake up last Wednesday morning and find snow on the ground. We have such a pretty view from our big picture window. Blithe spirit that I am when the snow doth fall, I fairly flew through the day.

By the way, I pulled a B- by "the skin of my teeth" in our first logic test. Biology and theatre arts test coming up this week. Were any of the comments in the *Falcon Flash* yours? It was interesting; I could have probably picked out a teacher for each comment.

This Pancake Dinner the choir is having is too much. You're going, of course. I'd love to be around school now; I can just hear the remarks made. Who do you suppose the Choir's own Miss Pancake could be? Pancakes are good, but there is always so much syrup, I get sick to my stomach. Do you find this so? So unfortunate for both of us.

I sent away for some pencils with "Lo-Babes" printed on them in gold! I know. You'd like me to save one for you!

Oh, would you do me a large size favor? Please and thank you. I need the dimensions of the LD stage. Like depth, height, width, and any other statistics that are readily available. Do you think you could get them from Mr. Fickes for me? Have to design a set for theatre arts class.

Well, if I can find myself out of this mess I'm in, I'll do some of my logic problems. I really should do some studying. I mean that's what college life is all about, isn't it? "Study and think. Study and think. Remember JTB, and study and think.[13]

November 7, West Chester

Thanks for the *Falcon Flash*. Can't say too much concerning the faculty column.

Jane wrote and said she's going to come to PA along with Pam over Christmas vacation. Haven't seen Pam for a year.

My parents came down yesterday—they had to pick up the youngsters near Media at a train station. It seems that they and another couple spent the weekend in NYC. Must be nice!! At least they stopped in West Chester **before** they picked up the crew. Was too upset to ask any details as to why my brother was allowed to spend money going there! Did I tell you that he's switching to pre-med to become a vet?

November 7, Boston

I'm currently engrossed in *Neuroses and Human Growth* by Karen Horney. What an abortion to good reading! – all 380 pages worth which I was supposed to have read for tomorrow. HELP! I'm on only chapter 4.

Well, mid-terms didn't turn out too bad. As of Nov. 4th my GPI is 2.56. Possibly I can raise that somewhat with finals. However, it isn't as bad as I had feared.

Things are really loused up for T-giving. As it looks now I won't be home until late Wed. evening of the 23rd. Don't know when I'll get to see you. Probably Thurs. sometime unless you go home. I hope not. In any case, I'll call you Wed.

I've been in a much better humor lately since all the tests are past. At long last I had a date with Jan last Friday night. Thursday of this week I hope to see *Marat/Sade*. Possibly over the weekend *Holly Golightly* with Mary Tyler Moore and Richard Chamberlain. Not sure if I can get tickets for that yet.

My roommate is out partying tonite. He decided to splurge and party on a week night for a change. He'll be sorry this weekend. We have off Veteran's Day so it'll be a long one.

I guess by now you're buried with work from school and the play. Hope the play is going OK. It's the only good play that school has per year. You got a comment on your choice of the play by the "right" person up here. Color you complimented! I'm thinking of you.

I'd better get back to neuroses. Sorry the letter is so short but I just wanted you to know I CARE.

Love, b

November 9

I made two cast changes Monday night. I removed friend Charles from *Arms and the Man*. Completely took him out; he was, you may recall, the lead. Jack Brandt is taking that role now, and Tom Hughes is taking Jack's role. Rehearsal went beautifully last night without Charles.

Just now saw paper dresses advertised at Pomeroy's. It was only Monday night that I threw away the order form for ordering one for myself from New York. I'm so glad now, that I didn't order one. It would have been a novelty from NY, but not from Pomeroy's.

Brendan Behan's *The Hostage* is playing at the Arena House on Nov. 23rd. Shall I make reservations? Or would you prefer *Zhivago*? Can't remember if you've seen it yet.

Parent Visiting Night is next Monday. It always hits the week of the play. Also grades are due and report cards go out.

My pantry shelves were nailed in place last night. Delighted!

I have an interview at LVC next Wednesday. Kids in the play are going to Hershey High today to try to be fit into military uniforms they have.

I am enclosing a copy of an underground newspaper, printed outside of school by a group called the Blue Guard. I think it's a fine idea. Another neat announcement on the Daily Bulletin was that seniors will be allowed into the football game at the stadium Friday night as guests of the Athletic Association.

November 11, Boston

Hurray for Veteran's Day!! Read some biochem this afternoon. Of course, I don't understand a damn thing I read. Well what's another C-? Check the picture enclosed of the *B.U. News* Editor. People wonder why the news is so radical this year. Who bases intelligence on appearances?

Finally received a letter letting me know that everything is still under control at Wesleyan. I guess he'll break the news about transfer to his father over vacation. There is some talk about Penn State and U. of Pennsylvania.

Currently I'm struggling with some unknown disease. I went to a lab yesterday for tests. Won't know the results until about next Wed. Cripes! Till then I could die. Doctor says possible kidney or urinary tract infection. That's all I need now. Meanwhile they haven't given me anything for back pain so I'm going to start eating Excedrin.

Tonight I go see *Holly Golightly*; will continue this letter when I return.

2:00 a.m. The show was very enjoyable. The trouble is I'm now very confused because of it. As usual, I wish you could have been with me. As soon as the overture began I got the chills up my spine which I haven't felt for a long time. I'm very tired so I'll explain when I continue the letter tomorrow.

Saturday. An ugly day with rain. Didn't do any work today. We didn't get up in time for dinner so we wasted time going out. Then, as we do every Sat., we cleaned the room.

Last night I got that old feeling that I could really be something in the legitimate theatre. However, I don't think I have enough guts to try. Who knows what will happen.

Tonite will be spent studying. If I soon don't get out of this dormitory, I'm going to go crazy. It's a real morgue this weekend since everyone went home for the long weekend. Only 10 more days – P.S. I got you a *Playbill*.

Love, b.

November 12, Delaware

Feel terribly raunchy this afternoon. Can't study—or should I say I am not in the mood to study zoology so I thought I would rationalize, which convinced me I could write you a letter.

If I remember correctly this is the week of final play practices in preparation for Saturday night. I was trying to think how it would turn out. Instead I will just say I hope the performance is up to your expectations.

I still have one more bluie—zoology, before I can start traveling back to Pennsy. Then, too, I have this damn research paper for psychology. I have taken n^{th} number of notes in OWU's libes. In fact, I am finished there except to look in Vital Statistics of our country. So consequently I will have to go to Ohio State U. in hopes they have more pertinent information on my subject.

So those two things plus other incidental scholastic things have kept me going through this dull and cold month. I also have been tutoring this sixth grader, a project of the OWU YMCA. I doubt that he and I will accomplish much (A pathetic soul who is flunking currently math, English, spelling and heavens knows what else!) but it is a change of pace for this one.

I also am in a Thursday night discussion group in Columbus made up of Wesleyan and Ohio State students. It is very interesting and fulfills my need of stimulating conversation which is rare on college campuses.

In your last letter you mentioned the *Falcon Flash* in which several students voiced their opinions regarding the faculty. When I was home Lee showed me the issue and I was amazed/shocked myself. I couldn't believe the kids would be allowed to say such crap.

I'm sorry but I had to laugh when I read that the choir is having a pancake dinner. That was Maggie's favorite project when I was in choir, except we refused to have one. Obviously she has her new children around her thumb and the administration, too.

I guess the news of my transfer has spread near and far by now. I still hope to go through with it. By now, I have adjusted to the fact that I must, although every once in a while I get these pangs of conscience that I shouldn't go. But don't panic, I will!

I am now a sophomore in college because I am not as keyed as I was last year at this time. Now, it is just a time to forget one's studies for a while which I can't deny is appealing at this point.

My psychology course is finally "coming around" so that I can enjoy it like I wanted to. The term is turning out quite well for me except the old accumulation won't be what I had hoped for with the usual A's.

Thanks for the goodies in the last letter.

P.S. I like your yellow mail box.

November 13

After a victory over Middletown Friday night, upon its return to LD the band marched through the halls of the school!

We held rehearsal this afternoon. Those who weren't on stage were cutting out large letters to spell "The Falcons Fly Highest" and we pinned them to the green stage curtains.

Big field trip to the State Library on Tuesday. On Wednesday I'll accompany a group on the ACES trip. Mr. Croll will be worry-warting all day, yet efficient with this field trip.

November 19, Boston

Your play is now over. Sincerely hope everything went OK. I imagine you're still partying with the cast. (Sorry; couldn't resist.) With taking a lead role and saving the day, Hughes must be even more unbearable now. He sure is the life of the party!

I write this letter with very confused emotions. I'm very anxious to go home, very apprehensive about a bio test next Tuesday, laden with nostalgia of the days of the Senior Class play with you. This semester has undoubtedly been the most confused period of my life besides my Senior year and my renaissance after the "church days."

Well, whenever you're down and out, the only way is up. New axiom I heard, "Whenever life hands you a lemon, make lemonade." Came from a psych. lecture. Speaking of psychology the Plymouth car commercial (sorry, ad) is Freudian.

I flunked my last bio quiz. Next week isn't going to be any better since it's right before vacation. That always louses me up. Unfortunately, I have seen *Dr. Zhivago*. We'll think of something else to do. The movie is great. Please try not to miss it.

I hope to talk to you about a few things over vacation. Depends on my mood while I'm home. If

I'm too busy trying to see everyone you know what will happen. Must control myself!! I also must do some social sciences. See you next Thursday (maybe Wed.).

Love, B.

November 20

Just a note here about the play. Would you believe that the bed fell apart in the first ("opening night") performance???? (You don't think Charles rigged it, do you?) Thank heavens the cast just did some ad libbing until they got back "on book." The audience went along with it, thank heavens. Frankly, I am still laughing (and grateful); the cast really were together, a well-oiled machine, relieved without Charles.

Arms and the Man Cast

November 26, Springfield

Just a note while I'm sitting here at the desk in the lobby. My roommate hooked this paper. This place is really swinging this week-end. There must be something like five girls left in the dorm. I know I'm the only one on my floor. Norm and Lin next door left me their AM-FM radio (to keep me company) with a note and two oranges. Went to see *Lilith* Thursday night. Fairly good movie. Wednesday night I went to Vespers. One of the most beautiful Thanksgiving services I've ever seen. Thanksgiving Day I gorged myself with shrimp cocktail, turkey, dressing, potatoes, and gravy, salads (Waldorf and tossed), and pumpkin pie and strawberry short cake, and fruit and nuts. I really didn't eat all that—just a little of each.

Other than that, nothing exciting has happened since I talked to you Sunday night, except I added a new specimen to my biological collection—water fleas or Daphnia as scientists prefer. I'm not sure if I live in a room or a lab anymore. I know I have trouble finding my bed at night. Hope I get some mail today. By the way, I'm now officially an English major. Next term I have geology, English novel, and Themes & Traditions (required course). I have a feeling I let myself have it. Can you imagine the reading?

I'm now engaged in a royal battle with the Registration Dept. over the conversion from the old to new system. I think I'm being cheated in credits. Tell you about it at Christmas. Got a letter from Elinor this week. Now I understand what you meant about Paul and all. Mother still hasn't said much about Christmas. Talked to her Thursday. Gee, I wish it would snow today. Well, bye.

November 26, Texas

I really enjoyed that little school spirit builder you sent to me. What really made me bust a gut was those "flushed proverbs," and "Where is Homer Plummer." It is about time that not so everyday occurrences take place around that dull funeral parlor of a school.

Remember when your class was doing ballads? It was about the time I was home on leave. I confess that I had a hand in writing Mary's ballad. We never did anything like that in our business English classes. It seemed that we hardly ever diverted from the nouns, pronouns, and all that common junk. It seems that you always have new and fresh ideas for your classes; even when you taught 9th grade English your classes were always interesting. Enough with the compliments already! I don't want you to get a big head.

It's about to rain so I better get to the post office. Write back soon. Almost forgot to ask, what is the exact date of Commencement?

P.S. Heard from John. Still complaining. Writes a lot about Mary, but don't tell her!

November 28, State College

I'm sorry I haven't gotten in touch with you before this. Beaver and I had planned to get over to see you before I came up to school, but we didn't get to it. Maybe we can get over during my Christmas vacation, and you can finally get to see Lori.

She is growing so much now and always changing, for the better. I only get home on the weekends, and she's cuter every time. I've been reading some books this term. Not especially superb classical literature, but I have been reading. I've gone through about six or seven novels and paperbacks. I also look through the "New York Times Book Review" to see what sort of books are coming out. I even find some that I might enjoy reading, but I can't really afford to pay at least $5.00 for a book. It's bad enough paying for text books.

Classes are going fairly well this term. I expect to get anything from a 2.00 to a 2.73. If I want a 2.73, I'll have to do a lot of work before finals, and this is the eighth week. But I still do have a chance. Beaver is going to start taking classes at HACC in January. She has a strong yearning to go to college. I believe some of it is to show people that she does have the ability and intentions to go to college. Sometimes it makes me glad and sometimes it makes me sad, but if that's what she really wants, there is no reason for me to stop her.

I hope we get to see you before Christmas; however, if we don't, let me take the opportunity now to wish you a "Merry Christmas and Happy New Year." We'll try to get over before Christmas.

November 28, Kentucky

To start things off I am sorry I didn't write before this but I am pretty busy down here and you can believe that. I don't know for sure if you will get this letter or not because I don't know your address but I hope you do.

How are you doing with school and how is good old LD coming along? Are you keeping the coronet polished up? I sure hope so!

Just about the only things we ever do down here is think about home and things that we used to do! Like going to school and fooling around.

I remember your English class very well. Are they still as cool as they were? Don't forget to write before Christmas or I won't be here. I'll be home for Christmas and after that who knows.

Did I tell you before I left that I was getting married at Christmas. Yep.

You wouldn't believe the haircuts they give you down here. The first time I got my hair cut I got a sore throat and a cold and besides that it feels and looks funny.

The food down here is worse than LD. I heard LD beat M-town this time in football.

I just got back from a pretty full day. I got up at 5:30 and just got back and it is now 12:30 at night and man, am I ever tired.

Right now I've got to clean my rifle before I can go to bed so I better get with it. So I'll say Good bye and God bless you always.

Remember Dorty.

November 29, Springfield

It's six o'clock in the morning. Still very dark out. And it's snowing. Guess I'm a real jerk, huh? But I was sitting here looking out the window and I wanted to remember to tell you not to forget to shake your fir trees off this winter when it snows so the limbs won't break. This will make two snowfalls and it's only November.

What really bugs me is that we can't get out of this building until seven o'clock and have to be back in by eleven. I never get a chance to walk in the snow at the best times. I bet you never knew how much I prowled Park Avenue at nights, did ya? That's all right, neither did my Mother.

I think I'll marry the first man who says, "I hate summer," not that I hate summer. But if he hated summer then he'd really have to love winter. How's that for a piece of logic?

Guess that's all I wanted to tell you. The snow has stopped. We accumulated about 3 or 4 inches. Enough to satisfy me. Seemed strange swimming on such a day. Want to go to the library, so I'll mail this on the way. Don't forget about the fir trees.

December 1, Boston

My biochem lab test today was impossible. It was so bad I started laughing hysterically in the middle of it. I've done that once before. It was actually absurd. Tonight to relieve some of the tension a bunch of us went downtown to see the Commons and Jordan Marsh. It was fun playing with the toys. The city is unbelievably beautiful at Christmas. Still no snow though. I also got tickets for *The Messiah* next weekend. Very excited about that.

As usual these three weeks until Christmas will be hell. I'm locking myself up this weekend. HELP!!! I'll be home the 16th sometime late afternoon. Over Christmas if you're playing anywhere I'll maybe get to hear you. Things won't be as hectic!

Hate to think of classes tomorrow.   Love, b.

Chapter 8 Endnotes:

1.   Almond bars were featured on the card.
2.   Their apartment building.
3.   A reminder again that this was a time before grade inflation.
4.   The front of the house is romanticism (usually the most attractive area); the back porch is realism (typically utilitarian); the garbage can, particularly the inside contents, is the underside of life, the naturalism.
5.   I was playing at supper clubs for my own entertainment as well as the extra earnings.
6.   A British film with leading actors John Mills, Michael Caine, Ralph Richardson, 1966.
7.   This means that humans don't see what we don't want to see.
8.   "The Girl from Ipanema."
9.   "Nothing in biology makes sense except in the light of evolution," an evolutionist/biologist.
10.   Referring to Darien, Connecticut (and all other towns similar to this, meaning "across America")
11.   Charles Raisch, new to the school, a maverick, a handsome "lady's man."
12.   It opened circa 1963.
13.   This is being quoted from an ode I wrote for this class, "Upon the Graduation of Friends."

Chapter 9

Changing

January 1967 to December 1967

The things that I could see I now can see no more

Intimations of Immortality
Wordsworth

January 7, Springfield

I find it hard to begin this letter. Letter writing requires one to be selective, yet so much has happened since I last saw you that I'm at a loss as to where I should begin.

You might be happy (for me) to know that I'm on the right track heading in the right direction once again. Ta Da! With two English courses, I'm on familiar ground and happy to be so. They appeal more to my romantic nature. Hmmm. In fact, my one professor won my heart over the very first day when he declared he was a romantic and felt the world would be better off if more people were likewise. (Something you don't often hear.) I absolutely love the course, in spite of the torture of getting up for an eight o'clock every morning.

My other English course is British Novels. Taught by Dr. Merrill, who is forever smiling. It's nauseating to see him smile so. The other nauseating thing is Samuel Richardson's *Pamela*. It is a five word novel: virtuous, innocent, dutiful, humble Pamela. Ugh.

As for geology, it's half-bearable. I'm in love with my geology lab instructor, Bob Minning (the very way he introduced himself). Dr. Thomas Gerrad is our lecturer, also very young. So as you see, I'm very satisfied with my courses and am anxious to do well in them. The time I spend on them is unbelievable. I've done nothing else this past week except read. I haven't even written my mother as of yet.

I got a postcard from Elinor (from Nassau) this week. She said she thought of me and how much I'd enjoy Nassau. How I hate her and I can hardly wait to hear every detail.

My own adventure to Jeff's was memorable. I got sick (sick, sick) in her driveway. I had such a headache on the bus, I thought for sure I was dying. Which doesn't make me any too anxious to come home this Easter. Just the word "bus" makes me vehemently ill. As for my first train ride, I thoroughly enjoyed it. I flitted from car to car in a manner unlike me. We had arrived at the station none too early and hopped on (if you can imagine me hopping on with my bag and baggage) as the train was pulling away—the novel way of boarding a train.

After much ado, we finally plopped ourselves down beside two service men. No sooner had we settled ourselves when the conductor fell "kerplunk" in my lap as the train made a great "kerbam." The incident aroused the laughter of the whole car and I blushed. If we hadn't drawn enough attention to ourselves already, Jeff then decided she wanted to find some guy she knew would be on this train. So we went traipsing back some ten cars (being thrown from one person, or wall, to another!) whereupon I was asked for my ticket by some frightfully mean old man; this meant retracing all my graceful steps. When I finally joined up with Jeff again, she had found her friend and I BRAVELY decided to go on exploring by myself.

When I got to the club car (with my virtue still intact, for the train was swarming with service men and college guys), I felt I had gone far enough. But Jeff decided she wanted one more glass of wine before she left New York State. So back to the club car. As we were buying our drinks, some guy (an Army captain) made some smart remark to us to which I smartly answered back and we struck up an acquaintance. So there we were drinking, laughing, and composing poetry. It was New Year's Eve all over again. We stayed with them for quite a while until they asked us to join them in their cabin, whereupon we promptly fled. We're both so unbelievably brave—to a certain extent. On the whole it was a great adventure and I hated to get off the train.

Then there's New Year's Eve. Fun, but hardly what I had in mind. In fact, would you believe I spent New Year's Eve singing "Nearer My God to Thee" in an $80,000[1] home (built on a mountain overlooking an Indian reservation) that had a swimming pool in its basement and toilets with warm water rinse (no toilet paper necessary). Yes, there was your Lois Mae singing her heart out with a church book in her hand, neatly snowed under. Every time I turned around these kind-hearted, well-meaning people kept filling my wine glass.

Jeff has got to have the most remarkable friends I have ever encountered. How I ever fit in among them makes me wonder.

Forgive me if I rattled on so about my last adventures. I feel rather like Pamela and her letters, but the people I met were such delightful talkers I had to share them with somebody who would be interested in my point of view.

January 9, Boston

9:15. (Help!) As finals approach the days get longer and the nights become much too short. I begin to wonder if I'll ever make it to the 17th.

Received your notes; thanks, they are very helpful and very, very much appreciated. You're always there...

Nothing exciting has been happening except that Boston police found $5,000 worth of drugs in our Union one day and $1,000 the next. It is becoming a well-known fact that B.U. is becoming one of the biggest distribution centers in Boston for the "stuff." Harvard still has the corner on the market. Needless to say, B.U. is crawling with Federal agents. Sure is exciting to be in the middle of things.

I'll be home the 17th. Make reservations for *Zhivago* for Wed. or Thurs. of that week if you can. Dale might be coming down that weekend. I'm anxious for you to meet her.

January 10, Boston

Tomorrow is our first exam and finally I have become panic stricken. It's the test on *Major Barbara*: one essay, an open book.

Have a chance to go to New York and Washington the first 3 days of Intersession. If you can hold out on the *Zhivago* tickets, do. My plans are not yet definite. If you have already ordered or picked up the tickets and can, cancel them. If you can't cancel, let me know and I'll be home. After all, either way, Washington or *Zhivago* will be very enjoyable.

Shocked myself tonight. I was discussing this situation with friends and found myself hesitating about telling them, when they asked, who was getting the tickets. I told them Carol. I can't figure out for the life of me why. Ken guessed who, since he knows Carol is in Richmond. Damn that confuses me! If only I could straighten out my feelings on us! Well, such is life. Must study. Love, b.

January 11, Fort Dix, New Jersey

I just received your letter today. I guess it took a pretty long time for it to get transferred up here. By the way, I am back in school again up here in Fort Dix.

I finished Basic about a month ago and now I am here for training. (Some fun. But not my idea of it.) I don't have a fiancée anymore. She is now my wife and a private secretary at Dauphin Deposit and Trust Co. in Harrisburg.

You said it's hard for you to imagine how I look with short hair. How do you think I felt every morning when I looked in the mirror to shave.

Since you are an English teacher, you should hear some of this language. You wouldn't believe it because I don't.

Things are starting to get easier. In two weeks I'll be getting my orders to go to my permanent unit. It will probably be in Germany. I hope, because if I don't go to Germany the only other place they are sending guys is to the rice patties of Viet Nam. And I sure don't want to go there.

Sometime when I get home I am going to stop at school and try to see you. I hope you don't mind. Well, I better go for now. I hope you can write again soon.

January 11, West Chester

I finally have a few minutes to take time to write—sure has been hectic around here. My most wonderful experience is almost over. I'm finding it hard to accept the fact that I have to pack all my belongings and leave friends and students behind at Sun Valley.

I want to tell you about the boner I pulled last week. My 5th period health class (the whifty ones) were trying to get the best of me so I figured it was time to lay down the law. I went into the classroom early and gave everyone the eyeball as they noisily walked in. When all were seated I walked slowly over to the door. Thought that slamming the door would give the effect of disturbance. I pulled the door and slammed it on my left index fingernail!!! At this point I didn't know whether to scream due to the agonizing pain, go to the nurse, examine the fingernail myself, calmly begin teaching about the nervous system, or else finish giving the class hell.

But believe it or not—they're my favorite health class and it really makes me mad when they are the center of complaints in the faculty room.

I am taking my co-op out to dinner Tuesday night. It's a West Chester student teacher tradition if the co-op proved to be tremendous. Mrs. Mawby is tops as far as I'm concerned and she certainly made student teaching something I'll never forget.

Write—all mail greatly appreciated!

January 13

Dear Barry/Mary Martyr,

You wrote: "If you can't cancel, let me know and I'll be home."

You wrote: " —either way, Washington or *Zhivago* will be very enjoyable."

What I am saying in response is, "Go ahead to NY & DC, silly. Just don't be so dramatic about it. It's fine; we can go to the movie any time."

I sensed a disaster as soon as I saw two letters from you, one being Air Mail. I just hope this reaches you in time to allay your fears.

Further, don't worry about straightening out your feelings for me.

On a lighter note, the LDHS Talent Show will be held this afternoon. It promises to be pretty good. However, every time I see a talent show I picture you sitting on a park bench there on stage....

I had hoped to see Captain Bill this evening. Now, when he calls I'll have to tell him I can't meet him as I am going up home. I think I feel more embarrassed than anything.

I'm also terribly upset about Bill Peck. The end is in sight. There's a benefit basketball game here for him tomorrow night. He so wants to make an appearance. If he's able (which is doubtful) he'll be brought by ambulance. I don't think I could bear to see that. I've been crying over that unfairness—that such a virile life be wasted to that. My God, he's only in his late 20s.

Forgive me! I'm a bit distraught. See you when you get home.

Love, J.

January 1967, Fort Worth

Things around here are fairly dull during the week, but lately, on weekends, I manage to make the scene in Fort Worth, Texas, and, believe me, that's where the action is! While I'm down there on weekends, I stay at my buddy's house. Two weeks ago when I was down there I met a cute girl. We went out New Year's Eve and had a blast. She is a freshman in college and (get this) she majors in ENGLISH. I broke the news to her that I was just a dirty old GI, but, ah ha! it turned out that her father had just retired from the Air Force as a Major. All in all, the whole thing is pretty great, and by the way, guess where I'm going this weekend. You guessed it. Fort Worth.

I haven't heard from John in a while. I think he's teed off at me. I was supposed to send him

Mary's graduation picture. I wrote the letter and told him, here's the picture. Well, would you believe I forgot to put the picture in the letter. I haven't heard from him since.

January 14, Springfield

Tonight is odds and ends night, so guess where that puts you? What a week this has been study-wise. Next Friday we have our first test already! I can't get used to the idea. I finally finished *Pamela, or Virtue Rewarded*. It presents a rather interesting theme, how to get a Mercedes without really trying. I figure if she can do it, I can, too. Hang on to my virginity, and sell it in the highest market.

Next we turn to *Shamela* and *John Andrews*. These satires should be more to my liking—cool and cutting. Did I tell you I found a book called *The Fat Little Girl*. I had to buy it. Pictures in it are terrific.

I was thinking tonight if I'm real good and lose ten more pounds, I'll treat myself to a trip to Dayton sometime. Wish Kirkus was still around. Would love to go to Columbus. Looking for things to do to counteract the studying.

Last night I saw *Rebel Without a Cause* for the tenth time. I have to laugh; that really sounds like evidence that I'm studying, doesn't it? Would you send me the guys' addresses? I would like to send them a valentine.

I remember that I wanted to tell you about this co-ed gym class I got myself into. At the time we were registering, I thought it sounded like a nice idea. It wasn't until we met in our first class that I realized what a fool I had been. Bowling and billiards. Seems I never in my life had picked up a bowling ball. A perfect chance to make a perfect fool of myself in front of some of the most suave guys on campus. Well, I didn't do too badly making a fool of myself. Only slipped and fell as I was releasing a ball. How dumb. But I picked myself up, dusted myself off, and rolled 2 strikes in a row. I thought, "There!"

It's really ugly and cold out now. I wish summer was here, so bad. I keep thinking of cruises in the Caribbean, Latin American music, and warm summer sun and cool moonlight breezes. Elinor said in her last letter that she thinks I should go if I ever can scrape up the money and she was putting in her application early to go as a companion.

January 18, Kentucky

Well, it's time for some more letter writing since we have the rest of the day off. I finally got my orders and you guessed it; they are for Viet Nam. We leave about the end of February. Today we had special classes on Viet Nam. They said we are supposed to get about a 15 day leave before we go, but it's not for sure yet. But they better arrange it or I know about 500 guys that will be AWOL and I'll be one of them.

How are things at LD? I heard the faculty basketball team made some money for Mr. Peck's hospital bills. I think that was real nice of the school to do that. How is Mr. Peck?

I guess I told you Hoke was in the Navy Reserves and right now he is at the Great Lakes for a month and the way his mother talks he hates it. But wait till he has to go for his two years. He won't know what to do.

Well, I guess that's about it for now. I hope I get a chance to stop at school before I go but if I don't, good luck and God bless you always.

January 20, Springfield

No mercy have I. First, I make you feel like a real rinky-dink by writing two letters to your one and now, to add insult to injury, I immediately **answer** your letter. I'm afraid it's my old inconsistency showing through again. You ought to know, it's either feast or famine with me. Don't try to keep up with me. I hardly expect it. (My mother is still beating her head against the wall.)

Hey, that sounds like a great selling formula: Pamela + slim shape + all my other virtues = one choice, desirable gal. You peddle it around your neighborhood and I'll see what I can do out here. By spring we ought to have something really hot going. Funny. I get the feeling people like you and my family are trying to save me from the straits of spinsterhood. Elinor keeps telling me to have fun and mother encourages it, too. They've got my mind so twisted that every time I see a guy I keep thinking in terms of marriage material. Makes me want to hit myself. I'm panicked enough. Hate to think myself that old already.

Nevertheless, tonight I'm going to try my hand at a blind date once again. This time it's a Wright-Patterson (Air Force Base) refugee, with his own car. Do I smell danger signs? Nothing like a loved-starved Air Force lad to keep you on your toes. And I'm not really sure I can take another challenge today after that Shakespeare exam this morning.

Guess what my latest trick is? Sunday night just after I finished telling my parents everything was fine, I pulled one of my Lois Mae specials; in fact, I pulled a whole coffee pot full of boiling water on my lap. There is **no** pain like a burn. I sat for four hours with ice on my ~~leg~~ thigh (sounds sexier), when I decided I couldn't do that all night. So Linn drove me up to the Health Center around 11 o'clock. They did a real good job on me—my thigh looked two sizes larger. Anyway, all that's left now is one big beautiful scar.

Nothing's funny about *Rebel Without a Cause*. Can't be if I have seen it for the 10th time. Tom really does look like James Dean, doesn't he? At least what I would imagine him to look like at that age. Certain movements and expressions. Were you two going together when the movie first came out?[2]

Jeff and I just celebrated our third week of rigorous diet this afternoon with a heaping hot fudge sundae. It's all over – Shazam!

If ever I was in the midst of utter turmoil, this week was it. We had our rooms painted. Yesss, I can feel the headache coming back. At least the walls don't look like gopher-gut-green anymore. They now look like gopher-gut-green once-over-white. If you can imagine that, you can imagine how I feel about its appearance!

Sunday: You only live once, but all in one night? Friday night we went to see a foreign film called *The Shameless Old Lady*. Saturday night we left here at 7:30 for a party in Dayton. By 10:30 when we still hadn't found the place, we had our own party. Now to fill you in on my date. He spoke Pennsylvania Dutch perfectly. And he was s..l..o..w, by that I mean mentally slow, though he was slow otherwise also, so no big problems. I walked all over him—cut him up right and left—and he stood there, smiling, "half a bar of chocolate runnin' down his fingers."[3]

Your prolific friend, Pamela

January 29, West Chester

Before I forget—here are some acting schools that Jane mentioned for your student. She said that the NY Times would have the addresses as to where to write for information: American Academy, Theatre Wing, Neighborhood Playhouse, and Stella Adler. She also suggested that this guy should write to Charles (the director at Mt. Gretna) and try to get summer work at the playhouse or get in touch with her and she could write to him.[4]

Had a wonderful time in New York. Spent Saturday night (five of us girls) in Jane's apartment. She showed us a good time! Got to bed at 4 a.m. and was rudely awakened by her parrot who sounded like a rooster at 7:30 sharp!

Dread the thought of going to classes tomorrow. Gotta fight those damn lines in the bookstore again. Can't wait to get out of this place—only four months yet!

January 31, Boston

It's a beautiful night—cold and snowing. I was listening to Streisand and music from *Zhivago* and suddenly missed you like crazy.

Things look pretty bleak this semester. Of the 2 courses I've had I dislike both. Economics is going to be an extreme bore. My philosophy course is impossible; thank God it's only 7 weeks.

Dale met me at the airport. She looked beautiful. Her hair up and the fur coat do it every time. We're contemplating this week-end at the Cape. All depends on my funds. Albee's *A Delicate Balance* is opening here the 13th with the New York cast. Hope I can see it.

Dale asked Ken about you. Seems she's worried. I must prepare myself for the inevitable confrontation. Take care. Love, b.

February 1, Fort Dix

Hello from Fort Dix, that wonderful place in New Jersey. I guess I'll be here for about two more weeks before I find out what my orders are for sure.

Little Walter gets home this weekend from his monthly cruise in the Navy. I saw him about two weeks ago and he doesn't like it very much.

How's Lower Dauphin? I kinda wish I was back there right now. Not because I like school but it would be better than this. Anything would be.

I was home last weekend and it was cold up there. I hope you don't mind these letters but they're not too often. Well, I guess that's about it for now, so I'll say good-bye and God bless you always.

February 2

Chalk one up for me! Charles returned a test paper (We had gone over them in class after I had corrected them.) on which was written "S- - -." (He, of course, had spelled out the word.) As I was recording the grades, I came upon this. I marched (literally) down to B-3 and called him out, calmly requesting an explanation. He calmly gave one. What could I say but to simply ask him to eradicate the word which he obligingly did. Anyhow, he handled it so respectfully that I accepted the explanation.

The next day Mrs. Lanshe said to me, "Charles thinks you're the coolest thing since icebergs. (Of course, this could very well be a pun on his part!) He says you're the first real teacher he's ever met." Fancy that.

I went to Clearfield over the week-end. I told Jeanie that I would bake brownies for her school's Valentine's Day party.

How are things with Dale?

Lois sent Tom (for his birthday) a box of stationery in which all of the envelopes bore her address! It was beautiful!

Have you decided about Easter vacation yet? Let me know. I think we should plan something wild and wonderful. If we have no "snow days" I'll be free Thursday–Monday. Maybe we can go on a day trip.

February 3, West Chester

Well, I'm ready to graduate right now and begin my teaching career! I seem to be having a little bit of difficulty accepting the fact that I'm listening to a professor once again. I really miss teaching a lot—think maybe I'll push graduate school ahead for a while!

I was talking to the student teachers who replaced us at Sun Valley—they hate the place and seem disappointed, which hurts me more than it would otherwise. Of course Sun Valley isn't the greatest school system but then they should at least give it a good ole West Chester State try. The one who took my place plans to try to revolutionize the P.E. Department. She'll probably be shot down mighty quick!

Jane sent me an application for Farmingdale (New York) School System and wants me to apply. There's a definite opening—starting salary is $6,500. However, I'm quite hesitant about even applying even though it sounds inviting. Decisions!!

My brother got his grades which weren't too good, which makes it bad for the draft and also greatly limits his possibilities of considering transfer. Sure would like to have heard my parents' reactions. I believe from the sounds of things that they weren't very pleased.

Almost have the "Esperanto" paper that you sent figured out—interesting.

Tomorrow I take the practical exam for my basketball official's rating. I am not looking forward to being placed on display like that, but it certainly would be nice to get my rating because then schools would have to pay me the standard fee for officiating.

February 5

I know how thrilled you aren't with the *Falcon Flash* per se, but you'll find my poem contained in this issue. Have fun with the *Flash*, but don't even try to explain it to anyone at BU!

Great news for LD High! There's to be a new choir director for next year. Miss Gluck hasn't (yet) resigned. I guess if she stays she'll teach general music. Nothing like news such as this to brighten one's day!

I find it interesting and somewhat amusing for Dale to have asked Ken about you and me. I'll be curious to hear how you handle "the inevitable confrontation." Simply tell her without elaboration. Short and sweet.

The next eight days are rather full. I'm playing at the Empress Room (lounge of Quality Court Motel) near Carlisle Monday through Thursday, 9-1. Friday my mother and Jean are coming down and Saturday all of us go to Philadelphia for my graduation. Sunday we all go to DC to visit my sister. Monday the two return to Clearfield. I collapse.

"Once in a while, will you try to give one little thought to me, Though someone else may be nearer your heart."

Love & stuff, J.

February 6

Bill Peck died Saturday. I didn't hear until this morning. It's funny, no matter how much it is expected, the news seems unexpected. There will be only a memorial service (tomorrow at 4:00) at the EUB church—no funeral, no viewing. Burial to be tomorrow at the convenience of the family. My heart is heavy.

February 8, West Chester

I received two A's in student teaching and a B in practicum. My accumulative average last semester was 3.87 which brought my overall from a 2.86 to a 2.99 (disheartening to say the least). Wanted to tell you the results just in case I don't make it home this weekend due to the snow blizzard. We're snowed in down here.

Went sledding tonight using Slater trays with the new Assistant Dean of Women—she's young and just recently graduated from a college out west. Acquired a few bruises but it was fun in the process and a great way to relieve all the tension within the system that has been building up since semester break.

My former roommate signed her contract for a position at L.D. She has to wait until the school board meets before a definite decision will be made. Evidently LD gave her the royal treatment when she was interviewed because she really seemed impressed.

Better get some philosophy and government read before hitting the sack. I'll give you a call if I get home—depends on how clear the roads are by then.

February 9, Springfield

Rather interesting issue of the *Falcon Flash* you sent. What's this I read about the Blue Guard, the hungry i, Gestapo action, *Flush Gazette*!?!! Sounds like the Underworld is masterminding an overthrow of some kind.

As for navy (wool) LD jackets...

I must tell you of the unexpected letter I got last week—from your daughter, no less. I was really tickled by it. She began, "On January 20th one of my front teeth came out." I must remember to send her a valentine.

Guess WHO I saw recently? Sir Tyrone Guthrie! A real treat. Boy, did he have a smooth way of cutting the people of Springfield down. I felt proud of myself when I recognized him as a group of us were filing out of the dining hall. My mouth must have dropped as he walked by, because one of the professors attending him smiled and gave me a wink. Of course, I was the only one to be so honored.

I also saw *Alfie* the other weekend. In the advertisements he didn't much turn me on, but wow! It's a movie every woman should see. Have you? When you do, tell me if he reminds you of someone we know.

Last Saturday I went to Dayton. It's only $2.50 round trip, so I might go again when it is warmer. (The other morning it must have been a whole 5 degrees! No kidding.) I met this guy there and we had fun in spite of the cold.

We're registering already for next term. I'm still having problems with this term, let alone to be thinking about the next one. I best not get onto that subject, but I'll say many's the day I want to lie down and die. The trouble is I don't really want to give up, but I don't know how long I can endure. No one can really help me, but me myself, and it's getting so I can't help myself. 'Nuff said.

Something this week made me think of our trip to New Hope. It would be nice if we could go there or somewhere else this summer.....

P.S. Thank you for relating the news of Mr. Peck's death. I purposely avoided asking it in my letters.

February 11, Boston

I guess by now you're in the thick of your graduation celebration. Congratulations are in order. Now to start on the next degree.

A pretty dull Saturday night. Can't afford to go out since my budget has been pretty tight lately.

Very sorry to hear about Bill Peck. Sure as hell makes me wonder what life is all about.

Lee told me about Maggie over Intersession. I meant to say something to you. It seems the choir has been giving her some trouble. Too bad they couldn't have seen what she was when I started the first "revolution." Oh, the joys of being a martyr. The good news does wonders for me. In fact, I had another nightmare about her last week. First in a long time. I dreamed I was beating her. Repressed hostilities as Uncle Sigmund would say.

A guy from RPI[5] is staying in our room this weekend. He's dating a friend of mine. It's been like living in a sardine can.

Dale and I are floundering. Partly because of my indecision and her uncontrolled imagination. The 24th will probably be our last tour de force! (Hope that's the right word.) We're going to see Bill Cosby and Nina Simone. It's a muscular dystrophy benefit; Mayor and Governor will be there. We're going as friends of the fraternity (nice to have connections). We'll be seated right behind the dignitaries and the fraternity. Damn, I like that!

The inevitable confrontation ended in disaster. I think I need a public relations man. Dale is insanely jealous of you. Her damn imagination blew our relationship into a mad, passionate love affair. Since she had experienced something similar she expected me to be involved in one also. She couldn't comprehend the type of platonic relationship we have. She hit me with lines like "You won't fully love me until you know you don't love her," etc. Things gradually became worse. I had to keep telling her our relationship is indefinable. That didn't help.

Then last weekend we had an open house. She saw your picture. I purposely didn't remove the picture because I deliberately wanted her to realize I had nothing to be afraid of or ashamed of and also the fact that with me go the accessories. (good word, huh?) We proceeded with the usual "program" of an open house. It was only afterwards that she blew up, saying, "It's like she was sitting there watching over us." Of course I laughed which I shouldn't have done. I told her, "I'm sure she would approve." She (Dale) did piss me off. I finally told her that this crap had to cease and proceeded to yell at her. She's such a kid! Such a woman, but yet a kid. I told her that she'd better stop letting her imagination run wild and think rationally.

The whole situation sort of shook me in a way. She had turned our relationship into something ugly, something which we kept it above. It (the "horror show") brought back unpleasant memories of my senior year. It brought to the surface so many of the things about our relationship which were at first hard for me to accept. But worst of all it created more doubt in me about my feelings. I just keep hoping they're an "adolescent fantasy." The whole thing's hard to explain in a letter. I'll explain everything more fully over spring vacation.

This week some kids in our room were selling magazines. They asked if "she" (your picture) was my girl. Well, I couldn't resist anymore. I said, "Yes." (male ego, you know!) Since I'd never see them again I figured it wouldn't hurt. They then asked me if you were a Playboy bunny. I kid you not. I told them **No.** Chalk another one up for you. Then later in the week you got another regular compliment."

What you wrote about Mr. Peck for the *Flash* was well received. However, I forgot it said Mrs. on it. Much to my surprise no one here knew you were married. That brought on another barrage of questions. Damn, I can't win.

Last week-end I saw the movie *A Man and a Woman*. Most beautiful movie I've seen in a long time. It was the grand prize winner at the Cannes Film Festival. I bought the record the day after, I was so impressed. $5.14, no less! If you get a chance, see it under any circumstance.

Wish I could celebrate your graduation with you tonight. Thinking of you. Love, b.

February 13

A Valentine: Drawing of two creatures, the smaller one on a ladder to be the same height as the one standing. Message inside: "Ours is a strange and wonderful relationship!" J.

February 17

I'll start this now but who knows when I'll finish. Ten minutes left of 2nd period study hall. Light snow has begun to fall. Although at the moment it does not appear to be threatening, the forecast promises 2-4 inches. Yesterday was the real beauty—winds up to 50 mph.

I don't know if *A Man and a Woman* has been in this area or not, but I'll watch for it.

Did I tell you that I received a Valentine from my 7th period class? How about that?

I hope things are straightened out with Dale. (I'm trying to sound sincere but don't really feel too empathetic.) I'm a bit disappointed that she can't accept your position. But, as you say, there are social compensations. Just drink deeply and learn all you can from whom you can.

I can't help but compare your situation to *In Praise of…* We should, I guess, just accept that fact of Dale's youth. Emotionally (for lack of wanting to use a more precise term) she is not ready to understand the overall situation of a relationship like ours. Of course, there's bound to be a certain amount of jealousy—every young, inexperienced woman senses her own lack. I sensed it in myself until I was made to realize that through experience I had come to know myself and find my own worth. True, I lack much, but I am more confident in what I do possess. Only a sense of acceptance and fulfillment can bring that. And, of course, all that comes with age and experience.

You yourself are rather exceptional in being able to "see the best of both worlds." You also fit well into both roles. For your age you have mature insight. This is one of the traits that I admire in you and why we get along so well. And we do, you know. Don't question, just accept and enjoy. Don't worry about what may develop. You can learn from all your relationships just as you teach all with whom you associate.

(An hour later: I just re-read this. Boy, does it sound stuffy and pedantic!)

Your Friend and Counselor

February 19, Boston

I hate Sundays. Slept late until 1:30 and then to lunch. By that time the day was wasted and I don't feel like doing a damn thing although I'm up to my neck in books to read— three to be exact in the next week and a half. *Utopian Essays* by Goodman, *We* by Eugene Zamaitin, and the *Bhagavad Gita*.

Last night Dale and I and a bunch of other friends were at a dinner party at the home of my last year's rhetoric prof (the fired one). Was great fun. The kid who drove had his dad's Toronado with MD plates. On the way home we were stopped by the police because they thought it was a stolen car. The girls were almost late for their curfew because of the delay.

Thanks for calling Wed. It was good to talk to you.

If you have any notes on *Walden II* I'd appreciate the help. Well, nothing else new, so I'll go check my dryer.

Love, b.

February 24

I have a stupid head cold. (Please note—the cold, not the head, is stupid.) It's blowing snow, it's cold outside, it's drafty in here, and I wish there was a good fire roaring. Hell, with this cold I have, even my eyes are foggy.

I have been reading like crazy all week. Got little else done. Virtuously I read two books on education. Following this was a poor biography of Disraeli (I'm curious about him, guess I'll have to get a better biography.) Finally I got into some interesting reading—little-heard-of titles that may appear to sound melodramatic, but I found all "hit the spot." You must borrow at least two of them—they're relatively short, esp. the play (only one act), *Mrs. Dally Has a Lover* (play), *The Prime of Miss Jean Brodie* (novel about a teacher's influence on her favorites), and *The Lonely Passion of Judith Herne* (poor soul spinster). I am planning to begin *The Dollmaker* this evening. With my own activities curtailed with this weather, I'm forced to return to my former means of vicarious experiences.

You remember Aaron (Bunk) Rhoads, of course. Did I tell you he's back from Scotland? He stopped in after school on Tuesday. Quite a talker, most of it intelligent.

I'll look for *Walden II* notes. I should have something.

March 11

A note card:

I am a bit pressed for time; therefore, I'm just writing a short note. To try to comment on your last letter (re the week-end) would take pages, so rather than risk being misunderstood (you know how letters are!), I'll wait till you're home and we can have a good long tête-à-tête.

Has Dale read *In Praise of…*?

I guess you figured I could find nothing worthwhile on *Walden II*. You're right.

Looking forward to the holiday.

Phaedra

April 11

Since I've been reprimanded for not writing, I'll answer this letter like immediately. And to think I mailed a letter to you just this morning—and it wasn't even a reply to one from you!

I think the swim trunks are smashing. Why hesitate? I really think you'd look good in them. Serially. Do you think Dale will allow you to bring them to Homelyville?

On another topic, if your funny mind and Dale's suspicious aspersions bother you about your paper, why not change your topic? Or to add fuel to the fire tell her I wrote a paper last summer on *Tea and Sympathy* in which you figured!

I very much liked your quotation from *The Harrad Experiment*.[6] By the way, did you like the book?

I heard about the "Love-In" in Boston. Sounded harmless enough on the radio report.

Did you watch the Academy Awards? I was well enough pleased with the winners. How about you? Wasn't Julie Christie darling? (Pun intended.) I also saw *Blow Up*.[7] Actually I was disappointed. It seemed so slow moving.

Hey—can you get me the album "If You Go Away?" Don't mail it (if you get it), but I'll send you a check for the amount.

Have started in earnest on Commencement. We are doing a Choralogue with a speaking and a singing choir and at least on the surface Miss Margaret Martyr is being cooperative. Will you be able to attend? I'd like you to see it and critique it. June 6th. I'll get you a ticket.

Love, J.

April 21

Am enclosing the lastest issue (tho' a couple of weeks old) of the *Falcon Flash*. Note the "H-wing" poem by Dodie Crousore.

I'm going up to Clearfield after school today. Plan to go to Pittsburgh shopping on Sat. It's forecast to rain, but I can hope otherwise.

Next week I'm booked to play at the **Holiday Inn in York** (Monday-Wednesday). That's long enough with teaching.

Wish I could do as the students do—come into school anytime from 10 to 1.

I went to the Arena House for the opening of *Irma La Douce*. It was fair.

Speaking of plays, this year LD surely will be remembered for the class plays. The Junior Class revised their script when parts of it were "re-written" *during the performance*. I am glad I wasn't the director! And, of course, the senior class play last fall (*Arms and the Man*), as a period comedy (1894), was not the typical high school play....either behind the scenes or on stage! (Did I tell you the bed collapsed at dress rehearsal?)

I am enclosing a reprint which may help re *In Praise of....* The page was larger than the copy machine, so it didn't come out perfect. It still should be worthwhile. The article I sent you last year was from *Saturday Review*. You could find it by looking in the *Reader's Guide* under either the author's name or the book title. Another play you might consider is *Mrs. Dally Has a Lover*—it's only one act. I can mail it to you if you'd like.

I'll be thinking of you this week-end. Envy, envy.

Mon Dieu! All this talk of study. Yes, yes, I am impressed. At the risk of sounding stuffy—Keep going!

April 27

Re *Mrs. Dally.* I did not purposely underline the passage in the copy I sent you to use in your report. It just happened to impress me as I was reading the play before you asked me to send it:

"...people got ways of talking to each other to avoid talking to each other"

—people speak superficially. They don't really connect. They talk on an impersonal level to avoid confronting each other. That is why I underlined it. As Aaron Rhoads says, "We really don't hear what the other person is saying. We are too occupied with what we're going to say next."

The rest of the line from the play is, "Every once in a while somebody talks to somebody else. I mean talks; I mean really cares enough to truly fully involve one's self." (Reminds me a bit of Thornton Wilder's *Our Town*.)

Friday

I had hoped to attend the "happy hour" cocktail party at Hotel Hershey last night—it was 9:00-10:00, but the FFA banquet at LD lasted until 10:15. Can you imagine sitting in the cafeteria seats [small, backless, round stool-like seats attached to tables] from 6:45 to 10:15? Well, we did, many with great difficulty! J.

May 2

I especially appreciated your letter today. It cheered me after a sad farewell. I saw Bill Allen this evening for likely the last time. Tomorrow is his final day at the military airport. I haven't been seeing him, but we did want to say good-bye. God—it certainly isn't easy. So little—and yet so much—to say.

Today really was an emotional one. I had a near showdown with Miss Gluck in Activity Period in Mr. Osevala's office. I believe I told you that she had refused to allow the choir to sing "Try to Remember" for Commencement—this happened two weeks ago. Yesterday I arranged to use Room D5 and sent the group there to practice "Remember" on their own.

Today Gluck told the choir that she would not practice any Commencement music until things were straightened out. The kids were up in arms and came storming into my room 3rd period. I sent them to Mr. Osevala. He heard them out and said he would check into it. So we three adults met. She was completely unyielding and said that if "Remember" and also a solo by Jack Brandt are used, she would not direct anything, just wash her hands of the program completely. Mr. O. tried to compromise—to let me practice "Remember" with the seniors. No dice. I held out on the premise that the lyrics of these two songs are an integral part of the program. There the problem still stands.

Later, Mr. Taylor was told to offer her three choices:

1. She will do all the songs.
2. She will do all except the two in dispute and I will do those.
3. She will drop out completely and I will direct all of the music.

Upshot: She agreed to do all of the music; however, near the end of 2nd period some of the choir members came bopping in to my room, saying that Miss G. had dismissed them early after singing through two songs that were completely unrelated to Commencement music. ... (and since when can students be "released" from their classes and allowed to wander?)

Last week I scheduled today's Activity Period for a meeting with the 35 honor students. On **this morning's daily bulletin** is an announcement of a full senior class meeting during Activity Period. Oops!

The guidance counselors and I have just about concluded that our "Charles" is manic-depressive and perhaps paranoid. Mrs. Douglass has been having a number of counseling sessions with him and has advised psychiatric care. Off the record she said his heterosexual life is fantastic. I almost can believe that, just by his appearance some mornings. I do wish you could meet this almost unbelievable young man.

In order to wear my hair like Vanessa Redgrave's I would have to get a hairpiece described as a "fall," just as she had in the movie. It's a thought~~~~.

Your quotation "the first symptom of love in man is timidity, in woman is aggressiveness" is correct—for adolescents; it certainly is not in **experienced** persons (of either sex). I still say subtlety is the key. Unquote.

The Agitator

May 17

Believe it if you will—but Maggie, the mad hatter (your remarks about her have been so apt!) is out and I am in for Commencement. Miss Gluck is to make her <u>room</u> available for us to practice Commencement. Yet a part of me feels sorry for her. We'll be putting the entire Commencement program together next Wed, Thur., Friday afternoons. Can you come?

I'll just wait until I see you to fill you in on the details.

Cheer up and study. It will soon be over.

Saw *Ulysses* last week. I thought it was fine.

J.

In this Fall of 1967 the Class of 1965 began their Junior year in college.

September 11

Last evening I couldn't believe that I actually had to go back to school this week. There have been many changes. For example, I am presently "on duty" in AGL[8] which is now known as the Periodical Reading Room where students may come from study hall to do desultory reading of magazines and newspapers. They are permitted to "talk in a normal tone of voice." I don't know what constitutes "normal." I hate it. You know me—run a tight ship and a QUIET study hall. I am naming this period "Student Happy Hour."

My schedule is the worst it's ever been. Straight through without any break until 7th period. Five straight classes, this reading room duty, and only then a heavenly free period, which I will lose any time there is a pep rally, assembly, class meeting, or any other extra event. The classes are now 49 minutes in length. We are to be here in the morning at 7:30, ready to roll.

Because the day officially ends at 3:30, we're expected to stay until after the students have gone. So the taxpayers now have the 8-hour day they had lobbied for—and then some. Lunch period is also shorter by about three minutes. Every other week I'm on split lunch. Today I ate at 12:25. I was really hungry, not having had anything since 6:30.

Public Speaking is something else. Some students are scheduled for Monday, Tuesday, Thursday; some for Monday and Tuesday; some for Monday and Thursday; and some for Tuesday and Thursday. It is totally unmanageable.

Oh, yes, the Senior Class Play. As you may recall, it is always the week after the last football game and the week before Thanksgiving. This year we are playing 11 instead of 10 games. You've guessed it. The last football game falls on the Friday night scheduled for the play. Mr. Taylor's secretary said he probably moved the play back to Saturday not realizing that the Senior Play is 2 nights and, even if it weren't, it **is** usual to have a dress rehearsal the night before the performance. Who can ask seniors to miss their last high school football game? Further, this would immediately eliminate band members, football team, and cheerleaders from even a minor role in the play.

The eight-period day begins next week. I've still refused to take a class or club for eighth period. Too exhausting.

For a change of pace, how is your world? Rather than ask a string of inane questions, I'll just wait for you to tell me all.

Miss talking to you,

J.

September 12

Second unhappy day in the "Student Happy Hour" room. If I stay in this room with this study hall much longer I might end up hating all teen-agers (former students excepted).

Was delighted at receiving your letter yesterday. Put a bright spot into an otherwise lusterless day. I know what you mean about feeling like a freshman again. That's the way it was with me when I went from DuBois Campus to Penn State Main Campus my sophomore year.

Have you ever heard of the play *Our American Cousin*? It was the play attended by President Lincoln the night he was assassinated. Mr. Bomboy told me today that he and his family saw a performance this summer. He seemed to have been quite impressed. It's a melodrama. I'll send for a copy to read.

I couldn't help but be struck by the contrast in the two letters I received yesterday—yours, of course, and one from Jack. You lightly say, "Well, be of good faith." His was a two-page testimonial on just that—how he found faith late this summer. He was so sincere—it was like nothing I had ever read before. I'm afraid I'm at a loss as to how to reply to such a letter.

Don't—Repeat—Do Not, under any circumstances, permit yourself to fall into a depression. Do not even think about it. Fight it. Good grief, dammit it, you know and I know that you've got what it takes. Get in there and fight. Let me handle the depression!

Luv, JTB

September 16

As an indication of how my situation is, it is just early evening (6:25) and already I'm settled in! Jeanie and Tom headed for Clearfield this morning, leaving me with the usual week-end chores.

LD's football team has two wins out of its first two games. Last week's contest with Susquenita was not a league game, but last night's was a real victory. We beat Middletown 13-6. Pre-season predictions listed M-town in 1st place, Mechanicsburg in 2nd, and LD in 3rd in the league. At last the sportswriters recognize us as contenders. You can see how our beating Middletown helps. Next week we meet Mechanicsburg. If we take them, there should be no stopping the Falcons.

Good to see B.U. winning today.

I like the sound of "Theories of Film." You should do well in that course.

Guide for the Married Man does look quite entertaining. I saw about the last half-hour of it this summer. There was a sneak preview.

Marat-Sade is playing at the Uptown Theatre. Even though I haven't seen it, I'm not too interested. I feel as if I'm tired of it and hearing of it. Know what I mean? There has been too much hype.

I've been feeling depressed all week. Everything seems so futureless. The long school day is really getting to me. Seems as if I have no time to myself. I'm hardly home till it's time to prepare dinner and lunch packing and dishes! I'm tired enough to start getting ready for bed. I've been going to bed at (choke!) 10 p.m. to arise at 5:30 a.m.

Jeanie seems to be adjusting better than anyone. I guess I can be glad of that. Kids really take things in stride. Of course, she still was quite eager to go to Clearfield today.

Mr. Osevala asked me to sponsor a Debate Club. I hated to say "no" to him, but I had to. The following day he asked me if I would co-sponsor with Miss Zeiters. I still declined. I know no more about debating than what's in our speech book. Sure, I got away with it, teaching it, but to coach a team for competition, no thanks! And the travel time to other schools for debates would be difficult with Jean's school schedule.

Nothing decided on the play. Can't find *Our American Cousin*.

Fondly,

Lil' Mary Darkness

September 21

It seems at times as if we're both full of depression and gloom. How I wish we were closer in distance to vent. Of course, then we'd both probably be morose. Coming back from lunch today I sat down at my desk and was just about to throw away some paper when what should I spy in the waste basket—a Krackel bar wrapper. I could have cried. Instead, I laughed at the whole situation here.

Damn, I wish I could see *Phaedra* again. I still want to see it some time with you. And *A Man and A Woman*. You know, I really feel torn between two cultures. I know I view these movies in a different light than most adults my age, yet I certainly can't be all that different. Talk about being born 10 years too early. This especially rang true when I read your letter referring to the three different people for three different needs. You don't know how much I wanted to say, "Let's talk about these." What a damn predicament. It's absurd for by fulfilling two needs, I'd forfeit the original position I now hold in your life. It's ironic, isn't it?

And to think I can't even say these things to you. Why is it we can often write what we can't say to each other? Perhaps it is because in a letter there is a delayed reaction; in other words, I don't have to immediately face the consequences of what I'm saying. In a letter I know you don't have to answer me if you can't, where silence in **conversation** can be devastating. Someday we'll figure this out and laugh about it.

What a bother to be further burdened with Dale. She's hanging herself if only she knew it. If only you could really tell her firmly what's what, just once, it should cure her. It's enough that she's parasitic upon you, but yet to bite the hand that feeds her. Oy!

Correct me if I'm wrong, but Mantells are celebrating? Their anniversary?! Mein Gott: if you can face that, "you're a better man than I am, Gunga Din."

I like your coat. I don't even have to see it. I love it just from your description.

September 27

It's 2:35 on a warm, balmy afternoon and it would be great to be almost anywhere but here. I especially would like to be home as this is Lo's last week at home. As I mentioned over the phone we moved the table from the farm into my house on Sunday. Except for not having dining room chairs the room now rather resembles a dining room. Then Monday night Lo painted over the mural in the living room!! No more mural. I now have a white wall. It's not black and white wallpaper—yet, but it **is** an improvement.

She also changed the furniture arrangement. **Then**~~~(isn't all this house talk exciting to you?) last night we cut out the living room curtains and I actually started to sew them. I just might have curtains by Christmas, considering all this is done by hand. It's amazing what she and I can do when we get together to work. Neither of us can seem to move as much without the incentive of the other. I'll probably just vegetate on the house projects between now and Christmas.

We lost a heartbreaking game with Mechanicsburg. They won in the last few minutes. Crushing. We should bounce back this week against Redland.

P.S. Thursday
A dreary, cloudy day today. I searched all my *Show* magazines plus some *Look, Life*, and other sundry papers and magazines—no luck on a picture of Bardot. Lois said she had one and it should be on its way to you today.

Love, J.

October 3, Indian Rocks (Charles Raisch[9])

Cher Madame Ball,
Are you still waiting for Godot?

In case you're interested in things down here from your level, Siddhartha and Steppenwolf are in my world lit. course with Dr. Peter Meinke.[10] It is so groovy here; it is *sans existe pas*. I'm taking Logic 101, French 201, World Lit 201, and CORE 101. This CORE is great. In it we read about 20 books from all angles of Western Contemporary Thought: *Notes from the Underground, In the Penal Colony, Waiting for Godot, Portrait of the Artist, The Bear, The Stranger, Dynamics of Faith, The Undiscovered Self, Essential Works of Marxism, Man in the Modern World, The Nature of Illusion, On Liberty*, etc. We see films such as *The Pawnbroker, Juliet of the Spirits, and Who's Afraid of Virginia Wolfe*.

We listen to the Minneapolis Symphony, etc., plays, art, lit, happenings, Zen Meditation. It's about 20 humanities courses rolled into one. And they do it all well. The lecturers are mixtures of

Steve Allen, Tim Leary, Hugh Hefner, Paul McCartney, Betrand Russel, and Christ. You sorta want to settle down and rap with the PhDs.

I can't tell you how sure I am that I've found my element. Of course, on the side, I mop floors in Beta Complex, give golf lessons at Indian Rocks Country Club and bus tables at Lum's, but like John Arbuckle used to say, you get what you pay for.

I go sailing during the day and roam from a lecture to a play, to a film, to a class, to the library, to the language lab, its *mon repaire* at will. You don't **have** to go to anything. No attendance required. No rolls, no absentee slips, and the word "cutting" doesn't exist in any form.

I wish I could keep my body and mind and stay here forever thinking everything over, absorbing and expressing opinions and ideas. I only hope I can stay four years. The people around me are strange, they're doing everything I am, saying a lot of the things I say and I can't find any of that needed contrast between me and the f--- -offs. There are none.

I am studying at least 8 hours a day outside of classes, etc. I really am and everybody can talk about the shit I studied as well as or better than I can. This never happened to me before. I mean if I really got into something nobody could touch me, but now. Jesus le Crist.

So don't sit around and let your muscles soften and arteries harden.[11] The world has enough geriatrics. Get back to those mental pigmies and moral nondescripts. Shape their little minds, expose them to your personality. I think of you often, *mais je ne sais pas pourquoi.* I sing of in praise of older women.

Prolifically, Stephen Dedalus.[12]

October 9

Sorry if this card arrives late. I was all set to call you Saturday evening till Judy assured me it wasn't really your birthday. Here I had baked a cake (choc. with choc. icing) for you and was going to describe it to you. I had visions of calling you away from a sumptuous dinner at the Mantells. Judy and I like 2 clods from Homeleyville calling you at the plush party of White Plains. Anyhow, we enjoyed your cake.

Well, he broke down. I actually received a letter from Charles. Can you believe it? I'll let you read it when you are next home.

Postmarked October 17

This letter was folded and sealed with this message to the recipient on the outside of the fold:

"**Do Not Open** this until you have time to sit down for a while after reading it."

As you know, some people will do almost anything to get out of something tiresome or unpleasant, like my teaching schedule this year. Guess what my method is? The last thing you'd ever expect from me. Yes, my dear Barry, it is pregnant. (What are you doing—fainting, crying, or laughing?) I've tried all three. None of them help. I am stunned, to say the least. Remember the unexplainable chills and fever I had in August? Surprise!

I plan to teach until Christmas. I still expect to have my big Christmas Open House. That will be my swan song. After that, I go into seclusion, hibernation, or anything else you care to call it.

Very few people know of this but I can't hide the fact much longer. I've been meaning to tell you for some time, but just didn't have the nerve, I guess. Anyhow I didn't want you hearing it from someone else.

Reactions have been varied: my sisters are in sympathy; my mother thinks it's fine; Jeanie is thoroughly delighted—"I never thought I'd ever have a brother or sister." ("Neither did I, kid; neither did I.") Mr. Osevala said, "I never would have thought it;" Mr. Taylor, after the initial shock, "I'm so happy for you. We always regretted that we only ever had Tommy;" Lois is elated (could kill her, but thank God she helped me keep my sanity when I first knew it); Judy, "Can't wait to check out its growth and bone structure" (Eck!); Upon hearing the news, Dr. Hoerner simply said, "She can't be!"

My husband hates me and is very resentful. He has hardly spoken to me since we knew. Is insanely concerned about finances and is completely unconcerned about me personally. Hasn't asked me once how I'm feeling and will make no attempt to help me. Acts as if it's entirely **my fault**!!! Like I did it all myself just to be mean. Sure! I will admit it was a long shot, when you consider how little time we do cohabit. Needless to say, he hasn't approached me since!

I plan to tell the play cast this week. While I don't exactly "look pregnant" yet, I am "thicker" through the middle and I can't bear (pardon the pun) to have people think I'm just letting myself go and am putting on weight. I'm so very "draggy" (tired-type) and as I had to tear out of the auditorium last Wednesday evening (and head for the lav!) and as I sit rather than <u>emote</u>, I think it fair to warn the cast. Also in that way word will get around to my classes without my having to (1) make a general announcement, (2) make them guess, or (3) play coy. The worst part is that I can't stand to appear lazy and, believe me, I spend more time sitting behind my desk than I ever dreamed of. And you know how I love my lectern!

In conclusion I might say simply that I'm resigned to my fate. While I never would have <u>chosen</u> this, I'm rather stuck. The hardest part is that I'm alone because Tom refuses to recognize the facts. He ignores me even more than usual and offers no support. What else is new?

(To be said nasally to you: "Don't worry, honey—I still love ya!)

J.

Friday, October 27

I was wondering how you could have known so soon about my being at your house. I found out last night from Judy that you called home shortly after (she and) I left. I had stopped to tell her of my visit to the OB and decided that was a good time to scoot across the street to pick up a dog license application for Bond. So that is why I was there. Your dad asked me if I was taking a leave of absence. He had heard that LD was looking for a teacher for College Prep English and he figured it must be for me as I have all College Prep. So I told him the reason.

Re the b. c. pills. My main reason for not taking them is (or rather was) that there were too many years involved. After all, I was 21 when Jean was born; that would mean I would have had to take them for about 20 years which is a bit risky. The <u>longest</u> time usually suggested is 5 yrs. The problem is that <u>after</u> taking the pills for a period of time, one is usually <u>more</u> fertile (Heaven forbid!). Also, until recently, they were rather expensive and it hardly seemed worth the money (and the ever present questionable risk) when I needed protection very, very infrequently. Who wants to bother (or take the risk of the side effects) when one is seldom participating? A third reason was that I take so many headache pills that I didn't want to add more pills to my system. Also, the b. c. pills make some people anxious and lead some to gain weight (heaven forbid). So, I did have my reasons. However, after this baby, I'll be first in line, although I probably needn't worry for a while as I'm sure Tom won't approach me <u>ever again</u>.

The play is well under way. I only wish my enthusiasm were. I have a good, cooperative cast, but it's a drain on me to get out to rehearsal night after night. I don't have a student director or stage manager. No one approached me for the position and I didn't feel like looking. What does bother me is the costuming. None of the boys has anyone to make a costume. I asked Emily Keller to take care of it (she's the Class Advisor). She said OK, but <u>nothing's</u> been done. I know from experience not to count on other people, but this year I really don't have the strength to do it all alone. Not that I'm ill. Just more tired.

As of today they still have no one to take my place after Christmas. Wonder where all these people are—the 500 who, as Dr. Hoerner claims, are begging to get in at LD.

Went up home last week-end where my mother pampered me and cooked all sorts of delicious things. So pleasant.

My student teacher started yesterday. I do believe she'll work out nicely.

Judy claims that Ken is returning to B.U. Is that true? Might this not complicate certain (Dale) relationships?

How's the apartment? Are you getting weekly maid service as promised?

Love, The Same Ole JTB

November 2, 1967

You can, no doubt, guess from the use of this paper that I'm in school. My student teacher is in charge this period and we're listening to (mmmm) Richard Burton's *Hamlet*. Mesmerizing.

The senior class play is moving along nicely. I have a good cast, dependable in learning their lines. However, they're lax in rounding up costumes. They seem to be depending upon others. Mrs. Keller, who weeks ago assumed the responsibility, is finally meeting with them today.

Tom took Jean to Park Avenue to go Halloweening Monday night. That's the night I told them was H-town's assigned time. Guess what? It wasn't, as they were told by people whose homes they visited! Trick or Treating was Tuesday night. Poor souls.

November 8

Help! May I unburden myself? Things are starting to fall in on me. Of course, "the play's the thing." The lines are being nicely memorized, but without much feeling. I'm upset, but not as much as I should be under the circumstances. I can't believe that they seem to think the costumes will magically appear. I take that back. It really shouldn't be their responsibility.

One of the cast members (Al Larsen) is also on stage crew and, as Mr. Fickes told him, with bemusement as only Bob Fickes could display, "You are the only stage crew member to date to be in the National Honor Society." Hats off to both!

As always, grades are due next week. Also, the annual Parents Open House is Monday night. We were told today that requisitions for general supplies are due Nov. 20 (for next year). I have articles to write for the newspapers re the play. I have, on top of this, a Master's Thesis to rewrite. You likely remember that I corrected the basic grammar for this teacher last year. Of course, at the time I knew it was generally poorly written, but hesitated to be so blunt. You know how thin-skinned he is! So here I am, stuck.

One of my leads just asked if he could be excused from practice next Monday. He obviously expected me to explode. I didn't. I must really be slipping! But really, rehearsals are going well with this devoted cast.

On Monday Mr. Taylor asked me to stay until Jan. 19 when a girl graduating from Millersville would be available. I agreed, not wishing to turn down the money. Also, that would give me a full semester. Today, Mr. T. told me that Dr. Hoerner had signed a young man from Shippensburg. He graduates Nov. 19 and will begin here after Christmas. He is to come in the week of Dec. 11 to observe, and the week of Dec. 18 for me to supervise him. As my student teacher will be here yet the week of Dec. 11, B-1 will be quite crowded with teachers.

I have a parental conference with Nancy Alleman's parents tomorrow. She refuses to come to my class because of the Hamlet soliloquy. She sees no point in memorizing it. She believes that one should not do anything (s)he does not believe in—that one should do nothing simply at another's command. Fine! But she seems unable to accept the consequences.

I won't begin to go into the home situation. Let's just say I am being basically ignored as usual. Know anyone who desires a slightly pregnant adult companion for basic conversation?

I haven't even answered Charles' letter yet. I've started it 3 different times, but that's it. I had a letter from John Seavers last week—he's coming (from Syracuse U.) for the play!

November 12
Hi, Sweetie,

Well, this is the week. The final countdown until the climax Saturday night of *She Stoops to Conquer*. Pray that we don't go down to defeat; the students are psyched and I am very pleased with their understanding of the play and their commitment throughout the process. I just hope the audience is ready for an Eighteenth Century comedy of manners. It really is a good play and I'm pleased with the cast, their commitment, and their performance. Solid all around.

She Stoops to Conquer

Oliver Goldsmith's

SHE STOOPS TO CONQUER

November 18, 1967
8:00 P. M.

Lower Dauphin High School Auditorium

308

I don't believe I'll make the big splash on stage this year for a curtain call. Lately I seem to have been the only director who has. Maybe it is a bit amateurish, but then, I've always felt it rather fit the occasion~~~

By now I'm sure you've heard of Lauren and Walt's event of Nov. 24th. I guess their "blessed event" is due around May. Just think, we can compare notes all winter! I believe Judy is greeting this with very mixed emotions. See what you miss by being in Boston?

My sister Jo Ellen and my mother were here for the week-end. Tom and Jeanie went to Clearfield so that worked out well. We went to Allentown shopping on Sat. Would you believe I didn't buy any clothes?!! Bought Christmas stuff and 2 items for the bathroom —a gold shelf and a beautiful waste basket. Now, all I need is new lights and the bathroom will be complete. I want at least one room ready for Christmas.

Can you be available December 16th or 17th to help prepare for the Christmas Open House Sunday night the 17th?

Guess what's opening at the Uptown? *A Man and a Woman.* Think you might work it in your schedule over Thanksgiving? We're going to Clearfield Friday night or Saturday morning. No school Monday, November 27th.

We still haven't had any snow. Saving it for you.

Love, J.

November 28

Hi, Sweetie (As you know, I hate that term, but somehow can't resist using it occasionally in jest [said with a twang].)

'Fore I forget—I'm sending you a magazine under separate cover. It's called *Theatre Crafts*, unavailable on the newsstands, although perhaps you might be familiar with it via class or the library.

Today is ACES tour groups. I'm headed with my group to (sound of trumpets, please!) Hershey Chocolate Corporation. You can imagine my enthusiasm.

Mary Alice (my student teacher) thinks you're sharp. ("Cool" may have been the word. I'm not sure.) So do I!

C. Leonard stopped by yesterday. Apparently he didn't know my "condition" as he added, "I stopped by to make mad, passionate love to you for 4 to 5 hours." What a creep! Somehow I felt ill the rest of the afternoon. Mary Alice about died when she saw him. After he left she asked me who that horrible person was. She couldn't believe seeing him here—said he is always hanging around Lebanon Valley campus and in the student lounge. Voyeur-type, no doubt.

Went shopping for bathroom lights yesterday. Found some I like but wanted to double-check my wall measurements. They'll work, so I plan to pick them up today.

I've decided to change the date of my Christmas Open House to Thursday, December 21st. Can't bear not to have you there. Please tell everyone with whom you come in contact – or have Dale tell your friends....

Love, J.

Wednesday, December 13

Things are a bit crowded here this week with three teachers in B-1. Actually, today is Miss Hostetter's last day of service. I really hate to see her go. It's hard for me to realize that soon I, too, shall be gone from my hallowed B-1 and my own platform stage! Oh, well, for now I hear the beat of a different drummer.

Hurry home so that I have a shoulder to lean on. I need a different channel.

Lois gets home late tomorrow night. I'll probably see her on Friday. We plan to decorate on the week-end. Hope we get some help from the other adult living in my house.

Christmas Holiday spirit—where are you?

Paranoidly yours, J.

Chapter 9 Endnotes:

1.   Comparable to $450,000 in today's market.

2.   Yes. We saw it in Chicago.

3.   Peter, Paul, and Mary, "Talkin' Candy Bar Blues."

4.   Another example of how difficult it was to get any kind of information on possible careers or career preparation. The young man in question wanted to major in theatre and didn't have any idea of where to begin. Further, this is an example of how adults helped with advice and contacts for young people they didn't even know.

5.   Rensselaer Polytechnic Institute.

6.   An interesting premise at the time, sold a huge number of copies, but now very "dated."

7.   *Blowup* won the Grand Prix du Festival International du Film, the festival's highest honor. Story of a fashion photographer who unwittingly captured on film a murder.

8.   The General Lab in A-wing.

9.   This young man requires a bit of background. He arrived at Lower Dauphin as a new student in the fall of 1966. Handsome, more cosmopolitan than our typical student, he obviously had more sophisticated experiences in his background than did the conventional Lower Dauphin student. I believe his father was a golf pro, although I don't recall ever meeting either of his parents. Charles appeared to be well-read compared to the usual male high school senior. A bit outspoken, he appeared to be one who had depended upon his charm to get through life. He auditioned for the Senior Class Play (perfect, it seemed, for the lead of the Chocolate Soldier in *Arms and the Man*). However, he was a disappointment in not having the discipline to learn his lines and, more importantly, attend rehearsals. His presence and habits were a distraction at rehearsals and the other students were, I sensed, just waiting to see how I would handle the situation. Such tension is not good anywhere, but it was especially disconcerting in our situation. I had to let him go well into rehearsal, replacing him with a much more practiced young man who delivered a most commendable performance. The play was successful and no animosity seemed to be retained by Charles. I believe he was used to bluffing through his charm, but really meant no harm by his unorthodox view of responsibility.

    After high school graduation, Charles returned whence he had come, to Florida and enrolled in college from which I had this letter. I did not hear from him again until many years later when we connected through emails and a couple of telephone calls when we tried to arrange to meet at a time when he was taking his daughter to college (perhaps Bucknell). However, in true Charles style, he never completed the plans. At least he goes down in my list of unforgettable characters.

10. An America poet of some note.

11. I was barely out of my twenties.

12. The protagonist of James Joyce's autobiographical novel *A Portrait of the Artist as a Young Man* (1916) and a central character in his novel *Ulysses* (1922).

Chapter 10

Metamorphosing

January 1968 to June 1969

O wonder! How many godly creatures are there here!

How beauteous mankind is!

O brave new world, That has such people in't.

The Tempest

Shakespeare

Historically 1968 was a landmark year because of the high number of protests and riots. Leslie Gelb of Harvard perhaps summed up the opinions of many adults at the time when he wrote, "1968 just blew away my self-confidence about what I thought I knew."[1]

Dorothy Rabinowitz, cultural columnist for *The Wall Street Journal*, recounts, "For an intellectual, the Sixties mark the end of all standards, all history. The most infuriating part of it was the denigration of all that came before."[2]

Tom Hayden, American social and political activist, author and politician, who was director of the Peace and Justice Resource Center in Los Angeles County, California, noted, "The sixties began with a kind of moral awakening that was translated into direct action by a new generation seeking to be central to our country's history and the world's history; 1968 was like a tornado year, with a lot of forces that became a vortex."[3]

Shelby Steele, African American author, columnist, documentary film maker, and a Robert J. and Marion E. Oster Senior Fellow at Stanford, said, "It all began in 1968 when white America lost its moral authority."[4]

In 1968 there were 7 million students in college, at a time of generous student loan programs, state and federal subsidies that greatly reduced tuition, corporate, philanthropic, and family support. While this fact appears to be positive, it provided crowd-following protestors who were easily-led and uninformed.[5]

Among the most remembered events, including killings and riots—and for which the latter half of the 1960s is most remembered—are the following:

1965

- August 1965: Watts Riot, Los Angeles, California

1966

- July 14, 1966: Richard Speck killed 12 student nurses.

- August 1, 1966: Charles Whitman shot 12 people from the U. of Texas Tower.

1967

- There were 164 eruptions in 128 cities, Newark and Detroit being the worst.

- October 1967: 50,000 protesters marched on the Pentagon.

- Beginning in March of 1967, protests and a take-over at Columbia University continued through April 1968.

1968

- January 1968: Tet Offensive, Viet Nam

- April 4, 1968: Approximately 130 uprisings followed the assassination of Martin Luther King.

- April 29, 1968: Approximately one million college and high school students took part in a national college student anti-war protest.

- August 1968: Major protests occurred at the Democratic convention in Chicago and in Grant Park and Lincoln Park.

1969

- October 15, 1969: Many national "teach-ins" sprouted.

- November 15: The first nationwide Viet Nam War Moratorium was held in Washington, DC with an estimated 600,000 demonstrators.

Collectively, during **1968-1969** there were well over a hundred politically inspired campus bombings, attempted bombings, and incidents of arson. In the spring of 1969 alone, three hundred colleges and universities, holding a third of American students, saw sizable demonstrations, a quarter of them marked by strikes or building takeovers, a quarter more by disruption of classes and administration, a fifth accompanied by bombs, arson, or the trashing of property. Revolt was everywhere, including a major series of uprisings at Berkeley and its surrounds.[6]

The most notorious disturbances, however, were the six days of riots in 1968, which first erupted in the nation's capital, following the assassination of civil rights leader Dr. King who had been shot while standing on the balcony of his room at the Lorraine Motel in Memphis, Tennessee.

Violence and chaos followed each and all of these uprisings, with (mainly black) protestors flooding out onto the streets of major cities, primarily in black urban areas. Over 100 major U.S. cities experienced disturbances, resulting in roughly $50 million in damage. In total, the assassination riots affected at least 110 U.S. cities; Washington, Chicago, and Baltimore were among those most affected.

In Chicago both rioters and police were particularly aggressive, and the damage was severe. More than 48 hours of rioting left 11 Chicago citizens dead, 48 wounded by police gunfire, 90 policemen injured, and 2,150 people arrested. Two miles of Chicago on West Madison Street were left in a state of rubble.

Then again, in August during the Democratic National Convention, Chicago became a place of political protest, resulting in clashes with the authorities.[7]

Thirty-nine people died in the above nationwide disturbances.

━━━━━━━━━━━━━━━

During this turbulent time most of the Class of 1965 reached the age of 21. The Class of 1964 was being graduated from college, ready to make their mark, with the events of calendar year 1968 having had a stronger influence on these young adults than anything else before or since. Not only had the world changed for them, but they now faced both the draft and greater competition in the job market than had any class before or following them.

It was this entire generation, pushed by their parents, who also changed the perception of college as an elite privilege to one of expectation, if not necessity. As noted in an earlier chapter of this book, part of this change of view toward the *need* for college is that the colleges and universities, which in the early to mid-1960s had gone on a major expansion streak, could now foresee that once the "enrollment boom" slowed to a bubble, they would have to find a way to keep the dormitories and classrooms filled. Thus, the colleges developed marketing strategies for **recruitment**, rather than "selection," through the same route as advertisers used—by manufacturing a need: "Your children *need* a college education to succeed in today's job market."

The number of letters written by The English Students decreased for the usual reasons. Reaching their comfort zone in sharing their lives with new friends and with increased confidence in themselves, they did not need the "support" of home. They were becoming quite independent—whether it was resources for their assignments or advice on courses. Thus, with each passing year, they were further removed in all ways from high school, busy in expanding their own worlds.

Fortunately for the continuation of representing this decade through letters, one of the students saved my letters beginning in 1967, so these serve to capture some of the events and flavor from my personal view to complement the earlier chapters in providing the tempestuous history of the times and in the lives of those who lived through them.

Back home in the quieter small town of Hummelstown—a world much different from what most of the collegians were experiencing, I continued with my Christmas Open House, which remained popular and would continue as a base for friends to see one another for another twenty years.

Circumstances changed in my own life as well in the last two years of this decade, and both the students and I discovered that the times, indeed, were changing.

1968

Come gather 'round people
Wherever you roam
And admit that the Waters
Around you have grown,
And accept it that soon
You'll be drenched to the bone
If your time to you
Is worth savin'
Then you better start swimmin'
Or you'll sink like a stone
For the times they are a-changin'[8]

Early to mid-January 1968

In case you're not sure, yes, this paper is hot pink. If it were white, the cost of the writing tablet would have been 20 cents; this was 69 cents. Outrageous. Only a fool or a show-off would buy it.

Today is a typical uneventful day in the life of homebound JTB. Saw Dottie this morning, then went to church to practice music at the organ for her wedding to Jack. When Jeanie came home from school we went to the shopping center to find birthday gifts for her dad. Do you know how impossible it is at this time of year to find men's mufflers and handkerchiefs?

I had a very nice letter from Kirk, thanking me for the hospitality at Christmas and complimenting me on the house. Always good to hear from the gang, infrequent as it often is now.

Did you happen to watch Rowan and Martin's *Laugh-In* on Monday night? It was pretty funny, though just a bit in poor taste in a few remarks. I'm looking forward to *Laura* tonight.

Tom has been wearing his new white knit hat every day. He seems to like it in spite of a number of comments from his friends, all of which I believe he relished sharing with me as most were teasing remarks. Yours will soon be finished. (Maybe you both will wear them only when I am around…..)

Hope your classes are at least stimulating. I am reading *The Spire* by Wm. Golding.[9] It's strange.

Sometime in later January

Just some odds and ends to brighten a bleak January…

I sent *The Graduate* (paperback) to Charles, asking for his opinion but not commenting on the book myself. I didn't want to give him any fodder.

You got out of town just in time. We had a miserable ice storm Saturday night and Sunday morning. Even churches were closed.

I will write "for real" soon.

February 2

It's Groundhog Day. That's the best I can come up with for excitement this week. For the record, the groundhog in Punxsutawney saw his shadow (I think they are lying), but the one in Quarryville did not.

Be **sure** to remind me to tell you about Dottie and Jack's wedding. I can do better justice to it by telling rather than writing.

Have you seen the magazine *Pace*?[10] Lo sent me a couple of issues. Looks like a pretty good mag. Aimed at young adults.

Re the knit cap I sent you. The bottom (the cuff) should be pressed. I didn't press it as I thought you should decide, depending upon fit, if you need a full or half cuff.

Incidentally, my feelings won't be hurt if you really don't like it.

What's a good book for me to read? I just finished *The Spire* but, unfortunately didn't care much for it. I get bored with vague writing styles. I think many authors are just incoherent. Let's return to short, simple, and to the point. Perhaps I'll try it again sometime since it received such great reviews.

The shelves in the study were started this week. The carpenter is to return Monday to finish. Slowly but surely!

Did you catch either *Elizabeth & Essex* or *Of Mice and Men*, both this past Wednesday? What an evening of good viewing!

Bye for now, J.

February 12, a Valentine

Front: "Have you ever stopped to think of the scandal our relationship could cause…?"

Inside: "… if we just tried a little harder?"

Is that a zip code I spy on your envelope? It is the first one I have seen used. Cool!

February 20

No luck here on finding information on your Russian poet. I asked Venus to look through the mags I gave her, so we'll see if she finds anything.

Why, oh why, do those insensitive newsmen go to the front (in Viet Nam) to interview those poor soul American military men with questions such as "How does it feel to be facing death all around you every day?" and "How do you feel when one of your buddies is killed?" Things like that should not be asked and certainly not aired. They are exploiting these young soldiers in a war no one understands.

Are they advertising prices for the movie *Funny Girl*? I understand that top seats are going for $7.50 in NY. That's about what they charged for the live performance! I can't see paying prices like that for a movie, especially since I saw Streisand do the show in person on Broadway four years ago!

Hurrah! My technical services are in demand. I'm proof-reading a master's thesis for a client (through Mrs. Connelly).

According to the English students, my replacement in B-1 is doing very little teaching. What irks me is that Dr. Hoerner thought this young man was so great and we will never know otherwise, for how is something like this revealed? The students won't complain, as either they're glad to get out of the work or they simply don't realize that they are missing something.

Your remark about Sundays brought back memories. How I hated Sundays when I was in college. In fact, I still dislike their vagueness.

You can be looking for another small, homey-type package. I'm sending you some homemade caramels.

March 13

Did you get to Homelyville over the week-end? We were late starting back from up home on Sunday in case you called. I guess Olmsted operates on radar or you wouldn't have gotten off the ground. Visibility must have been near zero. It's snowing or raining right now. Glad I'm not going out.

I received an odd letter from Pam Rainey. It had been written February 24th and mailed March 11th. Apparently she's living at home and working somewhere in the area. I like her; she has a quirky, often self-deprecating, sense of humor.

Sometimes I ask myself if I will ever be real again. All of this is such a haze.

The *Cosmo* article you sent me was most entertaining. Real and objective. Shall I return the clipping to you?

My round dining room table and cherry chest were delivered last Friday to the tune of $116. I don't think you'll recognize Grandma's table from the farm! What a wonderful item to have and how kind of Kirk to allow me to purchase this prior to the public sale. Now, of course, I want chairs, a chandelier, paneling, wallpaper ad infinitum!

Write and tell me what a great time you had in St. Thomas so I can suffer.

Love & stuff,

Ducky Waddles

March 14

By now I hope that all of the problems of last term at Shippensburg are forgotten. At least the spring term offers hope (end-of-year kind of faith!)

How is this term course-wise? I think it's twice as difficult taking rough courses in the spring, but I guess they can't be avoided.

Harold (or do you call him Howie as so many at Ship do?) stopped in Monday afternoon with the news that he's been separated from Ship. He didn't appear to be at all upset which is a good attitude. Seems now to be interested in the Peace Corps. Knowing how well Harold gets along with people, I think he'd be great in this line of work. He said that he rarely sees you so you must be off studying in your room.

Do you see much of Joan Hetrick? I've been wondering what her plans are. She seemed to be uncertain when I spoke with her at Christmas.

You asked what I've been doing with my time. Not nearly enough. I had so many projects planned. After all, I figured I had three good months (Jan., Feb., March) to work. Ha! I had forgotten how the body just doesn't function as one is used to. I had done so much over the summer that I assumed I could keep up a good pace.

I wasn't prepared to be so fatigued and lately so cumbersome! I tire so easily. I couldn't believe that I who always was constantly moving, never resting, could come to a reverse state of inertia. Alas, it is true. My only major project has been to refinish a washstand to use as a baby chest. However, I have been knitting and reading. Most evenings I just sit! I can't believe that it is me—I who rarely watched TV before. Oh, well, I guess I'll soon again have more than enough to do.

I enjoyed your mention of Kirk's putting Union Deposit on the map. I had the same thoughts when Barry told me Kirk's average. Then when I read it in the paper, I didn't know whether to laugh or cry—the article listed his address as Hershey rather than Union. Alas!

You asked me about Jeanie. Actually she would prefer a girl, as would I, but only because that is what I am used to. I have selected names, but as there is always the possibility of last minute changes, I'll wait before I say.

Always good hearing from you!

March 27, Temperature 70s!

Can it be possible that this is the first I've written since your return? Please forgive me. I've been nesting.

Actually I was runnin' (term loosely used) around most of last week. Lois was home. Need I say more? Anyhow, I finally got to *Gone With the Wind*. Loved it even more than the last time I saw it a hundred years ago. We also made our usual pilgrimage to Aumen's to look at wallpaper books. Found what I wanted for the dining room. As a result, our style plans for that room have completely changed.

It looks as if the living room might have to wait one more year. Can't see putting up wallpaper without getting new carpeting. Also we've decided that the white sofa will have to go. I'm hoping that by next year I can convince Tom to have a den or something in the basement where he can have the sofa and TV.

Harold is coming up this evening to babysit. Jeanie, of course, is thrilled. Tom is taking me to see *The Graduate*. What concerns me (not really) is his reaction to the film. I'm sure you and I are already pre-cast in the roles.

Are you going to let me read your essay on *Tea and Sympathy*? Someday we'll probably get reckless and expose all our writings which are based on or refer to our—what, friendship? Anyhow, I found your last letter particularly enchanting.

April 4

Hi Sweetie,

I'm depressed. Real kind of me to write to you in such a state, huh? I have been doing things to keep busy 'cause I can't just sit. I'm afraid I'll have to go back to work to save my sanity. I thought it might work but I'm just not a home person.

Of course, I'm expected to return to work in the fall. Really, I have to because we can't live comfortably on one salary. Know anyone who would be available to care for a five-month-old starting in September?

Went to York; I had never been there to shop. It's quite a nice city. There is a men's store there, Gregory's, listed in *Gentlemen's Quarterly*. They had some beautifully tailored suits and a Nehru-style jacket such as Sammy Davis, Jr. wears. You need one!

The Graduate was funny, but not very flattering to either generation.

April 11

Hi, again,

Still holding on. I wanted to last till next Monday so I'm halfway there.

So what's your professional opinion of the Academy Awards? I can't comment on most of the choices because I've seen so few of the movies, so I'll comment on people instead. Streisand gets the award for Miss Grotesque and Double Ugly. She needs a classic hair style, not a bramble bush. Also, did you notice that the stage was dimmed and that her entrance was the only one spot-lighted? I like Natalie Wood's hair. I didn't like Faye Dunaway's. I would like to have seen more Raquel. Really. Did you catch the music for Dame Edith Evans—"There's Nothing Like a Dame."

Warren Beatty must have been in a state of shock. Everyone expected *Bonnie and Clyde* to sweep the Awards, didn't they? Only Sammy Davis could have saved "If I Could Talk to the Animals," and he did. How I dislike that song! One of the most unnecessary songs I've ever heard. "Bare Necessities" was also poor. I thought Angela Lansbury's number, all things considered, was best. Lainie, gorgeous though she is, is too taken with herself.

Did you notice there were very few extremes in fashion? Actually some of the men out-dressed the women. Claire Bloom's black and white was smart. Patty Duke's remark that her mother would not permit her to see *Valley of the Dolls* fell flat—for many reasons. I liked the acceptance speeches of George Kennedy and Rod Steiger. Paul Newman is so choice I'll even forgive him for chewing gum. It struck me that Diana Carrol and Michelle Lee are look-alikes. I loved Angie Dickinson's gown with the open midriff, but my award for the choicest of the evening—the stunning simplicity of the striking Anne Bancroft.

Kept thinking about you yesterday, wondering how your TV production was going. How did it?

Love, Me (somewhere in this body)

April 19

♪ "Today is the day they give babies away with half a pound of tea."

No, I'm not cracking up quite yet, but today is supposed to be my day. Surprise. Of course, the day isn't over yet!

Actually, I'm booked into the hospital for next Tuesday at 7:00 a.m.—if the toad hasn't moved of its own accord by then. Tuesday they'll induce labor. Doesn't that sound like fun? At least by this time next week the worst should be well behind me.

As usual, day-to-day events are just that. Quite mundane. I took Harold into H-burg on Monday to help him select a suit. His fraternity's big week-end is this week-end and he needed a suit for the dance.

Went to see *Planet of the Apes* last night while Harold stayed with Jeanie. It was a good movie. I was pleased with myself as I had anticipated the "surprise" ending and you know we like to be right.

Have you decided anything about Hershey's Public Television Station yet? They could use some fresh ideas from what I've observed lately.

Weather-wise it's been just about perfect. Everything is in blossom and bloom. I'm really enjoying it. I guess I've never had time to notice Spring before.

Finished *The Arrangement* last week. I didn't really like it. Why don't you suggest something good I can read? I'm now about one-quarter of the way into *Anna Karenina* by Tolstoy. I had almost forgotten what good writing is.

The most unexpected people turn up around here. Last Thursday Bob Norris stopped by briefly.

Love, Soon-to-be-Me!

April 24

Surprise! We have a son and I am in love with this darling newborn. He, of course, is beautiful, but you've never seen such a thunder-struck father in your life. I think of all the creatures in the world a son was the last thing he expected. It was a relatively short labor—two hours. They allowed fathers in. Poor Tom almost didn't make it—during the first 15 minutes he went pale and I had to send for the nurse for him! They revived him with smelling salts and he left.

Love, Ms. Almost Slender!

May 7

I suppose today is "Cram Day" for you with an exam tomorrow. Or are you still relaxing?

Nothing new here since I talked to you on Saturday. Venus *et famille* were here last Thursday eve. She had just returned from Boston and looked sharp with whitish eye shadow. She brought a very good-looking pewter mug on which was engraved the baby's first name and birthdate. Of course, I love it.

As I have nothing more of interest to add, I'll not waste your time. Back to your books and studying.

Glad you called Saturday. Looking forward to your homecoming.

P.S. Know anything about the book *August is a Wicked Month*? Seems to be popular, but from what I read about it, it didn't appeal to me.

May 27

Just read your letter. For some reason I always feel "reassured" after receiving the first letter after your return from time at home. Somehow it seems to verify that everything went well during our seeing each other here, as I often have feelings of anxiety after your "good-bye."

Your grades are beautiful and you're beautiful for earning them. I'm ecstatic! This should please your parents as well.

Funny how you worried of my reaction to your "period of doubt and searching" (sounds like a religious trauma, doesn't it?). I felt the same way about your reaction to my pregnancy. I almost felt uncomfortable—until we talked and everything was still the same. Won't it always be so with us? Just for the record, no, I wasn't alarmed, etc., with your news. Interested, yes, because you are important to me and what happens to you is you. I'm glad you felt that you could tell me about it.

Always, J.

June 10th, 17th, or 24th

So glad you're becoming accustomed to handling complaints in your summer job. What would you like to hear about first? Domestic Relations? Children? Housework Syndrome? Persecution Personified? Or the weather, which, by the way, is delightful?

Come home. I need a real live male to talk to. I need one who understands and cares. Gordon Putt called last week and I almost imprisoned him on the phone. I just laughed last week after the doctor (six-week, post-natal check-up) said, "No restrictions. Resume normal activity." Well, I am back to normal, but for the record, make it normal **inactivity**!

Company has all gone and my household is slowly returning to my routine. A bit more frantic, to be sure, but under control. Baby Ross eats five times a day @30 minutes to an hour each time, but he is such a delight. Add to that feeding time, of course, beaucoup diaper changes, more laundry, plus regular chores. Days just come and go and Mary Martyr continues!

Wish you'd been here the night of Commencement. My hair was in long curls in a cascade—all my own hair (Note vanity here)—and I loved my dress. I had borrowed it from Nan.

Have you seen any of the girls there wearing WHITE JEANS? I got a pair and just love them.

Jeanie has been taking flute lessons (in a group) at South Hanover Elementary School. Today I decided I'd take her and just wait for her in the car rather than make a return trip. I glanced around the parking lot and saw my counterparts. I felt like running away. My saving grace—at least my hair was not in rollers and I was not wearing sneakers as the others were. The baby usually sleeps while we wait; he is so good-natured.

Take care of your roomies; I have mixed feelings about that situation. Sorry.

June 27

It's 8:00 p.m. on a rainy, dreary, lonesome-type Thursday evening.

We had rain all day, but at least my morning was brightened by a visit from Kirk. Guess he's making his rounds. He's always so pleasant and I enjoyed seeing him.

Lo and I have been running hither, thither, and yon to lumber companies looking for a corner cupboard and unpainted paneling. Of course, the cupboard we liked best (from seeing the pamphlets without prices listed) turned out to be the most expensive. And unpainted paneling is practically unheard of anymore. I mean, like nobody buys unpainted when all this "nice, modern, finished" paneling is available. But Lois and I don't want nice, modern, etc.! Then, too, we want to "build in" the cupboard. She's game, so I guess I'll be, too.

I've been working like a laborer (only without pay or even breaks) this week. I put the final coat of paint on the louvered doors (or was that last week?) and am deep into painting the powder room. It's quite a job as I'm so slow and meticulous.

Yesterday Jeanie and I had lunch at Lebanon Treadway Inn as guests of Lois Mae. It was great to get out. Lo's mother baby-sat.

Tom is going on a scuba diving trip this week-end. They're camping out Sat. night. At first he thought he might take Jean, too, but I guess there'll be no one to watch her while they're diving.

Poor Harold is in the Army. He was drafted and left June 7th. I found this out from his father whom I called. I hadn't heard from Harold for awhile and wanted to know what had happened. Something more must have.

Kirk tells me that Carol and her roommate are coming in for the Fourth of July week-end. Maybe that will solve your date dilemma. Hope so. If not, there's always Lo & I.

I had a letter yesterday from Harold. I don't believe he's too happy. He said boot camp is like pledging, only three times worse. Poor soul.

I like this:

"I shall choose friends among men, but neither slaves nor masters. And I shall choose only such as please me, and them I shall love and respect, but neither command nor obey. And we shall join our hands when we wish, or walk alone when we so desire."

Ayn Rand

July 11

Here is your friendly malcontent again. Twice in one week yet! And the week isn't over. I may write twice more. So there.

I stayed up late to watch Tiny Tim on Johnny Carson last night. He still is unbelievable. I enjoy him in a way (for a short time), but when my own Tiny Tom got me up at 5:30, I really wondered if watching the program was worth the loss of sleep last night.

Ever since you called my attention to dark blue shirts, I've been noticing them on the newscasters on television. Yes, you should definitely have one!

How are you doing with the course you are taking? Hang in there, as they say. Think of the advantages. (This, of course, is Pollyanna speaking.)

Lois is falling hard for her guy Ben.

July 12

I drove over to Lebanon this evening to see Lois. What a lovely summer evening—just pleasant perfect summer.

This morning I had nothing special scheduled, just routine daily chores and by noon I was jittery so I had to begin a new project. It's frightening to realize that I must constantly keep myself busy. Most people can relax occasionally. Is the Protestant Ethic that deeply etched in me? Anyhow, I started sanding the painted chairs I had bought some time ago. I really hate to sand; in fact, I hate all of the steps of preparation for the actual painting. I just like to paint.

Started to read *The Fixer*. I'm into it only about 50 pages, but I think I'll like it. Finally finished *Anna Karenina* early this week.

Any possibility of your coming in for Ann's wedding? I really want to go and thought that maybe you and I could trail along with Lois and Ben.

Ann stopped by here yesterday afternoon for a visit and to see the baby. She looked so pretty, and she's always so sincere and unaffected. She spoke well of you, that you have always been someone she could really talk to.

August 8

Hmm, just read your letters. Shall I reply in kind, or just ignore the sarcasm? (Gee, you know I am back to myself when you read this, right?)

OK, let's do hear it from the angle of repression. Or, better yet, let's try regression. If your "friends" bother you that much, whatever are you going to do when you have major problems in the big outside world? Oh, dear, the results of a sheltered life. To quote, "That's not the way things exist." Have you switched apartments yet? That might help make things better.

Good luck with your big production. Break a leg!!

Next time you are home remind me to show you the old-fashioned high chair, the one Lois' parents refinished for the baby, and with a cane seat. It is choice!

Sorry I didn't write last week. People kept coming into my room during my planning period and between classes. I finally tracked down Mr. Bomboy and told him I was withdrawing my name from consideration as chair of the department—and felt an immediate sense of relief.

September 4

School Days, School Days....

Spent most of the day preparing a new vocabulary notebook. Jon Glass stopped in to see me at school about 7:45. He really looks good. Quite handsome. He has one more year in the service, then he may go to Australia.

I am glad to hear you say you are happy. At least that is one of us! And you say you are eager to start back! How depressing. No, not really. Beginning your senior year should be full of great anticipation so be joyful!

September 13, Houghton, New York

Dear Mrs. Ball,

How are you? I'm sorry that I didn't have a chance to stop in & see you, but those last days before leaving for NY were very hectic.

I am very much involved within my "individual course of human events," since we last talked in the beginning of the summer. As a result of the summer I am not a full-fledged music major anymore; rather I'm what is called a liberal arts music major. Linda is fine and continuing her oboe major.

I don't know if you heard about Tom Conrad, Bill Grubb, Glenn Snavely, and Jay Ebersole, but all left their respective schools.

Are you directing the Senior Class Play again? If so, any ideas yet? Plays and public speaking are two things I really miss here.

October 31, Houghton, New York

Please forgive me for not writing until now and also for not calling this past summer. I'll try to explain a little. I have been helping my mother. We moved into one of our apartments the beginning of August and things changed; however, it was so hard for me to come back to school and leave her alone; she doesn't even drive. My uncle brought her up this past week-end; she looks good but she is very, very lonely. I'm looking forward to Thanksgiving vacation.

I'm still picking up the pieces spiritually and emotionally, but I'll make it; the Lord has been good to me.

School is rough this year but I like it. Oboe is going very well, my teacher is quite pleased and prospects are good for an A. Frankly, I'd be very well satisfied to play oboe for the rest of my life.

Are you back teaching again? I hope so. How is Baby Ross? I'll bet he's spoiled by now.

Love in Christ,

September 16

It was great, wasn't it? Streisand la grande. I was almost mesmerized. It was just as it should be for her. Just sing. The "natural habitat" setting had it all over her usual fancy sets in the studio. How did you like the first gown? It was a sort of natural-skin or peach color. She even, for the most part, handled the audience well. A few remarks were "too cute," but she wasn't aloof as might be expected from all of the adverse publicity about her ego-centricity. "He Touched Me" was particularly moving—it almost brought tears to my eyes. Even her "People" was real. I was completely absorbed, and I don't even like the song. Make that past tense. Her delivery last night sold it.

And "Silent Night." As I recall, last Christmas when she sang it, I didn't like it. Last night it was beautiful. The verse to "Second Hand Rose" was poor—she was parodying her own parody. You did see the show, didn't you? Tell me you did. I searched my files for your new phone number. Did you give it to me yet? I so felt like calling last night—even during the program. I wish there would be some way to "copy" the television program so that I could watch it again. Somehow it seemed that we should be sharing that show. Streisand seems to be us.

Enjoyed your card, especially your own version. So true.

I'm becoming acclimated to working again. Routine soothes the soul or something. Or maybe it's just that work dulls the senses, making one numb to crude reality.

How's the senior year going so far? My lord, to think I was married before my senior year in college!

Haven't seen Judy for a couple of weeks. Have you?

See, you **can** do things like carpentry. You've been hiding this talent! Of course, maybe you really shouldn't have told me. Think how you can help Lois and me here. Seriously though, I've just about been convinced to **hire** all work done after this recent delay. Still my dining room sits.

September 20

So I hain't writin' enough, eh? Sorry to disappoint. Maybe all was forgiven when I sent my letter of Monday to you. That and your letter probably crossed in the mail.

Another lonely week-end looms ahead. Of course, I'm so glad that I don't have to go to school, but staying home only brings work of another kind. No relief in sight. This is not Mary Martyr, but rather Polly Practical who still yearns to be idealistic or perhaps a bit of a romantic.

Bought a couple of new dresses yesterday so that perked me up to a degree, except they're not exactly school dresses so I'll probably never wear them.

Baby Ross continues to be the light of my life. Without the children there'd really be no spark in my life at the moment. Jeanie is such a sweetheart and helps out more than I ever expected.

Had a somewhat encouraging (?) note from my mother. She said something like, "Of course you're busy, but you'd be just as busy if you were home all day, and besides, you wouldn't be earning anything." Hate to say it, but she is right.

September 20

Hiya Sweetie,

Guess what! We got the word. We must be stationed in our classrooms during every Activity Period; that is, unless we're assigned for an activity somewhere else. The administration even published a list with everyone's name and where (s)he is to be every day during 8th period. Even Mrs. Sandel is listed with the word "Library" written in for each day. It's so asinine. JTB is scheduled for B-1. If we want to go anywhere—even just to another classroom—we must first report to the Sr. High Office. I don't know about permission to use the restroom. Speaking of that, I really feel ridiculous that people, esp. young men who are taller than I am, must ask my permission to go to the lav. I'm tempted to make a general announcement to the effect that if anyone wants to leave the room, he should just simply leave!

I have a George Wallace poster in my room. Did I tell you? It's been there for a while, but just this week Mr. Osevala told me that "several" (probably one) parent(s) called about it. He didn't ask me to take it down, but to give "equal billing" or pictures of other candidates. I then got out a picture I have of Beowulf (actually it's Grendel) and had it lettered "Beowulf for President." So you see I haven't completely given in.

Still me. (Written on the flap of the envelope is "Cellblock B, Room 1")

October 4

Dear bar,

Have you completely given up on receiving a letter from me? This week has been MAD. Been typing tests in the few "free" moments at home.

Can't stand my hair. Had it done yesterday. More or less straight, slightly turned under at the bottom. Feel like Prince Valiant.

The paneling is all on the walls and I have finished the first coat of paint. There is hope.

October 10

I'm sending for information on taking a group to England to study next summer. I know I'll never go but it's nice to think about. At least I'll have the information. Maybe the following year…or maybe just go myself. Or I may think of going to Italy.

Looked in a second-hand store for dining room chairs. No luck. Did I tell you I plan to have my 13 yards of white velvet made up (finally) into drapes? I'm going to call a seamstress about it this afternoon.

Try to enjoy your party. I'll be wishing it were I spending your 21st birthday with you. At least now you're your own man in the eyes of society. You've always been so in mine.

Re the birthday card. I just didn't feel like sending a funny one. Guess I'm becoming sentimental.

Me

P.S. Want to go along to Europe as a co-chaperone? Wouldn't that be groovy?

October 17
Dear bar,

Watching a movie on Shakespeare. It's OK, but it's in black and white.

Later:

Your letter reached me yesterday, almost a week after you wrote it. What happened? Was it misplaced over the week-end during the partying? (almost laughing)

Speaking of which, your letter has me worried. You sounded so depressed. Are you still so disposed? This letter didn't sound like a regular-type depression. You sound as if you need someone to talk to.

You know, you say that it bothers you that you can't financially compete with your associates. No, I'm not going to say "Money isn't everything," cause we both know otherwise. However, remember that many of your friends' parents are first generation nouveau riche. Why can't you be the same? You haven't yet started on a career. Who knows what job and business opportunities you'll have? There's money to be made in television, you know.

Or consider another possibility—marry money. Not all wealthy girls are like neurotic Dale. Make contacts; that's what your Boston friends are for. Your Hummelstown friends just "are."

Keep up the good fight. You know damn well you can pull it off. When you want to relax from your role, come to H-town and hide and regroup. Then back to the field refreshed!

Love and thoughts, J.

1:40, October 21 — Progress Report

The day has gone from good to middling to poor to nil. The opening session of "In-Service" had students pantomiming a typical school day. Rather corny idea, but very well executed. This was immediately followed by slides showing scenes of school. I'll tell you more about it when I see you, as you might be able to use the idea sometime. REMIND ME.

Second session was a movie, CBS News, *Road Signs on a Merry-Go-Round*. It was good, with a neo-Christian slant, based somewhat on the ideas of Martin Buber, the philosopher of *I and Thou*. You should have been here to see it. Good discussion material.

After lunch was a so-so movie on *Creativity*. Keynote speaker right before lunch was poor. Boring. Full of clichés and educational jargon. I had planned to attend a session going on right now on *How to Turn Kids On*, but everyone who was going started down the hall carrying ash trays. It seems that they were all going to smoke in B-2. I'm not about to sit through a smoke screen, thank you.

In one of the sessions today was a man who, at first glance, looked very much like Bill. It really gave me a turn, especially after having seen the *Road Signs* film. I know after what I've said of the movie, that seems crazy, but so many things of that movie reminded me of him. I think about him a lot, but I can't really tell anybody about it.

November 1

Dear bar,

At last a moment free. I've been having student and teacher conferences all week during free periods and activity periods. It's now 1st period Friday and my student teacher is handling the class. She's competent but not as "in command" as Mary Alice was.

I've been working at home all week on painting my Hi Fi and the large mirror above the mantel. Perhaps I did mention that I'm doing them over in antique white.

November 7

Glad you called last night. I had been upset earlier in the evening—one of those "feel-sorry-for-self" moods. Those moods really are a waste; I lost an hour and a half of good time by just sitting and later crying. Of course, that also leads to puffy eyes. Isn't that appealing, though?

Tom recently decided to sell $4,000 worth of stock as, he said, this would be a good tax year (one salary) in which to sell. I gullibly signed (the stocks were in both names) and several days later he re-purchased the stock in his name only. I've become so angry that I can't even talk to him.

November 14

Dear bar,

It's the middle of another dreary week. At least, however, there has been variety in the weather! Woke yesterday morning to the sound of howling wind and the sight of falling snow. "If winter comes….

I imagine you had another good week-end in New York! When are you going again?

Right now I am bored, but more than that, I'm annoyed with myself for being so. I guess I'm really better off if I do keep jumping. I'll have to find some more projects. Right now I'm tired of painting, although I should get busy antiquing the white pole drapery rods I bought for the living room. One of these days the draperies will be delivered and I won't be ready for them.

We're going to Clearfield this week-end. I don't know whether to say "Whoopee" or "Ugh." Mixed feelings. How I hate to pack. However, I must go as I've made an appt. to have Ross-pie's picture taken. Same photographer who did the portrait of Jeanie that I like so well.

Took a group to HACC on Monday. It was the first visit to the campus for me. Actually it's not too impossible. Student body didn't look much like college type, but then I'm not too sure what the typical college type looks like. Guess I'm using all of you as a (high) standard by which to measure.

What about Thanksgiving? May I count on a particular evening? I thought perhaps I should arrange in advance for a baby sitter or shall we just have our usually enjoyable à maison tête-à-tête pour deux?—Nothing fancy in the French. Just means an evening at home for two. We could try again for a fire—this time I'll remember which way the vent opens.

Happy thoughts of you. J.

November 20

And a cheery 8:00 a.m. to you! Now to more pleasant thoughts. Quick, JTB, there **must** be **something** pleasant to write about. I'm thinking.

OK—we have three school days off for Thanksgiving, making a beautiful, 5-day holiday. I hope to clean the basement, a most formidable task. It has almost reached the point of no return. Especially as Mother commented that the basement does not look like the rest of my house. Also, I actually felt embarrassed when Jeanie took the sitter down to play pool. Wonder if I could possibly make the one area livable—as a playroom for two children. That goal should spur me on!

November 21

Well, what a pleasant surprise to go home yesterday to find another letter from you. That's two for this week.

Funny, using this pen recalls the time about last October when I wrote to you about expecting (Ross). It's strange how things—objects or sounds or smells—remind us of events.

Ross has such a bad cold. I feel so sorry for the poor little soul. He doesn't understand why he can't breathe through his nose and he really becomes annoyed. I'm taking him to the doctor today.

Class play is tomorrow night. I have somewhat mixed emotions, but mainly I'm relieved I'm not involved this year. Seems odd not to be.

January to June 1969

The music in her heart she bore, long after it was heard no more

I sometimes think that there was so much turmoil in every aspect of life in 1968 that many of The English Students were on edge and "wiped out" as they approached dealing with their senior year and were concerned about their futures—grad school, first jobs, and, for some, marriage.

As they entered 1969, most were in their last semester, a few doing student teaching. Almost without exception all were in their early twenties, had made their mark in college (or military service or employment), and some also had become parents. While many returned for the Christmas Open Houses for another 18 years, their need for my guidance greatly lessened, as well it should.

January 13

Sorry I missed saying "Good-bye." We didn't get back home until nearly ten o'clock. Feel bad I couldn't "send you off" for your last semester!

I spent money!!! In Washington. You see, there is this marvelous little boutique gift shop in Falls Church that is open on Sundays…

I bought two absolutely perfect pictures. I thought they'd look good in Ross's room except that he doesn't yet have a room; he is still sharing mine as Tom still hasn't left. However, last night about 10:30 Tom told me that he thought he'd take a room in Harrisburg. He thinks it best that we live apart for a while. He was practically astonished that I wasn't upset. I really kept my cool. You would have been so proud of me! I don't think he could believe that I was agreeable, and he was on the verge of changing his mind.

I asked him "When?" and he said sometime this month. I told him that I thought he should go right away. I could sense his panic. I told him he could go this evening.

He then had to ask me what I thought about the whole situation, so you know how calm my reaction had been to that point. I simply told him that I believe that people should do what they want to do, if at all possible. He wanted to know what I wanted him to do. I said, "I don't want you to want to go, but I can't change that, so if you think you should leave, then that's what I want, etc."

January 20: Washington Inauguration Festivities, 10:30 a.m.

Kirk called last week to ask if I would write two letters of recommendation for him. Of course, very happy to do so.

I thought there was supposed to be an Inaugural Parade in DC. So far I've seen only the president's car. In honesty, I'm having difficulty in staying awake!

January 20, Naples, Italy[11]

Your letter was a pleasant surprise; it was just like you were talking to me. When I left you last, I was rattled just being near you, but no wonder, with shipping out. I am sitting here listening to radio Luxemburg, drinking vino rosato and thinking about you. To say that I've thought about you a lot is the understatement of the last decade and will be of this one as well. I wish you were with me here.

January 27

How could I have forgotten to mention last evening that I took Ross to Mary Sachs on Saturday to buy him a snowsuit (for next winter). I loved myself prancing up the street carrying a box labeled *Mary Sachs*.

Guess who has himself a room in Harrisburg? In fact, he's taken a room at the same place he lived 10 years or more ago. I'm not exactly sure what he hopes to prove. Also, as Thursday is his birthday, it's rather fitting, don't you think? What he says he wants is for me to become more dependent upon him. I say that his leaving would hardly make me dependent. Ridiculous. Tired dealing with it.

February 1, Naples

I just read your letter that likely came by boat. You said you might come to Europe for Easter. Lord knows I would like to be with you here. If you do, we can take some side trips to Rome and Florence.

Yes, I remember Gully Jimson and *The Horse's Mouth* and you, and seeing you the night of your summer party after a separation of several months. And then, it was two and a half years, and that is too long.

With the electricity out here, I am now down to one candle, so should quit writing. And I am like you (in more ways than you know) in that I don't like the rain and the wind and the storming unless I'm in to stay with someone, and I haven't been with the one someone in a long time. What I think could fill a book, our book.

February 3

Howdy, Mr. Graduating Senior,

We had a freak-out in the girls' lav today. J. Dxxxxxx appeared to be on a bad trip. She became combatant and had to be strapped onto the ambulance stretcher. How's that for a farmer school?

Finally I found the Jerry Vale record I'd been looking for, "With Pen in Hand." My mother actually discovered the record—in Clearfield yet!

Had a nice letter from Dave Lidle. I'll answer when I get a chance. Finding time for anything is becoming more **insane** and **inane** by the day.

Your graduation portrait is perfect. I showed it to my mother who said, "He looks like an English baron." What more could one want?

How was your week-end? I hope you were able to enjoy it. I want to know all the places you went.

Musical is plodding along. I'm slightly bored with it at this point, but that is typical some years. Things will pick up once they know their lines!

February 21

Wherever in the world did you find the Valentine? Never have I seen a more perfect, oops! **suitable** card.

I wish you could see Ross at this moment. He's sitting in my maple rocker (the one I had as a child) actually rocking himself; then resting, then crossing his ankles and holding his hands; occasionally looking around at me and "talking"—trying different sounds and tongue positions. To top it all off, he has a "fresh haircut." Perfect picture of a miniature old man.....

Looking forward to Saturday night.

I rearranged the living room, always a pick-up on a gloomy winter day.

February 27, Germany

Longfellow, Liz Taylor, and I just shared a birthday; I am younger than the poet, but the same age as Liz. I could meet your plane here if you come and we can fly back to Naples. I still haven't been to Pompeii or Capri. I'm waiting for someone important to show them to. I hope this can be arranged.

March 17

I think I'm going into a nervous collapse. Two fellows are here "repairing" my refrigerator. They are the same two who installed the infamous air conditioner of last summer. The kitchen is now a sight—melting food all over the place. Ten minutes ago the refrigerator door fell off and actually **dropped** to the floor. Of course, I had washed the floor and waxed it on Saturday.

On a much happier note my living room wallpaper is on order. $130 just for the paper. I got so carried away that I also ordered $80 worth of paper for Jean's room: three walls and ceiling covered with flowers; the fourth wall and closet in a co-ordinating narrow stripe. Should be darling.

Today I went to Bowser's and bought a studio couch. It's to be placed in the study where the card table now is. It separates into two sleeping units which could be helpful. Also saw other dining room chairs I liked. Will wait to check with Lo on those, since she has a good eye and seems to know immediately what I end up liking.

I have a smashing idea for Commencement. Using slides and movies, narrated in either a running commentary or with "one-liners," quotations, if possible. Slides and movies of school events, elementary school through senior prom with a "projected future" segment. What do you think? To retain a flavor of the traditional, we'd have opening (salutatorian) and closing (valedictorian) addresses.

How was your session on Friday? Am thinking of you. Surely spring will soon arrive. Has Boston Commons blossomed yet?

Love you in spite of all travails on all sides of both of us.

March 14, Naples

Monday we leave by military aircraft for Wiesbaden for the basketball tournament. I assume your plans fell through on your trip to Europe or maybe you just didn't make any plans. I wasn't much help, because I was never sure of my own schedule. We will be here through Easter Sunday…wish you were here.

March 22, Wiesbaden, Germany

Right before I left Naples I planted a lot of geraniums and I hope they survived. I like to fiddle with growing things. Didn't Faust conclude that working with the land was better even than Helen of Troy? Not sure I would agree with that. Hope to have a letter from you waiting for me back in Naples.

April 1, Germany

I find it so interesting to hear you talk about your various classes and their closeness to one another and your own class reunions from high school. Since graduating from high school at the age of 16, I don't think I have seen any of my high school classmates. I left the day after graduation to work in a gypsum mine, and then later from one college to another before and after enlisting. I liked your last letter. You sure have a hold on me. I miss the classes at University Center and I miss you.

April 2, Germany

If you want to visit a real Italian grocery store, there is one near the train station in Harrisburg. Last time I was there I got sidetracked about my interest in an English teacher and, forgetting her phone number from our classes at the Center, I spent a lot of time driving by her house and finally waited for the blasted school to open again after the holidays, hoping to see her there.

April 24

Dear soon-to-be-graduated,

Do you realize that as I hung up the phone last night my clock stopped? Figure that one out. I'm really excited about going to the Prom. Feel like a senior wallflower who just snared an import. Going with you seems like the plot for a short story—like four years late or something.

Did you happen to see the special drama *This Town Will Never Be the Same* Wednesday night? Somehow it didn't come off. It tried to put two themes in a weak plot and neither worked.

5ᵗʰ period Study Hall: I'm afraid Craig just hanged himself. From a discussion of Ayn Rand evolved (how, I don't know) comments on love; then someone mentioned the love or sex act and why one particular person goes to bed with another particular person. One of the girls said a man pursues and/or goes to bed with the one who reflects what he thinks of himself. In other words, how a man views himself is shown by the type of women he chooses. I thought, "Aha! Craig will probably promote this idea."

Instead, he violently objected. He implied that when a girl "gives in," a guy thinks less of her. (I personally had thought that this idea died in the past ten years. Am I wrong?) I can't wait to challenge him with this statement he has made publicly. He stopped after class to ask if I were free 6ᵗʰ period. I'm not.

Everything Craig says or does seems to have sensual overtones. There is a Freudian term for people like that, isn't there? For example, when he asked me to sign his absence excuse today, he handed me a pen and said something like, "Just try this pen. Doesn't it have a nice feel to it? It writes so smoothly (or something like that)." I just said, "I don't like ball point pens. There is something cheap about them."

I have been telling everyone you've been accepted at Columbia (and Temple). All are properly impressed.

April 22

Today is Senior Day. That means that the seniors are teaching, replacing the fogie faculty. For us, it's been boring, except for two things: (1) This morning Aleda and I took off for two periods to go to the neatest new dress shop on the square. I found a number of darling clothes, but didn't buy **anything**....yet. (2) Craig is role-playing as a Guidance Counselor, so I made an appointment. I went in requesting a schedule change; I asked to drop English. We talked for about 45 minutes. Kept his cool and didn't mention his book report.

Decided to give a note to Craig's homeroom teacher and asked him to stop by in B-1 to discuss his book report—if he wanted to. I said that if he didn't want to, to just let the subject drop. I'll keep you posted, if I may.

Mr. Heistand spoke to me today about **you**. He said you've really matured and he was **quite impressed** with your manner and appearance. He said he felt that you used to have a chip on your shoulder (in h.s. when you were in his class), but he says you now exude (my term here) confidence. A first base hit!

What do you think of the Streisand critique?

Mr. Osevala just stopped by to tell me to go to East Hanover to see a performance of their school play on Wednesday morning. I'm not sure of the purpose. Perhaps to view budding talent. Or maybe he was invited and can't leave our building.

Speaking of budding, have they planted spring in Boston yet? I love this time of year, especially "on the farm."

I need an adult in my life to relate to. Really no time to talk to adults at school.

Check out this clipping on Streisand's appearance at the Oscars:

> "Speaking of see-throughs, I thought Barbra Streisand made a spectacle of herself and a farce out of fashion by appearing at the Academy Awards Monday night in a black tulle see-through pants outfit by Arnold Scaasi. She bared more than her soul—quite a bit of her derriere.
>
> "Her outfit consisted of a black sequinned bra and bikini with a sheer layer of paillette-dotted tulle covering (?) her body and extremities. The star who got an Oscar for *Funny Girl* sure looked like a funny girl. All Hollywood is talking about her new high in bad taste."

No designer, not even Arnold Scaasi, should let a client, especially a famous one, make a fool of herself in an outrageous outfit.

Graduation and a New World for the Class of 1965

By the end of May 1969, most of the Class of 1965 had been graduated from college, as well as those having finished other career programs such as Nursing School. It was a new world for all of them—jobs, marriage, and/or grad school!

The last communication I had this final year from The English Students was a note card, summarizing and closing this chapter in their lives. It came from Boston.

Friday, May 2

Will be home Tuesday.

The Graduate

Chapter 10 Endnotes:

1   Brokaw, Tom. *Boom! Talking About the Sixties*, p. 138.

2   Brokaw, p. 502.

3   Witcover, *The Year the Dream Died*, p. 470.

4   Brokaw, p. 325.

5   Compare this to the present time, fifty years later.....and the same situation.

6   Gitlin, pp. 342-343.

7   Wikipedia and hundreds of supporting sources.

8   Composed by Bob Dylan in the aftermath of the Washington march.

9   Golding was described in *Show* magazine's April 1964 issue as "probably the most imaginative, inventive, and original writer to appear in the English language since the war [presuming WWII]. The sale in hard cover was modest; later it became a *must* read and soon replaced J.D. Salinger's *Catcher in the Rye* as the literate college student's equivalent of the letter sweater."

10 A highly regarded magazine aimed at the 18-34 year-old audience, founded in 1964 and published through the remainder of the 1960s. An interview by Star 14 (a television station in Kingston, South Africa) with Robert Fleming, one of the founders of *Pace*, tells of the reunion of the founders in Kingston in 2014. The magazine is now available online. Outstanding writers.

11 Sent from the Naval Support Activity Naples, a United States Navy military complex, located in Capodichino, Naples, Italy. It is home to U.S. Naval Forces Europe and the U.S. Sixth Fleet.

Reflections

The real voyage of discovery consists not in seeking
new landscapes but in having new eyes.[1]

Remembrance of Things Past
Marcel Proust

Diary of a First Year Teacher

September 5, 1960, Labor Day

This week-end I went by *TWA* and *American Airlines* to Boston (Harrisburg/ Newark / Boston and Return, $64.60) where Harold Whitney met me. Lunch at a restaurant named *KEN'S*, later *THE MEADOWS*, a supper club, and ended at *ARMAND'S*. Next morning on to Cape Cod to a collection of cottages with friends of my Cousin Noel.

However, it was so crowded in the cottage to which we were assigned that we slept on the beach in sleeping bags. (First time ever being in a sleeping bag. First time ever sleeping on a beach. Later shifted to sleeping in cars.[2] Was this really me?) Harold was embarrassed and offered to try to find other accommodations; Noel seemed to think this hospitality was typical. Being Labor Day, rooms were at a premium and the cottage was packed to the roof by those who had arrived earlier. As an out-of-town guest without a car there was little we could do. Saw some real[3] beatniks at Provincetown. A full-out New England Clambake that evening (Saturday). Monday I flew back on Eastern (4-engine, jet prop) and then Allegheny from Newark to H-burg.

September 6, 1960

First day of school for the teachers. Introductions and a tour of the building. Everything new and shiny, but they are still working on getting it finished! Postponed opening. Didn't really get to meet people personally.

September 7, 1960, First day of faculty meetings

There are many young teachers—and many of them single. It looks promising. The school is really something. Although it isn't complete, it will be neat! My room (C-3) is painted light gray which I like. My textbooks are there but I haven't had a chance to look over them yet. Ate lunch at the Cocoa Inn with three other young women teachers.

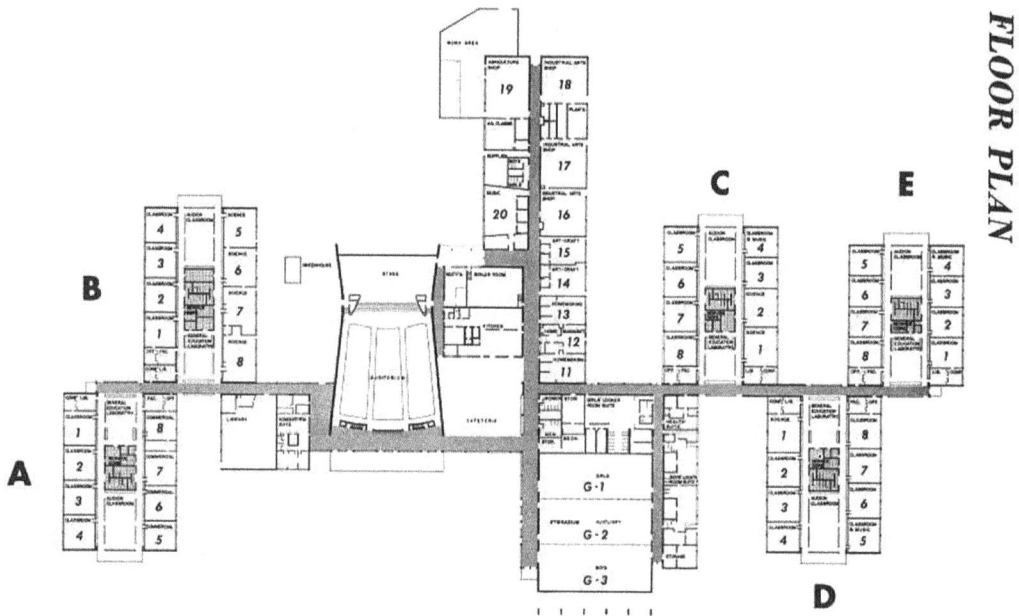

FLOOR PLAN

LOWER DAUPHIN HIGH SCHOOL

Left at 2:45 to get to the store, then home to start a cake. Barbara Thacik, Warren, and Ken McGillis arrived. After dinner we headed for H-burg and went to the dance at the American Legion. What a blast. There were two alternating bands and we were really having fun. Cut Ken's birthday cake when we all came back.

September 8, 1960

Faculty met from 9:00 to 9:45. We were free until 1:00, so Rosalie Bowers and I came here for coffee and cake. We talked and seem to hit it off real well. Talked with one of the young men, athletic and tall. He asked if I was married as he was looking at my ring-less hand yet calling me Mrs. Ball. So I explained that I was separated.

September 11, 1960

Ken brought a doll house he had made, a perfectly darling replica of a house. Invited me to a House Party at State.

September 12, 1960

First day of school with the students. Too many. Already I don't have enough desks. Nor do I have enough books even for the sections that are supposed to have them. Long, dragged-out day. If I only knew what to do with the three sections without books. Of course, the library isn't open so I can't make use of that yet. Duplicating services not available until October, so can't design work sheets. I'll figure something out—something to get their attention. I just hope I don't regret coming here.

September 15, 1960

School's becoming a little more routinized now. The mornings are the worst. As soon as it hits 11:00 (lunch) I'm fine. Four straight classes in the morning, lunch, class, free period, class, activity period (six classes a day plus activity)

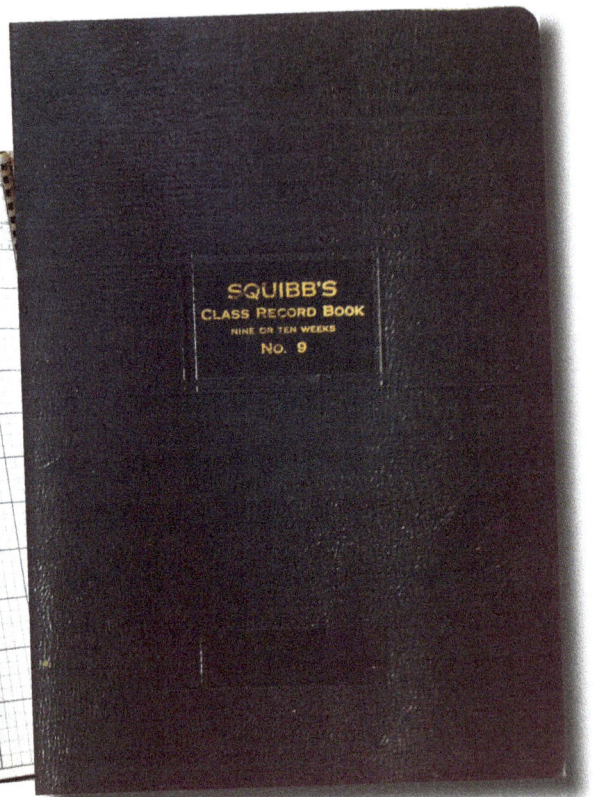

= SEVEN ASSIGNED PERIODS. The lit. books for sections 1, 2, 3 arrived. And I had the first smile from a student today; his name is Harold Snyder, very tall for a ninth grader, tallest in the class.

Week-end in New York City: travel by train. Governor Clinton Hotel. Cocktails in the Lounge Friday evening; Saturday Times Square, Empire State Bldg., Radio City Music Hall, Song Without End movie, then to a lounge; Sunday was Rockefeller Center, St. Patrick's Cathedral, and The MET (art museum)!

October 7-9, 1960

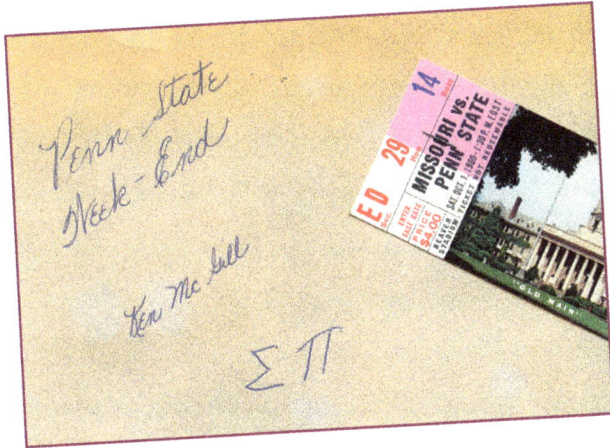

Homecoming Week-end with Ken at Penn State. (Much different than the last House Party I attended as a high school senior and stayed in the home of a professor.) State lost to Missouri, 21-8.

October 10-11, 1960, Monday and Tuesday

Teachers Institute in Harrisburg. I drove on the 10th, taking Sandy and Joan. Jim Middlekauf had asked us to his place for lunch, but we didn't go. He suggested we meet at Abe's at 2:00. We made tentative plans to go to Sandy's tomorrow afternoon. Jim was to round up the gang.

Early evening Jim came to the apartment (it was a mess with correcting papers). He said he had talked to the guys and they wanted to have lunch at Jim's again and then go to the afternoon meeting. So that cancelled out our earlier plans. Jim stayed till after 8:00 just talking.

October 12, 1960

Jim came over to my room 8th period to tell me he had not stopped last evening because he was late getting out of football practice. He mentioned that he later drove by with one of his players in the car and waved.

Had a letter from Harold Whitney. He said he loves me. I wish I knew what to do. Too busy to think about it.

October 13, 1960

Jane Mellin Smith, the Choral Director, came thundering into C faculty room in a whirl, assigning every one of us who happened to be there a task for the first school musical! Mine was to be the orchestra, she said as she laughed. Play piano for rehearsals; for performance we will have two pianos and a drum.

October 14, 1960

Harold Whitney in town. He is staying at the Simmons Motel in Hershey. He went to Gettysburg Friday night; Saturday morning we toured the battlefield, then went to DC to see the Lincoln Memorial and Washington Monument. Back to Hummelstown to wait for Cousin Noel to pick him up.

October 17, 1960

PTA tonight; tape recording on "Brainwashing." Gang then went to Martino's for "Faculty Tea." Danced with Bill Peck, Jim Middlekauf, and Carl Stanitski. Home by 11:30. Bill brought me from Martino's to my car I had left in the parking lot at school. I like him; he reminds me somewhat of John Elensky—tall, blond, funny, athletic. There is a dance at the school in November. A number of faculty have already volunteered to help. Phys. Ed. is going to give basic dance instruction, both in classes and, if necessary, also at the dance.

October 21, 1960

What a good football team we have! Crowds are large and playing our home games in the Hershey Stadium is so neat. A lot of faculty in attendance. We have passes. We also have opportunities to work in the ticket booth (for pay) if we would like. Gee, almost like working at the Rex Theatre back home!

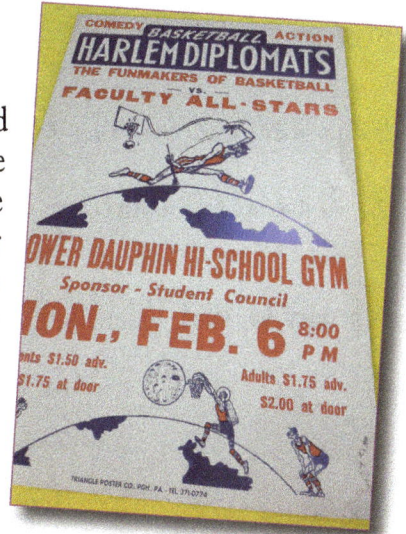

By November a men's faculty basketball team had been formed to play against other faculty teams in the area and, because of the number of cage stars[4] LD had, the team also was able to schedule an exhibition game with the Baltimore Colts. Over two years their record was 25-2, their only losses at the hands of the Harlem Satellites and the Albright College Club Team. Of course, they needed cheerleaders and four of us volunteered.[5]

December 31, 1960

Not unexpectedly, given our camaraderie as a new young cohort of teachers, we went to the Lawton Legion for the New Year's Eve celebration, arranged by Bill Peck, who likely is a member. No one thought to ask.

January 5, 1961

Oh, dear, it never occurred to me that there are mothers who don't sew, even though mine did not. We had Mrs. Buterbaugh! Anyhow, I made an assumption that Harold's mother could make his costume as the Maharaja. Wrong. However, she was kind enough to say she would make sure a costume is produced for him.

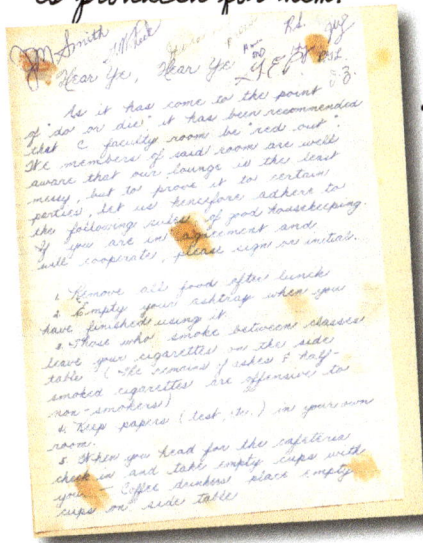

January 11, 1961

Trouble in the faculty room!! A hand-written announcement posted and signed by faculty members stated that while C Lounge was the least messy of all of the Faculty Rooms, Five Rules were being put into place, including the emptying of ash trays and not leaving the remains of cigarette ashes behind. Everyone signed it. I am glad. Those of us who don't smoke find the cigarette odor offensive.

February 14, 1961, Valentine's Day

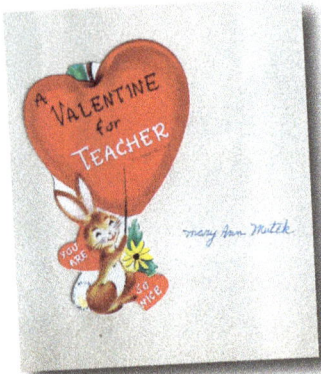

This morning I found on my desk the same style of penny Valentines that we had had at South Side in the 1940s. I kept as a memento the first one to land on my desk today; it was from Mary Ann Mutek with its message: "A Valentine for Teacher: You are so nice!"

March 3, 1961

The high school chorus sponsored a Mardi Gras Ball— costumes required! What a great time, grand fund-raising idea, and super morale builder as we struggle with the effort (more than some realized) required to produce a school musical with a totally inexperienced cast and crew. We are flyin' high with no parental complaints that I am aware of. Considering this is a very conservative area, it is surprising. I am sure some of the more conservative/moderate parents are a bit concerned about doing a musical—and a Mardi Gras Ball! At least there were no "scanty" costumes—at the Ball or for the Musical, as *Good News* takes place at a college and the students can wear their own street clothes. (Also there is no money for costumes.) A number of Freshmen are in the chorus! Rehearsals are going well.

Sometime during the spring the eighth grade sponsored a dance, the Spring Thaw, and the following year as ninth graders they held the Sweetheart Swing.

April 21, 1961

The Junior High Theatre Club presented its one-act play this evening. Harold's costume—complete with the high turban—was all I had hoped it would be. We had a good crowd in attendance.

May 20, 1961, Good News!

Dress rehearsal last evening went well and the curtain went up on "Good News" at 8:00 p.m. this evening with great anticipation. None were disappointed. (Of course, I had never seen a high school musical, so had nothing to compare this to, but I thought it was outstanding!)

June 7, 1961, Last Day of School

I felt sorry to see my ninth graders leave. However, they were ready and look forward to high school. A small cadre of them chanted as they left the building this afternoon: "High School Here We Come!" However, this was more mocking than serious.

CAST
(In Order of Appearance)

Tom Marlow	John Eckenroth
Patricia Bingham	Marilyn Miller
Flo	Carol Sanders
Windy	Barry Thompson
Slats	Lee Moyer
Millie	Emily Trefz
Babe O'Day	JoAnn Eshenour
"Beef" Saunders	Paul Orlowsky
"Pooch" Kearny	John Hall
Bill Johnson	Gene Espenshade
Sylvester	Bob Achenbach
Constance Lane	Carol Bixler
Bobby Randall	Gerald Wampler
Charles Kenyon	Larry Shertzer
George	Bob Gibble
Jim	Jerry Brinser
Ben	Jim Erb
Pete	Bryan Deimler
Girl	Ginny Stroman
Gatekeeper	Fred Harner

College Girls .... Dorle Porter, Mary Ann Umberger, Donna Wagner, Carol Flacken, Marilyn Shertzer, Donna Whitmoyer, Donna Curry, Norma Fink, Diane Breckenmaker, Judy Miller, Barbara Fisher, Gloria Shertzer, Roberta Espenshade, Mary Ann Bashore, Betty Musser, Charlotte McCoy, Vivian Lewin, Kathy Shendler, Joyce Wolf, Wilma Espenshade, Marilyn Deimler, Connie Nichols

College Boys .... Gene Hertzer John McKee, Ken Willard, Ken Miller, Don Green, Barry Free, Richard George, Mike Stauffer, Larry Eshenour, Jim Simmons, George Chellew

Dancers .... Judy Ramser, Carol Kashee, Cynthia Aldrich, Barbara Olson, Charles McKee, Jim Erb, Ken Willard, Jim Simmons

The entire action of the play takes place at Tait College, a co-ed school in a small town just far enough south for lovely warm weather in October.

Act I

Scene 1.	The Campus
Scene 2.	The Dormitory
Scene 3.	The Campus

(Intermission 10 minutes)

Act II

Scene I.	The Sorority House
Scene II.	The Gateway to the Stadium
Scene III.	The Locker Room
Scene IV.	The Hole in the Fence
Scene V.	After the Game
Scene VI.	The Sorority House

Judith Ball	
Roberta Espenshade	
Dave Bikle	Piano
	Drums

Musical Numbers

Act I

Opening Chorus: Learning, Learning	Students
He's A Ladies Man	Flo & Girls
Dance	Dancers
Flaming Youth	Babe, Millie, Flo, Slats, Windy
Dance	Babe
Happy Days	Tom and College Boys
Just Imagine	Connie, Patricia and Millie
Dance	Cynthia Aldrich and Jim Erb
The Best Things in Life Are Free	Tom and Connie
Nothing in Life is Free	Beef
On the Campus	Flo, Windy, Millie, Sylvester and Students
Patter Song	George
The Varsity Drag	Flo, Windy, Millie, Sylvester and Students
Dance	Dancers
Baby! What?	Babe and Bobby
Lucky in Love	Tom and Connie
Tait Song	Students
Lucky in Love	Connie and Students

Judy Sener, at that time a sophomore who had been doing some babysitting for Jane Smith during the school year, spent the summer at Mt. Gretna with Jane, continuing in the role as baby sitter as Jane did summer stock at the Gretna Playhouse, notably *Plain Betsy*, where she stopped the show every night with her solo. Many of the students who had been in *Good News* went to see the show. I did, too! Twice!

GRETNA PLAYHOUSE
Summer Season 1962
Monday, July 30 through Saturday, August 11
Nightly Except Sunday—8:30 P. M.
Gene P. Otto, Jr.
Presents
Vivienne Cooke   Ruth Webb
in
"Damn Yankees"
Book by George Abbott & Douglass Wallop
Music & Lyrics by Richard Alder & Jerry Ross
Production Under the Direction of Charles F. Coghlan

Choreographer   Musical Director
Joseph Masiell   Richard L. Kline
Settings   Lighting
Robert de Mora   Ken Kuhn

"Damn Yankees" is presented through arrangement with MUSIC THE-
ATRE INTERNATIONAL of New York City.

CAST
(In Order Of Appearance)
JOE BOYD (LATER CALLED JOE HARDY) .... FRANK C. BORGMAN
MEG BOYD .... RUTH WEBB
MR. APPLEGATE .... JOSEPH MASIELL
SISTER .... PAT SULLIVAN
DORIS .... DORIS SCOTT
JOE HARDY .... JOHN MINTO
HENRY .... RICHARD ERICKSON
SCHOVIK .... BILL DE LAND
SMOKEY .... MICHAEL ARQUETTE
LINVILLE .... PETE ROMAN
VAN BUREN .... LEONARD FREY
ROCKY .... JIM McKOY
GLORIA THORPE .... JANE MELLIN SMITH
LYNCH .... JOHN WITTEL
WELCH .... LEO BADIA
LOLA .... VIVIENNE COOKE
MISS WESTON .... O'BEAN FIEDLER
COMMISSIONER .... RICHARD HIRSCH
MR. HAWKINS (POSTMASTER) .... KEN KOTHE
SUSIE .... DONNA WALMER
JACKIE .... CAROL KASBEE
PEGGY .... LINDA ADAMS
TEDDY .... MICHAEL SCHROPP
FREDDIE .... DENNIS STICK

ORCHESTRA
PIANOS .... RICHARD L. KLINE
                                                                              CAROL ESHELMAN
PERCUSSION .... ROBERT MORRISON

COMING ATTRACTIONS ON CHANNEL 8

Monday, August 13, 10:00 p.m.
JAPAN: EAST IS WEST—Social changes in Japan
discussed

Wednesday, August 15, 10:00 p.m.
ARMSTRONG CIRCLE THEATRE—Story of one man who
escaped Nazi tormentors

Friday, August 17, 9:30 p.m.
THE INDISCRIMINATE WOMAN—starring
Carol Lawrence and Dane Clark

Sunday, August 19, 11:50 p.m.
ADVENTURES IN PARADISE (premiere)—Gardner
MacKay as ship's captain in Pacific paradise

Monday, August 20, 9:00 p.m.
LUCY-DESI COMEDY HOUR—Fred MacMurray
and his wife June Haver are guests.

Monday, August 20, 10:00 p.m.
THRESHOLDS FOR TOMORROW—Effects of
science on your life explored.

Friday, August 24, 9:30 p.m.
THE LONELY WOMAN—Ameri-
can woman's fight against loneliness dramatized.

WGAL-TV
Channel 8

July 11-July 24, 1961

Flew to California and did most of the tourist sites in the Los Angeles area, arranged by sister Kay, who interfaces with many venues in her position at TWA. The awe-striking moment for me was a visit to Griffith Observatory, location of "Rebel Without a Cause," where I confirmed that my first impression of this movie in 1955 really had been a defining moment. I also saw for the first time on stage "Bye, Bye, Birdie" at the Civic Light Opera House; absolutely loved it!

Itinerary for July 11-July 24, 1961:

✓ July 11 – fly over Grand Canyon

✓ July 12 – Olvera Street; Chinatown

✓ July 13 – Farmers Market; Hollywood and Vine; Dino's; Le Crazy Horse; Villa Nova

✓ July 14 – Knotts Berry Farm; stage coach

✓ July 15 – *Bye, Bye, Birdie*; Riverside Drive; Walt Disney Studio

✓ July 16 – Movie Stars homes in Beverly Hills; Santa Monica; Long Beach; L.A. Harbor; Marine Land; Pacific Ocean

CURTAIN CALL
LOS ANGELES CIVIC LIGHT OPERA ASSOCIATION
ROBERT F. HASTINGS, PRESIDENT
24TH ANNUAL SEASON   EDWIN LESTER, GENERAL DIRECTOR

BYE BYE BIRDIE

- ✓ July 19 – Griffith Observatory, Park & Zoo
- ✓ July 20 – Warner Bros. Studio: Maverick, Hawaiian Eye, 77 Sunset Strip
- ✓ July 21 – Disneyland
- ✓ July 23 – Hollywood Bowl: Laurel Canyon

Labor Day, September 1961

All ready for tomorrow; I understand this class is a good one, many bright kids. Eighth grade teachers hated to see them leave D-wing.

By the second year of teaching I began to understand the phrase "born ten years too soon." I liked these young people in my classes and I could identify with them, smiling to myself as they found their way—something my generation had not been able to do until we were well into our twenties.

October 9, 1961

Eighth grade teachers were right. This IS a good class. Many bright students who seem to be hard workers for freshmen. Funny, Mrs. Lanshe said her eighth grade top section this year looks like a good group, but not as many stars as last year's classes had. However, she likes them and expects they will do well overall. And she has already identified some to make a good junior high newspaper staff.

October 14, 1961

The musical "Fiorello" is playing at

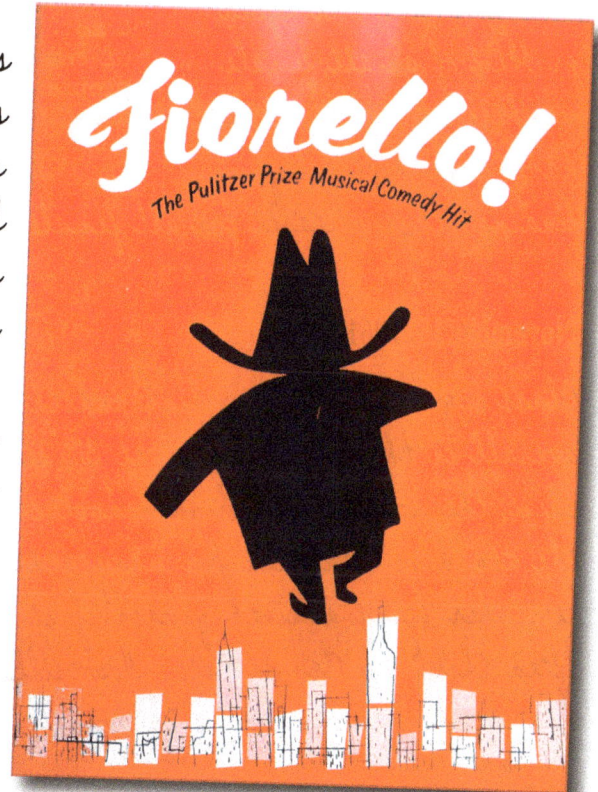

Fiorello!
The Pulitzer Prize Musical Comedy Hit

the Hershey Theatre, attracting a number of LD students who had stars in their eyes after being in Good News. And in November a group of us are going to see the Ice Follies at the Hershey Arena ice rink.

October 15, 1961

There was an article in the school newspaper about the Modern Theatre Club for which I am advisor:

"The Club is discussing the current musicals on Broadway, the most recent discussion being "West Side Story." We have a challenging problem of an all-female membership and will have some difficulty in finding plays suitable for all females."

> ### MODERN THEATRE CLUB
> The Modern Theatre Club, which meets Monday activity with Mrs. Ball, in discussing the different musicals that appeared on Broadway.
> They have a special problem of an all female attendance. The club will have some difficulty in finding plays suited for them.
> Lately the main topic of discussion was the musical "The West Side Story." The members of the club hope to see the movie when it comes to Harrisburg.
> Something to look for is their current project of compiling a list of the T.V. programs appropiate for Jr. High students. This appears in the C.General Lab.

November 15, 1961

Class sizes are still too high and this ninth grade class is the largest class overall in the whole school at 319 students. I am beginning to see myself in them, the way my own high school class was—all eager, the brightest class the teachers had seen for many years (as they later told some of us). How well I remember being a ninth grader; just like the proverbial yesterday. I still often think of Mr. Sabbato. How silly he must have thought we were. And how we had such crushes on him.

December 4, 1961

Jane has opened the musical this year to a few more hand-picked students from the ninth grade she thinks will add to the ensemble for "The Boy Friend." And since the kids are wearing some of their own outfits, they will fit in (with a bit of added 1920s flair) with the setting of a college campus.

Harold Snyder has a featured role in the show and he is only a sophomore! I hope these kids realize how wonderful it is to be in a musical—something I always had longed for. Well, at least I can enjoy being part of this one.

Cast
(in order of appearance)

Hortense	Barb Olson
Maisie	Donna Walmer
Dulcie	Barb Fisher
Fay	Marilyn Miller
Nancy	Mary Ann Umberger
Polly Browne	Carol Bixler
Marcel	Mike Stauffer
Pierre	Robert Gibble
Alphonse	Larry Eshenour
Madame Dubonnet	Alice Wiest
Bobby Van Husen	Gerry Wampler
Percival Browne	Lee Moyer
Tony	David White
Lord Brockhurst	Harold Snyder
Lady Brockhurst	Vivian Lewin
Gendarme	Kenneth Miller
Waiter	Brian Deimler

Dancers

Marilyn Seitzinger
Carol Kasbee
Judy Rainey
Mary Ann Umberger
Marilyn Deimler
Lynn Weeks
Audrey Roland
Donna Walmer
Kathy Lenker

Charles McKee
Barry Stopfel
George Wagner
Bobby Gibble
Jim Simmons
Darrell Howard
Earl Williard
Gerry Wampler
Don Green

Student Choreographers:
Carol Kasbee

Student Director	Charles McKee
Student Musical Director	Mary Ann Bashore
Stage Managers	Mike Stauffer
	Anna Dibeler
	Judy Sener

Ensemble

Dianne Breckenmaker
Peggy Weaver
Judy Ramsey
Susan Flocken
Karen Fair
Eleanor Kauffman
Norma Fink
Donna Curry
Gloria Verdellia
Portia Kirkpatrick
Bryan Deimler
Mildred Goss
Linda Banks
Nancy Brandt
Carol Heisey
Kathy Lenker
Joanne Kettering
Judy Miller
Charlotte McCoy
Kathy Sheeder
Ann Seaman
Marilyn Shertzer
Sally Walters
Betty Musser

Chester Morris
Jim Erb
George Chellew
Karl Bell
Dennis Patrick
Bill Campbell
John Burtner
Jack Musser
Bob Baumbreh
Paul Orlowsky
Elaine Learch
Nancy Smith
Kenneth Miller
Don Green
Don Page
Frank Pratt
Barry Thompson
Mike Krosevic
Don Miller
Terry Mills
Sam Lehman
Tom Hauer
Harry Dworchak

Musical Numbers
Act I

Overture	
	Judith Ball & Roberta Espenshade .... Pianos
	Lester Stucky .... Drums
Perfect Young Ladies	Hortense and Girls
The Boy Friend	Polly, Girls, Dancers and Ensemble
Won't You Charleston With Me	Maisie and Bobby
Fancy Forgetting	Mme. Dubonnet and Percy
I Could Be Happy With You	Polly and Tony
Soft Shoe	Carl Kasbee and Barry Stopfel
Repraise-The Boy Friend	Ensemble

December 17, 1961

A group of us held a Faculty Christmas House-Hopping Party tonight with guests traveling to three separate Open Houses (mine included).

These kinds of faculty socials continued through the first several years, but gradually diminished as faculty married. New social alliances formed around marriages and, before too long, families. I didn't really fit in.

The Culture of Lower Dauphin

During the third year (1962-63) an emerging culture of the school began to shape just who we would be as an institution. One of the most important elements for success was that both students and faculty were vested in making the school vibrant because they had had a voice in its formation.

Many years later Mr. Kenneth Staver, after becoming the Dean of Students, credited the success of Lower Dauphin High School to several factors, including the student leadership in the early classes, "In the Class of 1963 were a good half dozen students who were 'out of this world'—especially Bobby Gibble, Joyce Keener, Fred Shope, Carol Flocken, and Vivian Lewin. Mrs. Lewin was a driving force with this class and the high school in general in bringing things together." He then looked directly at me and said, "The next class like that was your Class of 1965. What is really unusual was to see two such groups separated by only two years. Such classes would not be seen again until your first 'English Enrichment' in the early 1970s when you patterned that program on the success of your teaching and working with the Class of 1965 for three years."

He further noted, "In the early years the full support of Hummelstown (in all ways) was critical to the district's success." Additional factors were that the officers at Olmsted Air Force Base paid tuition to send their children to Lower Dauphin and this district began to be viewed as "the school of choice" for those moving to the area. When the Medical Center began to grow, we had our share of students from these families as well.

He added, "Our vocational agriculture program was another factor, particularly the leadership training it provided to those like Russ Cassel, Jay Brandt, Galen and Jay Kopp (who was the first president of the FFA), and countless others. It was a loss when we no longer could financially justify continuing the program."

He continued, "Another crucial factor was providing activity buses, transportation for those who lived in the townships; in fact, these buses were critical to both the athletic and music programs. This also helped those teachers who were willing to offer enriched, specialized programs both as part of their curriculum and in extra-curricular activities.

"Further positive factors were the formal study and travel experiences such as managed by David Smith and the AIFS program; field trips to see great art and architecture and performances; unusual offerings such as Archeology, Longitudinal Studies, the early years of English Enrichment when it was your vision and under your direction; and the personal mentoring many teachers provided, such as the Christmas Open House you hosted for alumni home from college as well as arranging for the school's inviting these students to visit classes and talk to the students here about the various colleges they were attending. And it helped when they said they had been well-prepared at Lower Dauphin."

Later in a conversation initiated by Mr. Staver on September 15, 2009 after he had read the articles the Lower Dauphin Alumni Association had been running in *The Sun* relative to the then upcoming Golden Jubilee in 2010, he asked me what the Association was doing regarding the school musicals, "because it was the musicals that played a crucial role in setting the direction for the kind of high school Lower Dauphin would become." He noted that Jane Mellin Smith was determined to do a musical the first year with students who were just getting to know one another in a school community where musicals had never before been performed. Many citizens from the town and the townships were skeptical of such an undertaking and had no idea that they could enjoy such a stage production. However, both Mr. Emerich and Mr. Taylor saw the value of this endeavor and supported the efforts.

Mr. Staver continued with a smile, "Here she was, just charging ahead. It was all her influence that made this happen. She never had the space needed for music classes or a chorus rehearsal. She taught from a cart and never had a classroom or any other permanent space. She even held classes in the cafeteria—we were so crowded for space, even from the beginning."

"Doing a musical was the catalyst in elevating the culture of the school. It brought something to this area that hadn't been before. More importantly, what came out of all of this was the fact that it was the musical that first year that put music and art on the same table as English and Latin."

He continued, "What you did in your classroom with enrichment activities and what Jane did with the musicals gave us the foundation for the pursuit of a liberal arts education for the students. It is what led to scheduling chorus and band during the day, as areas as important as any other subject. Then when Marie Bergan came in the 1970s and created an orchestra literally from scratch, she added to the importance of music and culture for the district."

Finally and unexpectedly, came these words from this estimable member of the Greatest Generation who was directly addressing me, a member of the Silent Generation, "High school students in the 1960s and 1970s had the most extraordinary female teachers, such as you—**educated women who at any other time in history would have entered other professions. These students were very lucky**."

The High School

From My Diary

April 10, 1963

Mr. Emerich stopped by my classroom and asked if I would consider moving to the high school next year for the premier assignment of teaching three sections of British Literature, one or two sections of American Literature and one or two sections of Public Speaking!!!! It is the absolutely best assignment in the whole school! The icing on the cake is that I would be reunited with the Class of 1964 and the Class of 1965. This also includes managing the speakers for Commencement and directing at least two class plays.

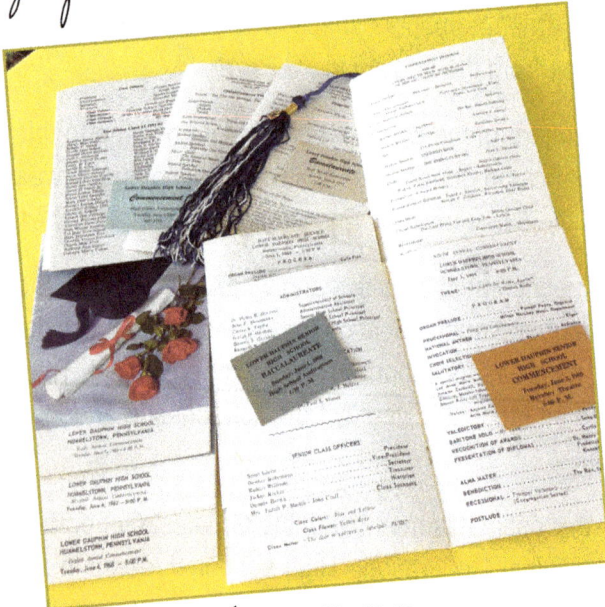

Commencement, 1963

A nice, typical high school Commencement. I enjoyed it and took mental notes since I will be involved with Commencements beginning next year. In addition to students, there was an invited speaker, the President of California State College.

August 29, 1963

I LOVE my new classroom, B-1. Spent a lot of time this week setting things up, arranging items on my desk and trying out, of all things, a lectern!!!! The front of the room is elevated about a foot above the rest of the room.

It is a large space designed as a small stage. With only my desk, chair and lectern on it, it works so well to be able to see everyone. It is the best classroom in the building. Oh, and there is a door in the back of the room that leads directly into the B-Wing Faculty Room lunch area. How convenient!

I am excited to see my classes, since I already know them from ninth grade. I wonder how many of them will faint to see me, anticipating another year of what they probably consider a lot of work!

September 3, 1963

Judy Sener stopped by after school; she was in her glory at leaving for West Chester and her enthusiasm was a welcome sight.

December 29, 1963

I sensed that tonight would be among the last of the "original faculty" parties when I held a Christmas Open House at my home, 9:00–11:00 p.m., complete with formal printed invitations.'

April 17, 1964

"The Falcon Flash" did a profile on me, since I am new to the high school, noting my philosophy of teaching: ... "trying to interest her students in loving knowledge, and understanding the world we live in today and in trying to show them through literature we can learn to understand other people, as well as ourselves."

The Theme for Commencement 1964 was "Pathways to Life." The student organist was Carol Kauffman, a junior. Of interest, the Honor Students were noted as those "with a 'B' average or better for three years." There were 35 names out of 179 members of the class, not quite 20%, an indicator that grade inflation was not as prevalent as it later became.

LOWER DAUPHIN HIGH SCHOOL
Hummelstown, Pennsylvania
June 2, 1964

COMMENCEMENT PROGRAM
Theme: "Pathways to Life"

Organ Prelude		Carol Kauffman
Prelude e' Fugue in a minor		Bach
Prie' re a' Notre Dame		Boellmann
Trumpet Voluntary		Purcell
Class Processional	Pomp and Circumstance (congregation standing)	Ed Elgar
Our National Anthem	(congregation standing)	Audience
Invocation	(congregation standing)	Rev. John E. Patterson
Student Speaker	The President's Welcome	Randall Maurice Kahler
Student Speaker	Conduct and Courage Lead to Honor	Joanne Faye Kettering
Music	America - Our Heritage.....Steele	Senior Concert Choir
Student Speaker	Faith and Wisdom Lead to Maturity	George Edward Chellew
Student Speaker	Perseverance and Knowledge Lead to Success	Karen Lee Fair
Music	Give Me Your Tired, Your Poor......Berlin	Senior Concert Choir
Recognition of Award Winners		Curtis S. Taylor
Presentation of Diplomas	David J. Emerich, Supervising Principal	
	James L. Helsel, President Joint Board	
Alma Mater		Senior Concert Choir
Benediction	Lord Bless You and Keep You......Lutkin	
Recessional	Pomp and Circumstance......Ed Elgar	
Postlude	Pilgrims Chorus......Wagner	

June 29 – July 3, 1964

Attended the World's Fair near New York City. Wonderful experience, especially the House of Tomorrow, the Unisphere, and the Belgian waffles. On July 1 saw Barbra Streisand in "Funny Girl" at the Winter Garden Theatre. Smashing!

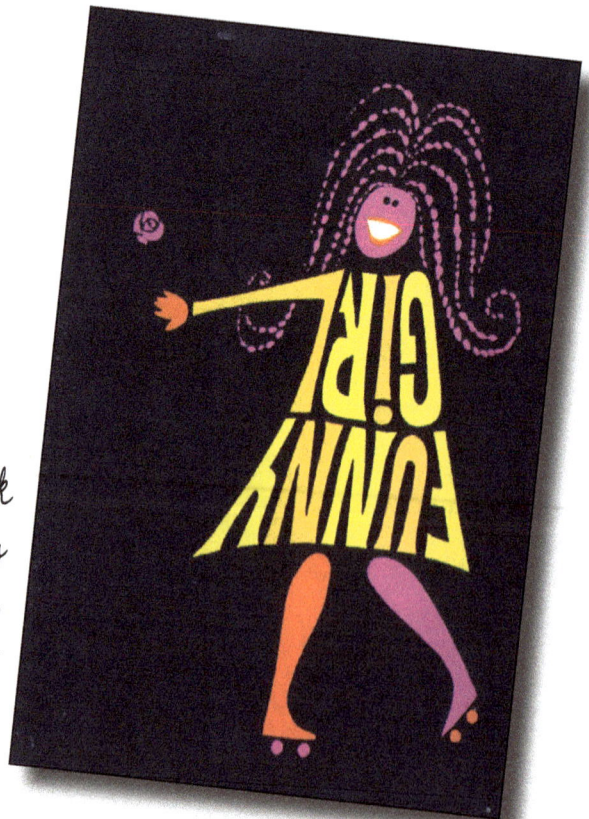

September 8, 1964

The first day back to school. My focus was totally on the students rather than seeing any colleagues for a lot of reasons. I am now in a Master's Program that meets on Saturdays, many of the faculty who were new in the fall of 1960 are now married and starting families, the Stanitski twins are gone, and, truthfully, in a high school there is little opportunity to build close friendships with other adults.

September 23, 1964

Just returned from taking a group of students to see Richard Burton in "Hamlet" at the State Theatre, delivered through a process called Electronovision which broadcasts the performance from the stage of the Lunt-Fontanne Theatre in NYC.[7] Outstanding.[8]

It wasn't long before it was <u>very clear how isolated teachers are,</u> each in his/her own classroom for most of the day. There is no "gathering at the water cooler" for teachers as was typical in business offices. Many of us rarely left our classrooms; by law we were/are responsible at all times for the students assigned at any given time, so even a restroom break was/is problematic, let alone an exchange of pleasantries or quick chat with a colleague.

Further, schedules change every year and sometimes every semester, so lunch periods change as well and teachers rarely see the same cohorts in the lunch room from one semester or year to the next. And extra-curricular activities generally involve only one adult and any number of students, so there is no adult conversation there, either.

Through the years B-1 was a refuge for students who needed a friend, a protector, a confidante, or just a safe haven. Later, as they moved into adulthood, many of these students became my friends. I am sure some of the other faculty experienced a similar friendship with students, but it was not something we discussed.

November 10, 1964

I took a group of students to the State Theatre to see the film "Macbeth" with Maurice Evans and Dame Judith Anderson. Stunning.

Little did I know that in the late 1970s Dame Judith Anderson would take the lead role of *Hamlet* in a touring company who performed in the Lower Dauphin auditorium the evening our English Enrichment group returned from an stirring three-day excursion as guests of Craig College (a member of the first English Enrichment cohort) at West Point where, among many events, we saw *A Midsummer Night's Dream* and had rooms at the famous Thayer Hotel, with a bonus of examining its Gothic Revival architecture as part of our classwork.

November 17, 1964

I received a reply from Robert Swartley, a teacher at Lower Dauphin, who had moved to Bristol, PA as a guidance counselor, responding to my request for information to help some students who needed guidance on applying to college.

This is just one example of the colleagues we had at LD, some for a short tenure, and the assistance offered by them, even though our students typically had no idea that we were gathering information to help them. Bob's generous assistance would make a difference for some of our students of how to apply to colleges. In fairness it probably should be noted that with the unprecedented number of mid-decade Baby Boomers, guidance counselors everywhere were no doubt overwhelmed; in any case, students often turned to teachers for help.

"I enjoyed talking to you last evening. It is always nice to know that someone remembers you. People sometimes do forget, you know. The information on L.D. students is always welcome. You and I are much alike in our feelings about the young people that we once taught.

About our young friend; she should write to the Dean of Admissions and ask for the forms she needs. Also, she should take the SAT and three specific Achievement Tests. The college may require her to take the OAIS test also. She then should see Mrs. Beers about the Occupational Aptitude Interest Survey test. I have information here which says she must take this test. Also have her inquire about the Parents Confidential Statement.

I haven't forgotten about David; just didn't get around to checking information yet for him. Also, if it can be done at an appropriate time, say "Hello" to your classes for me.

Yours Truly, Bob

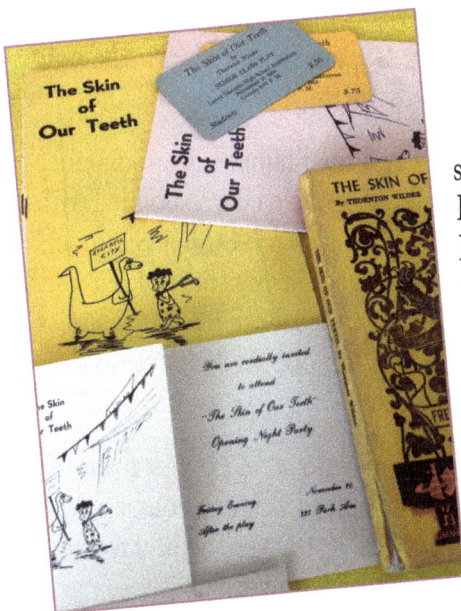

In November 1964 I began to extend hospitality to the students I had as seniors by holding an "Opening Night Reception" in my home for the cast and crew of the Senior Class Play, for which I was the faculty director. The students also held their own cast party the following night, marking the first time a play at the high school was offered on two consecutive nights.

March 11, 1965

Department Chairs were announced. I am the youngest.

365

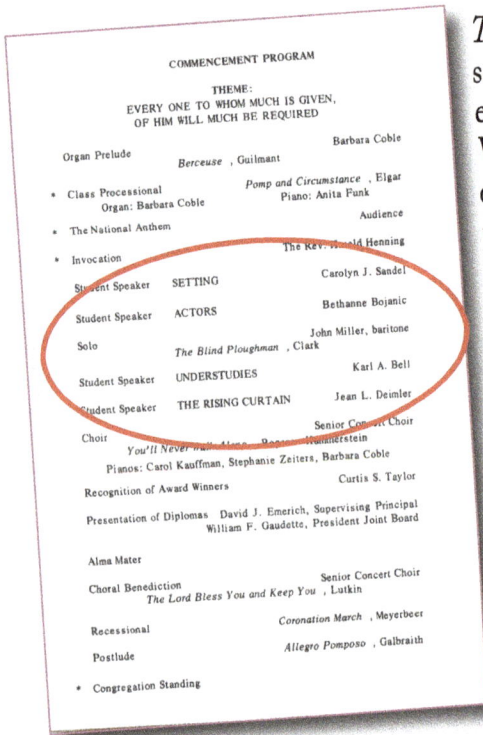

The English Students

This competitive graduating Class of 1965 finished their high school grade point averages with three seniors sharing the same exact final score, so, rather than drawing lots, we honored three Valedictorians, and a Salutatorian. Imagine the chances of this occurring! Preparing four distinct orations with a common theme based on their class motto, we were only beginning to discuss some variations to graduation programs, ideas that would expand through the following years.

Further, the colleges were full at the time, while trying to accommodate this massive onslaught of enrollees; even two of our three Valedictorians had to accept their second choice of colleges. (Of the top four students, two later earned PhDs and one a JD.)

This class had, indeed, been extraordinary in all regards, just as Mr. Staver later noted. I gifted several of the graduates with *The Readers' Guide to Literature* or *Merriam-Webster's Collegiate Dictionary*.

The last English class of The English Students was a celebration, as was appropriate after sharing four courses (three years of English and a public speaking course) with some of them. To celebrate the event I prepared a farewell—*Ode Written Upon the Occasion of the Graduation of Friends*. The only resemblance to fine poetry was its title in imitation of William Wordsworth.

In the fall of 1965 my daily focus moved to the Class of 1966, while I maintained correspondence with the Classes of '64 and '65. As each class headed to college and military service I corresponded with many of them and sent homemade baked goods, notes, books, news clippings, and other reminders of home. Because there were no electronic means by which to do research, I had my share of requests from them as to where particular information might be found, mailing to the college freshmen copies of reports they had written for my classes, and loaning books. However, not one student ever ask me to review assignments he/she had written for various college assignments.

What was most validating for me was the number of these students who were exempt from the traditional college "freshman comp" class and who were assigned to advanced English courses. Also gratifying was to hear from some that their "American Lit." and "Brit Lit." notes were helpful to them in their history classes, as well as in their literature—and some philosophy—courses.

In addition to taking classes on my way to earning a Master of Science degree the following year, in the fall of 1965 I began a three-year adventure (and supplemental income) for myself—and using a stage name—by performing with piano and vocals at various area supper clubs.

At the high school, I continued serving as advisor in many areas, including the Senior Class Play, *Ten Little Indians*, with H. Michael (Mike) Strite as Student Manager. Mike was very capable and had interest in both sports and the arts. Not many high school plays can boast a football team starter as their student manager. And his father drove a Morgan which provided a lot of fodder for banter!

Senior Class Play

CAST

(In Order of Appearance)

Rogers	Steve Lower
Mrs. Rogers	Jan Calhoon
Fred Narracott	Dale Espenshade
Vera Claythorne	Bev Bolton
Philip Lombard	Walt Sener
Anthony Marston	Rick Lenker
William Blore	Gary Lentz
General MacKenzie	Ray Tritch
Emily Brent	Pam Rainey
Sir Lawrence Wargrave	Mel Lingle
Dr. Armstrong	Ron Good

Prompters	Verna-Miller
	Marsha Mountz

Director	Judith T. Ball
Student Director	H. Michael Strite
Scenery and Lighting	Robert R. Fickes

Lower Dauphin High School Auditorium

November 20, 1965   Curtain 8:00 P. M.

TEN LITTLE INDIANS

CURTAIN: 8:00

368

Friends from British Literature, Commencement, Baccalaureate, Falconaire, Musical, B-1 Classes & Otherwise

You Are Cordially Invited to the

Nineteenth Annual Christmas Open House

T—Please help to spread the word

Merry Christmas, ... and Jay! ... I'm having some ... friends in on ... -ber 29th around ... p.m. I hope ... can join us ... share some ... memories ... have a happy ... day!

... ith Witmer

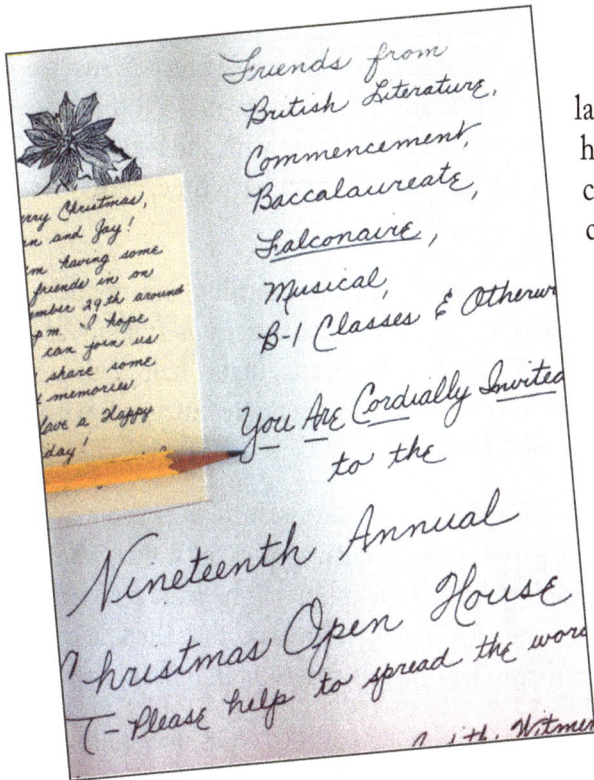

When "The English Students," as Barry Stopfel '65 later dubbed them, came home for Christmas break, I hosted a Christmas Open House so these collegians could catch up with one another in an appropriate, celebratory social setting.

I continued to hold annual Christmas Open Houses for former students with the last one held in 1986[9], marking more than twenty years. In June of 1986 I accepted a principalship at Lower Dauphin High School, later becoming Assistant to the Superintendent. To this day, I attend class reunions to which I am invited and retain a friendship with many of those in classes of the mid-to-late 1960s.

In February 1966 I offered to the senior class a non-credit, symposium course on the Humanities, held every Monday evening in my home during second semester. It was structured, well-attended, and productive. I don't think any of the students had ever before experienced that kind of forum for discussion, but I felt it was important for them to learn how to do this before they left for college. According to an article in *The Hummelstown Sun*, topics were to include "What are reformers and critics attacking in society?" "Can man master himself?" and "Why have men rebelled and revolted?"

trophy.

• • • • •

A humanities course, initiated by Mrs. Judith T. Ball, senior English teacher was begun recently for the benefit of students interested in the branches of learning concerned with man (languages, literature, philosophies, etc). Senior class college prep students meet together on Monday evening from seven to nine o'clock for the course.

Activities at the meetings vary from small-group discussions to speeches and lectures by the students. Samples of topics proposed were "What are reformers and critics attacking in society?", "Can man master himself?" and "Why have men rebelled and revolted?"

The program is voluntary. No grade or credit is given for the course.

At the close of the course the group gave me roses with the following message, "Each of these roses represents a symposium meeting where we were encouraged to grow, challenge, and be challenged, and by this, we learned. We extend our sincere thanks to the person we feel really deserves to be called teacher." I believe my students would agree that I opened my skills, my home, and my heart to them, and in that order.

Taking graduate courses kept me grounded and afforded friendships with adults in these classes. One in particular was Captain William Allen, career military, who became a close friend and debate partner in our grad class discussions. He was also a good source for ideas for reading material "the college students" had asked me for.

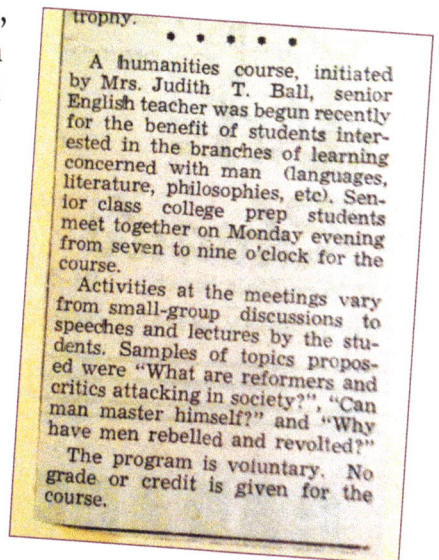

On June 24, 1966, he wrote, "As for books and plays with some ideas: *Tea and Sympathy*, maybe *You Can't Go Home Again, Youngblood Hawk, Sweet Bird of Youth*, and a few others that I'll think of after you don't need them. I'll try to remember to bring you *The Republic* along with the issue of *The New Republic* that has Stephen Spender's review of Sylvia Plath's poetry. If you have time, check the article in *Saturday Review* on a new national anthem."[10]

Taking such graduate courses helps teachers in many more ways than just "learning" information. It helps keep us connected to those in other fields and provides us with class discussions and out-of-class conversation that affords a window into a world that is filled with cohorts. It also helps balance our thoughts and experiences and serves as a reminder of what we as teachers are entrusted with. Friendship and scholarship with adult colleagues is a pleasant leveler.

What such experiences do not answer, however, is how to balance relationships with peers and with students. What makes such a relationship as I had with these students, atypical as it was, work? Through the years I often asked myself what happened at Lower Dauphin High School to have produced such a relationship between a teacher and her students. Further, I marvel that the Class of 1965 maintained a stronger bond between and among themselves than is common in most classes.

Part of the reason for my closer relationship with the high schoolers of the sixties may be that I was Class Advisor for the Class of 1965 for their years in high school, as well as their classroom teacher for, in some cases, four courses. During the 1960s alone, I directed six plays (five of which were not typical teen-age productions) and worked with three musicals. I designed six creative Commencement programs, including scripts for speaking choirs and dramas during that decade and coached twice as many valedictory and salutatory addresses—and this was just the extra-curricular events. Was that enough to cause the close friendships that resulted? Or was there something more?

We had many adventures, intellectual, artistic, and social, during those short and spectacular four years together and, as I came to know a core of these students over this period of time, so I came to know myself better, and wanted to be surrounded by and share with those who also were interested in finding themselves, and who wanted to understand life and its meaning, both in the 1960s and many years beyond.

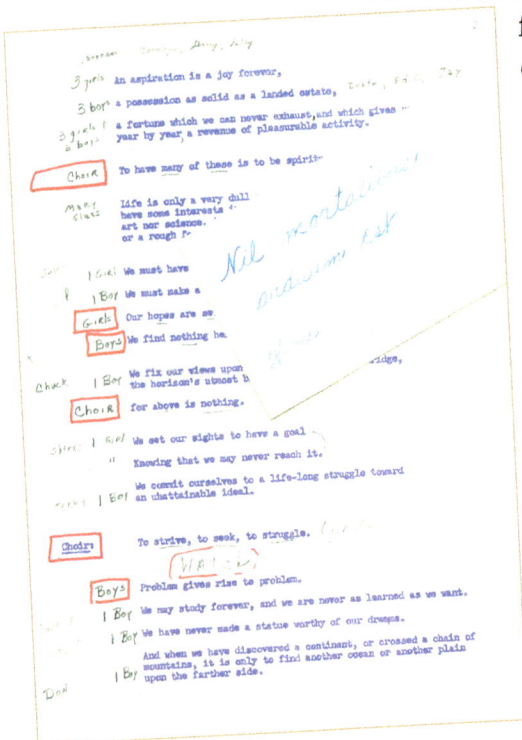

And as an amateur archivist I saved programs from football games and plays, copies of the *Falcon Flash* and *The Falconaire*, scripts from speeches, selected homework papers, grade books, bulletin board displays, signs the students made, newspapers and magazines, greeting cards, and wedding invitations, all indicators of what we had thought, studied, experienced—and cared about. Just as the school day does not end at the dismissal bell, so our intertwined experiences continued, and in some ways were made richer, through the thread of the passing years.

Every time I come upon the photograph of those on stage for *The Skin of Our Teeth* (Thornton Wilder) I wonder if many other schools have managed to produce that play, to say nothing of Edward Albee's "The Sand Box," "Ten Little Indians" (Agatha Christie), "Our Town" (Wilder), "Arms and the Man" (George Bernard Shaw, 1894), and "She Stoops to Conquer" (Oliver Goldsmith, 1773). Further, I see a composite of those in the casts whose influence remains strong in the narrative of Lower Dauphin and the wider community.

Twenty-five years following graduation, together we (a committee of former students) formed the Lower Dauphin Alumni Association which has been a grand addition to the school through the archives it maintains and the displays it places in the huge walk-in showcase constructed through donations by Alumni and curated by a member of the Class of 1965.

Twenty years following that—again mainly assisted by those who were graduated in the 1960s, we celebrated the school's fifty-year anniversary, appropriately named "The Golden Jubilee"—yearlong, culminating in a blow-out week-end celebration of football, tours, and a gala. All of this, along with fifty years of history, was included in the 500-page story of the school: *Loyal Heart Proclaim: The First Fifty Years of Lower Dauphin High School*, marshaled by those same dazzling, dependable English Students.

Loyal Hearts Proclaim
Lower Dauphin High School: The First Fifty Years

These, indeed, have been distinctive times, even singular sensations……and we can add to that list weddings, performances, additional community projects such as building a library and a field house, multitudes of letters, and ordinations, including that of the Reverend Barry L. Stopfel whose investiture made international headlines.

Barry Lee Stopfel

Kind, witty, caring, bearing with grace his being arbitrarily banned from the high school chorus room in the spring of his senior year, quietly wearing his integrity, maintaining balance in a skewed world, **Barry Stopfel** was most interested in directing and communications. In addition to performing in the school musicals, he also did summer stock where he grew up very quickly, but with quietly absorbing all he could about musical theatre. He served as Student Director of the Senior Class Play, *The Skin of Our Teeth*, and solely directed Edward Albee's "The Sand Box."

Like many of his peers he had a dream, even as he sluffed off assumptions that he would become a minister in the Brethren Church, torn between serving in the ministry and finding a place in the entertainment industry. He entered Boston University, alarmed, as most of his classmates were with their own perceived lack of readiness, that he didn't have "the right stuff." Well, he more than had what was needed, unexpectedly claiming a place in history. And few knew the role he played in ministering to those suffering from AIDS, when at the time there were more rumors than data on this medical scourge.

Barry loved Boston and traveling to New York at any opportunity. About one event (Movie Premiere for *The Oscar*) he wrote, "…sitting across from me at the premiere were Elke Sommer, Edie Adams, Stephan Boyd, Eleanor Parker, Joseph Levine, and Edith Head." Self-effacing, he added, "It was sort of depressing taking the MTA back to a dormitory."

He later recalled, "In that year we still had weekly bed linen change, free dry cleaning, and maid service … jackets and ties were required for dinner. Come to think of it, I haven't lived as luxuriously in all the following years. I'm grateful that I lived and drew it all in, for, as the sages say, it would be a tragedy to come to die and discover that one had never really lived."

After earning a BA from Boston University and an MA from Columbia University, Barry became a marketing communications executive in New York City and began his studies for his Master of Divinity degree from Union Theological Seminary. Before entering seminary he had been the Director of Marketing for the Joffrey Ballet.

Today the Reverend Barry L. Stopfel is an Episcopal priest, the author of numerous published articles and a book, *Courage to Love*, the story of a committed gay relationship. He was ordained in 1991 by a Bishop who had been tried for heresy by an ecclesial court, both events garnering wide coverage by the press. Barry now makes his home in South Carolina. For all his success, he remains humble and self-effacing, posing a philosophical question, "Do you have any insight into why I seem to periodically and willingly, maybe even masochistically, throw myself into an emotional Cuisinart with a mixture of dislocation and loneliness?"

I responded, "Yes."

He recently wrote to me, "My years at LD are forever framed in the nature of our relationship. It was one that swept me up in ways that few high school students would ever know. On both our parts it was a relationship that was an exploration of land beyond the norm, the permitted, the blessed. We both gained much from our friendship as we covered terrain that was rebellious, expansive, thrilling, courageous, and for me often beyond any words I could conjure. It was infused with passion, desire, self-discovery, and intellect. It was, therefore, holy and soulful. It was of the stuff that the Greek philosophers taught when they spoke of the highest values and attributes of the human heart and mind. Now, there's an education."

Barry was one of the three students who knew me best, who saw beyond the role I held as a professional. The relationship between us was a strong, but chaste, friendship in which we could joke at our own expense, especially after he was graduated from high school. We shared a simpatico matched only by that between Lois and me, yet different.

It likely is evident that there was a deep caring between us, a universal love, an affection of common interests, and even benevolence. And, most important, a great respect. It was not a romantic relationship and to say it was maternal would not be at all accurate. Platonic, yes, but more like a very rich fondness. He once wrote to me, "Among your most powerful influences upon me was the synthesis of eros and intellect.

Who else but Barry could have understood when years later he wrote, "Your fudge is unparalleled," and I replied, "That is because a measure of your thinking it is that it is a Proustian memory."

Through the years of our friendship we have tried to define its bond, but have never risked framing it entirely. Through the years, he has termed this relationship far better than I ever could, perhaps because I still am struggling with what I sense is a haunting sensation through the journey that made me feel that I had not fully carried my part of the friendship. I can't explain it, but it is almost as if there is something I feel I need to either apologize for or fulfill.

Later, as an Episcopalian priest, Barry confirmed, "To teach and listen to the other(s) because one cares about the outcome is something others pick up on consciously or otherwise. I have discovered over the years that love and relationship above doctrine is the most powerful message. The power of priesthood is in my humanity—perhaps it is so for teachers as well.

More recently he wrote, "As you say, our lives were and remain entwined. I would add that our love and friendship continue expanding beyond ourselves, ever-giving of life in ways we do not understand. As I reflect upon it, although I would not have had the word at the time, our bond was generative."

Harold Lee Snyder

The second student with whom I had a strong bond was **Harold Lee Snyder**, the first student with whom I made direct eye contact the first week of the first year of Lower Dauphin High School. The tallest boy in his ninth grade class, Harold was also one of the most quiet, reserved, and unfailingly polite. I could to this day identify the desk at which he was seated and can recall looking out over the sea of 37 faces, all new to that building and many to each other and certainly to most of the teachers. I was introducing new course material and trying to put the students at ease, full of trepidation myself, only a handful of years older than those who were facing me. And then there was the hint of a smile from the tall, lanky boy in the center of the room, who at 14, no doubt also was wondering what this class, this day, this year, and this high school would bring. I glanced at him and he smiled, the beginning of a friendship that was to last for 53 years.

Harold was cast as an Indian Maharaja in the first play I directed. Although I never met Mrs. Snyder, I remember Harold's coming up to me after play practice to tell me his mother did not know how to make a costume for the role he was to play. That is all that was said, and the following week, with a soft smile this young man, again after practice, assured me that a costume would be forthcoming. I had always hoped to thank Mrs. Snyder in person, as I silently had thanked her many times not only for arranging to have a costume made, but for rearing such an extraordinary son, one who was comfortable wherever he went.

Harold also was in the school musicals, always in a featured role, and, in an even more specialized role, was the first Lower Dauphin falcon mascot, wearing a costume covered with fabric cut with pinking shears to look like feathers (for what did we know about commercial costumers in those days?) and a large, heavy papier mâché headpiece in which he almost suffocated.

After high school Howie headed off to Shippensburg College. I sent him what his roommate and fraternity brothers laughingly called Care Packages—the first of many to the English Students—with homemade cookies and fudge. After 3½ years at Shippensburg, Harold, just like the young men who had left college and high school to serve in World War II, went into the service without fanfare, always comfortable in his own skin, even in Viet Nam.

As an adult Howie became a member of our family, just as he became the welcomed member of so many other families, for all who knew him would agree as to how well he fit into any family, any group, any place. Harold assimilated into the events in all of our homes, better even than some members of our own families.

When I was scheduled to chaperone a small group of students to Italy one spring in the early 1980s, one of the students canceled at the last minute and Harold filled in, becoming a surrogate big brother to the entourage, intuitively sensing when to be the adult and when to befriend any one of the group of youngsters. What I most remember, however, is that, as the lone adult male in our entire entourage of school groups, he was given the best of the rooms in our rooming houses; then, without hesitation, he would turn it over to me, taking the room without the hot water or the room without heat, and did this as a matter of course. This is only one of his many, nameless acts of kindness and unheralded consideration.

He came to our home every Christmastime and in 2001 my family and I hosted a 55th year birthday party for him, complete with dinner and live music for 40 guests.

Through the years Harold Snyder was steadfast. Even during times when we might not have seen each other regularly, I always knew he was only a phone call away. He was one of the few people—and probably the only one outside of the family—who was unfailing from the day I first met him. He helped me many times and was with us through our family tragedy with visits, offers of help, flowers, cards, dinner—and so much more when much of the time I was numb.

We had no idea that ten years later we would lose him to Agent Orange, and we were not ready for his leave-taking. I wanted only to again see him enter my home with a smile and a gentlemanly, "Hello, how are you?" I wanted to be able to say, as I did the very last time I saw him in hospice care, "I love you, too, Howie."

With heavy heart, I delivered the eulogy at the funeral, noting the heart-wrenching devotion of Howie's best friend from childhood, Byron Wyld, and Byron's wife, Beverly, who every day had walked the last, sorrowful journey with our dear Howie.

Lois Mae Downes

The third in this trilogy of young friends with whom I shared a closer friendship than typical, is **Lois Mae Downes**, who lived in the same block of the duplex Tom and I moved to during one of the times of residing in the same household. Although she was the youngest in her family, in many ways Lois was an old soul with great insight.

On the other hand, as the youngest child of her parents, Lois at times reminded me of a changeling child. She, of course, honored her parents, but, as is often the case, I believe they weren't always sure how to guide this spot of joy who had come late into their lives. I also believe the fact that Lois's brother, whom she revered, was my age helped her parents and siblings understand a friendship between Lois and me.

Like Barry and Harold, Lois was remarkable in being able to maintain a collegial friendship, as well as a mentee-to-mentor relationship, with me, but never as a proxy parent-child. She was wise beyond her years, unfailingly well-mannered and respectful, yet with each passing year with more leveling of the ten years that separated us in age.

Lois had a keen sense of humor as well as an ability to assess others privately, but rarely shared her personal viewpoint. She was an artist in her essence and inherently talented. She had an abundance of what I lacked, an "eye" for design, and it is she who enhanced my bulletin boards—and my own art choices—once she felt comfortable offering to assist. It was easy for me to enjoy her company and to rely on her advice when I was planning displays or redecorating. I especially relied on her after Tom and I purchased a house. It was Lois who helped me make it a home.

She "soaked up" all experiences, which were enhanced because of what she brought to every encounter. She was keenly observant of people but not judgmental. Most surprising in a young person was that she seemed to take every experience as a way to learn. Those who didn't know her might think her shy (and if she is reading this, she is probably even now laughing), not realizing that what she was doing was carefully assessing all of the information. She was a loner by choice, so I easily identified with her personality.

She loved the woods and—something I didn't know until she told me in a letter from Wittenberg—would take walks around our neighborhood late at night when all was still, especially if it had snowed!

Lois was one who wanted to "learn"—with a "liberal arts" heart, who admittedly sought a college education not so much to be credentialed in a field, but just to "be educated." When she wrote this in a letter I could hear my high school self saying almost the same words, that I wanted "to *learn*."

It bothered her when people—especially her parents—asked her what kind of career she wanted after college. Set design would have been an apt choice! I remember being delighted that she had the confidence to "join" stage crew at Wittenberg, because I had had to "steel myself" to audition for only the pit orchestra at Penn State, when I really wanted to audition for an on-stage role.

It was particularly a marvel—and a necessity--that she had the maturity and wisdom to be friends with Tom as well as with me; I think we all were sensitive to the tension in the household and often Lois's presence served as a kind of leveling.

And self-critical! Oh, my. With Lois I learned to laugh at both of us with our similar idiosyncrasies.

In some ways she knew me better than anyone else did. Case in point was a postscript to a letter she wrote to me, "Don't think my non-existing comments on your letters means they're unappreciated. We sense each other's reactions anyway. Read you loud and clear."

And, I, dear Lois, wish I had read you more clearly when you drifted away. I miss you. I can only hope that you will do what you suggested I do, in a letter when you wrote, "You have sense enough to let me bare my soul and go on about your business as if you had seen nothing. Thanks." Perhaps I can return the favor someday.

The Epicenter

What most clearly struck me about the 1960s generation as a whole was their ease with one another, particularly their ability to establish and maintain friendships. I am sure, like all young people since time immemorial, they had their moments of doubt (their letters from college attest to that), but there was always a sense of confidence in them not seen in previous generations of youth. Part of it likely was the fact that their parents had lived through the hard times of World War II, becoming what Tom Brokaw has called "the greatest generation." I also believe that their parents instilled in them the idea of **possibilities**, that they would have choices their parents never had.

But turning to the central question I have been asked many times: "During the 25 years you spent with students in your classroom, how did such strong bonds form and continue with students in the 1960s, particularly with those from the mid-1960s classes?"

As I searched for the answer, I came to believe part of the cause was the spate of protests of the times, on campuses and in many other places where young adults gathered. A key example is the campus protests between March of 1967 and April of 1968 at Columbia University, as these uprisings changed forever the nature of education, the power dynamics among administration, faculty, and students, and the right to free speech.

Barry Stopfel, who had participated in those protests at Columbia, recently reminded me of the far-reaching impact these demonstrations had had, affecting all education systems, spreading to many campuses and even trickling down to high schools. Perhaps this had been the underlying catalyst supporting the stand I took, often against the status quo and sometimes, but far less often, against the administration.

Perhaps, as Barry suggested, my relationship with these English Students was part of my own "coming out" narrative, influenced by my rebellion against the silence and my still-suppressed rage at the underestimation of women before and during these early years of teaching. In short, these protests likely had a very strong effect of providing courage and a platform for the way I taught.

I further credit my Liberal Arts education which generated a different product than did traditional Teacher Education programs. My university degree was expansive in literature, philosophy, history, and the sciences. As such, my entire approach to learning was deep in content and heavy in dialectics/analyses. The common theme in student comments, both spoken and written, reflects that my classes had the opportunity to explore, to reason, and to make connections. Most of what students wrote about these classes included descriptions such as "—who knows how to make a subject interesting. There was never a dull moment in your classes;"[11] "…you offered all of us a much broader education than just from the books;"[12] and "…you opened the door to understanding."[13]

I also discovered that I had much more than only a desire to teach well. The anthologies I chose for the American and British Literature courses, when the choice became mine to make, were intended as college texts, and I prepared for classes with precision and intensity, never depending on just the textbook. The class lectures and discussions were formal with a dash of levity, as the students would find in their college courses, the content honed and accurate (based on the extended research and materials I prepared), and the lively discussions of the materials were current and relevant. (My lecture notes alone—after culling eight drawers of file cabinets when I left the classroom—still tightly fill two bankers storage boxes.)

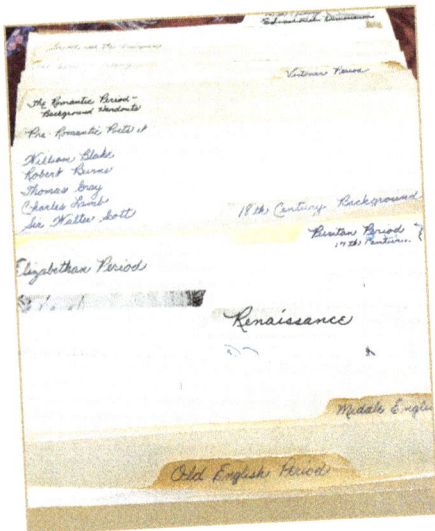

Many of The English Students later commented that what they had learned in our English classes prepared them better than any of their other high school courses. A remembrance from Ann Landis is representative of similar reports I still hear from students. Ann recalls, "Linda Alleman sat at my left in your class and I remember her telling me that the boy she was dating was in college, and he told her that the material she was getting in her high school English class was similar to that he was learning in his college classes. That really impressed me!"[14]

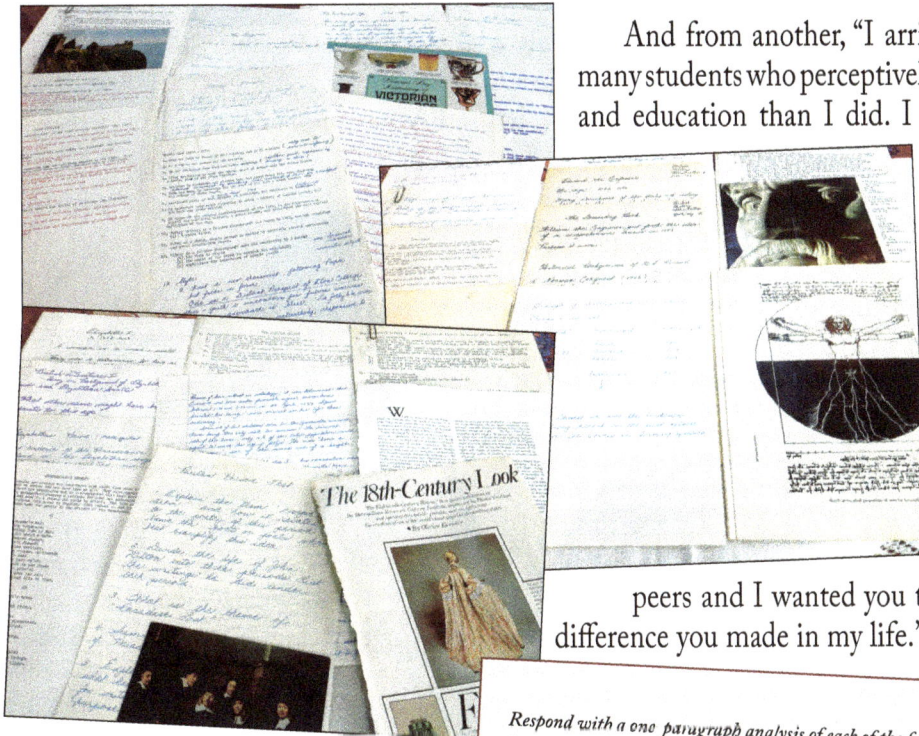

And from another, "I arrived at my college with many students who perceptively had better preparation and education than I did. I soon realized that was not the case when after writing my first English assignment, I was asked to join the "honors" English class. …the writing and comprehension skills and the introduction to the cultural arts put me far ahead of my peers and I wanted you to know how much of a difference you made in my life."

My efforts were directly aimed at delivering what I believed was important for students to know and to be able to do, and do well. It perhaps took some audacity to champion for what I saw worked in the classroom, but my students of the '60s demonstrated success and that emboldened me to campaign for what became the award-winning English Enrichment immersion course of the 1970s, patterned on the philosophy of the British Literature course of the 1960s, that personal involvement and high standards of scholarship produce better results in understanding, synthesizing, and writing.

Respond with a one paragraph analysis of each of the following three arguments, showing how the reasoning is false in each.

1. I just can't understand why Claire won't buy a yearbook. Anyone who won't buy a yearbook doesn't have real school spirit. Think of being able many years from now to look back on all of the good times we had in high school. Claire seems to have enough money for clothes and pleasure. I guess she just isn't like the rest of us.

2. Why Joe should call me conceited I just can't understand. But then what can you expect from someone who comes from a family like his. They're the biggest snobs in town. With people like that you never know where you stand. They're for you one day and against you the next. I really don't know how Joe's father made all that money; he doesn't seem smart enough to me.

3. In the modern business world it's either kill or be killed; you've got to be tough or they'll really take you. It's just like politics. Politics has always been crooked and always will be. As some fellow once said, "Nice guys finish last." You've got to be nice, all right—nice and mean. Otherwise you end up at the bottom of the heap."

Identify the fallacy or fallacies in each of the following arguments. Explain why each is a fallacy and consider how it can be corrected.

1. I have a headache and I feel tired. I think the heat and the humidity must be the cause.

2. Don't support the mayor's plan to build a new airport in King County. His primary motive is to get re-elected.

3. **Interviewer:** Does your country plan to invade your neighbor to the east of you?
   Diplomat: We are in favor of all peace-loving democracies.

4. I haven't read J. D. Salinger's latest novel, but I know it's good because I've enjoyed all his other ones.

5. "These men (economists) can take facts and figures and bring them together, but their predictions are not worth any more than ours are. If they were, they would have all the money and we would not have anything." (Bernard Baruch)

6. There are two kinds of people in the world, slaves and masters. All of us are one or the other.

379

My relationship with the 1970s Enrichment Students was, of course, not identical to that of the 1960s English Students. However, the result for both groups was high academic success *for* them as well as friendship *with* them. There was a positive rapport with students in both decades, but I believe that the significant issue with those in the 1970s is that I was primarily their *mentor*, whereas in the 1960s I had *identified* with the students. These mid-1960s students were who and what I had wanted to be in high school, but could not be because of the stultifying culture in the 1950s.

Thus, my more recent quest for understanding all of this led me back to the 1950s to find the early underpinnings of my later relationship with the 1960s Boomers.

Influence of the 1950s

In my own small town high school in the mid-1950s, a limited number of us had tried to take the road less traveled, sensing there had to be more to life than what we were experiencing. However, there was nothing in the 1950s specifically to prepare us for living in the 1960s—or for any other particular way to live: no script, no training, and no direction. We had only ourselves with no way to know how to find the information we weren't even sure existed.

Later, I realized that we had felt slighted by the world of the 1950s because we had missed the excitement of being teens, as in our world teenagers didn't count for much. Looking back I see we had the desire to be a part of the future, but we were not sure yet about breaking barriers, as we had had no experience or guidance (to say nothing of *permission!*) in doing so. We had the longing to do what the youth of the 60s later would be doing, but we didn't know what it was they would be doing or how to do whatever "it" was, *because we had not formulated any means by which to succeed in anything significant.* And any serious thought of rebelling had never occurred to us.

Although we didn't know it at the time, in retrospect it seems as if the whole period of the fifties had been a preparation for the 1960s generation. Or it may be that we were meant to serve as a kind of inert topsoil that protected the seeds of the 1960s generation germinating below our cover. Perhaps that is the role we were being prepared for, but who would want a role in which one would be only loam?

We, of course, could not identify with any of this at the time of our own youth, as there had been no precedent for the upheaval the 1960s would bring. It would not be until the explosion on the screen of *Rebel Without a Cause* that those of my generation would begin to realize we had missed an opportunity to speak out when we had been teens, and, even at best, would not have known what to say.

Thus, instead of the rebellion we might have created, we found ourselves destined to provide the support or guidance to the generation that would fulfill who we had wanted to be, but were not.

In contrast to our own floundering because of the vitiating 1950s culture, the classes of the mid-1960s seemed to know that they were in a new era, one that they would own. As a member of the Class of 1965 wrote in 2010 as he reflected on their high school years, "We had the opportunity to challenge the status quo and the world. *We wanted to be a part of the new culture* and we were attracted to the young teachers because of their enthusiasm to help us get there,"[15] confirmation of what was said above, that we were the potting soil for those in high school in the 1960s.

This Class of 1965 also noted its own dichotomy: "We were a split generation. We had early influence of the fifties (e.g., know your place, wait your turn, be respectful of your elders), but lived in the sixties world where we had the opportunity to challenge the status quo and the world. It was truly a culture shock for some of us. We revered 'the new' and avoided 'the old.' We were raised to value change. We wanted to be different, we wanted to be recognized. There was optimism in America, and the desire to provide opportunities for all people. We were part of that culture—even if we did not know it at the time."[16]

The Class of 1966 was even more sure than the Class of 1965 had been as to where they thought they were going. In their 2010 memoir[17] the Class of 1966 wrote, "At the end of our first day of school we headed home, listening to Elvis on our transistor radios, and we couldn't get home fast enough to watch American Bandstand."[18]

Most important, however, despite the delay of a decade, some of my own generation wanted to be active in the transformation of the sixties society more than just by observing. No, I didn't want to "be one of the students." I was very clear in my mind that I was the adult, but I wondered if maybe I could serve as a guide, a conscience, an advisor, and/or a friend. It was a big order to balance, but possible to do, since the teachers I had most admired in my own high school had done that—they engaged with us, but we (and they) knew the boundaries without the need for any discussion. I wanted the same kind of relationship I had sensed from them, but thought I might have more to offer than what my own teachers were able to give in the cautious and repressed 1950s.

For example, my own ninth grade English Teacher was exceptional. Nine or ten years older than we were, Mr. Sabbato lived with his parents who owned a small private airport. He engaged with us, assigning interesting topics to think and write about, discussing what we read in terms we understood, while asking thoughtful questions. He even took (in his own car) a group of us to see plays staged by the community theatre group in the town where he lived, six miles from our hometown.

He listened to us and guided us without our feeling that we were being "told what to do." He invited us to his parents' home and he chaperoned our freshman class picnic (likely as part of his assigned duty, but we didn't know that). Mostly we liked him because he respected us for who we were at 14 and 15. We trusted him. I saved the writing assignments I did for his class as a reminder of my admiration of him and of his "style" in commenting on our written work.

The Choral Director, new our sophomore year, and perhaps 10 years older than those in my class, was the proverbial breath of fresh air. He had been a professional musician prior to teaching (playing trumpet in dance bands and for major recording studio orchestras) and was very "cool." (Think Miles Davis and Dave Brubeck.) During his second year as our choral director he determined that our Christmas concert would be a cantata instead of the usual slate of holiday selections, and he made sure we understood its importance musically. To set a serious tone the evening of the performance, the boys wore suits and the girls wore gowns—a first for a choral concert in my hometown. We still talk about this event and we still believe we own Handel's *The Messiah*.

On the lighter side, Mr. Johnstone formed a "jug band" (four students, the band director, also new to teaching, and the choral director himself, totally out of his usual *savoir faire* character but seeming to enjoy the contrast). We consumed at least two dozen turkey dinners that holiday season from Thanksgiving to New Year's, as nearly every organization in the county invited us as their program feature. And "Arch" once took a carload of us to a college fifty miles from home so that we could hear the Robert Shaw Chorale in concert.

He also offered an elective course on "Music Theory." We had no idea what music theory was, but a handful of us scheduled it just because we were sure he knew things about music and the outside world that we did not, but just *might* learn about.

Our Chemistry teacher was another brilliant guide for us. He served as our tenth grade homeroom teacher—AND for our senior year—for ten students whose last names were at the end of the alphabet and for whom, in our senior year, there was no room in the traditional Senior Homeroom which held space for up to 90 students. I was indignant at being "left out," after waiting *my whole life* to attain a seat in Senior Homeroom! I think Mr. Bordas understood, even though I was the only one who raised a fuss because this was so important to me, and I felt that no one cared about what I considered an essential tradition, if not a legacy. My grandmother and my great aunt, my five aunts, my mother, and my older sister[19] had all been graduated from **Senior Homeroom**. However, no one offered a solution, and I was "brushed off."

Other than not wanting to deal with this personal obsession of mine, this special teacher always listened to us and then offered advice when needed. He also told us when he thought we were wrong. Forget the Table of Elements! We were learning life lessons.

Many decades later, shortly before his death, this chemistry teacher telephoned me several times just to talk, and I went to visit him in his assisted living apartment in Indiana County. He had only one high school yearbook on his shelf of text books and novels which included those he had written, and this yearbook was the one from my graduating class for which I had been the editor. He wanted me to have it.

Our Algebra I and II teacher, older than our parents, was a force, serving as an advisor to Tri Hi Y, carrying her lunch, as we did, in order to hold meetings during the 59 minute lunch break (there was no cafeteria and students either went home, to a restaurant, or carried a lunch), and staying after school to help students with their math homework. Mrs. Briggs was demanding, but in a way that we knew what we were learning—service and commitment—was important. I loved her.

The pair of teachers (both graduates of our high school a generation earlier) who guided us through an amazing, original Choralogue (speaking choir) for our Commencement program were unforgettable in their dedication, letting each graduating class plan its own program, its own Senior Shelf Day production, and the Class Picnic. In our high school were also traditions surrounding the yearbook (the advisor was also a graduate years prior), including limited, but permitted, creativity! We had pride of place and took gratification in our work. That was as important to us as the subject matter we had been taught. We somehow learned that traditions guided us, but did not rule us.

Then there was the Art Teacher who had tried, unsuccessfully, to help us understand, if not quite yet appreciate, Salvador Dali and Surrealism. He is remembered for his outburst when a student was coughing and was not able to suppress the sound. In total haughty exasperation, the teacher told the student to leave the room, and, to this day, I can hear Mr. Chadderdon loudly and firmly declaring, "I will have no tuberculars in this room!" A print by Dali displayed on a wall in my home is in tribute to this teacher who piqued my curiosity as an eighth grader to understand visual arts.

I never thought that I was patterning myself on any one of my own high school teachers, but as I write this I am seeing the nucleus of the way I approached my own classes and students, although what I offered was more of the college model, with far more rigor than was expected by my own teachers. The teachers in that small school in Curwensville were very influential in forming my work habits and code of responsibility, and what I carried from them into my own classes at Lower Dauphin was an expanded work ethic, the importance of engaging the students, high expectations, and acceptance—with creativity mixed in among the traditions, which in Lower Dauphin in the 1960s we were building.

I believe my passion for understanding and using the authenticity and life experiences of the authors whose work we studied was a strike against the silence I had lived with during the 1950s and my resentment at being confined in a stifling environment (albeit not even identified at the time).

That is not to say that my quest for an education was not supported in high school with the best they could offer; the problem was the limitation. I tasted possibility, but could not identify it and when asked why I wanted to go to college, I could answer no better than "I want to learn," and a Liberal Arts curriculum sounded like it had possibilities.

I spent my first year of college on the DuBois campus of Penn State. I had not wanted to go to DuBois, but, because of lack of finances, I was too late in applying to Penn State's State College campus.[20] Their dorms were filled, and freshmen were not permitted to commute, which was a moot point since I had no transportation. When I stomped around declaring, "I'll stay home rather than go to DuBois," my high school chemistry teacher set me straight in no uncertain terms. As a result, my freshman year at DuBois was the best year of my college life.

The following years at "main campus" (the self-important term that still stings as it diminishes the stellar education DuBois Undergraduate Campus provided) fueled my muffled rage at the then prevailing practice of most universities' underestimation and diminution of women, later stoked even more by some of the stifling restrictions I faced as a teacher, the small town gossip, and the thwarting of some of the many initiatives I was bringing to the high school—both in my teaching and in extra-curricular activities.

There was never any doubt about my intelligence (member of Mensa) and my skill as a teacher, coach, director, advisor, and mentor, yet there was a dismissiveness rendered to all female teachers. I watched several women being criticized and blamed by administrators before these teachers could recount their own narrative of whatever the issue was. I watched teaching schedules reflect the personal whims of some administrators who had the power to reassign at will, even to the detriment of the students who would be short-changed by some of the altered assignments. In the minds of some male administrators all English teachers were interchangeable.

As a personal example, parents requested that their children be placed in my classes, as my skill and integrity became legend; however, little, if any, support was given if a principal sensed even a slight infraction. One year I was assigned to teach several sections of non-academic, general English classes (instead of the college preparatory) because the year before I had refused to follow this administrator's arbitrary rule of "turning a name tag" in the morning upon arrival because I saw this order as unnecessary, unprofessional, and demeaning. (There already was in place a process to telephone if one were to be absent.)

I also watched as men were selected to be sent for advanced degrees and administrative certification. I resented this, although not fully knowing at that time that they had been singled out for these favors. There was no pathway for applying. All of a sudden one of the men would be leaving school early, being given a lighter teaching load, sent to a college campus during the summer with everything paid, or placed in an administrative capacity without any previous announcement of vacancies.

I personally recall how surprised—and grateful—I was on the Friday morning of my evening wedding in 1972 when the superintendent came to the door of my room to tell me I could leave early (at noon). Not at all to diminish his kind offer, but I was unaware just how many of the men had been rewarded with "extra days" for a wedding trip, vacation trip, or other digressions.

It was not until years later that I realized all the favoritism that had been given (rarely for women). Of course, all of these arrangements were made behind closed doors. So, I dug in and became entrenched in my classes and all of the extra programs and activities for which I held responsibility.

I poured my energy into creating new academic programs, including the development of the aforementioned and generally-celebrated English Enrichment program in the fall of 1971, a team-taught, three-year, sequential program designed to meet the needs of highly motivated, academically superior, self-directed students, and based on the success of the top academic sections which I had singly taught in the mid-60s. The structure for English Enrichment was interdisciplinary and, as noted earlier, garnered national recognition.[21]

As the first English Enrichment Class looked forward to college, the following letter best captures the essence of what the EE experience was.

West Point, July 6, 1974

Of all my senior high work, English Enrichment has had the greatest impact. As a three-year, continually building, learning experience, EE is unmatched at LD. It has made me so aware of my grammar that I continually correct myself whether I'm writing or just talking with a group of guys. Our literature studies have made me much more wary for the subtle meaning, the second-level of a novel. I try not to "look for things that aren't there," but three years of EE have made me appreciate symbolism and morals and themes and the like. This awareness has made many a dull book—at the literal level—a joy to read when pondering its full significance.

I hope you accomplish all your goals for the next year. I'm sure you'll return to LD just as—if not even more--prepared and enthusiastically ready. It also was that special chemistry between you and Mr. Z. that made our class click when it did. I sometimes think of Mr. Zeigler as a delightfully impish, well-read Uncle, but because of your reserve and bearing, your knowledge and wit, I often think of you as my Intellectual Mother.

I shall return in December and will let you know what happens at West Point a few times before that. I've written most of my school chums that the saddest part of graduation is leaving behind old school friends, and that applies to faculty members as well.

God Bless, CC

Where I saw a need, as a teacher or later as an administrator, I proposed bringing innovations both to the classroom and the high school—and later district. I initiated any number of endeavors, from Gifts from the Graduating Classes, Advisory Boards, Family Awards Dinner, and various clubs, to an endless number of programs and initiatives, including an active Alumni Association.

The Connection

As for the Class of 1965, I have always said I "grew up with this Class," beginning with a request from the supervising principal to "move with them" to the high school in the fall of 1963, where, in addition to being their classroom teacher, I became their Class Advisor, director for their plays, pianist for their musicals, coach for their speeches, director of their Commencement program, and mentor in general. They were mine and I was theirs.

Perhaps vicariously I was enjoying the freedom that came with the Baby Boomers. But, above all, I was a teacher, and wanted the experience of my students to be the best I could make it and the best they could deliver in return. And, in a way, finding myself, I wanted to be part of a core of students who were interested in finding themselves and who wanted to understand life and its meaning.

As noted, another factor of the high school success of these classes was that many of the teachers of this cohort were of the Silent Generation who themselves had come from solid, middle class families. Further, there was an assembly of teachers at Lower Dauphin in the 1960s not usually found in schools—more than half were first year teachers and most of the others were the best of a strong cohort from the small, local high school that had closed. What is fascinating is the balance of veteran and neophyte, yet the novices were totally respectful of the experience of the seasoned ones and the teachers with years of experience were uncritical and accepting of the greenhorns.

Further, the high school population initially was almost exclusively white, middle-class students whose parents found themselves on the cusp of cultural change, with only a few who were not sure they welcomed it. Initially, some parents were to some degree uncomfortable because they didn't know any of the new teachers. Other than that, there was an overall parental respect for the faculty.

It also must fairly be said that as a wider (beyond Lower Dauphin) cohort the classes from the 1960s had more opportunities than any other mixed socioeconomic group in history to that point. They came from parents of the most respected generation (The Greatest Generation), grew up pampered and protected (but not spoiled), had a critical mass, and were the recipients of probably one of the best mix of faculty, as noted above, one could ever collect under our American system of education.

Another positive factor is that the planning for the new school had been measured, with some board members who might be called radical and others who might be viewed as fogyish. There were successful businessmen and attorneys and physicians from Hummelstown mixed with rugged, practical, mainly working class conservative men from the townships.[22] From all indications when Lower Dauphin High School opened there were not yet any hints of the social protests to come, and some of the changes caught everyone by surprise, including the mid-sixties students themselves.

It is also likely that the impact of the Class of 1965 (white emerging middle class townies and farmers' kids at LD) was a unique convergence of particulars within a larger framework of the decade. As Barry Stopfel later described, "It was one particular class of small town kids who made a significant mark on both the school and the community because they had an expansive freedom to observe, speak their minds, critique, and create." Importantly, they also were among the last classes of their type, before the protests of the sixties changed forever the nature of education.

The astute participant-observer who recently asked me some of these details posed an interesting supposition, "A Class of 1965 at Hummelstown High School would have been vastly different from the Class of 1965 at Lower Dauphin High School. The cultural experience of all of us was blasted wide open as a result of the formation of LD. It is unfortunate that a study could not have been conducted to compare the authentic Lower Dauphin Class of 1965 to a mythical Hummelstown High School Class of 1965."[23]

This 1965 class member continued in his probing, "So what actually made the difference? In what ways did the wide cultural sweep of change in the sixties shape lifestyles, relationships, and attitudes? And why did not all of the class members embrace the opportunity? I sense that, of all the students at the center of the convergence, in the end some of them simply recreated their parents' ideals, yet with a zest and flair that freedom of experimentation permitted."

My response is that even the latter (bringing a zest and flair to recreating their parents' ideals) would have enhanced their lives. However, I could not dispute that there was a core of students, as there often is in any class, who best reflect the societal trends of which history is made.

More recently I was asked the following questions posed by this same Socratic examiner:

1. You once said that you believed that the Class of 1965 would rule the world. What led you to make that comment?

2. Which students most influenced your view?

3. What did they do or think or say that led you to have faith in your observation?

4. How did this shape you?

These were powerful questions—although impossible to answer. My reactive response to the first question was, "Observation, Intuition, and Experience"—and, of course, there is the fact that there were so many of them! I then added that I discovered in this cohort a passion for life and learning, along with a drive to do well, and, as a short-term goal, to be accepted by a good college.

There was no sign in the leaders of this pack of being over-confident, but I liked their "persona being shown to the world." They seemed to know they were preparing for a great adventure, and I was in awe of that. Further, their fundamental enthusiasm for life was evident.

To provide a list of names would result only in overlooking some of those who were very influential but not vocal, so I will focus on their general characteristics. For the most part their public personalities exuded confidence. It was the letters they wrote that suggested their vulnerability and I found that fascinating from the perspective of one who grew up keeping everything and every thought to oneself.

For this memoir, however, one must be content to consider only the relationship between one teacher and her students, one that was grounded in a short and spectacular four years, continued through letters for much of the following four years, then settled into comfortable friendship of various depths and lengths, with formal class reunions every five years.

This journey of teacher and students also supports the premise of a 2014 *New York Times* article, "Teaching is Not a Business," concerning current trends toward what journalist David L. Kirp terms "impersonal disruptive innovation." He takes issue with the belief that the solution for education is high stakes reading and math tests as the *single* metric of success. He decries what he terms "doing an end run" around inherently complicated and messy human relationships, because he sees these relationships as central to the educational process.

What is needed, Kirp proposes, are actions that foster *bonds of caring between teachers and their students.*

He provides a litany of changes in school systems through the years—all of which failed. Then he stresses that what counts in a good education is the forging of a *relationship based on mutual respect and caring* between teacher and student. He further cites various programs that demonstrate that the personal touch is crucial. He concludes that while technology can be put to good use by talented teachers, it is teachers themselves who must take the lead. He emphasizes, "The process of teaching and learning is an intimate act that neither computers nor markets can hope to replicate and that there is simply no substitute for the personal element."[24]

Importantly, Kirp is not alone in his thinking. From the mentoring of Socrates→ Plato→ Aristotle until the present day we have seen the positive results of the guidance and mutual respect between teachers and their students, and *we still can't convince the naysayers who continue to misunderstand how central human relationships are to the educational process.*

Mrs. Esther Hivner, the teacher who personally visited the home of every one of her fourth graders and took each pupil, one at a time throughout the school year, to lunch at a local, family-run restaurant, is representative of a teacher who is engaged with her students and sees each of them as an individual. Mr. William Peck, who established a club for young men and took groups of them to events, including a college football game, on his own time and often at his own expense; Mr. Cleon Cassel, who welcomed wrestling team members who were struggling to survive into his own family; and Mrs. Margaret DeAngelis, herself Class of 1965 (McDevitt), who sheltered and saved many vulnerable students—all are examples of teachers in the Lower Dauphin system who have made a substantial impact on young people and who understood the value of engagement.

The importance of relationships at any level of teaching cannot be oversimplified. It is what makes us human, even though teachers may never know which seeds are taking root. As Biblical wisdom goes, it is ours to plant thoughtfully and deliberately and to not worry about the harvest.

Looking more closely at the importance of relationships, let us think of the various levels of interaction, from a world view narrowed to 76 million Americans, then to a singular collection, which we identify as a smaller cadre of Lower Dauphin graduates (1960s), then to one central class (1965), then to those who were in any way involved in its Senior Class play, and, from that, down to a select group within that class (1965) of like-minded individuals who serve as exemplars (Symposium Society being the general term, although not all exemplars were members). Let us further view this as a description of the Baby Boomers, based on historical markers, as a class of students who attended high school in the 1960s in a small town in south-central Pennsylvania.

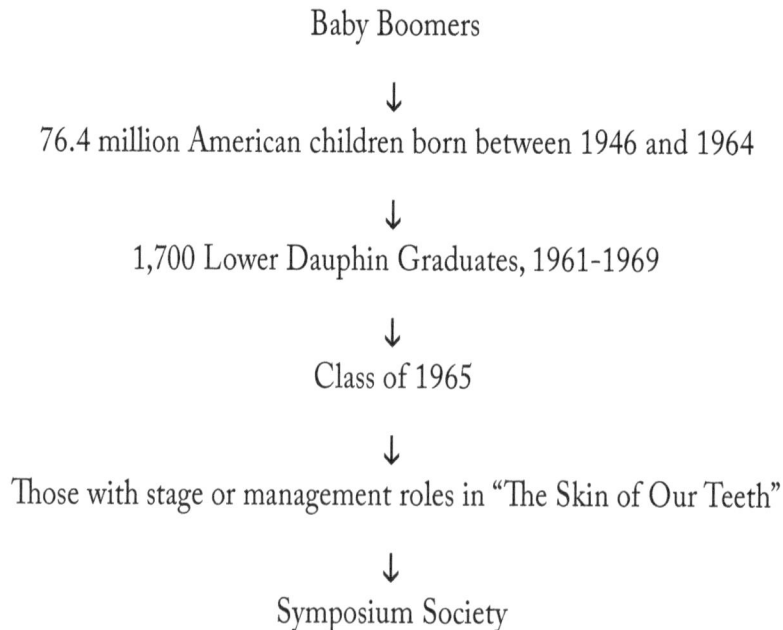

Baby Boomers

↓

76.4 million American children born between 1946 and 1964

↓

1,700 Lower Dauphin Graduates, 1961-1969

↓

Class of 1965

↓

Those with stage or management roles in "The Skin of Our Teeth"

↓

Symposium Society

It has been suggested that the photos of those on stage for *The Skin of Our Teeth* (Senior Class Play) is "a composite of those whose influence remains strong in the narrative history of Lower Dauphin and the wider community." While many would agree with this supposition—which certainly holds merit, such a study would require a very different, quantitative research than what is offered here. Thus, what is used in this qualitative reflection is fifty years of knowledge, observations, memories, impressions, and conversations of and with those directly or indirectly involved.

Further, narrowing the focus also provides a way to pay homage to a group of students who were most active in their class through music, sports, and/or other school programs and activities. While the group was fluid, it includes those who consolidated this power in flashy, fun, and creative ways extending far beyond the classroom.

One of the more memorable "flashy, fun, and creative" ideas of this class was the formation of what was named the **Symposium Society,** the first secret club on record at Lower Dauphin and established by members of the Class of 1965. Its purpose was social with overtones of organized intellectual activities which those not in the Society thought were a cover for their enviable, but decorous parties, desirable in the sense that everyone else wanted to be invited to these events.

In reality the Symposium Society was a classic, even issuing coveted membership cards, commercially printed for this purpose. The members will remember the Farm House, the stream, and the white banners created from bedsheets which to this day are brought out and displayed on the fence of a property belonging to the originator of the club, upon the occasion of their class reunions and other related, very special events. A one of a kind declaration, to be sure!

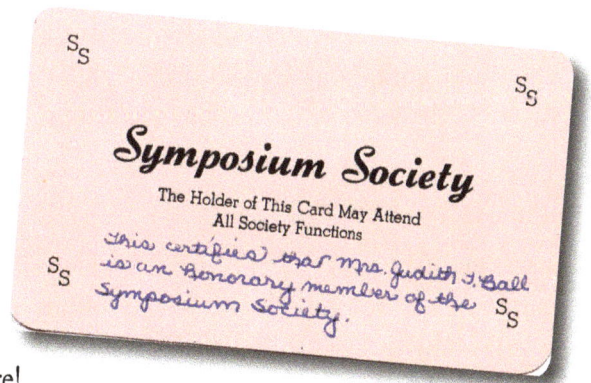

While I carry an honorary membership card, I attended only a few of the Symposium social events, and only for short courtesy visits. I went for three reasons—the honor of being invited, the trust and friendship this exemplified, and as part of a left-over 1950s longing to have had such a group among my own classmates.

Another organization, this led by the Class of 1967, was a pioneer male group, the self-styled **Blue Guard,** composed of mainly senior lettermen and/or class leaders. Rather than an organized club, the Blue Guard was a group who focused on school spirit. Armbands were sold and were to be worn on game day to signify school spirit (and exclusivity!). Anyone could purchase an armband, but the members of The Guard sat together at athletic competitions with an avowed mission of increasing school spirit. The Blue Guard also published a limited-edition, underground newsletter. (See Blue Guard Announcement in Chapter 5.)

The **Culture Creeps** were the intelligentsia of this same class (1967), a group who sat together at lunch discussing their interests—what they were reading and what music they were listening to. They enjoyed one another's company and keen intellect. At first offended by the name given to them by others, they came to embrace it. What set this group apart from many other "loner" groups is that they learned an early lesson about being true to oneself.

A few years ago, this group held a private reunion (arranged for by a member [Class of '66] of the family of one of the four) of their friendship to which I was invited, and which I considered an honor.

Part of the *raison d'etre* of all three of these groups was the eternal quest to be wanted and to be a part of a group of people into which one is accepted. To my knowledge, none of these cadres were mean-spirited and all had serious intentions.

The Class of 1965

Early on, the Class of 1965 began developing one of the cultural mandates of the sixties to redefine the nature of relationships between and among individuals, families, communities and beyond—the beyond now being manifested in their community, family, and class projects. Further, by virtue of their age, members of the classes of the 1960s are now the community leaders, and by their tendency to be selective, they choose only the areas in which they believe they can make a difference (and, in a few cases, control).

I see evidence of this in our common hometown, theirs by birth, mine by choice. Even today, I rely on their involvement for projects in which I, too, am engaged, such as producing the Golden Jubilee of Lower Dauphin High School (a yearlong celebration with a major culminating weekend event); fund-raising to build a town library; founding an alumni association; fund-raising to build and maintain a huge, walk-in showcase in the lobby of the high school; replacing a missile of historical value that had been illegally taken out of the school building; establishing a trust fund for scholarships; offering directories of alumni; purchasing folding chairs for winter sports use; and fund-raising to build a sports complex, with plans to raise money for a bronze statuary of the school mascot to be placed on the grounds of the high school.

These class members, most active in the Lower Dauphin Alumni Association, also were engaged in various celebrations of homecomings, locating losers/finders of class rings and yearbooks, mounting of a large falcon mosaic, a field banner, honoring alumni at homecoming, recognizing record-holders, and publishing the 500-page history of the high school, *Loyal Hearts Proclaim; The First Fifty Years of Lower Dauphin High School*, in which is memorialized the culture of its nascent years, and which even includes a listing of LD graduates who married fellow LD graduates. (It will come as no surprise that the list of married couples from the Class of 1965 is the longest.)

In **1997** (their 50th Birthday) I wrote this about the Class of 1965:

"I do hope you all realize what wonderful, special, joyous, creative people you were and still are. Perhaps the sheer numbers of you led to your carving out individual niches; however, I rather think it was a caring for one another that was the key. That caring is still there, as evidenced by your continuing close contact with each other."

In **2005** I wrote a letter to them upon the occasion of their 40th Class Reunion:

"You are part of history, not just as "boomers" but as trend-setters and leaders in every walk of life. …The sixties was a time of optimism, especially for the privileged young who believed there were no limits to how comfortable and powerful and healthy and happy they could be. …High school teachers saw you as energetic, bright, ambitious, and—an observation they had never before encountered— they saw you as very comfortable with one another, a social phenomenon no previous generation had enjoyed. …You displayed a sense of confidence not seen before in youth. I told you that your generation would rule the world. And you do. That power and desire to make your own way on your own terms has not changed. You are idealists, but willing to work for those ideals. And you have succeeded."

In **2012** I wrote the following:

"Nationwide the Class of 1965 was noted for its many achievements and the Lower Dauphin Class of 1965 was no exception. Taking a back seat to no one, they were multitudinous in number (colleges were becoming jam-packed with this raft of baby boomers), they were bright (the best class ever in the experience of many of their high school teachers), and they had a veneer of confidence. They seemed to know that they would soon be taking charge of the world and, over the next fifty years, they did."

Ode Written Upon the Occasion of the Graduation of Friends

Hail to thee, fifth period!
Group who has persevered
Against the ravages of classes
And the teacher you may have revered!

Since I have known you all four years
You'd think that I will soon shed tears?
I might have shed a few, my dears,
But I'll be myself and just make jeers!

Four years is long enough, I guess,
To culminate this lovely mess,
If truth were with you, you'd confess
You really wish the time'd been less!

However, now the time has arrived
And I shall show how I've connived
To reveal the secrets of you all;
So come along and hear J. T. Ball

I could start alphabetically
But that would sound pathetically;
So I'll just ramble, one by one,
And you must listen to catch the fun.

Marjorie worried all year through;
She fretted and cried a wee bit, too.
Now that it's over she can shout
"Hip! Hip! Horray! I'm finally out!"

Kirk's bright and shining face looked up
Holding wonder like a cup.
I thought he viewed my lectures as keen
Till I watched his attentions turn to Jean.

Jean, however, remained true blue
And never let her grades fall through;
She learned just how to juggle time
For dating, studying, and sampling wine.

Stanley, better known as Goose,
Had better watch out for that noose;
He's been so wrapped up in dating Motts
His grades have suffered lots and lots!

Vivian, on the other hand,
Tried hard to help her buddy Stan;
Perhaps the trouble, if I may be smart,
Was that they listened to just the heart?

Bonnie sits there so sedate
I wonder what it is for which she waits;
She never says an unkind word …
At least not one that I have heard.

Kathy's secret wish, I hear,
Is to murder someone very near;
Perhaps by waiting until after lunch
She can follow what was once a hunch.

Lo-Babe has suffered all year long
Tolerating just what I've done wrong.
She sighed at my attempts to draw
And often wished for a great big saw.

John, known to all of you as Jack
Is praying he never will come back
To English class, his bane in life;
He often wishes for a knife.

Poor Tom who tries so very hard
To always keep up his lowered guard
Against the slings and arrow of fate
While trying to love and not to hate.

Lynn, who continually questions
Would prefer to make suggestive suggestions.
Unfortunately she must curtail
For fear of her mother's keen assail.

Stumpy, whom I must call Bill,
Would like very much just to be nil;
Every day at eleven he feels he's in heaven
....Or is it instead in hxxx?

Karl, who for reasons unknown is "Bugs,"
Really needs what is just found in jugs.
He is fond of Lit., but won't admit,
For fear of all those slugs.

Ruth Ann, who with teaching is illusioned,
Her friends fear she's had a contusion;
They say the blood's rushed from her head
And she badly needs a transfusion.

And lovely Ann, what will become of you?
If you're away from the shop, what will you do?
Your hair will go straight and grow darker, too;
You'll rush right home, crying, boo hoo hoo.

Speaking of hair, Larry, you'll be in a stew
When you hit boot camp; you'll get a crew.
I'll bet then you'll shout and jump all about
And may even give in to some brew.

Watch out, State! Here comes Joe!
You'd best be prepared to Go, go, go!
Old Main will cringe as he starts his binge
Of studying, always just so.

Carol Zerfoss finally will be alone
As she or sister will leave home.
The football team will miss her scream
And the crowd will walk out and bemoan.

Dennis, who always is so quiet,
Will change and soon cause such a riot.
He'll break all rules for good little schools
And to M. G., well, he may even defy it!

Fay is another whose still water runs deep;
I'll bet each rule even she doesn't keep;
She's mysterious, never deleterious,
Some day into her diary we will peep!

Bill Campbell's thoughts I have discovered
Are not always of the best;
For last summer said, "I wish she'd drop dead,"
And you see I'm still here giving tests.

At Stevie's house there is always noise;
I guess because she invites the boys
And girls, though not the police
Who come anyway just for the joys.

Take John Miller, that's if you can,
To him you've really got to hand
The credit, for he has the luck
Of getting along with our Miss Gluck.

Geesaman just loves poetry;
For him it offers notoriety.
Late at night, always Lit. to fight
And he surely maintains his propriety.

Lauren, whose favorite class is Lit.,
Though she's quite unwilling to admit
That she loves it 'cause she can bare her claws,
And throw her cronies quite into a fit.

Don I should have saved for last
As we seldom see him in this class.
But that might be mean; it's almost obscene
How much he would just like to pass.

Nancy, though not in Fifth Period,
Is with me for reasons so myriad;
It's the third year in class and also homeroom
She's to be pitied, and we might a tear add.

Mary Ann shone forth so brightly
Performing dancing almost nightly;
We won't forget her flashing smile
Which brightened the stage up for awhile.

Carol Kauffman is going to West Chester
And I'll bet she'll soon be the best there;
She can liven up the place, really set the pace
…I just hope they permit her to stay there.

Barry is our guest today
Because as you all know …
He's had to leave F20A
And he has nowhere else to go!

John Enders who runs out of gas
So very often that it may seem
The reason just must be a lass.
Let's hope he does not run out of steam.

Bethanne's so used to being first
I thought she should be last.
We're still waiting for the bunny dance;
So, Go! …before the time has passed.

You now have heard this tale of glee
That was not meant diabolically.
I really think you're all the best …
But remember, there's much truth in jest!

Now, as you go along life's way
And reflect on dear L. D.
Remember who would always say,
"Study and think!" Yes, remember J. T. B.

In **2015** they celebrated their 50th Class Reunion, still fond of one another.

They describe themselves thus: "We were the generation who grew up with television. We grieved the death of President Kennedy. We eventually went to war against North Viet Nam. We were raised to have opinions and we let them be known. We had the draft and the lottery numbers—but they were for military duty and not for professional sports or fortune. We fell in love, drove too fast, and danced the night away—yet had our school work ready for the next day."[25]

They were described by *Time* magazine in 1965 as being "on the fringe of a golden era of introspection with a fixation on self." Boomers were said to be idealists, later in life surprising even themselves.[26]

From The English Students

And so we come to the most difficult part of this journey, one I do not have the power to fully answer, for few of us can truly evaluate and analyze ourselves. I don't know how to define how I was viewed by The English Students, but I would hope it included "teacher," "friend," and "mentor." I will admit that I had to learn to laugh, as the personality of those of my own Silent Generation is one of seriousness, and while I viewed the journey of learning as a serious matter, I had to work on using a little humor through the process. Further, I never viewed those in my classes as my surrogate children; that would have been insulting to all of us. Therefore, it is probably best to use the actual words The English Students themselves have used to describe me.

I am told the image that comes to the minds of most of The English Students is of my standing at my desk or behind the lectern on the raised platform in B-1 speaking to a specific section of English Students.

1963 [27]

I distinctly remember crossing the threshold of C-3 for the first time, never realizing how much I would be influenced by the teacher within. She attracted me from the very beginning by her youthfulness, which was tempered with a manner that bespoke experience. A little above average height, her five feet, seven inches lent a dignity and poise to her demeanor which commanded respect. There was an aloofness about her which was not unfriendly; a severity not vacant of humor, an air of assurance which was not arrogant, a subtle effervescence that was not boisterous, a strength not physical. These initial impressions of my Freshman English teacher were soon proved correct.

In the days that followed, my admiration for her as an individual and as a teacher grew. She attracted teenagers and gained their friendship and trust without once descending from the pedestal of authority. Possessing a keenly sarcastic sense of humor, she could enliven her remarks with a clever witticism. However, it was her sincerity that earned my greatest respect. She took her responsibility seriously, which suggested spending much time outside of school in preparation.

This sense of duty, coupled with originality, was manifested in the very course she taught. Using the textbook only occasionally, she supplemented its material with additional information from other sources. To increase our word power, spelling and vocabulary, tests were given weekly. For the first time writing came easily to me. Perhaps this was the result of the unique methods she introduced to help us choose topics. One such method was the use of music to provide a mental picture or an idea about which we wrote. Book reviews were not infrequent and yet a new and different format was provided for each. The *Practical English* magazine and our teacher's creativity served as guides in an extensive newspaper study. An introduction to philosophy and logic terminated the course which was the most enjoyable and worthwhile one that I have yet experienced.

The story of this teacher and her influence on my life does not end here, for, as Henry Brooks Adams said, "A teacher affects eternity; we can never tell where the influence stops." I, like all of her students, have been indescribably affected by her example and in the near, but still dim future, our lives, reflecting her beliefs and her character, will in turn influence those around us.

Collectively, most of those who were "The English Students" under my guidance say...

As a teacher you...

✓ are inspirational. You strive for that every time you stand in front of a class.

✓ understand how central human relationships are to the educational process.

✓ teach while listening to what the learner is saying because you care about the outcome for both.

✓ invite us to see and to share the many truly exciting experiences we are enjoying, while at the same time you are enriching what we are learning.

As a role model for students you...

✓ have been a most important influence on students' leadership style and approach to problem-solving.

✓ inspired students to put forth their best effort and to develop the confidence to excel.

✓ demonstrated that comprehension skills and the cultural arts put The English Students ahead of peers who were not your students.

✓ always held high expectations for us and for yourself.

As an individual person you...

✓ honored the ageless authority of classic values, yet in action undermined a variety of cultural attitudes.

✓ have devoted yourself to being a meticulous and heartfelt archivist not only because the history is important to preserve, but also because you are passionately engaged in an unfolding future.

✓ have a keen ability to synthesize Eros and Intellect.

✓ pushed against many boundaries, making life choices that sometimes placed you on the margins; you were representative of your own world of the 1950s, but not completely in it. In total, you are among the most remarkable of women and both pieces have intriguing possibilities.

Very recently one of The English Students made perhaps the most basic but profound observation when she wrote this about me, **"She totally believed in us."**[28]

To these summative comments I reply,

When I signed on for this adventure in a basement office on the Hummelstown Square in the summer of 1960, deciding whether to accept an offer from Mechanicsburg or from this new school, I thought of Robert Frost, and chose to take the offer to be part of a new school by taking "the road less traveled," with no idea of how powerful the journey would be for me.

Despite a few roadblocks along the way, I was given the freedom to produce results in and out of the classroom whether it be a recited soliloquy, a simulated 18th Century Coffee House in B-1, a "day at Walden Pond," (aka the Staver Farm), creative yearbooks, memorable, personalized graduations, fieldtrips with a purpose, challenging academics, a field house, or an Alumni Association. I held high expectations, to which The English Students rose.

And as Gore Vidal once said, and one of The English Students copied on an index card and mailed to me a few years following his graduation, "In a sense, the only purpose of life is the creation of a self; and what matters, finally, is the sum total of all one's attempts."

I would like to think I have provided a bit of each English Student's sum total, for they have provided much of mine.

Reflections Endnotes:

1   *Marcel Proust, Remembrance of Things Past.* The only true voyage of discovery would be to possess other eyes, to behold the universe through the eyes of another, of a hundred others, to behold the hundred universes that each of them beholds, that each of them is.

2   And the LAST time ever.

3   (authentic)

4   Jack Goepfert, former semi-pro; Jim Bishop, Millersville; Frank Capitani, Gettysburg; Bill DeLiberty, LVC; Bill Peck, Shippensburg.

5   Betsy Will, Jean Eckman, Mary Lewin, and the author.

6   These were formally printed in the print shop under Gordon Putt's supervision where during activity periods, students were eager to print invitations and announcements for actual events.

7   According to *SHOW* magazine, October 1964, this was shown in only 1,000 theatres and for only four showings in each theatre on September 23 and 24.

8   Many, many years ago I began saving journals and magazines with articles that I wanted to keep relative to my teaching, thinking that someday I would want this information to write about these English Students or to use in future classes. At that time, we had no idea that, in the future, most information would be at our finger tips through search engines, with some exceptions, one being that magazine articles are not necessarily retained in electronic data-bases.

> (Burton's portrayal of Hamlet can still be seen in Vox, which recounts his delivery and is still thrilling to hear, "… it's clear you're witnessing an astonishingly intense, once-in-a-lifetime performance.")

> *Show Magazine*, June 1964, went beyond this basic review, noting that directed by John Gielgud (ultimate Shakespearean actor), the play is staged as if it were an empty stage. "The physical size is deceptive; this Hamlet is enormous in size, a vast space which only a play larger than life could fill. Burton's delivery is beyond that of any other actor: Gielgud's voice (the voice of Hamlet's father's ghost) is a symphony orchestra; Burton's a solo instrument played at a jam session.'" The drama reviewer effuses, "This Hamlet soars to manic fury, plummets to depressive self-derision. …he is a Hamlet such as I have never seen before." No wonder many of the English Students noted this Shakespearean drama as the highlight of their Senior year in British Literature. (See Section II, "The Scrapbook.")

9   One was planned for 1987, but canceled because of the accidental death on November 28 of Tod H. Witmer, the son of the author's husband, Walter C. (Wally) Witmer.

10   See ericbrahinsky.com/starspangled.html.

11   Dale and Steve

12   Karl

13   Don

14   Email from Ann Landis Kopp to the author, July 17, 2012.

15   *Loyal Hearts Proclaim*, p. 114.

16   *Loyal Hearts Proclaim*, pp. 114-115.

Reflections Endnotes continued:

[17] "Reflections from the Class of 1966," *Loyal Hearts Proclaim.*

[18] *Loyal Hearts Proclaim,* p. 116.

[19] My high school references are based on the strong, matriarchal structure that was my heritage. My paternal grandmother and her sister had no brothers; my maternal grandmother had four sisters (and only one brother); my mother and her four sisters had no brothers.

[20] In the spring of my senior year, unknown to me until many years later, the school superintendent approached my paternal aunt (sister of my father from whom my mother was divorced) and told her of my need, "Of all Catherine's four daughters—all good students—if you can see your way to help, Judith needs to go to college." Aunt Mary Alice Thompson Jackson Crunk made it possible, completely paying for my college education and providing what I needed.

[21] *Loyal Hearts Proclaim,* p. 154.

[22] The larger Jointure Board included one female, Mrs. Anne Staver, from East Hanover Township.

[23] (Author's note: Since the trend and necessity of size was toward consolidated schools, it would be nigh to impossible to make a comparison of a new Lower Dauphin and a smaller high school class in another location.)

[24] Kirp, David L., a professor at the University of California, Berkeley and the author of "Improbable Scholars," in *The New York Times,* August 17, 2014, p. SR4.

[25] "Reflections from the Class of 1965," *Loyal Hearts Proclaim.*

[26] Strauss and Howe, *Generations.*

[27] June 10, 2017: In paging through scrapbooks from the 1960s I quite unexpectedly came upon a typed profile written by a student who had written this as an assignment. I share it as to how I was perceived in 1963.

[28] Ruth Ann Graybill, July 17, 2017.

The music in my heart I bore,

Long after it was heard no more.

The Solitary Reaper
William Wordsworth

SCRAPBOOK

FALCONAIRE

'62 Falconaire

FALCONAIRE '63

The 1960s
Lower Dauphin High School

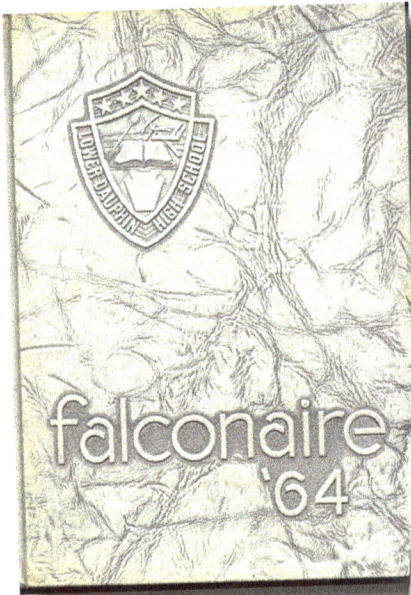
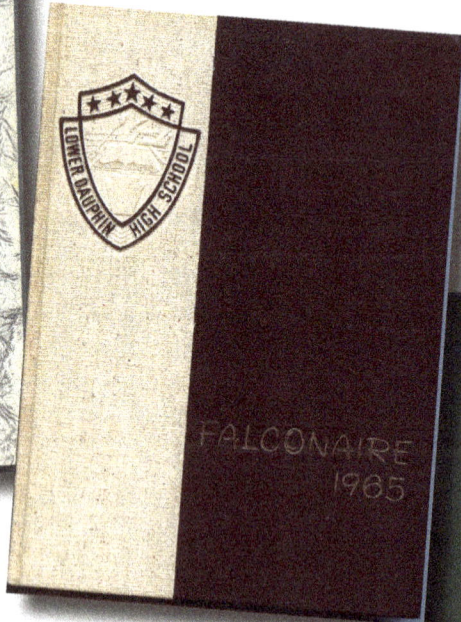

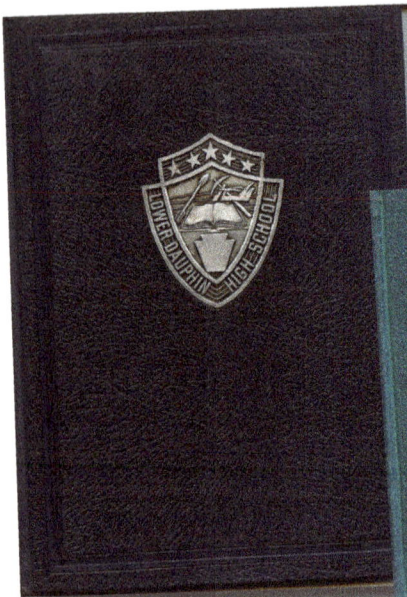
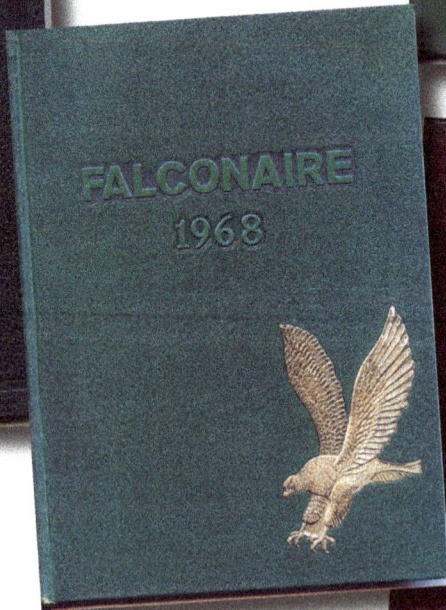
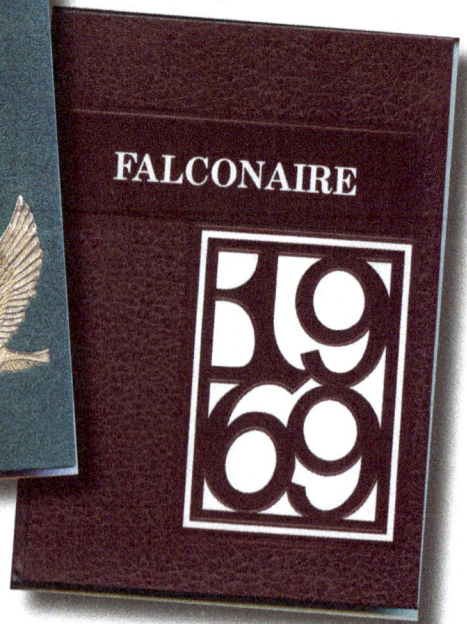

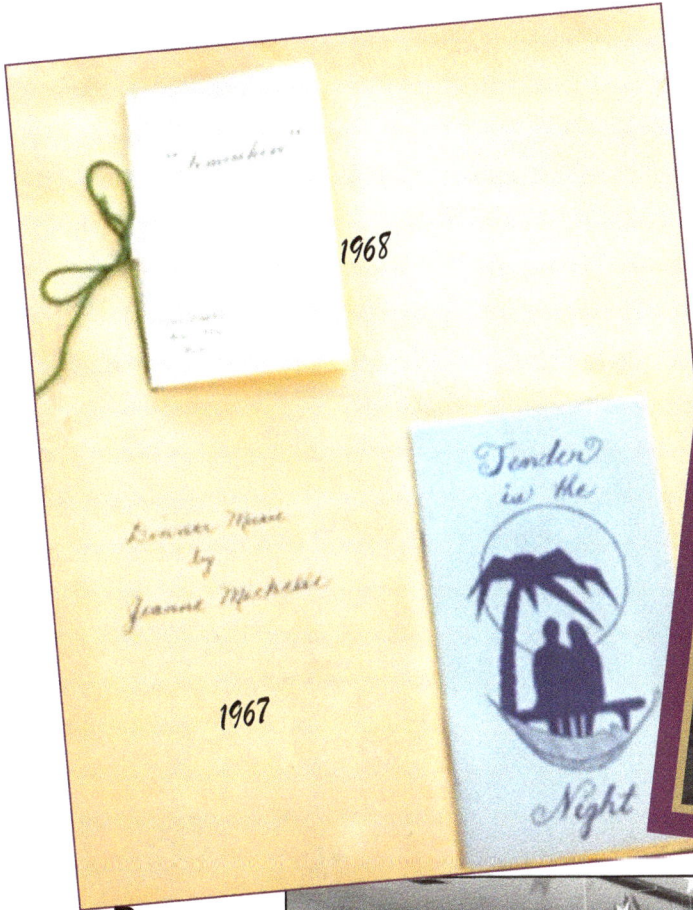

1968

Dinner Menu
by
Jeanne Michelle

1967

Tender is the Night

P
R
O
M

1
9
6
5

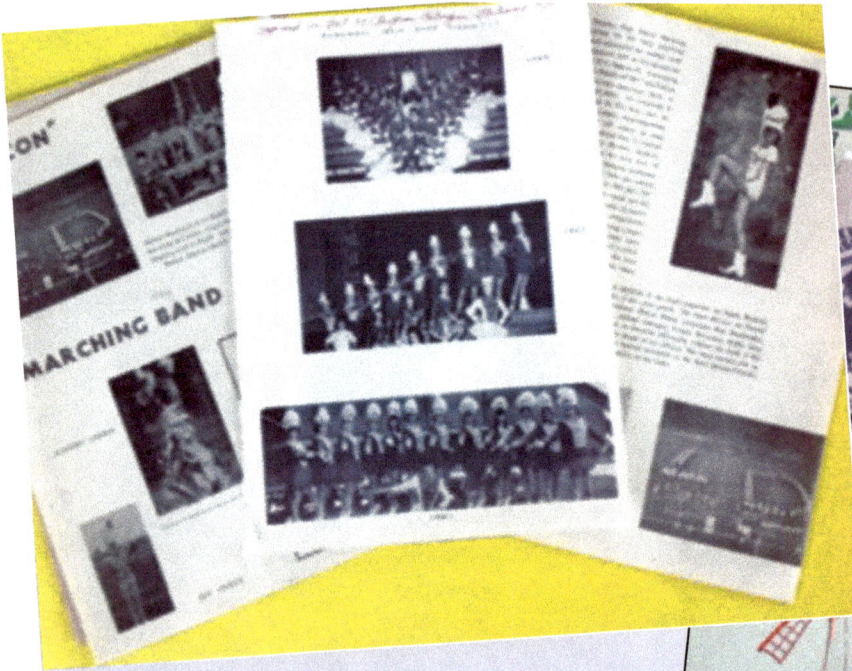

Jeannine Lehmer

BAND CAMP PLANNED FOR SECOND YEAR

The Nonettes

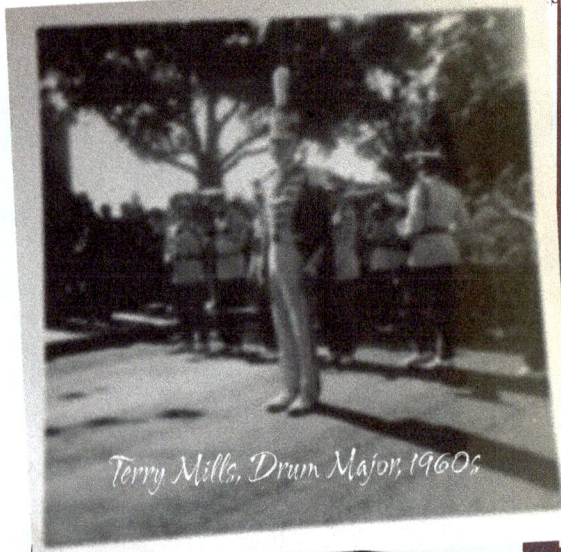

Terry Mills, Drum Major, 1960s

Ninth Grade Play

LOWER DAUPHIN HIGH SCHOOL MARCHING BAND

The Lower Dauphin High School Marching Band is composed of 72 playing members and 18 band front members for a total of 90 marching personel. The Falcon Band has taken first place in the PMEA Christmas parade in 1965, second place in the Olmsted Marching Band contest in 1965 and first prize in the Progress Firemen's Parade in 1966.

The band is under the baton of Mr. H. William Nixon. Mr. Nixon received his BS degree in Music Education from Lebanon Valley College and his M.Ed. degree in Music Education from the Pennsylvania State University.

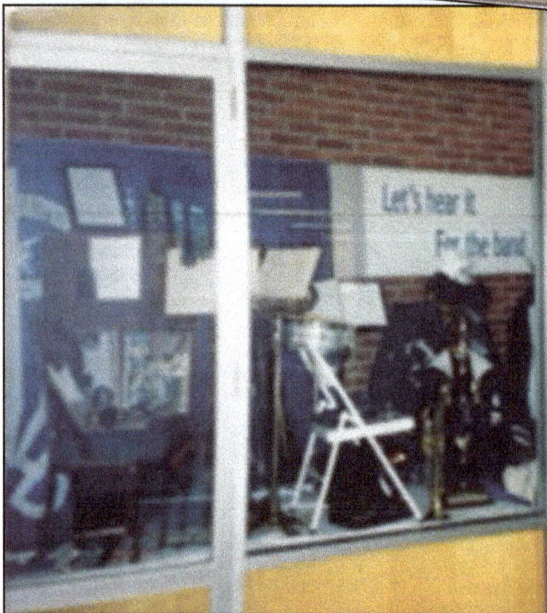

LDAA
Display
Case

411

Golden Jubilee Committee, 2008 - 2010

Dr. Judith T. Witmer, Jubilee Chair
Susan Petrina '65, Co-Chair, Alumni Week-end
Betty Musser Radle '62, Co-Chair, Alumni Week-end
Randy Umberger '65, LDSD Liaison
Dr. Jeffrey D. Miller '85, Time Capsule Project

Kyleen Fisher Bender '61	Kathy Saltzer Peffer '73
Barbara Olson Bowser '62	Kathy Weber '74
Carol (Janie) Baker Wenrich '62	Sheila Pankake Vandernick '88
Kathleen Convery '64	Denise Little '89
Ann Landis Kopp '65	Nicole Cassel '96
Dr. Janet Calhoon '66	Bill Minsker, Faculty
Martha Wrzesniewski Bossler '66	Margaret DeAngelis, Faculty

Alma Mater

Lower Dauphin, School Edi...
Vict...
Praises to...
Echo th...
Ever strivin...
Eager, ...
Help us keep our standa...
Seeking friendsh...
Hono...
We will proudly serve th...

Music by Prowell...
Lyrics by Elaine Harris Sulkey '63

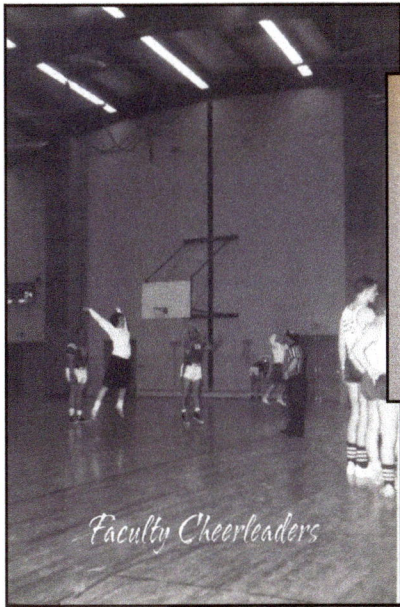

Faculty Cheerleaders

Faculty Cheerleaders

Jean Eckman   M. R. Lewis
Betty Hill   Judi Gall

Carl Stanitski

Women's Faculty Basketball

Faculty Basketball

Bill Peck - Faculty Basketball

Rotary

Sports Banquet

LOWER DAUPHIN
HIGH SCHOOL

Friday - May 23, 1969
6:30 P.M.

7th and 8th GRADE WRESTLING

Weight	Team I	Team II
Heavy	Jack Ruggles	Bob Plouse
145 lb	Randy Umberger	Barry Lehew
127	Bill Stump	Joe Hill
120	George Wagner	Barry Boykin
112	David Sheaffer	Dennis Coffman
103	James Sanders	Norman Cobaugh
100	Paul Weaver	Norman Keim
95	Barry Heffelfinger	Martin Remsburg
90	Randy Riffey	Arthur Goodling
85	Mike Remsburg	Dan Dorsheimer
78	Ed Boyer	Steve Lower
75	Bob Hess	Aaron Neidig

Richard Lyter vs the winner

64 CHAMPIONSHIP TEAM — Members of the Lower Dauphin High School Harrisburg Are
tling League Division I championship team in 1963-64 were, not in order in the photo, Aar
g. Bob Hess, Harold Shellenhammer, Jim Sanders, Bill Pinkerton, Gary Barb, Rick Gloc
Bhone. John Williams, Stu Wagner, Dennis Neidig, Randy Kahler, Randy

Wrestling Tournament

DISTRICT CHAMPIONS — 1964

Lower Dauphin High School "Falcons"

1961 Champs

Arbor Day 1965

Homecoming

Early Majorettes

LD Missile

418

Notice of Carol Channing Visit to LD

FACULTY: There is a 90% possibility that Broadway star, Carol Channing, will perform at Lower Dauphin, 7th period on Friday, January 12.

We realize that this notice is short only because we had not been fully informed ourselves. Her specific arrival time is uncertain so that there may or may not be an assembly called sometime during 7th period.

We know that you would appreciate seeing "Dolly" herself and would hate to pass up the opportunity of having her visit our school.

Thank-you for your consideration.

ENGLISH DEPARTMENT

David J. Emerich

WFIL-TV
46th & Market Streets
Philadelphia 39, Pa.

AMERICAN BANDSTAND
with Dick Clark

American Bandstand is holding a reservation for you to visit the program on WED JAN 2 1962

Dick Clark

Nº 19221

NOT TRANSFERABLE - VOID IF SOLD - SEE REVERSE SIDE

Curtis S. Taylor

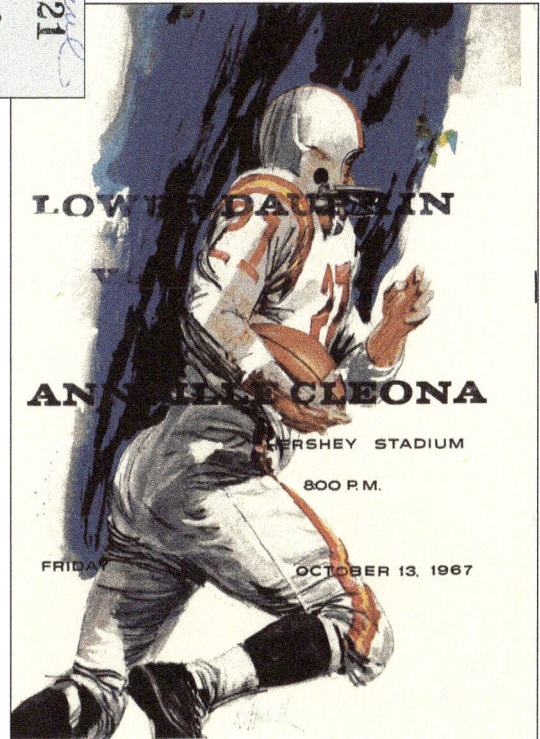

LOWER DAUPHIN
vs
ANNVILLE CLEONA

HERSHEY STADIUM

8:00 P.M.

FRIDAY   OCTOBER 13, 1967

Halloween

9th grade party

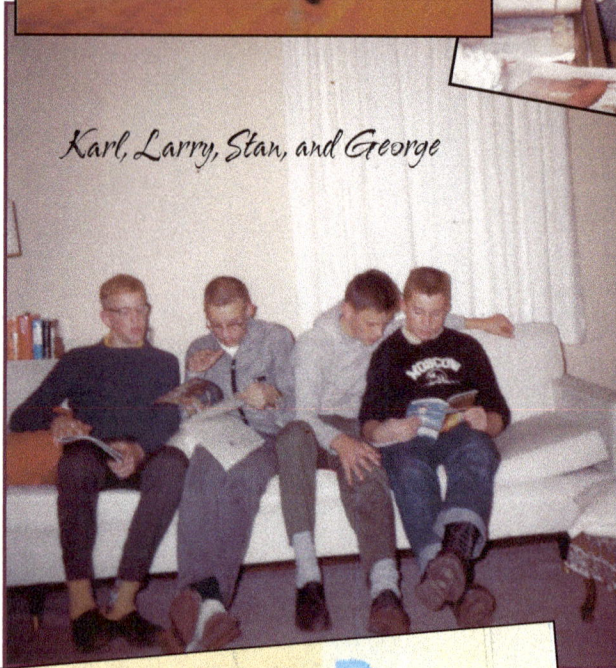

Karl, Larry, Stan, and George

The Original Falcon
Mascot 1963

MARDI GRAS BALL
MARCH 3
B-11 RM.

Byron Wyld, Howie Snyder, and John Burtner

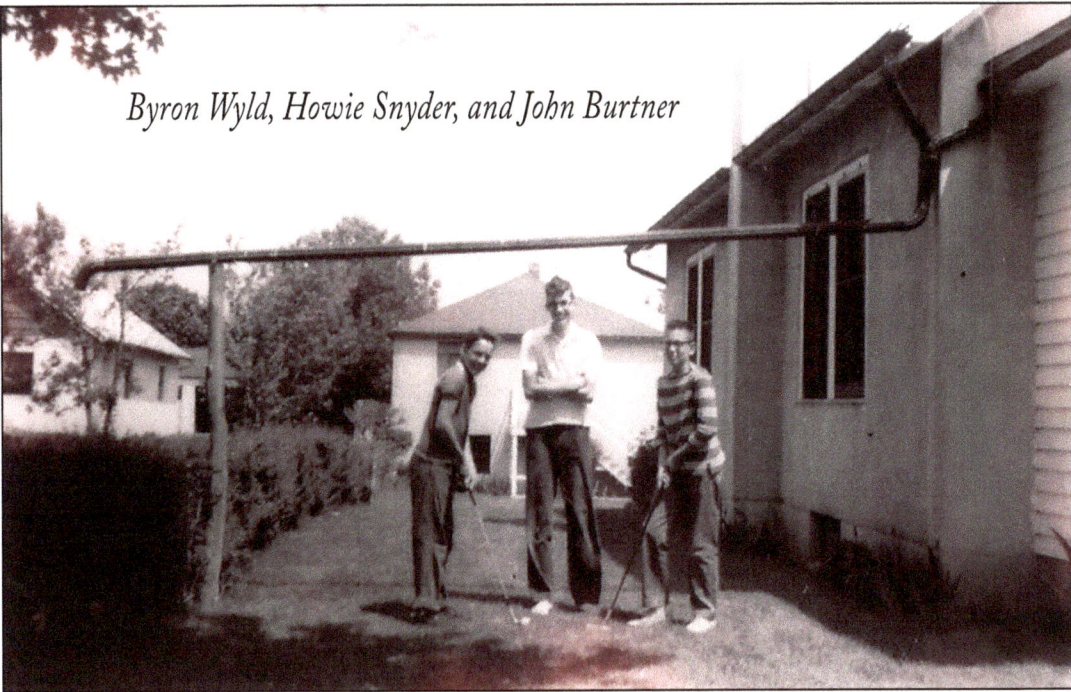

PROGRAM

Organ Selections .... Kenneth Miller

March of the Toys .... Victor Herbert
Silent Snow .... Harry Budka
Clock in the Toy Shop .... Lemon & Kullak
Yuletide Festival .... arr. by Warrington
    Lower Dauphin Band ----- Prowell M. Seitzinger, director

Festive Rounds
Christmas Bells .... Robert Farver
Goodnight to You All
Balladiers
    Accompanists: Judy Peterman, Linda Lash, Barbara Coble

Carol of the Bells .... Ukranian Carol
Merry Christmas .... Davenport
Joseph Dearest, Joseph Mine .... Old German
Dona Nobis Pacem .... Unknown
Glee Club
    Accompanists; Stephanie Zeiters, Linda Boyer

Gesu Bambino .... Pietro A. Yon
Honor Soloist: Alice Wiest

Silver Offering:
    German Carols .... German Club
        Helen Yount, director

Processional ..... *Joy to the World* ..... by Marcell

Deck the Hut With Coconut .... adapted by Sterling & Grant
    Dennis Mulligan .. Bongo drums   Betty Musser .. Maracas

T'was the Night Before Christmas ....Darby, Scott, & Simeone
    Robert Gibble, Dennis Patrick, Mildred Goss, Marylin Miller,
        Gerald Wampler, Thomas Hauer, Carol Bixler

My Favorite Things .... Rogers & Hammerstein
    Christmas Ballet .... Falconnettes
        Lower Dauphin High Choir
    Accompanists: Kenneth Miller, Roberta Espenshade

The Christmas Song .... Torme–Wells
Choir and Band

Dream of Peace ....
Combined Choirs

Angels We Have Heard on High .... French Carol
Recessional

Falconnettes

Linda Bell	Linda Leese
Nancy Bolash	Christine Maulfair
Valerie Braun	Vivian Motter
Mary Daub	Bonnie Sassaman
Linda Farver	MaryAnn Shertzer
Joyce Hostetter	Linda Shope
Pat Kerstetter	Connie Wolfe
Sandra Kreiser	

Christmas Program 1961

Hall Pass

The Unknown Side of Love

There is no pain when hate is here,
There is no hurt when trouble is near,
There is no pain when death I fear,
There is no hurt when burden I bear.

Though mortal wounds may end its beat,
the heart feels but ephemeral pain, a pain of mercy
and a pain of purpose;

But the heart and pain of love is merciless;
Hate, trouble, death, and burden cause no pain like this.

In that ephemeral pain of death there is
peace everlasting,

but the peaceless pain of love is forever
without passing.

by Ruth Glocker

Please
Return this
revised by Craig Trotch

The Eve of St. Agnes

It was chilly on the Eve of St Agnes
The owl was cold even though he
has thick feathers
The hare limped because he also was
cold
And the flock was silent
The Beadsman's hand were cold while
he fiddled around with the rosary beads
he was praying!
Past the Virgin Mary's picture while he
said a prayer,
Then took his lamp and rose from praying
He rose in his usual meager manner
and passed the dead
He passed many praying thinking on their
ill-at-ease mind
He turned north to go out and heard
music from party below.

Essays. Using the attached paper, answer the following.

I. Quote either the soliloquy or the poem you were required to memorize.

II. What period of English Literature most appealed to you and why?

III. What poem was your favorite and why?

Extra Credit: In this space, draw a self-portrait of how you feel at this moment.

You may now collapse

Personality Plus

Few people have the school record my friend has: five schools in nine years! These range from a one-room school on Round Top to the modern Lower Dauphin Jointure.

Second oldest of the seven children in the family, she has five younger brothers and sisters. This, along with babysitting, has given her experience with children. While babysitting, our classmate frequently is the victim of all the unpleasant pranks her charges can devise. She tells how once they tried to lock her outside the house. When she brings books to study, the youngsters are almost certain to hide them and make her search for them.

Of the several incidents in her life which my friend will never forget, one of the earliest she remembers is having been locked in a playhouse along with her cousin. The open door was suddenly blown shut by a gust of wind. When they discovered it was locked, my friend hit upon the effective but quite expensive solution of breaking the window. On the way out (through the window of

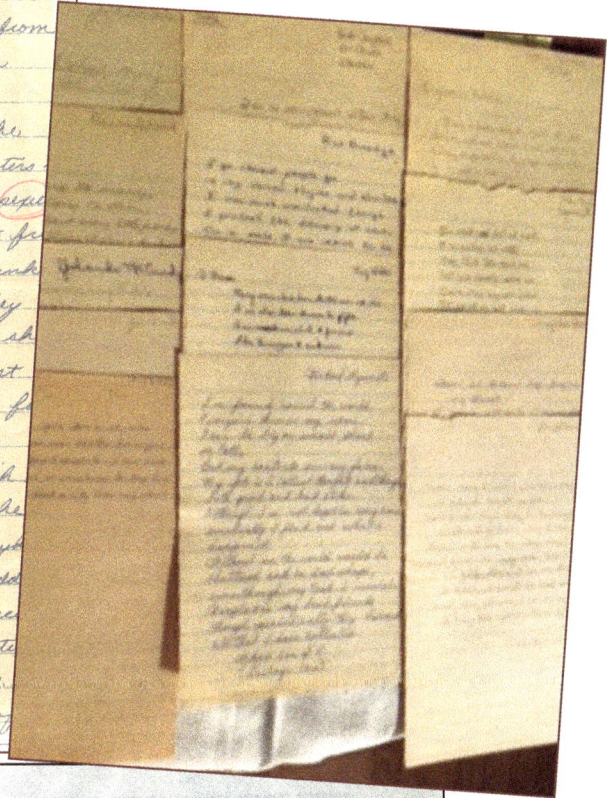

A COLLOQUY ON THE OCCUPATIONS
During the Medieval Period

Betsy Daisler
English II
Sept. 19, 1966

The following dialogue, written in Modern English, was structured after Abbot Aelfric's amusing "Colloquy on the Occupations", written in Latin during the late Tenth Century. The occupations discussed here are those uniquely a part of the Middle Ages, rather than those of the Anglo-Saxon Period.

1

Student: Don't you think we could delay our lesson until tomorrow and have a discussion?

Teacher: And what would you discuss?

Student: That doesn't matter. But if we chose a worthy subject, would you agree? Discussions are a part of learning and education, and we know that if it is not a good one, we will have to return to the books.

Teacher: What do you mean? What is your occupation?

Student: I am a monk, a scribe in the monastery. Every day I work in the scriptorium and copy manuscripts by the hour. Sometimes in many months or even many years, I complete an entire Bible or book. We are all very dedicated to the work because we know our dear Lord himself is pleased with our work.

Teacher: What type of work do your companions do?

Student: They work at a variety of trades and in many offices. Some are saints, some squires, some pages; others are minstrels, peasant friars, bowmen, doctors, masons, hunters, millers, glass-

---

It is generally thought that during the medieval era the cooking was done out of necessity and that foods were simple and basic. This was true for the peasants and lower classes. However, the rich, upper-class lords and barons were often guilty of overeating and drinking. England, at this time, was a great nation for eating, and even greater for drinking. The food of the serfs was poor and coarse. They barely survived on small quantities of fish, salt pork, soup, coarse black bread, cheese, and porridge.

An example of the food that the poor consumed is given in the poem, "Piers Plowman."

Bread and thin ale are for them a banquet,
Cold flesh and cold fish are like roast venison;
A farthing's worth of mussels, a farthing's worth
Of cockles,
Were a feast for them on Friday or fast-days;[1]

In the early times of cooking, especially in the summer, cooking was done outside. This was good enough for boiling and roasting, but not for baking. The lord of the manor would establish a common bakery where all of his tenants could get their bread baked for a small charge.

---
[1] L. F. Salzman, English Life In The Middle Ages (New York, Oxford University Press, 1960), p. 28.

THE PREPARATION AND TYPES
OF FOODS USED IN THE
MEDIEVAL HOMES
by
Wendy Daisler

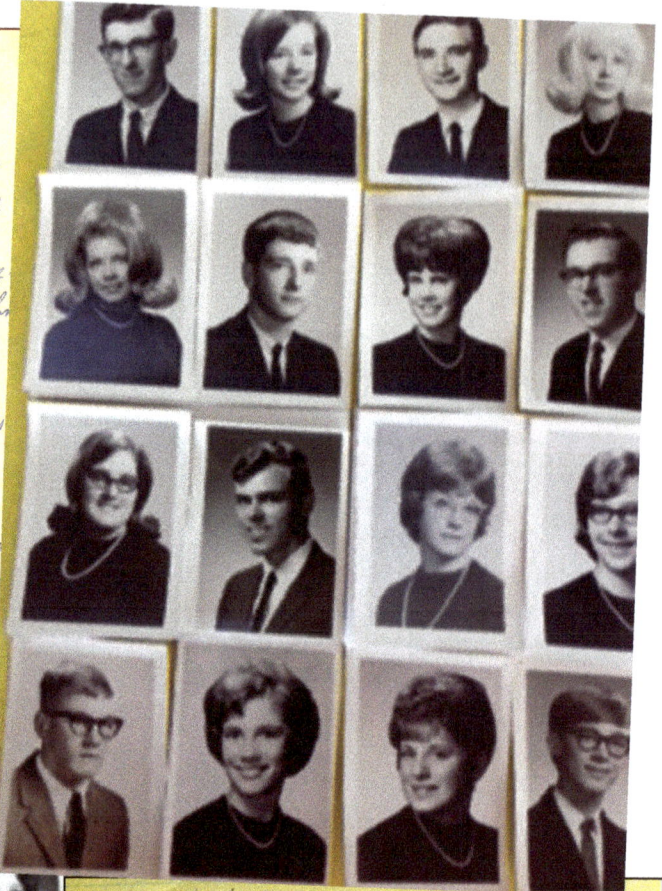

That orbed maiden with fire laden whom
 mortals call the moon
Glides glimmering o'er my fleecelike floor
 by the midnight breezes strewn
And wherever the beat of her unseen feet
 Which only the angels hear
May have broken the woof of my tent's
 thin roof, the stars peep behind
her a peer
And I love to see them whirl and flee
Like a swarm of golden bees
Till I widen the rent in my wind-built
 tent
And calms rivers, lakes and seas
Like strips of the sky
 fallen through me on high
Are each paved with the moon and
these.

Oh hell, you're beautiful, and I'm
intelligent so let's cut the crap
That also
↑ works in ↑
reverse

Craig Tritch
In Praise of Older Women
Stephen Vizinczey
Contemporary Canada Press
copyright 1965
224 pages

Novel

1 He ① enjoys his life best when spend
intimate company of women. Each cha
another encounter or affair (usually the
with all sorts of females.

He ~~had~~ experienced much in his
experinced all the inhumanities of the
World War and ② accompanying graft. ← some
in the war he learned to live for
pleasures. The war also showed him the
people will succumb to. to make a l
had his ④ first experience (fellatio)

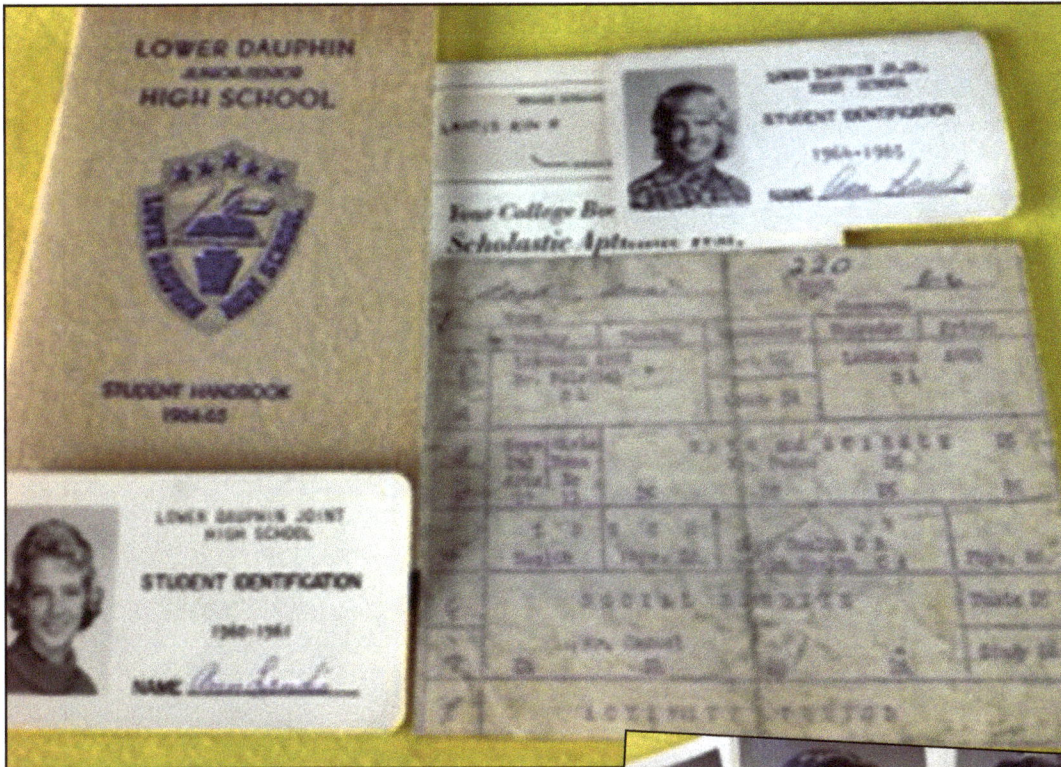

427

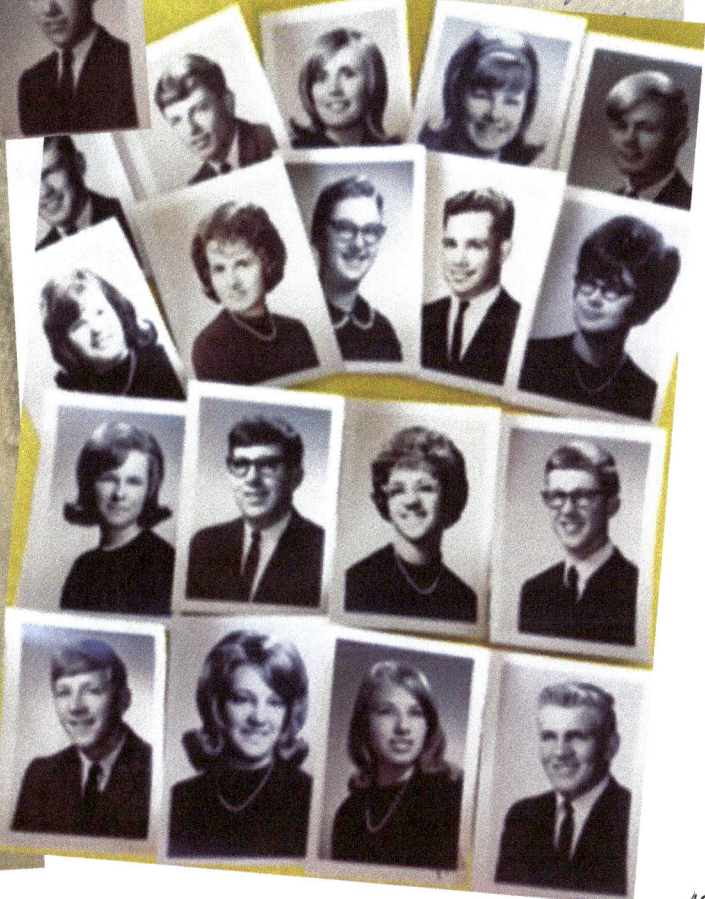

Book Report
Captain Danny Spi
Gladys Malvern

... Lake - 1965
... Julian Messner, Inc., New York

(... 11)

Molokai
...tion
...ncott Co

...Molokai gave me a
...erstanding of how
...his priests act out
...t faith and devo
...and his work
...splayed throughou
...count of Father
...e and his work
...leper colony un

The Life of Sir
Fleming
André Maurois
1959
E. P. Dutton and
293 pages
biography

Insights
1. Alexander Fle
decided to ded
life to fight
it was this
and purpose
him going
years of dis
and defeats.

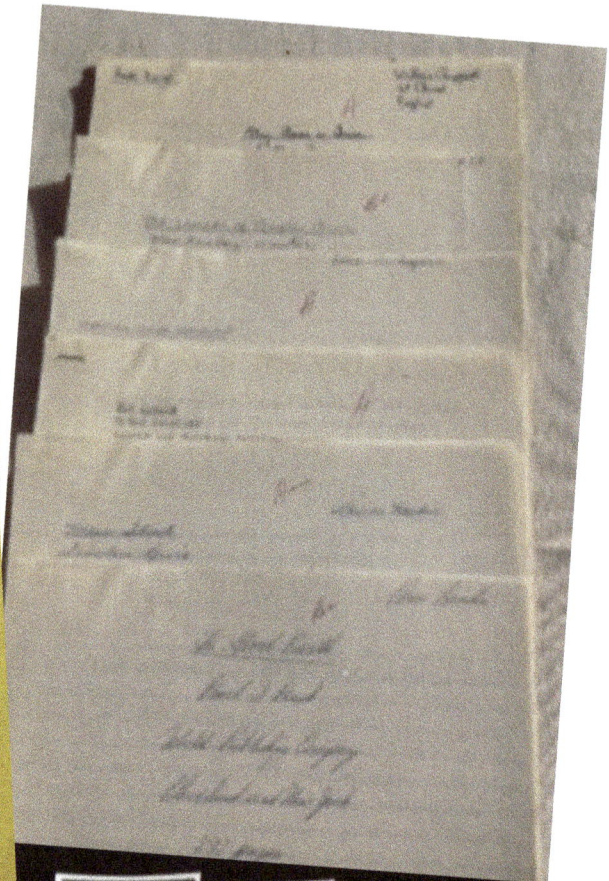

SCHOOL RULES – LDHS

LEAVING THE SCHOOL BUILDING
No student is permitted to leave the school building for any reason, unless authorized by the Principal.

DETENTION
Students will be assigned to detention by the Assistant Principal or Principal for truancy, class cutting, chronic tardiness, and major disciplinary offenses.

FIRE DRILLS
Fire drills at regular intervals are required by law and are an important safety precaution. It is essential that when the first signal is given, everyone obeys orders promptly and clears the building by the prescribed route as quickly as possible. The teacher in each classroom will give the students instructions.

THE CAFETERIA
The school cafeteria is maintained as a vital part of the health program of the school. To encourage good nutrition, a well-balanced lunch is offered at a reasonable price.

The lunchroom management and your fellow students will appreciate your cooperation in:

Depositing all lunch litter in waste baskets.

Returning all trays and utensils to the dishwashing area.

Leaving the table and floor around your place in a clean condition for others.

No food may be taken from the cafeteria.

SMOKING
Students are not permitted to smoke at any time in the school building, on the school grounds, or within the area surrounding the school grounds. This applies to all school-sponsored activities as well as the regular school day. Violation of this rule constitutes a serious offense, and possible suspension from school.

DRESS
We take pride in the appearance of our students. Your dress reflects the quality of the school, of your conduct, and of your school work. All students are expected to dress and groom themselves neatly in clothes are suitable for school activities.

THE SCHOOL AND THE LAW
Any unlawful act taking place on school grounds or busses not only makes the student subject to penalties which the courts may prescribe, but also will result in suspension or dismissal from school.

Pep pills, marijuana, LSD, and other stimulants are not only illegal, but may result in permanent physical and psychological damage and are usually the first steps towards drug addiction. Students are warned against their use. Anyone found possessing, selling, or buying drugs of any kind on school grounds will be placed in police custody.

WRITTEN AND PLANNED BY THE LOWER DAUPHIN SENIOR HIGH STUDENT COUNCIL OF 1969, RICK BURRIDGE, PRESIDENT.

SHORT STORIES

A Collection by the Junior Class
1964
1st Period English

Prim and Proper	Kirk Seibert
Clean Out Your Sewer	Lauren Haskin
Forget Me Not	John Enders
Disillusioned	Jean Deimler
A Man's Dignity	Bethanne Bojanic
The Three Generations	Karl Bell
Secret Agent #203	William Campbell
The Discovered Discoveries	Joe Hill
Then But Eight	William Stump
Present Imperfect	Lynn Sandel
Canaan Land	Ruth Ann Graybill
The Unwelcome Visitor	John Miller
The Hard-Learned Lesson	Carol Kauffman
The Revenge of Big Ben Williams	John J. Manura
Nothing But the Usual Stuff	H. Thomas Hauer
A Shadow	Kathy Verdelli
Friends Much?	Vivian Motter
The Mad Universe	Larry Lausch
To Go, or Not to Go	Stephanie Zeiters
Star of Gold	Ann R. Landis
Father, Forgive Me	Lois Downes
The Answer Will Come	Nancy Bolash
International Troublemaker	Larry Geesaman
Self-Confidence	Carol A. Zerfoss
Realization	Dennis Patrick
Everything for Mary Ann	Fay Zeiders
Promise Me This	Bonnie Fink

Falcon Flash

IT'S JUST MEMORIES NOW

FESTIVAL TIME A...

FALCON FLASH
LOWER DAUPHIN

OCT. 2, 1963 — VOL. 3, NO. 1

F.F.A. Works In Summer Months

Falcon Flash Staff Meet in Summer

New Teachers Make Debut At Lower Dauphin

NOVEMBER 13, 1963 — FALCON FLASH — 3

Concert Choir Begin Practice

P.S.A.T. Tests Taken Oct. 19

HOMECOMING QUEEN TO REIGN AT YOUTH FESTIVAL

Merry Christmas

FALCON FLASH
LOWER DAUPHIN

DECEMBER 20, 1963 — VOL. 3, NO. 3

Christmas Musical Held For Public

Assembly Held For Lettermen In Senior High

Lower Dauphin FHA Hosts to C. D. East

Strawser Earns Title

FALCON FLASH
LOWER DAUPHIN

FEBRUARY 20, 1964

Gym Team Performs For Students

Honor Society Inducts Members

7th Grader, Contest...

FALCON FLASH
LOWER DAUPHIN

APRIL 17, 1964

Classes Gain On The Job Experience In Model Office

Band To Be In Competition...

FALCON FLASH
LOWER DAUPHIN

MAY 28, 1964

Seniors Go To School

Clubs Elect Officers

434

Fall '61

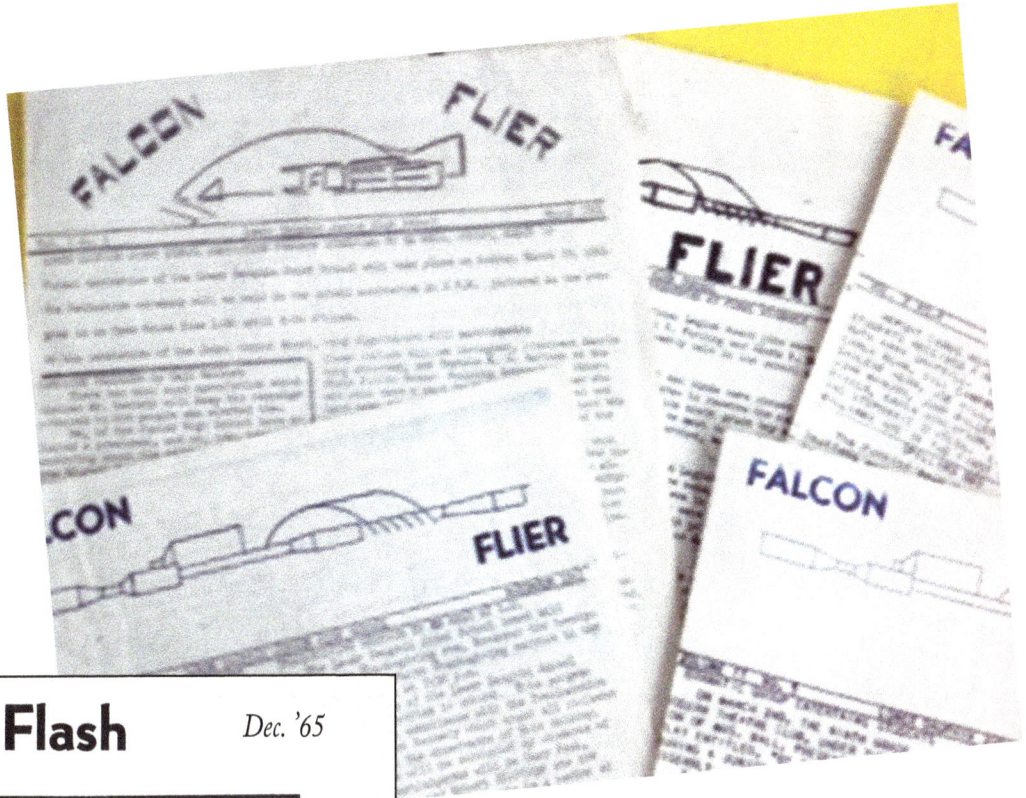

Falcon Flash

Dec. '65

Fall '64

Either defend or reject the manner in which
Shakespeare handles the conclusion of _Hamlet_. If you
disagree with Shakespeare's treatment of the ending of
the play, explain why and how you would revise the final
If you concur with Shakespeare's ending explain why you
agree. Utilize characterization, plot, theme and
structure from _Hamlet_ to either support or repudiate the
conclusion of the play. I will also be evaluating your
paper in terms of logical development and grammar.

GOOD LUCK....

In what words does the king virtually
order Hamlet's arrest?

sc ii

What attitude does Hamlet immediately
adopt again toward Rosencrantz & Guildenstern?

sc iii

Is the king justified in taking defensive
measures to save himself from Hamlet?

sc iv

What would you say is the key sentence
in Hamlet's argument with himself in
his soliloquy?

sc v

What state of mind does the king betray
in his speech alone with the queen, beginning
"O, this is the poison of deep grief"?

sc vi

What do the last three lines of the scene
about Horatio's character?

sc vii

What does the long conversation between
the king and Laertes show of the character

Act III, sc ii and iii

1. Give a brief synopsis of the King's
soliloquy

2. What are your feelings toward the King
in this scene?

3. In what way does this scene reveal
the character of Hamlet?

4. What may be the consequences/results
of Polonius' death?

5. How does Hamlet compare the two
kings?

6. Is Hamlet too severe with his mother?

7. What is achieved by the entrance
of the ghost?

8. Is there anything you'd like to ask
about Act III?

QUIZ: BACKGROUND ON PLAY (pp. 50-86)

1. What is meant by Shakespeare's "First Folio"?

2. Shakespeare's plays are divided into Histories, Comedies and Tragedies. What
is _Hamlet_ and why?

3. A good play needs four component parts. "Character" is one of them. What
are the other three?

does the image have on the novel play? on the audience?

3. Critics have disputed the character of Hamlet for centuries. Assume the role
of critic and comment "critically" on Hamlet's insanity, his reluctance to
avenge the death of his father, and Hamlet's relationship to Ophelia. Does
Hamlet's hesitation to act make him a weak character? Does Hamlet's relationship to Ophelia reflect Hamlet's inability to deeply love. Be sure to
document and support your position with quotes and incidents from the play.
Be specific.

...like all Elizabethan dramatists, used four kinds of speech.
"Rhymed verse" is one of them. What are the other three?

...meant by "Shakespeare's Universality"?

Hamlet is considered to be the most interesting play ever written.

The story of Hamlet in some form is 700 years old.

AS A "REVENGE PLAY:"

Vengeance was a pious duty laid on the next of kin.

1. Crime, usually murder
2. Discovery of the murderer by the avenger
3. Impediments to revenge
4. Triumphant conclusion, murderer destroyed
5. Since playgoers liked gore, the avenger and a half dozen others must perish in the last act.
6. Usually included at least one ghost and one mad scene.

Hamlet dominates all the other characters on stage as no other Shakespearean hero does.

His personality is not revealed by himself, but by the other characters.

His personality is not revealed by himself, but by the other characters.

TRAGEDY: This is the story of Hamlet's heroic struggle against insurmountable odds.

STRUCTURE

Introductions

HAMLET QU

1. Rich gifts wax poor when givers

2. For this relief much thanks: '

3. O, that this too, too solid fle Thaw and resolve itself into a

4. ...there is nothing either

5. What's Hecuba to him, or h That he should weep for he

6. If this had not been a gen burial.

7. The serpent that did sti Now wears his crown.

8. The lady doth protest t

9. This is the very ecsta

10. I am satisfied in natur I stand aloof

11. Alas, poor Yorick!

12. And let those that pl

13. My words fly up, Words without tho

Responses to Reasoning: Fallacies and Syllogisms

1. The first problem can be made into a simple syllogism by disregarding extraneous comments. If we set up a syllogism composed of a major premise, minor premise and conclusion, it would appear in the following order:

Major Premise: All normal people buy yearbooks.

Minor Premise: Claire won't buy a yearbook.

Conclusion: Claire is not a normal person.

The argument viewed in this form is easily proved false because the major premise is not a true statement. There are many people who are perfectly normal and still do not buy yearbooks. The other argument used which implies that Clair has plenty of money for other things may also be false. She may have just enough money for the basic pleasure with none left for what she considers trivial.

2. In this second example we can again recognize a simple syllogism. It can be stated in the following form:

Major Premise: Snobs are unpredictable.

Minor Premise: Joe is a snob.

Conclusion: Joe is unpredictable.

From the above conclusion we find a plausible reason for Joe's calling the writer conceited. Joe is unpredictable and thus goes through many moods. This whole deduction is based on the premise that snobs are unpredictable and is thus false because all snobs are not necessarily unpredictable. In reference to the last sentence we can again say this is not valid because one doesn't have to be smart to be rich.

In the modern business world it's either kill or be killed; you've got to be tough or they'll really take you. It's just like politics. Politics has always been crooked and always will be. As some fellow once said, "Nice guys finish last." You've got to be nice, all right—nice and mean. Otherwise you end up at the bottom of the heap."

3. The basic syllogism in the third paragraph can be presented as follows:

Major premise: Modern business is tough.

Minor premise: We are in business.

Conclusion: We are tough.

Again the fallacy of deduction occurs in the major premise. Not all modern business is kill or be killed. The example used of politics is an assumption or opinion made by the speaker without validity of relationship to business. The whole deduction is based on a false major premise. Therefore, it is not valid.

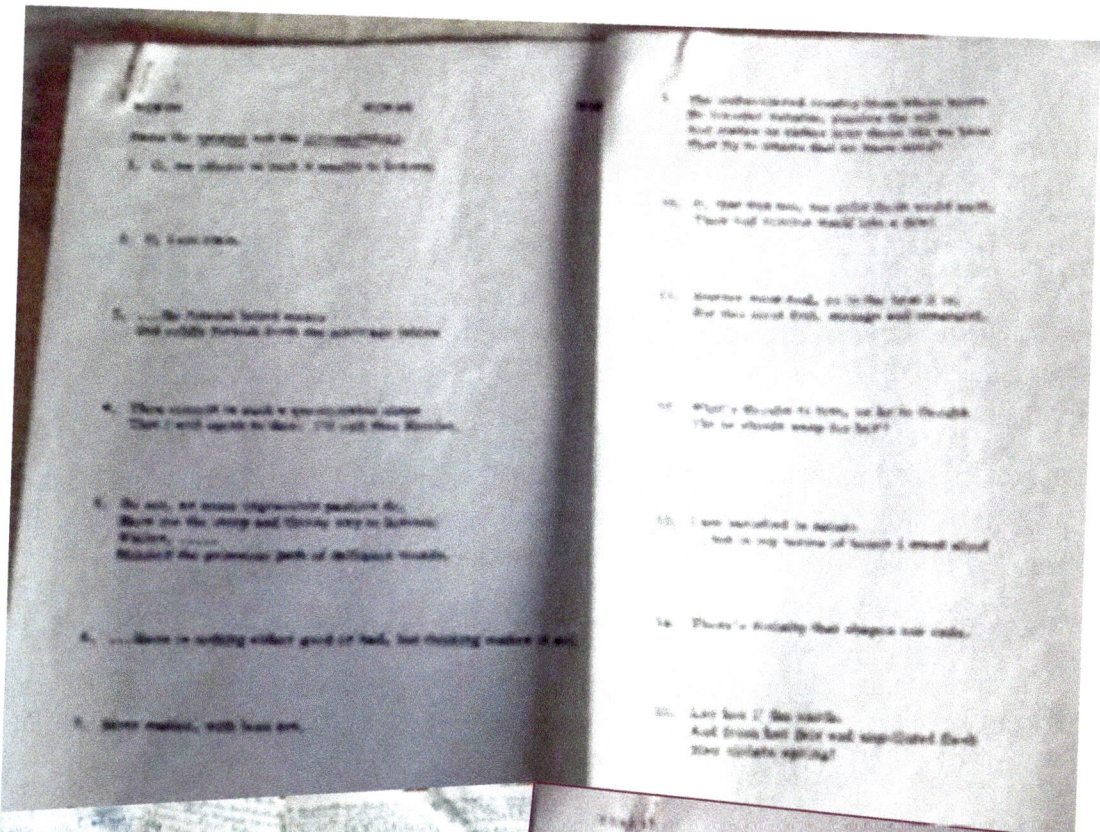
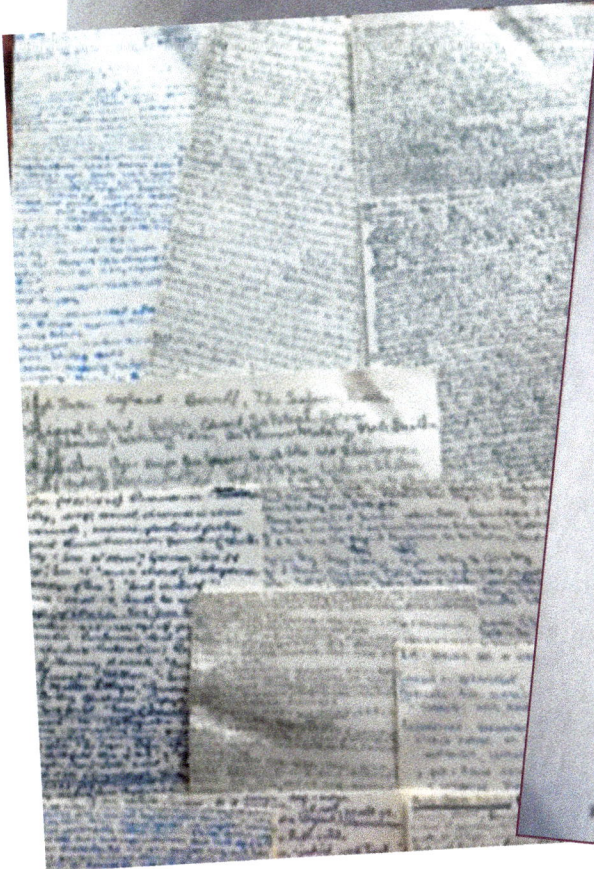
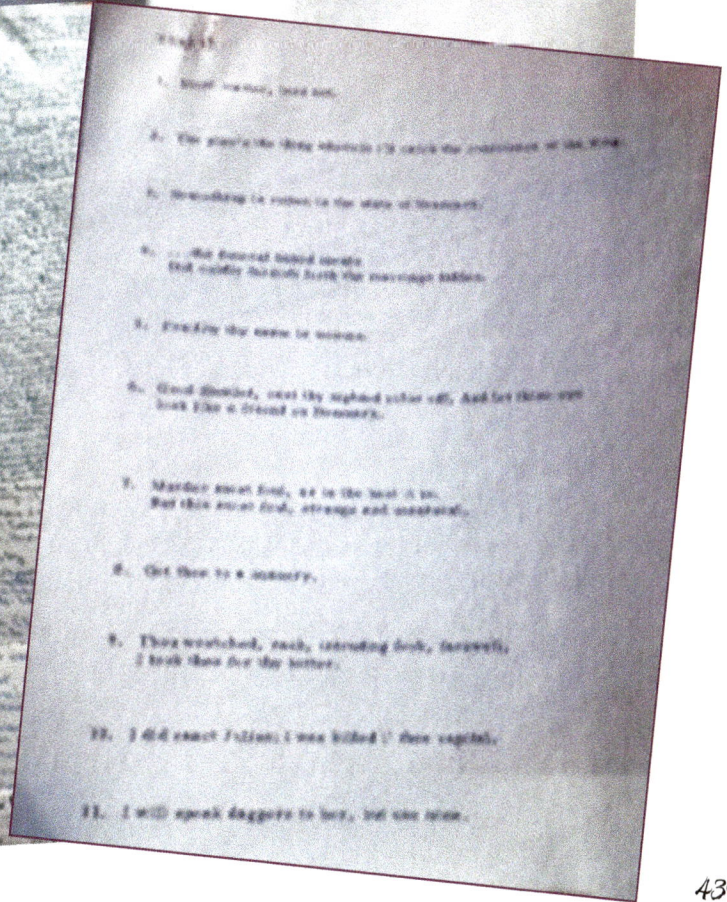

12th Grade English
Final Exam
1965
5th period

Answer all questions on the attached paper. There is more paper for those who may need it. When you have completed the test, put the papers in order, put the test sheets on top, attach the paper clip. Make sure your name is on every sheet and that the pages are numbered.

Do not panic! Think through each question and get your answer organized in your mind before you begin writing. You may draw upon any resource of your reading experience where applicable. These questions are geared to evaluate your overall comprehension of literature.

GOOD LUCK!

I. Select one theme in literature and trace it throughout all of the periods of literary history in which it (the theme) was used. Show how this theme was used by the writers of each period. Select either one of the following suggestions OR use one of your own choosing. Be specific in your essay.

    A. Nature
    B. Heroes
    C. War
    D. Love
    E. Hate
    F. Patriotism
    G. Freedom
    H. Man's inhumanity to man
    I. Religion
    J. Carpe diem

II. Answer two of the following. Cite examples of poems, essays, short stories, or novels to support your answers. (You are not necessarily restricted to English literature.) Be specific and analytic.

    A. Is escape from the modern world possible? Is it desirable?
    B. What is the ideal life?
    C. What is success? How may life be lived successfully?
    D. How should death be approached?
    E. What is the main criticism of contemporary civilization? Do you agree? Defend your answer.

III. Choose one of the following and discuss intelligently.

"The Relationship Between Literature and _____"

    A. Politics
    B. Art
    C. Society
    D. Economic Movements or Ideas
    E. Religion
    F. Philosophy
    G. History

IV. Discuss the following:

    A. This is the way the world ends, This is the way the world ends, Not with a bang, but a whimper.

    B. It is only by careful watching and absolute sincerity that we follow the path that is destined for us, and, no matter how tragic that may be, it is better than the tragedy we bring upon ourselves.

    C. To be truly happy is a question of how we begin and not of how we end, of what we want and not of what we have.

    D. There is nothing either good or bad, but thinking makes it so.

    E. Beauty is truth, truth beauty—that is all ye know on earth, and all ye need to know.

V. OPTIONAL. If you believe you have not done well enough on the previous questions, you may try this one. Those of you who have adequately answered the previous questions or are running short of time, omit this one.

Considering all of the periods of literature we have covered this year, select the one most meaningful to you. Discuss the characteristics of the literature of the period, cite examples of the literature, and tell why you like this period best.

Sample – 1965 Students Letters to Themselves

Dear Ann,

Well, here I sit in English Class after taking the last exam in Spanish. Boy, I'm glad that's over. Mrs. Ball says I'll get this back in 5 years. Well, we will see. I graduate June 8, 1965!!! In that time I intend to go to school, major in history and become a teacher. By that time I hope to have my own horse, gone water skiing, visited Canada, and I don't plan on being married. I'm dating Jay Kopp now, and I wonder if I'll be dating him then. I have dated him for 3 years and 8 months now.

I weigh about 135 lbs. and I'm 5' 4 ¾ tall. I hope I am thinner and my hair is still blonde in five years. Today I'm wearing mother's old blue cotton straight shirtwaist and my beloved charm bracelet. Mrs. Ball is wearing a lovely spaghetti-strap sundress.

Lauren Haskin is on my right, Karl Bell, right diagonally, Carol Kauffman in front, Vivian Motter beside, Linda Alleman back diagonally left, and Nancy Bolash came in and sat behind me to write this.

Today I believe in trying to lose weight, no cheating, drinking or smoking. I've never had intimate relations with a member of the opposite sex, mainly because I've never let myself get in such a situation and I don't believe in such actions before marriage.

I believe very definitely in God and go to church. I'm a bit fascinated by "plain" people and I love farming. Tonight I must iron, maybe watch television and sleep 'cause I'm tired. Beat is more like it.

When I see this again, who knows what or who I'll be.

Favorite record: "Crying in the Chapel," Elvis Presley

Reading The Yearling by Rawlings

This week-end Jay and I are going to ride Galen's horse & double with Galen to play golf in Lititz.

Daddy is thinking about revamping our farm into a horse farm.

Mother's working in the shop.

Jill has Robyn Lynch over for company now.

Rick is just plain know-it-all Rick! I wonder if he'll ever get to States.

Also I wonder who I'll meet in college.

I want to read Gone With the Wind.

This is fun sitting here jotting down ideas!!! Seems dumb, but fun!

We're at peace now, though there is trouble in South Viet Nam, and Johnson is President.

End of Year Evaluation, Steve Schell, 1965

1. I am sorry to say that all the activities I've been in have not been worthwhile at all to me. This year Student Council, as in the last three years, has been nothing more than a group gathering mainly because every   time a suggestion is made or a wish is asked it is killed by the higher authorities. This practice has been very   detrimental to Student Council. Also, the advisors have entered the realm of members and instead of mainly advising, they speak up about everything and usually take up much time.

   Varsity Club has been nothing more than a money-making club and interest was nil. Future Teachers Club, because all clubs started late this year (Why?), never got off on the right foot and as a result was boring.

2. a. During the year we have discussed U.S. edu. system problems and our own problems. One must agree that to be an administrator or teacher is not an easy task and that the primary purpose for High School is Education for all, but this philosophy of equal edu. for all, and the same edu., must be remedied. Today the students are not satisfied with what they are getting; they want more of a challenge and a somewhat faster pace, in other words, an individualistic approach. No one can say that the U.S. edu. system comes second to any but to be the best is not enough; we must continue to better our best and the above philosophy will and must be altered.

   b. One idea I have may seem absurd, but I feel that if the seniors were given special privileges (spelling's horrible, I know), there would exist a greater respect for being a senior. Right now it means nothing more than one's last year. A special room could be set aside for recreation and other small things used as special to seniors would be good.

3. I enjoyed very much the historical approach to lit. It served as a good review and I learned a lot. Your way of teaching is hard, but very good. I feel ready for college.

4. There wasn't enough writing at all. This was one downfall of High School here. I didn't do enough research for certain classes. Much more writing is necessary.

Off the record!
   Between you and me, the incident that took place with those poppers it would be appreciated if the truth was known. No doubt everyone does something in the last couple of days. It's our last chance, but what happened yesterday with Mr. Croll was blown up as much as what propaganda is. We were told he had a burned hand, that the poppers were firecrackers (they're not; [they are] the same as party poppers) and that it was a great crime. Let it be known that Mr. C's hand was not damaged one bit. I called his home to find out and he admitted that nothing had happened and even laughed when one parent went to his home last night. We got caught. That's the breaks, but what has gotten around to others (you have no doubt already heard) is worse than what we did. I consider you a friend and wanted at least you to know what goes.

   Thanks.

Student End of Year Responses

"I liked the way you taught the course. Last year I did not learn much english."[1]

During my first five years in the classroom, I asked the students to complete an informal evaluation as the concluding portion of their Final Exam. I saved all of these to return to them "someday." These reviews, as well as other assignments I have kept, will be returned—at least to the Class of 1965—at their next Class Reunion so that we will have come full circle in close to sixty years.

The Editorial Contributors read through all of these responses (but not the final exams) and selected a representative sample. We have identified the responders by only their initials.

Used with Ninth Grade (1961 and 1962): Please give your evaluation of this course—your likes and dislikes, and any suggestions and comments you may care to make. Feel free to express your views. This will not affect your grade in any way.

Used with Seniors (1964-1966): Please answer the following questions. Don't worry; I won't get a chance to read these papers until your final grades have been recorded. I would like truth without malice.

1. As Seniors, what school activities have been most worthwhile and which least?
   - Sports for all the good reasons. (BS)
   - Wrestling because of learning to get along and gain confidence. (JK)
   - Mr. Peck and Boys Club.

2. If you could make one or two changes in the school, what would you do and why?
   - Students would have more incentive to earn better grades if final exams were exempt. (CS)

3. What part of this year's English program have you liked best and why?
   - You were very fair with us. (JL)
   - A fine course with offered much challenge; I have learned a lot. You made things interesting. (LL)
   - Learning to write letters (9th grade). (AG)
   - Learned the most in Lit. Class, even though I was afraid to come to class in the beginning of the year.
   - The newest literature books are the best and should be used in all classes. (NB)
   - The best, most complete, and worthwhile course LD offers. (LH)
   - The most interesting course as it was rare that the term "routine" could be used.
   - I liked the course very much but I didn't study. (LC)
   - Poets and authors, because they are strange and fascinating. (RW)
   - I liked that you could laugh along with us.
   - Having the class first thing in the morning gave me a pleasant outlook on the day and the less interesting classes that followed. (AL)

4. What part have you liked least and why?

- Weekly vocabulary because I do not care for words very much. (MG)
- I don't specifically care for your sardonic, sarcastic, caustic, and sometimes unbearable attitude toward me. Yet, I've enjoyed English and have evidence that your course is profitable as my College Board scores show. Thank you. (JH)
- There is nothing I liked least because it is my problem that I am just too damn lazy. I like the way the class was handled and sorry that I didn't have any others like it. (MO)
- I felt the final exam was way out. (RL)
- I liked the writing process least. (CK)
- The students were at fault as we talked too much. (HS)
- Grammar, as a student learns all he will ever need in the first eleven years. (VM)
- There was sometimes favoritism shown.
- The smart-alecky kids in 9-1. (CH)
- Literature background material belongs in history class. (EM)
- Choir with its stupid merit and demerit system. (SP)
- In all honesty choir was rotten, the whole affair. (RM)
- Having student teachers. (WG and others)

5. Have you any constructive criticism for improvement?

- No; just destruction! (GW)
- We rushed too fast to really enjoy what we read. (RT)
- Sometimes assignments were too long and it was tough keeping up.
- Improvement could be made if you did not have everything so set. Let the students make up their minds about their senior year and do away with Executive Council. This didn't collect seniors' ideas any better than letting each senior have his say. (KW)
- I have gained a lot even if my grades don't show it. I took College Prep English with my Commercial Course because I knew it would help, as my junior year in English was wasted. You have left a lasting impression. (KZ)
- More time should be spent on events and ideas than on the authors and their ideas. (HB)
- Do away with vocabulary words that are impossible to pronounce and to learn. (RC)
- I feel teachers' attitudes, dress, and manner of speech should be more modest and conservative, not stifling or stern. The moral decadence and apathy of Americans is growing to alarming proportions and I believe it is partly the obligation of the Educational system to better this condition at every opportunity. (FR)
- More recent quotations on tests and more interpretation of them. (BS)
- I have no criticism as the two years I spent in this class have been excellent college previews. (FZ)
- There should be more practice writing paragraphs, essay, themes, critical analyses, etc. (LS)
- Nothing to add for improvement; we have a much more comprehensive course than a neighboring school and what we did with the multitude of material presented was up to us. (AL)
- English is NOT HALF BAD. (RG)
- Um, well. Maybe don't try so hard to fool your kids into thinking you are not on their side… (PR)
- Hamlet would have been better if we had read it for enjoyment rather than work. (RG)

General Comments:
- Enjoyed FFA and being a class officer because these activities provided training in leadership, organizing and speaking before people. (MH)
- I hate English, period! A couple of years, OK, but not 12! (DG)
- We should be able to go to the Guidance Office without a pass, "because many of us less fortunate ladies have many problems."
- Sports were best, along with friends who led me to interest in other activities. (BS)
- Loved the unique bulletin boards; they are really sharp! (MS)
- Usually English doesn't interest me, but the way your classes are is a blessing. (KS)
- I still think that the soldier was alive in "Soldier from the Wars Returning." (TB)

"Soldier from the wars returning" – A. E. Housman

Soldier from the wars returning,
Spoiler of the taken town,
Here is ease that asks not earning;
Turn you in and sit you down.

Peace is come and wars are over,
Welcome you and welcome all,
While the charger crops the clover
And his bridle hangs in stall.

Now no more of winters biting,
Filth in trench from fall to spring,
Summers full of sweat and fighting
For the Kesar or the King.

Rest you, charger; rust you, bridle;
Kings and Kesars, keep your pay;
Soldier, sit you down and idle
At the inn of night for aye.

And, my favorite comment came from JM whose father served on the School Board: "The way a course is taught is an important part of the course and I believe that the teacher of this course should get a raise in salary."

(Endnotes)
[1] Yes, this comment was written by one of the students.

B-1
Juniors

C-3
Class of 66

C-3

The English Students Class Rolls

1960-61

6 sections, 211 students

9-1 (33 students)
Banks, Linda
Byers, Janice
Chellew, George
Clark, Larry
Crick, Gerald
Davis, K. Louise
Fair, Karen
Farling, Michael
Flocken, Susan
George, Richard
Glocker, W. Rick
Green, Donald
Heisey, Carol
Johnson, Sandra
Kauffman, Eleanor
Kettering, Joanne
Kopenhaver, Robert
Lenker, Kathy
Miller, Kenneth
Moyer, Lee
Mudd, William
Neidinger, John
Roland, Audrey
Seitz, Glenn
Sharp, Judith
Smith, Nancy
Snyder, Harold
Verdelli, Gloria
Walborn, Gail
Walmer, Donna
Wert, Betty
Williams, Bruce
Wyld, Byron

9-2 (35 students)
Badman, Elsie
Blanchard, Susan
Broadwater, Dale
Buck, John
Burtner, John
Deaven, Donald
Deaven, Harriet
Dibeler, Anna
Dixon, Todd
Engle, Jeff
Fink, Joseph
Gluck, Marilyn
Hershberger, Larry
Horton, Allen
Johnson, John
Kantz, Susan
Klinger, Ted
Lenker, Bertha
Loser, Tom
Miller, Donald
Painter, Ruth
Peters, Denise
Rainey, Judith
Rhone, James
Ross, Delores
Saylor, Victoria
Seesholtz, Sandra
Shelley, Barbara
Taylor, Thomas
Taylor, William
Walters, Sally
Weaver, Bonnie
White, T. David
Redcay, Ralph
Warner, Anna

9-3 (38 students)
Barnhart, Pat
Barb, Gary
Bartholomew, Lynda
Bartholomew, Sharon
Brandt, Nancy
Caldwell, Allen
Carlson, Raymond
Convery, Kathleen
Ernst, Fred
Etnoyer, Donald
Fabian, Nancy
Goss, Mildred
Harman, Kathy
Hitz, Elvin
Hyde, Maradell (didn't finish)
Kahler, Randy
Kirkpatrick, Portia
Kling, Dennis
Kreiser, Gerald (didn't finish)
Krosevec, Michael
Lawson, Susan
Lower, Richard
McNeal, Barbara
Neidig, Dennis
Newlin, Marsha
Pintarch, George
Reigle Robert
Rine, Terry
Rosensteel, Leslie
Shandor, Frank
Shutt, Larry
Snavely, Susan
Vint, Gary
Watts, John
Warg, Eileen
Weaver, Peggy
White, David
Hosler, Joseph (A-2)

9-5 (39 students)
Baumback, Jeffrey
Burrows, Larry
Clark, Joyce
Coble, Jacob
Daniels, Clair
Duble, Sandra
First, Jan
Fisher, Catherine
Geesaman, Thomas
Green, Bonnie
Hetrick, Vera
Horst, Frances
Houser, John
Hubbard, Charles
Judy, William
Lehman, Donald
Linnane, John
Mack, Joseph
Myers, Ken
Mumma, Wayne
Nauss, Karen
Leeser, Kathy
Ney, Stuart
Patrick, Carl
Propst, Faye

Puzuk, Liga
Rhoads, Linda
Santarelli, Jack
Shuey, Wayne
Smith, Anna
Smith, Janet
Snyder, James
Snyder, Sylvia
Spillers, Earl
Steckman, Ronald
Tschudy, John
Whitehaus, Donald
Witmer, Dorothy
Wright, Victoria

9-6 (36 students)
Bechtel, Donna
Berkebile, Dale
Blose, Yvonne
Brandt, Jay
Burrows, Dayne
Cobaugh, Geraldine
Daub, Mary
Dieffenderfer, Earl
Diffenderfer, JoAnn
Fies, Elaine
Foreman, Annette
Horst, Harold
Horting, James
Krodel, Barbara
Martin, Joy
Miller, Anita
Moyer, Mary
Myers, W. John
Nowickie, Stanley
Oberholtzer, Victoria
Olson, Patricia
Patton, Diana
Reisinger, Betty
Rhoads, Carol
Roush, Reba
Sassaman, Bonnie
Schildt, Robert
Shifflett, Robert
Shull, Edward
Shull, Mary
Stauffer, Harry
Templin, Joseph
Wagner, Carl
Wagner, Luke
Weikel, Kenneth

Yinger, Vance
9-7 (30 students)
Bechtel, Doris
Bechtel, Joseph
Bechtel, Kenneth
Carlson, Dennis
Clair, Oscar
Cobaugh, Edwin
Conrad, Kay
Dettling, Minnie
Diegel, Mildred
Detwiler, Barbara
Good, Marlin
Grogan, Robert
Hosler, Beatrice
Koppenhaver, Lester
Kreiser, Eileen
Leach, Kenneth
Lehew, Jack
Martin, Jean
Mateer, James
McLaughlin, P. Gene
Pheasant, Craig
Resinger, Betty
Robertson, Lynn
Sandy, Dianna
Shifflet, Mildren
Stoner, Brian
Theurer, Barry
Theurer, Larry
Wallish, Carol
Williams, Ken

1961-62

159 students

1st period (35 students)
Badman, Edith
Baker, Ken
Bauder, Harry
Baumbach, Robert
Beaudrias, Mary-Paul
Bonawitz, George
Boyer, Linda
Brubaker, Mark
Coble, David
Derr, Carol
Dorsheimer, John
Fawber, Peggy
Geesaman, Lawrence

Gerlach, Karen
Glass, Jon
Harper, Jane
Haskin, Lauren
Heinzman, Joseph
Heueisen, David
Kalback, Karen
Landis, Ann
Laush, Larry
Lewis, Richard
Mateer, Joseph
Means, Jack
Plecker, William
Reed, Marsha
Reish, Debbie
Shilling, Robert
Skinner, Michael
Walker, Linda
Walters, Linda
Warble, Luke
Welker, Karen
Zerfoss, Karen

4th period (26 students)
Adams, Francis
Chiffo, Sandra
Cobaugh, Virginia
Ensminger, Joseph
Good, Sandra
Grasser, William
Gruber, William
Hoffer, Glen
Hostetter, Joyce
Kolaric, Judith
Lingle, Marlin
Martino, Ruth
Meyerhoffer, Bruce
Mutek, Mary Ann
Risser, Joann
Seibert, Irvin
Shertzer, John
Singer, Ronald
Sweigart, Arthur
Updegraff, Norman
Walters, Carolyn
Watts, Shelby
Weaver, Paul
Whitemoyer, George
Winters, Linda
Wolfe, Connie

5th period (30 students)
Barb, Gary
Bechtel, Betty
Behm, Carla
Bittinger, Pamela
Books, Patsy
Byers, Patricia
Clouser, Linda
Coble, Jacob
Coffman, Dennis
Cooley, Joel
Derr, Donna
Fegley, Brenda
Fenner, Frances
Gordon, Kenneth
Haldeman, William
Heisey, Arthur
Hetrick, Marlin
Hoover, Galen
Keller, Marjorie
Lehman, Robert
McNeal, Loretta
Neidig, Aaron
Pankake, Michael
Sanders, James
Santarelli, Maxine
Shaffer, David
Trissler, Karen
Via, Ronald
Wolfe, Barbara
Zerphy, Gerald

6th period (37 students)
Aucher, Dianne
Barb, Donna
Bickle, Robert
Carlson, Dennis
Crist, David
Davis, Loretta
Dean, Michael
Fink, Marlene
Fisher, Jane
Fox, Mary
George, Richard
Hall, Edgar
Heller, James
Hess, Robert
Hoffman, Mary
Horting, Lynette
Huff, Jo-Ann

Johnson, Pat
Kimmel, Susan
Livering, Earl
Martin, William
McNeal, Lorraine
Noel, Earla
Pace, Sherry
Peffley, Dolores
Plouse, Robert
Rhine, Sally
Ruggles, Jack
Snyder, Sharon
Stauffer, Jean
Stipe, Sandra
Taylor, Lynn
Umberger, Randy
Wagner, Errol
Weaver, Grace
White, David
Zechman, Anna

7th period (31 students, top section)
Bassett, Judith
Bell, Karl
Bojanic, Bethanne
Bolash, Nancy
Campbell, William
Deimler, Jean
Downes, Lois
Enders, John
Fink, Bonnie
Graybill, Ruth Anna
Hauer, Thomas
Hill, Joseph
Kauffman, Carol
Kreider, Donald
Manura, John
Miller, Doris
Miller, John
Mills, Terry
Motter, Vivian
Park, Marjorie
Patrick, Dennis
Perkin, Robert
Rhoads, Thelma
Sandel, Carolyn
Seibert, Kirk
Shertzer, Mary Ann
Stump, William

Waters, George
Wisniewski, Stanley
Zeiters, Stephanie
Zerfoss, Carol

1962-63

159 students, 9th grade, Class of 1966

2nd period (34 students)
Bashore, Anna
Boozer, Linda
Boyer, Edward
Brandt, Geraldine
Diegel, Charles
Espenshade, Gerald
Fegley, Yvonne
Fernback, Louise
Gepfer, James
Getz, Gloria
Hummer, Gary
Hitz, Galen
Landis, John
Lewis, Shirley
Miller, Kathy
Nichols, George
Pinkerton, Susan
Rhine, Fay
Rine, Thomas
Rogers, James
Scheetz, Bonnie
Seibert, Shirley
Shaffer, Dale
Shellenhamer, Georgine
Shirk, Richard
Smith, David
Straining, Chester
Spitler, Dale
Taylor, Carol
Venneri, Frank
Warner, Jean
Walters, Carolyn
Wheeler, Robert
Zeller, Linda

3rd Period (29 students)
Brown, Marie
Carlson, Robert
Day, Gerald
Dehmey, Earl

Espenshade, Dale
Fisher, Robert
Gingrich, Carol
Goodling, LaVern
Halterman, Barry
Heller, Edwin
Hess, Dennis
Hetrick, Harold
Hoffer, William
Lewis, Shirley
Long, Randy
Lutz, Nadine
Patrick, Carol
Pickel, Richard
Plecker, William
Potteiger, JoAnn
Rider, Ray
Shellenhamer, Robert
Shope, Linda
Teets, Rodney
Toomey, Terry
Wright, Francis
Wright, Robert
Wright, Sherman
Slick, Barbara

4th Period (34 students)
Baum, Lois
Calhoon, Janet
Campbell, Constance
Comitz, Ruth
Eshleman, Joseph
Espenshade, Kenneth
Garrison, Hubert
Geesaman, Sharon
Girvin, Wandy
Good, Richard
Gordon, Linda
Gourley, Ronald
Grubb, Paul
Hickey, Debbie
Holman, Janet
Hooton, Robert
Jeronis, Alice
Johns, Harold
Johnston, Ray
Lash, Linda
Leininger, George
Miller, Verna Jean
Minnich, Karen

Morrow, Sandra
Pheasant, Patty
Rainey, Pamela
Ratcliff, Lester
Rider, Keith
Shemas, Margaret
Spahr, William
Tomazin, Robert
Tritch, Vernon Ray
Walmer, Beverly
Williams, John

6th Period (29 students)
Adams, Linda
Alleman, John
Alther, Sharon
Barb, Calvin
Baumbach, Sharon
Behney, Charles
Bellaman, Paul
Blouch, Jessica
Cumor, Tonia
Ebersole, Gary
Forry, Susan
Gaudette, Richard
Gonse, Sharon
Goodling, Arthur
Heffelfinger, Barry
Hess, Ronald
Hoffer, Alvin
Leonard, Carl
Kromer, David
Moyer, Susan
Peiffer, Linda
Rhoads, Sandra
Saksek, Karen
Schmink, Dianne
Shifflett, Marilyn
Toberman, Jon
Weber, Linda
Umbrell, Donald
Wrzesniewski, Martha

7th Period (33 students)
Aldrich, William
Bedeaux, Timothy
Bell, Barbara
Brandt, Gayle
Carlson, Robert
Diodato, Darrell

Fetrow, Donna
Gonglowski, Joseph
Hand, Michael
Hartwell, Mary
Hershberger, Dennis
Jackson, Robert
Kassman, Linda
Kreiser, Sharon
Martincheck, Stephen
McNaughton, Joyce
Miller, Mary
Neagle, Karen
Petroski, Frank
Roger, Betsy
Roy, Geraldine
Sener, Walter
Shellenhamer, Harold
Shubert, Cheryl
Sipe, Pamela
Stauffer, Barbara
Stees, Nancy
Strite, Mike
Wagner, Evans
Walkup, Fred
Weaver, Barbara
Wherry, Michael
Wright, Sandra

1963-64

1st period, 11th grade, Juniors, American Lit, 28 students
Bell, Karl
Bojanic, Bethanne
Bolash, Nancy
Campbell, William
Deimler, Jean
Downes, Lois
Enders, John
Fink, Bonnie
Geesaman, Larry
Graybill, Ruth Ann
Haskin, Lauren
Hauer, Thomas
Hill, Joe
Kauffman, Carol
Kreider, Don
Landis, Ann
Lausch, Larry
Manura, John

Miller, John
Motter, Vivian
Patrick, Dennis
Sandel, Carolyn
Seibert, Kirk
Stump, William
Verdelli, Kathleen
Zeiders, Fay
Zeiters, Stephanie
Zerfoss, Carol

3rd period, 12th grade, Class of 1964, Brit. Lit, 24 students

Backenstoes, Becky
Banks, Linda
Chellew, George
Convery, Kathleen
Davis, Louise
Deaven, Harriet
Fabian, Nancy
Fair, Karen
Gluck, Marilyn
Green, Donald
Kauffman, Eleanor
Kopenhaver, Robert
Lawson, Susan
Lenker, Kathy
Peters, Denise
Roland, Audrey
Sharp, Judy
Snyder, Harold
Verdelli, Gloria
Walborn, Gail
Walters, Sally
Wert, Betty
Williams, Bruce
Yoder, Suzanne

4th period, 12th grade, Brit. Lit., 29 students

Brandt, Nancy
Dibeler, Anna
Dixon, Todd
Engle, Jeff
Farling, Mike
First, Jan
Flocken, Susan
George, Richard
Harman, Kathy
Hershberger, Larry
Horton, Allen

Kahler, Randy
Lenker, Bertha
McNeal, Barbara
Neidinger, John
Newlin, Marsha
Painter, Ruth
Rainey, Judy
Rhone, James
Seitz, Glenn
Shelley, Barbara
Shenfeld, John
Skinner, Sally
Smith, Nancy
Taylor, Bill
Walmer, Donna
Warg, Eileen
Weaver, Bonnie
Wyld, Byron

6th period, 12th grade, Class of 1964, 18 students

Bartholomew, Sharon
Baumbach, Jeff
Brewer, Steve
Broadwater, Dale
Burtner, John
Clark, Larry
Cruys, Melody
Deaven, Donald
Etnoyer, Donald
Glocker, Rick
Johnston, Sandra
Kantz, Susan
Kirkpatrick, Portia
Lower, Richard
Moyer, Lee
Shandor, Frank
Shearer, James
Wagner, Steward

2nd, Public Speaking, seniors, 19 students

Monday & Wednesday
Banks, Linda
Brandt, Nancy
Convery, Kathy
Fair, Karen
Green, Don
Harman, Kathy
Johnston, Sandy
Kantz, Sue

Kopenhaver, Bob
Lenker, Kathy
Moyer, Lee
Peters, Denise
Sharp, Judith
Skinner, Sally
Snyder, Harold
Verdelli, Gloria
Weaver, Bonnie
White, David
Yoder, Suzanne

6th period, Public Speaking, 15 students (12 seniors, 3 juniors)

Broadwater, Dale
Burtner, John
Chellew, George
Farling, Mike
Glocker, Rick
Henriksson, Linda
Kahler, Randy
Kauffman, Carol
Leeser, Kathy
Neidinger, John
Newlin, Marsha
Rhone, Jim
Walmer, Donna
Walters, Sally
Zeiters, Stephanie

1964-65

1st period, 12th grade, 16 students

Baker, Kenneth
Baumbach, Robert
Bolash, Nancy
Frantz, Allen
Martz, Judith
Mateer, Joseph
Mills, Terry
Mitchell, William
Pinkerton, William
Rhoads, Aaron
Rhoads, Thelma
Skinner, Michael
Stare, Ronald
Stopfel, Barry
Szymborski, James
Warble, Luke

3rd period, 34 students
Badman, Edith
Bauder, Harry
Blouch, Donna
Bonawitz, George
Boyer, Linda
Breed, Donald
Fake, Edward
Fisher, Patricia
Geesaman, Miriam
Givens, Janet
Grubb, Betty
Heinzman, Joseph
Herr, Darlene
Hetrick, Joan
Horton, Darlene
Keim, Norman
Lepperd, Rita
Lyter, James
Means, Jack
O'Donovan, Michael
Reed, Frank
Rider, Sandy
Schell, Steve
Schmink, Darlene
Shemas, John
Shimko, Carol
Smith, Fred
Teufel, Ronald
Tonkin, Robert
Walters, Linda
Welker, Karen
Wert, Linda
Wolfe, Gregory
Zerfoss, Karen

4th period, 29 students
Braun, Valerie
Brightbill, Pauline
Brooks, Sandra
Cassel, Russel
Chilcote, Dorothy
Coble, David
Dorsheimer, John
Good, Dale
Grubb, Samuel D.
Heueisen, David
Hoffman, Sylvia
Hubler, Michael
Keith, Judy

Kennedy, Sharon
Kienzle, Elizabeth
Knouse, Yolanda
Lidle, Steve
Mader, Elaine
Matrisian, Richard
Musser, John
Mumma, Linda
Page, Wanda
Petrina, Susan
Ritchie, Linda
Smith, Clayton
Wallish, James
Weaver, Richard
Werner, Judith
Wise, Linda

5th period, 31 students
Alleman, Linda
Bell, Karl
Bojanic, Bethanne
Campbell, William
Deimler, Jean
Downes, Lois
Enders, John
Fink, Bonnie
Geesaman, Larry
Graybill, Ruth
Haskin, Lauren
Hauer, Thomas
Hill, Joseph
Kauffman, Carol
Kreider, Donald
Landis, Ann
Lausch, Larry
Manura, John
Miller, John
Motter, Vivian
Park, Marjorie
Patrick, Dennis
Sandel, Carolyn
Seibert, Kirk
Shertzer, Mary Ann
Stump, William
Verdelli, Kathleen
Wisniewski, Stanley
Zeiders, Fay
Zeiters, Stephanie
Zerfoss, Carol

6th period, 13 students, Mon. and Wed., Public Speaking
Bell, Karl
Bojanic, Bethanne
Deimler, Jean
Downes, Lois
Enders, John
Geesaman, Larry
Graybill, Ruth
Heinzman, Joseph
Hill, Joseph
Matrisian, Richard
Mills, Terry
Motter, Vivian
Verdelli, Kathleen

6th period, 12 students, Tues. and Thurs., Public Speaking
Alleman, Linda
Bauder, Harry
Chilcote, Dorothy
Heueisen, David
Mader, Elaine
Kienzle, Elizabeth
Konecney, Diane
O'Donovan, Michael
Shickley, Richard
Stopfel, Barry
Teufel, Ronald
Zechman, Anna

1965-66

3rd period, Brit. Lit., 27 seniors
Baum, Kathleen
Baum, Lois
Beahm, Loren
Bolton, Beverly
Campbell, Connie
Comitz, Ruth
Eshleman, Joseph
Garrison, Hubert
Geesaman, Sharon
Girvin, Wanda
Good, Richard
Gonglowski, Joseph
Grubb, Paul
Johns, Harold
Kreiser, Sharon
Lee, Kitch

Leininger, George
Maxwell, Mary Lou
Miller, Verna Jean
Morrow, Sandra
Pheasant, Patty
Rainey, Pamela
Ratcliff, Lester
Rider, Keith
Shemas, Margaret
Spahr, William
Williams, John

4th period, Brit. Lit. seniors, 23 students
Bell, Barbara
Bohner, David
Calhoon, Janet
Funck, Dorinda
Gibble, Greta
Good, Ronald
Gourley, Ronald
Grubb, Ken
Johnston, Ray
Kassman, Linda
Lenker, Rick
Minnich, Karen
Nale, Sylvia
Petroski, Frank
Roy, Geri
Stare, Richard
Stauffer, Audrey
Stees, Nancy
Tritch, Ray
Walmer, Beverly
Weber, Curtis

5th period, Brit. Lit. (English IV), Class of 66, 22 seniors
Aldrich, William
Bedeaux, Tim
Bixler, Sandy
Brandt, Gayle
Cassel, Marshall
Day, Gerald
Espenshade, Dale
Espenshade, Ken
Gladney, Wanda
Hershberger, Dennis
Hess, Ronald
Jackson, Robert
Katzmire, Jack

McNaughton, Joyce
Oleynik, Gregory
Schwartz, Kandee
Shellenhamer, Georgine
Shubert, Cheryl
Tomazin, Robert
Wagner, Evans
Wrzesniewski, Marty
Tesno, Jean

7th period, Brit. Lit English IV, 27 students
Alther, Sharon
Barnhart, Kay
Brown, Marie
DeCelle, Florence
Forry, Susan
Goodling, Art
Hand, Mike
Hipple, Marie
Hoke, Walter
Hoover, Cheryl
Hostetter, Shirley
Knaub, John
Long, Randy
Miller, Kathy
Mitchell, Marilyn
Newcomer, Deloris
Nichols, George
Patrick, Carol
Rogers, Sallie
Scheetz, Bonnie
Shoop, Barry
Shuey, Linda
Sipe, Pam
Wheeler, Virginia
Wherry, Mike
Wright, Sandy
Yinger, John

Public Speaking, Wed and Fri (1st or 2nd period). 16 students
Bell, Barbara
Bolton, Beverly
Calhoon, Janet
Comitz, Ruth
Eshelman, Joe
Girvin, Wanda
Gonglowski, Joe
Good, Richard
Good, Ronald

Leininger, George
Lenker, Rick
Lentz, Gary
Maxwell, Mary Lou
Rainey, Pam
Spahr, Bill
Williams, John

Public Speaking, Tuesday and Thursday, 8 students
Cassell, Marshall
Lingle, Mel
Lower, Steve
Martz, Pat
Schock, Al
Schwartz, Kandee
Shellenhamer, Georgine
Snavely, Robert

1966-67

Seniors, Brit. Lit
1st period, 31 students
Bonawitz, Donald
Brandt, John (Jack)
Brubaker, Nancy
Carlson, Hazel
Carroll, Rogie
Criswell, Elaine
Dowhower, James
Espenshade, Karen
Fies, Barbara
Fureman, John
Geesaman, Connie
Geesaman, Gale
Glass, Mary
Hallman, Marilyn
Henriksson, Iris
Kantz, Sally
Kolak, Charlene
Kreider, Kenton
Krodel, Hervie
Leach, Linda
MacLeod, Ronald
May, Almeda
Miller, Janet
Miller, Miriam
Mull, Jane
Olvis, Diane
Reed, Jason
Schock, Al

Shenk, Eric
Shertzer, Shirley
Witmer, Donna

3rd period, 27 students
Bistline, Sharon
Brown, Carl
Carroll, Dennis
Conrad, Thomas
Crousore, Doris
Deimler, Wendy
Ebersole, Jay
Engle, John
Granzow, Anne
Grubb, William
Hughes, Faye
Hughes, Thomas
Kraft, Eric
Light, Jan
Lingle, Linda
Parmer, Edward
Patrick, Sharon
Rhoads, Charles
Sandel, Betsy
Schmick, Albert
Seaman, Rosemary
Seavers, John
Shifflet, Karen
Staver, Charles
Stroman, C. Bradley
Williams, Judy
Yancheff, Michael

5th period, 23 students
Frantz, Sandy
Gall, Barbara
Gehring, Anna
Ginder, Steve
Gruber, Mary
Hein, Terry Ann
Heisey, J. Ray
Hinkley, Scott
Hoffer, Don
Hooven, Marilyn
Jeffries, Patricia
Lidle, David
Matrisian, Paul
Mersing, Sandra
Miller, Larry A.
Raisch, Charles
Snavely, Robert

Stepp, Gary
Thomas, Cheryl
Umberger, Sandra
Wallish, Gary
Witmer, Kenneth
Woodard, Roger

7th period, 24 students
Alexander, James
Bechtel, Mary
Chapman, Cindy
Di Eleuterio, Nadine
Engle, Carol
Finnen, Michel
Folk, Terry
Gruber, Sherry
Hagy, Georgia
Holmes, Dayton
Kadish, Candace
Kadish, Keith
Landis, William
Martin, Mary
Miller, Joan
Prodromidou, Kate
Ranck, Darlene
Reitz, Donna
Sheehan, Peggy
Shenk, Donna
Snavely, Glenn
Stauffer, Carol
Teets, David
Tice, Landis

Public Speaking, 15 students
Brandt, John (Jack)
Fureman, John
Hughes, Faye
Hughes, Thomas
Kolaric, Al
Krafft, Eric
Krodel, Herbie
Lingle, Linda
Peiffer, Don
Peiffer, Ron
Prodromidou, Kate
Raisch, Charles
Ropel, Mark
Schmick, Al
Seavers, John

1967-68

(The gradebook was not returned to me by the substitute teacher who taught 2nd semester.)

Words from Al Larsen after their 50th reunion:

After the event, I realized there was a certain irony for you and your interactions with the classmates who were at the reunion. It is this. Of course, you taught primarily the college prep folks. Those people, went off to school and then many went even farther to live. That is, they now live farther away, as a group, than the class as a whole. Those who come to our reunions tend to be those who live close by. So, it struck me that a large percentage of the folks you taught weren't there, and a large percentage of those who were there were the ones you didn't teach. I never thought about that dynamic ahead of time—but I'm pretty confident about the correlation. The result was that you knew fewer of us than we would have expected. I wish more of the group you knew had been there, as it would have been more enjoyable for you, in terms of the social aspects of the evening. Well, so be it. Everyone appreciated your coming, a special treat and something we had never done in our previous gatherings. Most importantly, we all got a lot out of your observations, whether we were in your classes once upon a time or not.

I'll remember this one.

Thanks.

Al

1967 – 68

The following were confirmed with Al Larsen:
Alwine, Joyce
Bell, Elaine
Boyles, Susan
Duncan, Susan
Fink, Richard
Fisher, Karol
Funck, Linda
Furman, Janice
Gingrich, Elnoise
Imhof, Hank
Jones, Connie
Larsen, Al
Lesser, Ann
Mateer, Betsy
Messinger, James
Rhoads, Ann
Ricker, Liz
Robertson, Larry
Ruhl, Pat
Seibert, Lee
Stees, Bill
Wolfersberger, Jeff
Zeiters, Russ

1968 – 69

1st period, Brit. Lit., English IV, 24 students
Aldinger, Barbara
Arehart, Margaret
Bell, Thomas
Blough, Richard
Ebersole, Paul
Eckert, Lana
Eisenhour, Joanne
Fisher, Marilyn
Forry, Jean
Frascella, Mike
Geesaman, Mary
Gleim, Scott
Heisey, Richard Lee
Hostetter, Karen Long
Konecny, Conrad
Light, Steve
Robertson, Dennis
Shemas, Robert

Spillers, Diane
Thomas, Bonnie
Thompson, Patricia
Via, Joyce
Walters, Doug
Wise, Richard

4th period, Brit. Lit, Class of '69, 16 students
Bolton, Wendy
Burkholder, Ron
Caldwell, Annette
Detweiler, Greg
Gregor, Mark
Hartwell, Tom
Hughes, Barbara
Kline, Linda
Lehman, Miriam
Lehmer, Jeannine
Rowan, Gale
Ricker, JoAnn
Ruiz, Blanca
Snyder, Lois
Witmer, Sandra
Gaydos, Larry

5th period, Brit. Lit., 28 students
Barry, Jeanne
Bassett. Kerry
Bell, Susan
Broadwater, Jane
Brown, Dennis
Burridge, Rick
Campbell, Sue Ann
Collins, Linda
Cosey, Barry
Frantz, Don
Good, Scott
Granzow, Laurie
Holman, Helen
Imhof, Marsha
LeVan, Debbie
Logan, Fay
McCurdy, Anne Marie
Messinger, Jane
Oellig, Bretta
Peck, Jeannine
Rathfon, Susan
Smink, Marsha
Stees, Bonnie
Topper, Jeff

Tritch, Craig
Weber, Tom
Williams, Robert
Wywadis, Rachael

7th period, Brit. Lit, 27 students
Barnhart, Quinn
Baum, Dennis
Cichan, Linda
Crick, Susan
Druffner, Richard
Ebersole, Beverly
Fies, Shirley
Finnen, Peggy
Getz, Kathy
Hixon, Pat
Kienzle, Sandy
Krodel, Harold
Kveragas, Ann
Landis, Howard
Lehman, Garry
Long, Cindy
Lutz, Stewart
Lytle, Debbie
Rine, Edward
Schock, Sharon
Sheehan, Mike
Veigle, Carol
Wagner, Wendy
Walker, Kenneth
Warble, Dennis
Wenrich, Sandy

Public Speaking, 17 students
Bell, Mary
Bolton, Wendy
Caldwell, Annette
Davenport, Audrey
Engle, Adrienne
Engle, Carol
Fedora, Ann
Good, Scott
Granzow, Laurie
Holman, Helen
Ruiz, Blanca
Smink, Marsha
Snyder, Lois
Staver, Julie
Williams, Robert
Wywadis, Rachael
Yoder, Charles

The B-1 Pilgrims

Since the three-year program was begun,
We've laughed, we've cried,
We've lived, we've died;
We've suffered all, and we have won!

A varied package, we did meet
Unknown acts of skill and feat.
Hammers, shaped, culled, and honed.
Some glimmered faintly; others shone.

Let us greet the pilgrims, one by one,
Before the sun its course has run.
We first met one without a sin
So with a Hall we will begin.

Tom, Tom, the pianist's son,
Stole a year and away he run;
But he returned to chime right in
To set us straight with pious grin.

Carol once distinguished her bearing—
Provoking, "Is that a wig you're wearing?"
Abashed, abashed, this quiet lass
Has become a real favorite of the class.

Dan, the woodsman, serene and strong,
Always sang his private song.
Months went by, his shyness waned
And, golly gee, he once profaned!

Phil ...
"Oh, sorry I didn't get this finished."
But our love for you has not diminished.
Each class needs a gadfly, a wit,
And for baiting, you are just a hit.

"People aren't like that," said Ken,
"I know from watching in my pen."
No pretense, fraud or even sham.
"I guess that's just the way I am."

Dave gets the prize for most improved.
His verbal density is best in-grooved.
From just "that Jones boy" he became
Smooth and polished in his fame.

Sally each year was coaxed to stay
And reached her hey-day this past May.
When Craig blew one on a test,
Sally's put-down was the best.

Paul's quiet reserve is just a cover
For an ardent campsite lover.
In his studies he's the same—
Inwardly powerful, seemingly tame.

Asides are the forte of our friend Ray.
If we only had heard what he did say!
Courageous, dependable, and true;
He cleaved the Falcon staff in two.

Laden with feelings of inferiority,
Gina oft showed superiority.
Confidence grew, talent shown through
As she led the silent majority.

Randy, always armed with retorts,
Would rather play in woodland forts.
He came to class just to pass,
Hoping we would be overcome by mort(s).

Laurie, conscientious and true-blue
To what, though, we never knew.
Her quietness while in the class
Was quite unlike the sportive lass.

"What did I miss?" was Mark's common query
Of a dubious fact he was often leery.
The Press and Journal brought him fame;
A vivisectionist he was called by name.

We named her "Annie" to her chagrin,
This virtuous lass, free from sin.
A worker, diligent and neat,
Endears herself to all she meets.

Bowser asks himself each day,
"Why, oh, why, did I ever stay?
I had hoped to best her, I detest her."
As for him, I wish him away!

Frank found his calling in the spring,
When with caterpillar voice he began to sing.
And now he smiles, his smile beguiles,
And his noises make him a real ding-a-ling.

Craig, as usual, has the last word,
Above us all he will be heard.
His voice isn't loud, his manner is slick,
And what he says does always "click."

So here you have them all together,
Through many a storm they have weathered.
We love you all, rise or fall,
You'll remain in our hearts forever.

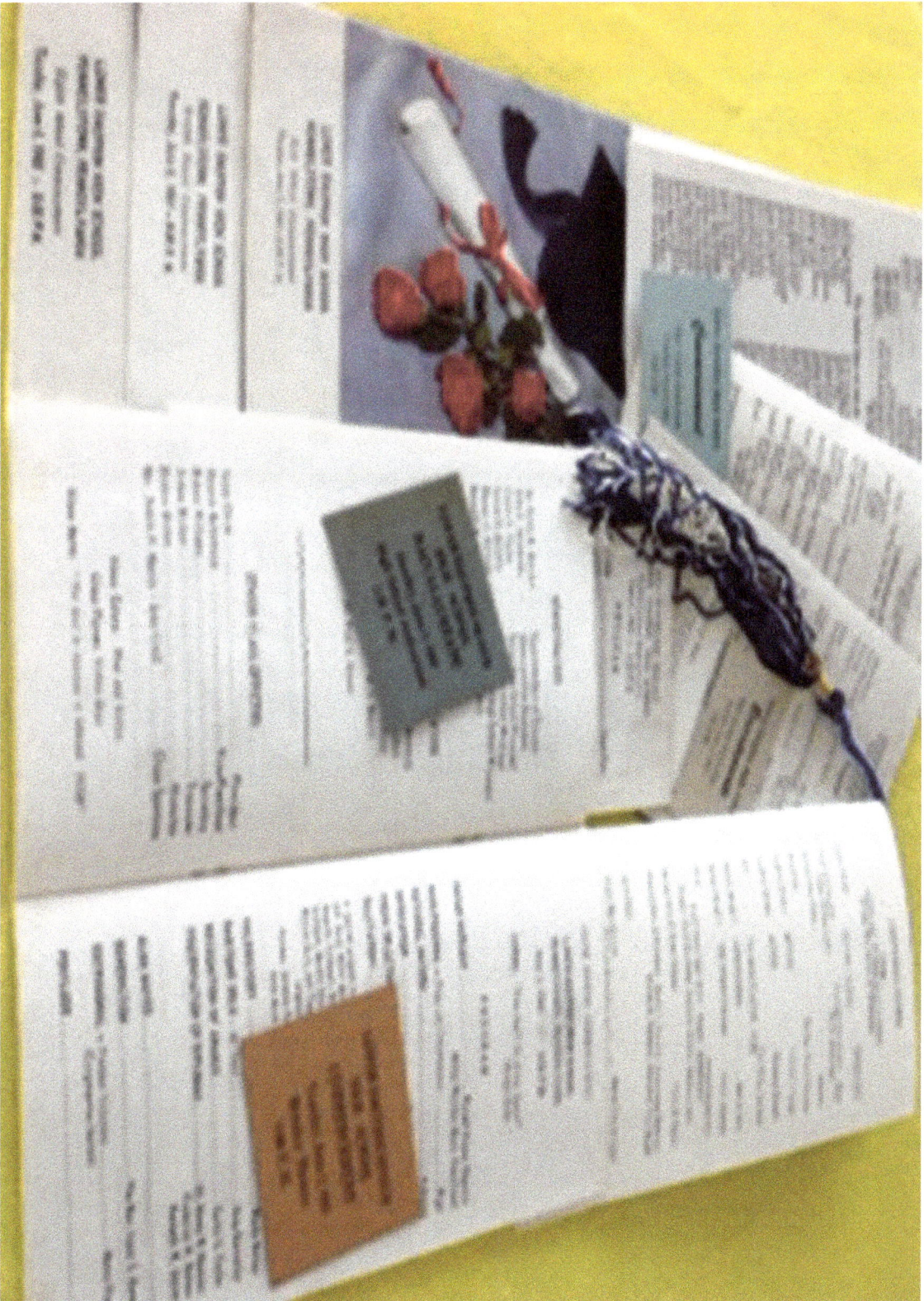

contact. It involves us as graduates for the mere reason that we are here
tonight, and we are here tonight because for twelve years we have enjoyed
opportunities and advantages of which 700 <u>million</u> people in the world today cannot
avail themselves. It involves the people with whom we come in contact
simply because they are a part of the society which has given us these
opportunities.

But bear in mind, we are given just that--opportunities, not the
finished products. One of the ways we can repay society is by using these
gifts to create a <u>well-made</u> finished product. The young person with a
God-given mind and the limitless possibilities for success in the United
States today who refused to use the potential within and around him
offends the timeless code of noblesse oblige.

John D. Rockefeller, Jr. said, "I believe that every right implies
a responsibility; every opportunity an abligation; every possession a
duty. We must be conscientious in the use of our rights, our opportunities,
and our possessions. In this we must eventually project beyond ourselves
to others. Our lives and our interests must be exprospective rather than
introspective, centering on people outside the self-centered "me." We
must be concerned enough to share with others less fortunate than ourselves,
out of the riches we have received and in proportion to them.

Pause and consider a moment. The world really doesn't owe you and
me a thing, and we? -- well, we owe the world quite a lot.

Carolyn Sandel, Salutatory address
June 8, 1965

SALUTATORY ADDRESS

BETSY SANDEL

June 6, 1967

Members of the clergy, administration and school board, faculty,

parents, and friends:

The Lower Dauphin High School graduating class of 1967
welcomes you to its commencement exercises. Through the use
of a speaking choir and several musical groups we shall present
a number of significant themes. However, the major idea pervading
the entire choralogue is that realization that man must strive
for something beyond himself. Taking a realistic view of life,
he must accept the fact that he may never reach this goal; but
always, in order to maintain his own dignity, he must strive,
search, and struggle. Horace, a Latin poet who lived a century
before Christ, shaped this idea concisely when he said "Nil
mortalibus arduum est." Nothing is too high for the daring of
mortals.

In order to achieve any kind of nobility, we as individuals
must first of all make a commitment. We must accept the truth
of the statement "In ourselves our future lies." We must consider
and put trust in the all-encompassing force we call God. In
other words, it is necessary to maintain jointly a self-dependence
and a faith in the forces beyond our control which help to shape
our destiny.

While constatnly looking forward, we must occassionally
look back on the road we have taken. Dag Hammarskjold, former
UN Secretary-General, once wrote: "We cannot afford to forget
any experience, not even the most painful." Such reflection gives
us stronger insight into the future we are making for ourselves.

With courage we must look forward. The road ahead will
undoubtedly have as many perils as the one we are leaving behind.
But the rewards are great indeed for those who would persevere.
As the writer of Proverbs urged many centuries ago: "Let your
eyes look directly forward, and your gaze be straight before you.
Take heed to the path of your feet, then all your ways will be
sure."

SOPRANO Carolyn, Sherry, Sally

3 girls An aspiration is a joy forever,

3 boys a possession as solid as a landed estate, Dusty, Ed O., Jay

3 girls & a fortune which we can never exhaust, and which gives
3 boys year by year, a revenue of pleasurable activity.

Choir To have many of these is to be spirit...

MARY Life is only a very dull
GLASS have some interests
art nor science.
or a rough f...

Almeda 1 Girl We must have

Ed P 1 Boy We must make a

Girls Our hopes are se

Boys We find nothing he

✗

Chuck 1 Boy We fix our views upon   ...idge,
the horizon's utmost b

Choir for above is nothing.

Sherry 1 Girl We set our sights to have a goal

" Knowing that we may never reach it.

TERRY 1 Boy We commit ourselves to a life-long struggle toward
an unattainable ideal.

Choir: To strive, to seek, to struggle. (get louder)

WATCH

Boys Problem gives rise to problem.

Jack E 1 Boy We may study forever, and we are never as learned as we want.

M, K2 ? 1 Boy We have never made a statue worthy of our dreams.

And when we have discovered a continent, or crossed a chain of
mountains, it is only to find another ocean or another plain
Don 1 Boy upon the farther side.

Nil mortalibus arduum est.

Hence

Commencement Script 1967

462

Commencement 1967
A Class Choralogue

Nil mortalibus arduum est.
(Nothing is too high for the daring of mortals.)

A Choralogue is a group performance of a written work that can incorporate single voices, small groups, and a larger "choir." Such performances can also incorporate songs by the choir or by selected voices. The Choralogues produced by Lower Dauphin High School from the late 1960s through the 70s were written by a selected committee of seniors and their teacher. The first performance, by the Class of 1967, was a creation of Judith T. Ball (Witmer) whose own Alma Mater is the only school of record who still utilizes this style. The content of the script is based on passages from literature.

Choir: Commencement!
         A wonderful word!
         A shining, long-to-be-remembered, night!

Salutatorian Address: Elizabeth Sandel

Choir: I saw a man pursuing the horizon,

         Round and round they sped.

Boys: I was disturbed by this; I accosted the man.

Carl: "It is futile," I said,

         "You can never --- "

Choir: "You lie," he cried, and ran on.

Song: The Impossible Dream

Jay & Karen: We live in an ascending scale when we live happily, one thing leading to another to another in an unending series.

Dennis: There is always a new horizon for forward-looking men, and although we dwell on a small planet, immersed in petty business and not enduring beyond a brief period of years, we are so constituted that our hopes are inaccessible, like stars, and the term of hoping is prolonged until the term of life is finished.

Diane: To be truly happy is a question of how we begin and not of how we end.

Choir: Of what we want, and not of what we have.

Carolyn, Sherry, Sally: An aspiration is a joy forever,

Dusty, Ed, Jay: A possession as solid as a landed estate,

All six: A fortune which we can never exhaust, and which gives us, year by year, a revenue of pleasurable activity.

Choir: To have many of these is to be spiritually rich.

Mary: Life is only a very dull and ill-directed theatre unless we have some interests in the piece; and to those who have neither art nor science, the world is a mere arrangement of colors or a rough footway where they may very well break their shins.

Almeda: We must have an interest.

Ed: We must make a commitment.

Girls: Our hopes are set high.

Boys: We find nothing here below.

Chuck: We fix our views upon the summit of a craggy ridge, the horizon's utmost boundary.

Choir: ....for above is nothing.

Sherry: We set our sights to have a goal, knowing we may never reach it.

Terry: We commit ourselves to a life-long struggle toward an unattainable idea.

Choir: (increasing in volume)   To strive, to seek, to struggle.

Boys: Problem gives rise to problem.

Jack: We may study forever, and we are never as learned as we want.

Mike: We have never made a statue worthy of our dreams.

Don: And when we have discovered a continent, or crossed a chain of mountains, it is only to find another ocean or another plain upon the farther side.

John: "Tell me," said he, "Where can it be—this land of El Dorado?"

           "Over the mountains of the moon,

Carl: Down the Valley of the Shadow, Ride, boldly ride,"

           The man replied,"--if you seek for Eldorado."

Choir: Nothing gold can stay.

Girls: A man saw a ball of gold in the sky;

Choir: He climbed for it.

Girls: And eventually he achieved it

Boys: —it was clay.

Choir: Yet man continues in his search.

Marilyn: "I must go down to the seas again, to the lonely sea and the sky."

(Pause)

Dennis: We know not why, but man must strive.

Girls: I may!
Boys: I might!!
Choir: I must!!!

Wendy: If you will tell me why the fen appears impassable, I then will tell you why I think that I can get across it if I try.

Jack Brandt: My Task

Don: Whatever the dream and the search involved, man must know that of and by himself alone, he cannot succeed.

Carol: But if ye have faith as a grain of mustard seed … nothing shall be impossible unto you. All things are possible to him that believeth.

Choir: The Lord is my shepherd.

Jane: I will lift up mine eyes unto the hills, whence cometh my help. My help cometh from the Lord, which made heaven and earth.

Soprano Girls: Seek, and ye shall find;

Alto Girls: Knock, and it shall be opened unto you.

John: He who, from zone to zone, Guides through the boundless sky the certain flight,

In the long way that we must tread alone, Will lead our steps aright.

Nancy: Nothing in life is more wonderful than faith—the one great moving force which we can neither weigh in the balance nor test in the crucible.

Girls: Faith is the substance of thing hoped for, the evidence of things not seen.

Choir: Where there is no hope, there can be no endeavor.

3 boys: Columbus found a world, and had no chart,

Save one that faith deciphered in the skies.

Jack: And I said to the man who stood at the gate of a new kind of life; "Give me a light that I may tread safely into the unknown." And he replied, "Go out into the darkness and put your hand into the hand of God. That shall be to you better than light and safer than a known way." So I went forth, and finding the hand of God, trod gladly into the night. And He led me towards the hills and the breaking of day in the lone East.

Group: Canst thou by searching find out God?

Karen: As man strives he comes to realize how much a part of God he is. He may suffer anguish, he may fail at any point along the way, but he will ultimately find fulfillment, a becoming, if he will but believe and accept the divine help of God.

Choir: I believe; therefore, I am.

Song: I Believe

Choir: We must practice our beliefs.

Linda: There can be no happiness if the things we believe in are different from the things we do....

Choir: We must act, and know reality.

Ed: We are the ones to act. We must carry out our beliefs. No one can walk the road for another. Depend not on another; rather lean upon thyself; trust to thine own exertions ...true happiness consists in self-reliance.

Choir: This above all:

Mixed voices: To thine own self be true, and, it must follow, as the night the day, Thou canst not then be false to any man.

Ann: For a man must stand alone. He is responsible for his own actions. He must make those actions worthwhile. He must set a goal for himself to follow. He must move ahead. He must strive.

Il faut que je cherche pour trouver, mais pas pour trouver ce qu'on cherche.

Terry: What is it that makes one man succeed and another fail? The one who succeeds is the one who has tried. Many fear to try because they know they will make mistakes.

Es irrt der Mensch, so lang er strebt.

Marilyn: Unless we err, we will never come to understanding. If we wish to begin life, we must begin it at our own expense. We will find that our choice is sometimes not between "right doing" and "wrong doing," but between a greater and a lesser evil. We strive, but we do not fear because a good man is still conscious of the right way.

Choir: Our goal:

Jack E: To scale life's topmost heights through toil and strife.

Choir: Only then will man be truly fulfilled; only then will man be truly worthy.

Jack B: He only merits freedom, merits life, who daily has to conquer them anew,

For life is for the one who will earn it. The reward is in the struggle.

466

Choir: To strive, to seek, to find.
Nothing is too high for the daring of mortals!

Song: Reprise, The Impossible Dream

John: I am a part of all that I have met.
What I am is a result of what I have done.
What I become shall depend upon the roads I choose to travel.

Betsy: Two roads diverged in a wood, and I ...
I took the one less traveled by,
And that has made all the difference.

Choir: Let us look back upon that road.

Anne: If the days grow dark, if care and pain press close and sharp on heart and brain, then lovely pictures still shall bloom upon the walls of memory's room.

Song: Try to Remember

Janet, Carol, Ed, Don: For memory has painted this perfect day with colors that never fade, and we see at the end of a perfect day, the soul of a friend we've made.

(Music softly playing in the background)

Choir: Remembrance of things past.

Boys: Our struggle for victory.

Dusty: The time you won your town the race
We chaired you through the market place;
Man and boy stood cheering by,
And home we brought you shoulder high.

Karen: Through many hours of hard work and practice, the class of '67 has compiled one of the most outstanding athletic records in the school's history. In the process we have had a championship cross-country team and girls' basketball team, as well as a regional champion wrestler. Many of our distinguished performers will be continuing in college and all who participated will look back and remember their struggle for victory.

Choir: The thrill of opening night.

Jack: Speak the speech, I pray you, as I pronounced it to you, trippingly on the tongue.

John: What amateur thespian can forget the chill of panic as the curtain opened for the first time? What doting parent can forget the pride he felt at seeing his child performing on the stage? What student can forget the enjoyment of watching a classmate trying to be something he otherwise is not? These experiences are a cherished part of school life, and are to be remembered with a sad smile and a happy tear.

Choir: The compelling cadence of the drum.

467

Carl: Oh, what is that sound which so thrills the ear, Down in the valley drumming, drumming?

Jack: Who can forget the exhausting miles of marching or the long hours of indoor rehearsal? But always in the end, that inner self-satisfaction of a job well done.

And who can measure the rewards gained from friendships centered around the joy of music? Or who can describe that intense pride felt by the Falconettes and the majorettes as they strut behind those flags, flying in the breeze? No one can describe these things. But for those of us who have felt the excitement of a parade and the pressure of a concert, these feelings are very real. As the last cadence dies away, memories of our band will live on as a real part of each of us.

Choir: Voices blended in harmony.

Linda: There's no truer truth obtainable by man than comes of music.

Ann: Music and harmony are more powerful instruments than any other because they find their way into the inward places of the soul. Thus, it is that the memories of spring musicals and Christmas concerts and assembly choirs and county festivals and the annual chorus picnic have all become a part of us and will be a part of us forever.

Choir: Knowledge is power.

Miriam, Connie, Linda: Reading maketh a full man;

Three boys: Conference a ready man;

All six: and writing an exact man.

Betsy: All these things we have experienced in part in the laboratories and classrooms. From the B-7 physics room, to the typing rooms off the halls of A-wing, to the mathematics and economics classrooms in H-wing, each senior carries with him some knowledge gained and an experience with which he can better solve the problems of his future. Not one can truthfully say there was nothing given, nothing gained. The truth lies in our souls.

All six: This truth is manifested in courage.

Choir: Courage to learn, to create, to work.

Diane: The courage when we took our first examinations, plunged through the line with our stalwart football tacklers, steadied our voices when we made our first speeches, and held back the tears as we watched another classmate win the award we so ardently desired.

Choir: Courage to strike forth and ignite others with our spirit.

Dennis: From such courage comes enthusiasm, the zeal, the "go" that leads us on to accomplishment. It is the "school spirit" that spurs the Falcons to victory, that puts snap in the cadence of the band as it marches down the field, that rocks the grandstand with its fervor.

Choir: Courage to pursue our ambitions, to face the daily tasks of maturity.

Nancy: The coward never started; the weak died on the way; only the courageous came through.

Charles Staver: Valedictory Address

Song: Halls of Ivy

Choir: We leave

Betsy: And take a part of you with us.

Choir: We leave

Charles: And leave a part of us with you.

Song: The Impossible Dream

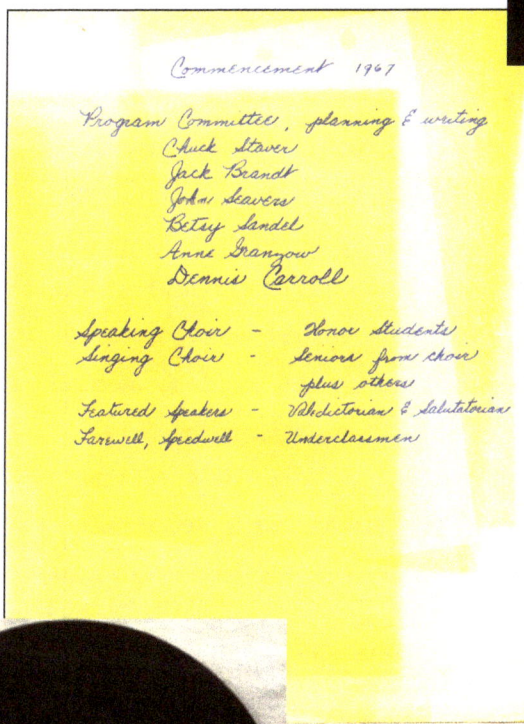

Commencement 1967

Program Committee, planning & writing
  Chuck Staver
  Jack Brandt
  John Seavers
  Betsy Sandel
  Anne Granzow
  Dennis Carroll

Speaking Choir — Honor Students
Singing Choir — Seniors from choir
                plus others
Featured Speakers — Valedictorian & Salutatorian
Farewell, Speedwell — Underclassmen

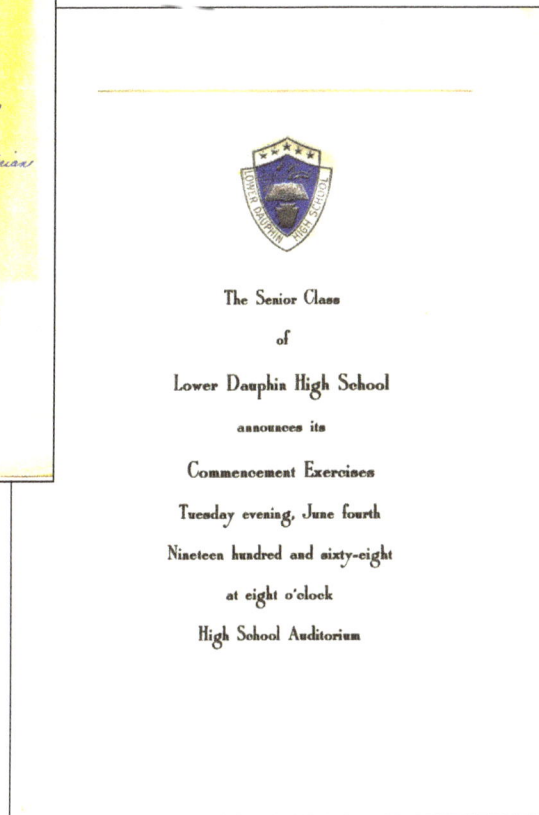

The Senior Class

of

Lower Dauphin High School

announces its

Commencement Exercises

Tuesday evening, June fourth

Nineteen hundred and sixty-eight

at eight o'clock

High School Auditorium

Tonight, too many of us are thinking in terms of an end; a final event. Tonight is a beginning. We stand this evening on the threshold of a vast frontier. The prospects for the future are fascinating and frightening. Instead of looking eagerly forward, many of us may dwell too long on a tearful glance backward.

Traditionally, this night has been one of acknowledgement of a task accomplished but I like to see it more as a realization of a goal and an anticipation of things to come. It is from this point that we go on, not powered by what we have done, but by what we can do. There is a future ahead for each one of us. Tonight is the first major plateau on the road into that future. For all of us it is a start.

I do not mean, in any way, to render these past eighteen years insignificant. The years have served us well. They have been happy years; perhaps some of the happiest we will ever have. But enjoyment is not all that these years have given us. We have learned from them. I am not referring to classroom instruction alone. The simple daily experiences we have had are just as important. Each day has revealed something new to us--both in the understanding of ourselves and others. This understanding that we have gained is very often disregarded. Many people value factual knowledge more than insight into people. Those who do fail to realize that this insight is essential in the understanding of life itself. And this understanding can come only from within yourself. Your mind must determine for you your basic ideas concerning life; the ideas that mold your future. It is in this that you preserve

your uniqueness. For this reason you should cling to your
convictions, for by holding on to them, you maintain a hold
on yourself. It is by seeking the answer to the questions,
"Who am I?" and "What do I want to become?" that growth is
possible.

Growth is relative to the goals each individual sets
for himself in life. Nothing reveals more about the inner
self than your dreams and goals. Make them speak well of you.

The realization of our hopes and desires lie in the
future. It is in the future that we will search for the
solutions to our problems and the fulfillment of our dreams.
We are the chief architects of our future. With vision and
creativity we can design a structure of which we will be
proud.

I suppose I should wish you success, but I would like
to wish you something more important. So I am going to wish
you meaning in your life. And meaning is not something you
stumble across, like the answer to a riddle, or the prize
in a treasure hunt. Meaning is something you build into your
life.

It is my task tonight as the representative of the class
of 1969 to say goodbye to the institution that has given us
the skills we will use in shaping our lives, goodbye to those
who have helped us along the way, and goodbye to the life of
a high school student. Though we will never be students in
this high school again, what we became here will always be a
meaningful part of what we are.

Mrs. Ball

⑥

Annette

It's strange to think that as we passed through these doors/ and trafficked these halls, everything we are now was promised in us as we were then./ Some tell us we have changed, and surely in some ways we have./ But just as surely was this the source of all we have become and just as surely what we shall become must grow from what we are now./ Those days seem short and long ago and much of what happened then we won't remember./ But they will always be with us and play their part/in how we think and what we do./

Bob

"Though nothing can bring back the hour
Of splendor in the grass,/ of glory in the flower,
We will grieve not, rather find
Strength in what remains behind."/
✗ ⑤

Craig

We needed that strength. For timid but excited we ventured into the larger world of junior high./ Bolstered by a nucleus of friends we expanded and explored/ ourselves, our thoughts,/ and new fields of knowledge./ We soon learned all there was to know and were eager to welcome the challenge of high school--/ some of us already armed with philosophies and ambitions--out to change the world--/ "To dream the impossible dream, To fight the unbeatable foe."/ Each of us firm in the conviction: "I am the master of my fate. I am the captain of my soul."/ Wendy

Anne Marie

In high school we came into the wondrous world of new discoveries./ We came to know the glory of ourselves and our existence. As our understanding grew, we could feel the

Commencement 1969
A Class Choralogue

You Can't Go Home Again

Thomas Wolfe

A special program written by Anne Marie McCurdy; arranged by Wendy Bolton and Anne Marie McCurdy; photographed and produced by Wendy Bolton, Annette Caldwell, Don Frantz, Larry Gaydos, Mary Ann Geesaman, Laurie Granzow, Marsha Imhof, Jeannine Lehmer, Steve Light, Anne Marie McCurdy, Blanca Ruiz, Jeff Topper, Craig Tritch, Bob Williams, and Rachael Wywadis; originated and directed by Judith T. Ball. The program was enhanced by music and photographs shown on the theatre's screen. (Note that the slides were matched to the dialogue. Further, the script here below is among the final versions; it is not complete. Included with these notes was a direction from Craig Tritch, "All of the happenings should be related to how they are preparing us for success in life and should tie in with our groovy motto!)

Annette:

It's strange to think that as we passed through these doors/and trafficked these halls, everything we are now was promised in us as we were then. We have changed in many ways, and what become will grow from what we are now. Those days seem short and long ago and much of what happened then, we won't remember. But the experiences will always be with us, continuing to play their part in how we think and what we do.

Bob:

> "Though nothing can bring back the hour of splendor in the grass, of glory in the flower.
> We will grieve not, but rather find strength in what remains behind."

Craig:

We needed that strength. For timid but excited, we ventured into the larger world of junior high. Bolstered by a nucleus of friends, we expanded and explored ourselves, our thoughts, and new fields of knowledge. We were eager to welcome the challenge of high school…some of us already armed with philosophies and ambitions—out to change the world. And "to dream the impossible dream, to fight the unbeatable foe" and to embrace new experiences.

Wendy:

"I am the master of my fate,

I am the captain of my soul."

Anne Marie:

In high school we came into the wondrous world of new discoveries. We came to know the glory of ourselves and our existence. As our understanding grew, we could feel the promise and the power of the words of Ayn Rand:

> "I am a man. This miracle of me is mine to own and to keep, and mine to guard and mine to use, and mine to kneel before!"

"It is my eyes which see, and the sight of my eyes grants beauty to the earth. It is my ears which hear, and the hearing of my ears gives its song to the world. It is my mind which thinks, and the judgment of my mind is the only searchlight that can find the truth. It is my will which chooses, and the choice of my will is the only edict I must respect. Many words have been granted me, and some are wise, and some are false, but only three are holy: 'I will it.'"

Bob:

From this love and respect for our minds comes the great quest for knowledge—the thrill of learning—the ambition to make ourselves all we can be.

> "Teach me half the gladness
>
> That thy brain must know,
>
> Such harmonious madness
>
> From my lips would flow
>
> The world would listen then, as I am listening now."

Teachers respond to this need of ours and those who understand and who help us, we love. Teachers are a vital part of this noble, exciting, and enjoyable endeavor. They share in and contribute to our successes and failures.

Laurie:

Successes---failures---all of it we love and welcome. We are Youth, and all the wonder, glory, passion, and pain of Youth are ours.

Larry:

Youth, large, lusty, loving. Youth full of grace, force, fascination.

Annette:

Day, full-blown and splendid; day of immense sun, action, ambition, laughter.

Bob:

High in young pride you hold your head high and you meet the rush of roaring days and new experiences.

Craig:

Youth. "In this moment there is life and food for future years."

Larry:

But sometimes the glory and nobility escape us and there is doubt in our youth—the joy and the struggle in the discovery of ourselves. We explore the meaning of our existence and search the eternal question of "Who am I?" groping toward fulfillment in its infinite revelations.

Larry:

We learn to love the uniqueness of our identity and learn to follow the directives of our individual minds.

Wendy:

"Resolve to be thyself; and I know that he who finds himself loses his misery."

Anne Marie:

"And no man understands any greatness or goodness but his own, or the indication of his own."

Laurie:

"If a man does not keep pace with his companions, perhaps it is because he hears a different drummer. Let him step to the music which he hears, however measured or far away."

Annette:

Love for ourselves grows into love for others. We go beyond ourselves into the diverse worlds of those we know, those we can love. We form friendships—laughing, living, in the mutual enrichment.

Larry:

The give and take of friendship wakens and develops new parts of our ever-growing selves. There is excitement in the interplay of minds, wills, hearts.

Bob:

"I am a part of all that I have met."

Ann-Marie:

"Remember that every man is a variation of yourself. No man's guilt is not yours, nor is any man's innocence a thing apart."

Craig:

"No man is an island, entire of itself; every man is a piece of the continent, a part of the man … any Man's death diminishes me because I am involved in Mankind."

Annette:

This is a time to feel our oneness with all. This is a time to love, to care, to live.

Wendy:

But we already too well know that this is also a time for uncertainty, for questioning. We falter in our progress, we wonder, we despair, we search.

> "Whither is felt the visionary gleam?
> Where is it now, the glory and the dream?
> The things which I have seen, I now can see no more."

To falter is not to fall—and youth carries its own magnificent strength. In a moment we are glibly ready and eager to live life to its fullest—our deep and overwhelming knowledge of its value is not so easily defeated.

Bob:

Our zealous energy bursts past the bounds of school and comes alive in new forms—wild, intense, dynamic, calm, laborious, competitive.

Backstage where so much comes to life—like the Senior Class play! And the Band where lots of hard work establishes an esprit de corps. Of many clubs, such as chess—intense and absorbing. And always the money-making projects to boost the economy.

Craig:

Sports constantly made demands on players for top performance, and they develop integrity, self-reliance, and initiative. You learn to work in teams without becoming consumed by the group.

Larry:

Upon the fields of friendly strife are sown the seeds that upon other fields on other days will bear the fruit of victory.

And when it is over, and all the days of planning have resulted in either a glorious burst, or occasional disappointment, the details of these experiences will remain in our hearts…although we know it will never be the same. We accept that we can't go home again.

Rather we embrace that each moment that lies before us holds opportunity, and the greatest joy, the consuming joy that is to be found now, by living now, by laughing now, by loving now.

(Music: *The Age of Aquarius*)

The evening's program also included the Senior Choir singing *The Road Not Taken* and a baritone solo by Greg Detweiler

The Salutatory Address was delivered by Anne Marie McCurdy.

The Valedictory Address was delivered by Wendy Bolton.

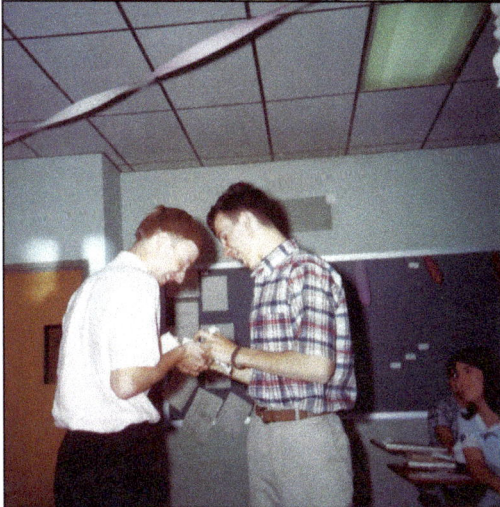

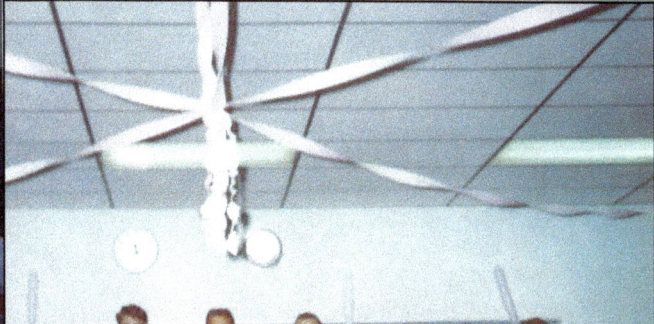

Class of 1965 Picnic

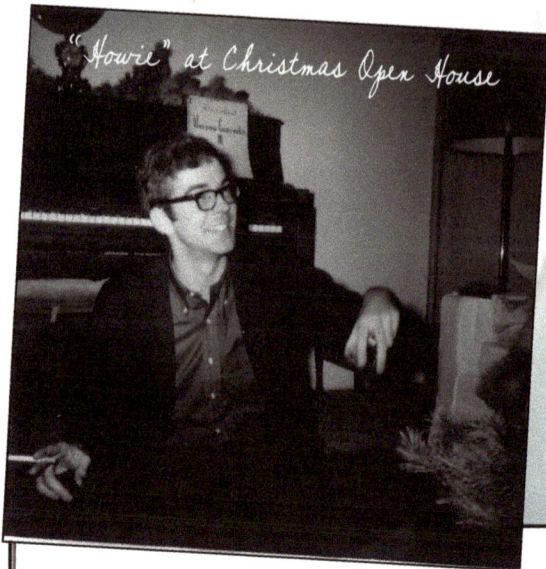

"Howie" at Christmas Open House

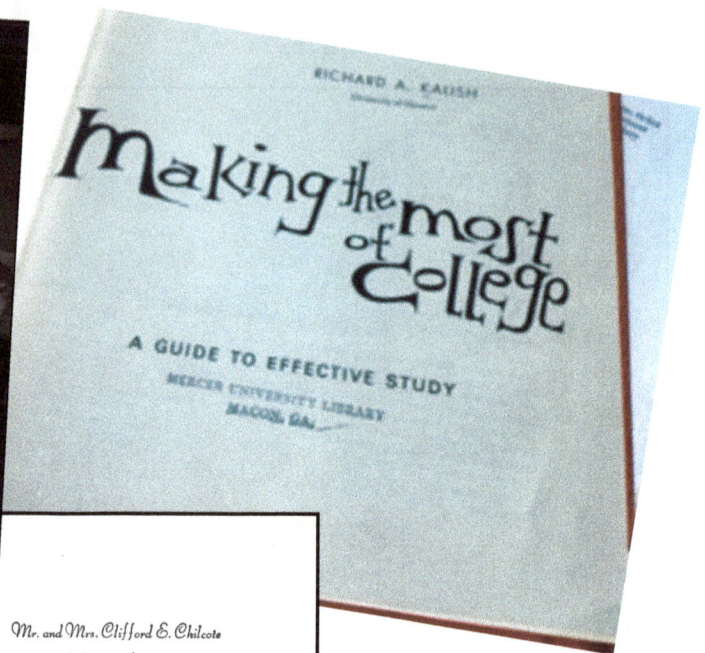

RICHARD A. KAUSH
University of Illinois

making the most of college

A GUIDE TO EFFECTIVE STUDY

MERCER UNIVERSITY LIBRARY
MACON, GA.

Mr. and Mrs. James Richard Landis
request the honour of your presence
at the marriage of their daughter
Ann Rebecca
to
Mr. Jay Howard Kopp
Saturday, the third of August
nineteen hundred and sixty-eight
at one-thirty o'clock
Zion Lutheran Church
Main and Rosanna Streets
Hummelstown, Pennsylvania

Mr. and Mrs. Clifford E. Chilcote
request the honour of your presence
at the marriage of their daughter
Dorothy Mae
to
Mr. Jack W. Means, Jr.
on Saturday, the twenty-seventh of January
Nineteen hundred and sixty-eight
at six o'clock
Christ Lutheran Church
75 East High Street
Elizabethtown, Pennsylvania

Philip and Marsha
Reed Bentley

Anne Harper Benton
and David Benton

George and Kim
Benjamin

[...] and Ruth
Brubaker

Bill Campbell

David Cobbs and
Sylvia Huffman Cobbs

Dennis and Maryann
Shertzer Coffman

Lauren Hankin
[...] and Trish
[...]

[...] Cobaugh
[...]

Jeff Davidson

[...] Boyer
[...] and Galen
[...]

[...] and Min Fake

[...] Fornbach

[...] Ann Graybill
and Frank Graybill '70

[...] and Elie
[...]

[...] Hauer

[...] Shindler Henry
and Ray Henry '61

Carol Kauffman
Mahler

Carol Zarfoss Knight

Ann Landis Kopp and
Jay Kopp '62

Judy Werner Lyter
and Gary Lyter

Lorraine McNeal
Mayers

Dorothy Chilcote
Means and Jack
Means

Judy Wofford Miller
and Dan Miller

Kathy Ernst Miller
and Marvin Miller

Loretta McNeal
Miller

Linda Mumma Mills

Maryann Mutok Mull
and Stanley Mull

Stevie Zeiters Nordai
and Fred Nordai

Evelyn Walkup Rye

Wanda Page

Dennis Patrick and
Linda Heffleger
Patrick '64

Karen Zarfoss
Penman

Susan Petrina

Donna Blough
Rehman

Linda Wise Rodgers
and Don Rodgers

Elaine Muder Royer

Brenda Fegley Sarao
and Michael Sarao

Joyce Hostetter
Schmidt and Chuck
Schmidt

Jean Deimler Seibert

Jean Stauffer

Bill Sturm

Jim Szymborski and
Lynn Taylor
Szymborski

Ron Teufel and
Debbie Teufel

Ron Vio

Errol Wagner

Sharon Kennedy
Williams and Bruce
Williams '64

Greg Wolfe and
Johnette Wolfe

Class Advisors

Gerald & Evelyn
Brittain and Dr.
Judith (Bul)Witmer

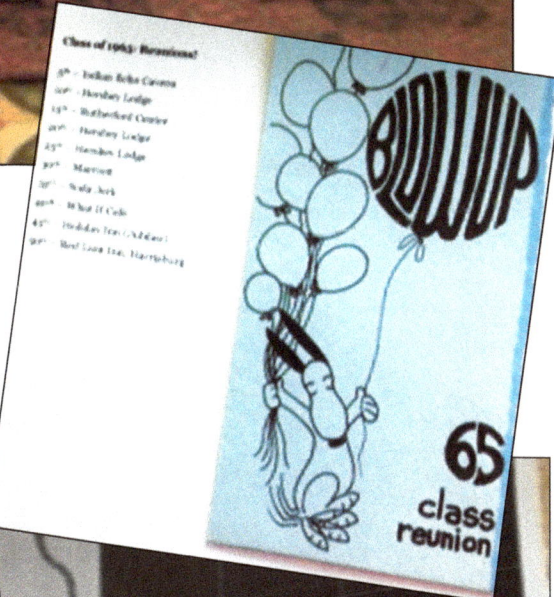

Class of 1963 Reunions!

5th — Indian Echo Caverns
10th — Hershey Lodge
15th — Rutherford Center
20th — Hershey Lodge
25th — Hershey Lodge
30th — Marriott
35th — Scala Jerk
40th — What If Cafe
45th — Holiday Inn (Jubilee)
50th — Red Lion Inn, Harrisburg

BLOWUP
65
class
reunion

Hershey Lodge

Golden Jubilee
Lower Dauphin High School
1960 - 2010

LD
50
**Lower Dauphin
Alumni Association
LD Alumni Golden Jubilee**

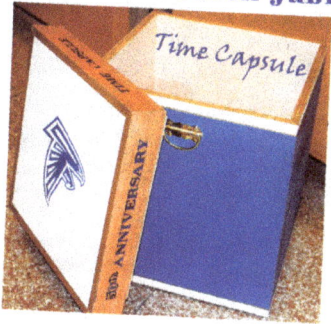

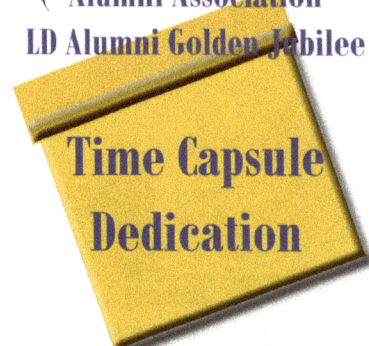

Time Capsule

50th ANNIVERSARY

**Lower Dauphin High School
Saturday, October 2**

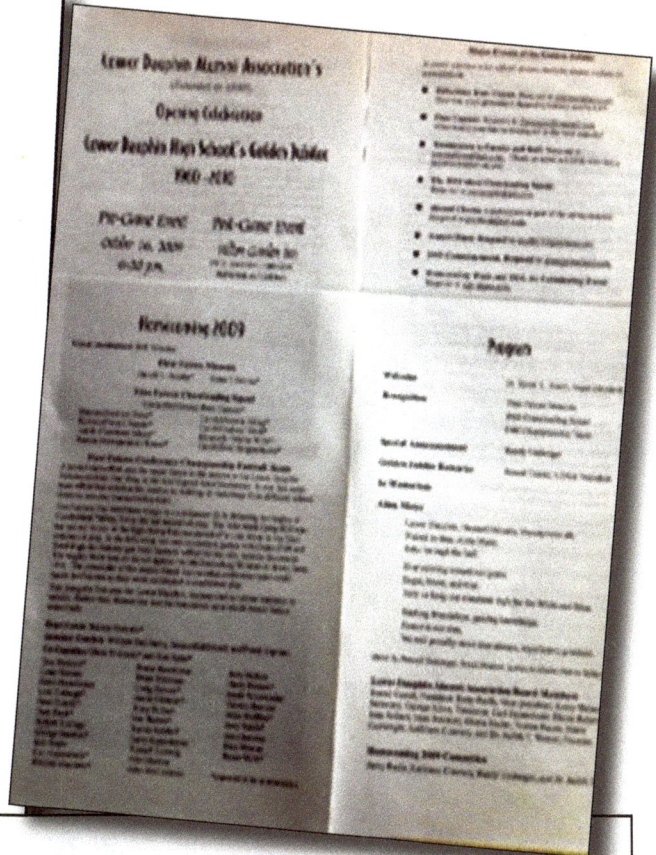

Golden Jubilee Committee, 2008 - 2010

Dr. Judith T. Witmer, Jubilee Chair
Susan Petrina '65, Co-Chair, Alumni Week-end
Betty Musser Radle '62, Co-Chair, Alumni Week-end
Randy Umberger '65, LDSD Liaison
Dr. Jeffrey D. Miller '85, Time Capsule Project

Kyleen Fisher Bender '61	Kathy Saltzer Peffer '73
Barbara Olson Bowser '62	Kathy Weber '74
Carol (Janie) Baker Wenrich '62	Sheila Pankake Vandernick '88
Kathleen Convery '64	Denise Little '89
Ann Landis Kopp '65	Nicole Cassel '96
Dr. Janet Calhoon '66	Bill Minsker, Faculty
Martha Wrzesniewski Bossler '66	Margaret DeAngelis, Faculty

Alma Mater

Lower Dauphin, Onward Falcons,
Victory over all;
Praises to thee, Alma Mater,
Echo through the hall.
Ever striving toward our goals,
Eager, brave, and true;
Help us keep our standards high for the White and Blue.
Seeking friendships, gaining knowledge,
Honor is our aim;
We will proudly serve thee always, loyal hearts proclaim.

*Music by Prowell Seitzinger, Band director;
Lyrics by Elaine Harris Sulkey '63*

LD
50
**Lower Dauphin
Alumni Association
LD Alumni Golden Jubilee**

**Time Capsule
Dedication**

**Lower Dauphin High School
Saturday, October 2**

Father	(Yr. Grad.)	Mother	(Yr. Grad.)	Child 1	(Yr. Grad.)	Child 2	(Yr. Grad.)	Child 3	(Yr. Grad.)
Issac Albright	'35			Doris Albright		Betty Albright	'65		
		Geraldine Heisey	'41	William Calhoon	'61	June Calhoon	'66	Janet Calhoon	'66
Morris Engle	'32			Robert Engle	'61				
John Hall	'40	Jean Eshenhour	'41	John Hall	'61				
		Lucille Shertzer	'33	Lawrence Shertzer	'61	Michael Shertzer	'63	Marilyn Shertzer	'63
Clayton Smith	'32	Thelma Kreiser	'35	Elizabeth Smith	'61	Clayton (Bo) Smith	'65		
Carl Stoner	'34	Blanche Hale	'34	Ronald Stoner	'61				
Marlin Stopfel	'39	Mildred Starry	'35	Marlin Stopfel	'61	Barry Stopfel	'65		
		Whilimine Ludwick	'38	Virigina Stroman	'61	Bradley Stroman	'67		
				RobertStuckey	'61				
		Marybelle Goshert	'32	Mary Jane Dibeler	'62	Anna Deibler	'64		
Norman Fisher	'43			David Fisher	'62				
		Gladys Shoop	'36	Larry Klink	'62				
Oscar Fors	'42	Louella Shepler	'30	Ronald Mark	'62				
		Emilie Diffenderfer	'38	J. Philip Mathias	'62	Susan Mathias	'66		
Carroll Porter	'30			Carroll Porter	'62				
John Musser	'35	Margaret Hartman	'36	Elizabeth Musser	'62	Jack Musser	'65		
		Betty Deimler	'42	Thomas Shaeffer	'62				
		Josephine Spangler	'32	Darlene Tansky	'62				
		Ruth Miller	'31	William Walton	'62				
				Diane Breckenmaker	'63				
Miles Early	'41	Evelyn Coopet	'40	Marie Early	'63				
		Marion Shuey	'34	Robert Johnson	'63				
Philander Rainey	'38			Patricia Rainey	'63	Judy Rainey	'64		
		Lucille Shertzer	'38	Michael Shertzer	'63	Marilyn Shertzer	'63		
		Mildred Sanders	'38	Michael Shifflet	'63	Karen Shifflet	'67		
Clarence Stauffer	'36			Michael Stauffer	'63				
Earl Strite	'34			Joseph Strite	'63	Thomas Strite	'66		
Charles Wolfe	'34			Patricia Wolfe	'63				
		Rozella Deaner	'42	Bruce Wyld	'63	Bryon Wyld	'64		
		Zelma Zinn	'39	Thomas Blose	'62	Yvonne Blose	'64		
Lester Fair	'36			Karen Fair	'64				
		Lucille Walters	'35	Michael Farling	'64				
		Alma Fisher	'46	Marabell Hyde	'64				

Father	(Yr. Grad.)	Mother	(Yr. Grad.)	Child 1	(Yr. Grad.)	Child 2	(Yr. Grad.)	Child 3
Ray Lenker	'39			Kathy Lenker	'64	Richard Lenker	'66	
Jay Ney	'39			Stuart Ney	'64			
Edward Reigle	'36			Robert Reigle	'64			
Raymond Smith	'35			Nancy Smith	'64			
Melvin Baker	'38			Kenneth Baker	'64			
Ammon Bell	'33	Esther Sell	'38	Karl Bell	'65	Elaine Bell	'68	
		MaryBolton	'39	George Bonawitz	'65			
				William Campbell	'65	Susan Campbell	'69	
Guy Davidson	'39	Evelyn Ferguson	'33	Jeffrey Davidson	'65			
Paul Deimler	'30	Arvilla Kautz	'31	Jean Deimler	'65			
William Fox	'31	Evelyn Sowers	'31	William Fox	'65			
		Esther Slough	'34	Thomas Hauer	'65			
		Dorothy Brightbill	'43	Carol Kauffman	'65			
William Martin	'43	Dorothy Hoerner	'34	Bill Martin	'65			
		Genevieve Bistline	'36	Vivian Motter	'65			
John Patrick	'40	Kathryn Witmer	'30	Dennis Patrick	'65			
Rudolph Petrina	'40	Ethel Harro	'39	Susan Petrina	'65			
		Jane Stroman	'44	Thelma Rhoads	'65			
				Carolyn Sandel	'65	Betsy Sandel	'67	
				Evelyn Walkup	'65			
Raymond Zeiters	'41			Stephanie Zeiters	'65			
Carroll Zerfoss	'37	Helen Thomas	'37	Carol Zerfoss	'65	Karen Zerfoss	'65	
Robert Bolton	'38	Esther Kline	'43	Beverly Bolton	'66	Bradley Bolton	'66	
				Marie Brown	'66			
Clifton Hartwell	'35			Mary Harwell	'66	Thomas Hartwell	'69	
Marshal Mountz	'37			Marsha Mountz	'66	Gregory Mountz	'68	
		Alice Zimmerman	'47	Linda Shope	'66			
		Thelma Shepler	'42	Michael Stritte	'66			
		Helen Wyld	'42	Rev. Curtis Weber	'66	Linda Weber	'66	
		Nelda Ludwig	'42	Thomas Hughes	'67			
Charles Bistline	'41	Eleanor Beck	'38	Sharon Bistline	'67			
Harold Hoffer	'45	Mildred Brandt	'45	William Hoffer	'67			
		Zelma Rupert	'30	Faye Hughes	'67			
				Jan Light	'67	Steven Light	'69	

Father	(Yr. Grad.)	Mother	(Yr. Grad.)	Child 1	(Yr. Grad.)	Child 2	(Yr. Grad.)
		Violet Martin	'45	Mary Martin	'67		
		Faye Gingrich	'50	Charles Rhoads	'67		
James Slough	'43	Sara Jane Buser	30	John Seavers	'67		
		Mae Graybill	'44	Linda Slough	'67		
Harold Hainley	'35	Martha Markey	'46	Nancy Alleman	'68		
Kenneth Imhof	'46	Dorothy Clark	36	Robert Baxter	'68		
		Helen Hixon	47	Thomas Hainley	'68		
		June Stroman	'44	Hank Imhof	'68		
Jack Rhoads	'44	Rachael Stoner	'38	Russell Zeiters	68		
				Susan Nisley	68		
		Melba Rathfon	'38	John (Jack) Rhoads	'68		
		Verna Youtz	'38	Robert Schultz	'68		
		Anna Mae Enders	'47	Bradley Warble	'68		
				Jeffrey Wolfensberger	'68		
		June Stroman	'44	Russell Zeiters	'68		
				Wendy Bolton	'69		
Fred Bolton	'36	Mildred Fisher	'39	Rogie Carroll	'69		
Roger Carroll	'46	Jean Keogel	43	Bonnie Gipe	69		
				Marsha Imhof	69		
William Rathfon	'45	Virgina Fors	'48	Susan Rathfon	'69		
Earl Wenrich	'41	Pauline Shuey	'44	Jeff Topper	'69		
				Sandy Wenrich	'69		

References and Bibliography

1919-1929, *The Tatler* newspapers/magazines, Hummelstown High School.

1930-1960, *The Tatler* yearbooks, Hummelstown High School.
....

1920, *The Breeze*, Clearfield High School.

1939, *The Echo*, Curwensville High School.

1940, *The Echo*, Curwensville High School.

1942, *The Echo*, Curwensville High School.

1944, *The Etonian*, Elizabethtown College.

1946, *The Ingot*, Steelton High School.

1947, *The Etonian*, Elizabethtown College.

1947, *Quittapahilla*, Lebanon Valley College.

1949, *The Etonian*, Elizabethtown College.

Aldridge, John W. (1969). *In the Country of the Young*. NY: Harper.

American Red Cross Journal, January 1964.

Bailey, Thomas A. (1976). *Voices of America*. NY: The Free Press, Macmillan.

Bell, Daniel. (1960). *The End of Ideology*. Glencoe, IL: Free Press.

Breines, Wini. (1992). *Young, White, and Miserable: Growing Up Female in the Fifties*. Boston: Beacon Press.

Brodeur, Paul. "The Teen Scene: A Hard Year's End," *SHOW Magazine*, December 1964.

Brokaw, Tom. (2007). *Boom! Talking About the Sixties*. NY: Random House.

Campbell, David N. (2005). *Silent Celebration: The Generation That Transformed America*. Lulu.com.

Carlson, Elwood. (2008). *The Lucky Few: Between the Greatest Generation and the Baby Boom*. NY: Springer.

Cohen, Rich. (2016). *The Sun and the Moon and the Rolling Stones*. NY: Spiegel and Grau, Random House.

Douglas, Susan J. (1994). *Where the Girls Are: Growing Up Female with the Mass Media*. NY: Random House.

Ehrenreich, Barbara. (1989). *Fear of Falling: The Inner Life of the Middle Class*. NY: Pantheon, Random House.

Ehrenreich, Barbara. (1983). *Hearts of Men: American Dreams and the Flight from Commitment*. NY: Anchor Press, Doubleday.

Eisler, Benita. (1986). *Private Lives: Men and Women of the Fifties*. NY: Franklin Watts.

Ellwood, Robert S. (1997). *The Fifties Spiritual Marketplace: American Religion in a Decade of Conflict*. New Brunswick, NJ: Rutgers University Press.

Evans, Harold. (1998). *The American Century*. NY: Alfred A. Knopf.

"Face of the Future," *Look,* December 25, 1964.

Falcon Flash, February 20, 1964. Lower Dauphin High School.

Falcon Flier, June 1961. Lower Dauphin Junior High School.

Farber, David. (1994). *The Age of Great Dreams*. NY: Hill and Wang.

Foreman, Joel, ed. (1997). *The Other Fifties: Interrogating Midcentury American Icons*. Chicago: University of Illinois Press.

Franzosa, Susan Douglas. (1999). *Ordinary Lessons: Girlhoods of the 1950s.* NY: Peter Lang Publishing.

Gitlin, Todd. (1987). *The Sixties: Years of Hope, Days of Rage*. NY: Bantam.

Goodman, Paul. (1960). *Growing Up Absurd*. NY: Vantage Books, Alfred A. Knopf, Inc.

Handy, Bruce. "This is Cinerama," *Vanity Fair*, April 2001.

Huntington, Samuel P. (1981). *American Politics: The Promise of Disharmony*. Boston: Harvard University Press.

Huntington, Samuel P. (2007). *The Clash of Civilizations and the Remaking of World Order*. NY: Simon and Schuster.

Jezer, Marty. (1982). *The Dark Ages: Life in the United States, 1945 – 1960.* Boston: South End Press.

Joseph, Peter. (1974). *Good Times: An Oral History*. NY: William Morrow.

Kaledin, Eugenia. (1984). *Mothers and More: American Women in the 1950s*. Boston: Twayne Publishers.

Katz, Donald. (1992). *Home Fires*. NY: Harper Collins.

Kett, Joseph E. (1977). *Rites of Passage: Adolescence in America, 1790 to the Present*. NY: Colophon Books, Harper.

Kleban, Edward. (1976). "One Singular Sensation," *A Chorus Line*. Tams-Witmark.

Know Your Schools. (June 1969). Lower Dauphin School District.

Leckie, Will and Barry Stopfel. (1997). *Courage to Love*. NY: Doubleday.

Lewis, Magda Gere. (1993). *Without a Word: Teaching Beyond Women's Silence*. NY: Routledge.

Life at 50 Years, Special Anniversary Issue, Fall 1986.

Life Bicentennial Issue, 1976.

Light, Paul C. (1988). *The Baby Boomers*. NY: Norton.

Lingeman, Richard. (1970). *Don't You Know There's a War On?* NY: G. P. Putnam's Sons.

Lynd, Robert S. and Helen Merrell Lynd. (1937). *Middletown in Transition*. NY: Harcourt, Brace.

Miller, Douglas T. and Marion Nowak. (1975). *The Fifties: The Way We Really Were*. NY: Doubleday.

Modell, John. (1989). *Into One's Own: From Youth to Adulthood in the United States, 1920-1975*. CA: University of California Press.

Morison, Samuel E. (1965). *History of the American People*. NY: Oxford University Press.

Palladino, Grace. (1996). *Teenagers: An American History*. NY: Basic Books.

"Picture This: 1951," *Temple Review*, Fall 2002.

Riesman, David with Nathan Glazer and Reuel Denny. (1950). *The Lonely Crowd*. NY: Doubleday Anchor Book/Yale University Press.

Roszak, Theodore. (1969). *The Making of a Counter Culture*. NY: Doubleday.

Sann, Paul. (1979). *The Angry Decade: The Sixties*. NY: Crown.

Schrum, Kelly. (2004). *Some Wore Bobby Sox: The Emergence of Teenage Girls' Culture, 1920-1945*. NY: Palgrave Macmillan.

Strauss, William and Neil Howe. (1991). *Generations: The History of America's Future, 1584 to 2069*. NY: William Morrow.

Strauss, William and Neil Howe. (1997). *The Fourth Turning: What Cycles of History Tell Us About America's Next Rendezvous with Destiny. An American Prophecy*. NY: William Morrow.

Unger, Irwin & Debi Unger. (1998). *The Times Were a Changin'*. NY: Three Rivers Press.

Wakefield, Dan. (1982). *Under the Apple Tree*. NY: Delacorte Press.

Wakefield, Dan. (1992). *New York in the 50s*. NY: Houghton Mifflin.

Wallechinsky, David. (1986). *Midterm Report: The Class of '65*. NY: Viking Press.

Wasserman, Dale. (1964). "The Impossible Dream," *Man of La Mancha*. Tams-Witmark.

Witcover, Jules. (1997). *The Year the Dream Died: Revisiting 1968*. NY: Warner Books.

Witmer, Judith T., Editor/Feature Writer. (2012). *Bicenquinquagenary of Hummelstown*. Picture Perfect Publishing.

Witmer, Judith T. (2013). *Loyal Hearts Proclaim: The First Fifty Years of Lower Dauphin High School*. Yesteryear Publishing.

Author's Brief Biography
Dr. Judith Thompson Ball Witmer

Education: BA in English Literature, Penn State; MS in Science and Humanities, Temple; Doctorate in Administration, Temple; Graduate Credits, Harvard

Professional Work History

- Director, Capital Area Institute for Mathematics and Science, Penn State Harrisburg
- Owner, Educon Consulting and Yesteryear Publishing
- Project Manager, PA Department of Education
- Evaluator, Hershey Medical Center and other entities
- Consultant and Program Designer, Milton Hershey School
- Speechwriter for various national presenters
- Editor for the U.S. Department of Education's *National Arts Standards*
- College Professor (Adjunct: Temple, Millersville, and Penn State)
- Assistant to the Superintendent; High School Principal for Academic Improvement; Director, Coalition of Essential Schools; English Instructor (Initiated English Enrichment, Developed Special Topic Courses; Department Chair)

Community Service

- Co-Chair, fundraising for Lower Dauphin School District's Field House
- Chair, Editor and Chief Contributor for *Bicenquinquagenary Book*, 250th Celebration of Hummelstown's Founding
- Chair, Golden Jubilee, celebrating the first 50 years of Lower Dauphin H.S.
- Chair, fundraising to build the Alexander Library in Hummelstown
- Chair, fundraising for imposing Alumni Display Case
- Member, Harrisburg Public Schools Foundation
- Founding Board Member of the Lower Dauphin Falcon Foundation
- Chair, Board of Pennsylvania Governor's Schools of Excellence
- Founder and Member of the Lower Dauphin Alumni Association

Selected Honors

- Lower Dauphin Falcon Foundation Honoree for Lifetime Service
- Penn State DuBois Outstanding Alumna
- Class of 1965, Life Service Award
- Lower Dauphin Alumni Association, Initial Honoree
- Scholarship established by the Class of 1965
- Dissertation Award, Association for Moral Education, Harvard
- Mensa International
- Outstanding Classroom Teacher
- Outstanding Freshman, Penn State DuBois
- Outstanding Attainment in English, Penn State

Administrative Contributions to LDSD

Initiation and development of several Student Assistance Programs, including an early plan for coping with crises; creation of Student Advisory Board; redesign of Student Forum; initiation of plan and process for Class Gifts to the school; design for New Teacher Induction Plan; proposal for School Governance/Fairness Committee; institution of Senior Awards Family Night; founding of Secondary and Elementary Parent Advisory Boards; formation of student Spirit Club in response to negative incidents; establishment of administrative committee for professional supervision & evaluation

Extra-curricular Service to LDHS

Director/Producer of 8 school musicals; Director of 7 plays and other performances; Advisor for 7 Yearbooks; Director/Producer and Script-writer for 24 student-centered Commencement Productions and 24 Baccalaureate Programs; Initiator of Junior Class Marshals and Alumni participation in Commencement; Advisor to various clubs and the Class of 1965; Dinner music for several proms; Editor and Voice of Daily Announcements at LDHS, 27 years.

Dr. Judith T. Witmer
Annotated (Top Ten of 22 Published Books)

1. *The B-1 English Students*, 2018

This work is a celebration of all Baby Boomers, those who were members of the Classes that were graduated from Lower Dauphin High School in the 1960s, and, especially to a specific class in a distinctive high school. The Class of 1965 was not only a singular sensation in and of itself, but was in a very special place which in many ways seems to have been built especially for the Boomers, providing just the nurturing they needed to come of age.

2. *A Son's Letters to His Father, WWII*, December 2016

Based on letters written by a young soldier during World War II, A Son's Letters to his Father is compelling reading. Bill Calhoon, Class of 1941, Middletown, Pennsylvania, who could have grown up in your hometown, was described by an early reviewer of the book as a regular GI, a simple man who understood the complexity of the war in which he found himself, not having any idea that he would not see his wife or as-yet-unborn child until the little boy was three years old. Bill was faithful in writing to both his wife and his father despite the fact that soldiers' letters were censored as to war campaigns and locations. However, because the letters are masterfully narrated in the context of the history, today's reader, with even a limited knowledge of WWII, is immersed in the daily coping on the home front and the events in the Philippines as they were happening.

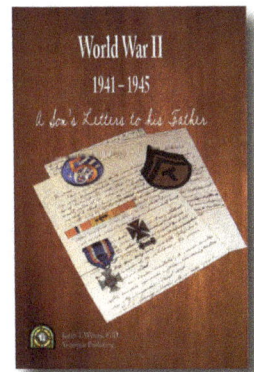

3. *I Have Always Loved You*, the story of an enduring friendship and belated romance. Private printing, July 2016.

They were so much alike in their youth without realizing it at the time. From the first day they met in elementary school, there was a simpatico—whether intellect or humor or suppressed attraction—between them. They were twin personalities with a polarity that ebbed and flowed, almost but never quite touching—like two magnets that moved on the same plane but did not meet.

They were connected by a psychic destiny, almost telepathic in their encounters, which revived what had been harboring in both of them for almost six decades. No one would believe that this reunion took most of a lifetime to be realized, for better or for worse, in sickness and in health, to love and to cherish.

4. Narrative Genealogy of the Thompson Sisters, January 2016

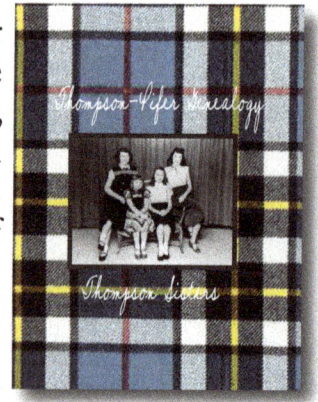

This annotated genealogy traces the lineage of four sisters through their two sets of grandparents from the time these ancestors landed in the 17th Century on the east coast of America from England, Germany, Scotland, Ireland and The Netherlands. There are four maternal and four paternal lineages included here, one of which connects the sisters to the 11th Century and William the Conqueror. Names and dates of births, marriages, and deaths are all listed with many generations' lineages enhanced by personal stories and anecdotes that remind us of the struggles and very human characteristics not included in typical Family Trees and not always found in genealogies. Although this is a narrative, not a family tree, it includes all ancestries.

5. *The Story of Kate and Howard,* July 2015

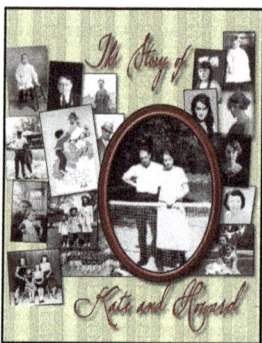

This is not a typical biography, but rather a collection of history, remembrances, experiences, explanations, and tributes to Kate. It contains the genealogies of both Kate and Howard, who they were and who they became, scenes of childhood, unpleasant—but necessary—familial lawsuits, and, perhaps, understanding and forgiveness. Excerpts from Diaries, as well as letters among family members, are inserted here just as they were written, without editing.

6. *Loyal Hearts Proclaim,* December 2013

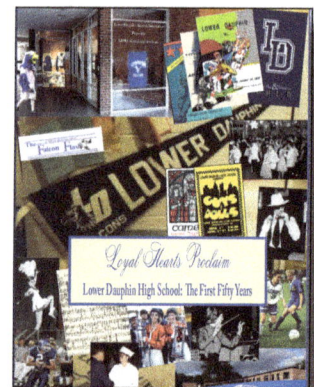

At first glance, Lower Dauphin might just look like most other high schools in the United States, its most distinguishing feature being its sprawling configuration, chosen by the planning board because there was generous acreage in the purchase. Another distinguishing feature was what it did not have—and that was a football field in a state where football was king. The Board had determined that a stadium would not be built until the library shelves were filled.

Over its history LDHS has offered a premier vocational agriculture program, study and travel abroad; field trips to see great art and architecture and performances; unusual offerings such as archeology, longitudinal studies, and English Enrichment.Producing a musical the first year elevated the culture of the school, putting music and art on the same table as English and Latin, providing the foundation for a liberal arts education. And so it began....

7. *Growing Up Silent in the 1950s: Not all Tailfins and Rock n Roll*, Dec. 2012

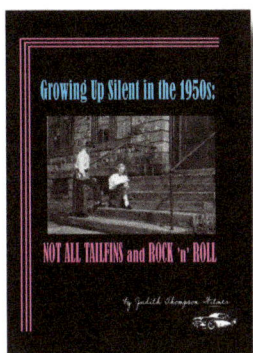

While most of the popular books written about the 1950s focus on the "pop" culture of the decade, Growing Up Silent considers the difficulties of growing up in a society that expected its youth to always "be good." This book is an investigation of the factors that created such a generation as they were—a generation, despite the suppression, that history has shown to be responsible and productive. Silent is well-researched and the author, Class of 1955, writes with historical accuracy. Enlivening the book are reflections by members of the Silent Generation, through diaries, scrapbooks, interviews, and personal narratives from an era described as a time with "unimaginable restrictions."

8. *All the Gentlemen Callers: Letters from a 1920s Steamer Trunk*, March 2012.

Shortly after completing the biography of my Aunt Jessie Pifer, I opened her steamer trunk (the high school graduation gift from her parents in 1924). Expecting that the standing trunk would make a charming photograph, I set it upright and opened it, to best display its set of five drawers in graduated sizes on the right. In opening the bottom drawer to give depth to the view of the trunk's interior, I found a dozen letters, tied with a white ribbon, which turned out to be from Jessie's high school and college girlfriends.

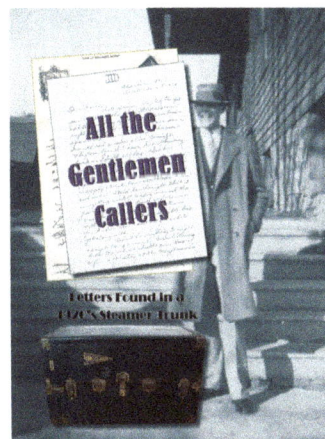

Under that small bundle was a cache of more than 100 letters, dating from 1924 to 1938, some tied together, others loose, but all addressed to "Jebbie" and all from her suitors during that period of her youth. Providing a candid and personal view of the social history of the times, the letters cried out to be used in a book, placed in the framework of history from 1920-1940, providing a firsthand account of daily travails of life nearly a century ago, expressing a parallel to modes of communication of then and now, displaying emotions familiar to all generations, and revealing the love and devotion of All the Gentlemen Callers for one particular beauty—dashing, independent, fashionable, and remembered as the vibrant Jebbie, Belle of the Class of 1924.

9. *Jebbie: Vamp to Victim: The True Story of Miss Pifer*, December 2011

Jessie Beverly Pifer (Jebbie) was a real person, as real as the reader, and as complicated yet vulnerable as most human beings. Jessie, like your aunt, or perhaps your mother or grandmother or even you yourself, was a full human being who lived, laughed, and loved. She grew up in a small town and went from being the stunning and stylish girl with all the gentlemen callers to becoming a town legend. She was lively and witty, popular and, in some ways, eccentric, but she was, above all, an independent person who asked help from no one.

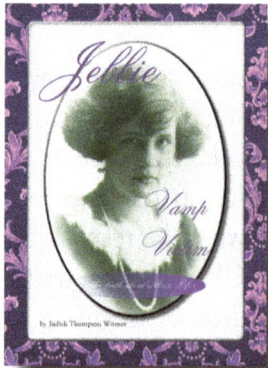

The book follows Jessie throughout her life, providing a keen historical perspective of the 20th Century. The reader is drawn into this family as they not only become products of the era, but also are caught in a web of deceit. Laughing with Jessie and living with her family makes the tragedy of betrayal and elder abuse, when it occurs, all the more real and unforgiving.

10. *I Am From Haiti: The Story of Rodrigue Mortel, MD*, A Biography, Mortel Foundation, December 2000. (French edition, *Je Suis D'Haiti*, 2002.)

Rodrigue Mortel, a Horatio Alger Awardee, in addition to many other accolades, grew up in abject poverty in Haiti and never forgot his homeland. Following a stellar career as a gynecologic oncologist, he was the fire-starter for the creation of the Cancer Center at the Milton Hershey Medical Center, as well as the founder of a tuition-free school in Haiti. I traveled with Dr. Mortel to his homeland during the writing of this book.

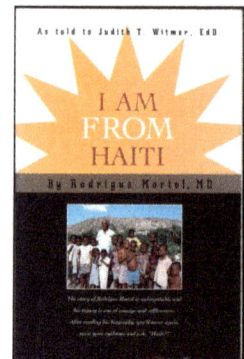

www.ingramcontent.com/pod-product-compliance
Lightning Source LLC
Chambersburg PA
CBHW050405110426
42812CB00006BA/1809

9 780099 779563